Your All-in-One Resource

On the CD that accompanies this book, you'll find additional resources to extend your learning.

The reference library includes the following fully searchable titles:

- *Microsoft Computer Dictionary*, 5th ed.
- *First Look 2007 Microsoft Office System* by Katherine Murray
- Windows Vista Product Guide

Also provided are a sample chapter and poster from *Look Both Ways: Help Protect Your Family on the Internet* by Linda Criddle.

The CD interface has a new look. You can use the tabs for an assortment of tasks:

- Check for book updates (if you have Internet access)
- Find links to helpful tools and resources
- Go online for product support or CD support
- Send us feedback

The following screen shot gives you a glimpse of the new interface.

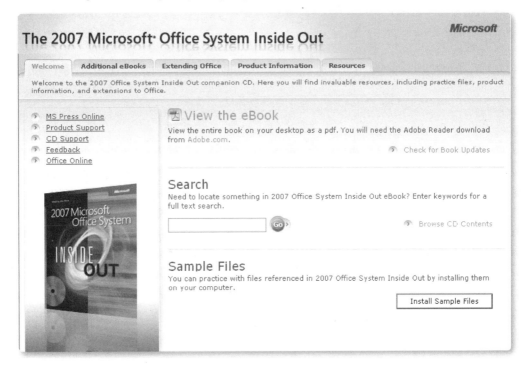

Windows® SharePoint® Services 3.0 Inside Out

Errin O'Connor

PUBLISHED BY
Microsoft Press
A Division of Microsoft Corporation
One Microsoft Way
Redmond, Washington 98052-6399

Library of Congress Control Number: 2007939310

Printed and bound in the United States of America.

1 2 3 4 5 6 7 8 9   QWT   2 1 0 9 8 7

Distributed in Canada by H.B. Fenn and Company Ltd.

A CIP catalogue record for this book is available from the British Library.

Microsoft Press books are available through booksellers and distributors worldwide. For further information about international editions, contact your local Microsoft Corporation office or contact Microsoft Press International directly at fax (425) 936-7329. Visit our Web site at www.microsoft.com/mspress. Send comments to mspinput@microsoft.com.

Microsoft, Microsoft Press, Active Directory, ActiveSync, ActiveX, Expression, Front Page, IntelliSense, Internet Explorer, MSDN, Outlook, Visual Studio, Win32, Windows, Windows NT, and Windows PowerShell are either registered trademarks or trademarks of Microsoft Corporation in the United States and/or other countries. Other product and company names mentioned herein may be the trademarks of their respective owners.

The example companies, organizations, products, domain names, e-mail addresses, logos, people, places, and events depicted herein are fictitious. No association with any real company, organization, product, domain name, e-mail address, logo, person, place, or event is intended or should be inferred.

This book expresses the author's views and opinions. The information contained in this book is provided without any express, statutory, or implied warranties. Neither the authors, Microsoft Corporation, nor its resellers, or distributors will be held liable for any damages caused or alleged to be caused either directly or indirectly by this book.

Acquisitions Editor: Juliana Aldous Atkinson
Developmental Editor: Sandra Haynes
Project Editor: Victoria Thulman
Editorial Production: Custom Editorial Productions, Inc.
Technical Reviewers: David Robinson and Sean Childers
Cover: Tom Draper Design

Body Part No. X13-24195

This book is dedicated to the men and women of the United States armed forces, to whom we owe a great deal.

Contents at a Glance

v

Table of Contents

What do you think of this book? We want to hear from you!

Microsoft is interested in hearing your feedback so we can continually improve our books and learning resources for you. To participate in a brief online survey, please visit:

www.microsoft.com/learning/booksurvey/

What do you think of this book? We want to hear from you!

Microsoft is interested in hearing your feedback so we can continually improve our books and learning resources for you. To participate in a brief online survey, please visit:

www.microsoft.com/learning/booksurvey/

Acknowledgments

First and foremost, I would like to thank Carol Donnelly for her steadfast support throughout the writing of this book. She kept me on track, kept me mentally sane, and kept the long hours with me throughout this long, long project. When I contemplated trying to jump out the second floor window to do a cannonball into the pool to relax, her wise counsel kept me in the chair and writing. When I began talking to my mouse and asking it opinions on the grammatical rules around *affect* or *effect*, she would bring me a soda to relax.

At Microsoft Press, thanks to Vicky Thulman, the project editor, and Sandra Haynes, the development editor, for their confidence, encouragement, patience, and assistance.

Thanks to the entire team at StudioB and especially my agent, Neil J. Salkind, whose experience and professionalism were always extremely refreshing.

This project took me several months of very long nights and weekends while maintaining a very busy SharePoint consulting practice. I found respite in the Jim Rome Show's daily podcasts. Romey's humor and the XR4TI Crew, who were assuredly kept on point by Mr. Automatic (the best contestant Blind Date's ever had), and Jay Stew always kept me laughing.

Most of all, thanks to you, the readers, who make a marathon effort such as this both possible and worthwhile. I hope the book meets your expectations and that we meet again come the next release of this powerful platform.

About the CD

 The companion CD that ships with this book contains many tools and resources to help you get the most out of your Inside Out book.

What's on the CD

Your Inside Out CD includes the following:

- **Complete eBook**   In this section, you'll find an electronic version of *Windows SharePoint Services 3.0 Inside Out*. The eBook is in PDF format.

- **Microsoft Online Resources**   A catalog of helpful online resources for Microsoft Windows SharePoint Services 3.0 (WSS 3.0), Microsoft SharePoint Server 2007, Microsoft Office SharePoint Designer 2007, SQL Server 2005, .NET Framework, and Microsoft Windows Vista.

- **Links to Reference Documents, Files, and Material**   These links will point you to a collection of files that are referenced within the book. Files such as the full installation file for WSS 3.0, the WSS 3.0 Quick Reference Guide, WSS 3.0 Applications Templates, the Microsoft Best Practices Analyzer for WSS 3.0, and many more.

- **The Links (URLs) Listed in the Chapters**   Here's a catalog of the links that were referenced throughout the book. They are sorted by chapter for easy navigation.

- **Contacting the Author**   Here you'll find several ways to contact the author as well as links to the WSS 3.0 dedicated site on *EPCGroup.net*. Errors, omissions, corrections, and frequently asked questions will be posted on this site, along with free Web Parts and solutions that were developed for the readers of this book.

> **Note**
>
> Please note that the links to third-party sites are not under the control of Microsoft Corporation, and Microsoft is therefore not responsible for their content. Nor should their inclusion on this CD be construed as an endorsement of the product or the site.
>
> Software provided on this CD is in only the English language and may be incompatible with non-English language operating systems and software.

System Requirements

The following are the minimum system requirements necessary to run the CD:

- Microsoft Windows Vista, Windows XP with Service Pack 2 (SP2), Windows Server 2003 with SP1, or newer operating system

- 500 megahertz (MHz) processor or higher
- 2 gigabyte (GB) storage space
- 256 megabytes (MB) RAM
- CD-ROM or DVD-ROM drive
- Microsoft Windows or Windows Vista–compatible sound card and speakers
- Microsoft Internet Explorer 6 or higher
- Microsoft Mouse or compatible pointing device

Support Information

Every effort has been made to ensure the accuracy of the contents of the book and of this CD. As corrections or changes are collected, they will be added to a Microsoft Knowledge Base article. Microsoft Press provides support for books and companion CDs at the following Web site:

http://www.microsoft.com/learning/support/books/

If you have comments, questions, or ideas regarding the book or this CD, or questions that are not answered by visiting the site above, please send them via e-mail to:

mspinput@microsoft.com

You can also click the Feedback or CD Support links on the Welcome page. Please note that Microsoft software product support is not offered through the above addresses.

If your question is about the software, and not about the content of this book, please visit the Microsoft Help and Support page or the Microsoft Knowledge Base at:

http://support.microsoft.com

In the United States, Microsoft software product support issues not covered by the Microsoft Knowledge Base are addressed by Microsoft Product Support Services. Location-specific software support options are available from:

http://support.microsoft.com/gp/selfoverview/

Microsoft Press provides corrections for books through the World Wide Web at *http://www.microsoft.com/mspress/support/*. To connect directly to the Microsoft Press Knowledge Base and enter a query regarding a question or issue that you may have, go to *http://www.microsoft.com/mspress/support/search.htm*.

Conventions and Features Used in This Book

This book uses special text and design conventions to make it easer for you to find the information you need.

Text Conventions

Convention	Meaning
Abbreviated menu commands	For your convenience, this book uses abbreviated menu commands. For example, "Choose Tools, Forms, Design A Form" means that you should click the Tools menu, point to Forms, and select the Design A Form command.
Boldface type	**Boldface** type is used to indicate text that you enter or type.
Initial Capital Letters	The first letters of the names of menus, dialog boxes, dialog box elements, and commands are capitalized. Example: The Save As dialog box.
Italicized type	*Italicized* type is used to indicate new terms.
Plus sign (+) in text	Keyboard shortcuts are indicated by a plus sign (+) separating two key names. For example, Shift+F9 means that you press the Shift and F9 keys at the same time.

Design Conventions

> **Note**
> Notes offer additional information related to the task being discussed.

Cross-references point you to other locations in the book or other sources that offer additional information on the topic being discussed.

INSIDE OUT   This statement illustrates an example of an "Inside Out" problem statement

These are the book's signature tips. In these tips, you'll get the straight scoop on what's going on with the software—inside information on why a feature works the way it does. You'll also find handy workarounds to different software problems.

TROUBLESHOOTING

This statement illustrates an example of a "Troubleshooting" problem statement

Look for these sidebars to find solutions to common problems you might encounter. Troubleshooting sidebars appear next to related information in the chapters. You can also use the Troubleshooting Topics index at the back of the book to look up problems by topic.

Sidebar

The sidebars sprinkled throughout these chapters provide ancillary information on the topic being discussed. Go to sidebars to learn more about the technology or a feature.

Introduction

People working together is a key element in the success of any organization. Only through the cooperation, interaction, and collaboration of its members can an organization multiply its efforts and become stronger and more productive.

Much of this collaboration is, of course, face-to-face—we work together in pairs, in informal groups, in targeted meetings, and even in large assemblies. And when we can't be face-to-face, we speak by telephone, teleconferencing, instant messaging, and e-mail. Although these methods are personal, immediate, convenient, and efficient, we sometimes need a more permanent record of our thoughts, our preparations, and our statements. For that, we've historically resorted to paper trails, file folders, and electronic media such as Microsoft Office Word documents, Microsoft Office Excel spreadsheets, Microsoft Office PowerPoint presentations, and Web pages.

To be useful, of course, documents of any kind must find their way to the people who need them. Traditionally, they've followed one of four routes:

- **Mail**   Gets the immediate attention of its recipient, but it creates duplicate copies of each document for each recipient; it requires the sender to anticipate who might need a document; and it's awkward for long-term storage.

- **File Systems**   Provide medium-term storage for documents and (usually) a hierarchical scheme for organizing them in some sort of folder structure. Unfortunately, most computer file systems maintain very little data about the documents they store, often providing just a cryptic file name and the date the file was last updated. Metadata, or data about data, is mostly nonexistent in the standard file system. Searching for documents by content or by property (such as author, title, keyword, or version) is slow and resource-intensive.

- **Databases**   Provide excellent long-term storage and search capabilities, but only by splitting documents into discrete data elements. As such, they usually store the data content of highly structured documents, and not the documents themselves.

- **Libraries**   Combine, in many respects, the file system and database approaches. A library stores whole documents, not just their structured data content, and it provides a database of information about the documents it stores. This is a powerful approach, but it often suffers from a lack of scalability. Either the library can't accommodate the massive number of documents a large organization can generate, or its indexing, search, and retrieval mechanisms aren't granular enough. For example, they start generating search results in the thousands or tens of thousands.

Taken individually, none of these approaches meets all the requirements for quick, easy, accurate, and efficient collaboration throughout an organization. Vendors, systems integrators, and organizations have therefore tried combining these approaches in various ways, hoping to multiply their benefits and cancel out their deficiencies.

Presenting Windows SharePoint Services 3.0

Microsoft's approach to collaboration and document management answers the short-comings of all past and present approaches. It centers on two products named, collectively, SharePoint Products and Technologies—those two products are Microsoft Windows SharePoint Services 3.0 (WSS 3.0) and SharePoint Server 2007.

Microsoft Windows SharePoint Services 3.0 (WSS 3.0) is built on the Windows Server 2003 platform and conforms to the Windows Server 2003 licensing model. Using these services, you or any authorized team member can create specialized Web sites for sharing information, developing group documents, organizing meetings, and generally fostering collaboration among team members. The key components of these Web sites are lists and libraries.

- A SharePoint *list* contains rows and columns of data, much like a standard database table. SharePoint lists, however, are much easier to create and maintain. They're great for collecting and sharing fielded information such as contact lists, calendars of events, or custom information of any kind.

- A SharePoint *library* is similar to a list, except that it exists solely to store a collection of documents. Each list item describes one document, providing information such as the file name, the file title, the date last modified, and the person who last modified the document. SharePoint libraries can retain multiple versions of each document, and they support change control through document check-in and checkout. WSS 3.0 supports special library types for pictures and for Microsoft Office InfoPath forms.

Organizing these lists and libraries into team Web sites places most administration and content management in the hands of team members who are close to the work and familiar with the subject matter. This avoids the bureaucracy and the waiting times that are typical of strictly centralized administration. But at the same time, Microsoft provides all the tools that centralized administrators need to keep the installation under control and running smoothly.

Team members can access SharePoint Web sites by using either a browser or a Microsoft Office 2003 or Microsoft Office 2007 application. Individuals on teams can configure lists and libraries to record whatever information they want, and they can easily create shared work areas for documents, projects, and other work in progress. Members can sign up to receive change notifications by e-mail. These features go way beyond anything traditional file sharing can provide. The file share is a thing of the past!

You can also use WSS 3.0 as a development platform for creating custom collaboration and information-sharing applications. For example, third-party or in-house programmers can access SharePoint sites by using Web services or readily accessible application programming interfaces (APIs). In addition, you can develop custom Web pages by using SharePoint Designer 2007, and custom SharePoint objects and solutions with Microsoft Visual Studio 2005.

SharePoint Server 2007 is an application that runs on the WSS 3.0 platform. For most organizations, its most important features are enterprise content management, search, workflow, and enterprise-wide collaboration. SharePoint Server 2007 also provides a personal Web site for each user, called a My Site. I like to refer to this as the Corporate MySpace.

SharePoint Server 2007 also has the ability to connect and search other business applications such as SAP by using the Business Data Catalog.

Both of these products integrate smoothly, almost effortlessly, with your existing Microsoft software. The platform is Windows Server 2003 or Windows Server 2008; the Web server is Internet Information Server (IIS); security integrates with Windows domains or Microsoft Active Directory directory service; and both the run-time environment and development platform are Microsoft .NET Framework version 2.0. All Office 2007 programs function as SharePoint clients. You can even e-mail–enable SharePoint lists and document libraries. Microsoft Project Server 2007 runs on WSS 3.0, and SharePoint Server 2007 integrates with BizTalk Server 2006. The list goes on and on.

Both WSS 3.0 and SharePoint Server 2007 make extensive use of Microsoft SQL Server 2005. If you are using a single server deployment, then you can either go with the Windows Internal Database or install SQL Server on the stand-alone machine along with the other components.

Scalability is never really going to be an issue with WSS 3.0. If usage demands, you can create as large a farm of Web servers as you like and spread the database load across as many SQL servers as you like. The back up and restore functionality has been drastically improved in this latest release of SharePoint.

Who This Book Is For

This book addresses the needs of anyone who uses, designs, installs, administers, governs, or programs WSS 3.0. It begins with an overview of the product and how a successful SharePoint initiative should be planned and implemented. I have used my past 6.5 years of SharePoint consulting experience to provide you with a best practices approach for successfully implementing SharePoint within any organization. This is helpful so that any audience can see the big picture of an entire SharePoint implementation project. The book ends with an explanation of detailed SharePoint programming techniques, best practices, and information about how to get your new implementation off the ground. In between, the material is organized in order of increasing detail and complexity. This means you can read until you learn what you need at the moment, and then continue as the need arises.

Alternatively, you can approach the book randomly, on a sort of "need to know" basis. The index and table of contents will guide you to the specific information you need.

Even in its initial release, WSS 3.0 integrates tightly with an extremely wide range of Microsoft software. This book, however, is a complete guide only for WSS 3.0, with some detailed information about SharePoint Server 2007. It presumes that if you're interested in the interface between WSS 3.0 and, say, Microsoft Office Outlook, then you already know how to use Office Outlook. The same is true for the other Microsoft Office programs, for Windows Server 2003, Microsoft SQL Server 2005, and for Visual Studio 2005. This book also gives you a great deal of information about using Share-Point Designer 2007.

How the Book Is Organized

This book consists of seven parts, organized in order of increasing complexity and specialization. The early chapters, for example, meet the needs of the widest and least technically curious audience: team members who use WSS 3.0 via Internet Explorer or Microsoft Office 2007 on a daily basis. Later chapters address the needs of more specialized workers, such as Web designers, power users, administrators, and software developers.

Here are the titles and specific coverages of each part:

- **Part 1: Overview and Concepts**   In this part, Chapter 1, "Introducing Windows SharePoint Services 3.0," introduces the basic features and mindset of WSS 3.0. For comparison, Chapter 2, "Introducing Microsoft Office SharePoint Server 2007," describes an overview of a SharePoint enterprise deployment and Share-Point Server 2007.

- **Part 2: End-User Features and Experiences**   This part explains the features team members are likely to use the most. Chapter 3, "Using the Built-In Features of Windows SharePoint Services 3.0," explains how to work with SharePoint sites by using a browser, and Chapter 4, "Using SharePoint with Microsoft Office 2007," explains how to access SharePoint sites from Microsoft Office 2007.

- **Part 3: Creating, Designing, and Configuring Sites, Workspaces, and Pages with a Browser**   Chapter 5, "Creating SharePoint Sites, Workspaces, and Pages," explains how to create, design, and configure new SharePoint sites, workspaces, and Web pages by using only a browser. Chapter 6, "Designing Lists, Libraries, and Pages," explains how to create, modify, and manage SharePoint lists and libraries, again using the browser interface.

- **Part 4: Creating. Designing, and Managing Sites and Working with SharePoint Designer 2007**   A lot of functionality and options are available for you to consider when properly creating, designing, and managing SharePoint sites. Also, with the release of SharePoint Designer 2007, you have a very powerful tool to use for site customization and the creation of custom functionality. With all of this information, it takes six chapters to properly explain.

  Chapter 7, "What's New with Templates and Design," explains how SharePoint Designer 2007 can create, open, add pages to, export, import, back up, and restore SharePoint sites. It also goes into creating no-code solutions such as custom workflow. Chapter 8, "Creating and Formatting Web Part Pages," then explains how to create and modify Web Part pages, which are special Web pages that display the output of SharePoint software components called, logically enough, Web Parts.

Chapter 9, "Creating and Modifying Basic Site Features," explains how to create and modify basic site features as well as how to modify SharePoint site navigation. This chapter also discusses the use and creation of site templates in relation to how to properly use master pages.

Chapter 10, "Creating Data Sources and Data Views," explains how to design, create, and modify SharePoint lists and libraries. Chapter 11, "Using WSS 3.0 Web Parts," explains how to properly use WSS 3.0's out-of-the-box Web Parts. Chapter 12, "Managing Site Content," explains how to manage SharePoint content and how to properly keep your site's content up-to-date and relevant.

- **Part 5: Installing Windows SharePoint Services 3.0**   In this part, Chapter 13, "Planning and Installing Windows SharePoint Services 3.0," explains how to plan for and then install WSS 3.0 in the most common scenarios. It goes into requirements gathering and the choices you have concerning the proper server configurations. Chapter 13 also discusses the extranet capabilities of WSS 3.0 as well as information on language packs. Chapter 14, "Backing Up, Restoring, and Migrating Sites," then explains how to back up and restore SharePoint sites. It covers information on SharePoint disaster recovery plans for your organization, migrating sites, and third-party backup and restore tools you should consider.

- **Part 6: Administering SharePoint Services**   An organization running WSS 3.0 can delegate administration at the physical server, virtual server, site collection, or site level. If your duties fall into any of these categories, this part has something for you.

Chapter 15, "Administering a SharePoint Server," explains how to properly administer a SharePoint server. This chapter covers topics such as server monitoring, how to use applications such as Microsoft Operations Manager or System Center Operations Manager 2007, and using SQL Reporting Services with SharePoint.

Chapter 16, "Managing Site Settings," explains how to administer an individual SharePoint site or site collection. For the most part, these are functions that administrators of individual sites or site collections will use. Chapter 17, "SharePoint Central Administration," explains how to use SharePoint Central Administration's Operations and Application Management pages. This chapter is geared toward site collection and server administrators because these pages control almost every aspect of your organization's WSS 3.0 implementation.

- **Part 7: Developing Web Parts in Visual Studio 2005, SharePoint Best Practices, and Maintaining Your Implementation**   This part provides four chapters of interest to software developers who want to learn SharePoint development techniques and want to develop new components such as Web Parts for WSS 3.0. This part is also geared toward administrators because it covers SharePoint best practices, content type configuration, and limitations, as well as how to maintain a healthy SharePoint environment. Chapter 18, "Advanced Design Techniques," explains a number of techniques that are useful when designing Windows Share-Point Services 3.0 sites. The topics that are covered in this chapter will assist you in following best practices development techniques to help you and your organization get the most out of this powerful platform. Chapter 19, "Beginning Web Part Development," explains Web Part development, information on how to configure a development environment, the SharePoint object model, and a number of other detailed development topics. Chapter 20, "Additional SharePoint Best Practices," explains SharePoint best practices to help you successfully implement many different areas of your WSS 3.0 deployment. Chapter 21, "Getting Share-Point off the Launch Pad," concludes with instructions for getting your new SharePoint implementation off the ground with topics concerning SharePoint training and communications.

If this strikes you as quite a range of topics, you're right, and it indicates the popularity that WSS 3.0 enjoys among Microsoft products and technologies. SharePoint is becoming one of the hottest software solutions available. It is also becoming one of the hottest IT skill sets on the market. With this kind of promise, it's no wonder you're interested in WSS 3.0.

PART 1
Overview and Concepts

Introducing Windows SharePoint Services 3.0

O ver the past several years, organizations across the globe have been investing more time, effort, and capital into connecting their people and managing their information. Portals have become extremely popular within organizations to assist their user base in storing and accessing content while simultaneously linking the organization's departments and teams together in a way that offers users a familiar Web-based experience. Portals have enabled employees with very different roles to have a hand in enhancing the company's overall collaborative nature. Microsoft's SharePoint Products and Technologies suite, which primarily consists of Microsoft Windows SharePoint Services 3.0 (WSS 3.0) and Microsoft Office SharePoint Server 2007 (MOSS), has emerged as the platform to be reckoned with in the portal and collaboration arena.

Windows SharePoint Services 3.0 enables organizations of all sizes to deploy robust solutions within their enterprises that will help their people stay connected regardless of size, geographic location, and most importantly their available IT budget.

Whether the organization is a *Fortune* 500 company or a start-up, SharePoint offers an easy-to-use Web-based interface that is fully integrated with Microsoft Office, offering authorized user access to the documents and information they need to help them be more effective at completing the task at hand. SharePoint Server 2007 extends the capabilities of Windows SharePoint Services 3.0 by providing functionality such as enterprise search, robust storage and auditing policies, and flexible organizational management tools.

Windows SharePoint Services 3.0 is built on the Windows Server 2003 platform and conforms to the Windows Server 2003 licensing model, which enables organizations who already own Windows Server 2003 to take advantage of the powerful collaboration features without having to purchase additional licensing. If enterprise-wide records management and enterprise search are major requirements of your deployment, then SharePoint Server is a platform that you should definitely consider. If your goals are less complex, then Windows SharePoint Services 3.0 is the robust and cost-effective platform you should strongly consider.

Windows SharePoint Services, all by itself, is powerful, flexible, and easy to use. The rest of this book, therefore, explains how to make the most of this amazing component that comes free with every copy of Windows Server 2003.

The remainder of this chapter provides a brief overview of Windows SharePoint Services 3.0, how to customize and enhance it, how it works with the Microsoft Office system, and how to develop entirely new SharePoint applications. Later chapters will explain these topics in much greater detail.

> **Note**
>
> You can download Windows SharePoint Services 3.0, both the standard and 64-bit versions, at *www.microsoft.com/technet/windowsserver/sharepoint*. Installing Windows SharePoint Services 3.0 over any beta or trial edition of SharePoint Server is not supported.

Presenting Windows SharePoint Services

At a high level, Windows SharePoint Services 3.0 consists of five principal components:

- Software that provides database services, document management capability, security and access control, and administration features built on the ASP.NET 2.0 platform

- A Web delivery mechanism, consisting of one or more Internet Information Services (IIS) Web servers

- A Microsoft SQL Server database

- Software components called Web Parts that execute on the Web server and display information and content in portions of a Web page called Web Part zones

- Sample collaboration and meeting templates (site templates)

Table 1-1 lists the templates that come with every copy of Windows SharePoint Services 3.0. With new and improved functionality in version 3.0, these collaboration and meeting templates continue to be ideal for information workers in corporate environments. People use these same templates more than ever to create Web sites for professional and charitable organizations, schools, social clubs, sports teams, churches, youth groups, and almost any other kind of group you can think of. This same platform can also be utilized to develop custom applications of any kind.

Table 1-1 Collaboration and Meeting Templates Supplied with Windows SharePoint Services 3.0

Template Name	Template Description
Team Site	A site for teams to quickly organize, author, and share information. It provides a document library and lists for managing announcements, calendar items, tasks, and discussions.
Blank Site	A blank site for you to customize based on your requirements.
Document Workspace	A site for colleagues to work together on a document. It provides a document library for storing the primary document and supporting files, a tasks list for assigning to-do items, and a links list for resources related to the document.
Wiki Site	A site for teams to brainstorm and share ideas. It provides pages that can be quickly edited to record information and then linked together through keywords.
Blog	A site for an individual or team to post ideas, observations, and expertise that site visitors can comment on.
Basic Meeting Workspace	A site for planning, organizing, and capturing the results of a meeting. It provides lists for managing the agenda, meeting attendees, and documents.
Blank Meeting Workspace	A blank meeting site for you to customize based on your requirements.
Decision Meeting Workspace	A site for meetings that track status or make decisions. It provides lists for creating tasks, storing documents, and recording decisions.
Social Meeting Workspace	A site for planning social occasions. It provides lists for tracking attendees, providing directions, and storing pictures of the event.
Multipage Meeting Workspace	A site for planning, organizing, and capturing the results of a meeting. It provides lists for managing the agenda and meeting attendees in addition to two blank pages for you to customize based on your requirements.

These templates give users the flexibility to accomplish fast-paced and effective collaboration on documents, meetings, events, projects, discussions, and ideas. A Web site that can be created in a matter of minutes would be ideal in the following situations:

- When project team members have many recurring meetings throughout the year where agendas, meeting minutes, and related project-specific documentation differ from meeting to meeting

- When a specific document exists that requires feedback from a large audience but will require granular security so that only document owners will be able to perform update features

- When an ad hoc meeting is called to discuss a specific topic and this information must be retained and collaborated on throughout a period of time.

- When a series of Web sites need to be created for different departments so that specific content can be disseminated throughout an organization but still remain secure based on each member's role.

These collaboration and meeting templates are ideal for members of a department or project who need to retain version control on their documents; conduct discussions; and track tasks, issues, and agendas. Massive file shares are becoming a thing of the past, and with this new technology, users can keep their content up to date and collaborate in a secure, controlled environment. With site quotes, file exclusion lists, improved governance, and advanced administration features, Windows SharePoint Services 3.0 can accommodate thousands of sites within an organization.

> **Note**
> Microsoft has also released 40 additional application templates that address the needs and requirements of specific business processes or sets of tasks in any organization. A link to twenty site admin templates and 20 server admin templates is available on the companion CD *(http://www.microsoft.com/technet/windowsserver/sharepoint/wssapps/templates/default.mspx)*.

With the improvements in Windows SharePoint Services 3.0, it is safe to say that this powerful platform is now a true .NET application, leveraging the full capabilities of Microsoft ASP.NET 2.0 while core components such as the Web Part Framework and Web Virtualization are now being provided by the .NET runtime. These improvements at the most granular layers of SharePoint give it the ability to be a robust platform for Web-application development and administration. Developers have vastly improved the object model and added new namespaces for new features while at the same time placing a high priority on backward compatibility with Windows SharePoint Services 2.0.

The new content management capabilities of Windows SharePoint Services 3.0 are made possible by the addition of two new tools: content types and site columns. A content type is really a reusable collection of settings that you can apply to a certain category of content. Content types enable organizations to better manage the metadata of a document or item type in a centralized manner. Site columns provide a centralized and reusable method for defining column definitions while eliminating the monotonous work of reproducing the column for every list in which it needs to reside.

For more information about content types, refer to the section titled "Working with Content Types in a List or Library" in Chapter 6, "Designing Lists, Libraries, and Pages in WSS 3.0," and to the section titled "Defining the Proper Content Types and Metadata for Your Enterprise" in Chapter 20, "SharePoint Best Practices."

Users now have the ability to edit the Top Link bar and the Quick Launch and easily navigate using breadcrumbs, which will show users the path to the current page. Administration in Windows SharePoint Services 3.0 allows for improved backup and restoring of sites as well as the configuration of service account credentials. There is no longer the need to use the standard IIS tools to enable or disable anonymous authentication because you now utilize the SharePoint Central Administration to fully enable the authentication for anonymous access.

> **Note**
>
> The Quick Launch can now easily be customized to meet the specific needs of the site on which it resides. For more information about the Quick Launch, refer to the section titled "Quick Launch" in Chapter 16, "Managing Site Settings."

Some of the most frequently asked questions by users of Windows SharePoint Services 2.0 centered on why item-level security was not available. SharePoint administrators all over the world are now happy to know that item-level security is available with Windows SharePoint Services 3.0, and that it allows for powerful content management across any SharePoint environment.

Figure 1-1 is an example of setting custom permissions on a single document in a document library.

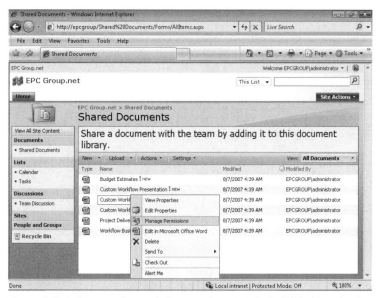

Figure 1-1 A document's permissions can be set at the individual item level.

Windows SharePoint Services 3.0 gives users the ability to attach a business process to an item to maintain control of the item during its entire life cycle throughout SharePoint. Workflows can be user initiated or automatically initiated based on an event within SharePoint such as an addition or change.

Users can also receive updates about lists and libraries with Really Simple Syndication (RSS) feeds. Users can receive periodic updates about selected lists and libraries—as well as other resources like news sites and blogs—in one central location like an RSS reader or feed aggregator.

With features such as item-level security, new digital rights management capabilities, improved Microsoft Office Outlook integration, and workflow support, Windows SharePoint Services 3.0 is positioned to deliver a powerful set of features and functionality to all who implement it within their organization or enterprise.

Sites and Workspaces

Team Sites have become the most popular and well-known application feature of Windows SharePoint Services. With the added functionality and robust site administration features included in the release of Windows SharePoint Services 3.0, these collaboration and meetings sites can now take care of the needs of most any organization. Within minutes, a new site can be created for an organization's department, project, or collaboration need. Figure 1-2 shows the home page of a new Team Site.

The Top Link bar represents the site's overall structure by default, but in WSS 3.0 it can be customized to meet the site's exact needs. The Quick Launch, which now resides on all pages by default, provides fast access to the most frequently used pages or subsites, and it can be easily customized out of the box to meet almost any navigational requirement. In a new Team Site, the Web Parts for Announcements, Calendar, Site Image, and Links display by default, but within minutes—and without extensive technical or programming knowledge of the product—an experienced SharePoint user can modify the page to meet the needs of the organization.

Figure 1-2 shows the standard Team Site template's navigation with the Top Link bar reflecting the site's overall structure at the top of the page and the Quick Launch providing fast access to lists, libraries, and other sites.

A great new feature of Windows SharePoint Services 3.0, which will be described in detail in later chapters, is the capability to quickly save a site as a template. After a SharePoint user has finished modifying and building-out a SharePoint site, the site and its content can be saved as a template. Anyone with the appropriate permissions can then create a new, identical site that matches the content, layout, and navigation of the template, a feature that is ideal for organizations needing to create multiple sites that are very similar in nature. This approach can save hours of manual work and effort.

Figure 1-3 shows the standard Team Site template's navigation after it was modified via Site Settings.

Chapter 1

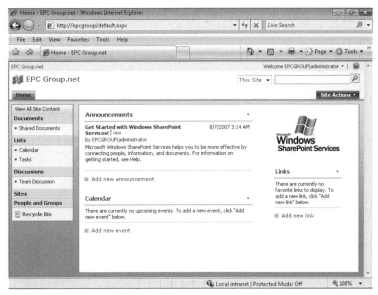

Figure 1-2 This is the default home page for a Team Site running on Windows SharePoint Services 3.0.

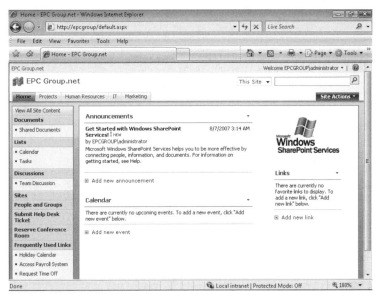

Figure 1-3 This is the default home page for a Team Site after the navigation was modified to meet the specific needs of the team. Links to other organizational sites were added on the Top Link bar, and the Quick Launch was updated with links that team members frequent.

Document, Form, Picture, and Wiki Libraries

Document libraries are the most popular feature in SharePoint for storing and editing content. There has been a vast improvement in list functionality in Windows SharePoint Services 3.0. By coupling this improved functionality with the improved integration features of Microsoft Office 2007, team members will be able to have a complete collaborative experience every time they access SharePoint.

A SharePoint site can contain any number of document, form, picture, and wiki libraries. With the popularity of sites like Wikipedia, users find that wikis provide a technology that is not only easy to use, but that also brings people together in an "open editing" format. Windows SharePoint Services 3.0 wiki libraries are a perfect addition to the powerful set of tools already available at our WSS 3.0 fingertips.

With the addition of content types and the integration with Microsoft Office 2007, document libraries enable organizations to abandon their existing file shares for SharePoint's robust and secure content management features. Document libraries give the user the ability to create a new document or upload one or more existing documents into the library. After a user chooses to create a new document, the computer will load the required Microsoft Office program and enable the user to begin creating or editing content.

> **Note**
>
> Users can take advantage of the Explorer view in a document library to drag and drop multiple files at once into a document library.

SharePoint administrators can block certain file types or set upload limits within sites and libraries.

For more information about file type exclusion and overall SharePoint governance, refer to the section titled "Site Governance and Best Practices" in Chapter 5, "Creating SharePoint Sites, Workspaces, and Pages," and to the section titled "Site Governance" in Chapter 12, "Managing Windows SharePoint Services 3.0 Site Content."

The Shared Documents page shown in Figure 1-4 is a typical listing of the default document library.

Form libraries allow for the storage of XML-based business forms like a new employee form or a sales purchase order, as shown in Figure 1-5. Microsoft InfoPath forms are easily managed using a form library.

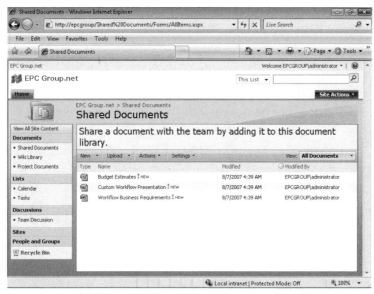

Figure 1-4 A SharePoint site can accommodate any number of libraries.

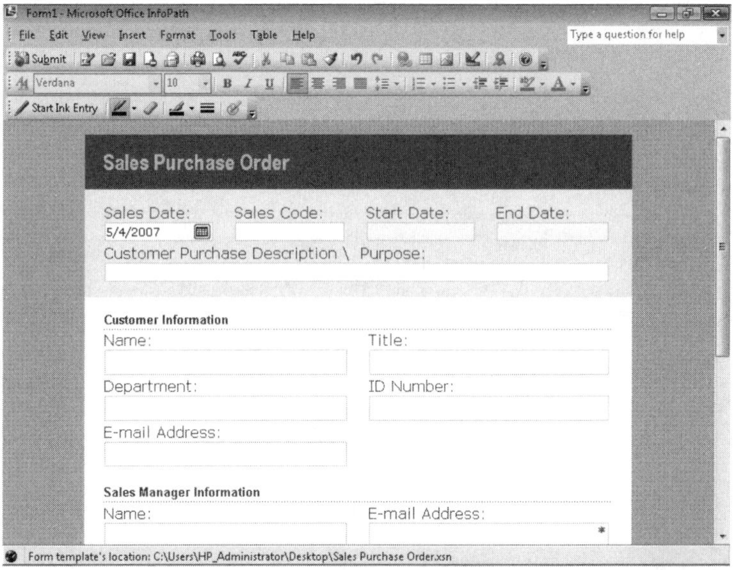

Figure 1-5 An example of an InfoPath form that was accessed from a form library.

Picture libraries enable users to store and share pictures, and they contain special functionality for managing and displaying pictures such as thumbnails and slide shows.

For more information about using picture libraries, refer to the section titled "Using Picture Libraries" in Chapter 3, "Using the Built-In Features of Windows SharePoint Services 3.0."

A wiki page library, as shown in Figure 1-6, enables users to view and manage an interconnected collection of wiki pages that supports tables, hyperlinks, pictures, and wiki linking. The wiki library has a built-in WYSIWYG (what you see is what you get) editor and is primarily a place where members of a virtual community can add or edit any wiki page at will. They can also interject or modify content without any security restrictions to allow for a more collaborative and open user experience. Figure 1-7 shows the version history page of a wiki page library after modifications were made to the library.

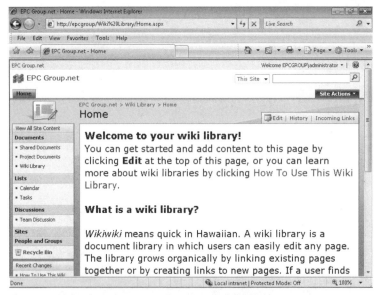

Figure 1-6 This view shows a newly created wiki page library.

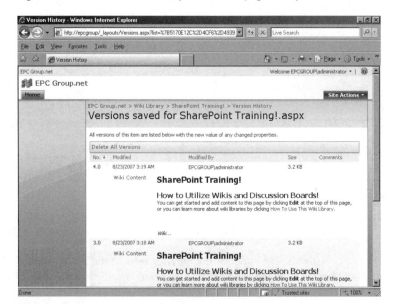

Figure 1-7 The version history page of a wiki library.

Web Parts, Web Part Pages, and Web Part Zones

SharePoint Web Parts are individual software modules that reside in containers on the page called Web Part zones. As mentioned previously, site templates contain a default set of Web Parts, but specific business needs will quickly require Web Parts and content to be added, moved, or deleted. Thankfully, SharePoint users in the organization are not all required to have development experience or extensive technical ability to use a SharePoint site. Windows SharePoint Services 3.0 offers a collection of Web Parts out of the box to allow for robust collaboration within your organization's sites without the need for custom development.

Figure 1-8 shows some of the Web Parts available to users in Windows SharePoint Services 3.0.

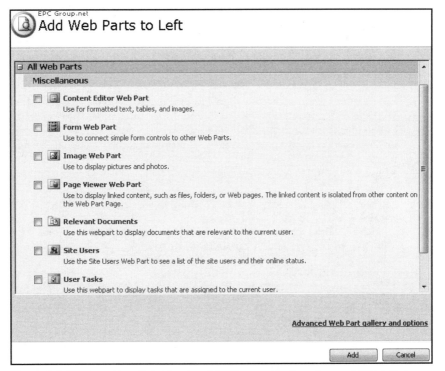

Figure 1-8 Windows SharePoint Services 3.0 offers a collection of powerful Web Parts.

Web Part pages, which can be identified by their .aspx file extension, are a special type of Web page that contains one or more Web Parts. Web Part pages consolidate data into a dynamic information portal that is built around a common interest or task. Web Part zones vary by the template that the user is viewing, and Windows SharePoint Services 3.0 allows for the creation of new Web Part pages with a variety of templates.

With the recent release of Microsoft Office SharePoint Designer 2007, it is easier than ever for experienced users to build powerful no-code solutions within SharePoint sites. With Windows SharePoint Services 2.0, users too often experienced compatibility issues on pages that were customized via Microsoft FrontPage 2003. The reason this issue occurred is as follows.

SharePoint pages, by default, are "ghosted," which means the layout template is stored on the SharePoint front-end Web server's file system. "Un-ghosted" pages are those where the layout and content are stored within the SQL database. A ghosted page will become un-ghosted once the page or its properties have been modified by a program such as FrontPage 2003, which can cause not only performance issues but also upgradability issues to Windows SharePoint Services 3.0.

Office SharePoint Designer 2007 and ASP.NET 2.0 have made significant progress in resolving this type of issue, but it is still important to follow a set of SharePoint development best practices when editing or modifying SharePoint pages within your environment.

For more information about customizing Web Part pages and custom Web Parts, refer to the section titled "Creating Custom Templates" in Chapter 9, "Creating and Modifying Basic Site Features in WSS 3.0," and to the section titled "Creating a Web Part" in Chapter 19, "Beginning Web Part Development."

A site administrator or site designer can easily customize a site by adding specific Web Parts, document libraries, and lists to the site to meet the exact requirements of the organization. Multiple Web Parts can be stacked into the available zones, but it is important to keep in mind the usability issues that may arise when users are forced to scroll down or across a page to view content. In Figure 1-9, a site administrator has added four Web Parts onto the page.

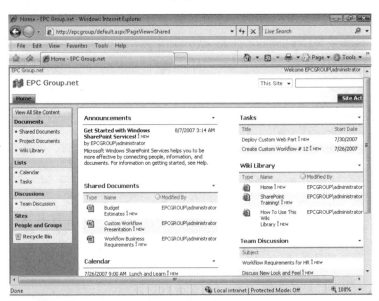

Figure 1-9 The site administrator has added multiple Web Parts to the page to meet the requirements of a specific department.

For more information about Web Parts and customizing sites, refer to the section titled "Creating and Configuring Basic and Web Part Pages" in Chapter 5, and to the section titled "Using Built-In Web Parts" in Chapter 18, "Advanced Design Techniques."

Reviewing Key Scenarios

The following sections detail some possible scenarios in which you might use Windows SharePoint Services 3.0. These are abbreviated introductions provided to illustrate how this new technology can assist you and your organization in meeting your collaboration, knowledge management, intranet, content management, and business process needs.

Sharing Information

Windows SharePoint Services 3.0 document libraries now have the capability to offer robust Web-based content management functionality to enable you to replace your existing file-sharing solution. For example, WSS 3.0 document libraries can:

- Provide item-level security on all of your documents.

- Use SharePoint's built-in workflow capabilities to attach a business process to a document.

- Provide robust version control for your documents and content.

- Offer departments and project teams a way to organize their documents in Web-based, easily accessible systems.

- Offer check-in and check-out capabilities so that multiple users can make simultaneous changes while also retaining comments from each user as to the changes that were made.

- Alert capabilities on documents to notify users when changes, updates, additions, or deletions occur.

- Display flexible, customizable views of each document library's contents.

- Provide content approval functionality for managing major and minor versions of documents.

SharePoint sites can use a calendar list to store important dates so that site users can keep up to date on important events and receive alerts when new information is added to the list. A contact list can be added to a site to centrally track team members, subject matter experts, customers, or other important contact data in an easily viewed and accessible manner.

A links list Web Part can be added to enable users to add links to other important SharePoint sites, external Web sites, or any other URLs that may be relevant to the team. Discussion boards can be very useful to site members when they store best practices and lessons learned, or they pose a question to other members who may have input on the topic posted.

SharePoint has now all but rendered obsolete the old method of dumping multiple files into a file share. The robust search features of SharePoint enable users to perform searches for documents as well as the document's related content type or metadata. By utilizing Adobe's PDF iFilter, users can also search against PDF documents stored within SharePoint document libraries.

SharePoint sites are easy to use "one stop shops" for securely storing and accessing your content, providing information to other users, and accessing existing knowledge that your organization already owns but may not be fully exploiting because the current tools do not allow for internal sharing of the information.

Collaborating Within Teams

Windows SharePoint Services 3.0 libraries provide functionality to enable team members to set alerts on documents so that they can be notified of any changes. Figure 1-10, for example, shows a default document library named Project Documents, and a team member has selected the file Project Scope.docx and clicked the drop-down arrow. (The file name is a Microsoft Office Word document, as can be seen from its Microsoft Word icon.)

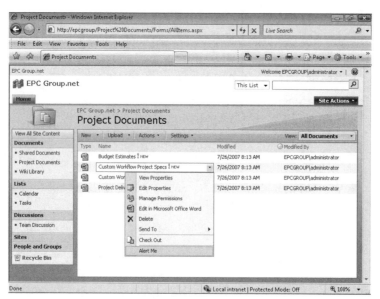

Figure 1-10 A user can select the name of the file and click the drop-down arrow to view the available functions.

Here are the functions of each command in this drop-down list.

- **View Properties** Displays a Web page that shows all available descriptive data for the document, as well as other available options: Edit Item, Delete Item, Manage Permissions, Manage Copies, Check Out, Alert Me, or Approve/reject Item. This page also shows the date/time stamp for Created and Last Modified as well as the associated user.

- **Edit Properties** Displays a Web page where you can modify the descriptive data for the current document as well as choose an option to delete the item. This page also shows the date/time stamp for Created and Last Modified as well as the associated user.

- **Manage Permissions** Displays a Web page where you can manage the permissions for the document. The page description describes the inheritance status for the document. You can choose to Manage Permissions of Parent or Edit Permission. If Edit Permissions is selected, the permission inheritance will be broken and you will be able to create unique permissions for this object.

- **Edit In (Appropriate Office Application)** Starts the appropriate Microsoft Office application and tells it to open the current document. The default application for which the document would be opened would change based on the document type. For a document with a file name extension of .docx, the option would read Edit In Microsoft Office Word.

- **Delete** This option removes the current document from the library.

- **Send To** Enables users to send a document to other locations or perform some additional actions. The Send To options are as follows: Other Locations, E-Mail A Link, Create A Document Workspace, and Download A Copy.

- **Approve/Reject** When this content approval setting is applied to a library, a file that has been changed remains in a pending state until it is approved or rejected by someone who has permission to approve it. If the file is approved, it is assigned an Approved status in the library, and it is displayed to anyone with permission to view the library.

- **Check Out** Locks the library copy of the document so that no one except the user who checked it out can update it. Once the check-out is in effect, a check-in command appears in this position.

- **Version History** If Document Version History is enabled within the library, this option displays a clickable listing of all versions that are currently available. This listing includes the version number, last modified date, the person responsible, the file size, and the Approval Status as well as any related comments. From this page, you can delete all versions, delete draft versions, or restore previous versions.

- **Alert Me** Displays a page where you can choose the users who will receive e-mail alerts and how frequently they will receive them whenever certain selected aspects of a document change.

One new exciting capability of Windows SharePoint Services 3.0 is found in the Alert function. It still enables you to set alerts for yourself, but with the new Alert capabilities, you can specify other users or e-mail addresses that will also receive the alerts, as shown in Figure 1-11.

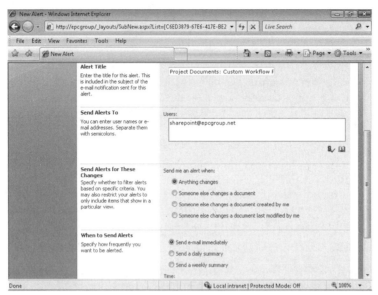

Figure 1-11 The New Alert page opened by selecting Alert Me from the drop-down menu, showing the different alert options available.

A user can create a new document workspace around any document in a document library. The user simply needs to highlight the document, select Send To from the drop-down list, and then click Create Document Workspace, as shown in Figure 1-12. A new document workspace is created for storing the primary document and its support files, as shown in Figure 1-13.

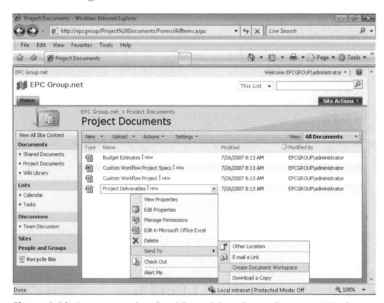

Figure 1-12 A user can select Send To and then Create Document Workspace.

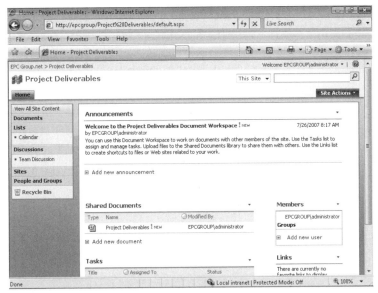

Figure 1-13 A new Document Workspace was created via the Send To option in the drop-down list.

Integrating with Microsoft Office 2007

Windows SharePoint Services 3.0 integrates with Microsoft Office 2007 via Web Services and application interfaces that enable users to directly interact with information stored in SharePoint sites. (See Table 1-2.) There is no need to manually download content because users can open and edit documents directly from SharePoint sites. Users running Windows Vista can save documents directly from Office 2007 via a Windows Vista mapped network location.

Table 1-2 Integration of Office 2007 Applications and Windows SharePoint Services 3.0

Office 2007 Application	Windows SharePoint Services 3.0 Integration
Word 2007	Users can edit a Word document directly from a SharePoint document library.
Excel 2007	Users can edit an Excel document directly from a SharePoint document library.
Outlook 2007	Users can view contact lists and calendars stored on Windows SharePoint Services sites, as well as create and manage sites for editing documents and organizing meetings.
PowerPoint 2007	Users can edit a PowerPoint document directly from a SharePoint document library.

Table 1-2 **Integration of Office 2007 Applications and Windows SharePoint Services 3.0**

Office 2007 Application	Windows SharePoint Services 3.0 Integration
Access 2007	Users have the ability to easily track and report information with drastically improved design capabilities in Access 2007 without having extensive database design experience. This data can be stored in Windows SharePoint Services 3.0 lists and made easily accessible and auditable.
InfoPath 2007	Users have the ability to create powerful and dynamic forms and make them readily available to the organization via the form libraries in Windows SharePoint Services 3.0.
Groove 2007	Users can synchronize to a Windows SharePoint Services 3.0 document library. The users can collaborate on the files in Groove and then publish back to SharePoint when the files are finalized.
SharePoint Designer 2007	Users can use the powerful tools of SharePoint Designer to deliver compelling and attractive SharePoint sites and quickly build workflow-enabled applications and reporting tools on the SharePoint platform, all in a managed environment.
OneNote 2007	Users can set up shared notebooks in which team members can view, add, and edit information. Notebooks can be stored in a shared document library where multiple users can simultaneously access shared notes and contribute to them on an ongoing basis.

Saving Documents Directly from Microsoft Office 2007 to SharePoint

With Windows Vista, users can save documents directly from Microsoft Office 2007 into SharePoint document libraries. Figure 1-14 shows a user mapping a network location directory to a SharePoint document library. Figure 1-15 shows a user performing a Save As command in Word directly to a mapped network location of a SharePoint document library.

Populating Additional Metadata Within a Microsoft Office 2007 Application

If a user is saving a document directly from a Microsoft Office 2007 application into a SharePoint document library, the user may be prompted to go to the Document Information Panel, as shown in Figure 1-16, to fill in additional metadata or content type information about the document, as shown in Figure 1-17, especially if the document library has required properties.

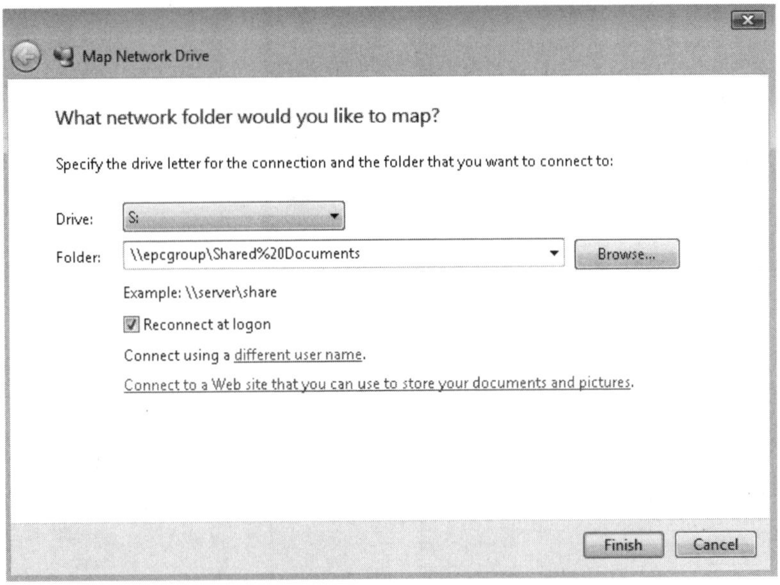

Chapter 1

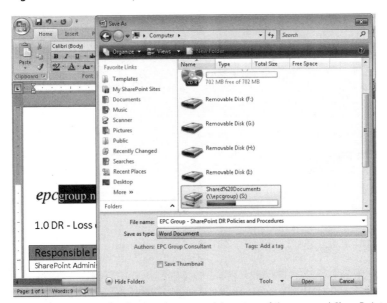

Figure 1-14 How to set up a network location to a SharePoint document library.

Figure 1-15 In Word, selecting the network location of the mapped SharePoint document library after having clicked File, Save As.

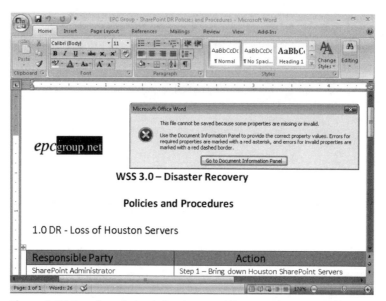

Figure 1-16 How Save As loads the document library and prompts with an error message because some of the required fields are missing.

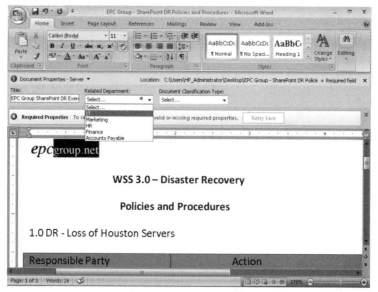

Figure 1-17 The document information panel in Word is requesting additional information about the document. You must also populate all required properties, which will be reflected by the Required Field flag.

Viewing and Editing Datasheets

Users who have a Windows SharePoint Services–compatible database program installed on their computer will have the option to view or edit a list item in a datasheet view. The data is opened in an Excel spreadsheet–style editor that supports such commands as add row, copy, paste, and file-down. Edit In Datasheet is extremely popular with SharePoint users and allows for quick and powerful editing. It also provides rich options for filtering and sorting. Figure 1-18 shows the Edit In Datasheet option in use.

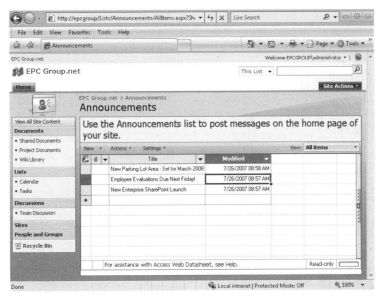

Figure 1-18 The Edit In Datasheet view allows for an editable spreadsheet format that is convenient for bulk editing and quick customization.

Creating a SharePoint List by Importing an Excel Spreadsheet

With Windows SharePoint Services 3.0, users can create a new custom list by importing an existing Excel spreadsheet directly into SharePoint. Figure 1-19 shows how to create a custom list based on an existing Excel spreadsheet.

Editing Pictures in a Picture Library

Users can view and edit the contents of a picture by selecting Edit from the Actions menu within a SharePoint picture library. After clicking Edit, Microsoft Office Picture Manager will load and enable the user to edit the currently selected picture. This application can receive bulk downloads from a SharePoint picture library, transmit bulk uploads to a picture library, and perform global editing such as resizing, rotation, and color correction. Figure 1-20 shows a typical view of this application.

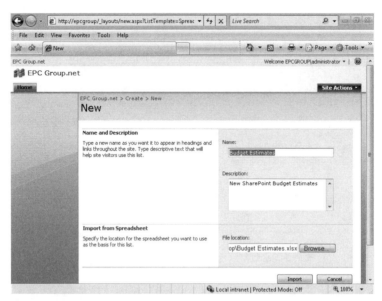

Figure 1-19 A user can simply import an existing Excel spreadsheet into SharePoint to create a custom list.

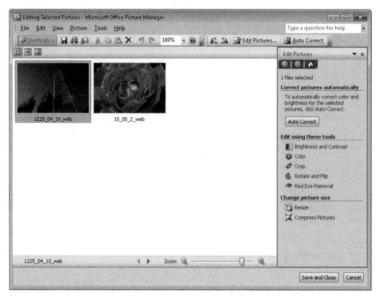

Figure 1-20 Microsoft Office Picture Manager can perform simple editing, bulk uploads, and bulk downloads on files in a SharePoint picture library.

A New Way to Share Attachments

E-mail has become a way of life for many, and the way we currently share attachments within our personal e-mail accounts does not always force us to think about the storage needs and traffic caused by these files. Within an organization, a user may send an e-mail out to 10 other employees with one attachment. One of the 10 employees who received the attachment decides to forward it on to 3 more employees who could also use the information. This situation can quickly lead to many individual copies of a file being stored in many separate locations. With all of these employees having a separate copy of the file, it can be hard to track which users may have viewed the file and forwarded it to others and what changes they have made to the file.

Windows SharePoint Services 3.0 enables users to store a file in a document library and then send a link to that file to other employees without having to actually attach the file to the e-mail. The document is stored in one central location, and the document's security can be easily managed within the document library. Version control keeps track of changes and updates.

Managing e-mail attachments in this manner can lower storage requirements within an organization as well as improve an organization's content management strategy. Figure 1-21 shows a user sending an e-mail to members of his team with a URL to an attachment in the body of the e-mail.

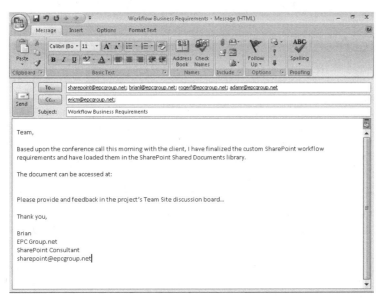

Figure 1-21 An Outlook e-mail with a URL to an attachment in the body of the e-mail.

Microsoft Project Server 2007 and Windows SharePoint Services 3.0 Integration

Project Server 2007's Project Web Access is built on Windows SharePoint Services 3.0 and the .NET Framework 2.0. This integration enables project team members to store project-related documents, track project issues and risks, and utilize workflow on specific project items. More than ever, organizations have the ability to customize Project Web Access because it is built on Windows SharePoint Services 3.0, which exposes all functions as Web Services. This also means organizations can take advantage of new features in WSS 3.0 such as item-level security, customizable navigation areas, and out-of-the-box workflow. With InfoPath 2007 integrated into a forms library, organizations can easily create an object like a project initiation form while using workflow to route the form's progress.

> **Note**
> You can add Project Server Web Parts to other Windows SharePoint Services 3.0 sites if they all reside within the same server farm as Project Server 2007. This does not require any additional site provisioning to the SharePoint sites.

Using Additional Development Tools

Windows SharePoint Services 3.0 is an amazingly powerful platform for the design of highly scalable Web sites that can meet your organization's needs, whether for an intranet or extranet solution. Using the SharePoint architecture model, a developer can save a tremendous amount of time and effort. Developing applications within the SharePoint framework gives the developer an enormous head start versus starting from scratch. The topics in this section introduce SharePoint Designer and provide an overview of custom SharePoint development in Microsoft Visual Studio 2005.

Customizing SharePoint Sites and Creating Custom Workflow

SharePoint Designer enables SharePoint users, with the appropriate permission levels, to create powerful collaborative sites without having to write code or be skilled in a development language.

Users now have the ability to create the custom reporting that SharePoint has been lacking over the past few years. They can also create powerful workflow within their site or application to automate business processes and simplify day-to-day tasks in their organization. To strengthen governance and standardization throughout the enterprise,

SharePoint Designer 2007 also enables control of the permissions that specify who can create or edit the organization's SharePoint branding.

> **Note**
>
> Microsoft offers a free RSS feed for SharePoint Designer 2007 to help you stay current on the latest tips, tricks, and how-to articles. The feed can be accessed along with other useful items at *http://www.office.microsoft.com/en-us/sharepointdesigner/ FX100487631033.aspx*.

The Workflow Designer

Many organizations have been attempting to implement workflows within their organizations, and many have failed. The Workflow Designer within SharePoint Designer enables your workflows to be as simple or complex as needed based on your business needs. The workflow can control almost any list item within Windows Share-Point Services 3.0 at any point in its life cycle by any workflow participants. Actions and conditions can be applied to certain steps within the workflow, which can be manually or automatically initiated based on a set of available events.

When you use Workflow Designer, you first determine the internal criteria of the work-flow and then use the tool to generate the necessary forms for the workflow initiation or possible related task. Once that is in place, you can use the tool to further customize the forms to meet your exact business requirements.

> **Note**
>
> Current FrontPage 2003 users who do not use SharePoint can use Microsoft Expression to design their non-SharePoint sites.

Figure 1-22 shows the Workflow Designer in SharePoint Designer initiating the process to design a custom workflow. Figure 1-23 shows the Workflow Designer prompting you to define a new step for the workflow and to define the conditions and actions that further define the new step.

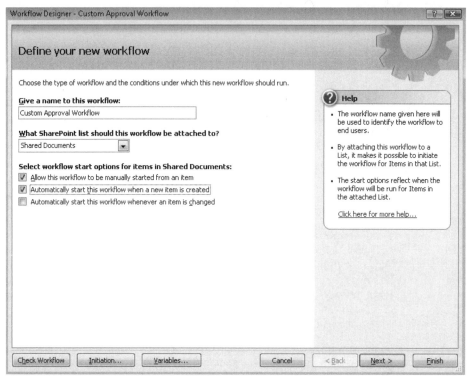

Figure 1-22 SharePoint Designer is initiating the process of designing a new custom workflow.

SharePoint Site Customization

SharePoint Designer allows for the creation of ASP.NET master pages that lay the groundwork for the overall look and feel of a SharePoint site. Master pages enable you to define standard page layouts for an entire site with common headers and footers, controls, menus, and banners. These ASP.NET master pages also allow for designer support in Visual Studio, which enables you to further take advantage of ASP.NET 2.0 user controls (ASCX controls) and Web server controls. Master pages enable users to position items shared by all pages such as copyright footers and approved company logos. With master pages, you can build-out a SharePoint site that contains multiple subsites in a matter of minutes, thus increasing productivity while maintaining design consistency and governance.

SharePoint Designer contains a WYSIWYG (what you see is what you get) editor that enables users to graphically view the page in real time as it is designed to properly position items such as tables, cells, and images. SharePoint Designer also contains powerful cascading style sheet (CSS) tools for managing style sheets, further promoting design consistency and enterprise governance.

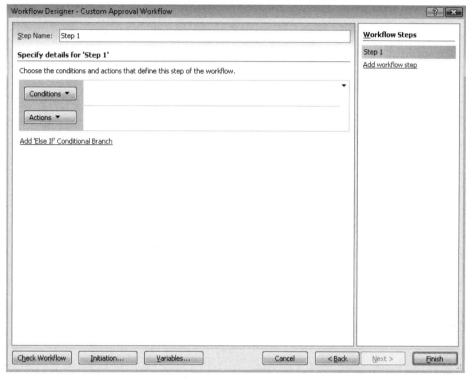

Figure 1-23 SharePoint Designer allows a user to create steps for the workflow and apply custom conditions and actions that further define each step of the workflow.

> **Note**
>
> The SharePoint Designer workflow functionality is built on the Microsoft Windows Workflow Foundation, which is a component of Microsoft Windows. It is important to note the same version of Workflow Foundation will need to be installed on both your computer and the server. You may be prompted to install Workflow Foundation the first time you create a workflow.

Developing Web Parts in Visual Studio

Windows SharePoint Services 3.0 along with SharePoint Designer gives organizations exceptional control over creating, modifying, and customizing SharePoint sites. Users can quickly create master pages, templates, and site layouts in a manner that can be controlled based on a user's current permission level.

There are many cases in which this degree of customization does not fulfill an organization's business requirements; more robust, in-depth development is required. Third-party Web Parts are available, but in many cases, a tailored solution must be developed. This is where Visual Studio comes into play to offer organizations a way to develop a solution to meet their exact needs. Visual Studio offers a platform to create items such as custom Web Parts, advanced SharePoint workflows, and many other specific solutions for any type of organization.

Microsoft offers assistance to developers of custom SharePoint solutions with items such as the Software Development Kit (SDK) for Windows SharePoint Services 3.0 and Visual Studio Extensions.

The Windows SharePoint Services 3.0 SDK contains information concerning the following technologies:

- **Web Part Framework** Create, package, and deploy Web Parts on SharePoint sites.

- **Server-Side Object Model** Work with individual lists and sites or manage an entire Windows SharePoint Services deployment.

- **Web Services** Use default Web Services or create custom Web Services to interact with Windows SharePoint Services from external applications.

- **Collaborative Application Markup Language (CAML)** Customize the schemas that define lists and sites, define queries for use with members of the object model or Web service, and specify parameters for use with methods in the Remote Procedure Call (RPC) protocol.

- **Master Pages** Specify all the shared elements of your site in the master page or pages and add content-page–specific elements to content pages.

- **Workflows** Create workflows that encapsulate business processes to be performed on items in Windows SharePoint Services and attach those workflows to specific items.

- **Custom Field Types** Create custom field types that conform to your business data. These custom field types can build on the base field types already included in Windows SharePoint Services and can include custom data validation, field rendering, and field property rendering and processing.

- **Information Rights Management (IRM)** Specify IRM for files located in document libraries and stored as attachments to list items. Create IRM protectors for your own custom file types.

- **Document Property Promotion and Demotion** Use the built-in XML parser to synchronize the document properties and list column data for XML documents. Create document parsers to do the same for your custom file types.

- **Search** Use the new Query object model and Query Web service to retrieve search results. Search in Windows SharePoint Services now shares the same SharePoint search technology used by SharePoint Server.

- **Workflow Developer Starter Kit** Assists solution providers and developers in writing custom workflows for Windows SharePoint Services 3.0 and contains Visual Studio project templates and sample custom workflow.

The various releases of Visual Studio Extensions for Windows SharePoint Services 3.0 contain the following tools to aid developers in building SharePoint applications:

- **Visual Studio Project Templates** For Web Parts, team site definitions, blank site definition, and list definitions.

- **Visual Studio Item Templates** For Web Parts, custom fields, list definitions, content types, and modules.

- **SharePoint Solution Generator** A stand-alone program that generates a Site Definition project from an existing SharePoint site. The Solution Generator enables developers to use the browser and SharePoint Designer to customize the content of their sites before creating code by using Visual Studio.

Customizing Site Actions and Settings

Windows SharePoint Services 3.0 allows for granular control over site permissions, appearance, design, content, and site administration for each and every SharePoint site.

> **Note**
> Available site settings may vary depending on a user's permission level.

To begin working with these settings, click the Site Actions link at the upper right of any page and then click Site Settings. This displays the Site Settings page, shown in Figure 1-24.

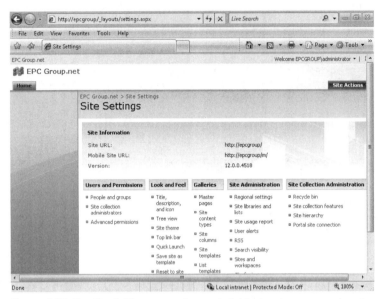

Figure 1-24 The Site Settings page allows administrators to manage almost every aspect of a SharePoint site.

Within Site Settings, there are several different categories of links divided into separate columns (see Figure 1-24). The options are described in the following list:

Users And Permissions:

- **People And Groups** Displays a list of current team members and provides links for adding, removing, or configuring users. This option enables site owners to control which users or groups of users have access to the SharePoint site.

- **Site Collection Administrators** Displays a list of site collection administrators who are given full control over all Web sites in the site collection. They may also receive site use confirmation mail.

- **Advanced Permissions** Displays a page to assign permission levels to users and groups as well as to create custom permission levels.

Look And Feel:

- **Title, Description, And Icon** Displays a page that enables site administrators to type in a title and description for the Web site. The title is displayed on each page in the site, and the description is displayed on the home page. The logo URL and description field enable administrators to associate a logo with the site and an optional image description.

- **Tree View** This page manages the site's left navigation panel. This gives administrators the options of enabling the Quick Launch and Tree View. Quick Launch displays site content in a logical manner, and Tree View displays site content in a physical manner.

- **Site Theme** Displays a page giving the administrator the ability to change the fonts and color scheme for the site. Applying a theme does not affect your site's layout and will not change any pages that have been individually themed.

- **Top Link Bar** Use this page to specify the links that appear in the site's Top Link bar. The Top Link bar can contain the overall hierarchy of the site, its subsites, or the overall SharePoint environment.

- **Quick Launch** Use this page to change the links and headings in the Quick Launch menu. Quick Launch can contain a list of libraries, discussion boards, and surveys as well as links to other SharePoint sites or external Internet sites.

- **Save Site As Template** Use this page to save your Web site as a site template. Users can create new Web sites from this template, which can save a tremendous amount of time and effort. The content of the site can also be saved within a new site template.

- **Reset To Site Definition** This page can be used to remove all customizations from a page (such as changes to Web Part zones or text added to the page). This feature can be used to reset to the version of the page included with the site definition.

Galleries:

- **Master Pages** Displays the master page gallery and gives administrators options to perform additional tasks such as storing new master pages. The master pages displayed on this page or gallery are available to this site and any sites underneath it.

> **Note**
> By default, SharePoint Server creates a master page gallery for every site. You can only create new pages with the page layouts stored in the master page gallery of the top-level site in the site collection.

- **Site Content Types** This page is used to create and manage content types. Content types visible on this page are available for use on this site and its subsites.

- **Site Columns** This page is used to manage columns on this site and all child sites.

- **Site Templates** Displays the templates available for use in this Web site. The templates in this gallery are available to this site and all sites under it. Default site templates are not shown.

- **List Templates** Displays the gallery containing the available list templates. List templates can be made available to sites by adding them to this gallery. The templates in this gallery are available to this site and all sites under it. Default list templates are not shown.

- **Web Parts** Displays the Web Part gallery and is used to store, retrieve, and preview Web Parts. The Web Parts in this gallery are available to this site and all sites under it.

- **Workflows** Displays workflows in the current site collection.

Site Administration:

- **Regional Settings** Displays regional settings such as locale, time zone, calendar settings, your organization's workweek, and the time format.

- **Site Libraries and Lists** Displays the option to customize lists such as announcements, calendar, links, shared documents, tasks, and team discussions.

- **Site Usage Report** Displays a page to view a detailed usage report for the Web site.

- **User Alerts** Displays a page to manage alerts for users.

- **RSS** Displays a page to enable or disable RSS feeds for the site collection.

- **Search Visibility** Displays a page that contains options to manage a site's search visibility.

- **Sites And Workspaces** Displays a page that shows the user the sites to which they have access below the current Web site. The user can also create a new site or click an existing site to view its contents.

- **Site Features** Displays a site's features as well as its activation status.

- **Delete This Site** Displays an option to delete the current site.

Site Collection Administration:

- **Recycle Bin** Displays a page that enables users to restore items that they have deleted from the current site. The page also gives the users the option to empty the deleted items that currently reside in the recycle bin.

- **Site Collection Features** Displays a site's collections features as well as their activation status.

- **Site Hierarchy** Displays a page showing all Web sites that have been created under the current URL.

- **Portal Site Connection** Displays a page that enables a user to specify whether the site should connect to a portal site.

> **Note**
>
> A site collection is a set of Web sites on a virtual server that shares the same owner and site administration settings. A site collection contains top-level Web sites with one or more subsites.

Windows SharePoint Services 3.0 Central Administration

When you install Windows SharePoint Services 3.0 on a computer, the setup program creates the SharePoint 3.0 Central Administration site that manages SharePoint settings for all of the virtual servers and site collections on the same server. This section introduces the functions available on this administrative server.

SharePoint Services 3.0 Central Administration controls every aspect of the Windows SharePoint Services server and can also affect other related servers and their SharePoint functionality. The Central Administration page shown in Figure 1-25 is the home page for SharePoint Services 3.0 Central Administration.

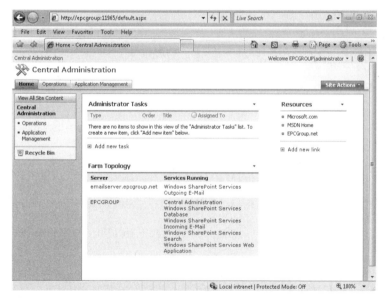

Figure 1-25 Server administrators use this page to manage the most global settings for a SharePoint installation.

There are two primary pages within the Central Administration: the Operations page and the Application Management page.

The Operations page contains links to pages that will assist you in managing your server or server farm. The Operations page is divided into six sections, which are described in detail in the following lists. It is shown in Figure 1-26.

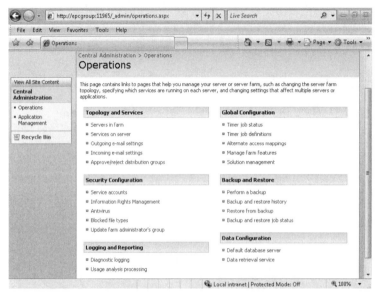

Figure 1-26 The Operations page in Central Administration.

Topology And Services:

- **Servers In Farm** Displays farm information such as the configuration database server, the configuration database name, and the version, as well as other relevant farm information.

- **Services On Server** Displays a list of services on the selected server as well as their status.

- **Outgoing E-Mail Settings** Displays a page from which you can configure e-mail settings for outgoing e-mail such as the outbound Simple Mail Transfer Protocol (SMTP) server, the From address, the Reply To address, and the character set.

- **Incoming E-Mail Settings** Displays a page from which you can enable or disable incoming e-mail, specify e-mail options, and configure the Microsoft SharePoint Directory Management Web Service.

- **Approve/Reject Distribution Groups** Displays a page from which you can configure the Directory Management Service Approval List.

Security Configuration:

- **Service Accounts** Displays a page from which you can manage the service accounts in the farm.

- **Information Rights Management** Displays a page from which you can specify the location of the Windows Rights Management Services (RMS).

- **Antivirus** Displays a page from which you can configure settings for virus scanning.

- **Blocked File Types** Displays a page from which you can disallow specific file types from being saved or retrieved from any site on this server.

- **Update Farm Administrator's Group** Displays a page from which you can specify farm administrators.

Logging And Reporting:

- **Diagnostic Logging** Displays a page from which you can configure error reports, event throttling, trace logging, and the option to sign up for the Customer Experience Improvement Program.

- **Usage Analysis Processing** Displays a page from which you can enable and configure usage analysis processing.

Global Configuration:

- **Timer Job Status** Displays a page showing timer job status.

- **Timer Job Definitions** Displays a page showing timer job definitions.

- **Alternate Access Mappings** Displays a page from which you can configure alternate access mappings.

> Note
>
> Each Web application within Windows SharePoint Services 3.0 can be associated with a collection of mappings between internal and public URLs.

- **Manage Farm Features** Displays a page from which you can manage SharePoint-wide features throughout the farm.

- **Solution Management** Displays a page with a list of the solutions in the farm.

Backup And Restore:

- **Perform A Backup** Displays a page that enables you to configure and perform backups.

- **Backup And Restore History** Displays a page that enables you to manage the history logs for backup and restore operations.

- **Restore From Backup** Displays a page to enable you to restore from an existing backup.

- **Backup And Restore Job Status** Opens a page to display the status of a backup or restore job.

Data Configuration:

- **Default Database Server** Displays a page from which you can set the default content database server.

- **Data Retrieval Service** Displays a page from which you can configure settings for data retrieval services.

The Application Management page contains links to pages that will help you configure settings for applications and the components that are installed on your server or within your server farm. The page is divided into five sections, which are described in detail in the following sections. It is shown in Figure 1-27.

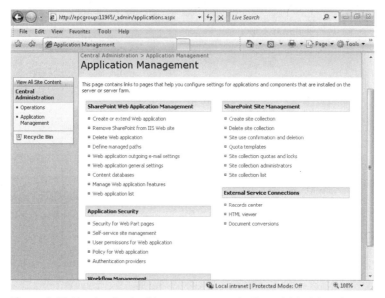

Figure 1-27 The Application Management page in Central Administration.

SharePoint Web Application Management:

- **Create Or Extend Web Application** Displays a page from which you can create a new Windows SharePoint Services application or extend an existing application to another IIS Web site.

- **Remove SharePoint From IIS Web Site** Displays a page from which you can remove Windows SharePoint Services from an IIS Web site.

- **Delete Web Application** Displays a page from which you can delete an entire Windows SharePoint Services application, including all of its content and settings.

- **Define Managed Paths** Displays a page from which you can specify which paths in the URL namespaces are managed by Windows SharePoint Services.

- **Web Application Outgoing E-Mail Settings** Displays a page from which you can configure the e-mail settings for this Web application.

- **Web Application General Settings** Displays a page from which you can configure settings applying to all Web applications.

- **Content Databases** Displays a page from which you can manage content databases for this Web application.

- **Manage Web Application Features** Displays a page from which you can manage Web application features.

- **Web Application List** Displays a page that shows a list of Web applications.

Application Security:

- **Security For Web Part Pages** Displays a page from which you can administer Web Part pages on your Web application.

- **Self-Service Site Management** Displays a page from which you can enable or disable Self-Service Site Creation.

- **User Permissions For Web Application** Displays a page from which you can configure the user permissions for a Web application.

- **Policy For Web Application** Displays a page from which you can configure policies for Web applications.

- **Authentication Providers** Displays a page from which you can configure authentication providers.

Workflow Management:

- **Workflow Settings** Displays a page that enables you to configure global workflow settings.

SharePoint Site Management:

- **Create Site Collection** Displays a page from which you can create a new top-level Web site.

- **Delete Site Collection** Displays a page from which you can completely delete a top-level site and any subsites of that site on this Web application.

- **Site Use Confirmation And Deletion** Displays a page from which you can require site owners to confirm that their Web site collections are in use. This page also allows for automatic deletion of unused Web site collections.

- **Quota Templates** Displays a page from which you can create or modify a quota template.

- **Site Collection Quotas And Locks** Displays a page from which you can change the quota template or individual quota values for a Web site collection. You can also clear a lock set by an application or caused by exceeding a quota.

- **Site Collection Administrators** Displays a page from which you can view and change the primary and secondary site collection administrators for a site collection. As site collection administrators, these users receive any quota or autodeletion notices and have full control over all content in the site collection.

- **Site Collection List** Displays a page with the list of site collections and their related information.

External Service Connections:

- **Records Center** Displays a page that enables you to connect to a Record Center by entering the URL and a display name for a Records Center server. Unless the Records Center is configured to enable records to be anonymously submitted, you must configure each Web application to use a domain user account.

- **HTML Viewer** Displays a page to view, change, and configure the HTML Viewer service.

- **Document Conversions** Displays a page that enables you to configure document conversions.

The Site Settings page is also available for Central Administration, as shown in Figure 1-28.

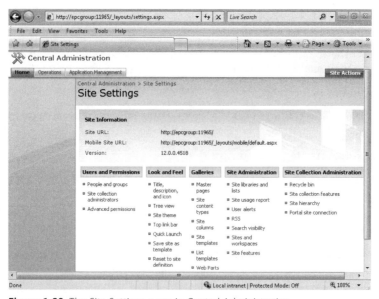

Figure 1-28 The Site Settings page in Central Administration.

The Windows SharePoint Services 3.0 Architecture

This section briefly introduces the internal structure of Windows SharePoint Services 3.0. The chapters in the later sections of this book will expand on this information.

Server Components

At the highest level, the design of Windows SharePoint Services 3.0 involves two components:

- **A front-end communication service (Web server)** This must be Internet Information Services 6.0 (IIS6) at a minimum. The front-end Web server receives and renders the requested information. If a server-farm topology exists, it is possible to load balance the front-end Web servers for performance, disaster recovery, or other related scenarios.

- **A back-end data store (SQL Server)** Database servers in a Windows SharePoint Services 3.0 environment store both environmental configuration settings and all content that exists within the SharePoint installation. It is possible for the database server to reside on the front-end Web server in a single-server installation environment. Database server clusters are also supported in Windows SharePoint Services 3.0.

> **Note**
>
> When a basic installation of Windows SharePoint Services 3.0 is performed, a Windows Internal Database is automatically installed by default, and options will be available concerning whether to perform additional database configuration actions.

> **Note**
>
> If SharePoint Server is installed within the server farm, the search and indexing services can be configured to run on a separate search server. Depending on the requirements, the search server can reside on a single server farm or across multiple server farms.

> **Note**
>
> It is possible for all server components to exist in a single server farm environment.

Chapter 1

Every SharePoint server makes use of at least two databases that serve very different purposes:

- A centralized configuration database to store configuration and site mapping information for your server, the virtual servers on the server, and the services within a server farm.

- A content database to serve as the file system for Web pages, pictures files, lists, tasks, contacts, events, document libraries, picture libraries, and all the other types of content that make up a SharePoint site.

As shown in Figure 1-29, the Content Databases page within Windows SharePoint Services 3.0 Central Administration allows for easy management of SharePoint content databases.

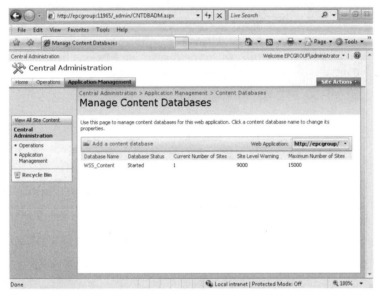

Figure 1-29 The Content Databases page within the Windows SharePoint Services 3.0 Central Administration allows for easy management of content databases.

With the improvements in Windows SharePoint Services 3.0 and its integration with IIS and SQL Server, the platform is extremely scalable. Whether your organization resides at one central location, or you have the need to scale between multiple cities within one country or globally across oceans and language barriers, Windows SharePoint Services 3.0 can be implemented within your organization in a scalable, distributed, and high-performing manner while still giving your organization proper disaster/business recovery and the service level agreements (SLAs) most enterprise applications require.

A great new feature of Windows SharePoint Services 3.0 is a centralized configuration and management model. This includes a centralized configuration database and two new services that automatically propagate and synchronize the centrally stored configuration settings across all of the servers within your server farm.

In Window SharePoint Services 2.0, farm settings had to be managed on a server-by-server basis. With Windows SharePoint Services 3.0, you can now centrally manage your server farm. If a new Web application is created on a Web server within your farm, the Web application is automatically propagated to all of the servers in the farm. Administrators no longer need to create and configure individual Web applications on each of your Web servers.

The two new services in the Windows SharePoint Services 3.0 central configuration model are the Windows SharePoint Services Administration service and the Windows SharePoint Services Timer service. The SharePoint Services Administration service works in conjunction with the Timer service, and it is responsible for making the actual configuration changes on each of the servers in your server farm. The SharePoint Services Timer service acts as the central nervous system for your server farm and is responsible for running timer jobs that propagate configuration settings across the farm.

With Windows SharePoint Services 3.0, a content database can scale to more than 50,000 site collections, although that would rarely happen. The content databases can scale to hundreds of gigabytes (GB), and the overall farm can handle several terabytes of content. However, it is important to consider disaster recovery performance when sizing your enterprise.

Windows SharePoint Services 3.0 Object Model

There have been significant enhancements in the Windows SharePoint Services 3.0 object model. The new features in WSS 3.0 have totally new namespaces while maintaining the Windows SharePoint Services 2.0 object model namespaces to ensure backward compatibility with existing code. Microsoft has gone to great lengths to enhance the 3.0 object model and to retain this backward compatibility, but it is important to note that old code may not function as expected in the new object model hierarchy.

A new namespace, *Microsoft.SharePoint.Administration.Backup*, provides members for backup and restore operations. The *Microsoft.SharePoint.Administration* namespace has been completely refurbished to allow for greater flexibility, whereas the new hierarchical object store provides a common framework so that all third-party applications can store and maneuver data. Windows SharePoint Services 3.0 has an extended events foundation that enables third-party applications to seamlessly implement or override WSS 3.0 events. WSS 3.0 also has powerful job services that enable administrators to set up timed jobs that execute during a certain time window or at specific intervals and can be distributed to work across several server farms.

SharePoint Web Services

Windows SharePoint Services 3.0 builds on existing Web services including services for copying files, portal search, authentication, and managing security. It also provides new methods for content type integration of Lists and Webs that allow for these methods to work directly with files in document libraries. The following are the available Web Services:

- **Administration** Provides methods for managing a deployment of Windows SharePoint Services, such as creating or deleting sites.

- **Alerts** Provides methods for working with alerts for list items in a SharePoint site.

- **Copy** Provides methods for copying items between locations.

- **Document Workspace** Provides methods for managing Document Workspace sites and the data they contain.

- **Forms** Provides methods for returning forms used in the user interface when working with the contents of a list.

- **Imaging** Provides methods that enable you to create and manage picture libraries.

- **List Data Retrieval** Provides a method for performing queries against lists in Windows SharePoint Services.

- **Lists** Provides methods for working with lists and list data.

- **Meetings** Provides methods that enable you to create and manage Meeting Workspace sites.

- **People** Provides methods for working with security groups.

- **Permissions** Provides methods for working with the permissions for a site or list.

- **SharePoint Directory Management Service** Provides methods for remotely managing distribution groups.

- **Site Data** Provides methods that return metadata or list data from sites or lists in Windows SharePoint Services.

- **Sites** Provides a method for returning information about the site templates for a site collection.

- **Search** Provides methods for remotely performing searches within a Windows SharePoint Services deployment.

- **Users And Groups** Provides methods for working with users, site groups, and cross-site groups.

- **Versions** Provides methods for working with file versions.

- **Views** Provides methods for working with views of lists.

- **Web Part Pages** Provides methods to send information to and retrieve information from Web services.

- **Webs** Provides methods for working with sites and subsites.

In Summary...

This chapter introduced Windows SharePoint Services 3.0 and the vast improvements that have been made since the release of Windows SharePoint Services 2.0 and SharePoint Portal Server (SPS) 2003.

Windows SharePoint Services 3.0 is a very powerful Web-based platform that will enable organizations to collaborate, store, and retrieve knowledge; build custom applications; and manage content—all on a scalable and secure platform.

The next chapter will introduce and explain the features of SharePoint Server, including enterprise-wide portal search, enhanced business process management and workflow, true enterprise record management, and several other powerful features that add to this already supercharged solution.

Introducing Microsoft Office SharePoint Server 2007

Microsoft Office SharePoint Server 2007 (MOSS) is an exciting new server application that organizations can use for enterprise content management, search, workflow, and collaboration. This application is part of the 2007 Microsoft Office system, and any features that are available in Microsoft Windows SharePoint Services 3.0 (WSS 3.0) are also available in SharePoint Server. However, SharePoint Server provides additional functionality and features that are perfect for large organizations that require a true content management platform. If your organization needs to connect with and search other business applications such as SAP, implement advanced business processes and workflow, and provide employees or users with their own personal Web page or My Site, SharePoint Server can provide all this functionality.

> **Note**
> When we refer to SharePoint Server in this book, we will always be discussing the Enterprise version.

Looking Back at SharePoint Portal Server 2003 and Windows SharePoint Services 2.0

Consultants who have implemented Windows SharePoint Services 2.0 (WSS 2.0) or SharePoint Portal Server 2003 (SPS 2003)—or users who have been intimately involved with its operation—will recognize that functionality which was lacking in previous SharePoint releases is now more than adequately supplied in WSS 3.0 and SharePoint Server.

The lack of SharePoint item–level security is a major issue in WSS 2.0 and prevents many organizations from using SharePoint as their content management platform. Questions concerning whether to use portal areas or team sites in SPS 2003 to store documents, the overall navigational limitations, the lack of workflow, and limited administrative functionality are all major issues in WSS 2.0 and SPS 2003.

Organizations that lack enforcement of enterprise SharePoint governance or standards, as well as those that make numerous customizations to sites via Microsoft FrontPage 2003, have caused major issues for many WSS 2.0 and SPS 2003 administrators.

Microsoft has addressed and resolved many of these issues and has added a treasure trove of new features and functionality with WSS 3.0 and SharePoint Server. Organizations of any size should strongly consider SharePoint for their Web-based collaboration and document management platform.

Benefits of Using SharePoint Server

SharePoint Server is a one-stop shop for an organization's collaborative needs. Users can access their My Site pages to manage and share information such as documents, links, tasks, and their Microsoft Office calendars in one central location. They can then navigate into any departmental or project site to search for information or documents within lists or document libraries. If they have a question that they think another SharePoint user in the organization can answer, they can post it on a discussion board for someone at any location to answer.

Consider a situation in which users need to find specific documents somewhere in the organization, but they are not sure where the files are stored or exactly which organization or department may own or store the documents. The search capabilities in SharePoint Server enable users to search for the files and get results in a matter of seconds. If users were to search for specific documents, they could again use the search feature in SharePoint Server to find the documents as well as go into the document library and view the documents' version histories to find out who has edited the documents or find out if the documents are in draft form or are major versions.

The content type functionality in SharePoint Server enables organizations to add metadata to documents, which can enhance the search feature in SharePoint Server and tie retention schedules to certain types of documents. Use of metadata assists an organization in better organizing its content and saving money on storage space, as well as lowering its legal liability by no longer storing data that it is no longer required to retain.

SharePoint Server allows for a true enterprise portal, which can also be used as an organization's intranet solution or Knowledge Management platform. Each department within the organization can have its own site, and SharePoint Server will allow for advanced searching of the documents stored within these department sites based on the security role of the user performing the search.

Organizations with offices all over the globe and multiple language requirements can use SharePoint language packs to provide content in a particular region's required language. The language packs enable site owners to create sites and related site collections in different languages so that content can be managed for each language across different sites. It is also possible for users to create a site or site collection based on a specific language's site template by choosing the language–locale combination when creating the site.

With proper infrastructure planning, SharePoint Server can scale globally to support hundreds of terabytes (yes, I said *terabytes*) of data, although disaster recovery times and service level agreement (SLA) requirements must always be taken into consideration. These topics will all be covered in detail throughout the rest of this book.

Though large organizations can use SharePoint Server to meet their collaboration needs, it is important to keep in mind that WSS 3.0 has functionality to handle the needs of most small- to medium-size organizations.

The offline capabilities of SharePoint Server enable users to use Microsoft Office Outlook 2007 to manage their work offline and then sync back with the server once they are back online. In later sections of this book, we will discuss powerful third-party tools that can help you use SharePoint Server offline.

As a consultant who has implemented SharePoint technologies in organizations both large and small throughout the United States, I am very excited about SharePoint Server and the features and functionality of WSS 3.0. The platform is enjoying growing popularity throughout the world.

It is rare for one platform to be able to serve organizations ranging in size from large manufacturing or oil and gas *Fortune* 500 companies to small organizations with 10 employees, but SharePoint is now that platform.

> **Note**
>
> The Office SharePoint Server Enterprise site collection features need to be activated before you can use features such as the Business Data Catalog, forms services, and Excel Services.

Reviewing SharePoint Server

This section will review the key features of SharePoint Server in detail. This chapter assumes that you already have SharePoint Server installed and running. You can find a link to installation instructions for SharePoint Server on the companion CD.

A quick-start guide appears within the Central Administration administrator tasks after the initial installation. This quick-start guide is helpful and covers:

- How to deploy SharePoint Server on a single server
- How to deploy SharePoint Server in a server farm environment
- More information about SharePoint Server deployments

Figure 2-1 shows the SharePoint 3.0 Central Administration page right after the initial installation, and Figure 2-2 shows the home page of a SharePoint site after the initial installation.

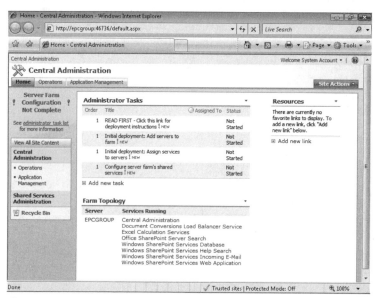

Figure 2-1 The Central Administration page of a newly installed SharePoint Server site.

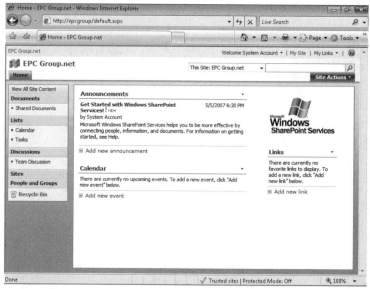

Figure 2-2 The home page of a newly installed SharePoint Server site.

My Site pages, shown in Figure 2-3, are personal sites that are available to users throughout the organization. Figure 2-4 shows the Site Settings page for an out-of-the-box SharePoint Server site.

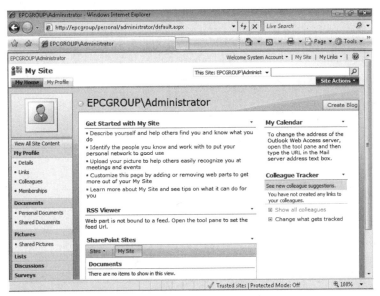

Figure 2-3 The My Home page of the out-of-the-box My Site.

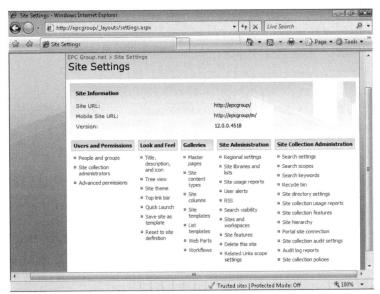

Figure 2-4 The Site Settings page for SharePoint Server, which is similar to the Site Settings page of WSS 3.0.

SharePoint Server Web Parts

SharePoint Server offers a number of powerful Web Parts that cover areas such as document management, collaboration, Office Outlook 2007 integration, and search. The categories of SharePoint Server Web Parts are as follows:

- Lists And Libraries, as shown in Figure 2-5
- Content Rollup, as shown in Figure 2-6
- Default, as shown in Figure 2-7
- Miscellaneous, as shown in Figure 2-8
- Outlook Web Access, as shown in Figure 2-9
- Search, as shown in Figure 2-10
- Site Directory, as shown in Figure 2-11

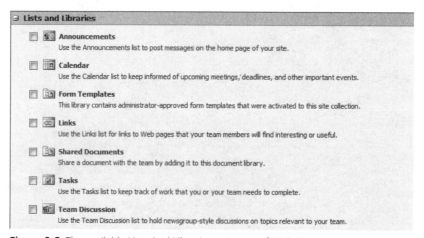

Figure 2-5 The available Lists And Libraries category of Web Parts.

Figure 2-6 The Content Rollup category of Web Parts.

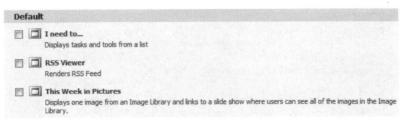

Figure 2-7 The Default category of available Web Parts.

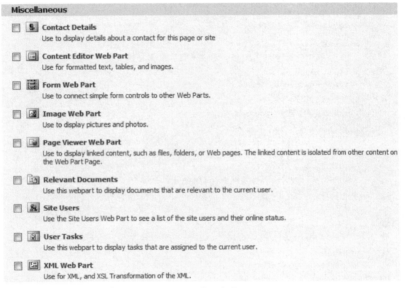

Figure 2-8 The Miscellaneous category of Web Parts.

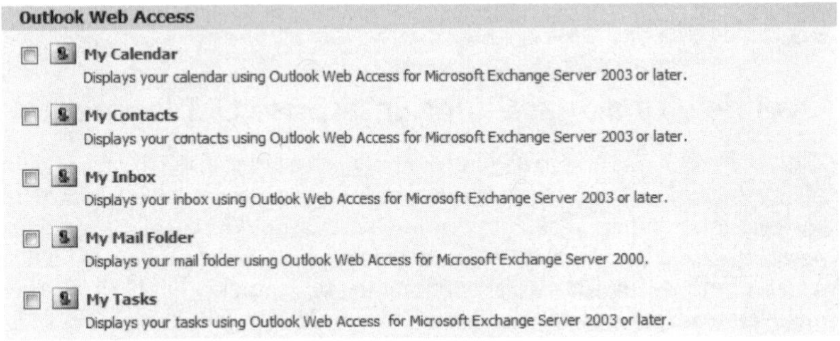

Outlook Web Access

☐ 🔲 **My Calendar**
Displays your calendar using Outlook Web Access for Microsoft Exchange Server 2003 or later.

☐ 🔲 **My Contacts**
Displays your contacts using Outlook Web Access for Microsoft Exchange Server 2003 or later.

☐ 🔲 **My Inbox**
Displays your inbox using Outlook Web Access for Microsoft Exchange Server 2003 or later.

☐ 🔲 **My Mail Folder**
Displays your mail folder using Outlook Web Access for Microsoft Exchange Server 2000.

☐ 🔲 **My Tasks**
Displays your tasks using Outlook Web Access for Microsoft Exchange Server 2003 or later.

Figure 2-9 The Outlook Web Access category of available Web Parts.

Chapter 2

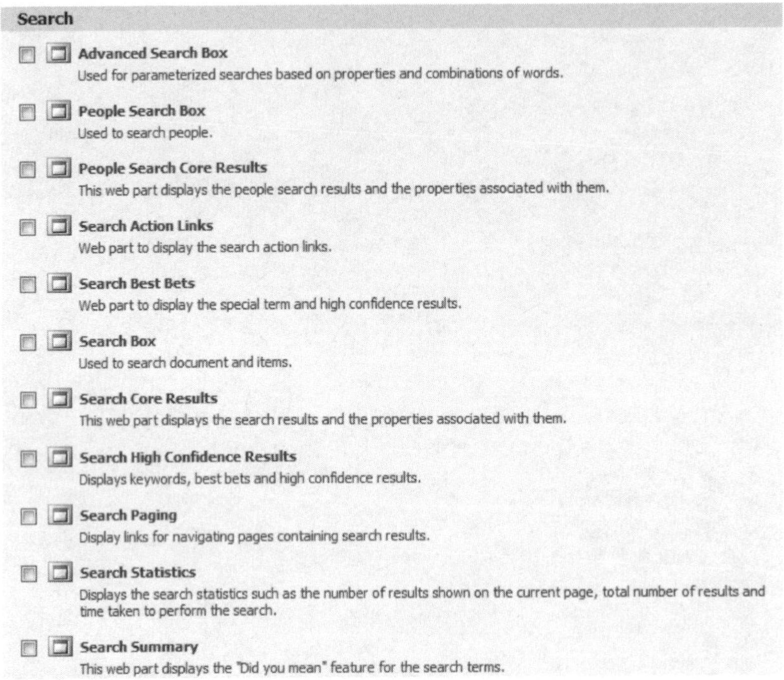

Search

☐ ⬜ **Advanced Search Box**
    Used for parameterized searches based on properties and combinations of words.

☐ ⬜ **People Search Box**
    Used to search people.

☐ ⬜ **People Search Core Results**
    This web part displays the people search results and the properties associated with them.

☐ ⬜ **Search Action Links**
    Web part to display the search action links.

☐ ⬜ **Search Best Bets**
    Web part to display the special term and high confidence results.

☐ ⬜ **Search Box**
    Used to search document and items.

☐ ⬜ **Search Core Results**
    This web part displays the search results and the properties associated with them.

☐ ⬜ **Search High Confidence Results**
    Displays keywords, best bets and high confidence results.

☐ ⬜ **Search Paging**
    Display links for navigating pages containing search results.

☐ ⬜ **Search Statistics**
    Displays the search statistics such as the number of results shown on the current page, total number of results and time taken to perform the search.

☐ ⬜ **Search Summary**
    This web part displays the "Did you mean" feature for the search terms.

Figure 2-10 The Search category of available Web Parts.

Site Directory

☐ ⬜ **Categories**
    Displays categories from the Site Directory

☐ ⬜ **Sites in Category**
    Displays sites in the Site Directory

☐ ⬜ **Top Sites**
    Display the top sites from Site Directory

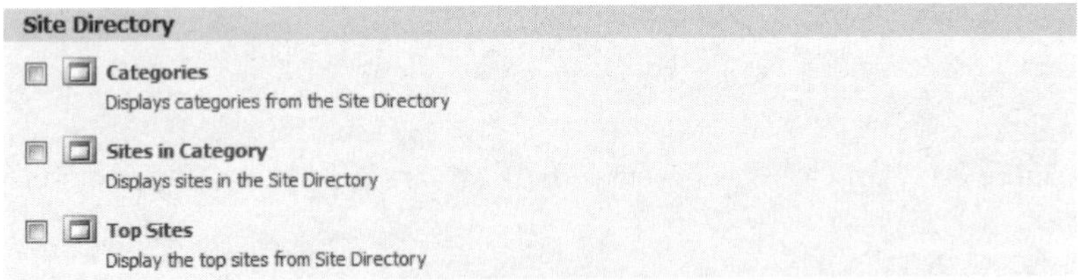

Figure 2-11 The Site Directory category of available Web Parts.

Overview of a SharePoint Enterprise Deployment

With the previous version of SharePoint Portal Server 2003, many organizations make the mistake of putting a system into production without the necessary infrastructure and information management planning and without a portal governance model in place. Once users within the organization start to use SharePoint and become comfortable with its interface and functionality, they quickly begin to see the benefits of the overall SharePoint environment. The resulting requests for team sites can quickly become difficult to manage. Once SharePoint is rolled out in an organization, its proliferation can be so drastic that often organizations are playing catch-up from day one. This is why the proper overall architecture of SharePoint and its deployment planning is so critical.

There are four categories of planning and SharePoint best practices that an enterprise should follow in any SharePoint implementation. These categories cover the items that are required for a successful deployment of SharePoint Server or WSS 3.0. The four categories of planning and SharePoint best practices are as follows:

- **Plan the detailed system design** The overall detailed server configurations of the deployment should take into consideration the overall user base, geographical considerations, and content and sizing. Whether the deployment is a single-server deployment or a large server farm with front-end Web servers, search and indexing servers, and SQL Server clusters, it is important to have an accurate architectural picture of your SharePoint deployment. This will help you to:

  - Acquire the necessary hardware to implement the physical architecture.
  - Have a good grasp of the best possible physical and logical configuration options.
  - Start designing and implementing a solid and highly available environment.
  - Efficiently plan the deployment of this new collaboration platform.

- **Plan the high-level design** When designing the SharePoint hierarchy of portals, sites, and subsites, you should take into account the navigational requirements of your organization. You should also start to consider the management of the content in SharePoint once the portal is rolled out to the user community. This will help you to:

  - Plan the overall portal and SharePoint approach.
  - Configure the navigational taxonomy.
  - Plan the team/departmental sites and subsites.
  - Gather the organization's business requirements.
  - Plan the initial management and staffing of the environment.
  - Develop an implementation plan.
  - Reassess storage requirements and future scalability based on any new requirements.

- **Plan the information architecture design** Planning the logical architecture and information management side of SharePoint consists of identifying the required metadata or content types as well as the tools that will be used to create and store content. Planning of SharePoint search is important in this phase, as is presenting the proper SharePoint terminology to the audience who will be using SharePoint and participating in its deployment. This will help you to:

  - Present a common language to the project team and organizational audience that will use SharePoint.
  - Plan the logical architecture for features such as My Site pages and specific portal landing areas.
  - Plan search and any specific search scopes, content sources, and scheduling.
  - Plan the security model in relation to the overall logical architecture.

- **Plan and design SharePoint governance** The overall governance of SharePoint is a critical piece of a SharePoint deployment. Consider not only SharePoint's branding and look and feel, but also quotas, file type exclusions, appropriate content policies, My Site management, and site provisioning. This will help you to:
    - Develop a governance model that includes the roles of the content owners and teams.
    - Develop an organizational communication plan.
    - Create portal standards, including development and security standards.
    - Set the organization's operational and content management processes.
    - Identify end-user support processes and tools.
    - Plan monitoring and compliance policies and procedures.
    - Manage user requests (new sites and custom development).
    - Create a style guide as well as SharePoint branding and a distinctive look and feel.

My Site Management

Office SharePoint Server My Site functionality enables users to have a dedicated personal site to manage all of their documents, content, and tasks. It also provides enhanced circles of collaboration with users that have similar skills and interests within the organization. My Sites in SharePoint really have two sites: a public site and a private site. My Sites can be an extremely powerful tool that organizations can take advantage of to vastly improve collaboration, but it is important to have policies and procedures in place to govern these sites. The nature of SharePoint is to encourage users to venture out into the organization and find important and relevant information as well as to help others find the content they are looking for in a timely manner. When I am in meetings with my clients, I sometimes refer to My Sites as the corporate My Space, as My Sites definitely encourage collaboration within an organization.

> **Note**
> Microsoft offers templates that can be downloaded from *http://www.microsoft.com/technet/windowsserver/sharepoint/wssapps/templates/default.mspx?*, for example, Role-Based My Site For Sales Account Managers. This link can also be found on the companion CD.

For example, consider the case of an organization with high turnover that wants to retain departed employees' knowledge and keep it readily available. My Sites is a fantastic tool that enables users to share this type of information. However, without the proper security model and content approval process in place, it is possible for confidential or private data to be posted in error to a large audience within SharePoint. With proper planning and My Site management, these types of issues can be avoided.

My Site templates and custom site definitions can be created to minimize these risks, but organizations should adhere to the following standards during their My Site rollout:

- All My Site Public View content must contain only work-related material. This includes work-related documents, discussions, pictures, links, calendar events, and related content.

- No My Site Public View content can contain any confidential or private data. If the organization would not allow all users within the company with a domain login to view this information, consider whether it should be on your My Site Public View.

- Content pertaining to human resources or legal is typically considered confidential and should not be listed on My Site Public View.

- Financial data must be reviewed prior to its posting on My Site Public View.

- Content on the private site must not contain personal audio files, inappropriate pictures, or other materials not allowed within the organization.

- All discussions or blogging done within a My Site must follow company policies and must not contain sensitive company material or defamatory comments about any person within the organization.

My Site has a public page called My Profile and a private page called My Home. Several Web Parts are built into these two out-of-the-box templates. Figure 2-12 shows the My Profile page of an out-of-the-box My Site.

Figure 2-12 The default My Profile page of a user's My Site page.

The out-of-the-box public My Profile page contains the following elements:

- **User Details** Shows information about the My Site user such as location within the organizational hierarchy as well as contact and other relevant information.

- **Recent Blog Posts** This Web Part shows the recent blog posts that have been submitted.

- **Documents** This Web Part displays lists of documents the user has created, saved, or modified on sites within the organization.

- **Colleagues** Shows a list of the colleagues the user is in contact with throughout the organization.

- **In Common With You** When users within an organization visit a user's My Site, this section shows what they have in common: which colleagues are mutual acquaintances, what managers are shared, and which memberships are held in common.

- **Memberships** This Web Part displays the Active Directory distribution lists and SharePoint sites for which the user is a member. This membership list can be customized by the My Site owner, who can pick and choose who gets to view the memberships and also which memberships, if any, are displayed.

- **Links** This Web Part displays links that the owner of the My Site would like to share with other SharePoint users.

Note

Users can restrict visitor access to information on their My Site by editing the membership list.

Figure 2-13 shows the My Home view of an out-of-the-box My Site private page.

The public My Home page contains the following:

- **Get Started With My Site** This Web Part enables you to customize your My Site and assists you in learning more about its capabilities.

- **RSS Viewer** This Web Part is new to SharePoint Server, and it works directly with Really Simple Syndication (RSS) newsfeeds.

- **SharePoint Sites** Users have the ability to add sites to the tabs across the top of the Web Part to allow for easy viewing of documents and tasks in those sites.

- **Recent Blog Posts** This Web Part shows the recent blog posts that have been submitted.

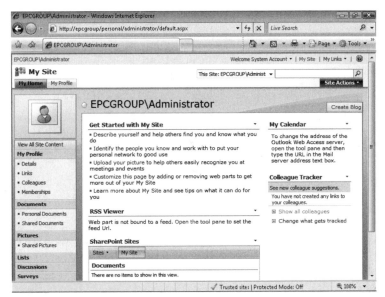

Figure 2-13 The My Home view of a user's My Site page, showing several of the available Web Parts.

- **My Calendar** This Web Part gives users the ability to display their Outlook calendars within their My Sites.

- **Colleague Tracker** Identifies users you are familiar with so that SharePoint Server can help you collaborate with them and view their current online presence via a status icon that will appear next to each colleague.

> **Note**
>
> My Site users can add colleagues to Colleague Tracker by manually adding them via the Add Colleagues page or by allowing SharePoint Server to suggest colleagues that it feels should be part of the user's Colleague Tracker list.

Managing Sites and Subsites

Planning and deployment of SharePoint sites and subsites is a detailed process that requires precise planning of the overall architecture, including items such as site collections and the overall SharePoint enterprise hierarchy (especially in large organizations). These topics will be covered in detail in later chapters of this book.

Managing sites and subsites is a critical piece of the puzzle in a successful SharePoint implementation. Which departments, projects, or teams will new sites be created for, and how will the security model be aligned with those sites? Once the new sites are created, who will manage the day-to-day content to make sure the sites stay relevant within the organization? What support model will be set up to provide maximum availability of the environment, and how will the organization's site provisioning model be implemented and enforced within the organization?

It is important to consider these questions beforehand so that once the sites are deployed and they begin spreading like wildfire, the organization can keep up with the sites and their content. WSS 3.0 gives site administrators the option of setting up Self-Service site creation, which enables users to create their own top-level Web sites without requiring them to have administrator permissions on the server or virtual server. However, this option is not viable within all organizations.

It is helpful if your organization puts site provisioning policies in place early on to answer questions such as who gets a new site and who has to use an existing site. Doing so ensures that either an automated process like Self-Service site creation can be configured or a Microsoft Office InfoPath 2007 new site request form can be developed for the organization. In most cases, a request process can be put in place so that a SharePoint administrator or group of administrators can handle new site requests by using organizational templates that are already in place.

A proper SharePoint security model is critical in SharePoint site management because administrators, designers, contributors, readers, and custom security groups should stay consistent within the organization. The one-off addition of SharePoint users to sites should be avoided whenever possible. However, there are always those situations in which a specific Active Directory group does not exist for the user or set of users who need to be added, and adding them individually to SharePoint is the only current option. Once SharePoint administrators start giving individual users permission to certain sites, or when permission inheritance is broken in a document library or list, the SharePoint administrator must separately keep track of these unique users, document libraries, and lists. This process takes additional administration time.

Note

SharePoint Server does provide for the support of federated authenticated scenarios. Information on configuring Web single sign-on (SSO) authentication by Active Directory Federation Services (ADFS) can be found on TechNet at *http://technet2.microsoft.com/ Office/en-us/library/61799f9a-da01-4c11-b930-52e5114324451033.mspx?mfr=true*.

The later chapters of this book will cover items such as overall infrastructure considerations, planning site collections, and planning security. Learning about these topics will help you align your organization with best practices that will provide a high level of performance and user acceptance and protect against the need to revisit these issues once the SharePoint environment is in production.

SharePoint Server Search

SharePoint Server can supply any organization with a powerful enterprise search solution that is reliable, scalable, and customizable. The search features return accurate and timely results that help to build on the collaborative nature of SharePoint Server, enabling users to find specific documents, people, or content. While enforcing the organization's SharePoint security permissions on the users' search results, SharePoint Server search enables users to span across organizational repositories regardless of departmental, functional, or global boundaries.

The search feature of SharePoint Server is extremely powerful right out of the box. It provides the user base with search tools that will help them find the content they need so that they don't waste time on searches that return unrelated and useless content. Users can take advantage of query suggestions, duplicate collapsing, and alerts on searches to enhance the overall search experience.

Figure 2-14 shows the Search Center site (without tabs). Figure 2-15 shows the People tab of the Search Center site (with tabs). It also shows Search Options expanded on the page. Figure 2-16 shows the All Sites tab of the Search Center site (with tabs).

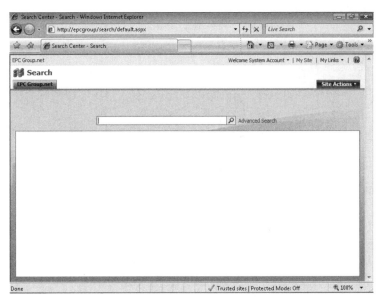

Figure 2-14 Perform a search for sites within the organization.

Chapter 2

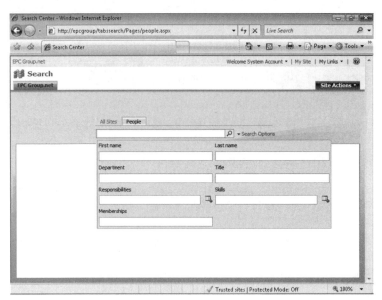

Figure 2-15 Perform a search for people within the organization.

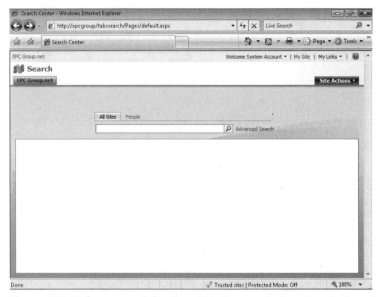

Figure 2-16 Perform a search for sites within the organization. You also have the option to click the People tab to search for people within the organization without having to load a new Search Center page.

SharePoint Server also offers an Advanced Search page that enables users to select more granular criteria for the search they are performing. Figure 2-17 shows the Advanced Search page.

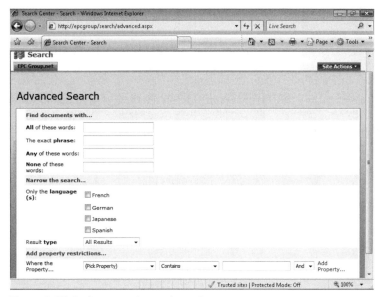

Figure 2-17 Perform an advanced search.

The search infrastructure can be expanded and configured to meet the requirements of any organization, including those that require multiple language support. The search feature can be customized so that users can use a preferred language to search content across the organization while still using the same familiar SharePoint interface.

> **Note**
>
> Microsoft offers six useful video presentations on SharePoint Server search, available from *www.microsoft.com/downloads/details.aspx?familyid=2751D5CD-8690-44B5-AE5C-D2769B227929&displaylang=en*. A link to this information is also available on the companion CD. The presentations cover enterprise search strategy and opportunities, SharePoint search extensibility, protocol handlers and iFilters, customizing and extending search in SharePoint Server, business data search, and SharePoint search deployment.

SharePoint Server will search SharePoint sites, file shares, Web sites, Exchange public folders, and Lotus Notes databases right out of the box, and you can also extend your search to third-party sources and file types. You can take advantage of its capabilities to find the right people in the organization without having to know which departments they work in or their specific job titles.

SharePoint Server can also search, index, and display information from your organization's existing relational databases, line-of-business applications, or other structured content by using the Business Data Catalog, which is discussed later in this chapter.

> **Note**
>
> It is important to note the search differences between SharePoint Server and WSS 3.0. In WSS 3.0, when you search on a SharePoint site, your query searches only the current site and any subsites below it. You cannot search across sites like you can in SharePoint Server unless you search from the root SharePoint site. The robust enterprise search capabilities of SharePoint Server highlight the limitations of WSS 3.0.
>
> If a search is performed on a WSS 3.0 site that is on the same server as the SharePoint Server instance, your search results will reflect only results from WSS 3.0 sites and subsites.

SharePoint Content Types

The content type functionality of WSS 3.0, which is a core element of this new version, offers organizations a robust solution to capturing metadata. It provides a better way to categorize SharePoint content in a centralized manner that is both easily configurable and reusable. Content types are collections of settings you can apply to a specific category of content. You can also apply retention schedules to content types, which allows you to keep content you are required to retain and to remove or eliminate content you no longer need. Content types are also organized into a hierarchy so that you can have one content type inherit its characteristics from another content type.

Content types enable you to assign specific metadata to documents of different types or from different categories, functions, divisions, or topics, which enhances SharePoint Search's content retrieval process. Workflow can be made available for items of a specific content type and triggered to begin based on a specific event or condition.

SharePoint administrators and site collection owners can easily manage content types because they are defined separately from any document library or list. Content types that are initially defined in the central site Content Type gallery for a site are referred to as site content types. When a content type is added to a specific library or list, it is referred to as a list content type, which is a child of the site content type from which it was created.

Site content types are available for use by any subsite for which a content type is assigned to one of its parent sites. If a content type is defined in the site Content Types gallery on a site collection's top-level site, it will then be available for use by all sites' libraries and lists in that site collection.

SharePoint enables organizations to have a standardized interface with which to collaborate on and manage content. Content types build on this interface by making sure that entire categories of documents and content are handled consistently within your organization. An owner or administrator can set up multiple content types within a site from which users can select when creating a new document.

Figure 2-18 shows a user clicking the New menu to create a new document from a list of available content types within a document library.

Figure 2-18 A site administrator has configured several content types from which users can select when creating a new document within a document library.

For more information about content types, refer to the section titled "Working with Content Types in a List or Library" in Chapter 6, "Designing Lists, Libraries, and Pages," and to the section titled "SharePoint Best Practices" in Chapter 20, "Defining the Proper Content Types and Metadata for Your Enterprise."

Overview of the Business Data Catalog

The Business Data Catalog (BDC) is a key feature of SharePoint Server that allows for powerful integration with your organization's existing link-of-business applications, SAP implementations, Siebel, or other databases via Web services. Several Web Parts related to the Business Data Catalog are available right out of the box and can be used to display this data without any custom coding or development.

The BDC is a shared service that enables organizations to merge existing data and Share-Point Server into a seamless platform that again offers organizations a one-stop shop for content and user collaboration. For example, you now have the ability to pull SAP data into a SharePoint list or use SharePoint search to find specific data from external data sources without the extensive custom development that is required in previous versions of both Windows SharePoint Services 2.0 and SharePoint Portal Server 2003. In previous versions, the effort it takes to bring these external systems into SharePoint is extremely extensive, but with the Business Data Catalog, merging this data requires much less effort.

The BDC consists of a metadata database and an object model that enables a simple object-oriented interface for business logic and methods to interact with the external data sources or line-of-business applications.

> Note
>
> The metadata database does not contain business data. Instead, it holds only metadata about the business application.

Chapter 2

The Business Data Catalog architecture is designed to coincide with roles within the organization that would all work together to bring external data into SharePoint. In some smaller organizations, a single resource may take on some or all of these roles, but in larger organizations, separate resources will more than likely be required depending on the size and scope of the external data source.

The identified BDC roles are the business analyst (BA), the metadata author, the Share-Point administrator, and the developer. The business analyst identifies the scope and business requirements of the external source that will be integrated with the BDC and then passes on those requirements to the metadata author. The metadata author then creates XML based on the BA's findings and hands off the XML to the SharePoint administrator, who adds the application definition to the BDC via SharePoint 3.0 Central Administration.

The final step is for the developer to use the BDC object model in conjunction with the SharePoint Server object model to create the business applications within SharePoint Server. But it is also possible to access the data in the BDC via the available out-of-the-box Web Parts.

SharePoint Server comes with several Business Data Web Parts, as shown in Figure 2-19, which require no coding and can be reused on virtually every site to which the organization makes them available. These Web Parts are:

- Business Data List
- Business Data Item
- Business Data Item Builder
- Business Data Related List
- Business Data Actions
- Excel Web Access
- IView Web Part
- WSRP Consumer Web Part

Note
The Business Data Catalog filter also filters Web Part contents based on the BDC values.

For more information, refer to the section titled "Introducing Business Data Web Parts" in Chapter 11, "Utilizing WSS 3.0 Web Parts," and to the section titled "Using and Customizing the Business Data Web Parts" in Chapter 18, "Advanced Design Techniques."

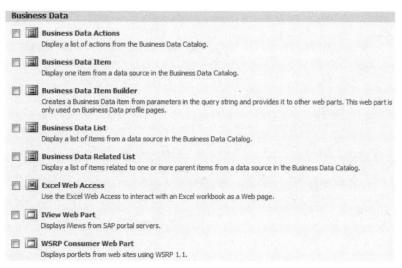

Figure 2-19 A list of Web Parts that are available right out of the box that work with the Business Data Catalog.

Excel Services Overview

SharePoint Server offers a powerful new feature called Excel Services to interact with Microsoft Office Excel 2007 workbooks securely and directly on SharePoint sites. In Chapter 1, "Introducing Windows SharePoint Services 3.0," we discussed how Share-Point document libraries and lists in conjunction with Outlook allow for a new way to share attachments. Embedding a URL into an e-mail that points to specific content will allow all users on the e-mail's distribution list to have access to the same file or pieces of content in a version-controlled, secure manner. Office Excel 2007 files are typically the most-used document type in an organization, followed closely by Microsoft Word (DOC/DOCX) and Adobe (PDF) files. Excel Services assists organizations by enabling them to have "one version of the truth" for Excel workbooks.

Excel Services is especially useful for Excel month-end reporting workbooks or similar Excel files on which a large number of users within the organization rely for specific summary data. When these users no longer need to receive Excel files as e-mail attachments, the organization avoids increased storage costs as well as possible security issues surrounding the release of sensitive data or intellectual property.

Not only does Excel Services in SharePoint Server allow for this type of central spreadsheet management, but it also offers other powerful features such as:

- **Excel Calculation Services** The main calculation engine for Excel Services that loads workbooks and performs calculations, interacts with Excel, and updates the displayed data in real time during browser sessions.

- **Excel Web Access** A Web Part that enables users to load Excel workbooks in a browser session without the user being required to have Excel 2007 or even Windows loaded on the desktop. This Web Part uses dynamic HTML (DHTML) and JavaScript to load the data. It does not require users to download any additional browser add-ons such as custom Microsoft ActiveX controls.

- **Excel Web Services** A Web service within SharePoint Server that provides an application programming interface (API) to build powerful custom applications based on an Excel workbook.

It is important to note that the cells in Excel workbooks cannot be edited in SharePoint Server Excel Services. However, the Excel Services component is still extremely powerful because it enables users to see the latest and most refreshed version of the content within a workbook at any particular time. Excel Services allows for powerful sorting and filtering of data and the use of a PivotTable report in which users can additionally sort and filter data, and expand or collapse levels within the PivotTable. Data can be recalculated on the fly by updating any available formulas or fields, and users can perform what-if analysis by temporarily changing cell values or update parameters.

Due to the vast improvements to Central Administration in SharePoint Server, the configuration of Excel Services is straightforward. To configure Excel Services, open Central Administration and go to the Operations tab, shown in Figure 2-20.

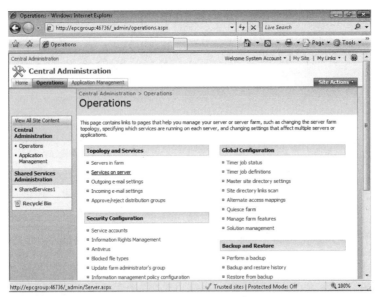

Figure 2-20 On the Operations tab of the Central Administration page, click Services On Server to begin configuring Excel Services.

You will need to start Excel Calculation Services because it is stopped by default. (See Figure 2-21.) Once Excel Calculation Services has been started, you will need to go to the Application Management tab and click Create Or Configure This Farm's Shared Services, as shown in Figure 2-22.

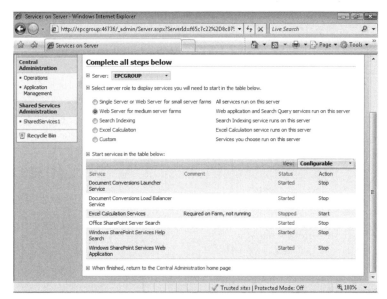

Figure 2-21 On the Services On Server tab, click to start Excel Calculation Services.

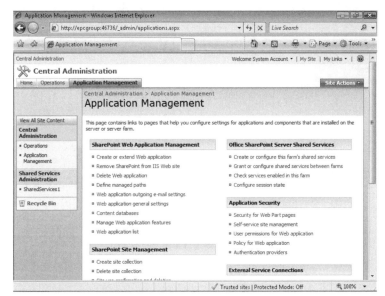

Figure 2-22 Click Create Or Configure This Farm's Shared Services to access the Manage This Farm's Shared Services page.

Within the Manage This Farm's Shared Services page, make sure a Shared Services Provider is configured within the environment and then select Open Shared Services Admin Site from its drop-down menu, as shown in Figure 2-23. The Shared Services Administration page will then load, as shown in Figure 2-24.

Note

If a Shared Services Provider does not yet exist, you will need to click New SSP to configure a new shared services provider.

Figure 2-23 Click the shared service that exists within the environment to open the available drop-down options that will take you to the Shared Services Administration site.

Within the Shared Services Administration site is a section labeled Excel Services Settings. You can configure specific settings, such as trusted file locations, as shown in Figure 2-24.

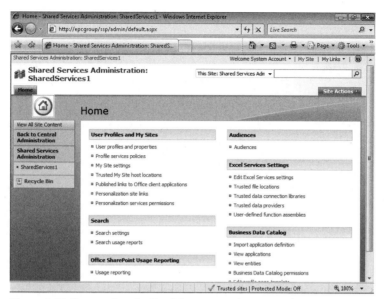

Figure 2-24 To complete the Excel Services configuration, SharePoint administrators can click the five links available within Excel Services Settings to configure items such as trusted file locations and trusted data providers.

SharePoint Server and Enterprise Content Management

Over the past few years, Microsoft has continued to improve its Enterprise Content Management platforms, and the release of SharePoint Server provides a Web-based solution to meet the organizational requirements of almost any organization. Since the release of Content Management Server (CMS) 2001, followed by CMS 2002, and then SharePoint Portal Server 2003, Microsoft has been working toward perfecting a Web-based collaborative content management system. SharePoint Server is now the flagship solution for managing enterprise content in a centralized, governed, fully searchable, and secure environment.

Organizations can easily create sites based on a specific need to connect not only their internal employees but also their partners, customers, and affiliates across a single platform with a common look and feel. SharePoint Server allows for an Internet or external-facing presence as well as an internal presence for content management for each department, team, project, or employee.

> **Note**
>
> Microsoft offers functionality and resources for migrating from CMS 2002 to SharePoint Server. Resources can be found at *http://msdn2.microsoft.com/en-us/office/aa905505.aspx*, which includes tools, white papers, and webcasts.

With SharePoint Server, new and powerful features and capabilities enable you to manage and share content with ease. Among these are:

- Robust new content type functionality that can define content fields, workflows, and events.

- Integration with ASP.NET 2.0.

- Easy site creation based on content types and templates.

- Workflow support built on the Windows Workflow Foundation.

- Robust publishing and version control (major and minor versions).

- Recycle Bin functionality that allows for the restoration of content that has been deleted.

- Significant enhancements in the Windows SharePoint 3.0 object model, the foundation for Web content management.

- Significant improvements in navigation.

- Improvements in Central Administration settings.

- Improvements in search to enable users to access content faster and more accurately.

- SharePoint Server Web-based authoring capabilities.

- Multiple language content management capabilities.

SharePoint Server also contains robust policy features for information management. They include:

- Content expiration (based on a retention schedule).

- Auditing (detailed auditable system of record capability).

- Document labels (auto-generated based on content type metadata).

- Document bar codes (generated unique IDs).

SharePoint Server also offers a Records Center site template that is designed to implement records management and retention with features such as record routing and policy enforcement.

Record routing allows for a document to be sent to a specific document library based on its type. The record routing table manages the logic behind the document's routing, and additional information can be attached to the document, such as the records audit history, which allows for quick and powerful auditing of all documents located in the Records Center site.

The policy enforcement capabilities of the Records Center site template are extremely powerful. The template offers the following features:

- Expiration of records based on their retention schedule. You can save valuable storage space within the organization's storage area network (SAN) or storage mechanism. In addition, this feature can lower the organization's legal liability because, in most cases, documents can be expired if they are past their retention life cycle.

- Bar codes are available to provide records with a unique graphical as well as a numerical value. The bar code's number is stored and indexed with the electronic version of the record. This can be especially useful when trying to manage both paper and electronic copies because organizations can reference the bar code on the paper copy of the record. This capability opens the door for SharePoint Server to begin to not only manage electronic copies of documents but also to assist in the management of paper copies.

- Auditing can be configured to log the operations that are performed on documents to see who is accessing the information stored in the Records Center site.

> **Note**
> Additional information on the design and configuration of the Records Center site can be found on TechNet at *http://technet2.microsoft.com/Office/en-us/library/03702c06-3e32-409d-ad8c-7e84eae386ba1033.mspx?mfr=true*.

Microsoft has made improvements over the years in the content management arena and has learned lessons from CMS 2001, CMS 2002, and SharePoint Portal Server 2003. Today, SharePoint Server is a platform that has built on the functionality of its predecessors and is at the head of its class. Many organizations are now migrating from their existing Documentum, LiveLink, DocuShare, or custom-developed content management platform into SharePoint Server.

INSIDE OUT   **SharePoint Server Receives Certification**

SharePoint Server received the U.S. Department of Defense 5015.2 Certification. On May 29, 2007, Microsoft announced that SharePoint Server had received this certification, which is endorsed by the National Archives and Records Administration. The 5015.2 standard on which the DOD certification is based serves as the benchmark for government and corporate organizations that manage records and documents.

Comparing SharePoint Server and Windows SharePoint Services 3.0

As discussed in Chapter 1, organizations of all sizes can deploy WSS 3.0 to increase collaboration by promoting quick and efficient information sharing within SharePoint sites. SharePoint Server extends the capabilities of WSS 3.0 by providing portal functionality, enterprise search, and the powerful enterprise records management capabilities we discussed earlier in this chapter.

WSS 3.0 is built on the Windows Server 2003 platform and conforms to the Windows Server 2003 licensing model, which enables organizations that already own Windows Server 2003 to take advantage of the powerful collaboration features without purchasing additional licenses.

SharePoint Server has a completely separate licensing structure, and Microsoft offers at least three different versions of the product, which can include or exclude certain features.

Table 2-1 compares the collaboration features of WSS 3.0 and SharePoint Server.

Table 2-1 Collaboration Features: WSS 3.0 vs. SharePoint Server

Feature	WSS 3.0	SharePoint Server
Real-time presence and communication	✓	✓
Social networking Web Parts		✓
Standard site templates	✓	✓
Wikis	✓	✓
Blogs	✓	
Calendars	✓	✓
E-mail integration	✓	✓
Task coordination	✓	✓
Surveys	✓	✓
Document collaboration	✓	✓
Issue tracking	✓	✓

Table 2-2 compares SharePoint platform features of WSS 3.0 and SharePoint Server.

Table 2-2 SharePoint Platform Features: WSS 3.0 vs. SharePoint Server

Feature	WSS 3.0	SharePoint Server
Customizable alerts and alert filtering	✓	✓
Task notification	✓	✓
RSS feeds	✓	✓
Consistent user experience	✓	✓
Extensibility of search		✓
Automatic breadcrumb	✓	✓
Quick Launch	✓	✓
Top Link bar	✓	✓
Recycle Bin	✓	✓
Backup and restore for the Volume Shadow Copy Service	✓	✓
Document libraries	✓	✓
Metadata	✓	✓
Content types	✓	✓
Application templates	✓	✓
Workflow	✓	✓
Tree view	✓	✓
Extensible site and list templates	✓	✓
Support for ASP.NET 2.0	✓	✓
ASP.NET master pages	✓	✓
Object model	✓	✓
Performance caching	✓	✓
Folder metadata	✓	✓
Web services	✓	✓
Version history	✓	✓
Major and minor version tracking	✓	✓
Item and folder-level access controls	✓	✓
Single sign-on		✓

Chapter 2

Table 2-3 compares Enterprise Portal features of WSS 3.0 and SharePoint Server.

Table 2-3 Enterprise Portal Features: WSS 3.0 vs. SharePoint Server

Feature	WSS 3.0	SharePoint Server
My Site		✓
Integration with the Microsoft Office 2007 versions of Excel, Word, Access, and PowerPoint	✓	✓
User profiles and profile storage		✓
Integration with Outlook	✓	✓
Site Manager		✓
Mobile device support	✓	✓
Portal site templates		✓
Roll-up Web Parts		✓
Site directory		✓
Search results	✓	✓
Integration with SharePoint Designer	✓	✓
Enterprise content sources		✓
People search		✓
Business data search	✓	✓

Table 2-4 compares Enterprise Content Management features of WSS 3.0 and SharePoint Server 2007 (Enterprise).

Table 2-4 Enterprise Content Management Features: Windows SharePoint Services 3.0 vs. SharePoint Server

Feature	WSS 3.0	SharePoint Server
Integration with Microsoft Information Rights Management		✓
Records repository		✓
Retention and auditing policies		✓
Document information panel	✓	✓
Legal holds		✓
E-mail content as records	✓	✓
Content publishing and deployment		✓
Slide libraries		✓
Policies, auditing, and compliance		✓

Table 2-5 compares business intelligence features of WSS 3.0 and SharePoint Server.

Table 2-5 Business Intelligence Features: WSS 3.0 vs. SharePoint Server

Feature	WSS 3.0	SharePoint Server
Excel services		✓
Business Data Catalog (BDC)		✓
Data connection libraries		✓
Business data Web Parts		✓
Report center		✓
Key performance indicators		✓
Filter Web Parts		✓

In Summary...

This chapter looked back at WSS 2.0 and SharePoint Portal Server 2003 (SPS 2003), provided a detailed review of SharePoint Server and compared it with WSS 3.0, examined best practices and deployment items around a SharePoint enterprise deployment; described the content management capabilities of SharePoint Server, and provided an overview of the Business Data Catalog and Excel Services.

This chapter compared the features offered in WSS 3.0 and SharePoint Server. It detailed how a majority of organizations can use Windows SharePoint Services 3.0 to provide a Web-based collaboration solution for their enterprise and showed that although SharePoint Server is a more robust solution for larger organizations that require portal and enterprise content management capabilities, WSS 3.0 is a powerful platform solution for many organizations throughout the world.

Part 2, "End-User Features and Experiences," which immediately follows this chapter, examines the end-user features and experience of WSS 3.0. For new SharePoint users, this part of the book offers a tutorial for the most basic features and details the new features that WSS 3.0 has to offer. For administrators and programmers, it illustrates the working environment that WSS 3.0 can deliver and how it can be customized to meet an organization's exact needs.

PART 2
End-User Features and Experiences

Using the Built-In Features of Windows SharePoint Services 3.0

This chapter explains how organizations can take advantage of the powerful built-in features of Microsoft Windows SharePoint Services 3.0 (WSS 3.0). The items discussed in this chapter are ones team members will use on a daily basis. These items will increase collaboration with other SharePoint users and also increase productivity on day-to-day tasks and activities.

This chapter addresses SharePoint site functionality around managing content in document libraries and lists as well as how to use discussion boards to increase knowledge management and collaboration. Issues and task tracking help team members stay on track with their current projects and initiatives, and team members can be alerted whenever items are updated or changed within their site.

Whether you're new to SharePoint or a seasoned SharePoint user, this overview of built-in features will help you get the most out of WSS 3.0.

The optimum computer environment for a SharePoint user exploring these features includes:

- Microsoft Internet Explorer 6 or 7 as the browser.

- A complete installation of Microsoft Office 2007. (Microsoft Office 2003 users will experience a similar but not identical experience.)

- The Windows Vista or XP operating system.

Sites and Workspaces Features

SharePoint sites and workspaces provide the following robust features and functionality that are available to any user within the organization who has a Web browser, network connectivity to the SharePoint server, and the proper permissions:

- **Document libraries** These are lists of stored files such as text documents and spreadsheets. Functionality such as check-in/checkout, major and minor version numbering and tracking, content-type support, workflow integration, and item-level security provide a much more robust solution for document storage than an ordinary file share. Content can be organized into folders, and offline synchronization with Microsoft Office Outlook 2007 is also available.

- **Discussion boards** Within a site, you can create discussion boards to provide a forum for conversations about any topic that may be of current interest to the team. Discussion boards are useful for day-to-day topic discussions as well as for knowledge management and capturing best practices and lessons learned within an organization. You can display messages in threads, or you can select a flat view and then sort the messages any way you want. You can also receive alerts when there is activity within the discussion board.

- **Picture libraries** This type of library is similar to a document library, except that each document is a picture, and the various picture library Web pages display the pictures visually. Built-in features provide several ways of locating, viewing, and modifying pictures. For example, you can display pages that feature clickable thumbnails, full-sized pictures, and slide shows.

- **Task lists** Track task information about current projects or events within the organization. Tasks can be assigned to users who can then receive e-mail alerts regarding their assignments. Outlook 2007 integration is also available with task lists.

- **Issue lists** Store and track information about issues on projects or initiatives within your organization. Issues can be assigned to users and groups. These lists notify users of issues assigned to them by sending out e-mail alerts.

- **Form libraries** This type of library is similar to a document library, but it is used to manage and store XML-based business forms such as those used by Microsoft Office InfoPath 2007. Form libraries can also be configured to receive content via e-mail. Within the form library settings, you can specify that the form should open in a browser so that users are not required to have Office InfoPath 2007 installed on their machines.

- **Surveys** Surveys collect feedback from users within the organization. They can be configured to ask users for feedback on a specific project or initiative. They can also be used for something like a satisfaction survey.

- **Alerts** Team members can ask to be notified whenever a specified document or folder changes. Windows SharePoint Services 3.0 detects such changes and sends the notifications by e-mail.

- **Wiki page libraries** Create a collection of wiki pages that are all connected within the wiki page library.

Using Team Sites and Related Subsites

Figure 3-1 shows a typical SharePoint team site, which contains the Windows Share-Point Services logo as well as Web Parts for announcements, events, and links that instantly retrieve and display up-to-date information from lists.

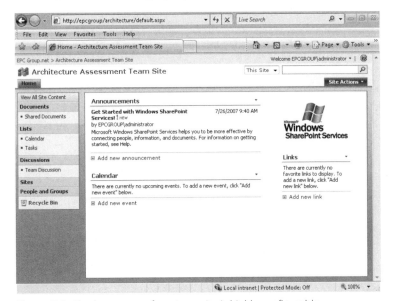

Figure 3-1 The home page for a team site is highly configurable.

The out-of-the-box template for a team site provides the following elements:

- **Top Link bar** Displays the fully customizable home page link for the current site.

- **Site Actions** A user with the appropriate permissions can display the Site Actions link, which contains a drop-down list to take a user to the Create, Edit Page, or Site Settings pages.

- **Search box** A search box at the right of the page enables users to search for content within the site and all of its subsites.

- **Quick Launch** The navigation pane on the left provides customizable links; by default, it contains the following links:

  - **View All Site Content** Links to a page containing all the site's content
  - **Documents** Links to a list of all the document libraries within the site
  - **Shared Documents** Links to the default document library that is created via the out-of-the-box Team Site template

- ○ **Lists** Links to a list of all of the SharePoint lists within the site
- ○ **Calendar** Links to the default events list that is created via the out-of-the-box Team Site template
- ○ **Tasks** Links to the default task list that is created via the out-of-the box Team Site template
- ○ **Discussions** Links to a list of all of the SharePoint discussion libraries within the site
- ○ **Team Discussion** Links to the default discussion list that is created via the out-of-the-box Team Site template
- ○ **Sites** Links to a list of all sites and workspaces within the site
- ○ **People and Groups** Links to a list of people and groups related to the site
- ○ **Recycle Bin** Links to the site's Recycle Bin

The Announcements and Calendar areas are Web Parts. They display recent additions to their respective lists and provide links to more detailed views. The Links area is a Web Part that provides hyperlinks that team members might frequently use. This data resides in a list named Links.

> **Note**
>
> Selecting Edit Page from the Site Actions menu provides an editable version of the page. You can then add to, remove, or rearrange the Web Parts that make up the site.

Using SharePoint Libraries and Lists

SharePoint sites and workspaces store virtually all information and content in lists. Many lists are available right out of the box, and SharePoint gives you the ability to easily create custom lists based on your specific criteria or even by importing a spreadsheet. A SharePoint list is similar to a database table and can contain either no records at all or a large collection of records with one or more fields. A list can record any combination of fields you wish to configure. Microsoft's technical description of a list is a collection of items displayed on a site.

A new team site automatically contains the following lists:

- **Announcements** Record informative messages for display on the site's home page.

- **Calendar** Maintain a list of upcoming meetings, deadlines, and other important events.

- **Links** Store URLs to sites that your team members will find interesting or useful.

- **Tasks** Maintain a list of assignments that your team members need to complete.

Each of these lists starts out with a different assortment of columns, but you can add, remove, and modify the columns in any list using nothing more than a browser. With Window SharePoint Services 3.0, you can now assign content types to these lists as well.

Chapter 6, "Designing Lists, Libraries, and Pages," explains how to create and modify Share-Point lists and libraries and goes into detail about applying content types to these items.

New List Functionality in WSS 3.0

Microsoft has added a significant amount of new list functionality in Windows Share-Point Services 3.0. The new functionality reflects lessons learned from previous Share-Point versions as well as feedback from SharePoint users.

E-Mail and SharePoint Lists and Libraries

SharePoint lists as well as document libraries can now receive e-mail. In the same way that you would e-mail another employee within your company, you can now add content to a SharePoint site by e-mailing a list. Your SharePoint administrator will need to enable this setting within your SharePoint environment and take into consideration a proper e-mail naming convention to properly manage this feature. But once this is done, discussion boards, announcements, calendars, document libraries, picture libraries, form libraries, and blog post lists can all receive content via e-mail.

Blogs and SharePoint

Blogs have become extremely popular, and organizations benefit from harnessing this technology as a means of expression and collaboration. With blogs, SharePoint users can collaborate on almost anything. From new ideas about how to improve productivity to suggestions about current projects to lessons learned, blogs can greatly benefit an organization. Blogs, or weblogs as they were originally called, are short but specific content posts that are typically displayed by date of creation. With almost any list in Share-Point, views can be created to display the data in whatever manner the user chooses.

With any technology that enables users to freely speak their minds or discuss information about the organization, it is important to have a governance model in place so that negative situations can be avoided before they occur and so users clearly understand the guidelines they must follow. SharePoint governance is covered in greater detail in Chapter 5, "Creating SharePoint Sites, Workspaces, and Pages," and Chapter 12, "Managing Windows SharePoint Services 3.0 Site Content."

Wikis

A wiki is a collaborative Web site that can be directly edited by anyone with access to it. As wikis became more and more popular, Microsoft recognized that this technology should be properly introduced into SharePoint to increase its already collaborative nature. Wikis allow for easy collaboration and sharing of information and ideas. Like almost anything in SharePoint, wikis can be searched so that no matter how many wiki entries a team may have, the entry of interest can be found in a matter of seconds.

RSS Feeds

Windows SharePoint Services 3.0 has introduced RSS (Really Simple Syndication) feeds into both lists and libraries to enable users to easily keep track of the content and information they have stored. RSS is an XML-based protocol that is used to syndicate information. You can also use RSS feeds to receive information and updates from news sites and other blogs.

Item-Level Security

Item-level security enables you to manage and modify permissions at the item, folder, file, list, library, or site level. In Windows SharePoint Services 2.0 and Microsoft Share-Point Portal Server 2003, the lack of this type of item-level security was a serious issue. Having to create a separate document library or list for each team or department that wanted to secure a specific set of content is cumbersome and causes sites to become disorganized. Now, a user with the appropriate permissions can configure security for a specific set of content in a matter of moments in a library or list. Figures 3-2 through 3-4 show you how to manage the permissions of a document.

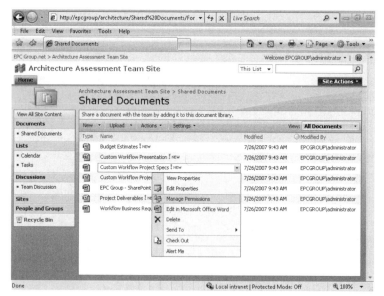

Figure 3-2 By selecting the drop-down list of a specific file and selecting Manage Permissions, you can access the permissions page for the document.

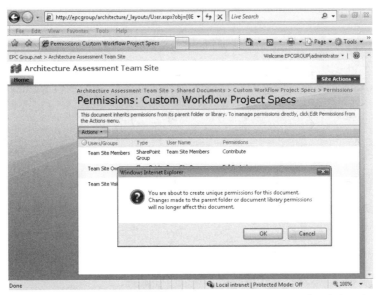

Figure 3-3 You can then select Actions and Edit Permissions to break the inheritance of the parent site and create unique permissions for this specific document. A warning message will appear notifying you of the inheritance break.

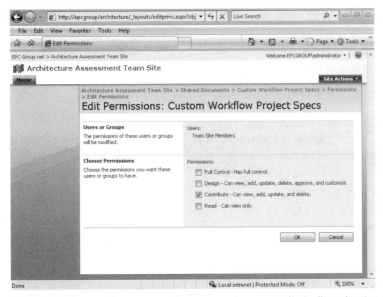

Figure 3-4 You can then manage the users and groups individually and assign them specific permissions based on your requirements.

Chapter 3

INSIDE OUT Keeping track of Unique Permissions

Unique Permissions is an exciting new feature but it can lead to problems. When you create unique permissions to a specific document library or list, the parent level site's permissions will no longer control the permissions in this list or library. Keeping track of these unique libraries is especially important for future auditing within your organization.

Viewing Lists and Lists Content

Clicking the Lists link within the Quick Launch of any site will display the All Site Content page with the Lists view applied (see Figure 3-5). This summarizes all the lists in the current site. Each list contains a different combination of fields, serves a different purpose, and provides different views.

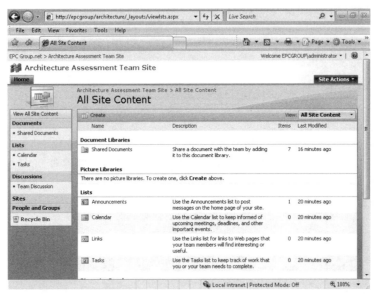

Figure 3-5 From the All Site Content page, you can select any list in a team site.

At the upper right of the page, the View drop-down list provides several filtering options: All Site Content, Document Libraries, Lists, Picture Libraries, Discussion Boards, Surveys, and Sites And Workspaces. The Lists view, for example, displays all lists that are not document libraries, picture libraries, discussion boards, surveys, or sites and workspaces (see Figure 3-6).

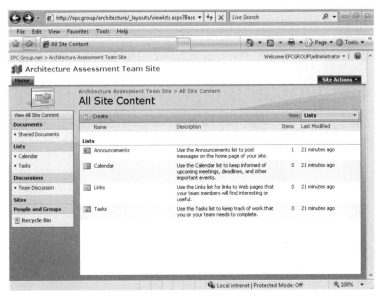

Figure 3-6 Lists view available on the All Site Content page.

Click the name of a list to display its content. For example, click Calendar to open the calendar (see Figure 3-7).

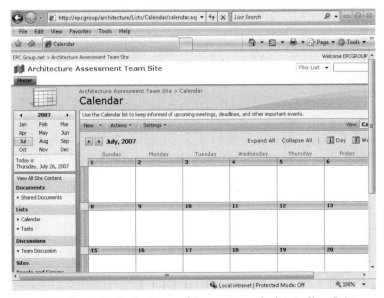

Figure 3-7 The Calendar list is one of the most popular lists in SharePoint.

Here's how the links on the Calendar list work:

- **View** At the upper right of the calendar is a drop-down list of views that can be selected: Calendar, All Events, Modify This View, and Create View. The default Calendar view displays the list in a gridlike calendar view, as shown in Figure 3-7. The All Events and Current Events views display filtered events in a list. You can easily modify the view you are using by selecting Modify This View. Create View allows you to create and save a custom view from a list of template options: Standard View, Calendar View, Gantt View, Standard View With Expanded Recurring Events, and Datasheet View.

- **New** Add a new item to the calendar.

- **Actions** This area provides the following commands for working with the Calendar list:

  - **Connect To Outlook** Synchronize items within Outlook 2007 so that they are available offline.

  - **Export To Spreadsheet** Download a Microsoft Office Excel Web Query file. Such files have an .iqy file extension that, by default, causes Office Excel to start. Excel then connects to the team site database and downloads the data for the list you requested.

  - **Open With Access** An item in a SharePoint list can be opened in Microsoft Office Access 2007, where users can create forms, reports, and queries using the data.

  - **View RSS Feed** Keep track of the list information via RSS feeds. You can use RSS feeds to receive periodic updates about the events.

  - **Alert Me** Display a New Alert page where you can specify the alert's title as well as the list of users to whom the alert's e-mail notification should be sent when there are changes to a specific item, document, list, or library.

- **Settings** This area provides the following commands to creating a new column or view for the list as well access to the list settings:

  - **Create Column** Add a column to store additional information about each item in the list.

  - **Create View** Create a view to select columns, filters, and other display settings in the list.

  - **List Settings** Access a page with options to manage list settings such as version settings, permissions, columns, views, workflow, and policy.

Additional options may appear depending on the type of list. A task list, for example, has an option for creating a Microsoft Office Visio 2007 diagram based on the list.

Updating List Content

Windows SharePoint Services 3.0 has built-in features for adding list items, viewing, editing, or deleting them, managing their permissions, and attaching alerts to them. To perform any of these actions, first display the list and then choose which of the following you'd like to do:

- To add a new item, click the New button on the list's toolbar.

- To view existing content in an item, hover over its name, open the resulting drop-down menu, and choose View Item.

- To edit existing content in an item, hover over its name, open the resulting drop-down menu, and choose Edit Item.

- To manage permissions on an existing item, hover over its name, open the resulting drop-down menu, and choose Manage Permissions.

- To delete a list item, hover over its name, open the resulting drop-down menu, and choose Delete Item.

- To add an alert on an existing item, hover over its name, open the resulting drop-down menu, and choose Alert Me.

Choosing either New or Edit Item displays a page like the one in Figure 3-8. For a new item, all the input fields will (of course) be blank or have default values. For an existing item, the item name will replace New Item in the heading, and each input field will contain its current value. There will also be time and date information as well as information regarding the creation and last modified times and the identity of the user that performed these actions. If a file was attached to the list item, the name of the attachment with an embedded link will appear along with a delete link next to the attachment.

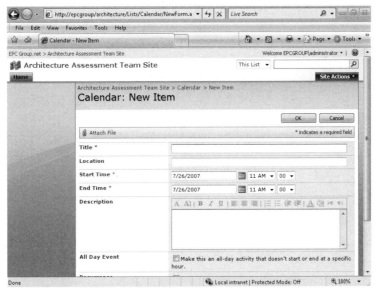

Figure 3-8 This page creates a new item in the Calendar list.

Versioning in Lists

With Windows SharePoint Services 3.0, you can track versions of list items. Each item's version is numbered and saved as part of the version history. Versioning is not enabled by default. To enable and configure versioning in, for example, the Calendar list, select Settings, then List Settings, and then under the heading General Settings click Versioning Settings. The resulting configuration page, shown in Figure 3-9, contains the following options:

- **Content Approval** The list administrator selects either Yes or No concerning whether to require content approval for submitted items.

- **Item Version History** The list administrator selects either Yes or No to determine whether a version is created each time you edit an item in the list. The administrator can choose to limit the number of versions to retain as well as the number of approved version drafts to retain.

- **Draft Item Security** The list administrator selects who can see draft items in the list. The administrator can choose from the following options:
    - Any User Who Can Read Items
    - Only Users Who Can Edit Items
    - Only Users Who Can Approve Items (And The Author Of The Item)

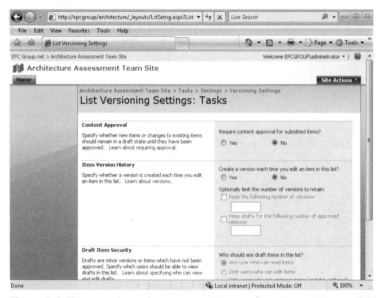

Figure 3-9 This page shows the version settings configuration options available in a task list.

Using Document Libraries

SharePoint document libraries store the majority of the content in SharePoint—including documents and spreadsheets—and can create, collect, update, and robustly manage files within organizations. A SharePoint document library is similar to a list on which every item must have an attachment. Document libraries also display key information about each file and provide many powerful features including version control; item-level permissions for libraries, documents, and folders; and built-in workflow.

Viewing Document Libraries

To work with a SharePoint document library, click the Documents link in the Quick Launch to display the All Content page for that site. The Document Libraries view will be applied. To view a specific document library, click the document library name on the Quick Launch.

Figure 3-10 shows the link to the Shared Documents library on the Quick Launch. The one document library shown in Figure 3-11—Shared Documents—appears automatically on every new team site. However, a single site can have as many document libraries as required by the team, department, organization, or user.

Figure 3-10 The Quick Launch, by default, contains a link to the Shared Documents library.

Here's how the links in the Shared Document library work:

- **View** At the upper right of the Shared Documents library is a list of views that can be selected. The All Documents view displays all documents and folders that currently exist in the library (see Figure 3-11). There is also Explorer View, Approve/Reject Items view, and My Submissions view. Modify This View allows for the modification of any of the existing views. Create View allows for the creation of new views. It is important to note that only users with the appropriate permissions can perform some of these specific actions. You must have Microsoft Office installed for the Explorer View to function properly.

- **New** Create a new document based on the available content type(s) or the document library's default document template.

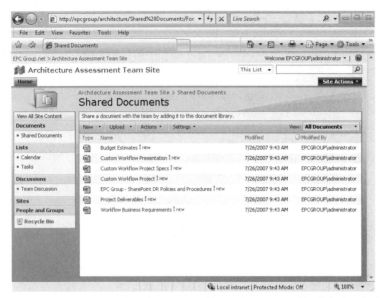

Figure 3-11 This is the Shared Documents library that is created by default with the Team Site template.

- **Upload** This area provides the following commands for working with the list:
  - **Upload Document** Upload a single document into the document library from your computer.
  - **Upload Multiple Documents** Upload multiple documents at once into the document library from your computer.

- **Actions** This area provides the following commands for working with the list:
  - **Edit In Datasheet** Bulk edit items by using a datasheet format.
  - **Open With Windows Explorer** Open the document library in a separate Windows Explorer window to allow for dragging and dropping files into this library.
  - **Connect To Outlook** Synchronize items within Outlook 2007 so that they are available offline.
  - **Export To Spreadsheet** Download an Excel Web Query file. Such files have an .iqy file extension that, by default, causes Excel to start. Excel then connects to the team site database and downloads the data for the list you requested.
  - **View RSS Feed** Keep track of the information via an RSS feed. You can use RSS feeds to receive periodic updates about lists.
  - **Alert Me** Display a New Alert page where you can specify the alert's title as well as the list of users to whom the alert's e-mail notification should be sent when there are changes to a specific item, document, list, or library.

- **Settings** This area provides the following commands to create a new column or view for the list as well as to access the list settings:
  - ○ **Create Column** Add a column to store additional information about each item in the document library.
  - ○ **Create View** Create a view to select columns, filters, and other display settings in the document library.
  - ○ **Document Library Settings** Access a page with options to manage document library settings such as version settings, permissions, columns, views, workflow, and policy, as seen in Figure 3-12.

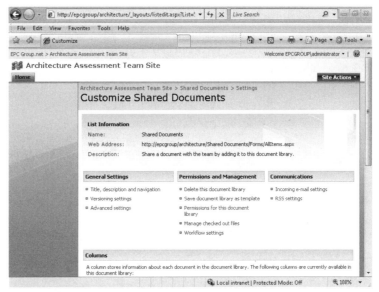

Figure 3-12 This is the document library Settings page, which allows the administrator to modify settings within a document library.

Each line in the main document area of a document library view page (see Figure 3-13) contains the clickable fields described in the list that follows.

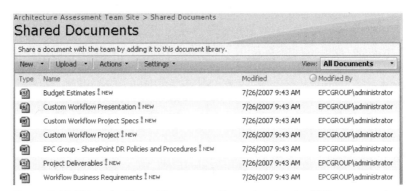

Figure 3-13 This is the Shared Documents library showing the All Documents view.

- **Type** Display an icon that indicates the document type. Clicking this icon opens the file for viewing. If the file is a type that the browser can display, the browser displays it. Otherwise, the browser treats the file as a download and starts the application that normally opens the given file type.

- **Name** Display the document's file name. Hovering over the name displays a drop-down list with these choices:

    ○ **View Properties** Display all available information about the document.

    ○ **Edit Properties** Display a page where you can modify the document's name, title, or other custom metadata or content-type information.

    ○ **Manage Permissions** Display a page where you can break the permission inheritance from the parent folder for the library and manage unique permissions for the item.

    ○ **Edit In <*application*>** Download a temporary copy of the document and open it in the associated application.

    ○ **Delete** Remove the document from the library.

    ○ **Send To** Send a document to another location. There are at least four Send To options, and users can also create custom Send To locations. The four Send To options provided are:

        ■ **Other Location** Create a link from the source document to the published copy so that whenever the document is checked back in, the author will be prompted to update the published version(s) of the document.

> **Note**
>
> Within the Advanced Settings of a document library, you can specify a custom Send To location. Doing so will allow you to specify a common place that documents or content may be published to.

        ■ **E-Mail A Link** Open Outlook 2007, or your default e-mail program, and place a link to the document into the body of the e-mail.
        ■ **Create Document Workspace** Create a new document workspace from the selected document that exists within the document library on the site.

> **Note**
>
> If this option is not available to you, it is possible that you do not have the appropriate permissions. Please contact the site owner to request permission to create workspaces on the site.

- **Download A Copy** Open or download a copy of the document.

○ **Approve/Reject** Approve or reject submissions. It is important to note that rejecting an item does not delete that item. Those users who know the exact URL of a rejected item can still view it. The available options for approve/reject are:

   - **Approved** This item will become visible to all users. The document libraries settings will determine whether this option is available to you.

   - **Rejected** This item will be returned to its creator and will not appear in public views. The document libraries settings will determine whether this option is available to you.

   - **Pending** This item will remain visible to its creator and all users with the Managed List permissions. The document libraries settings will determine whether this option is available to you.

> **Note**
>
> By default, a pending item or file is visible to its creator and to the people with permission to manage lists and libraries, but you can specify whether other groups of users can view the item or file.

○ **Check Out** Stop anyone but you from updating the document. (After you choose this option, it changes to Check In.) An administrator or list manager can activate or block this feature.

After a document is checked out, an additional item on the drop-down list appears. It is Discard Check Out, and it will check the document back in without any changes. After a document is checked out, select the drop-down list again and select Edit In *<application>* so that you can begin editing the document. After your changes are made, you can save and close the document. In the Check In dialog box, check in the file by clicking OK. You can also set the option Keep The Document After Checking In This Version? to Yes, which saves your changes to the document but keeps the file checked out to you.

○ **Version History** This option will not be present unless it is activated for the list. Display a history of updates to the document. This includes the version number for major and minor versions, the ability to restore or delete older versions and delete all or draft versions, along with date, time, modified by, document size, and comments. The next section will explain this feature in more detail.

Chapter 3

> **Note**
>
> Version control is disabled by default and must be enabled by the site owner or administrator as discussed above. It is a best practice to have version control turned on within all document libraries and to create document library templates. Rolling these templates out throughout your organization ensures that the proper settings are identical throughout the SharePoint environment.

- ○ **Alert Me** Display a New Alert page where you can specify the alert's title as well as specify the list of users to whom the alert's e-mail notification should be sent when there are changes to a specific item, document, list, or library.

- **Modified** Display the date and time when the last document update occurred.

- **Modified By** Show who last updated the document. Click a link to access a User Information page that shows information such as the user's account information, name, e-mail, About Me information, picture that they posted, departmental information, job title, and session initiation protocol (SIP) address.

- **Approval Status** Display the current approval status of the document: Approved, Rejected, or Pending.

Updating Document Libraries

Because each item in a document library must have an attached document, updating a document library requires procedures that are somewhat different from updating an ordinary list. The next five topics describe these procedures.

Creating a New Document and Adding It to the Library

Every SharePoint document library has a default document template that is selected at the time of the document library's creation, as shown in Figure 3-14.

The Microsoft Word template is selected by default, but a site owner or administrator can select from among several template choices.

When you click the New Document button in a toolbar of a library view, Windows SharePoint Services displays either the default document template or the list of content types that have been associated with the document library. Content types allow for the document library to have a single content type within the library that contains multiple item types or document types, of which each can have unique metadata, policies, or behaviors.

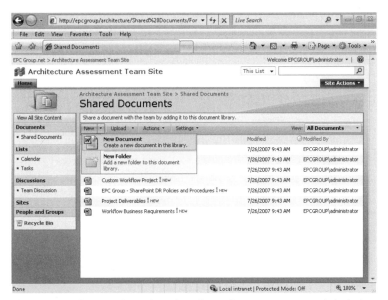

Figure 3-14 The New drop-down box shows the New Document default document type template.

> **Note**
>
> To allow for content type management within a document library, you select Settings, Document Library Settings, and then under the heading General Settings click Advanced Settings. Select Yes for Allow Management Of Content Types.

After content has been added to the new document and it is saved into the document library, SharePoint will automatically record your name, the date and time, and the type of document. If you selected a New Item that was associated with a content type, the metadata around that document will also be saved into SharePoint.

Adding an Existing Document or Documents to the Library

To add a document that already exists on your computer, network share, CD, or other location to a SharePoint library, click the Upload button on the library's list view toolbar. This displays two drop-down options to the users: Upload Document or Upload Multiple Documents (see Figure 3-15).

If the Upload Document option is selected, a screen appears to prompt the user to browse for the specific document (see Figure 3-16).

Chapter 3

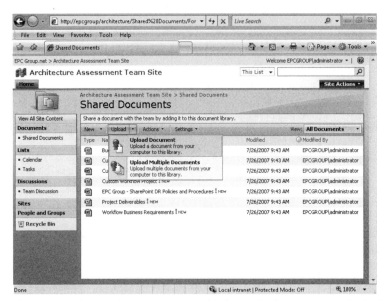

Figure 3-15 The user has an option to upload a single document or multiple documents into a SharePoint document library.

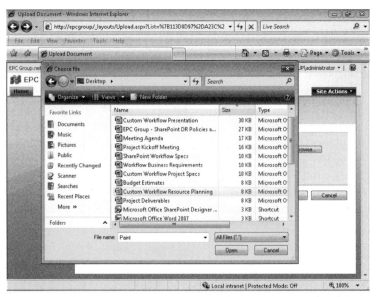

Figure 3-16 The user has an option to browse for a single document and upload it to a SharePoint document library.

From this point, the procedure varies depending on whether you want to add a single document or multiple documents.

After the user browses, finds the correct document, and selects OK, the following screen will appear to prompt for additional data (metadata) about the document. It is important to note that when additional content types or custom columns are created or applied to the document library, users will be prompted to fill in data regarding those additional fields (see Figure 3-17).

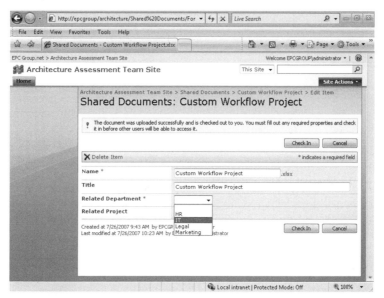

Figure 3-17 The user must populate the additional fields regarding the document properties.

> **Note**
>
> A red asterisk (*) next to a field on the Edit Properties page denotes a field that is required and must contain data before the page can be saved and closed.

After the fields are populated, the user must either select Check In to check the document into the library or Cancel to cancel the operation. After the document is checked into the library, its default status will be pending unless the content approval settings have been configured to make this not required (see Figure 3-18). The content approval settings for a library can be accessed by going to its Settings page and then clicking on Versioning Settings.

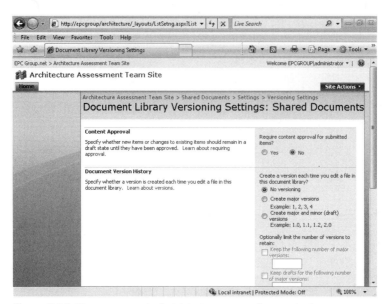

Figure 3-18 Site owners and administrators can configure whether content approval is required.

If the user selected Upload Multiple Documents, a screen will appear to prompt the user to browse for a folder containing the documents you wish to upload (see Figure 3-19).

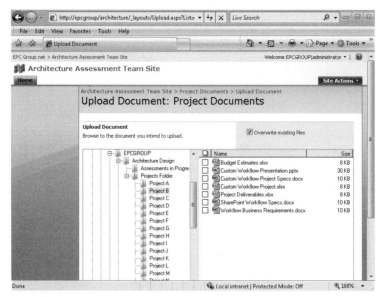

Figure 3-19 The user can upload multiple documents from the same folder.

Select the documents to upload and then click OK. You will receive a warning message telling you that you are about to upload multiple documents. Click OK to proceed. By default, the multiple documents you just uploaded will have a status of pending until they are approved.

Updating a Library Document

To change the content of a library document, follow the procedure outlined here:

1. Hover over the document name until a drop-down list appears.

2. If you wish, open the drop-down menu and choose Check Out. This locks the library copy of the document so that no one but you can update it.

3. Open the drop-down list again and choose Edit In *<application>*. This will download a temporary copy of the document to your computer and open it in the corresponding application.

4. Change and save the document within the application selected in step 3. This will update the copy in the document library, and you will be prompted to check the document back in as well as to provide comments regarding the changes you have made (see Figure 3-20).

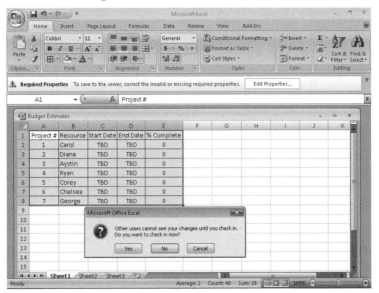

Figure 3-20 After saving the document, Excel prompts the user with options to check the document back in and provide comments about the changes.

If the application you are using to modify the document in the document library does not have the integrated capabilities of Microsoft Office 2007 and you are finished making your changes, check the document back in by opening the drop-down list and choosing Check In.

Updating the List Information for a Library Document

Here's the procedure for updating the library information (metadata) for a document. This has no effect on the document itself.

1. Hover over the document name until a drop-down list appears.

2. Open the drop-down list and choose Edit Properties. This will display a page with the library name, a colon, and the document title.

3. Change the values of any fields you like.

4. Click the OK button.

> **Note**
> You cannot edit the properties of a document while it is checked out and being modified offline.

Deleting a Library Document

To delete a library document, hold the mouse over its title, open the resulting drop-down list, select Delete, and click OK to confirm the deletion. If the SharePoint Recycle Bin is enabled, the document will then be sent to the Recycle Bin.

Versioning in Document Libraries

An administrator or site owner/manager can activate versioning, which is not enabled by default, by selecting Settings, Document Library Settings, and then under the heading General Settings clicking Versioning Settings. Versioning is the method by which SharePoint stores successive iterations of a document in a numbered format. Windows SharePoint Services 3.0 has three versioning options:

-   **No Versioning** Version control can be turned off, and all previous versions of documents would not be able to be retrieved and will be discarded. If you have a need for a temporary storage location for documents that are not important, you can utilize use this option. However, this it is not recommended for any other scenario.

-   **Create Major Versions** This versioning option uses numbered versions using a sequential schema (1, 2, 3, 4, and so on). It is possible to specify the number of major versions that SharePoint will store. Once a document is classified as a major version, all users who have access to the document will be able to view it.

- **Create Major And Minor (Draft) Versions** This versioning option uses numbered versions similar to Create Major Versions, but a major/minor numbering schema (1.0, 1.1, 1.2, 2.0, 2.1, 3.0, 3.1, and so on.). Versions ending with .0 are major versions, and versions ending with nonzero extensions are minor versions. Similar to major versions, it is possible to specify the number of major and minor versions that SharePoint will store. In this versioning scenario, all users with read permissions can view major versions of the documents, and you can specify which users may view the minor versions. This versioning scenario is very helpful when you want to have only major versions published to the greater audience and to limit who can see the drafts (minor versions) of content that is currently being developed.

If you select Version History from the library-item drop-down list, the Version History page displays the following options and information, as shown in Figure 3-21.

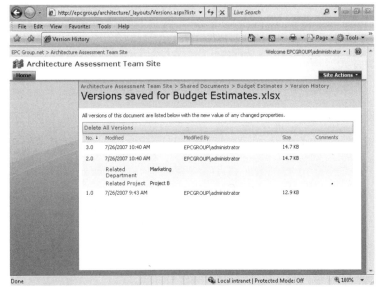

Figure 3-21 The Version History page displays and manages multiple versions of each document in a library. You could have additional options on this page depending on the versioning settings you have specified.

- **Delete All Versions** The user with appropriate permissions can delete all versions of the document.

- **Delete Minor Versions** The user with appropriate permissions can delete all draft (minor) versions of the document. Choosing this option creates a new copy of the document version and makes it the current version. (This will increment the current major version number by one.)

- **No.** The version number.

- **Modified** The time each version of the document was last modified. A user can hover over the Modified field of a version and access a drop-down list with the following items:

  - **View** Links to an additional screen, shown in Figure 3-22, to edit, delete, manage permissions, manage copies, or check in a version of the selected document.

  - **Restore** Restores a previous version and overwrite the current version. All changes to the current version are lost.

  - **Unpublish This Version** Unpublishes the version of the document.

- **Modified By** The user who last modified the document.

- **Size** Shows the file size of the version.

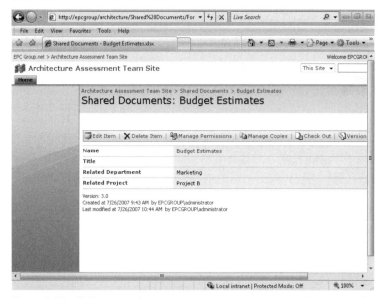

Figure 3-22 Clicking on a document version opens a screen with many useful management options.

Using Picture Libraries

Most of the content that organizations work with on a daily basis is textual in nature. Microsoft Office Word, Microsoft Office PowerPoint, Excel, and PDF files are the primary files that most organizations store, though some graphical files are stored as well. The SharePoint team site provides picture libraries to efficiently store, view, and retrieve graphical information.

Creating Picture Libraries

A new team site doesn't contain a picture library by default, but one can be easily created using the following procedure:

1. Open the team site in Internet Explorer and click Site Actions. Click the Create option on the Top Link bar. (Note that it is also possible to click View All Site Content on the top of the Quick Launch and then click Create.)

2. When the Create page appears, click the Picture Library link.

3. When the New page shown in Figure 3-23 appears, enter values for these items:

    o **Name and Description** Provide a short name to identify the library throughout the team site, and a description of the library's content or purpose.

    o **Navigation** Select Yes if you want a link to this library on the Quick Launch of the team site home page.

    o **Picture Version History** Select Yes if you want Windows SharePoint Services 3.0 to create a version every time someone updates a picture in this library.

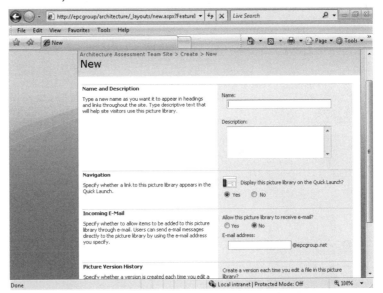

Figure 3-23 The page shows the options available for the creation of a new picture library.

Updating Picture Libraries

At this point, Windows SharePoint Services 3.0 will display an empty contents page for the new picture library, in a format similar to that of a document library. To begin adding pictures, click the Upload link and select either Upload Picture or Upload Multiple Pictures.

> **Note**
>
> If you have Microsoft Office 2007 or a Windows SharePoint Services-compatible image editor installed, such as Microsoft Office Picture Manager, an option to upload multiple files should appear when you click Upload.

The Upload Picture link displays the Add Picture page, shown in Figure 3-24, which is similar to the Upload Document page in the document libraries discussed earlier in this section.

For those that have the option available, select the Upload Multiple Pictures link. Once the editor is open, follow the instructions to upload multiple files into the SharePoint document library.

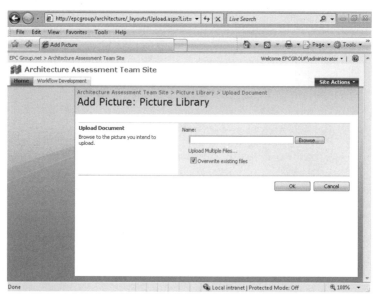

Figure 3-24 Use this page to upload a single picture to a picture library.

Viewing Picture Libraries

Figure 3-25 shows the contents of a picture library containing several pictures. By default the library displays a thumbnail view of the pictures.

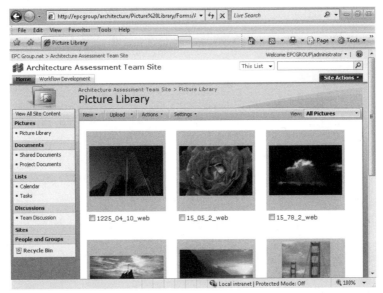

Figure 3-25 The contents listing for a picture library resembles that for a document library, but it contains additional controls for working with pictures.

To display the library contents in a different format, click one of these links in the View menu:

- **All Pictures** Displays three options to present the pictures in the All Pictures views, which are:
  - **Details** List the information for each picture in the library; doesn't show the entire picture, but just a thumbnail at the lower left of the screen.
  - **Thumbnails** Display a miniature version of each picture in the library. Clicking any thumbnail loads a larger version of the corresponding picture into the thumbnail page. Clicking the larger version displays the full-size picture alone in the browser window.
  - **Filmstrip** A horizontal series of thumbnails representing each picture in the library.

- **Explorer View** Lists the library contents in a format resembling Windows Explorer. This is available only when you use a Windows version of Internet Explorer.

- **Selected Pictures** Displays only those pictures whose check boxes you selected in an All Pictures view.

Here are some common actions you can perform from the All Pictures, Details view. Many of these actions are available in other views as well.

- Clicking the Type icon for any picture displays the full-sized picture—and nothing else—directly in the browser window.

- Clicking the name of any picture when the user is in the Details view displays a larger version of the picture in a formatted team Web page, as shown in Figure 3-26. This page will give you additional options: Edit Item, Delete Item, Manage Permissions, Manage Copies, Check Out, and Alert Me.

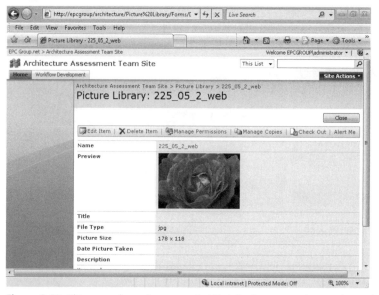

Figure 3-26 This page shows the expanded Details view page when a picture is clicked in the standard Details view.

As shown in Figure 3-27, clicking the drop-down menu for the name of any picture displays the following choices:

- **View Properties** All available information about the picture.

- **Edit Properties** A page where you can modify the document's name, title, or other custom metadata or content type information.

- **Manage Permissions** A page where you can break the permission inheritance from the parent folder for the library and manage unique permissions for the item.

- **Edit Picture** Start Office Picture Manager and tell it to open the picture for editing.

- **Delete** Remove the picture from the library.

Figure 3-27 Click the drop-down menu for a picture name to display a variety of picture management options.

- **Send To** Send a document to another location. There are at least three Send To options, as shown in Figure 3-28, and users also have the ability to create custom Send To locations:
  - **Other Location** Create a link from the source picture to the published copy so that whenever the picture is checked back in, the author will be prompted to update the published version(s) of the picture.

> **Note**
>
> Within the advanced settings of a picture library, you can specify a custom Send To location. Doing so will allow you to specify a common place that picture may be published to.

  - **E-Mail A Link** Open Outlook 2007, or your default e-mail program, and place a link to the document to the body of the e-mail.
  - **Download A Copy** Open or download a copy of the document.
- **Download Picture** Download the picture to your computer.
- **Check Out** Stop anyone but you from updating the picture (after you choose this option, it changes to Check In).

- **Unpublish This Version** Unpublish this version within the picture library (note that this feature will display only if versioning is enabled within the picture library).

- **Version History** Display a history of updates to the picture, including date, time, modified by, picture size, and comments.

- **Alert Me** Display a New Alert page where you can specify the alert's title as well as the list of users to whom the alert's e-mail notification should be sent when there are changes to a specific item, document, list, or library.

Figure 3-28 The Send To option enables you to send the image to another location, to e-mail a link, or simply to download a copy of the file.

> **Note**
>
> As is the case for other lists and libraries, versioning of picture libraries is not enabled by default. Activate it by selecting Settings, Picture Library Settings, and then under the heading General Settings clicking Versioning Settings.

- **Actions** This area provides the following commands for working with the picture library:
  - ○ **Edit** Open the picture for editing.
  - ○ **Delete** Remove the picture from the library.
  - ○ **Download** Download the picture to your computer.
  - ○ **Send To** Display an options box to insert the picture into an open file or to insert it into another Microsoft Office application.

○ **View Slide Show** Open a new window that displays the first picture in the library and has buttons to display additional pictures.

○ **Open With Windows Explorer** Open the document library in a separate Windows Explorer window to allow for dragging and dropping files into this library.

○ **Connect To Outlook** Synchronize items within Outlook 2007 so that they are available offline.

○ **View RSS Feed** Keep track of the information via RSS feeds, which can be used to receive periodic updates about the lists.

○ **Alert Me** Display the New Alert page so that you can request e-mail notification when someone changes or electronically discusses anything in the library.

- **Settings** This area provides the following commands to create a new column or view for the list as well access to the list settings:

○ **Create Column** Add a column to store additional information about each item in the list.

○ **Create View** Create a view to select columns, filters, and other display settings in the list.

○ **Picture Library Settings** Access a page with options to manage list settings such as version settings, permissions, columns, views, workflow, and policy.

Using Discussion Boards

A team site discussion board works a lot like an Internet newsgroup. Team members can post new messages, respond to existing messages, and view messages in their entirety or in condensed lists. Discussion boards also work great for sharing knowledge about best practices and lessons learned within the organization.

Windows SharePoint Services 3.0 team sites already have a discussion board called Team Discussion set up by default. The name, along with other properties of this discussion board, can easily be changed to meet your organization's exact needs. Additional discussion boards can easily be created.

Choosing or Creating a Discussion Board

To view an existing discussion board on a standard team site, click Team Discussion on the Quick Launch or the name of another existing discussion board. To view the entire contents of a site to find a specific list, click View All Site Content (located at the top of the Quick Launch). You can then select Discussion Boards from the View drop-down list to show all of the discussion boards in the site (see Figure 3-29).

To create a new discussion board, click View All Site Content, Create, and then Discussion Board in the Communication section. You can also click Site Actions at the upper right of the page and then select Create. When the Create page appears, select Discussion Board as above.

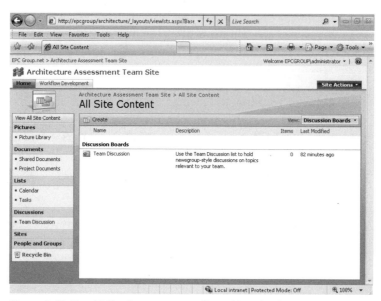

Figure 3-29 The All Site Content page is filtered here by the Discussion Boards view showing all discussion boards that reside on this team site.

Viewing and Updating a Discussion Board

To view or modify the contents of an existing discussion board, click the name of the discussion board on the Quick Launch or click View All Site Content and apply the Discussion Boards filter. Then click the desired discussion board. A list of the board's topic threads will open, as shown in Figure 3-30.

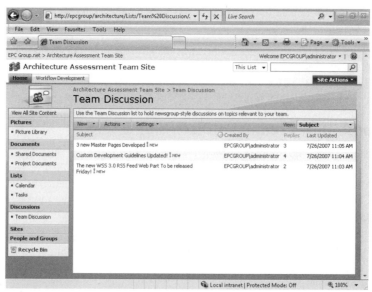

Figure 3-30 Click a discussion board name or icon to display a list of discussion threads.

The options available on this page are as follows:

- **View** Select a view to display the discussion board in the format you want.

- **New** Click New to create a new top-level message. This opens the New Item page, shown in Figure 3-31.

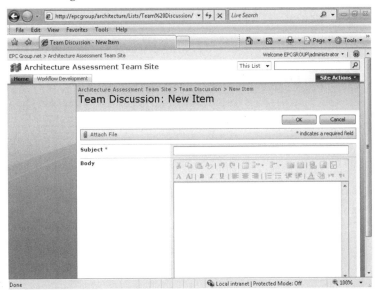

Figure 3-31 Clicking New on a board's list of discussion threads opens the New Item page. After you enter your subject and body and click OK, a new discussion thread will be started.

- **Actions** This area provides the following commands for working with the list:

    - **Connect to Outlook** Synchronize items within Outlook 2007 so that they are available offline.

    - **Export To Spreadsheet** Download a Microsoft Excel Web Query file. Such files have an .iqy file extension that, by default, causes Excel to start. Excel then connects to the team site database and downloads the data for the list you requested.

    - **Open With Access** Open an item in a SharePoint list in Microsoft Access, where users can create forms, reports, and queries using the data.

    - **View RSS Feed** Keep track of the information via RSS feeds. You can use RSS feeds to receive periodic updates about the lists.

    - **Alert Me** Display a New Alert page where you can specify the alert's title as well as specify the list of users to whom the alert's e-mail notification should be sent when there are changes to a specific item, document, list, or library.

- **Settings** This area provides the following commands to create a new column or view for the list as well as access to the list settings. Additional options may appear depending on the type of list.

  - **Create Column** Add a column to store additional information about each item in the discussion board.

  - **Create View** Create a view to select columns, filters, and other display settings in the discussion board.

  - **Discussion Board Settings** Access a page with options to manage list settings such as version settings, permissions, columns, views, workflow, and policy.

After clicking the New option and entering a new discussion item, the new item will appear as shown in Figure 3-32. Users can then respond to this new discussion topic.

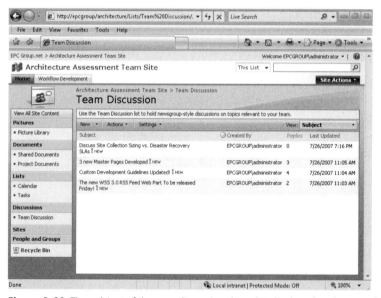

Figure 3-32 The subject of the new discussion thread is displayed at the top of the board's thread list.

To see the messages within a discussion thread, click the subject line. The messages in the thread will be displayed, as shown in Figure 3-33.

Figure 3-33 The messages in a discussion thread shown in Flat view.

- **View** There are several different options for viewing messages grouped under the View menu:
    - **Flat** This link appears only in Threaded view. Click it to toggle between a display of all messages and a display of top-level messages only.
    - **Threaded** This link appears only in Flat view. Click it to toggle between a display of all messages and a display of top-level messages only.
    - **Modify This View** Customize the current view's content, layout, and policies.
    - **Create View** Starting with any of several view-format templates, create a new view.

- **Posted By** Displayed only in Flat view, this shows the user that posted each discussion item and the post time. Click any entry in the Posted By column to display a detailed information page about that person.

- **Reply** Reply to the original post by using the discussion board editor. Reply also gives you the option to attach a file to your reply.

- **View Properties** This link on each message takes you to a page where you can perform the following actions:
    - **Reply** Reply to the message by using the discussion board editor. Reply also gives you the option to attach a file to your reply.
    - **Edit Item** Modify the current message. Depending on the settings in effect for the discussion board, this might be possible only for an administrator or the person who originated the message.

- ○ **Delete Item** Delete the current message. Again, this might be possible only for an administrator or the person who originated the message.

- ○ **Manage Permissions** Display a page where you can break the permission inheritance from the parent folder for the library and manage unique permissions for the item.

- ○ **Alert Me** Display a New Alert page where you can specify the alert's title as well as specify the list of users to whom the alert's e-mail notification should be sent when there are changes to a specific item, document, list, or library.

Using Task and Issue Lists

Task and issue lists in Windows SharePoint Services 3.0 enable users to keep track of their day-to-day activities related to both project and nonproject work. Users can track tasks and issues and receive automated alerts based on any updates or changes. These lists are ideal for users with busy schedules who can benefit from e-mail reminders and the centralized manner in which these tasks and issues can be managed.

Enterprise Project Management (EPM) software, such as Microsoft Project Server 2003, made these SharePoint task and issue tracking lists popular and proved how useful they are to keep track of project-related information.

Choosing or Creating a Task List

A Windows SharePoint Services 3.0 team site contains a default task list called Tasks that can be accessed from the Quick Launch. A user can also access task lists by clicking View All Site Content, which is located at the top of the Quick Launch, to view all available lists. Then select the desired task list.

To create a new task list, click View All Site Content, and then click Create. Alternatively, click Site Actions, and Create. When the Create page appears, look under the Tracking section and click Tasks. The New page opens, as shown in Figure 3-34, allowing you to create a new list.

You can find the following items on the New page:

- **Name** Enter the name of the new task list.

- **Description** Briefly characterize the list's content or purpose.

- **Display This List On The Quick Launch?** Choose Yes or No.

- **Send E-Mail When Ownership Is Assigned?** Choose Yes or No.

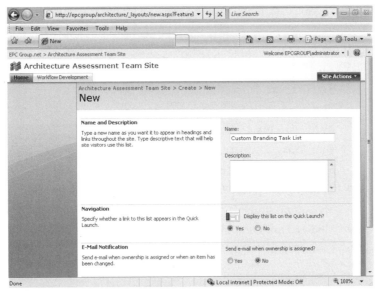

Figure 3-34 The New page, which is used for creating task lists and other lists.

Viewing and Updating a Task List

To view or modify the contents of an existing task list, click the name of the task list on the Quick Launch. Alternatively, click View All Site Content at the top of the Quick Launch and then click the desired task list for which you are searching. In Figure 3-35, the standard task list was selected.

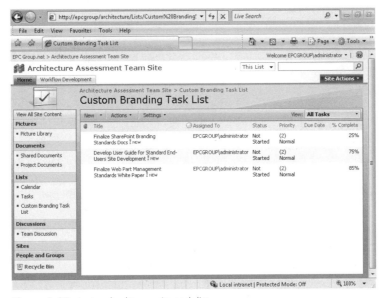

Figure 3-35 A standard team site task list.

Here are the options available on the page for tasks:

- **View** The View drop-down menu is located at the upper right of the screen. A user can select the following views of the task list:
    - **All Tasks** Display all tasks in the list.
    - **Active Tasks** Display all active tasks in the list.
    - **By Assigned To** Display tasks by Assigned To.
    - **By My Groups** Display tasks by My Groups.
    - **Due Today** Display tasks that are due today.
    - **My Tasks** Display tasks that are assigned to you.
    - **Approved/Rejected Items** Display approved and rejected items.
    - **My Submissions** Display tasks that you submitted.
    - **Modify This View** Modify the current view.
    - **Create View** Create a new custom view.
- **New** Create a new task item. Figure 3-36 shows the New Item page for a task list.

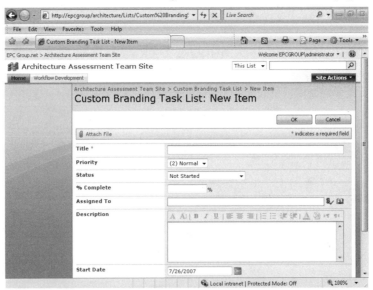

Figure 3-36 This page creates a new task item.

The following items are captured in the task list New Item page:

- **Title** The name of the new task.
- **Priority** The priority of the new task. The options out of the box are High, Normal, and Low.
- **Status** The status of the task item. The options out of the box are Not Started, In Progress, Completed, Deferred, Waiting On Someone Else.

- ○ **% Complete** The current percentage complete of the task.
- ○ **Assigned To** The person or persons assigned to the task.
- ○ **Description** A detailed description of the new task.
- ○ **Start Date** The date on which the task is set to begin.
- ○ **Due Date** The date on which the task is scheduled to be completed.

- • **Actions** This area provides the following commands for working with the list:
  - ○ **Edit In Datasheet** Bulk edit items by using a datasheet format.
  - ○ **Connect To Outlook** Synchronize items within Outlook 2007 so that they are available offline.
  - ○ **Export To Spreadsheet** Download a Microsoft Excel Web Query file. Such files have an .iqy file extension that, by default, causes a spreadsheet program such as Excel to start. It will then connects to the team site database and download the data for the list you requested.
  - ○ **Open With Access** Open an item in a SharePoint list in Access, where users can create forms, reports, and queries using the data.
  - ○ **Create Visio Diagram** Create an Office Visio diagram based on the content of the task list. This option will be available if you have Visio installed on your computer.
  - ○ **View RSS Feed** Keep track of the information via RSS feeds. You can use RSS Feeds to receive periodic updates about the lists.
  - ○ **Alert Me** Display a New Alert page, where you can specify the alert's title as well as specify the list of users to whom the alert's e-mail notification should be sent when there are changes to a specific item, document, list, or library.

- • **Settings** This area provides the following commands to create a new column or view for the list as well access to the list settings:
  - ○ **Create Column** Add a column to store additional information about each item in the task list.
  - ○ **Create View** Create a view to select columns, filters, and other display settings in the list.
  - ○ **List Settings** Access a page with options to manage list settings such as version settings, permissions, columns, views, workflow, and policy.

Creating an Issue List

A Windows SharePoint Services 3.0 team site does not have an existing issue list, but one can be easily created. A site administrator or site owner can click View All Site Content on the top of the Quick Launch and then click Create. Once the Create page loads, the user can scroll down under Tracking and click Issue Tracking to create the new issue list. You can also click site Actions at the upper right of the page and then select Create. When the Create page appears, scroll down to the tracking section, and then select Issue Tracking. The New page will appear, as shown in Figure 3-37.

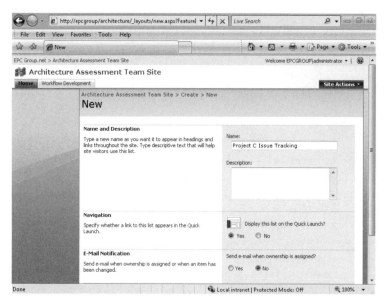

Figure 3-37 The New page for creating an issue tracking list.

Enter the following information when you create the new issue tracking list:

- **Name** Enter the name of the new issue tracking list.

- **Description** Briefly characterize the list's content or purpose.

- **Display This List On The Quick Launch?** Select Yes or No.

- **Send E-mail When Ownership Is Assigned?** Select Yes or No.

Viewing and Updating an Issue List

To view or modify the contents of an existing issue list, click the name of the issue list on the Quick Launch. Alternatively, click View All Site Content at the top of the Quick Launch and then click the desired issue list. On the page shown in Figure 3-38, the Project C Issue Tracking list was selected.

The options available on this page are as follows:

- **View** Select the view in which to display the issue list. The following views are available by default:

  - **All Issues** Display all issues in the list.

  - **Active Issues** Display all active issues in the list.

  - **My Issues** Display issues that are assigned to you.

  - **Modify This View** Modify the current view.

  - **Create View** Create a new custom view.

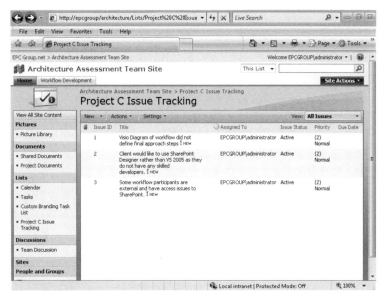

Figure 3-38 A team site issue tracking list.

- **New** Click this link to create a new issue item. Figure 3-39 shows the New Item page used for adding items to an issue list. The following items are captured in an issue list's New Item page:

  - **Title** The name of the new issue.

  - **Assigned To** The person or persons assigned to the issue.

  - **Issue Status** The status of the issue. The status defaults are Active, Resolved, and Closed.

  - **Priority** The priority of the new issue. The default options are High, Normal, and Low.

  - **Description** A detailed description of the new issue item.

  - **Category** A customized category selection. The defaults are Category1, Category2, and Category3.

  - **Related Issues** Select other issues that are related to the issue that you are currently creating or modifying.

  - **Comments** Enter comments about the issue.

  - **Due Date** The date by which the task is scheduled to be completed.

Chapter 3

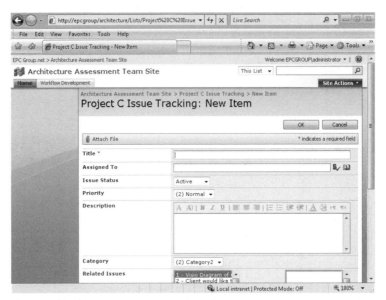

Figure 3-39 This page creates a new issue item.

- **Actions** This area provides the following commands for working with the list:
    - ○ **Edit In Datasheet** Bulk edit items by using a datasheet format.
    - ○ **Export To Spreadsheet** Download a Microsoft Excel Web Query file. Such files have an .iqy file extension that, by default, causes the spreadsheet program you have installed on your computer, such as Excel, to start. It then connects to the team site database and downloads the data for the list you requested.
    - ○ **Open With Access** Open an item in a SharePoint list in Microsoft Access, where users can create forms, reports, and queries using the data.
    - ○ **Create Visio Diagram** Create a Visio diagram based on the content of the task list. This option is available if you have Visio installed on your computer.
    - ○ **View RSS Feed** Keep track of the information via RSS feeds. You can use RSS feeds to receive periodic updates about the lists.
    - ○ **Alert Me** Display a New Alert page where you can specify the alert's title as well as specify the list of users to which the alert's e-mail notification should be sent when there are changes to a specific item, document, list, or library.
- **Settings** This area provides the following commands to create a new column or view for the list as well access to the list settings:
    - ○ **Create Column** Add a column to store additional information about each item in the list.
    - ○ **Create View** Create a view to select columns, filters, and other display settings in the list.

- ○ **List Settings** Access a page with options to manage list settings such as version settings, permissions, columns, views, workflow, and policy.

Versioning in Task and Issue Lists

Windows SharePoint Services 3.0 task and issue lists allow for the tracking of versions of items within the lists. Each item's version is numbered and saved as part of the version history.

Versioning in task and issue lists is not enabled by default. To enable and configure versioning on a list, select Settings, then List Settings, and then under the heading General Settings click Versioning Settings. The following options are available when configuring task and issues list versioning settings, as shown in Figure 3-40:

- **Content Approval** The list administrator selects either Yes or No concerning whether to require content approval for submitted items.

- **Item Version History** The list administrator selects whether a version is created each time an item on the list is edited. Optionally, the administrator can choose to limit the number of retained versions.

- **Draft Item Security** The list administrator selects who should see draft items in the list. The administrator can choose from the following options:

    - ○ Any user who can read items

    - ○ Only users who can edit items

    - ○ Only users who can approve items (and the author of the item)

I would recommend keeping a low number of versions, as shown in Figure 3-41.

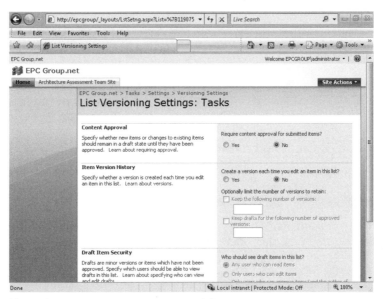

Figure 3-40 Versioning settings on a task list.

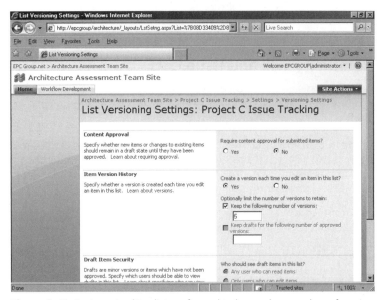

Figure 3-41 An issue tracking list configured to have a low number of versions.

Other Available SharePoint Lists

Windows SharePoint Services 3.0 has several other lists available out of the box that allow for robust collaboration within your organization. Some of the most popular lists are the announcements list and the contacts lists as well as a few other lists that are new with Windows SharePoint Services 3.0.

Announcements Lists

Announcements lists are used to share news, current initiatives, and status updates with your team as well as to provide timely reminders. For example, they could be very useful if your team members have an alert set on the announcements list to get automatically notified when an announcement is created or changed.

Choosing or Creating an Announcements List

A Windows SharePoint Services 3.0 team site has an existing announcements list called Announcements. This list can be accessed by clicking View All Site Content located at the top of the Quick Launch to view all available lists.

To create a new announcements list, click the View All Site Content link at the top of the Quick Launch and then click the Create link. You can then navigate down to the Communications section and click Announcements. You can also click Site Actions at the upper right of the page and then select Create. When the Create page appears, scroll down to the Communications section and then select Announcements. The New page will then appear, as shown in Figure 3-42.

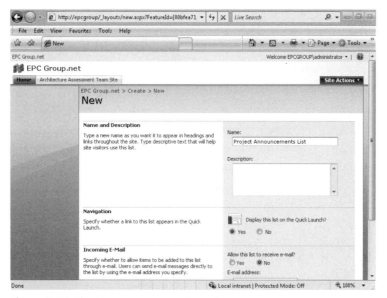

Figure 3-42 The New announcement creation page.

The following items are on the New announcement creation page:

- **Name** Enter the name of the new announcements list.

- **Description** Briefly characterize the list's content or purpose.

- **Display This List On The Quick Launch?** Choose Yes or No.

- **Send E-mail When Ownership Is Assigned?** Choose Yes or No.

Viewing and Updating an Announcements List

To view or modify the contents of an existing announcements list, click the link to the list in the Quick Launch. Alternatively, click View All Site Content and then open the announcements list from the available lists. See for example the list that has been opened in Figure 3-43.

Here's how to use this page:

- **View** Use the View menu to select one of the following format for viewing the announcements list:
  - **All Items** Display all items in the announcements list.
  - **Modify This View** Modify the current view.
  - **Create View** Create a new custom view.

- **New** Click this link to create a new announcement item. Figure 3-44 shows the New Item page for the announcements list.

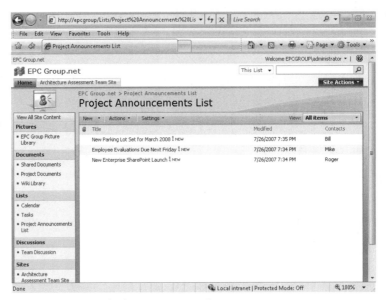

Figure 3-43   A standard announcements list.

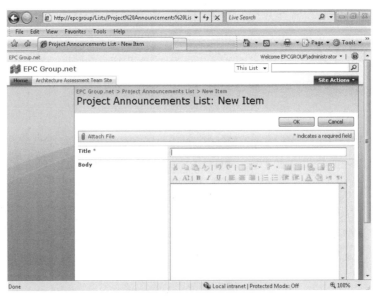

Figure 3-44   This page creates a new announcement item.

The following information can be entered on the New Item page:

- **Title**   Provide a name for the new announcement item.
- **Body**   Type the full text of your announcement using enhanced formatting with images, hyperlinks, and formatted text.

- ○ **Expires** If you would like the announcement to automatically expire after a specified date, type the date in the Expires box.

- **Actions** This area provides the following commands for working with the list:

  - ○ **Edit In Datasheet** Bulk edit items by using a datasheet format.

  - ○ **Export To Spreadsheet** Download a Microsoft Excel Web Query file. Such files have an .iqy file extension that, by default, causes Excel to start. Excel then connects to the team site database and downloads the data for the list you requested.

  - ○ **Open With Access** Allows for an item in a SharePoint list to be opened in Microsoft Access where users can create forms, reports, and queries using the data.

  - ○ **View RSS Feed** Keep track of the information via RSS feeds. You can use RSS Feeds to receive periodic updates about the list.

  - ○ **Alert Me** Display a New Alert page where you can specify the alert's title as well as specify the list of users to which the alert's e-mail notification should be sent when there are changes to a specific item, document, list, or library.

- **Settings** This area provides the following commands to create a new column or view for the announcement list as well as to access the list settings:

  - ○ **Create Column** Add a column to store additional information about each item in the list.

  - ○ **Create View** Create a view to select columns, filters, and other display settings in the list.

  - ○ **List Settings** Access a page with options to manage list settings such as version settings, permissions, columns, views, workflow, and policy.

Contact Lists

Contact lists within Windows SharePoint Services 3.0 store information about people on your project, on your team, or in your overall organization. Contact lists can be great for listing subject matter experts within certain departments so that people can contact the right person for their issue. Contact lists are also useful when you need to find a backup for someone who is on vacation or out sick for the day. It is also possible to update a list of all your key suppliers within Outlook 2007 or another compatible e-mail program that resides on your computer.

Choosing or Creating a Contact List

To create a new contact list, click the View All Site Content link at the top of the Quick Launch and then click the Create link. You can then navigate down to the Communications section and click Contacts. You can also click Site Actions at the upper right of the page and then select Create. When the Create page appears, scroll down to the Communications section and then select Contacts.

To view or modify the contents of an existing contact list, click its icon or title to display the contact list page, such as the list shown in Figure 3-45.

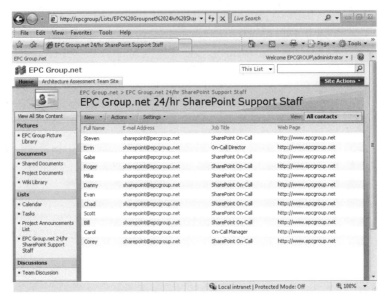

Figure 3-45   A contact list within a team site.

Here's how to use this page:

- **View**   Use the View menu to select one of the following formats for viewing the contacts list:
  - **All Contacts**   Display all items in the contacts list.
  - **Modify This View**   Modify the current view.
  - **Create View**   Create a new custom view.

- **New**   Click this link to create a new contacts list. Figure 3-46 shows the New Item page.

  The following information can be entered on the New Item page for the contacts list:
  - **Last Name**   Field for the contact's last name
  - **First Name**   Field for the contact's first name
  - **Full Name**   Field for the contact's full name
  - **E-Mail Address**   Field for the contact's e-mail address
  - **Company**   Field for the contact's company affiliation
  - **Job Title**   Field for the contact's job title

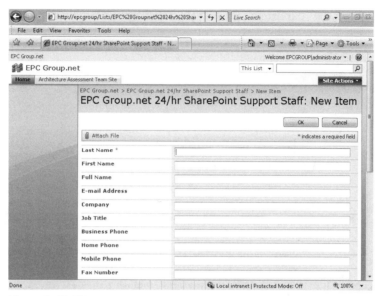

Figure 3-46 This page creates a new contact item.

- ○ **Business Phone** Field for the contact's business phone number
- ○ **Home Phone** Field for the contact's home phone number
- ○ **Mobile Phone** Field for the contact's mobile phone number
- ○ **Fax Number** Field for the contact's fax number
- ○ **Address** Field for the contact's street address
- ○ **City** Field for the contact's city
- ○ **State/Province** Field for the contact's state or province
- ○ **Zip/Postal Code** Field for the contact's ZIP code or other postal code
- ○ **Country/Region** Field for the contact's country or region
- ○ **Web Page** Field for a Web address that can be listed for this contact; a description field will make up the hyperlink to the URL
- ○ **Notes** Notes section regarding the contact
- **Actions** This area provides the following commands for working with the list:
  - ○ **Edit In Datasheet** Bulk edit items by using a datasheet format.
  - ○ **Connect To Outlook** Synchronize items within Outlook 2007 so that they are available offline.

- ○ **Export To Spreadsheet** Downloads a Microsoft Excel Web Query file. Such files have an .iqy file extension that, by default, causes Excel to start. Excel then connects to the team site database and downloads the data for the list you requested.

- ○ **Open With Access** Open an item in a SharePoint list in Microsoft Access to create forms, reports, and queries using the data.

- ○ **View RSS Feed** Keep track of the information via RSS feeds. You can use RSS feeds to receive periodic updates about the lists.

- ○ **Alert Me** Display a New Alert page where you can specify the alert's title as well as specify the list of users to which the alert's e-mail notification should be sent when there are changes to a specific item, document, list, or library.

- **Settings** This area provides the following commands to creating a new column or view for the list as well as access to the list settings:

  - ○ **Create Column** Add a column to store additional information about each item in the list.

  - ○ **Create View** Create a view to select columns, filters, and other display settings in the list.

  - ○ **List Settings** Access a page with options to manage list settings such as version settings, permissions, columns, views, workflow, and policy.

Wiki Page Library

The new wiki page libraries in Windows SharePoint Services 3.0 enable users to view and manage collections of wiki-linked pages that support tables, hyperlinks, and pictures. Wikis enable users to easily add, remove, or edit content with hardly any technical knowledge. A team site does not include a wiki page library by default, but one can be easily created. Alternatively, a user can create a new wiki site from the available out-of-the-box site templates.

To create a new wiki page library within an existing SharePoint team site, a site administrator or site owner can click View All Site Content on the top of the Quick Launch and then click Create. Once the Create page loads, navigate to the Libraries section and click Wiki Page Library. You can also click Site Actions at the upper right of the page and then select Create. When the Create page appears, navigate to the Libraries section and click Wiki Page Library. After you create the new Wiki Page Library, it will load and contain default content, as shown in Figure 3-47.

The following controls are available on the wiki Home screen:

- **Edit** Edit the wiki with a WYSIWYG (What You See Is What You Get) editor.

- **History** This will take you to the wiki library's Page History, which will show the library's history.

- **Incoming Links** This will take you to the wiki library's Incoming Links page, which will show the pages linked to the page.

Figure 3-47 A newly created wiki page library.

Updating a Wiki Page Library

To update the contents of the wiki library, open the library, and then click Edit in the upper right corner. A page similar to Figure 3-48 opens. You can now make changes to the content of the existing wiki that you feel are necessary to improve the wiki site. Multiple formatting tools are available, similar to those found in Microsoft Office Word. Wikis also have a check-in/check-out option so that users can lock a particular wiki while the edits are in progress and make comments once they check the wiki back in.

Wikis are powerful in that users can automatically view the changes that other users have made to a page. At the bottom of each page is last-modified information as well as the identity of the user associated with the modification. A History link is at the top of each wiki page (as in Figure 3-47 above), enabling users to view a color-coded modification history of the wiki page, as shown in Figure 3-49.

Chapter 3

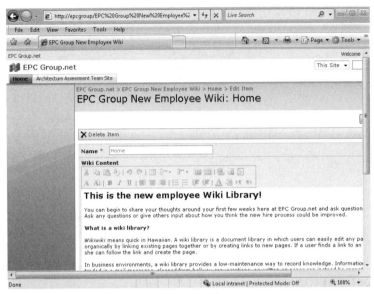

Figure 3-48 An existing wiki being edited by a user.

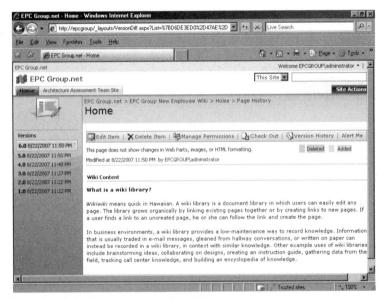

Figure 3-49 A wiki page modification history.

The following items are available on the page history screen showing the most recent version of the a wiki page:

- **Edit Item** Edit the current wiki page.

- **Delete Item** Delete the current wiki page.

- **Manage Permissions** Display a page where you can break the permission inheritance from the parent folder for the library and manage unique permissions for the item.

- **Check Out** Stop anyone but you from updating the document. (After you choose this option, it changes to Check In.)

- **Version History** Display a page showing all information regarding each modification along with the numbered versions of the wiki page.

- **Alert Me** Display a New Alert page where you can specify the alert's title as well as specify the list of users to which the alert's e-mail notification should be sent when there are changes to a specific item, document, list, or library.

- The All Pages view allows you to view all of the wiki pages that exist in the library as well as detailed information about each of the pages. Figure 3-50 shows the wiki library in the All Pages view.

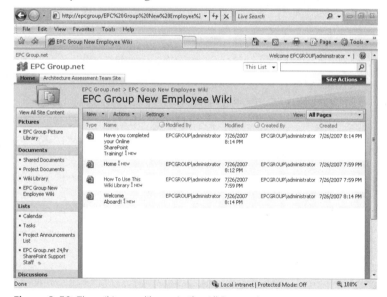

Figure 3-50 The wiki page library in the All Pages view.

Here's how to use the main wiki library page:

- **New** Create a new wiki page. Figure 3-51 shows a new page in the WYSIWYG editor.

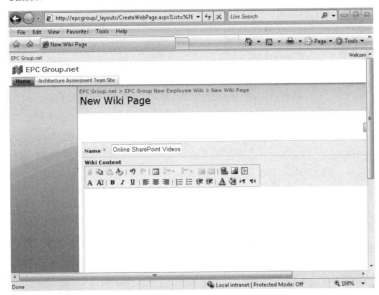

Figure 3-51 This is the New Wiki page.

The following items are available on the new wiki page:

- ○ **Name** The name of the new wiki entry.
- ○ **Wiki Content** The content for the new wiki; use the WYSIWYG (What You See Is What You Get) editor.
- ○ **Create** Save the new contents to the wiki page library.
- ○ **Cancel** Cancel the operation and return to the wiki page library Home.

- **Actions** This area provides the following commands for working with the wiki library:
  - ○ **Edit in Datasheet** Bulk edit items by using a datasheet format.
  - ○ **Connect To Outlook** Synchronize library items within Outlook 2007 so that they are available offline.
  - ○ **Export To Spreadsheet** Download a Microsoft Excel Web Query file. Such files have an .iqy file extension that, by default, causes Excel to start. Excel then connects to the team site database and downloads the data for the list you requested.
  - ○ **View RSS Feed** Keep track of the information via RSS feeds. You can use RSS feeds to receive periodic updates about the library.

○ **Alert Me** Display a New Alert page to specify the alert's title as well as specify the list of users to which the alert's e-mail notification should be sent when there are changes to a specific item, document, list, or library.

- **Settings** This area provides the following commands to create a new column or view for the list as well as to access the list settings:

    ○ **Create Column** Add a column to store additional information about each item in the library.

    ○ **Create View** Create a view to select columns, filters, and other display settings in the library.

    ○ **Document Library Settings** Access a page with options to manage list settings such as version settings, permissions, columns, views, workflow, and policy.

Surveys

Windows SharePoint Services 3.0 allows for the creation of Web-based surveys that allow you to poll the SharePoint user base easily. These surveys can assist users, managers, site owners, or others in making decisions, improving processes, rewarding special effort, and improving the SharePoint experience.

Creating a Survey

A SharePoint team site, by default, does not contain a survey, but one can be easily created. To create a new survey, click View All Site Content at the top of the Quick Launch and then click Create. You can then navigate to the Tracking section and click Survey. You can also click Site Actions, Create at the upper right of the Team Site page, then navigate to the Tracking section and click Survey.

The following items are on the page where you'll construct a new survey:

- **Name** Enter the name of the new survey.

- **Description** Briefly characterize the survey's content or purpose.

- **Display This Survey On The Quick Launch?** Choose Yes or No.

- **Show User Names In Survey Results?** Choose Yes or No.

- **Allow Multiple Responses?** Choose Yes or No.

Click Next. On the next page, you'll populate the first question, the question type, and other relevant information, as shown in Figure 3-52.

Chapter 3

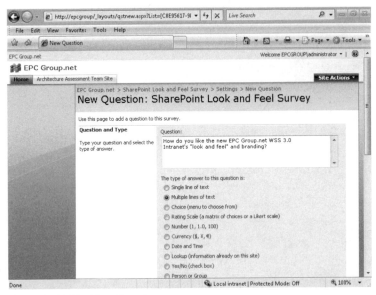

Figure 3-52 The New Question page.

The following items are on the survey's New Question page:

- **Question** Enter the name of the new survey.

- **Type (of answer)** Select one of the following formats for the answer to the question:
  - **Single Line Of Text** Columns that collect and display small amounts of text in a single line, including text only, combinations of text and numbers, and numbers that are not used in calculations (such as phone numbers).
  - **Multiple Lines Of Text** Columns that collect and display one or more sentences of text or formatted text.
  - **Choice** Columns that display a list of options.
  - **Rating Scale** A rating scale question consists of a question and subquestions that are rated on a scale such as 1 to 10. You will type a question into the Question box and then type a subquestion that supports the main questions with a number range to define the number of options that users can choose from.
  - **Number** Columns that provide a box in which you can type a numerical value.
  - **Currency** Columns that provide a box in which you can type a monetary value.
  - **Date And Time** Columns that store calendar or time-of-day information.
  - **Lookup** Columns that make it easy for you to select information that's already stored on a site.
  - **Yes/No** Columns that store true/false information.

- ○ **Person or Group** Columns that display the names of users or SharePoint groups.
- ○ **Page Separator** Insert a page break into your survey.
- • **Additional Question Settings** This section allows you to specify detailed options for the type of answer you selected.
  - ○ **Require A Response To This Question** Require an answer.
  - ○ **Display Choices Using** Display choices by using a drop-down menu, radio buttons, or check boxes (which allow for multiple selections).
  - ○ **Allow "Fill-In" Choices** Survey respondents can type their own selections.
  - ○ **Default Value** To not specify default values, leave this field blank. If you would like to specify a default value, the selection specified here would be the default for all new items. You can also select Calculated Value and then enter a formula to create the default value.
  - ○ **Branching Logic** This section allows you to specify if branching is enabled for this question. Branching can be used to skip to a specific question based on the user's response. A page break is automatically inserted after a branching-enabled question.
- • **Next Question** The survey saves the current question data and moves on to the next question.
- • **Finish** The survey saves the data of the current question and closes the survey. The user will be returned to the Survey Settings page.
- • **Cancel** Cancel the survey and return to the Survey Settings page.

After a survey has been created, it can be accessed using the Quick Launch. Figure 3-53 shows the main survey page for the newly created SharePoint Look And Feel Survey.

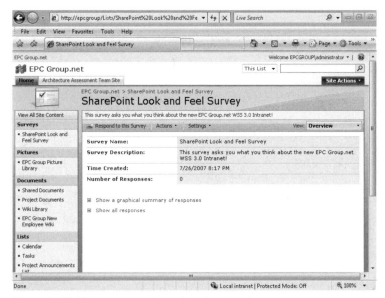

Figure 3-53 This new survey is ready to be taken by users.

The following items are available on the main survey overview page:

- **View** Use the View menu to select one of the following formats for viewing the contacts list:
  - ○ **Overview** Display an overview of the survey.
  - ○ **All Responses** Display all responses from users for this survey.
  - ○ **Graphical Summary** Display a graphical summary of the responses for this survey.
- **Respond To This Survey** This option starts the survey for the user.
- **Actions** This area provides the following commands for working with the survey:
  - ○ **Export To Spreadsheet** Download a Microsoft Excel Web Query file. Such files have an .iqy file extension that, by default, causes your spreadsheet program, such as Excel, to start. It then connects to the team site database and downloads the data for the list you requested.
  - ○ **View RSS Feed** Keep track of the information via RSS feeds. Use RSS feeds to receive periodic updates about the library.
  - ○ **Alert Me** Display a New Alert page where you can specify the alert's title as well as specify the list of users to which the alert's e-mail notification should be sent when there are changes to a specific item, document, list, or library.
- **Settings** This area provides the following commands to create a new column or view for the list as well as to access the list settings:
  - ○ **Add Questions** Add an additional question to this survey.
  - ○ **Survey Settings** Manage questions and settings for this survey.

Advanced List and Library Features

Windows SharePoint Services 3.0 has greatly enhanced the capabilities of the out-of-the-box lists. The following sections will briefly touch on a few of the advanced features in lists and libraries that are contained within Windows SharePoint Services 3.0.

Incoming E-Mail Settings

Lists and libraries in Windows SharePoint Services 3.0 can now receive and store e-mail messages and attachments. This feature can assist team members within the organization in archiving their e-mail or uploading the contents of a specific e-mail to a SharePoint list or library. E-mail that is sent to a SharePoint group can be archived so that entire teams can review a specific discussion without retrieving the messages from their mailboxes.

RSS Settings

Windows SharePoint Services 3.0 can now monitor RSS feeds from any SharePoint list including announcements, discussion boards, picture libraries, blogs, document libraries, form libraries, calendars, and surveys.

SharePoint administrators can enable RSS support within Central Administration at the Web application level so that RSS feeds can automatically be enabled throughout your SharePoint enterprise. Project managers who would like to be periodically updated about specific projects can receive RSS feeds from project issues tracking or task lists without having to browse throughout the specific project sites.

Data Calculations

Windows SharePoint Services 3.0 lists and libraries can now use formulas and functions to perform calculations on data. Data from multiple columns can be used, and formulas can be created to manipulate algebraic and logical expressions or date and time estimates concerning the content stored in any list or library.

Formulas can be as simple as =100+50, which adds 100 and 50, or more advanced, such as =[Income]*10/100, which calculates 10% of the value in the Income column.

Several formulas call built-in functions, such as this one, which would return Not OK if Expenses is greater than Income:

=IF([Expenses]>[Income], "Not OK", "OK")

This equation would return the day part of the date, which is 19:

=DAY("19-Mar-2007")

Formulas can also contain nested functions such as in this example:

=SUM(IF([E]>[O], [E]-[O], 23), [D])

In this formula, the *IF* function evaluates an expression and returns a value that the *SUM* function adds to the value in column D.

Data calculations in lists and libraries can use the following:

- Column references
- Functions
- Formulas with nested functions
- Formulas with constraints
- Calculation operators such as arithmetic operators, text operators, and comparison operators

Data calculation functionality is another useful resource that administrators can use to assist users in getting the most out of Windows SharePoint Services 3.0 lists and libraries.

Workflow in WSS 3.0

In the previous two chapters, Windows SharePoint Services 3.0 workflow has been discussed, and it will be further examined in detail in several future chapters. Chapter 7, "What's New with Templates and Design," discusses SharePoint Designers workflow designer, which is a great tool for creating WSS 3.0 workflows.

Workflows in WSS 3.0 are made available within lists or document libraries and can be used to attach business processes at the granular level of a document or list item. Workflow can be developed by users without development knowledge using a "no code" solution such as SharePoint Designer 2007, or they can be developed by senior .NET architects and developers using Visual Studio 2005 Designer for Windows Workflow Foundation. Windows SharePoint Services 3.0's architecture now allows for organizations to develop workflow solutions that are tailored to meet their exact needs.

Mobile Access in WSS 3.0

Windows SharePoint Services 3.0 enables users to access SharePoint content on mobile devices so that they are always connected to key business data. They can access discussion boards to view best practices or other key SharePoint lists and receive alerts when those lists are updated.

The following mobile browsers are compatible with WSS 3.0 (in the United States, United Kingdom, Germany, France, Japan, and Spain):

- Pocket Internet Explorer in Microsoft Windows Mobile for Pocket PC and in Smartphone

- The Nokia WAP 2.0 browser (xHTML only)

- Motorola Mobile Information Browser 2.2 or later

- Openwave UP.browser 6.2 or 7.0

- NTT DoCoMo: FOMA series

- The au by KDDI: WIN series

- SoftBank: 903SH,902SH,802SH,703N,703SH,703SH

- WILLCOM: W-ZERO3

Offline Capabilities in WSS 3.0

It is now easier than ever to take your SharePoint content offline while you are on the go. With Outlook 2007, users can work offline with content in libraries as well as certain lists such as contacts, tasks, calendars, and discussions. When you are able to connect back to the network, your files easily sync back up to the SharePoint server.

Access 2007 also has the ability to work with data from a SharePoint site that is offline. After links between Access 2007 tables and SharePoint lists are created, users can use Access 2007 to work with and analyze list data offline. Just like in Outlook 2007, once the user is reconnected to the network, the data can be synchronized back to the Share-Point server.

Third-party vendors are also developing robust offline solutions for SharePoint. Colligo and iOra are just two of the companies that have developed powerful offline solutions that are further helping organizations use SharePoint offline.

Information on Colligo's SharePoint offline solution can be found at *www.colligo.com*, **and information on iOra's SharePoint offline solution can be can be found at** *www.iora.com*.

The Recycle Bin

Item-level recovery has been a big concern for many users of WSS 2.0 and SPS 2003. With the new Recycle Bin in WSS 3.0, users can now easily recover deleted documents without having to send a request to the SharePoint administrator to have an entire site restored (as has been the case). When a document is deleted, it is sent to your Recycle Bin, as shown in Figure 3-54, similar to how a file is deleted in Windows Vista or Windows XP.

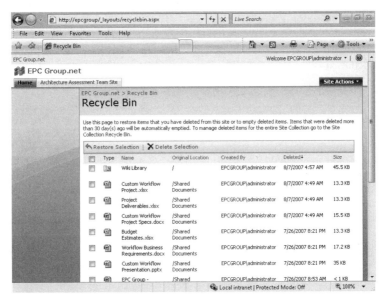

Figure 3-54 This is a site's Recycle Bin.

Users can periodically clean out their Recycle Bins, which will then send the file to the site collection Recycle Bin, where SharePoint sites' collection administrators can then manage the deletion of the document.

> **Note**
>
> By default, items that were deleted more than 30 days ago are automatically deleted from your Recycle Bin.

The Recycle Bin can store more than just your deleted files. If a site administrator accidentally deletes an important list or library containing critical business data, the deleted material can be retrieved from the WSS 3.0 Recycle Bin, which automatically stored it. SharePoint administrators can modify the retention schedule of the Recycle Bin to meet your organization's needs or can completely disable the Recycle Bin functionality.

Information Rights Management (IRM) and Windows SharePoint Services 3.0

Microsoft has developed Information Rights Management (IRM) to protect organizations' content and intellectual property. IRM enables security and access controls for content so that when a user attempts to access a protected file from a SharePoint document library, IRM will verify that the user does in fact have the rights to access the file. A license will then be given to the user allowing access to the content at the appropriate security or permissions level. IRM encrypts the file before the user actually downloads the content, which further secures the intellectual property and content of the file.

For more information on Information Rights Management, visit the site Information Rights Management in the 2007 Microsoft Office System at *www.office.microsoft.com/en-us/help/ HA101029181033.aspx.*

> **Note**
>
> IRM is enabled at the document library level but must be configured throughout the SharePoint environment for the functionality to propagate correctly throughout the enterprise. Also, IRM typically must be installed on each SharePoint front-end Web server throughout the organization.

Using Alerts

Alerts enable you to receive e-mail notification when information in lists or libraries is changed. Several criteria can be set before an alert is sent:

- Someone else changes a document
- Someone else changes a document created by you
- Someone else changes a document last modified by you

Alerts can be sent to users as soon as one of the previously mentioned criteria is met, or users can choose to receive a daily or weekly summary of the alerts. Users can also specify the time they would like to receive their weekly summary, which can be helpful for those with unusual working hours or limited connectivity.

There have been several alert improvements that make it easier to stay up to date on updates and changes within the SharePoint environment. In the previous SharePoint release, a major complaint from the user base has been that they are not able to set alerts for other users. Third-party solutions were developed to solve some of these issues, but most companies struggled with setting alerts for key individuals who did not have the time to manage their own SharePoint alerts.

WSS 3.0 now enables users to input the names or e-mail addresses of multiple users at once to properly manage the organization's alerts. Managers or resources in the field do not always have the time to go in and manage granular items such as an alert, so this new feature in WSS 3.0 is one that organizations can immediately benefit from.

In Summary...

Windows SharePoint Services 3.0 provides a wealth of functionality for working with lists and libraries. The improvements in WSS 3.0 greatly assist organizations in getting greater user buy-in. Many of the complaints SharePoint consultants such as myself receive regarding functionality limitations in the previous version have been addresses and resolved.

With the superior technology that this Web-based platform can offer organizations in a secure and governed environment, the standard file share will soon be a thing of the past.

The next chapter explains how Windows SharePoint Services 3.0 integrates with the applications in Microsoft Office 2007.

Chapter 3

Using SharePoint with Microsoft Office 2007

Chapter 3, "Using the Built-In Features of Windows SharePoint Services 3.0," explained how Microsoft Windows SharePoint Services 3.0 (WSS 3.0) enables you to use Microsoft Office 2007 programs from within SharePoint to edit your documents and content easily. It is also possible to work in the reverse manner with a Microsoft Office application to open and save files, collaborate with other users, manage alerts, and manipulate SharePoint sites without using a browser at all. Microsoft Office has improved its integration points for Web-based collaboration so that seamless editing of a document stored within SharePoint can occur without affecting the user experience in Microsoft Office.

These enhanced integration points also make it easier than ever for users to perform actions such as content type classifications or the population of certain metadata fields in a Microsoft Office application's document properties pane right before completing an upload. Such seamless integration points help improve an organization's overall content management strategy, which in turn improves search results from SharePoint and the user's information retrieval performance.

This chapter will walk you through how Microsoft Office applications can act as the client to Windows SharePoint Services 3.0. This chapter covers a wide array of the Microsoft Office applications including Microsoft Office Word 2007, Microsoft Office Excel 2007, Microsoft Office PowerPoint 2007, Microsoft Office Access 2007, Microsoft Office OneNote 2007, Microsoft Office Publisher 2007, Microsoft Office Outlook 2007, Microsoft Office InfoPath 2007, and Microsoft Office Groove 2007.

> **Note**
>
> Organizations that have implemented WSS 3.0 but are still using Microsoft Office 2003 or Office XP should experience no loss of functionality within their environment. If they have upgraded their previous Microsoft Office version to Microsoft Office 2007 but are still using Windows SharePoint Services 2.0, they will find some features and functionality that will not be as robust as they would be if they were using Windows SharePoint Services 3.0.

Opening and Saving Library Documents

Windows SharePoint Services 3.0 and Windows Vista offer several ways to save content directly into SharePoint. The File Open and File Save As dialog boxes are the most popular and well-known options for saving content, and they will continue to be the most popular methods to save content directly into SharePoint. To save content directly into SharePoint, follow these steps:

1. In any Microsoft Office program, choose Open or Save As from the File menu.

2. You now have a few options for locating the SharePoint site in which you would like to save your content. If you are a Microsoft Office SharePoint Server 2007 (MOSS) user, click My SharePoint Sites to view a list of SharePoint sites of which you are a member or in which you have published content. You can also click Computer, which is under the Favorite Links section, and double-click the saved network location of the SharePoint site you saved. In this example, I click Computer and double-click a SharePoint site that was saved as a network location. In Windows XP, you could click on My Network Places in the Save As dialog box to view the saved network places of any SharePoint sites. You could also type or paste the site's URL into the File Name box in the Microsoft Office application's Save As window.

INSIDE OUT   What do you do when the document library you need isn't listed?

If the SharePoint site you are looking for does not appear in My SharePoint Sites or in Computer, type or paste the site's URL into the File Name box in the Microsoft Office application's Save As window. This will then update the Save As windows with the available libraries for which you can save a document. Select the appropriate library and click Save.

3. The Save As dialog box should switch into Web view, displaying the site's content, which will display all the site's document libraries as well as all related sites and workspaces, as shown in Figure 4-1.

4. Double-click the library that you would like to open and then browse to the appropriate location within the library to save your file. In this example, the file is being saved at the top level of the document library, and the user is able to view the other files that exist within the library, as shown in Figure 4-2.

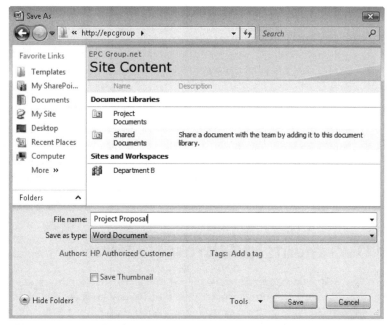

Figure 4-1 Microsoft Office applications enable a user to browse for the appropriate document library or site on which to save documents.

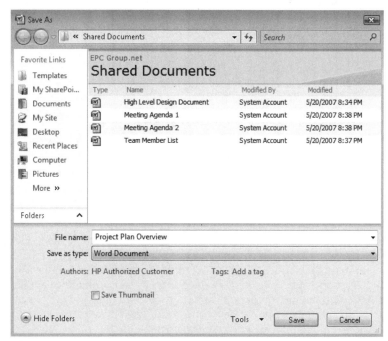

Figure 4-2 The Microsoft Office program will also display the contents of a SharePoint library to enable the user to choose the proper library location.

If you originally chose File Open, you would follow the same procedure as in steps 1–4, click either My SharePoint Sites or Computer or My Network Places in Windows XP, and select the saved network location of the SharePoint site. Once you find the appropriate SharePoint library, you can browse to find the file you would like to open. Once it is located, double-click the file.

If you chose Save As and want to overwrite an existing file, double-click that file. Otherwise, type in the file name you would like to assign to the file and then click Save.

Saving documents directly from Microsoft Office to SharePoint is a best practice for information workers because doing so allows for one copy to be stored within a document library or SharePoint site. This builds on the "one version of the truth" concept for content because you are not first saving it to your computer and then uploading it later to SharePoint.

Editing Documents in Microsoft Office

The vast array of applications offered in the Microsoft Office suite provides various ways of properly editing documents and content so that you can not only take advantage of the technology at your fingertips, but also allow SharePoint to interact and assist in editing and managing this content. Today's workplace is vastly different from that of just a few years ago, and the technology combination of SharePoint and Microsoft Office enables users to create content and quickly share it with other members of the organization. This can all be accomplished in a secure, Web-based environment that offers seamless integration with your favorite Microsoft Office applications.

When you edit documents with Microsoft Office and use the collaborative functionality found in SharePoint, you can cross departmental, cultural, and organizational hurdles to quickly receive feedback and additional ideas from a much larger audience.

Checking In and Checking Out

When editing files, a key feature available within the SharePoint and Microsoft Office suites is check-in and check-out capability. This feature enables a user to temporarily control a document's state while editing it to prevent other users from making simultaneous changes. This feature also populates SharePoint's version control and tracking mechanism to allow for granular document management of a single file within a library. A new version is created only when a file is checked back in, not every time a file is simply opened and closed.

Microsoft Office enables you check in files from within a document library and also directly from Office Word 2007, Office PowerPoint 2007, Office Excel 2007, or Microsoft Office Visio 2007. WSS 3.0 enables users of Microsoft Office applications to work with checked-out files on their local hard drive regardless of whether they are connected to the local network. When a copy is checked out, a copy is stored by default in the SharePoint Drafts folder in the My Documents folder on your computer. It is possible to customize the storage location to meet your organization's needs. If you are going to be traveling or are unable to connect to the network, this is a great way to quickly work with a file on your local hard drive while SharePoint keeps other SharePoint users apprised of the document's status.

When a file is checked out, other users will not be able to open it, and a special icon appears next to the file in the document library listing. Other users may be able to open a read-only copy of the file, but they will not be able to overwrite the file that is checked out. By default, SharePoint administrators can configure libraries to require users to check out files before editing them. Also, there is no need to worry about the transparency of the edits you are making while the document is checked out because they will not be accessible or viewable to anyone until the document is checked back into the library. Users can create comments based on their edits, which will be tracked in a document's version history within the document library.

A user can check in a file and select the Keep The Document Checked Out After Checking In This Version option to allow other users to see the changes that were made but to continue to leave the document in a checked-out state.

> **Note**
>
> If checkout is required within a document library, prior to editing being enabled, a user who wants to work on the file will be notified that the file is being checked out.

Checking Out a File from Within a Document Library

When you check out a file from a library on a WSS 3.0 site, you ensure that others cannot make changes to the file while you edit it. While the file is checked out, you can edit and save the file, close it, and reopen it. Other users cannot change the file or see your changes until you check in the file.

To check out a document so that only you are able to edit it, perform the following steps:

1. Within a document library, hover over a file name, click the corresponding drop-down list, and select the Check Out option, as shown in Figure 4-3.

INSIDE OUT   Picture library differences

If you are in a picture library, you will first need to click the file, which takes you into an additional properties page. Then select the Check Out option, as shown in Figure 4-4.

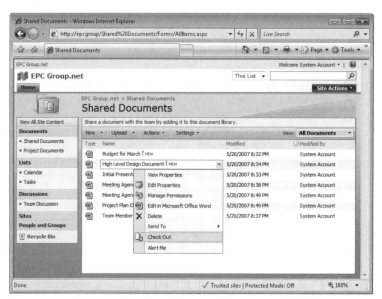

Figure 4-3 A user can select the Check Out option from a drop-down list within a document library.

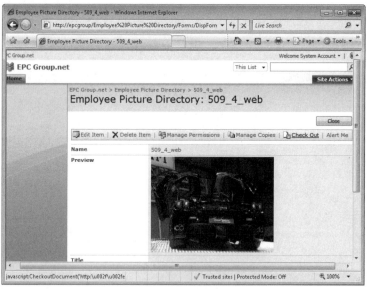

Figure 4-4 In a picture library, a user must click an image to enter the image's properties page. Then they select the Check Out option.

2. When you are working with a Microsoft Office application, a message box may ask if you would like to work with the file as a local draft (see Figure 4-5). If you select this option, the file will be stored in the SharePoint Drafts folder, as mentioned in the previous section. If you do not check this option, the local draft copy will be stored on the server while it is in a checked-out state.

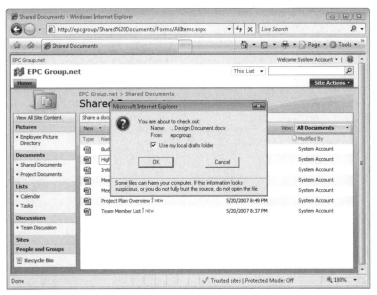

Figure 4-5 A user has the option of working with a file as a local draft copy that would be stored on the user's local hard drive.

Checking Out a File from Within Word, PowerPoint, or Excel

When a user has already used a Microsoft Office application to open a document that resides in a SharePoint document library, the following procedure can be used to check out that document for editing in Word, PowerPoint, or Excel. (Note that the checkout procedure for Office Visio 2007 is detailed in the section titled "Checking Out a File from Within Visio" later in the chapter.)

1. Within Word, PowerPoint, or Excel, click the Microsoft Office Button, shown in Figure 4-6.

At this point, what you see displayed depends on what default settings you have enabled within your Microsoft Office application. After clicking the Microsoft Office Button, you may see the Server option, which is the next step to check out a document. Or, your default view may not be set up to show this option. If you do not see the Server option after clicking the Microsoft Office Button, you will need to add it by clicking Word Options, Options, or the options of the Microsoft Office application you are currently in, as shown in Figure 4-6.

The Options menu (Word Options in this example) enables you to customize the application to your specifications. The Server button can be added to the application by clicking Customize. Then, on the Choose Commands From drop-down list, select All Commands. Scroll down the list until you find Server and then click Add to add the Server option to the drop-down list when the Microsoft Office Button is selected. You must close the application after you make this change and be authenticated to SharePoint for the option to display.

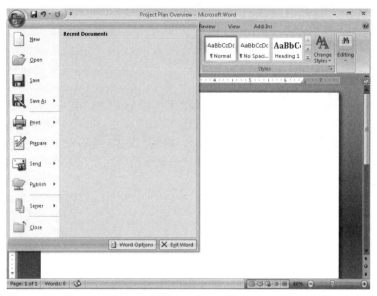

Figure 4-6 The new Microsoft Office Button is the single entry point and common denominator among most applications in Microsoft Office 2007.

INSIDE OUT   Just close and reopen to be sure

After adding the Server option, I recommend closing and then reopening the application. Then perform a File Open command and type or paste in the location of a SharePoint site. This will ensure that everything will work right the first time.

2. After clicking the Microsoft Office Button, click Server and then click Check Out, as shown in Figure 4-7.

3. After the Check Out option is selected, most users will see a message detailing where the checked out file will be stored during the check-out period. If this message box appears, click OK.

INSIDE OUT   Want to change where your temporary files are stored?

It is possible to modify the location where checked out files are temporarily stored while they are being modified. For example, to make this change in Word 2007, click the Microsoft Office Button and then click Word Options. You will then need to click the Save category of options and modify Server Drafts Location.

Figure 4-7 A user can select Check Out directly from within a Microsoft Office application to check out the file stored within SharePoint.

Checking In a File from Within Word, PowerPoint, or Excel

When you have already used a Microsoft Office application to open a document that resides in a SharePoint document library, and you have checked the document out, you can follow a process similar to checking out to check the document back in to SharePoint. Use the following procedure in Word, PowerPoint, or Excel to check in a document to SharePoint. (Note that the check-in procedure for Visio is detailed in the section titled "Checking in a File from Within Visio" later in this chapter.)

1. Within Word, PowerPoint, or Excel, click the Microsoft Office Button, shown in Figure 4-6. Click Server and then click Check In, as shown in Figure 4-8.

2. After the Check In option is selected, you may be prompted to enter comments about the edits that were made to the document. If the document library is configured to create major and minor versions, you may also be prompted for this information.

3. If you plan to keep working on the file, and if the Keep The Document Checked Out After Checking In This Version check box is available, you can select it.

> **Note**
>
> The Keep The Document Checked Out After Checking In This Version option is available if the library does not track versions, if the library tracks all versions in the same manner, or if you are checking in a minor version. The option is not available if you are checking in a major version or publishing a file.

Figure 4-8 A user can select to check a file directly into SharePoint from within a Microsoft Office application.

Checking Out a File from Within Visio

When a user has used Visio to open a document that resides in a SharePoint document library, the following procedure can be used to check out that document for editing. (You will not see the check out or check in options unless you have first opened a Visio document that resides in a document library in a SharePoint site.)

1.   Within Visio, click the File menu.

2.   On the File menu, click Check Out, as shown in Figure 4-9.

Checking In a File from Within Visio

When a user has already used Visio to open a document that resides in a SharePoint document library and has checked the file out, the following procedure can be used to check the document back in to SharePoint. (You will not see the check-out or check-in options unless you have first opened a Visio document that resides in a document library in a SharePoint site.)

1.   Within Visio, click the File menu and click Check In, as shown in Figure 4-10.

2.   After the Check In option is selected, you may be prompted to enter comments about the edits that were made to the document. If the document library is configured to create major and minor versions, you may also be prompted for this information.

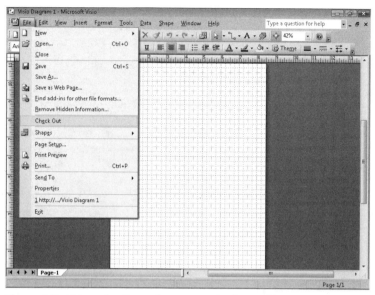

Figure 4-9   Visio makes it easy for users to check out a file.

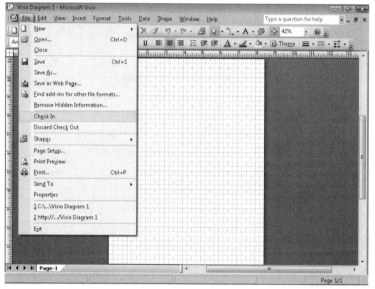

Figure 4-10   Visio makes it easy for users to check in a file to SharePoint that was previously checked out for editing.

3.   If the Keep The Document Checked Out After Checking In This Version check box is available, you can select it if you plan to keep working on the file.

Editing Content in Microsoft Office: Word, Excel, PowerPoint, and Publisher

Microsoft Office allows for similar editing of content in Word, Excel, PowerPoint, and Office Publisher 2007 files stored within SharePoint. Not only can users edit content in document libraries from within the Microsoft Office application, they can also use SharePoint's additional collaborative editing features, such as creating a document workspace, to enable a user to simultaneously work on content with other users. Microsoft Office applications can now initiate ad hoc knowledge management around a particular document or piece of content to gain insight from other users and take advantage of their best practices, lessons learned, or in-depth knowledge on a topic.

Working with Document Workspaces

As discussed in previous chapters, a document workspace site can be created to assist users as they coordinate and collaborate on the editing and development of a document. When a document workspace site is created, you not only get the standard check-in and check-out features that come with the seamless integration of Microsoft Office, but you also get additional functionality within the workspace site.

A document workspace's discussion board is a great place to receive input from other users on the content of a document the user is working on. A calendar is available to schedule meetings or events related to the document, and a task list is available to assign specific tasks to team members so that all items are properly tracked and completed. Combining all of this functionality with the out-of-the-box alert capabilities in a document workspace (as shown in Figure 4-11) provides a great environment for teams to develop extremely high-quality and well–thought-out content that a standard file share or static document sitting on a user's hard drive could rarely equal.

A user can also take advantage of the Microsoft Office application's Document Management pane, seen in Figure 4-12, which has five separate tabs with actions such as updating tasks or adding and inviting new team members to the workspace.

Adding a Site to Trusted Sites Zone

You may need to add your SharePoint site as a trusted site to resolve any authentication issues around the Document Information Panel or creating a workspace. To add sites to the trusted sites zone in Microsoft Internet Explorer 6 or 7, follow these steps:

1. Click on Tools and then select Internet Options.

2. Select the Security Tab.

3. Select the Trusted Sites zone.

4. Click on Sites. Type in or paste the URL of the SharePoint site you would like to be trusted and click Add.

5. When you are finished, click Close and then click OK.

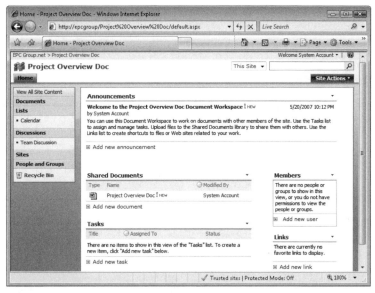

Figure 4-11 A standard document workspace created right from Word.

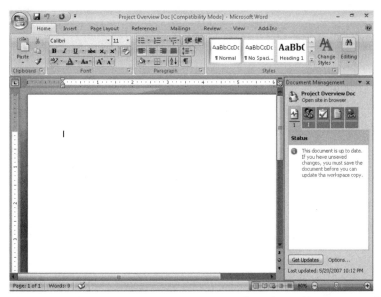

Figure 4-12 The Document Management pane's five tabs enable users to perform several different actions to update information in the document workspace.

An organization can place a retention policy on document workspaces so that once a Microsoft Office file's editing and team collaboration are complete, the document workspace can be deleted. Some organizations like to retain these document work-spaces for reference purposes or to view best practices or lessons learned on a specific document, or the organization may want them to be deleted after a specific time.

Document workspaces can be created from within a Microsoft Office application by performing the following actions:

1. Click the Microsoft Office Button and select the Publish option. Then select Create Document Workspace, as shown in Figure 4-13, to begin the creation of the document workspace.

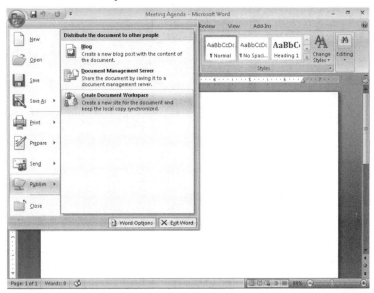

Figure 4-13 From within the Microsoft Office application, a user can select from a few simple options to begin creating the document workspace.

2. The Document Management pane will then load, requesting a user to specify the document workspace name as well as the location for the new workspace, as shown in Figure 4-14.

INSIDE OUT   Exclude default.aspx from the path

When specifying the location, it is important to not include the default.aspx page in the path you are providing. For example, the SharePoint path of *http://epcgroup/projects/default.aspx* failed during creation, but the path of *http://epcgroup/projects/* was successful.

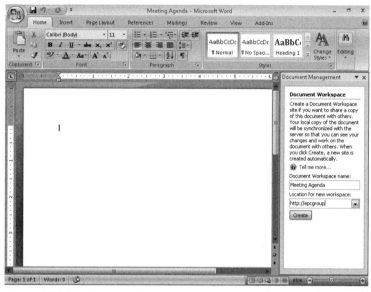

Figure 4-14 The Document Management pane prompts the user for the new workspace name and the location (that is, the SharePoint URL) for which the workspace will be created.

3. After the Document Workspace Name and Location For New Workspace fields are populated, click Create. The workspace will be created. Once this is done, the Document Management pane will have tabs available for workspace management, as shown previously in Figure 4-12. The Document Management tabs are Status, Members, Tasks, Documents, and Links.

> **Note**
>
> It is also possible to create a document workspace by simply sending an e-mail in Outlook. When a user sends a file as a shared attachment in an e-mail, the sender of that shared attachment will automatically become the administrator of the workspace, and all recipients of the message will become collaborative members of the workspace site.

Modifying Existing Document Properties

As discussed in previous chapters, WSS 3.0 offers robust content types and metadata capturing capabilities. At any time, the Microsoft Office applications can modify the content types and columns properties of Microsoft Office documents stored within SharePoint. Keeping your Microsoft Office documents' metadata current will enable search functionality in SharePoint to remain current and return accurate results to the organization's users.

To update a Microsoft Office document's properties within the application, you can perform the following actions:

1. Click the Microsoft Office Button, select Prepare, then select Properties, as shown in Figure 4-15.

Figure 4-15   At any time, a user can modify the existing properties of a document within the Microsoft Office application.

2. The Document Properties pane will load, and you will be able to populate the available options, as shown in Figure 4-16. Red asterisks mark the required fields.

If an organization has not configured any content types or custom columns, the user's options for populating a document's properties may be limited.

Integrating Excel with WSS 3.0

Excel is a powerful application that enables users to organize and analyze large amounts of data in files typically referred to as spreadsheets. In conjunction with WSS 3.0, users can manage their Excel files within document libraries and make the data within the Excel files securely available to users via a SharePoint list.

Excel makes it possible for users to create a one-way connection to data that resides in a SharePoint list so that once changes are made to that list, they can be automatically introduced to the Excel spreadsheet. With this type of one-way connection, the Excel spreadsheet will always be current, because the SharePoint site will overwrite any data in the worksheet with the latest SharePoint list data. This makes it easier than ever for users to avoid the pitfalls of e-mailing Excel attachments to multiple users, managing the retrieval of those updated files, and performing the daunting task of updating the "master" copy in an efficient and accurate manner.

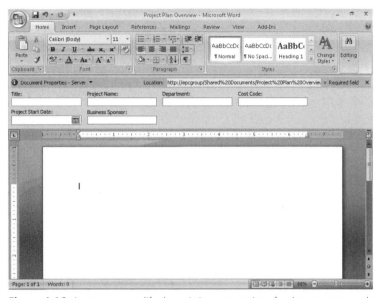

Figure 4-16 A user can modify the existing properties of a document to update a document's content type or metadata.

You have a choice about whether to have the data in the Excel spreadsheet updated after a change is made in a SharePoint list. If you want to keep it updated, a one-way connection can be created. If not, you can simply export the table data to a SharePoint site without creating this connection.

> **Note**
>
> When a user with Excel 2007 opens an existing Excel 2003 file, no loss of functionality will occur, and the experience will be identical to that of opening an Excel 2007 file.

Importing Excel Data into a SharePoint List

WSS 3.0 enables you to easily create a new SharePoint list based on an existing Excel spreadsheet. By following a few easy steps, you can import data into SharePoint and begin collaboratively managing your content in one secure area that helps promote the one version of the truth that SharePoint champions.

To import data, the user must have Excel or another SharePoint-compatible spreadsheet application loaded. To create a custom SharePoint list based on an existing Excel spreadsheet, perform the following steps:

1. Select Create from either the Site Actions or the View All Site Content page.

2. Select Import Spreadsheet, as shown in Figure 4-17, to begin the importation process.

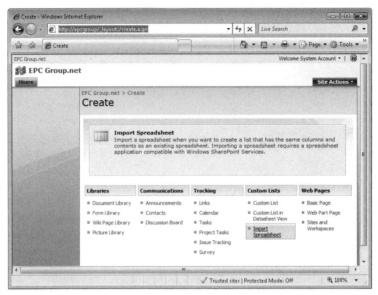

Figure 4-17 A user can easily create a new custom SharePoint list by selecting Import Spreadsheet from the Create page.

3. The New page will load, as shown in Figure 4-18. On this page, the user will need to populate the following fields:

- **Name** This will name the new custom list being created by the Excel file importation.

- **Description** The user can optionally specify a description of the new list.

- **Import From Spreadsheet** This enables the user to browse for and select the existing Excel spreadsheet to be imported into a new custom list.

Once the existing spreadsheet is selected, click Import to create the new custom SharePoint list based on your existing data.

4. Once the user clicks Import, the spreadsheet application installed on the user's machine will load and prompt the user for the following information, as shown in Figure 4-19:

- **Range Type** Select from three range types—Range Of Cells, Table Range, or Named Range.

- **Select Range** Select a range within the spreadsheet based on the type of range that was selected. Click the Select Range box to select a range of cells to import and then drag through the spreadsheet areas that you want to import. If the spreadsheet uses names to represent cells, in the Range Type box, click Named Range.

5. Once the Range Type and Select Range fields have been populated, click Import.

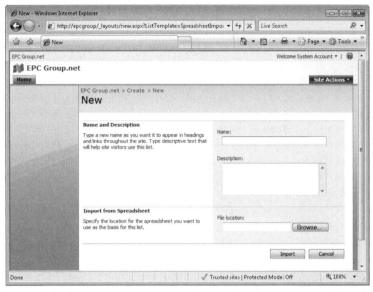

Figure 4-18 You can supply a name to the new list being created as well as a brief description. Then browse to the existing Excel spreadsheet and click Import to create the new list.

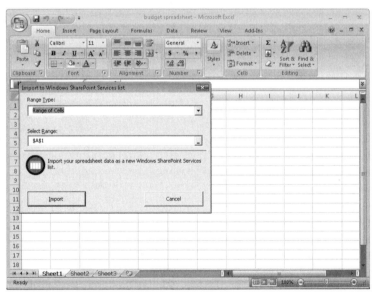

Figure 4-19 You will be asked to specify the areas of the spreadsheet that should be imported.

Windows SharePoint Services 3.0 importation functionality is powerful, but it is important to double-check all the columns and data within the new SharePoint list to ensure they were properly imported. After the list has been created, a user can view or change the data types of columns in the list by opening the list and selecting List Settings on the Settings menu.

Once on the Customize page, a user can view the new list's column names as well as their type and required status. To modify the settings of one of the columns, click the name of the column to modify, and the column's properties will be displayed for review, as shown in Figure 4-20.

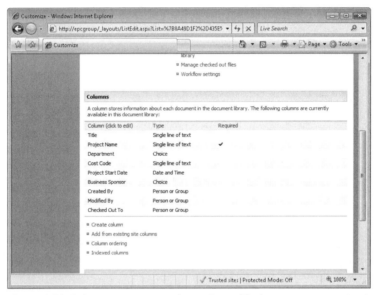

Figure 4-20 Column properties can be easily modified to meet an organization's exact needs.

Excel Services is a new technology that allows for some additional capabilities and features around the reuse and sharing of Excel data. It also provides a Web service for custom application development. However, it is only available in SharePoint Server 2007.

Excel Services provides SharePoint Server users with two primary ways of interacting with Excel data:

- Through an Excel Web Access Web Part, which offers real-time collaborative access to an Excel workbook via a Web browser

- Through Excel Web services, which offers a programming interface for the development of custom applications using a .NET Framework–compatible development tool such as Microsoft Visual Studio 2005

For additional information on Excel Services, refer to the section titled "Excel Services Overview" in Chapter 2, "Introducing Microsoft Office SharePoint Server 2007."

Integrating Office Access 2007 with WSS 3.0

With the release of Access 2007 and WSS 3.0, the days are over when you were forced to store an Access database on a shared network drive for use by multiple users. It is now possible to manage your Access databases and share their data in a much more powerful manner. Combining the collaborative nature of SharePoint and the powerful analytical features of Access will allow you and your organization to powerfully manage this data.

Integrating your Access databases with WSS 3.0 enables you to manage your data in a more centralized manner because you can manage the data by assigning different groups or team members specific permission levels based on their roles or access needs. The version control features of SharePoint can also be used to manage versions of the data, and the alert functionality can notify you of any updates or changes.

Another useful feature is the ability to create list views based on the items within the Access database. Similar to standard list views, these Access-related SharePoint views can display forms, queries, and reports. This integration enables users throughout the organization to securely view the Access database data in the familiar SharePoint.

Moving Access Databases into SharePoint

A user can move an existing Access database into SharePoint via the Move To Share-Point Wizard within Access. When a database is moved to a SharePoint site, lists are created within the SharePoint site that are linked back to the tables within the database. By moving a database into SharePoint and creating these lists, your team members can use these lists to update and manage the data as well as view the latest versions of any changes that have occurred. If your database contains several tables, which most Access databases do, links between these lists are created within Share-Point. These links are stored within the Access database along with the other standard Access items such as reports, forms, and queries.

> **Note**
>
> The Move To SharePoint Wizard is a powerful and easy-to-use tool, but when moving an existing database into SharePoint, you need to consider the database's size and the performance of your overall environment. If you begin the wizard and decide you need to cancel the procedure, click Stop.

To use the Move To SharePoint Wizard in Access, perform the following steps:

1. On the External Data tab, click Move To SharePoint, as seen in Figure 4-21.

2. Follow the steps in the resulting Move To SharePoint Site Wizard, including specifying the location of the SharePoint site to which the data should be moved. While the wizard is running, you can cancel the operation at any time by clicking Cancel or Stop.

Chapter 4

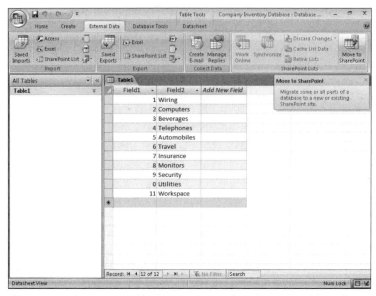

Figure 4-21 The Move To SharePoint Site Wizard can be accessed from the External Data tab.

3. After the wizard has completed, select the Show Details check box to view the specific details of the migration. Click Finish after the wizard has completed these actions to finalize the data move.

> **Note**
>
> If you receive a warning message during this process, the log table should be reviewed to make sure all of the data was properly moved and to see if any actions are necessary on your part to allow for a successful data move.

Publishing an Access Database to SharePoint

With Access, you can publish a database to a SharePoint site to allow other users to view it and still use Access to build reports, queries, and forms for the database. After you publish your database to SharePoint, Access will retain its SharePoint location in memory so that you do not need to locate the server when changes need to be published.

To publish an Access database to SharePoint, do the following:

1. Click the Microsoft Office Button, select Publish, and then click Document Management Server, as in Figure 4-22.

2. Specify the URL of the SharePoint site where the database should be published.

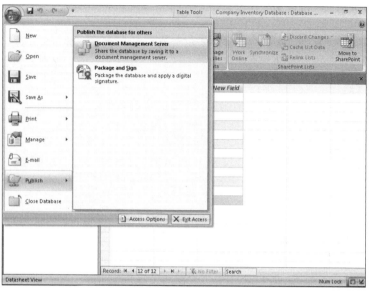

Figure 4-22 To publish a database to SharePoint, select Publish, Document Management Server.

3. Specify the library location, such as a document library, to publish the database to and then click Open.

4. Type the name for the database in the Name box and then select Publish.

Using Access to Work Offline with Linked Tables

Access enables users to work offline with data that has been linked to a WSS 3.0 Share-Point list. This powerful functionality is great for users who need to update SharePoint list data when they are not connected to the network or are out of the office. You can also use this offline feature to view and display your SharePoint list data to others in meetings and at offsite locations without server connectivity.

Users must first create links between their SharePoint lists and Access database tables before using these offline features. A link can be established if you move your database to a SharePoint site, as discussed previously, which will link the tables in the database to the SharePoint lists within the site. It is also possible to create the links between lists and Access by exporting the data from a list in a datasheet view within SharePoint to an Access database table.

Once the links between the SharePoint lists and Access database tables are in place, you can immediately start to work offline. A user can take the lists offline and work with them to update the data. When the user reconnects to the server, the data is synced back up to SharePoint, and the lists are then updated. There is no need to worry about other users updating the identical record within the SharePoint list while you are offline, because once you sync to the server, you are able to resolve any conflicts at that time.

Chapter 4

> **Note**
>
> Databases created by versions of Access earlier than 2007 do not support these offline features. If you have an Access database from a previous version and want to take advantage of these offline features, convert the database to the Access 2007 file format.

Placing SharePoint List Data Offline

A user can easily place the SharePoint list data offline for Access to use. If you have already published your database to a SharePoint site, save a local copy of the database to your computer prior to placing the list offline.

To place your SharePoint list data offline for Access to use, perform the following steps:

1. In Access, open the database that is linked to a SharePoint list.

2. On the External Data tab, select Work Offline, as seen in Figure 4-23. If you do not see this option, your tables are not properly linked to the SharePoint list, or the list may already be in an offline status.

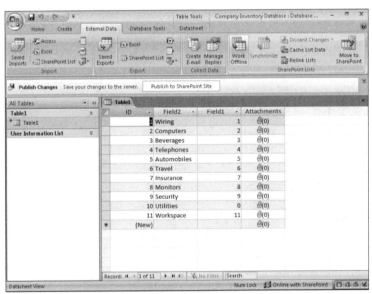

Figure 4-23 A user can easily place the data offline so that it can be viewed and updated regardless of the user's location or network access.

Placing SharePoint List Data Online

As easily as they can take a SharePoint list offline, as described previously, users can place SharePoint list data back online. When you place data back online and reconnect the linked tables, the synchronization process begins, updating to reflect any changes that were made while the list was offline.

To place your SharePoint list data online, perform the following steps:

1. Open the Access database that is linked to a SharePoint list.

2. On the External Data tab, select Work Online. If you decide that you do not want to save the changes that you made to the data while it was offline, you can select Discard Changes.

Synchronizing Offline Lists with SharePoint

If you want to keep your offline list offline but still synchronize the list's data with SharePoint, perform the following steps:

1. In Access, open the database that has been linked to the SharePoint list.

2. On the External Data tab, select Synchronize. Your data will start to be synchronized.

For additional information on the offline capabilities of WSS 3.0, refer to the section titled "Offline Capabilities in WSS 3.0" in Chapter 3.

Integrating Office OneNote 2007 with WSS 3.0

OneNote and WSS 3.0 enable users to share their notebooks with multiple users within SharePoint, where they can update a notebook's data in a secure and collaborative environment. The functionality of OneNote and WSS 3.0 is very similar to that of Excel and WSS 3.0.

The OneNote owner can specify the permission level for the notebook, allowing specific users to view the notebook and giving other users rights to contribute to the notes. Version history can also be enabled to track the changes that have occurred to the notebook, and users can set up alerts and even receive RSS feeds about the notebook.

Similar to the Move To SharePoint Site Wizard that was discussed in the section about Access, OneNote offers the New Notebook Wizard to enable users to easily create a shared notebook in SharePoint. When a notebook is shared, those with the appropriate permissions can contribute, and the changes will be automatically synced. OneNote also places an offline copy of the notes on each user's computer to allow for offline editing. Changes are synchronized when users go back online.

Chapter 4

Creating a Shared OneNote Notebook in SharePoint

Users can easily create a shared notebook within a WSS 3.0 document library. When the notebook is shared within the library, it becomes a folder, and each section of the notebook is stored as a file.

To create a shared OneNote notebook within SharePoint, perform the following steps:

1. From the Share menu, select Create Shared Notebook, as in Figure 4-24.

2. The New Notebook Wizard will start. Do the following:

    ○ In the Name box, enter the name for the shared notebook.

    ○ You have the option to select a color for the new notebook's cover, which will be displayed as the icon on the notebook's navigation bar.

    ○ In the From Template list, you have the option to select a template to be used for all the pages in the shared notebook.

3. After the fields in step 2 are populated, click Next.

4. Under Who Will Use This Notebook?, select Multiple People Will Share The Notebook, choose the On A Server option, and click Next.

5. In the Path selection box, enter the location of the SharePoint library where you want to store your notebook. Click Browse to browse for the proper SharePoint site and then click Select when it is located.

6. Send an e-mail to the users you want to notify about the new shared notebook by checking the Create An E-Mail With A Link To This Notebook That I Can Send To Other People check box and then clicking Create.

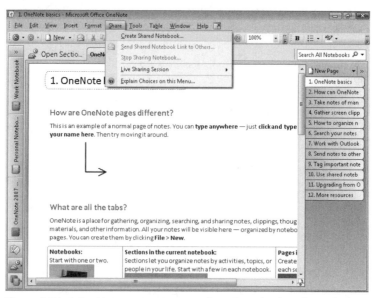

Figure 4-24 A OneNote user can create a shared notebook and specify the permissions of the users who can read or contribute to the notes.

> **Note**
> A user can also create a shared notebook by clicking New Notebook on the File menu.

Integrating with Outlook

The integration between Outlook and WSS 3.0 enhances collaboration and information sharing within your organization. Outlook enables users to access and update content as well as share information within SharePoint in many different areas. Users can maintain shared calendars, contacts, tasks, and even search for, preview, and edit documents right from within Outlook.

Outlook users can access shared calendars, which can be viewed within SharePoint and automatically updated when the Send/Receive command is run. When a SharePoint user assigns a task to resources within the organization, it will automatically appear on the user's Outlook To-Do Bar and daily task list within the calendar.

The following section goes into detail on the new, powerful features and functionality that the integration of Outlook with WSS 3.0 provides. This integration makes it easier than ever for users to stay up-to-date on current events within the organization.

Connecting Shared Calendars

Outlook and WSS 3.0 enable users to share calendar information throughout the organization in several different ways. A user can view a calendar from within Outlook or SharePoint and even view an overlay of the calendars for an all-encompassing view of event information.

Users can connect to and view multiple calendars simultaneously to check for possible event conflicts and have greater control over their schedules. This feature can also assist managers in proper resource scheduling and planning so as to avoid overbooking people.

Connect a SharePoint calendar to Outlook by performing the following steps:

1. From Internet Explorer, locate and open the calendar within the SharePoint site. If you can't find the calendar, you can always go to View All Site Content within a site and select the specific calendar you are looking for.

2. On the Actions menu within the SharePoint Calendar, click Connect to Outlook, as in Figure 4-25.

3. You will then be prompted to confirm that you want to connect the SharePoint calendar to Outlook. Select Yes to complete the calendar connection.

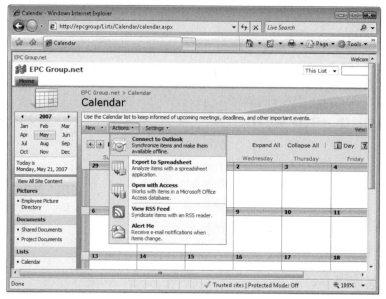

Figure 4-25 A user can easily connect a SharePoint calendar to Outlook.

> **Note**
>
> Calendars added from within SharePoint can be found in Outlook under Other Calendars.

Removing a SharePoint Calendar from Outlook

If you no longer want a SharePoint calendar to be linked to Outlook, follow these easy steps to remove the calendar from Outlook:

1. Within Outlook in Calendar, go to the Navigation pane. Under Other Calendars, select the calendar that you would like to remove from Outlook.

2. Right-click the calendar and then select Delete (*Name of the Calendar*) on the shortcut menu that is displayed, as in Figure 4-26.

3. You will then be prompted for confirmation of the removal of this calendar from Outlook. Select Yes. The calendar will no longer appear in Outlook but will still exist within the SharePoint site.

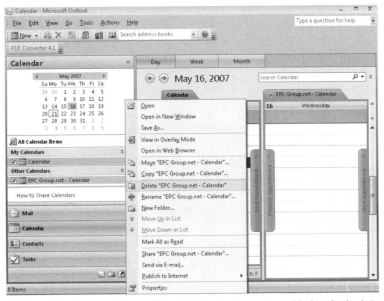

Figure 4-26 Just as easily as a SharePoint calendar can be added to Outlook, it can be removed.

> **Note**
>
> To remove the actual SharePoint calendar, talk with the SharePoint site owner, who will have the appropriate permissions to perform the deletion.

Adding SharePoint Calendar Events from Outlook

Users can add calendar events to SharePoint calendars without ever having to leave Outlook. The integration of these features saves users time and minimizes their use of computer resources because there is no need to open a Web browser or browse to find a specific calendar. It is even possible to drag event items between SharePoint calendars and an Outlook personal calendar.

Add an event to a SharePoint calendar from Outlook by performing the following steps:

1. Within Outlook, open the SharePoint calendar to which you would like the event to be added.

2. Within the Actions menu, click the type of event you would like to add to the calendar, as in Figure 4-27.

3. Enter the information about the event and then click Save and Close.

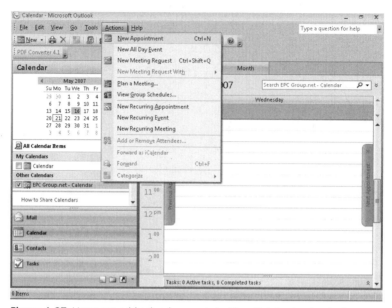

Figure 4-27 Users can add calendar events to SharePoint calendars in the same way they add items to a standard Outlook calendar.

> **Note**
>
> If the SharePoint administrator has enabled e-mail submissions to the site's list items, you can add an event to a SharePoint calendar by sending an e-mail.

Connecting Contacts to Outlook

Users can add contacts that exist within WSS 3.0 sites to Outlook and make changes while automatically syncing the entire process back to SharePoint. This is a great way to, for example, always keep your Outlook departmental or subject matter expert contact information up to date.

Adding SharePoint Contacts to Outlook

Add a WSS 3.0 contact to Outlook by performing the following steps:

1. Within Internet Explorer, locate and open the contacts list within the SharePoint site. If you are having trouble finding the list, go to View All Site Content and select the specific contact lists you are looking for.

2. Click Actions and then click Connect To Outlook, as in Figure 4-28.

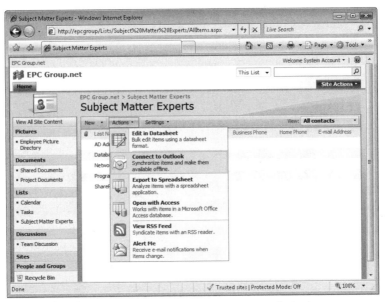

Figure 4-28 Users can easily add SharePoint contacts to Outlook.

3. You will then be prompted to connect the SharePoint contact(s) to Outlook. Select Yes.

> **Note**
>
> Just as calendars linked from SharePoint to Outlook appear under Other Calendars, these new SharePoint contacts are added under Other Contacts within the contacts in the Navigation pane.

Removing SharePoint Contacts from Outlook

Just as you removed a SharePoint calendar from Outlook, you can perform these easy steps to remove contacts from Outlook:

1. In Contacts, in the Navigation pane, under Other Contacts, locate the contacts folder you want to remove.

2. Right-click the folder and click Delete (*Name of the Contacts*) on the shortcut menu.

3. You will then be prompted to confirm the deletion. Select Yes. The contacts will no longer appear in Outlook but will still exist within the SharePoint site.

> **Note**
>
> To remove the actual SharePoint contacts list, talk with the SharePoint site owner, who will have the appropriate permissions to perform the deletion.

Tracking Updates and Notifications

Outlook has two powerful features that enable users to receive updates and notifications about changes that occur within WSS 3.0.

RSS feeds—Really Simple Syndication—are now available for users to subscribe to so that when changes occur in a SharePoint list or library, they receive periodic feeds right to Outlook.

The alert notification features of SharePoint are another powerful way users can be kept up to date on any content changes within SharePoint. Alerts are now much more configurable, and you can receive them at specific times or intervals. You can choose to be notified of any changes that may have occurred within a specific area of SharePoint, or alerts can be modified to deliver a more granular layer of detail so that the user is not inundated with alerts.

Subscribing to an RSS Feed from a SharePoint List

Users can subscribe to an RSS feed in SharePoint and receive the periodic information feeds from within Outlook. These feeds can be helpful in keeping a user informed about what is going on within SharePoint lists and libraries of special interest.

Subscribe to an RSS feed from a SharePoint list by performing the following steps:

1. From Internet Explorer, open the list or library on the SharePoint site. If you are having trouble finding the item, you can always go to View All Site Content within a site and select the specific list or library you are looking for.

2. On the Actions menu, click View RSS Feed, as in Figure 4-29.

3. On the RSS page that loads, click the Subscribe To This Feed link, as in Figure 4-30. When the prompt with the name of the feed appears, click Subscribe.

4. Navigate to your Outlook account. Under RSS Feeds, select the folder for your SharePoint list or library.

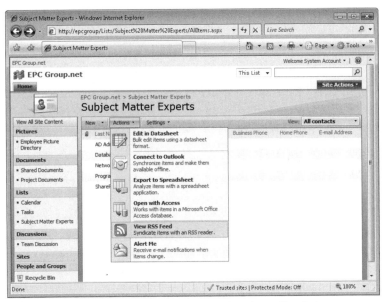

Figure 4-29 Users can subscribe to RSS feeds for a list in SharePoint.

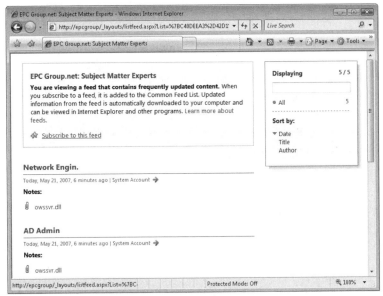

Figure 4-30 Users can then confirm the RSS feed subscription by clicking the Subscribe To This Feed link.

Chapter 4

Canceling the Subscription to an RSS Feed from Within Outlook

Users can cancel an existing subscription to an RSS feed for a SharePoint list or library about which they are no longer interested in receiving information directly from Outlook.

Cancel the subscription to an RSS feed from a SharePoint list or library by performing the following steps in Outlook:

1. In Mail, in the Navigation pane, select the RSS Feeds folder to expand it.

2. Highlight the RSS feed that you would like to cancel. Then select Delete.

3. When you are prompted to confirm the deletion, select Yes.

Creating an Alert for SharePoint from Outlook

Users can now create alerts for lists and libraries within SharePoint without having to leave Outlook. An Outlook user must have the appropriate permission level to create an alert for the list or library as well as the ability to connect to the SharePoint site.

Create an alert for a SharePoint list or library from within Outlook by performing the following steps:

1. From within the Navigation pane in Outlook, verify that the Mail tab is selected. Then click the Tools menu and select Rules And Alerts.

2. Select the Manage Alerts tab, seen in Figure 4-31, and click New Alert.

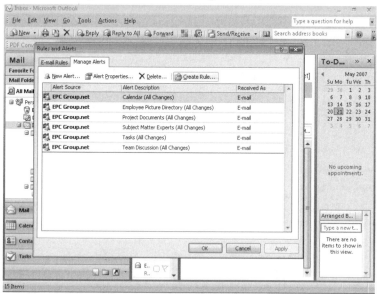

Figure 4-31 A user can create a new alert in the Rules And Alerts window in Outlook.

3. The New Alert dialog box will then prompt you to select the source of the alert that you want to create.

4. Select Open to open the SharePoint site's New Alert page. Select the list for which you would like the Alert to be created and click Next.

5. In the Alert Title section, type a title for the new alert. This title will be used in the subject line of all e-mail alerts to the user.

6. In the Send Alerts To section, enter the names of the users to whom you would like to send the alerts, or click the address book icon to browse and select the users' names.

7. Select the criteria for the new alert and then click OK to finish the process.

Canceling an Alert for SharePoint from Outlook

Users now have the ability to cancel the alerts they currently have created for lists and libraries within SharePoint without having to leave Outlook. The Outlook user must have the appropriate permission level to cancel an alert for the list or library as well as the ability to connect to the SharePoint site.

Cancel an alert for a SharePoint list or library from within Outlook by performing the following steps:

1. From within the Navigation pane in Outlook, verify that the Mail tab is selected. Then click the Tools menu and select Rules And Alerts.

2. Click the Manage Alerts tab and select the alert you would like to cancel. Click Delete.

3. If you are prompted to confirm the deletion, select Yes.

Opening or Editing Items from a SharePoint Site in Outlook

As seen in the previous sections, Outlook can be used as a central tool to perform many actions. It can also be used to connect directly to a SharePoint site to browse and edit content, and it also works as a great offline tool for users because they can work with SharePoint documents offline and then synchronize the content when they reconnect to the server. Outlook can be used as a Web browser for viewing SharePoint sites and content, which can save valuable time.

Connecting SharePoint Libraries to Outlook

When a user connects a SharePoint library to Outlook, the library will appear in a folder in Outlook called SharePoint Lists. This folder can be accessed to perform actions on the contained items much as e-mail is managed. When a SharePoint library is connected to Outlook, the data in the library can be synchronized with Outlook and can also be available offline, as discussed in the previous section.

Connect a SharePoint library to Outlook by performing the following steps:

1. From within Internet Explorer, open the library on the SharePoint site. If you are having trouble finding the library, you can always go to View All Site Content within a site and select the specific list or library you are looking for.

2. On the Actions menu of the SharePoint library, select Connect To Outlook, as in Figure 4-32. When you are prompted to confirm this connection, click Yes.

   It is important to note that the connection will be made at your exact location within the document library. If you would like to only make the connection within one of the folders of a document library, you can drill down into the folder and then make the connection.

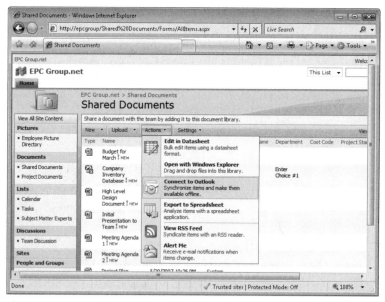

Figure 4-32 A user can easily connect a SharePoint document library to Outlook.

Removing a Connection of a SharePoint Library in Outlook

When users would like to remove the connection of a library in Outlook because they are no longer interested in the content that it contains, this task can be quickly accomplished by performing the following steps:

1. From within the Navigation pane in Outlook, verify that the Mail tab is selected. Expand the SharePoint Lists folder.

2. Right-click the folder you wish to remove and then click Delete (*Name of the Library*) on the shortcut menu that is displayed. When you are prompted to confirm the deletion, click Yes.

> **Note**
>
> To remove the actual SharePoint library, talk with the SharePoint site owner, who will have the appropriate permissions to perform the deletion.

Downloading a File Stored in a SharePoint Library to Outlook

Users now have the ability to download files to Outlook so that they can work on the files when they are offline and not connected to the organization's server. Outlook offline integration features with SharePoint are robust and extremely useful so that mobile users within the organization can have access to their content at all times.

New files added to a SharePoint folder that is linked to your Outlook should automatically download. If they do not, you can download a file from a SharePoint library into Outlook by performing the following steps:

1. Starting in Outlook, select the SharePoint Folder that is linked with your Outlook and that contains the file you want to download.

2. In the SharePoint Library Folder message list, in the Available For Download group, right-click the file that you want to download. If you would like to download multiple files at once, you can also hold down the Ctrl key as you select the files you'd like to download.

3. Select Mark To Download Document(s) on the shortcut menu that is displayed. If you have a connection to the server, the file will be downloaded. If the file does not download, click Send/Receive.

Removing a SharePoint File from Outlook

Just as users can download a file from SharePoint into Outlook, they can just as easily remove it. To remove a SharePoint file stored in Outlook, perform the following steps:

1. From within the Navigation pane in Outlook, verify that the Mail tab is selected. Then click the SharePoint Lists folder and select the library in which the file or files that you would like to remove reside.

2. In the message list, select the file that you want to remove (if there is more than one, hold down the Ctrl key while you click the file names).

3. Right-click the file selection(s) and then select Remove Offline Copy.

Opening or Editing a File Stored in a SharePoint Library from Outlook

Outlook 2007 now can open a file that is stored within a SharePoint library and even edit the file too. Users can now use Outlook for not only e-mail management but for content management as well. As a best practice, the file should be checked out from the SharePoint library prior to opening and editing it.

Chapter 4

A user can open or edit a file stored in a SharePoint library directly from Outlook by performing the following steps:

1. From within the Navigation pane in Outlook, verify that the Mail tab is selected. Click the SharePoint Lists folder and select the name of your SharePoint library, as seen in Figure 4-33.

2. Double-click the name of the file you would like to open. You may be prompted to verify the source of the file; click Open if it is the correct file.

3. If any updates were made to the file after you downloaded it from Outlook, you may be prompted to select whether you want to open the latest version of the file. Select either Yes or No, depending on whether you want to open the copy on your hard disk or the copy from the SharePoint server.

4. The file opens in the program in which it was created, if you have that program installed on your computer. Click Edit Offline in that program. Depending on the configuration of your SharePoint, you may be prompted for additional information such as links to the SharePoint Drafts folder on your computer or the offline editing options for your program.

5. You can now modify the file. Once you have completed your modifications, save the file as you usually do and then close the file.

6. If you are connected to the server and ready to update the file, select Update when prompted on closing.

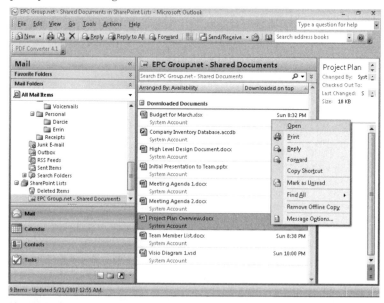

Figure 4-33 A user can view the files in a SharePoint document library that has been connected to Outlook and easily edit them in the Microsoft Office application with which they are associated. There is also a preview pane available to get a sneak peek at the document.

> **Note**
> The file will remain checked out and unavailable to other users until you check it back in.

For additional information on checking in and checking out files, refer to the section titled "Checking In and Checking Out" earlier in this chapter.

Searching for Items in SharePoint from Outlook

The preceding steps enable the user to connect to files and libraries as well as receive notifications and synchronize SharePoint and Outlook calendars. Another great feature that ties calendar, file access, and alert capabilities together is Outlook search capability. After SharePoint lists and libraries have been connected to Outlook, a user can start searching for them right away.

The search functionality described here is for users who have both Outlook and WSS 3.0 installed and configured within their environment. These search features use Instant Search and may require the user to download Windows Desktop Search 3.01 or newer from the Microsoft site at *www.microsoft.com/windows/desktopsearch/default.mspx.*

Once Instant Search is configured and running within Outlook, perform searches for content by following these steps:

1. From within the Navigation pane in Outlook, verify that the Mail tab is selected. Under SharePoint lists, select the name of the list or library you would like to search within.

2. In the Instant Search box that appears once you've selected the list/library you'd like to search, type your search text and press Enter.

3. To narrow your searches, you can enter additional criteria. In the Instant Search pane, click the Expand button.

Using Outlook 2007 to View and Create Tasks in SharePoint

Users can connect to SharePoint Task lists in the same way that they connect to SharePoint Calendars and Document libraries. This enables them to connect to all collaborative aspects of WSS 3.0 and helps them stay on top of their daily activities and planning. With the new Project task lists in WSS 3.0, users can take advantage of Gantt views, which can assist with managing project tasks in which they are involved.

Connecting SharePoint Task Lists to Outlook

When a SharePoint task list is connected to Outlook, task data in the list can be synchronized with Outlook and be available offline. When this task list is connected to

Outlook, it will appear in the Tasks Navigation pane under Other Tasks. Connect a SharePoint task list to Outlook by performing the following steps:

1. From within Internet Explorer, open the issues list on the SharePoint site with which you would like to connect. If you are having trouble finding what you want, you can always go to View All Site Content within a site and select the specific list or library you are trying to find.

2. On the Actions menu, click Connect To Outlook. When you are prompted to confirm the connection to Outlook, click Yes.

Deleting the Connection of a SharePoint Task List from Outlook

A SharePoint task list connected to Outlook can easily be removed by performing these steps:

1. From within the Navigation pane in Outlook, verify that the Tasks tab is selected. Under Other Tasks, select the task list for which you would like the connection to be deleted.

2. Right-click the task list name and then click Delete (*Name of Task List*) on the shortcut menu displayed (see Figure 4-34). When prompted to confirm the deletion, click Yes.

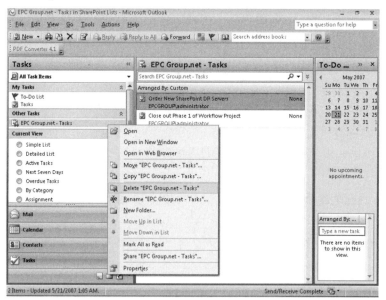

Figure 4-34 A user can easily remove a linked SharePoint task list that is no longer in Outlook.

> **Note**
>
> A user wishing to remove an actual task list from the SharePoint site should talk with the SharePoint site owner, who will have the appropriate permissions to perform the deletion.

Adding a Task to a SharePoint Task List from Outlook

Once the connection to the SharePoint Task list is created and the connection resides in Outlook, users can easily add new tasks to the list. To create a task, follow these steps:

1. From within the Navigation pane in Outlook, verify that the Tasks tab is selected. Under Other Tasks, select the task list to which you would like to add a new task.

2. On the New menu, click Task and enter the new task's information. Once you are done entering the information for the new task, click Save & Close to complete the operation.

Updating a Task on a SharePoint Task List from Outlook

Once the connection to the SharePoint task list is created and the connection resides in Outlook, you can easily update a new task for the list. To do so, follow these steps:

1. From within the Navigation pane in Outlook, verify that the Tasks tab is selected. Under Other Tasks, select the task list for which you would like to update a task or set of tasks.

2. After the task list opens, double-click the task you would like to update.

3. Once the task is open, update the content and settings of the task. When the task is updated, click Save & Close. Or, if the task is complete, click Mark Complete.

Using Office InfoPath 2007 with WSS 3.0

InfoPath enables users to gather information by offering a powerful electronic forms solution. WSS 3.0 allows for the storage and interaction of those forms within a SharePoint form library. A form library is similar to the standard document library, but it allows for the powerful management of XML-based business forms such as those created by InfoPath.

With InfoPath, organizations can quickly and accurately gather information from either a specific set of users or the entire organization by replacing existing manual paper processes with efficient online automated solutions. InfoPath can easily integrate with your existing business applications, and with WSS 3.0 you can send these forms to a much larger audience.

A major problem with InfoPath 2003 is that a large group of people within the organization cannot use the forms unless all potential InfoPath users have the InfoPath 2003 client installed on their machines. Many organizations have Microsoft Office 2003 and even have purchased the license for InfoPath 2003 but have not rolled it out to all the

Chapter 4

machines in their organizations. Therefore, it sometimes becomes a guessing game as to whether a form will work for all the users who are asked to use it. This is also hard on the help desk and IT staff, who sometimes have to quickly do a "one-off" installation for users needing access to the form.

Fortunately, this is no longer an issue with InfoPath 2007 and the form library's browser-enabled document option in WSS 3.0. Form libraries can easily display InfoPath forms as Web pages and can be sent to any SharePoint user within the organization.

> **Note**
>
> InfoPath Forms Services is another powerful new server technology that allows for robust management of InfoPath forms. This functionality is only available in Microsoft SharePoint Server 2007 Enterprise Client Access License (CAL) and separately in Microsoft Office Forms Server 2007.

Using Form Libraries

As mentioned previously, form libraries are similar to standard document libraries but exist for the specific purpose of managing XML-based business forms that InfoPath creates and publishes. Form libraries, seen in Figure 4-35, have options similar to document libraries. InfoPath users can simply upload the InfoPath form into the library, or they can publish the form via the Publishing option in InfoPath.

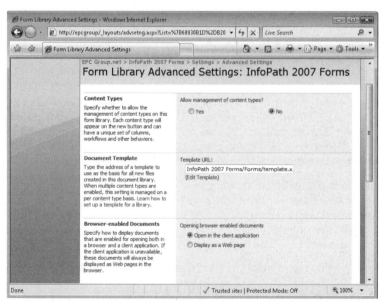

Figure 4-35 The form library is tailored to manage XML-based business forms and enables the InfoPath forms to be displayed via its browser-enabled documents option.

A SharePoint administrator can specify a particular InfoPath form as the form library's document template. They can then use its browser-enabled document option to display InfoPath forms within the Web page. This allows for seamless integration with SharePoint's Web-based collaboration platform. Form libraries also have the option to allow for content type management and version control. They inherit all the other powerful features that a standard SharePoint document library has to offer.

Uploading an InfoPath Form to a Form or Document Library in SharePoint

Users who have InfoPath forms they would like to store in SharePoint can use the standard upload capabilities in SharePoint to move the forms into the form library or document library. By clicking the Upload button on the library's List View toolbar, users can upload InfoPath forms that already exist on their computer, network share, CD, or other location to a SharePoint library. Clicking Upload displays two available drop-down lists: Upload Document and Upload Multiple Documents. The form library uses the same upload capabilities as the standard document library discussed in previous chapters. The user can also use the form library to store non-InfoPath documents as well as to assist in storing project-related documents used in the creation of the InfoPath form.

Publishing a Form Template from InfoPath to SharePoint

A user can publish a form template directly from InfoPath to a SharePoint form or document library in the same way that users can now save Word documents directly from Word into a document library. Before an InfoPath user publishes a browser-compatible form template, the Design Checker in InfoPath should be run to identify and fix any compatibility issues that the form's design might have prior to publishing. The Design Checker can be found on the Tools menu and is a great tool for final testing and review.

When InfoPath users have completed their forms and are ready to publish them directly to the WSS 3.0 forms or document library, they can do so by performing the following steps:

1. On the File menu, click Publish, as shown in Figure 4-36.

2. In the Publishing Wizard, select To A SharePoint Server With Or Without InfoPath Forms Services, as shown in Figure 4-37, and then click Next.

3. On the next page of the wizard, in the box labeled Enter The Location Of Your SharePoint Or InfoPath Forms Services Site, type the location of the SharePoint site and then click Next.

Chapter 4

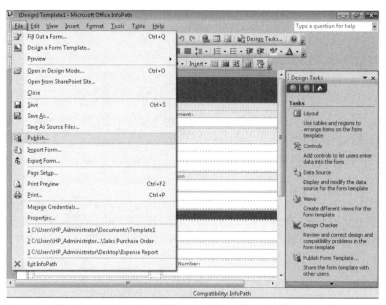

Figure 4-36 A user can easily publish an InfoPath form to SharePoint by selecting Publish from the File menu.

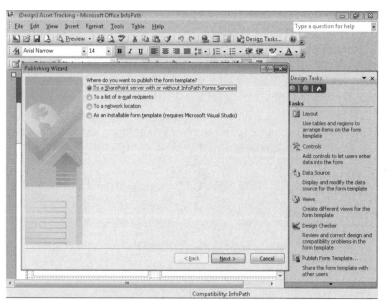

Figure 4-37 A user selects the To A SharePoint Server With Or Without InfoPath Forms Services option to publish to SharePoint.

4. On the next page of the wizard, select Document Library and then click Next.

5. On the next page of the wizard, select Create A New Document Library and then click Next.

6. On the next page of the wizard, type a name and description for the new document library and then click Next.

7. Choose the fields in the form template that you want to appear as columns in the default view of the document library. InfoPath may suggest a set of default fields; you can add, modify, or remove fields by clicking the Add, Modify, or Remove buttons and following the wizard's prompts.

8. On the next page of the wizard, verify that the information shown is correct and then click Publish. If the form is saved successfully, you will receive a confirmation from the wizard.

9. You have two options before clicking Close. To send an e-mail message with the form and form template to your users, select the Send The Form To E-Mail Recipients check box. To open the document library and test the process for filling out a form based on this form template, select the Open This Document Library check box. With this selected, the document library will open in a Web browser when you close the wizard. In the SharePoint page that opens, click New on the list toolbar, and a form based on this form template will open in InfoPath.

Working with Custom InfoPath Forms

WSS 3.0 can host a wide variety of custom InfoPath forms and make them securely available to the organization's SharePoint users.

Custom InfoPath forms developed in both SharePoint Designer 2007 and Visual Studio 2005 can be implemented in WSS 3.0. In addition, items such as custom workflow development can be implemented. However, the overall architecture of the environment must be taken into consideration when planning these custom forms.

> **Note**
>
> A great resource for InfoPath customization and related development best practices and free resources can be found at the InfoPath developer portal on MSDN at *http://msdn2. microsoft.com/en-us/office/aa905434.aspx.*

Working with Office Groove 2007

Groove is a powerful collaboration software program that brings people together regardless of their location or organization. Groove and WSS 3.0 together allows for an even greater collaborative environment in an already robust platform. With Groove, team members can create a working area right on their computers with only two clicks and invite other members to collaborate regardless of network or infrastructure concerns.

Chapter 4

Groove now includes key elements such as a Launchbar, workspaces, presence and communications, and alerts. Groove 2007 offers a new piece of functionality called the SharePoint Files tool, which provides access to several powerful features that enable Groove to store content in SharePoint document libraries.

SharePoint Files Tool

With the SharePoint Files tool, a person outside of the organization can access specific content within a SharePoint document library. The tool is also powerful offline, giving remote and mobile users an environment in which documents and content can be accessed, viewed, and updated while offline. The SharePoint Files tool is limited to mapping to document libraries in WSS 3.0 and will not function in the previous versions of SharePoint.

All of the standard features of the SharePoint document library are available to you, and version control can limit the risk of lost data that may occur due to the extremely collaborative and open nature of Groove. There are limitations to the SharePoint Files tool that must be taken into consideration—Groove does not support or recognize custom content types and columns or document library views. An organization can set up a separate site or WSS 3.0 instance to minimize any of these issues, allowing the Groove user base to take advantage of features in SharePoint while minimizing risk to the organization.

Groove synchronizes its data to maintain identical sets of content between the Groove SharePoint Files tool and the related SharePoint site and document libraries. Synchronizations can be done manually by the SharePoint administrator or designated Groove administrator, or they can be scheduled at specific times to take into consideration the backup schedule for SharePoint as well as the organization's other line-of-business systems.

In Summary...

Microsoft Office has powerful integration points with WSS 3.0 in every application within its suite. The combination of the two platforms enables organizations to create powerful content that can be widely shared in a secure manner within a standardized Web-based platform.

The next chapter begins Part 3, "Creating, Designing, and Configuring Sites, Workspaces, and Pages with a Browser," which details how to create SharePoint sites, workspaces, and pages with only a Web browser.

Creating, Designing, and Configuring Sites, Workspaces, and Pages with a Browser

With any Microsoft Windows SharePoint Services 3.0 (WSS 3.0) implementation, some of the most important parts of the initiative are proper planning, creation, and governance of the sites and workspaces as well as what the organization will allow the users to do within them. SharePoint can become so popular so fast that without proper planning, the IT staff and its business sponsors can be in a race to play catch-up to its growth and popularity even from its first day in production. I have personally seen several large *Fortune* 500 organizations roll out SharePoint without this proper planning, and in a short six-month time frame have thousands of sites without any real road map or governance model. Trying to bring things back under control after this occurs is costly to the organization not only in budget and resources but in credibility and user acceptance.

This chapter will go into detail on how to plan a SharePoint site structure and hierarchy as well as site creation and provisioning. It will also touch on site governance and best practices for SharePoint sites. Chapter 20, "Additional SharePoint Best Practices," will continue on this point and go into granular detail on SharePoint best practices on every aspect of a SharePoint deployment either large or small.

Within Windows SharePoint Services 3.0, a site is the basic unit for organizing content of all kinds. Sites contain groups of pages that work closely together, as well as libraries and lists that store documents and other kinds of information. Sites are also the basic unit for security administration, disk space management and utilization, user experience, and visual appearance.

Creating a SharePoint site is an easy process, which is why organizations need to plan for how much governance they would like to place around it. The previous chapter explained the convenience of creating document workspaces from within Microsoft Office 2007 applications, and Chapter 7, "What's New with Templates and Design," will explain options available to organizations for creating SharePoint sites with Microsoft Office SharePoint Designer 2007. Even so, the most common way of creating new SharePoint sites is through the browser interface, and that is the approach that this chapter explains.

Planning a SharePoint Site Structure and Hierarchy

Any WSS 3.0 implementation is going to have an overall site structure and navigational hierarchy. If your organization is just now implementing WSS 3.0, you may be able to avoid mistakes that others have made in past deployments. Some administrators create their site structure and navigational hierarchy directly from their companies' organizational charts, which is very straightforward because most users can easily identify with this structure, whereas others may follow a set of specific criteria or functional requirements. In some cases, there is no rhyme or reason whatsoever to the site structure, and SharePoint administrators find themselves desperately looking to bring it in line with organizational needs.

In any case, proper planning of structure and hierarchy in WSS 3.0 can result in an environment that excels in performance, usability, scalability, security, content-type management, and search features, just to name a few.

WSS 3.0 can accommodate thousands of SharePoint sites running on a single Web server, but it is up to the organization to properly plan its environment or modify the existing environment. Whether your users would rather browse for content or use Search to find it, this planning will help them efficiently find the right SharePoint sites and content. This section, therefore, provides guidance, best practices, and governance information on how to organize WSS 3.0.

Planning SharePoint Sites

SharePoint servers typically contain a large number of sites and subsites. Most organizations have sites for departments, projects, product groups, special initiatives, and individual employees. Depending on the current site creation and provisioning guidelines, within each of those sites could reside a large number of subsites as well. SharePoint seems to be one of those unique platforms that spreads like wildfire within the organization. Once users are exposed to another department's, project's, or team member's site, they are quickly on the phone or in Microsoft Office Outlook requesting one of their own.

This makes it imperative for the organization to have a way for organizing these sites. SharePoint sites reside in a site collection, which is a group of sites built on WSS. They all exist under a top-level site. This means you can have several different site collections and thus several different unique top-level sites. Before a site collection can be created, a Web application must exist, which SharePoint's Central Administration automatically takes care of behind the scenes. A Web application is an Internet Information Services (IIS) site with a unique application pool that can also have a separate database and authentication method. This is all invisible to the overwhelming majority of users, who will never need to know about the underlying technology.

WSS 3.0 is now a platform that can have both intranet and Internet facing sites. Organizations that are considering SharePoint as an intranet site can now also use SharePoint for external access. You can plan an intranet site or an Internet site in a very similar manner.

For example, if you only want to have a site for each department within your organization, you may have one site collection with a top-level SharePoint site and then a site for every department. The information technology department may receive a SharePoint site, but five teams reside within IT, each of which may also need a site. Each of these teams could get a subsite off of the main IT site, as shown in Figure 5-1. This site structure could look like the following:

- Top-level SharePoint site: *http://sharepoint*

- IT's team site: *http://sharepoint/IT*

- Help desk's subsite within IT: *http://sharepoint/IT/helpdesk*

- Development team's subsite within IT: *http://sharepoint/IT/development*

- Database team's subsite within IT: *http://sharepoint/IT/database*

- Network security's subsite within IT: *http://sharepoint/IT/networksecurity*

- Microsoft Active Directory directory service team's subsite within IT: *http://sharepoint/IT/activedirectory*

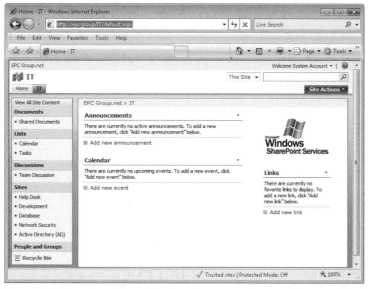

Figure 5-1 The information technology department has used the out-of-the-box team site template to created five subsites. The subsites are linked under Sites in the Quick Launch.

After your SharePoint site structure is laid out, you could apply specific security groups to each department and then more granular permissions to each subsite within the department for more targeted and sensitive material. Also, you could create a site template for each department so that when a new site is created for that department, it inherits a standardized look and feel and has specific document libraries and lists with predefined content types and columns.

Chapter 5

This is the type of planning that your organization can perform to have a best-practices deployment that is rock solid and will enable SharePoint to grow in a controlled manner.

Planning a Best-Practices Approach

For a best-practices approach to planning SharePoint sites, consider all available scenarios and information that you currently have regarding your organization and make that the basis of your creation and configuration strategy. When implementing this approach, also take into account the functional areas that site creation and deployment will require as follows.

User Considerations:

- How many users will be using the sites, and will they all be using the sites at the same time?

- What types of users are they, what permission levels will they require, and who will be the users you can rely on to manage sites content (that is, who are the power users)?

- What will be the users' access requirements, and will all of them have a domain login account? Will any require additional offline capabilities?

- Will Internet access to the site be necessary?

- Will there be multiple language requirements?

Site Collection and Hierarchy Considerations:

- How many site collections will be required?

- What will the root or top-level site's path be, and what will the subsites' paths be?

- Will all sites use the same top-level navigation?

- What will the Quick Launch display?

Site Content Considerations:

- What content types or columns (that is, metadata) should be configured within document libraries and lists?

- What Web Parts should be displayed within the sites?

- Will any custom lists need to be created?

Customization Considerations:

- Will there be a need for any custom workflows?

- Do we need to plan for the development of any custom Web Parts?

- Do we need any custom master pages, the page templates that define the common look and feel of the site? (Master Pages are discussed in detail in Chapter 7.)

Considering these items will allow your organization to properly plan site creation so that the user base will be able to access their content easily and get the most out of SharePoint as their daily collaboration and document-management platform. This type of planning is also important if you plan to use SharePoint for any custom application initiatives within your organization, either internal or external.

Planning Site Collections, Top-Level Sites, and Containers

As discussed earlier in the chapter, SharePoint site collections give you a way to manage groups of sites and have multiple unique top-level sites if necessary. A site collection begins with a top-level site and includes every site that falls within its hierarchy. Within a site collection, all sites can share these functionalities and configurations in common:

- Search scopes for SharePoint search

- Workflows

- Security groups

- Navigation bars for both the Top Link bar and breadcrumb navigation

- Content types within all document libraries, lists, and folders

- Lookup fields across all lists

Unique top-level sites can exist within separate site collections to enable SharePoint administrators to apply specific criteria within the top level. A top-level site does not inherit its navigation or permissions from another site because it provides its own navigational elements and permissions. However, the permission elements can be modified to fit the organization's needs. Separate top-level sites can be created within separate site collections if:

- The site requires unique or custom search scopes for the users.

- Specific workflows will be made available to users in a specific site collection.

- There are unique security requirements across SharePoint instances.

- Separate quotas, upload limits, and file exclusion lists will need to be applied to each SharePoint instance.

- There are disaster recovery or backup needs.

Document libraries and sites are sometimes referred to as containers in WSS 3.0. When rolling out a site, it is helpful to standardize the initial document libraries and lists it will contain. This way, the organization can apply the proper content types or custom columns to these document libraries so that they can capture specific metadata for documents. This planning will enhance the searchability of the content.

For deployments that have multiple language requirements, SharePoint administrators create sites based on a language-specific site template, causing all text on the specified sites or site collections to be displayed in the desired language. This enables the organization to have multiple languages within their SharePoint environment, all within one installation of WSS 3.0.

Chapter 5

For additional information on site collections, refer to the section titled "Planning Site Collections" in Chapter 13, "Planning and Installing Windows SharePoint Services 3.0."

Creating a New SharePoint Site or Workspace

Earlier chapters have explained how Microsoft Office programs can create sites and document workspaces. This section explains the more general procedure for using a browser to create SharePoint sites of any kind.

Creating a New SharePoint Site

Site administrators can easily create a new site by performing the following steps:

1. Click View All Site Content and then click Create on the All Site Content page. You may also be able to click Site Actions and then Create within any site, as shown in Figure 5-2.

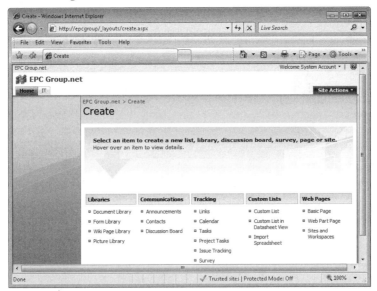

Figure 5-2 The Create page within a site enables users to create a new SharePoint team site as well as other libraries and lists.

2. Under Web Pages, click Sites And Workspaces.

3. In the Title And Description section, type in a title for the new site. The title is required. This title will appear at the top of the new site and in all navigational elements.

4. Optionally, type in a description of the purpose of your site in the Description box. The description box will also appear at the top of the site.

5. In the Web Site Address section, type a URL for your site. The initial part of the URL will be provided for you.

6. In the Template Selection section, click the tab that you want and then select the site template that you want.

7. In the Permissions section, select whether you want to provide access to the same users who have access to this parent site, or to a unique set of users. If you select unique, you can populate the permissions later.

8. In the Navigation section, select whether you want the new subsite to be visible in the navigation of its parent site.

9. In the Navigation Inheritance section, specify whether you want the site to inherit its Top Link bar from the parent site or to have its own set of links on the Top Link bar. This setting also affects whether the new site appears as part of the breadcrumb navigation of the parent site. If you click No, your subsite will not contain the breadcrumb navigation of the parent site.

10. Click Create.

11. If the Set Up Groups For This Site page appears, you need to specify whether you want to create new groups or use existing groups for visitors, members, and owners of the site. In each section, do one of the following:

   ○ If you select Create A New Group, either accept the automatically created name for the new SharePoint group or type a new name. Then add the people you want. Click the check mark icon to verify any names that you type, or click the address book icon to browse through your directory for more names. In the Visitors To This Site section, you can also add all authenticated users to the Visitors group, which by default provides the group members with permission to read the content on your site.

   ○ If you click Use An Existing Group, select the SharePoint group that you want from the list.

   If you have several SharePoint groups, the list may be abbreviated. Click More to see the full list or Less to abbreviate the list.

12. Click OK.

Other Available Options for Creating Sites

SharePoint sites can also be created in a variety of other ways. If you are a SharePoint administrator or developer with the appropriate access, you can take advantage of some of the other options that are available for creating SharePoint sites. Here are some of the options:

- **Create sites in SharePoint Central Administration** If you are a SharePoint administrator, you can create new site collections via Central Administration.

- **Create sites programmatically via the command line or with SharePoint Designer 2007** If you are a SharePoint administrator or developer, you can create custom code or sites via the command line by using the createsites command and its related arguments. You also have the option to create sites by using SharePoint Designer 2007. SharePoint Designer 2007 is discussed in more detail in Chapter 7.

Selecting the Right Template, Permissions, and Navigation Options

WSS 3.0 provides a wide variety of templates right out of the box. It's also easy to save an existing site as a custom template that can then be available while creating a new site or workspace.

You can select site and workspace templates when setting up a new SharePoint site via the Create page. The default templates that are included with WSS 3.0 are arranged under two tabs in the Template Selection area of the New SharePoint Site page.

On the Collaboration Tab:

- **Team Site** Select this site template when you want to create a site that teams can use to create, organize, and share information. The template includes a document library and basic lists such as Announcements, Calendar, Contacts, and Links. This is the most commonly used template in SharePoint.

- **Blank Site** Select this site template when you want to create a site with a blank home page that you plan to customize. You can use a Web design program that is compatible with Windows SharePoint Services, such as Microsoft Office Share-Point Designer 2007, to add interactive lists or any other feature.

- **Document Workspace** Select this site template when you want to create a site that helps your team members to work together on documents. This template provides a document library for storing the primary document and supporting files, a Tasks list for assigning to-do items, and a Links list for resources related to the document.

- **Wiki Site** Select this site template when you want to create a site where users can quickly and easily add, edit, and link Web pages. Wikis are a new feature in SharePoint that allows for easy and open sharing of SharePoint information.

- **Blog** Select this site template when you want to create a site where users can post information and allow others to comment on it. This is a great tool for knowledge management and capturing best practices and lessons learned.

On the Meeting Tab:

- **Basic Meeting Workspace** Select this site template when you want to create a site that helps you plan, organize, and track your meetings with the rest of your team. The template includes the following lists: Objectives, Attendees, Agenda, and Document Library.

- **Blank Meeting Workspace** Select this site template when you want to create a blank meeting workspace site that you can customize based on your requirements.

- **Decision Meeting Workspace** Select this site template when you want to create a site that is ideal for reviewing documents and recording any decisions that are reached at a decision-making meeting. The template includes the following lists: Objectives, Attendees, Agenda, Document Library, Tasks, and Decisions.

- **Social Meeting Workspace** Select this site template when you want to create a site that helps you plan and coordinate social occasions. The template includes the following lists: Attendees, Directions, Things To Bring, Discussions, and Picture Library.

- **Multipage Meeting Workspace** Select this site template when you want to create a site that provides all the basics to plan, organize, and track your meetings with multiple pages. In addition to two blank pages for you to customize based on your requirements, the template contains the following lists: Objectives, Attendees, and Agenda.

Save an Existing Site as a Template to Use During Site Creation

If you would like to save a current site as a template, you can do so with just a few clicks. This is a great way to save an existing site's content, design, and structure so that you can standardize future sites based on one you have already designed and approved. To save a site as a template, perform the following steps:

1. On the Site Actions menu, click Site Settings. Within any site, you may also be able to click Site Actions, Create.

2. On the Site Settings page, in the Look And Feel section, click Save Site As Template.

3. On the Save Site As Template page, in the File Name section, type a name for the template file (see Figure 5-3).

4. In the name and description sections, type a name and optionally a description.

5. In the Include Content section, select the Include Content check box if you want new Web sites created from your template to include the contents of all lists and document libraries in your existing Web site.

6. Click OK.

This site will now be in the list of available site templates under a new tab called Custom. This site can be used in your next new site creation.

Chapter 5

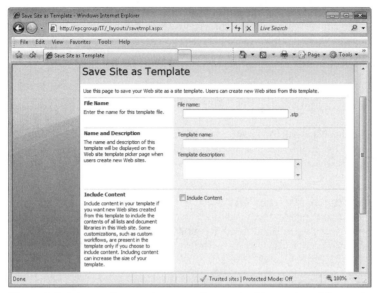

Figure 5-3 A site can be saved as a template to simplify creation of future sites.

Permissions and Navigation Inheritance

When you're creating a new site, you can allow it to inherit the permissions of the parent site. Alternatively, you can give it a set of unique permissions. If you decide to use the same permissions as the parent site, the permissions will then be shared by both the new site and its parent. If you give it unique permissions, you will then need to go into the People And Groups page within Site Settings and specify the users or groups for the site.

By default, SharePoint sites have the Owners (full control), Members (contributor), and Visitors (reader) groups available after site creation. If you give permissions to users directly, choose one of the following four permission levels:

- **Full Control** The user has full control of the site.
- **Designer** The user can view, add, update, delete, approve, and customize.
- **Contribute** The user can view, add, update, and delete.
- **Read** The user can only view the content of the site.

Navigation can also be inherited or unique based on the user's selection criteria during the site creation. If the user specifies that a site should inherit its Top Link bar from the parent, an identical Top Link bar will be displayed within the site. If it is not inherited, the link bar will have its own links and will also not contain breadcrumb navigation inherited from the parent site.

Next Steps for the New Site

After it's created, the new site is ready to be used "as is" by a user with the appropriate permissions to begin adding content and features to meet the needs of the organization. Libraries and lists can be created, and Web Parts can be added to the page to enhance the functionality of the site. Permissions can be modified to add or edit the permissions of existing users, and the Top Link bar and the Quick Launch can be customized to meet the site's exact needs.

A standardized training process should be developed to help new sites users become accustomed to SharePoint's features as well as the features that enable it to be integrated with Microsoft Office.

Self-Service Site Creation

WSS 3.0 gives SharePoint administrators the option of allowing self-service site creation so that users and groups can create sites as needed. Administrators create these sites in a new site collection, and users will need to be added uniquely to these new site collections. With planning, it is possible for organizations to track SharePoint site and resource usage back to the user or their department, and to customize the sign-up page for self-service site creation to track billing or other information.

Create a Top-Level Site by Using Self-Service Site Creation

Because it is disabled by default, the self-service site creation option must be enabled before the SharePoint administrator uses it. This can be done by clicking the Self-Service Site Management link on the Applications Management page of SharePoint's Central Administration. Once the option is enabled, an announcement with a link to create a site appears in the Announcements list on the site, as shown in Figure 5-4.

A user can create a site by performing the following steps:

1. Go to the top-level site in the site collection. If you are in a subsite of the top-level site, click the home page in the Top Link bar or the first site in the hierarchy of the breadcrumb navigation.

2. On the home page of the top-level site, look at the Announcements list. If you don't see an announcement for self-service site creation on the home page, display the full list by clicking Announcements. If you do not see the Announcements list, click View All Site Content and then look for Announcements under Lists.

3. In the announcement titled Self-Service Site Creation, click the URL for creating a new Web site. If you do not see the URL, click the announcement to open it fully. By default, the announcement is called Self-Service Site Creation, but this can be customized by the SharePoint administrator.

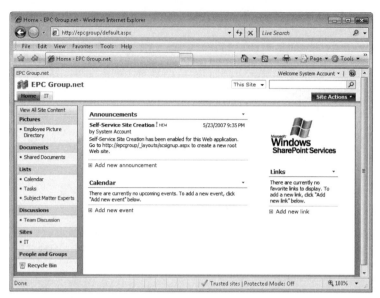

Figure 5-4 If self-services site creation is enabled, a link for creating a new site will appear in the Announcements list.

4. On the New SharePoint Site page, in the title section, type a title for your site. The title is required and appears at the top of the Web page and in navigational elements that help users to find and open the site. Optionally, in the description section, type a description of the purpose of your site in the Description box. The description appears at the top of the Web page and helps users understand the purpose of your site.

5. In the Web Site Address section, type a URL for your site. The first part is provided for you.

6. In the Template Selection section, click the appropriate template category tab and then select the desired site template. By default, there are two categories of site templates: Collaboration and Meetings.

The following five templates are available on the Collaboration tab on the New SharePoint Site page:

○ **Team Site**   Create a site that teams can use to create, organize, and share information. The template includes a document library and basic lists such as Announcements, Calendar, Contacts, and Links.

○ **Blank Site**   Create a site with a blank home page that you plan to customize. You can use a Web design program that is compatible with Windows Share-Point Services, such as Microsoft Office SharePoint Designer 2007, to add interactive lists or any other feature.

○ **Document Workspace**   Create a site that helps your team members to work together on documents. This template provides a document library for storing the primary document and supporting files, a Tasks list for assigning to-do items, and a Links list for resources related to the document.

- ○ **Wiki Site** Create a site where users can quickly and easily add, edit, and link Web pages.
- ○ **Blog Site** Create a site where users can post information and allow others to comment on it.

The following five templates are available on the Meetings tab on the New Share-Point Site page:

- ○ **Basic Meeting Workspace Site** Create a site that helps you to plan, organize, and track your meeting with the rest of your team. The template includes following lists: Objectives, Attendees, Agenda, and Document Library.
- ○ **Blank Meeting Workspace Site** Create a blank Meeting Workspace site that you can customize based on your requirements.
- ○ **Decision Meeting Workspace Site** Create a site that is ideal for reviewing documents and recording any decisions that are reached at the meeting. The template includes the following lists: Objectives, Attendees, Agenda, Document Library, Tasks, and Decisions.
- ○ **Social Meeting Workspace Site** Create a site that helps you to plan and coordinate social occasions. The template includes the following lists: Attendees, Directions, Things To Bring, Discussions, and Picture Library.
- ○ **Multipage Meeting Workspace Site** Create a site that provides all the basics to plan, organize, and track your meeting with multiple pages. The template contains the following lists: Objectives, Attendees, and Agenda in addition to two blank pages for you to customize based on your requirements.

Once you have made the appropriate template selection, click Create.

7. The Set Up Groups For This Site page will appear. You can then set up groups for this new site.

8. In each section of the Set Up Groups For This Site page, accept the automatically created name for the new SharePoint group—or type a new name—and then add the people or groups you want. Click the check mark icon to verify any names that you type, or click the address book icon to browse through your directory for more names. Then click OK.

Administration of Self-Service Site Creation

Self-service site creation can greatly assist in the proliferation of SharePoint sites, but it can negatively affect certain aspects of your SharePoint environment (such as security and performance) unless it is closely monitored. It is disabled by default and must be turned on individually on every Web application within the server farm.

It is important for organizations to follow certain governance best practices such as applying site collection use confirmation and auto-deletion to the site. These tools will send warning messages to owners of any site collection that has not had activity for a specific period of time. If the owner does not reply to one of four messages, the site will be deleted.

Chapter 5

It is also important to configure quota templates along with a secondary site collection administrator for sites to allow for a fixed amount of space that the site collection can use, and to designate another SharePoint administrator to assist in the monitoring of this feature.

Site Governance Best Practices

Site governance is a critical step in ensuring the success of your WSS 3.0 deployment. From an information management perspective, WSS 3.0 is extremely powerful and robust. When you add in Microsoft Office 2007, SharePoint Designer 2007, and the possibilities of customization in Microsoft Visual Studio 2005, you have a huge amount of territory to monitor and properly govern within the organization.

As we have discussed in the past few chapters, the collaboration and sharing aspect of SharePoint is one of its best features because it can get a large number of users within the organization involved and collaborating in many different ways. This feature needs to be controlled in a way that does not discourage the user base. I have personally seen many large SharePoint environments that have not had control and, as I mentioned earlier, it is much more time consuming and expensive to fix a problem that has already occurred than to prevent it. But it is never too late! This is one time when it is actually better to ask permission first rather than ask for forgiveness later.

Consider the following when planning your SharePoint site governance model.

Site and Workspace Governance:

- All pictures within a picture library should be periodically reviewed for content.

- Document libraries and lists should contain at least a few key content types (metadata fields) to assist the organization in managing enterprise content and improving search results.

- Site quotas must be set within each site.

- The utilization of power users or site content owners within your organization—on every site—ensures that content stays relevant and monitored.

- File upload limits should be set to 50 megabytes (MB). If there are specific requirements that require larger file uploads, the maximum allowable size is 2 gigabytes (GB).

- All site content should be periodically monitored for your specific set of banned words or phrases.

- List views should be limited to 2,000 items per site.

- Limit Web Parts to 50 per page.

- A SharePoint Change Management Plan should be developed and implemented.

Chapter 5

- Top-level navigation should be vetted and agreed upon by all stakeholders to allow for easy navigation through the WSS 3.0 environment.

- RSS (Really Simple Syndication) feeds should be limited to content related to the organization.

- Blogs must not contain defamatory content about the company or employees within the organization.

- Make sure all executive sites (concerning the CEO, CIO, CFO, and so on) and their related content are excluded from search except in public announcements or areas that are specifically set up to share their content (note that this could be relevant for human resources and legal as well).

- To improve standardization, site templates should be developed for departments or projects sites whenever possible.

- SharePoint Designer 2007 customizations should be strictly monitored and possibly controlled by specific groups within the organization.

- Develop a policy to answer these questions: "How does third-party SharePoint-related software get introduced within the organization? Who will approve it and who pays for the cost of the software, its testing, and its implementation?"

- A file-type exclusion list should be implemented within sites to avoid nonorganizational or possibly harmful files from entering the environment.

- Custom search scopes should be identified and created to assist users to quickly find their data.

- Version control should be turned on within all document libraries along with major and minor versions when the environment—for example, storage capacity—allows.

- Avoid breaking inheritance whenever possible from all subsites, libraries, and lists. A broken inheritance should be centrally documented and tracked.

- Site provisioning policies and procedures should be developed as well as consideration around a centralized site creation process or possible automated process.

Communications Governance:

- A central communication area should be set up for the entire SharePoint environment, for an intranet-type solution, or within each department or project site.

- All communications should contain the URL of the SharePoint site referenced in the communication.

- Responsibility for the organization's maintenance-related communications to the overall SharePoint audience should be established (who, when, where).

Navigating Among SharePoint Sites

Unlike the previous version, WSS 3.0 offers a wide variety of ways for users to navigate among sites. With its new features, an organization can easily use WSS 3.0 as a portal solution, although it lacks some of the features and functionality that Windows Share-Point Server 2007 offers in that arena. A few key elements of navigation include:

- **Quick Launch**   Displayed on the left side of most SharePoint sites directly below the View All Site Content link. The Quick Launch displays links grouped in different headings for quick access to a site's most popular items, whether a library, list, site, or any other item accessible via a URL.

- **Top Link bar**   Appears as one or more hyperlinked tabs across the top of all pages on a site. The Top Link bar is used primarily as an overall hierarchical structure of the site or sites for which it resides.

- **View All Site Content**   Appears as a link on the side of nonadministration sites directly above the Quick Launch. This link will take users to the All Site Content page, which displays links to all lists, libraries, discussion boards, sites and work-spaces, surveys, and the Recycle Bin for the site.

- **Tree View**   Similar to the tree view in Windows Explorer. Objects shown in the tree view are displayed in a hierarchy view, which will display libraries, lists, discussions, surveys, and subsites. Items that have objects within them will have an expandable view. Tree View is disabled by default, but can be enabled in Site Setting for a site.

- **Content breadcrumb navigation**   Provides a set of hyperlinks that the enable site's users to quickly navigate up or down to sites within the hierarchy.

- **Global breadcrumb navigation**   Provides hyperlinks that enable site users to link to various sites within the site collection. Global breadcrumb navigation is always visible in the upper-left corner of the page and will display the site's name.

New Navigation Features in WSS 3.0

One of the most powerful new features in WSS 3.0 is the ability to customize a site's navigation. One of the most frequent user complaints with the previous version con-cerned customization. Now you achieve customized site navigation in a matter of clicks by using out-of-the-box options.

Users can now customize the Quick Launch to display custom headers and links within those headers. The order in which they are displayed can also be customized. Users have the ability to create a link to anything that can be accessed via a URL. They can also edit or delete the existing out-of-the-box names that are created with the site template that was selected during creation.

> **Note**
>
> It is important to communicate to the site's user base that not all of the site's libraries, lists, and subsites will necessarily be displayed in the Quick Launch now that it is fully customizable. If the users are not aware of this, there could be a lot of needless calls to the help desk or to SharePoint administrators asking where a specific item may have gone. Users can always click the View All Site Content link to view all the content within a site.

Users can now also customize the Top Link bar in the same manner as the Quick Launch. A custom site hierarchy can be put into place within any site regardless of its location within another site or even a site collection.

Breadcrumb navigation is now available on all sites, enabling users to have a better sense on where they currently are located within a site's structure and then to move up or down the navigational tree within sites.

Configuring Sites and Subsite Navigation

As mentioned earlier in this chapter, users can now easily customize WSS 3.0's site navigation. It is important to map out a hierarchy and navigational structure that will work for your top-level site as well as the subsites below it that may be inheriting navigation from the parent site.

> **Note**
>
> All library or list items that are created are added to the Quick Launch by default. A user can go into an existing library or list item's list settings and, within its General Settings column, click Title, Description And Navigation. Within the Navigation section, there will be an item that says Display This *List/Library/etc*. On The Quick Launch. A user then has the option to either display or remove the item from the Quick Launch.

Displaying or Hiding the Quick Launch

The Quick Launch can be customized to meet the exact needs of your organization. It can even be hidden if necessary. If you would like to hide the Quick Launch, perform the following:

1.   On the home page for the site, click the Site Actions menu and then click Site Settings.

2.   In the Look And Feel column of the Site Settings page, click Tree View.

Chapter 5

3. In Tree View page, shown Figure 5-5, you have two options. If you would like to display the Quick Launch, select Enable Quick Launch. To display Tree View, select Enable Tree View. Clearing either check box will cause the associated feature to be hidden.

4. Click OK to commit the changes.

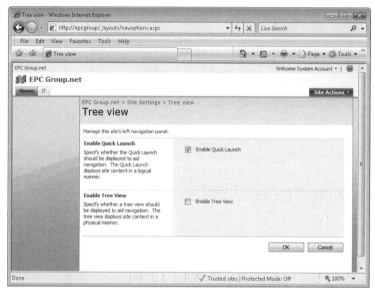

Figure 5-5 Users have options to display or hide the Quick Launch and to display or hide a tree view of a site.

Editing the Quick Launch

Users can add, edit, delete, and reorder items on the Quick Launch by using WSS 3.0 site settings features. To perform modifications on the Quick Launch, a user can do the following:

1. On the site's home page, click the Site Actions menu and then click Site Settings.

2. In the Look And Feel column, click Quick Launch.

3. Figure 5-6 shows several of the Quick Launch page options that users can choose from—adding, editing, or deleting a link.

   ○ To add a new link, click New Link. Type the URL and a description for the link and then, in the Heading section, select the heading that you want this new link to appear under. Then click OK.

   ○ To edit a link, click the Edit icon of the item you would like to edit. Make any necessary changes to the URL and description of the link and then click OK.

   ○ To delete a link, click the Edit icon of the item you would like to delete and then click Delete.

Adding, Editing, or Deleting a Heading

To add, edit, or delete a heading, perform one of the following:

- To add a new heading, click New Heading. Type the URL and a description for the heading and then click OK.

- To edit a heading, click the Edit button of the heading you would like to edit. Make any necessary changes to the URL and description and then click OK.

- To delete a heading, click the Edit button of the heading you would like to delete and then click Delete. Any link under this heading will also be deleted.

Changing Order

To change the order of items on the Quick Launch, on the Quick Launch page, click Change Order. The resulting Change Order page provides drop-down lists that allow you to change the order of the headings and links. Once you have made the desired changes, click OK.

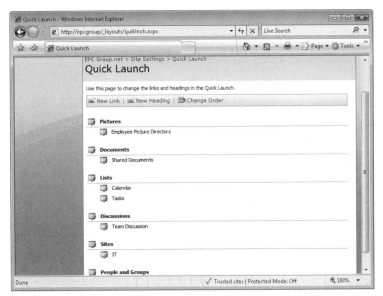

Figure 5-6 The Quick Launch configuration page enables users to make modifications to the Quick Launch.

Configuring the Top Link Bar

By default, when you create a new site, the site appears on the Top Link bar of the parent site, and the new site inherits the Top Link bar of the parent site. To stop using the Top Link bar from the parent site, you can change the setting at any time and use a customized Top Link bar for your subsite. To do so, follow these steps:

   1.   On the home page for the site, click the Site Actions menu and then click Site Settings.

2. In the Look and Feel column, click Top Link Bar.

3. Do one of the following:

- To create custom links for the site, click Stop Inheriting Links.
- To use the same links as the parent site, click Use Links From Parent.

Editing the Top Link Bar

If your site is using a unique Top Link bar, you can customize the links that appear on the Top Link bar for the site. Any sites created below the parent site can also be displayed on the Top Link bar, provided that the sites are configured to inherit the parent Top Link bar. You can also include links to other sites outside of your site collection. To do so, follow these steps:

1. On the home page for the site, click the Site Actions menu and then click Site Settings.

2. In the Look And Feel column, click Top Link Bar.

3. Do one of the following:

- To add a new link, click New Link. Type the URL and a description for the link.
- To edit a link, click the Edit button. Make any necessary changes to the description.
- To remove a link, click the Edit button and then click Delete. When you delete a link from the Top Link bar, any links contained under that link are also deleted.

4. Click OK.

Reordering Top Link Bar Links

You can change the order in which the tabs are displayed on the Top Link bar. Any changes that you make to the order of items on the Top Link bar are reflected in any sites that inherit Top Link bar navigation from your site. To change the order, follow these steps:

1. On the home page for the site, click the Site Actions menu and then click Site Settings.

2. In the Look And Feel column, click Top Link Bar.

3. Click Change Order.

4. In the Link Order column, click options in the lists to change the order in which the links appear on the Top Link bar.

5. Click OK.

Using Web Parts to Display Sites

Web Parts can be used within a site to display links to other sites or Web-based content. The standard team site template contains a Links list that is automatically placed within one of the Web Part zones on the site upon its creation.

The Content Editor Web Part enables users to add HTML content within a Web Part page. Users can also take advantage of this Web Part to link to different sites and content because it contains both a rich text editor (for users who do not have knowledge of HTML) and a source editor (for those who prefer to use HTML code directly). It also has a content link available for users to link to existing content.

> **Note**
>
> The Content Editor Web Part will be discussed in greater detail in the section titled "Proper Use of the Content Editor Web Part" in Chapter 12, "Managing Windows SharePoint Services 3.0 Site Content," and the section titled "Displaying the HTML with the Content Editor Web Part" in Chapter 18, "Advanced Design Techniques."

Configuring a Links Web Part

Any Web Part page can display a Links Web Part configured with links to any site or piece of content accessible by a URL. This Web Part typically displays links to parent sites and subsites, and it is great for displaying other frequently used links both internal and external to the organization.

Most sites contain a Links list, but if your site does not already contain one, click Site Actions, Create. Then click Links to create the new list. Alternatively, click View All Site Content, Create, Links.

To add a Links List Web Part to your site, do the following:

1. On the Site Actions menu, click Edit Page.

2. In Figure 5-7, you can see how the Web Part zones on your Web page are displayed. In the Web Part zone that you want to add the Web Part to, click Add A Web Part.

3. In the Add Web Parts dialog box, select the check box for the Web Part that you want to add to the page and then click Add to add the Web Part to the page.

4. Once the selected Links Web Part is added to the page, click Exit Edit Mode.

Once the Links Web Part is on the page, it will display any links that the list currently contains. To add a new link to the Links list, simply follow these steps:

1. In Web Part Edit Mode, click Add New Link.

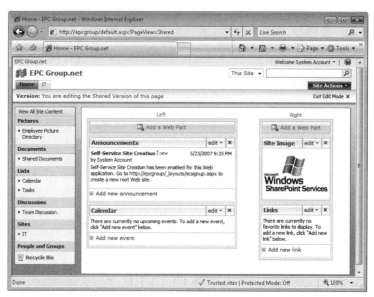

Figure 5-7 Web Part Edit Mode enables users to make and remove Web Parts on a Web page.

2. Specify the new link's URL in the dialog box, as shown in Figure 5-8. There is a link for users to test this new link to make sure it is valid before moving to the next step.

3. Give the link a description that will also become the link text.

4. In the *Note* field, add notes you would like to store concerning the link. The *Note* field will not be displayed within the Links Web Part.

5. Click OK.

Using a Links Web Part requires only one click. However, it does require you to build the links manually and remove them manually when they fall out of use. It is a good practice for a site's owner to periodically check all hyperlinks within a site to make sure they are still working and that they display relevant and valid content.

Using a Custom Web Part to Display Links

If the standard Links Web Part does not meet the needs of your organization, a few options are available. You could develop a custom Web Part, which will be discussed later will be discussed later in Chapter 19, "Beginning Web Part Development," or you could purchase a third-party solution Web Part that would meet your needs.

It is always best, especially when first rolling out your implementation of WSS 3.0, to try and use the features and functionality that are available to you right out of the box. But if these will absolutely not meet your needs, then a custom or third-party solution can bridge the gaps between your business needs and the available technology.

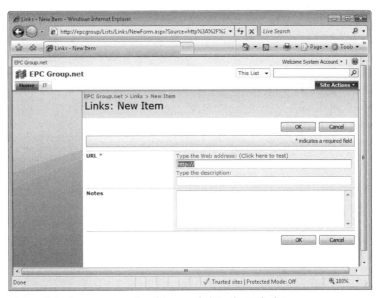

Figure 5-8 A user can easily add a new link to the Links list.

Creating and Configuring Basic and Web Part Pages

With WSS 3.0 and only a browser, a user can create a powerful set of sites and pages to meet a vast number of needs.

Creating Basic Pages

The simplest kind of page is an ordinary, basic page that contains no Web Parts or other special features. A basic page can be created by performing the following steps:

1. Click View All Site Content and then click Create on the All Site Content page. Alternatively, click Site Actions and then click Create within any site.

2. In the Web Pages category, click Basic Page.

3. On the New Basic Page form shown in Figure 5-9, in the Name section, type in a name for the new page. Selecting the Overwrite If File Already Exists check box causes an existing page to be overwritten if the page name is already in use. If you do not want to overwrite a page that already exists with the same name, leave this box blank.

4. Under Document Library, select the document library where this new page will be stored.

5. Click Create to load the Rich Text Editor, as shown in Figure 5-10.

Chapter 5

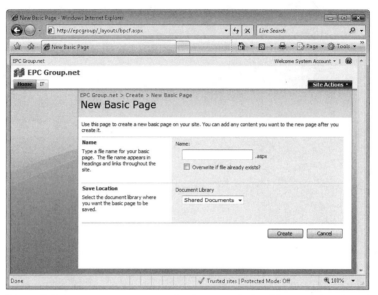

Figure 5-9 A user can create a new basic page, which will be stored in the selected document library.

6. Type whatever content you like into the Rich Text Editor. You can use the toolbar buttons to apply colors, fonts, text styles, alignment, and so forth. There are also buttons to insert hyperlinks, pictures, and tables.

7. Click Save to save the rich text content into your new Web page. WSS 3.0 will supply the standard top navigation bar and apply the site's default theme.

Links to the new page will appear in all standard views of the document library in which it resides. To provide additional links, add the page URL to one or more Links lists and then display the Links list on any Web Part page (such as the site's home page). A user could also add the link somewhere in a Content Editor Web Part as well.

You should be aware of two special precautions when using the Rich Text Editor to create a Web page. To change an existing page you created this way, open the page by clicking its link in the list where it resides and then click the Edit Content link at the upper right corner of the page.

- If you insert any pictures or hyperlinks, be sure to specify valid, complete URLs. In the case of pictures, for example, you might want to specify the full path of a picture in a SharePoint picture library. When users make the mistake of linking to local paths and drives, other users without the same access will be unable to load the files.

- When you have created a table, you can insert rows, columns, or cells, and you can merge or split cells. However, you can no longer modify table and cell attributes such as cell spacing, cell padding, and borders. If you make a mistake, you'll need to delete the table (and its contents) and then recreate it from scratch.

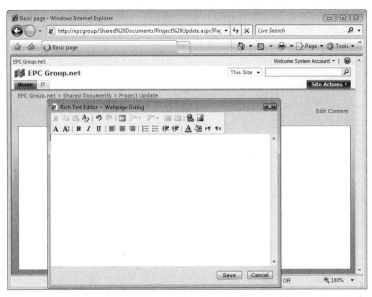

Figure 5-10 The Rich Text Editor enables users to begin adding content to the basic page.

For a more flexible way of adding pages to a SharePoint site, refer to Part 4, "Creating and Designing Sites Using SharePoint Designer 2007."

Creating Web Part Pages

Technically, a Web Part page is an ASP.NET file, and Web Parts are derived from Web Form controls. Using only a browser, you can easily create new Web Part pages. With Web Part pages, you don't have to fight the limited editing capability of the Rich Text Editor. Instead, Web Parts provide all the page content, and they are much more flexible and easy to configure.

To create a new Web Part page by using only a SharePoint site's browser interface, perform the following steps:

1. Click View All Site Content and then click Create on the All Site Content page. Alternatively, click Site Actions and then click Create within any site.

2. Under Web Pages, click Web Part Page.

3. On the New Web Part Page form, shown in Figure 5-11, type a name for the new page. Selecting the Overwrite If Already Exists check box enables you to overwrite the page if the name is already in use. If you do not want to overwrite a page that already exists with the same name, leave this box blank.

4. Under Choose A Layout Template, select a layout template to arrange the Web Parts in zones on the new Web Part page. You can add multiple Web Parts to each zone. If a Web Part is not added to a zone, the zone will collapse (unless it has a fixed width).

5. Under Document Library, select the document library where this new page will be stored.

6. Click Create, and the new Web Part Page will be created and then loaded in Edit Mode.

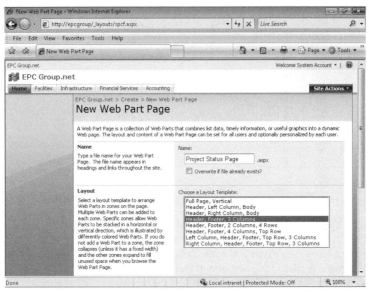

Figure 5-11 A user can create a new Web Part page with a specific layout. It will be stored in the selected document library.

Modifying Web Part Pages

You can also use a browser to add, reconfigure, and remove Web Parts in many Share-Point pages. These can include sites or Web Part pages that you created, or any page for which you have the proper editing and design permissions.

Web Parts are independent units of content designed to occupy part of a Web page. Web Parts have code that executes on the Web server, but they don't usually display page banners, signature lines, and other aspects of a complete Web page design. The page that contains the Web Part usually provides these elements. Web Parts reside in a Web Part zone that reserves space within a Web Part page for one or more Web Parts.

Web Parts share a set of common properties that are organized into different sections of the tool pane that controls the Web Part's appearance, layout, description, image icon, and so on. There are also Web Parts that contain custom properties that are displayed in the tool pane, either above or below the standard Web Part properties. Certain Web Parts have more properties than others, but most share common properties that make editing them easy.

WSS 3.0 stores either of two view settings for a Web Part:

- **Shared view**   You can add a Web Part to a Web Part page and then edit the Web Part page in a shared view. Shared Web Parts are available to all users of a Web Part page who have the appropriate permissions.

- **Personal view**   You can add a shared Web Part to your own personal view and then edit your view of the Web Part. The changes that you make to a Web Part while you are in a personal view are available only to you. Other users who did not make changes in a personal view continue to see the shared view of the Web Part.

Web Part Page modification can begin with only a few clicks of the mouse. For example, to move a Web Part from one zone to another, follow these steps:

1. On the Site Actions menu, click Edit Page.

2. Select the Web Part you want to move into a different Web Part zone and drag the Web Part to its new location.

3. When you are finished, click Exit Edit Mode.

In Figure 5-12, a user followed the preceding Web Part page modification steps on the standard out-of-the-box team site and moved the existing Web Parts into opposite Web Part zones. This was accomplished in a matter of seconds by dragging Web Parts into the different zones.

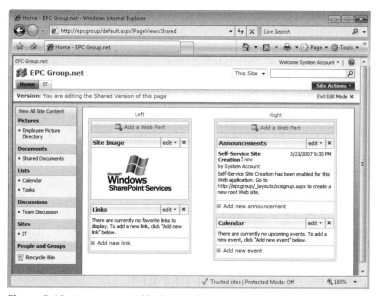

Figure 5-12 A user can quickly drag Web Parts into the different Web Part zones available within a site.

Adding Web Parts to a Page

Web Parts can be added to a page to meet the needs of the organization and ensure that the site captures all the functionality needed for optimal collaboration and document management. All new document libraries and lists that are created can instantly be added to the page and viewed as Web Parts.

Web Parts are stored within repositories called Web Part galleries. Web Part galleries contain all of the Web Parts available to the site that you are designing, and three or more galleries may be available to the user—the Closed Web Parts Gallery, the *Site Name* Gallery, the Server Gallery, and possibly others.

Adding a Web Part to a Web Part Page

Adding a Web Part to a Web Part page in WSS 3.0 can be quickly done by using the Add Web Parts dialog box. A user with the appropriate permissions level can do this as follows:

1. On the Site Actions menu, click Edit Page.

2. In the Web Part zone where you want to add the Web Part, click Add A Web Part.

3. In the Add Web Parts dialog box, select the check box for the Web Part that you want to add to the page, as shown in Figure 5-13.

    WSS 3.0's site templates provide a collection of Web Parts that are ready to use with your site. You can use these built-in Web Parts, customize them to suit your needs, or create new Web Parts and upload them for use throughout your site.

4. Click Add.

To determine which sites and Web Part pages your account permissions allow you to modify, click Site Actions and then Edit Page. If you do not see the Edit Page link within Site Actions and need to be able to modify a Web Part page, contact your SharePoint administrator to discuss permission settings for your account.

It is also possible to add a Web Part to the page by using the tool pane, which enables you to see all the available Web Part galleries that you have permission to view. You can use this method to add a Web Part to the page by doing the following:

1. On the Site Actions menu, click Edit Page.

2. In the Web Part zone that you want to add the Web Part to, click Add a Web Part.

3. When the Web Parts are displayed, click the Advanced Web Part Gallery And Options link, visible in Figure 5-13.

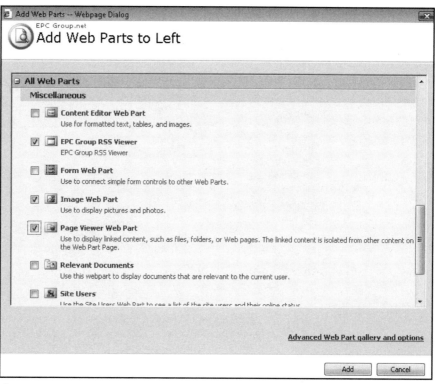

Figure 5-13 A user adds Web Parts to the site to meet the organization's exact needs.

4. The tool pane, shown in Figure 5-14, will enable you to do the following:

   ○ **Browse for a Web Part** At the top of the tool pane, click the drop-down list arrow and then click Browse. Click the gallery name to view a list of Web Parts that are available for that gallery. Click Next to view more Web Parts in that gallery.

   ○ **Search for a Web Part** At the top of the tool pane, click the drop-down list arrow and then click Search.

   ○ **Import a Web Part** At the top of the tool pane, click the drop-down list arrow and then click Import. You can now browse to a new Web Part file and upload it.

5. Click the name of the Web Part that you want to add, select the zone to add it to, and then click Add.

Chapter 5

Figure 5-14 A user can add Web Parts via the tool pane.

Creating a Personal View

You may be able to create a personal view of the page by doing the following:

1. At the top of the page, click Welcome *Your Name*, as shown in Figure 5-15, and then click Personalize This Page. The page should then load in Edit Mode, as shown in Figure 5-16. Please note how the version of the page is marked: You Are Editing The Personal Version Of This Page.

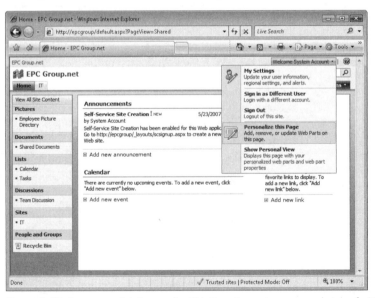

Figure 5-15 A user can click Personalize This Page to create a personal view of a Web Part page.

2. Add and remove Web Parts or modify their properties as needed. You also can customize the view of any List Web Part on the page. You can close the Web Parts when editing in Personal view, but you will not be able to delete them from the page.

3. When you finish, click Exit Edit Mode.

Figure 5-16 A user can edit the personal version of the page in Edit Mode.

In the future, if you ever need to delete the personalized changes that you made to a Web Part page, you can do the following:

1. At the top of the page, click Welcome *Your Name* and then click Reset Page Content.

2. You will then be prompted to confirm that the reset of the page was correct. If so, click OK. This will permanently delete the personalized view you previously created, and you will need to create a new personalized view if you ever need one in the future.

Working with Out-of-the-Box Web Parts

WSS 3.0 offers a wide variety of out-of-the-box Web Parts for you to use. The more familiar you become with SharePoint, the more you will be able to get out of these Web Parts. During the site creation process, users select the templates they would like to use to build their sites. These templates contain a preset number of libraries and lists that can automatically be placed on a Web Part page and used. These preconfigured List View Web Parts are as follows:

- **Announcements** The Announcements Web Part is great for posting news and other short pieces of information within a site.

Chapter 5

- **Calendar** The calendar is great for tracking events and team members' schedules. It can also be handy for tracking things like vacation time or who is out of the office today.

- **Links** Use the Links Web Part to post hyperlinks to Web pages that interest your team.

- **Shared Documents** Use the Shared Documents Web Part to share files from the default document library. This can be helpful if, for example, you need to post frequently used documents right on the site so that users can find them immediately and not have to browse for the content.

- **Tasks** Use the Tasks Web Part to assign a task to a member of your team, specify its due date and priority, and indicate its status and progress.

- **Team Discussion** Use the Team Discussion Web Part to provide a forum for talking about topics that interest your team. This Web Part is great for knowledge management and the capturing of best practices and lessons learned within an organization.

Another selection of Web Parts is the Miscellaneous category. These Web Parts are automatically available to all sites and Web Part pages. They are powerful and can be used to capture and display various pieces of information. These Miscellaneous Web Parts are as follows:

- **Content Editor Web Part** This Web Part is one of the most useful default Web Parts available. It can store formatted text, hyperlinks, images, and tables on a Web Part page. It is useful for rendering HTML content as well.

- **Form Web Part** You can use the Form Web Part to connect to and filter a column of data in another Web Part. Both Web Parts must run on the same server.

- **Image Web Part** You can use the Image Web Part to add a picture or graphic to a Web Part page. To more easily coordinate the image with other Web Parts on the page, you can control the vertical alignment, horizontal alignment, and background color of the image inside the Image Web Part by editing its custom properties in a shared view.

- **Page Viewer Web Part** You can use the Page Viewer Web Part to display a Web page, file, or folder on a Web Part page. You enter a hyperlink, file path, or folder name to link to the content.

- **Relevant Documents** You can use the Relevant Documents Web Part to display documents that are relevant to the current user.

- **Site Users** You can use the Site Users Web Part to display or add a list of users and groups who have permission to use a site. The Site Users Web Part automatically appears on the home page of a document workspace site.

- **User Tasks** You can use the User Tasks Web Part to display tasks that are assigned to the current user.

- **XML Web Part** You can use the XML Web Part to display Extensible Markup Language (XML) and apply Extensible Stylesheet Language Transformations (XSLT) to the XML before the content is displayed.

Configuring Web Parts

A Web Part's properties, such as the Web Part's title or border, are configured using the tool pane that was first shown in Figure 5-14. The tool pane enables users to specify widths for Web Parts as well as a number of other options to ensure the Web Parts mesh well with the rest of the page.

Editing a Web Part's Tool Pane

To edit a Web Part's tool pane, a user must have appropriate permissions. To edit the tool pane, do the following:

1. On the Site Actions menu, click Edit Page.

2. Click the Edit drop-down list on the title bar of the Web Part you would like to edit and select Modify Shared Web Part, as shown in Figure 5-17.

3. The Web Part's tool pane will then be displayed, as shown in Figure 5-18.

4. You will now be able to edit attributes such as Selected view and Toolbar Type, and you can open up the Appearance, Layout, and Advanced sections to modify many additional items.

5. After you are satisfied with your changes and are ready to close the tool pane, click OK. Alternatively, to view your changes without closing the tool pane, click Apply.

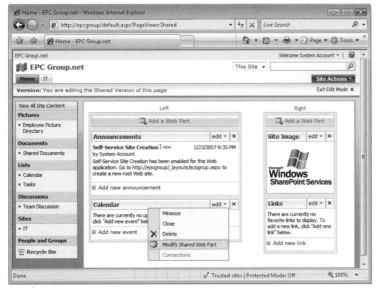

Figure 5-17 To display a Web Part's tool pane, click Edit and then Modify Shared Web Part on the selected Web Part.

Figure 5-18 A Web Part's tool pane allows for detailed editing of a Web Part's appearance as well as several other items.

Modifying the View of a List or Library Web Part

Users can change the view of any List View Web Part. To change the current view or create a new custom view when a List View Web Part is loaded onto the page, do the following:

1. On the Site Actions menu, click Edit Page.

2. Click the Web Part menu of the Web Part that you want to customize and click Edit. Then click Modify Shared Web Part.

3. In the tool pane, the Selected View drop-down list will be displayed. Directly below it, click Edit The Current View.

4. The Edit View page will then load, and in the Columns section, which you can see in Figure 5-19, you can choose to show or hide columns by selecting the appropriate check boxes. Next to the column name, enter the number for the order of your column in the view.

5. Directly below the Column section is the Sort section of the Edit View page. In the Sort section, as shown in Figure 5-20, choose how you want the information to be sorted. You can use two columns for the sort, for example, first by author and then by file name for each author.

6. Directly below the Sort section is the Filter section of the Edit View page.

7. In the Filter section, choose whether and how you want to filter the information, as shown in Figure 5-21. A filtered view shows you a smaller selection, such as items created by a specific department or with an Approved status.

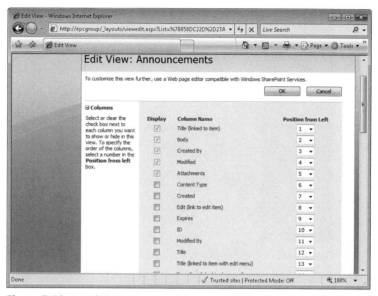

Figure 5-19 A Web Part's view can be customized to display specific columns based on your specific needs.

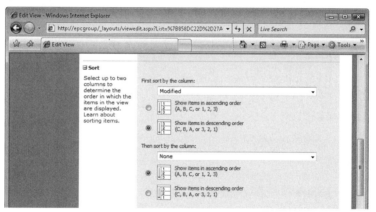

Figure 5-20 A user can sort the Web Part's view and even use two columns to sort if needed.

8. In the Group By section, you can group items with the same value in their own section, such as an expandable section for documents by a specific author.

9. In the Totals section, you can count the number of items in a column, such as the total number of issues. In some cases, you can summarize or distill additional information, such as averages.

10. In the Style section, select the style that you want for the view, such as a shaded list in which every other row is shaded.

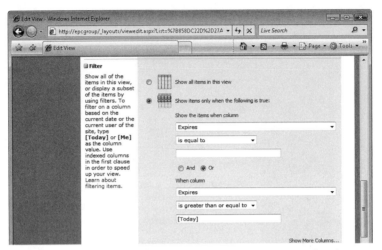

Figure 5-21 A user can filter the Web Part's view to display specific information in the Web Part.

11. If your list or library has folders, you can create a view that doesn't include the folders. This is sometimes called a flat view. To view all your list items at the same level, click Show All Items Without Folders.

12. If your list or library is large, you can limit how many files can be viewed in the list or library, or how many files can be viewed on the same page. In the Item Limit section, select the options that you want.

13. If you plan to view the list or library on a mobile device, in the Mobile section, select the options that you want.

14. Click OK.

In Summary...

This chapter explained the basics of organizing content on a server running WSS 3.0. This included planning a site structure, creating sites and site collections, planning site governance, planning navigational elements, choosing a visual appearance, and linking among sites once they exist. It then explained how to create your own Web Part pages, and how to add and arrange Web Parts that display your information the way you want.

The next chapter will explain how to create, modify, and display SharePoint lists and libraries by using only a browser.

Lists and libraries are the repositories for almost anything you want to keep in a Microsoft Windows SharePoint Services 3.0 (WSS 3.0) site. You design lists and libraries in relatively the same manner because their framework is similar. They are a powerful solution for organizations that currently store content from many different types of applications in many different locations. If you have a collection of straightforward spreadsheets you store and track on your desktop, it is much easier in most cases to import them into a SharePoint list so that they are now available to a larger audience but in a secure manner. Why type your content into static HTML pages or have five different mechanisms for collecting and presenting data when you can accomplish this in a flash and store the content in lists and libraries? Once you have stored the data, you can configure Web Part pages to display the lists and libraries in your SharePoint site.

You will soon discover that using SharePoint lists and libraries is much easier than handcrafting a never-ending series of spreadsheets and custom Microsoft Office Access databases, and it is certainly easier than coding your own custom Web pages from scratch. This chapter explains how to create lists and libraries, including not only the standard types that come with WSS 3.0, but also custom types you design yourself to meet your specific needs. It goes on to explain how you can then utilize WSS 3.0's powerful new features to display data via RSS feeds or even use workflows to automate specific tasks and receive content approval and feedback. The chapter also goes into detail about how you can use content types to standardize your organization's procedures for capturing metadata and managing information.

This chapter concentrates exclusively on using a browser to create, modify, and display lists and libraries. Microsoft SharePoint Designer 2007 can also perform these tasks, and Part 4, "Creating, Designing, and Managing Sites and Working with SharePoint Designer 2007," will explain that approach.

Creating Lists

Whenever you want to add data to a SharePoint site, or whenever you want others to do so, you should first locate the proper list (or library). If an appropriate list or library does not exist, a new one should be created.

> **Note**
>
> Whenever possible, it is important not to duplicate efforts in SharePoint when deciding whether to create a new list or library, or to use one that already exists. A little investigation about what is currently available can go a long way toward the "one version of the truth" philosophy.
>
> If a list or library exists that meets your needs, store your content there. But what if your SharePoint site doesn't contain a list or library that seems right for the type of information you need to store? WSS 3.0 list and library functionality is so robust that if you need new ones, you can create them with ease and without expert knowledge of the product. The next two sections provide guidance for new list and library creation.

Creating Built-In Lists

To begin creating a SharePoint list of any kind, open the site where you want the list to reside and then click the View All Site Content link at the top of Quick Launch. Then click Create. This displays the Create page, shown in Figure 6-1.

> **Note**
>
> It is also possible to access the Create page by clicking Site Actions and then clicking Create.

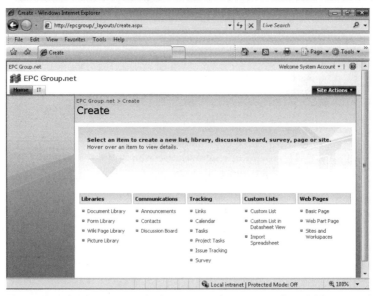

Figure 6-1 The Create page displays options for creating all available types of SharePoint lists, libraries, and pages.

The simplest lists to create are the built-in types that appear under the Communications and Tracking headings. Table 6-1 lists these types.

Table 6-1 Built-In SharePoint List Types

Type	Description	Interface to Microsoft Office Outlook?
Announcements	Stores news, status, and other short bits of information.	No
Contacts	Stores information about people your team members work with, such as customers or partners.	Yes
Discussion Board	Stores information regarding team discussions on any given topic and can be e-mail enabled. Information can be captured here such as a team's best practices and lessons learned. It is also great for knowledge management.	Yes
Links	Stores links to Web pages or other resources that you want to share.	No
Calendar	Stores information on upcoming meetings, deadlines, and other important events.	Yes
Tasks	Stores work items that you or your team members need to complete.	Yes
Project Tasks	Stores work items that you or your team members need to complete. Similar to the Tasks list, it also offers a Gantt view with progress bars.	Yes
Issue Tracking	Stores a set of issues or problems. You can assign, prioritize, and follow the progress of issues from start to finish.	No
Survey	Stores feedback from users within the organization. This list is a great tool for collecting and compiling feedback—such as an employee-of-the-month survey—and enables you to design custom questions for your audience.	No

Although many aspects of working with these and other list types are the same, each built-in list type has properties that you can't change. For example:

- You can't change the icon assigned to a built-in list.
- Each type of list has certain required fields that you can't delete. For example, you can't delete the *Title* and *Start Time* fields in a Calendar list.

Creating a New List from the Built-In Lists

Site administrators or those with the appropriate permissions can easily create a new list from WSS 3.0's available built-in lists by performing the following steps:

1. Click View All Site Content and then click Create on the All Site Content page.

2. Under either the Communications or Tracking headings, click the type of list that you would like to create, such as Issue Tracking or Project Tasks, as shown in Figure 6-1.

3. In the Name box, type in a name for the new list (this is a required field; see Figure 6-2). The name you type here will appear at the top of the list's page and will become part of the URL for the page and any related navigational elements.

4. In the Description box, type the purpose of the list. The Description field is optional, but it will appear at the top of the list in most views.

5. If you would like the new list to display in the site's Quick Launch, select Yes in the Navigation section.

6. If your organization has chosen to allow lists to be e-mail enabled, you may see an e-mail section as your next option (see Figure 6-2). If this option is enabled and you plan to e-mail enable this new list, select Yes under Allow This List To Receive E-Mail. Then, in the e-mail address box, type the address that you want people to use for the list.

7. As discussed previously, if an e-mail notification section appears, your administrator has enabled lists on your site to send e-mail notifications when list items are assigned. To enable the list to send e-mail to people when an item is assigned to them, click Yes under Send E-Mail When Ownership Is Assigned? This option is not available for all lists.

8. Click Create to finalize the new list creation process. The new list will then be created but will not contain any items, as shown in Figure 6-3.

> **Note**
>
> If you plan to e-mail enable a new list you are creating, the *Description* field is a great place to store the list's e-mail address so that it can be easily discovered by the user base.

> **Note**
>
> Organizations are slowly coming around to the idea of e-mail enabling lists. This powerful new technology can be a great tool for your team. If this feature is not currently enabled, ask your e-mail administrator if e-mail enabling SharePoint lists would be a possibility.

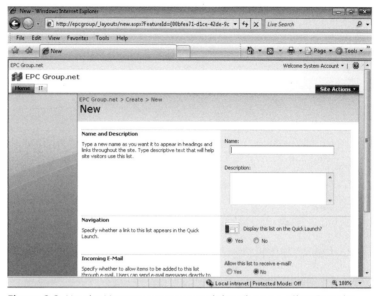

Figure 6-2 Use the New page to name and describe a new SharePoint list.

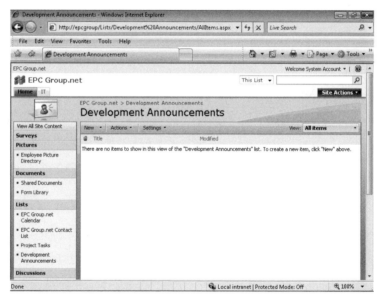

Figure 6-3 This new list has no items yet.

Once the list exists, you can enter data, create new views, display views in Web pages, or even modify the list's data fields and features. Sections later in this chapter will explain these procedures.

Creating Custom Lists

For maximum flexibility when creating a new list, choose one of the links under the Custom Lists heading. Here's how these links work.

- **Custom List**   This option displays the New page, shown in Figure 6-2, and then creates and displays a list with only the Title column displayed. Two columns are created behind the scenes to store information on the users who work with the content of the list: Created By and Modified By.

  In almost every case, you would use the instructions in the next section—"Modifying Lists"—to modify this starting point with additional fields and features.

- **Custom List In Datasheet View**   Like the previous option, this option displays the New page and creates a list with Title as the only column that is displayed. This option, however, opens the new list in the datasheet view so that you can view and modify list items in a tabular interface.

- **Import Spreadsheet**   Creates a list from data contained in a spreadsheet.

For more information about creating a custom list by importing a spreadsheet, refer to the section titled "Importing Excel Data into a SharePoint List" in Chapter 4, "Using SharePoint with Microsoft Office 2007."

Creating a List from a Template

WSS 3.0 enables users to create lists from templates so that lists that have already been proven to work within the organization—or those that contain customizations—can be easily reused. List templates can be imported and exported to different site collections and can be made available to a larger audience.

If desired, a list template can contain the actual content that existed within the list when it was saved as a template. It can also retain any of its views. You create list templates via the same process that you use when creating lists from built-in list templates, as detailed earlier in this chapter. The list templates will display as available links on the Create page, as shown in Figure 6-4.

Creating a Library

As discussed in earlier chapters, the main area for storing content in WSS 3.0 is a library. A library enables you to store, create, and manage files within your organization. If a library that meets your needs does not already exist within your organization, a new one can be created.

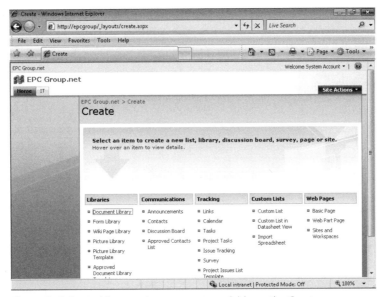

Figure 6-4 Several list templates are now available on the Create page.

Creating a New Library

Site administrators or those with the appropriate permissions can easily create a new library from WSS 3.0's available built-in libraries by performing the following steps:

1. Click View All Site Content and then click Create on the All Site Content page.

2. Under Libraries, click the type of library that you want, such as Document Library.

3. In the Name box, type a name for the library, as shown in Figure 6-5. The library name is required and will display at the top of the library page. It will become part of the library's URL and navigational elements.

4. In the Description box, you can optionally type a description of the purpose of the library. The description will appear at the top of the library page.

5. To add a link to this library on Quick Launch, verify that Yes is selected in the Navigation section.

6. If an Incoming E-mail section appears, your administrator has enabled your site to receive content by e-mail. If you want people to add files to the library by sending them as attachments to e-mail messages, select Yes. Then, in the e-mail address box, type the address that you want people to use for the library. Note that e-mail options are not available for wiki-page libraries.

7. To create a new version each time a file is checked into the library, select Yes in the Document Version History or Picture Version History section.

8. Depending on the type of library you are creating, a Document Template section may be available. It lists the compatible programs that are available as the default for creating new files. If content types are enabled, the default template is specified through the content type. In the Document Template section, in the drop-down list, select the type of file that you want to be used as a template for files that are created in the library.

9. Click Create.

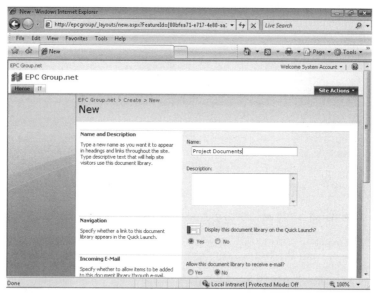

Figure 6-5 Use the New page to name and describe a new document library.

Modifying Lists and Libraries

You might find an existing list or library within your organization that would meet your needs if it only contained a few additional fields (that is, content types or columns). The topics in this section explain how to modify an existing list or library to better suit your needs.

INSIDE OUT   **Be cautious of not duplicating an existing storage location if one already exists**

As a consultant, I have been in numerous organizations where similar data was being captured on the same topic but within multiple lists or libraries on separate sites. The challenge is working with different users and groups to see if these lists or libraries can either be combined into a centralized one that contains all of the content types and columns or, if not, then how one or more of the lists or libraries can be modified to meet the organization's needs. Performing a quick proof-of-concept with a new list or library that contains all of the fields is sometimes a great way to show users that one centralized repository can work for the entire user base.

Modifying List and Library Settings

SharePoint lists and libraries are extremely flexible and customizable right out of the box. You can change their properties, behavior, security, appearance, workflow settings, and fields at will. To begin, display the list or library you want to modify and then click Settings. Select List Settings or Library Settings to display the customization page, shown in Figure 6-6.

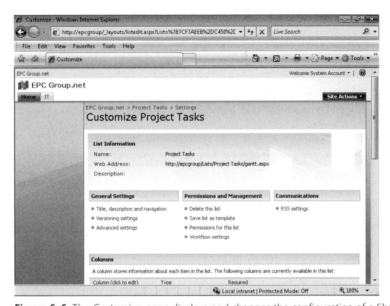

Figure 6-6 The Customize page displays and changes the configuration of a SharePoint list.

The next few sections explain how to use the commands on the customization page.

Updating General Settings

In WSS 3.0, three links are available under the General Settings header to enable a user to change the general settings for the list or library. These links are Title, Description And Navigation; Versioning Settings; and Advanced Settings. To change any of these items, click its link.

Updating Title, Description, and Navigation

To change the title, description, or navigation, click the corresponding link to display the List General Settings page, shown in Figure 6-7.

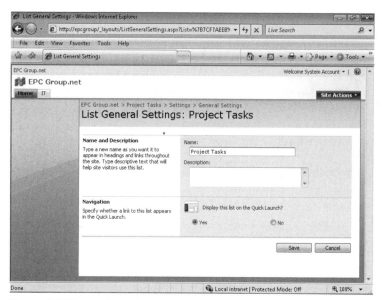

Figure 6-7 The List General Settings page displays and changes the title, description, or navigational settings of a SharePoint site list or library.

Once the List General Settings page is on display, make any changes you like to the following fields:

- *Name*   Type a name that will identify the list or library throughout the site.

- *Description*   Briefly describe the list or library's content or purpose.

- *Display This List Or Library On Quick Launch?*   Select Yes if you want Quick Launch on the site's home page to display a link to this list or library.

Versioning Settings in a List

To change the versioning settings in a list, navigate to the list, click its link, click Settings and select List Settings, and click the Versioning Settings link to display the List Versioning Settings page, shown in Figure 6-8.

Once the List Versioning Settings page is on display, make any changes you like to the following fields.

- *Content Approval*   Select Yes if you want to require content approval for items submitted to the list, or No if you do not.

- *Item Version History*   Select Yes if you want to create a new version each time you edit an item in the list. Optionally, you can then limit the number of drafts to be retained.

- *Draft Item Security*   Specify which users will be able to see draft items in the list. The available options are Any User Who Can Read Items, Only Users Who Can Edit Items, and Only Users Who Can Approve Items (And The Author Of The Item).

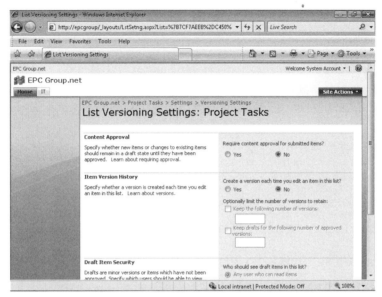

Figure 6-8 The List Versioning Settings page displays and configures the versioning settings of a SharePoint list.

Versioning Settings in a Library

To change the versioning settings in a library, navigate to the library, click its link, click Settings and select Document Library Settings, and click the Versioning Settings link to display the Document Library Versioning Settings page, shown in Figure 6-9.

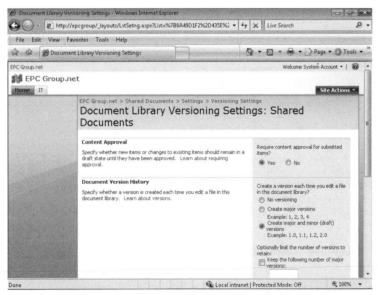

Figure 6-9 The Document Library Versioning Settings page displays and configures the versioning settings of a SharePoint library.

Once the Document Library Versioning Settings page is on display, make any changes you like to the following fields:

- **Content Approval** Select Yes if you want to require content approval for items submitted to the library, or No if you do not.

- **Document Version History** Select from No Versioning, Create Major Versions, or Create Major And Minor (Draft) Versions. Optionally, you can then limit the number of versions that are retained.

- **Draft Item Security** Specify which users will be able to see draft items in the library. The available options are Any User Who Can Read Items, Only Users Who Can Edit Items, and Only Users Who Can Approve Items (And The Author Of The Item).

- **Require Check Out** Specify whether users will be required to check out the documents before they can be edited.

Advanced Settings in a List

To change the advanced settings for a list, on the list's Customize page, click the Advanced Settings link to display the List Advanced Settings page, shown in Figure 6-10.

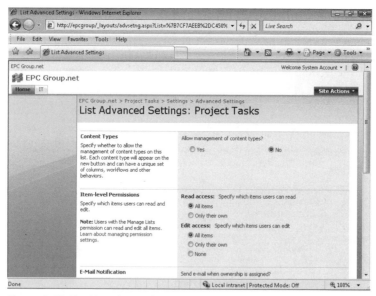

Figure 6-10 The List Advanced Settings page displays and configures the advanced settings options for a SharePoint list.

Once the advanced settings page is on display, make any changes you like to the following fields.

- **Content Types** Select Yes if you want to allow management of content types on the list. Select No if you do not wish to allow it.

- *Item Level Permissions* Specify which items users have either read or edit access. In the Read Access section, you can specify either All Items or Only Their Own. There is also a section for Edit Access. You can specify either All Items, Only Their Own, or None.

- *E-Mail Notification* Select Yes if you want to have the list send an e-mail when ownership is assigned to an item or when an item has been changed. Select No if you do not want the e-mail notifications to be sent. (Note: Some available options may vary depending on your overall environment settings.)

- *Attachments* Specify if users will be allowed to attach files to items in the list. Select Enabled if you would like to allow attachments in the list or Disabled if you do not wish to allow attachments.

- *Folders*   Specify whether you would like to display the New Folder command on the New menu within the list. Select Yes if you want to have New Folder displayed, or No if you do not wish to show this command. Changing this setting will not affect existing folders in the list.

- *Search* Specify whether the list should be visible within SharePoint's search results. Select Yes to allow the items to appear in the search results, or No if you do not wish them to appear. Users who do not have permissions to view the list items will not see them within the search results regardless of this setting.

Advanced Settings in a Library

To change the advanced settings for a document library, on the library's Customize page, click the Advanced Settings link to display the Document Library Advanced Settings page, shown in Figure 6-11.

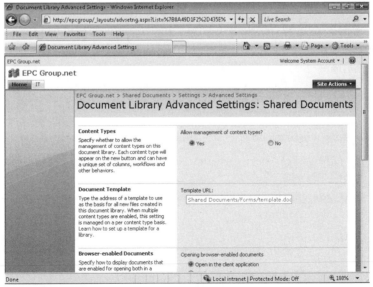

Figure 6-11 The Document Library Advanced Settings page displays and configures the advanced settings of a SharePoint document library.

Once the Document Library Advanced Settings page is on display, make any changes you like to the following fields:

- **Content Types** Select Yes if you want to allow management of content types in the library. Select No if you do not wish to manage them.

- **Document Template** Specify the URL of the template to use as the basis for all new files created in this library. If multiple content types are enabled, this setting is managed on a per-content-type basis.

- **Browser-Enabled Documents** Specify how to display documents that can be opened in either a browser or in a client application. Select either Open In The Client Application or Display As A Web Page.

- **Custom Send To Destination** Specify the destination name and URL of a custom Send To destination that you would like to appear on the context menu for this library.

- **Folders** Specify whether you would like to display the New Folder command on the New menu within the list. Select Yes if you want to have New Folder displayed or No if you do not wish to show this command. Changing this setting will not affect existing folders in the list.

- **Search** Specify whether the list should be visible within SharePoint's search results. Select Yes to allow the items to appear in the search results, or No if you do not wish them to appear. Users who do not have permissions to view the list items will not see them within the search results regardless of this setting.

Incoming E-Mail Settings

To change the incoming e-mail settings in a list or library, click its link to display the Incoming E-Mail Settings page. (Note: Some available options may vary depending on your overall environment settings.) Once the Incoming E-Mail Settings page is on display, make any changes you like to the following fields.

- **Incoming E-Mail** Select Yes if you want to allow items to be added to the list or library through e-mail. Select No if you do not wish to allow them. Also, specify the e-mail address of the list or library in the E-Mail Address box.

- **E-Mail Attachments** Specify whether to save attachments included with an incoming e-mail message as attachments to the item created in the list or library.

- **E-Mail Message** Specify whether to save the original EML file for an incoming e-mail message.

- **E-Mail Meeting Invitations** Specify whether to save e-mailed meeting invitations to this list or library.

- **E-Mail Security** Specify if the list or library's security settings will be used for e-mail to ensure that only users who can write to the list or library can send e-mail to it. The choices are to accept e-mail messages based on discussion board permissions or accept e-mail messages from any sender.

Deleting a List or Library

To delete a list or library, navigate to its Customize page and under the Permissions And Management category, click Delete This List or Delete This (*Library Type*) Library on the customization page of the list or library.

For the list, you will receive a prompt of either Are You Sure You Want To Send This List To The Site Recycle Bin or Are You Sure You Want To Delete This List.

For the library, you will receive a prompt of either This Document Library Will Be Removed And All Its Files Will Be Deleted. Are You Sure You Want To Send This Document Library To The Recycle Bin or This (*Library Type*) Will Be Removed And All Its Files Will Be Deleted. Are You Sure You Want To Delete This (*Library Type*) Library.

Users whose sites have the Recycle Bin enabled will receive the message about sending the list or library to the Recycle Bin, and those who do not have it enabled in their site will receive the dialog box that does not mention the Recycle Bin.

> **Note**
>
> The Recycle Bin is enabled within a site collection by default and can be configured in Central Administration at the site collection Web application level.

Saving a List or Library as a Template

WSS 3.0 enables users to save an existing list or library as a template so that users can create new lists from ones that are already proven to work within the organization or contain customizations that they require. List or library templates can also be imported and exported to different site collections. When you save a list or library as a template, you can specify whether to include the existing content in the template. Lists saved as templates are then made available in the List Template Gallery.

Saving an Existing List or Library as a Template

A list or library can easily be saved as a Template by performing the following steps:

1. Click View All Site Content and then click the link for the list or library you would like to save as a new template.

2. Click Settings within the list or library and then click List Settings or (*Library Type*) Library Settings to display the Customize page for the list or library.

3. Click Save List As Template for a list or Save (*Library Type*) Library As Template for a library.

4. In the File Name box, type in a file name for the new list or library template, as shown in Figure 6-12. This file name will be displayed in the appropriate Template Gallery.

Chapter 6

5. In the Template Name box, type a name for the new template. The template name field will be displayed on the site's Create page.

6. In the Description box, type a description for the new template. This description of the template will be displayed on the site's Create page.

7. If you would like the list or library's content to be saved in the template, so that new lists and libraries will automatically have the content available to them when they are created, select the Include Content check box. If you would like the template to be created without including the content, do not check this box.

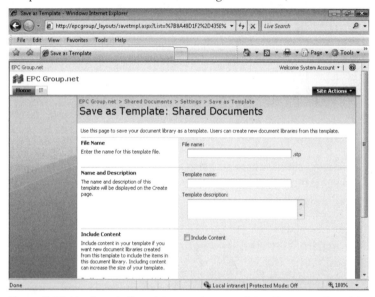

Figure 6-12 Use Save As Template page to save a list or library as a template.

> **Note**
>
> Templates neither save security settings nor apply them to new lists or libraries. Take this into account before including confidential content in a template.

Adding a Template to a List Gallery

If you have a list template file available to you and would like to add it to the Template List gallery, perform the following steps:

1. On the Site Actions menu, click Site Settings.

2. On the Site Settings page, in the Galleries section, click List Templates.

    It is possible that you may need to click Go To Top Level Site Settings in the Site Collection Administration column to see this link. (Note: Some available options may vary depending on your overall environment settings.)

3. On the List Template Gallery page, click Upload, as shown in Figure 6-13.

4. In the Name box, type the path to the template. Alternatively, click Browse.

5. Click OK to add an existing list template file to the List Template gallery.

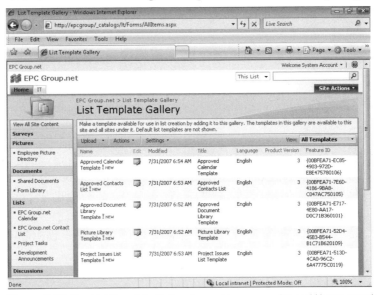

Figure 6-13 The List Template Gallery is used to manage list and library templates in the list and library template galleries.

Deleting a Template in the List Template Gallery

Users with the appropriate permissions can easily delete a template within the List Template gallery. To delete an existing list template, perform the following steps:

1. On the Site Actions menu, click Site Settings.

2. In the Galleries column, click List Templates. The List Template Gallery page will appear, as shown in Figure 6-13.

3. In the Edit column, click the Edit Document Properties icon for the list template that you want to delete.

> **Note**
> It is also possible to edit the properties of an existing list template on this page without having to delete the template.

4. Click Delete Item and then click OK to confirm the list template deletion.

Chapter 6

Changing Permissions for a List or Library

WSS 3.0 offers robust and granular management of the permissions for list and librar-ies. They can either inherit permissions from a parent site or object, or they can have their inheritance broken so that they can have unique SharePoint groups or permis-sions levels assigned to them.

> **Note**
> If a list or library's permissions are customized so that they no longer inherit permissions from a parent site or object, you can still reinherit permissions from the parent site or object at a later time.

It is a best practice to use Active Directory Security Groups or SharePoint groups to manage list permissions whenever possible. In some cases, though, you may have to break the parent's inheritance to manage a list. Within the SharePoint environment, it is good practice to track all lists, libraries, or items that have been assigned unique per-missions so that future permission updates to SharePoint can be appropriately applied.

Editing a List or Library's Permissions

To change the permissions for a list or library, a user with the appropriate permissions can perform the following:

1. Open the list or library.

2. On the Settings menu click List Settings or (*Library Type*) Settings.

3. On the Customize page, in the Permissions And Management column, click Permissions For This List / (*Library Type*) Library. The Permissions page will display all of the users and SharePoint groups associated with this list or library, along with their assigned permission levels.

4. If the list or library is inheriting permissions, you must first break the inheritance of the permissions before you edit permission levels on this list. To do this, on the Actions menu, click Edit Permissions and then click OK, as shown in Figure 6-14. If you would like to edit the permissions of the parent, you can click Actions and then Manage Permissions Of Parent, which will take you to the parent's permission area.

5. Select the check boxes for the users and SharePoint groups whose permissions you wish to edit.

6. On the Actions menu, select Edit User Permissions.

7. In the Choose Permissions section, select the permission levels that you would like to apply and then click OK.

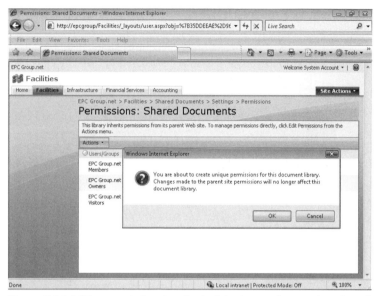

Figure 6-14 Editing permissions breaks the inheritance of permissions from the parent.

Adding Users to a List or Library

To add users to a list or library, a user with the appropriate permissions can perform the following steps:

1. Open the list or library.

2. On the Settings menu, click List Settings or (*Library Type*) Settings.

3. On the Customize page, in the Permissions And Management column, click Permissions For This List / (*Library Type*) Library.

   The Permissions page will display all of the users and SharePoint groups associated with this list, along with their assigned permission levels. If the list or library is inheriting permissions, you must first break the inheritance of the permissions before you can edit permission levels for this list or library. To do this, on the Actions menu, click Edit Permissions and then click OK. If you would like to edit the permissions from the parent, you can click Actions and then Manage Permissions Of Parent, which will take you to the parent's permission area to edit permissions.

4. On the New menu, click Add Users, as shown in Figure 6-15.

5. In the Add Users section, specify the users and SharePoint groups you want to add to the list or library.

6. In the Give Permission section, you can add users to an existing SharePoint group or give them permissions directly, as shown in Figure 6-16. Select one or more of the check boxes to give these users the permissions you want to apply.

7. Choose the permissions you want for the selected team members or groups and then click OK.

Chapter 6

> **Note**
> You cannot add a SharePoint group to another SharePoint group. If you are adding a SharePoint group, you have to select Give Users Permissions Directly.

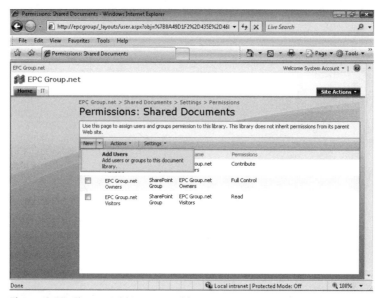

Figure 6-15 Choose Add Users to add users or groups to a list or library.

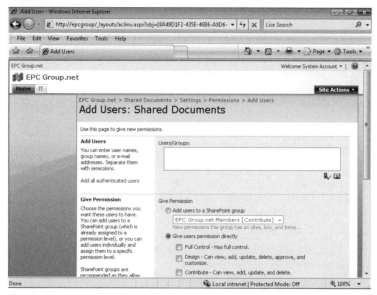

Figure 6-16 With the Give Users Permission Directly option, you can add users to the list or library without adding them to an existing SharePoint group.

Removing Users from a List or Library

To remove users from a list or library, a user with the appropriate permissions can perform the following steps:

1. Open the list or library.

2. On the Settings menu, click List Settings or (*Library Type*) Settings.

3. On the Customize page, in the Permissions And Management column, click Permissions For This List / (*Library Type*) Library.

   The Permissions page displays all users and SharePoint groups associated with this list or library and their assigned permission levels.

4. If the list or library is inheriting permissions, you must first break the inheritance of the permissions before you can edit permission levels. To do this, on the Actions menu, click Edit Permissions and then click OK. If you would like to edit the permissions from the parent, you can click Actions and then Manage Permissions Of Parent, which will take you to the parent's permission area to perform permission editing.

5. Select the check boxes for the users and SharePoint groups you want to remove from this list or library.

6. On the Actions menu, click Remove User Permissions and then click OK to remove the selected users and groups.

Workflow Settings

Workflows can be applied to lists and libraries much as templates or permissions can. Microsoft WSS 3.0 includes one predefined workflow by default. The Three-state workflow, which is designed for the Issue Tracking list, can be applied to a list or library. Additional workflows that are developed or purchased by the organization in the future can be made available and applied using the methods shown below.

Adding a New Workflow or Change the Settings of an Existing Workflow

To add a new workflow to a list or library, a user with appropriate permissions can perform the following steps:

1. Open the list or library.

2. On the Settings menu, click List Settings or (*Library Type*) Settings.

3. On the Customize page, in the Permissions And Management column, click Workflow Settings.

   If an existing workflow has been applied, you will go directly to the Change Workflow Settings page, and you must click Add A Workflow to go to the Add A Workflow page. If no workflows have been added, you will go directly to the Add A Workflow page.

4. On the Change Workflow Settings page, click Add A Workflow or click the name of a workflow to change the settings.

5. If you are adding a workflow, on the Add A Workflow page, in the Workflow section, click the name of the workflow template that you want to use. If you are changing the settings for a workflow, on the Change A Workflow page, change the settings according to the following steps:

   a. In the Name section, type in a unique name for the workflow you are adding, as shown in Figure 6-17.

   b. In the Task List section, specify a task list to use with this workflow. You can use the out-of-the-box tasks list or create a new one.

   c. In the History List section, select a history list to use for this workflow. This history list will contain and display all of the workflow events that occur during each instance of the workflow.

   d. In the Start Options section, specify how, when, or by whom the workflow can be started, and then click next. This may be limited if the workflow template does not support certain options. Major and minor versioning must be enabled to support some features.

   e. The Customize The Workflow page will then load so that users can specify and configure the additional options that are available to that particular workflow. After these fields have been customized to meet your needs, click OK.

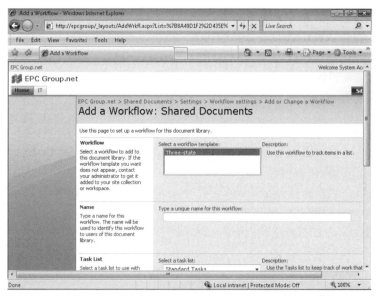

Figure 6-17 The Add A Workflow page enables users to add a workflow to a list or library.

> **Note**
>
> If you have a task list for a workflow that may contain any of the organization's confidential content, it is a best practice to create a new task list for this workflow rather that utilizing the out-of-the-box task list.

Information Management Policy Settings

WSS 3.0 now allows for the use of Information Rights Management (IRM) to protect and control content within a list. IRM can limit how list and library content is distributed and block specific content from being shared with others. IRM can restrict access to list content for a specific interval and can require users to confirm their login credentials to access or download specific content.

IRM is applied at a list or library level and uses an application called a *protector,* which is installed on the front-end Web servers, to encrypt and decrypt content within the list or library. You can restrict users' use of a file based on their security credentials.

> **Note**
>
> Before an organization can utilize IRM within its environment, the Microsoft Windows Rights Management Services (RMS) client with Service Pack 2 (SP2) has to be installed on every front-end Web server related to your SharePoint site along with the proper protectors. IRM must also be enabled within SharePoint's Central Administration.

Applying IRM to a List or Library

To apply Information Rights Management to a list or library, a user with appropriate permissions can perform the following steps:

1. Open a list or library.

2. On the Settings menu, click List Settings or (*Library Type*) Settings.

3. Under Permissions and Management, click Information Rights Management. Note that if you do not have this link available, it is possible that IRM is not enabled. IRM can be enabled in Windows Central Administration's Operation page.

4. On the Information Rights Management Settings page, select the Restrict Permission To Documents In This Library On Download check box to apply restricted permission to documents that are downloaded from the list.

5. Under Permission Policy Title, enter a unique descriptive name for the policy.

6. Under Permission Policy Description, type a description that people who use this list or library will see. This should help explain how they are to handle the documents or items.

7. You can now apply any additional restrictions to the documents in this list or library by specifying available IRM restriction criteria. After you finish specifying the criteria and specific IRM options for the list or library, click OK.

RSS Settings on Lists and Libraries

As discussed in Chapter 3, "Using the Built-in Features of Windows SharePoint Services 3.0," RSS feeds can enable users to receive periodic updates about specific lists in the organization without have to browse to a specific list to find this content. To change RSS settings for a list or library, navigate to its Customize page and click the RSS Settings link. Once the RSS Settings page is on display, make any changes you like to the following fields:

- *List RSS* Select Yes if you want to enable RSS for the list or library. Select No if you do not wish to enable it.

- *RSS Channel Information* Specify the channel elements that define the RSS feed. You have the options to truncate multiple line fields to 256 characters as well as to specify a title, description, and image URL.

- *Columns* Specify which columns to display in the RSS description.

- *Item Limit* Specify an item limit for the most recent changes for the RSS feed as well as the maximum number of days to include an item in the RSS feed.

Subscribing to an RSS Feed in a List or Library

To subscribe to an RSS Feed for a specific list or library, a user can perform the following steps:

1. Open the list or library.

2. On the Actions menu, select View RSS Feed, and the feed will load in your browser window.

3. On the page that appears, follow the instructions for how to subscribe to the feed. You may see a link called Subscribe To This Feed, which can be clicked to subscribe.

4. Closely follow any instructions you receive in the RSS reader, browser, or e-mail program you will be using to view the list's RSS feed.

Adding Columns to Lists or Libraries

With WSS 3.0, you can easily add columns to lists or libraries to capture additional information about the data. Doing so speeds up the information retrieval process. Out-of-the-box list templates contain certain default columns, but adding organizationally tailored columns can greatly improve the user experience in both browsing and searching.

You can add a custom column at almost any time, allowing users to choose from several column types, such as a single line of text, a calculated column, a drop-down list, or even a column that acts as a lookup for displaying data from other lists. WSS 3.0 now offers a site column—which is a reusable column definition or template—that users can assign to lists or libraries across a SharePoint deployment. Site columns are great for promoting the standardization of tested and proved formats across your organization.

Creating a Custom Column

To create a custom column, a user with the appropriate permissions can perform the following steps:

1. Open the list or library.

2. On the Settings menu, click Create Column.

3. In the Name And Type section, type the name you want in the Column Name box, as shown in Figure 6-18.

4. Under The Type Of Information In This Column Is, select the type of information that you want to appear in the column.

5. In the Additional Column Settings section, type a description in the Description box to help users within the organization understand the purpose of the column and what data it should contain. This description is optional but recommended.

6. Depending on the type of column that you selected, more options may appear in the Additional Column Settings section. Select the additional settings that you want.

7. To add the column to the default view, which people on your site automatically see when they first open a list or library, select Add To Default View.

8. Click OK.

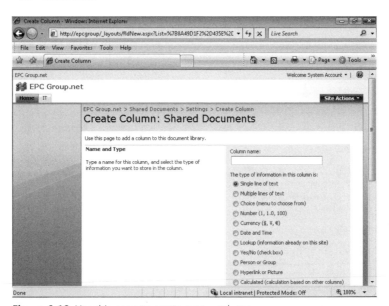

Figure 6-18 Use this page to create a new column.

Creating a Site Column

To create a site column for your organization that can be later used within a list or library, a user with the appropriate permissions can perform the following steps:

1. On the Site Actions menu, click Site Settings.

2. On the Site Settings page, under Galleries, click Site Columns.

3. On the Site Column Gallery page, click Create.

4. In the Name And Type section, type the name that you want in the Column Name box.

5. Select one of the choices under the heading The Type Of Information In This Column Is. Table 6-2 lists the available choices and the type of control each choice will display on input forms.

6. In the Group section, select the existing group in which to store the new site column, or create a new group in which to store the column.

7. In the Additional Column Settings section, select the additional column settings you would like. The options available in this section can differ depending on the type of column that you selected in the name and type sections. Then click OK.

Table 6-2 SharePoint List Column Types

Type of Information	Input Form
Single Line Of Text	Text box
Multiple Lines Of Text	Text area box
Choice (Menu To Choose From)	Drop-down menu, radio buttons, check boxes, or fill-in choices
Number (1, 1.0, 100)	A list of choices that team members rate on a numeric scale, such as 1 (low) to 5 (high)
Currency ($, ¥, £)	Text box
Date And Time	Combination of text box (for date) and drop-down lists (for hour and minute)
Lookup (Information Already On This Site)	Drop-down list
Yes/No (Check Box)	Check box
Person Or Group	Check box
Hyperlink Or Picture	(none)
Calculated (calculation based on other columns)	(none)

Calculating Column Values

WSS 3.0 can perform calculations to determine the value of a column in a given row. You can invoke such calculations in two situations:

- When initializing the form that will add a new list item.
- Every time you retrieve the list item. In this case, the column occupies no physical storage. Instead, WSS 3.0 calculates the value every time you request data from the column.

Calculations use formulas very much like those in Microsoft Office Excel. The input for calculations generally comes from system functions or from the columns in the list.

If there's any ambiguity as to the name of a function or column, or if the name contains any special characters, enclose the column name in square brackets. For example, the expressions FirstName and [FirstName] both refer to a column named FirstName because there's no function named FirstName. Most of the functions and operators from Office Excel are available to SharePoint. For example, to add the Number Present and Number Absent columns, you would code:

```
=[Number Present] + [Number Absent]
```

To combine text from two columns, use the ampersand operator. Here's an example:

```
=[Last Name] & "," & [First Name]
```

You can also use functions in formulas. This formula, for example, returns the weekday for the date in the Date Due column.

```
=TEXT(WEEKDAY([Date Due]), "dddd")
```

Changing and Deleting List Columns

To change or delete a column, click its name in the Columns section of the Customize page. This will display the Change Column page, as shown previously in Figure 6-18.

To change any other aspect of the column, correct the setting and click OK. To delete the column and all its data, click the Delete button at the bottom of the page.

Reordering List Columns

It's easy to reorder list columns in WSS 3.0. To change the order of columns within a list or library, go to the list's Customize page and under Columns, click Column Ordering to reorder the columns. After you have reordered the columns, click OK.

Working with Content Types in a List or Library

As discussed in Chapter 2, "Introducing Microsoft Office SharePoint Server 2007," WSS 3.0's new content-type functionality provides organizations with a powerful content-management feature for capturing metadata and categorizing content in a way that is both configurable and reusable.

Chapter 6

When content types are added to a list or library, it is possible for the list to contain multiple items of that type. A list or library within WSS 3.0 can contain a large number of item or document types, each of which in turn can have unique policies as well as metadata. The New command in a list displays all the content types that were added to the list, which means users can create new items of those types.

For more information about content types and their configuration, refer to the section titled "Defining the Proper Content Types and Metadata for Your Enterprise" in Chapter 20, "Additional SharePoint Best Practices."

Adding a Content Type to a List or Library

To add a content type to a list or library, it must first be configured to allow multiple content types. To ensure that the list or library you are configuring has this setting configured properly, navigate to the Customize page for the list or library, in the General Settings section click Advanced Settings, and in the Content Types section select the Yes setting for Allow Management Of Content Types.

Once this setting is properly configured, a content type can be added by a user with the appropriate permissions by performing the following steps:

1. Open the list or library.

2. On the Settings menu, click List Settings or (*Library Type*) Settings.

3. Under Content Types, click Add From Existing Site Content Types.

4. In the Select Content Types section, open the Select Site Content Types From drop-down menu to select the group of site content types from which you want choose a type, as seen in Figure 6-19.

5. In the Available Site Content Types list, click the content type that you want and then click Add to move the selected content type to the Content Types To Add List.

6. To add additional content types, you can repeat steps 4 and 5.

7. When you finish selecting all of the content types that you want to add, click OK.

Modifying the New Button Order or the Default Content Type

In WSS 3.0, it is possible to change the order in which content types are displayed on the New button for a list or library. When a list or library is first created, the first content type that is displayed on the New button will become the default content type. To change the default content type, a user must simply change the content type that is displayed first on the New button. There is also the option to either show or hide the content types that have been added on the New button.

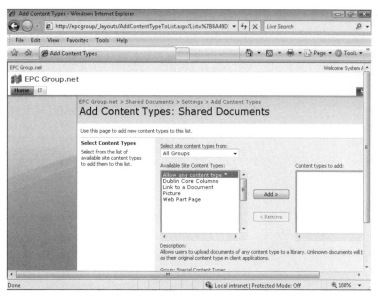

Figure 6-19 Use the Add Content Types page to add a content type to a list or library.

To modify these settings, a user with the appropriate permissions will need to perform the following steps:

1. Open the list or library you wish to modify.

2. On the Settings menu, click List Settings or (*Library Type*) Settings.

3. Under Content Types, click Change New Button Order And Default Content Type.

4. In the Content Type Order section, as seen in Figure 6-20, perform either of the following:

   ○ To remove a content type from the New button for the list, clear the Visible check box.

   ○ To change the order in which a content type appears on the New button, click the arrow next to that content type in the Position From Top column and then select the ranking that you want.

5. When you are finished modifying these settings, click OK.

For more information about content types and their proper utilization, refer to the section titled "Defining the Proper Content Types and Metadata for Your Enterprise" in Chapter 20.

Chapter 6

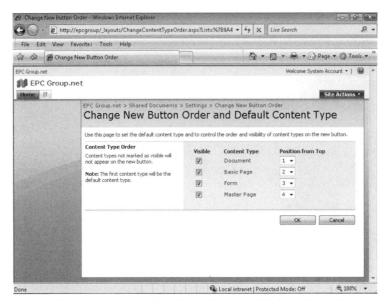

Figure 6-20 Use the Change New Button Order And Default Content Type page to set the default content type on a list or library and to specify the ranking of other content-type menu options.

Creating and Modifying List and Library Views

You'll often want to modify an existing view of a list or library or create a new custom list to meet your organization's exact needs. WSS 3.0 not only makes this a straightforward process, but it has several new features that make list views even more powerful.

Creating List and Library Views

If a task list is created to manage tasks for an initiative going on within an organization, a project manager will want to be able to easily view which tasks are assigned to specific teams or individuals without having to browse through every single task in the list. This is where a new list view could be created for each of the different teams or individuals. Doing this allows for quick viewing of only the needed tasks.

> **Note**
> When you create a new view, it will be assigned a unique URL. A link can be added to the Links List Web Part of a group's or team's SharePoint site to provide easy access to the customized view of the list.

You may also need to create views to display additional columns in the list that have been created, or to totals or specific column orders. Views also allow users to temporarily sort and filter the items in the list by choosing the name of a specific column and then clicking the arrow beside its name.

Creating a New List View

To create a new view in a list, a user with the appropriate permissions will need to perform the following steps:

1. Open the list or library.

2. On the View menu, click Create View, as shown in Figure 6-21.

3. Under Choose A View Format, click the type of view that you want to create, as shown in Figure 6-22.

4. In the View Name box, as shown in Figure 6-23, type a name for your view.

5. If you want to make this the default view, select the Make This The Default View check box. A list view can only be made the default view if it is a public view and if you have permission to change the design of a list.

6. In the Audience section, under View Audience, select whether you want to create a personal view that only you can use or a public view that others can use.

7. In the Columns section, you can show or hide columns by selecting the appropriate check boxes. Next to the column name, enter the number for the order of your column in the view.

8. In the Sort section, choose whether and how you want the information to be sorted. You can use two columns for the sort, such as first by author, and then by file name for each author.

9. In the Filter section, choose whether and how you want to filter the files. A filtered view shows you a smaller selection, such as items created by a specific department or with an approved status.

10. In the Group By section, you can group items with the same value in their own section, such as an expandable section for documents by a specific author.

11. In the Totals section, you can count the number of items in a column, such as the total number of issues. In some cases, you can summarize or distill additional information, such as averages.

12. In the Style section, select the style that you want for the view, such as a list in which every other row is shaded.

13. In the Folders section, for lists with folders, you can create a view that doesn't include the folders. To view of all your items at the same level, click Show All Items Without Folders.

14. In the Item Limit section, you can limit how many files can be viewed or how many files can be viewed on the same page.

15. The Mobile section sets the view for a list or library that will be delivered to users of mobile devices.

16. When you are finished, click OK.

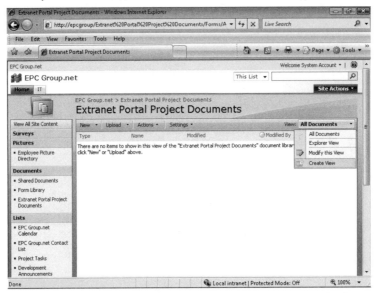

Figure 6-21 Begin defining a new view by selecting Create View under the View menu.

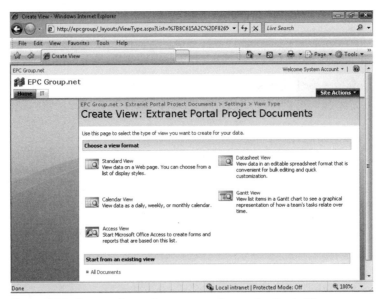

Figure 6-22 Choose a format for your new view on the Create View page.

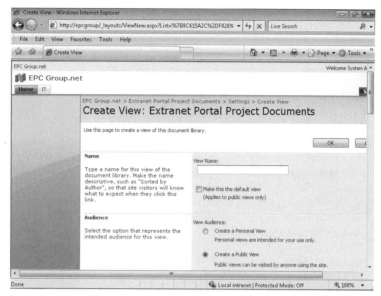

Figure 6-23 Configure the new view to meet your individual needs.

As Table 6-3 shows, the sections that appear on the Create View page will vary depending on the type of view you selected on the View Type page.

Table 6-3 SharePoint List View Settings

Section	Standard View	Datasheet View	Calendar View	Gantt View
Name	✓	✓	✓	✓
Audience	✓	✓	✓	✓
Columns	✓	✓		
Gantt Columns				✓
Sort	✓	✓		✓
Filter	✓	✓	✓	✓
Group By	✓			✓
Totals	✓	✓		✓
Style	✓			✓
Folders	✓	✓		✓
Item Limit	✓	✓		✓
Mobile	✓			
Time Interval			✓	
Calendar Columns			✓	
Default Scope			✓	

Chapter 6

> **Note**
> Users who have Microsoft Access 2007 loaded on their machines can create an additional view called an Access view, which is discussed in the following sections.

Modifying and Deleting List Views

Several views come right out of the box with a newly created list or library. You may want to modify these views or even delete ones that you know you will never use or others that have served their purpose. The process of modifying or deleting a list view is similar to that of creating a new view (described in the preceding section). After opening the view that you want to modify or delete, just click the View menu and click Modify This View. A screen will load with all the same options as the Add View page, and you can modify settings and then click OK. Or, to delete the view, click Delete.

Creating an Access View of a SharePoint List or Library

Users who have Microsoft Access 2007 loaded on their machines can create an additional view called an Access view. When you create an Access view, Access 2007 starts automatically.

To create a new Access view, a user with the appropriate permissions and with Access 2007 installed can perform the following steps:

1. Open a list or library.

2. On the View menu, click Create View.

3. On the Create View page, click Access View. Access will load, and you'll be prompted to save a local copy of the database that will contain your new view.

4. In the Save A Local Copy dialog box, browse to the location on your computer where you want to save the copy, type a name for the local copy in the File Name box, and then click Save. Access saves and opens the local copy and then the Create Access View dialog box appears.

5. In the Create Access View dialog box, double-click the type of view that you want to create. Access creates your new view and opens it.

6. You can customize your new view in Layout view, or you can switch to Design view. In Layout view, you can resize and rearrange the controls in your view, but you will not be able to add controls. In Design view, you can resize and rearrange controls, and you can add additional controls. However, Design view does not provide a data preview.

7. After you are finished with your customizations, on the Message Bar, click Publish To SharePoint Site to finish the operation.

Working with List Content

WSS 3.0 provides a variety of ways to work with lists and views, all of which require little effort or programming to set up. This includes displaying attractive input forms and reports. This section explains how these features work.

Working with List Content in Standard View

After a list contains all the fields you want, team members can view it or update it by:

- Clicking its link in Quick Launch if you chose to display this list on Quick Launch when you created or later modified the list.

- Clicking the View All Site Content link and then, under Lists, clicking the list name.

- Adding the list to a Web Part page.

Adding Items to a List

To add an item to a list, proceed as follows:

1. Open the list view using any of the methods previously provided.

2. Click New. When a New Item page like the one in Figure 6-24 appears, enter data into the list.

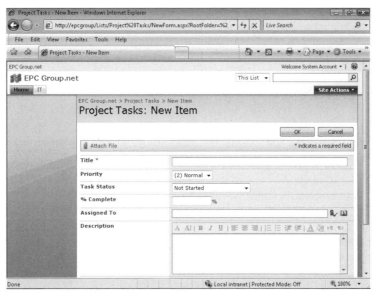

Figure 6-24 A SharePoint site automatically creates a data entry page like this for each list.

3. To save the data you entered, click OK.

4. To enter more data into the list, click New again as in step 2.

Changing or Deleting the Content of a List Item

To change or delete the content of a List item, a user with the appropriate permissions can perform the following steps:

1. Click the item's title (which should be a hyperlink).

2. When the item appears on its own page, click the Edit Item or Delete Toolbar button. Alternatively, move the mouse pointer over the item's title, click the drop-down arrow, and then choose Edit Item or Delete Item from the shortcut menu.

Working with Lists and Libraries in Datasheet View

If team members have Excel 2003 or Excel 2007 installed, they can create, modify, and delete content by using the datasheet view. To invoke this view, navigate to the list or library page, click the Actions menu button, and select Edit In Datasheet from the drop-down menu. Alternatively, if you have created a Datasheet view for the list or library, you can open that view as well.

The datasheet view provides users with an editing format similar to that of Excel so that they can edit large numbers of items at once. The view can also be useful for exporting data into an external application such as Excel.

> **Note**
>
> The datasheet view requires a program that is compatible with Windows SharePoint Services, such as Excel 2007, along with a Microsoft ActiveX control. If you do not have these installed or are using a browser that does not support running ActiveX controls, you will either get an error message or not see these options available to you.

Exporting Content to Spreadsheets

With WSS 3.0, you can export your list or library data to an external spreadsheet. If you have data that you would like to share with a user who does not have access to your list, or possibly with a user outside of your organization, this functionality enables you to quickly export your data into a spreadsheet in the exact or very similar format.

> **Note**
>
> I have had many users ask me why all of their fields are not getting exported properly when they click Export To Spreadsheet. Make sure that the view you are in contains all of the fields that you would like to have exported.

Exporting a SharePoint List or Library to a Spreadsheet

To export a list or library to a spreadsheet, a user with the appropriate permissions and a compatible spreadsheet program installed can perform the following steps:

1. Open a list or library.

2. On the Actions menu, click Export To Spreadsheet.

3. Follow the prompts from your spreadsheet program to open and activate the file. If you are using Excel 2007, you may receive a security query asking whether you want to enable a data connection. You may also receive a query from your spreadsheet program asking how you would like to view the data.

4. After you have selected the criteria about the export, click OK.

Viewing RSS Feeds

To view RSS feeds that you have subscribed to within WSS 3.0, you can use a RSS reader such as Microsoft Internet Explorer 7 or Office Outlook 2007. There are also many free RSS readers that you can download from the Internet, for example, NewsGator, RSS Bandit, FeedReader, SharpReader, RSSReader, and many more.

Creating Discussions

A SharePoint discussion board is a list that supports newsgroup-style dialog. Discussion boards can be as open as you like, but they also have features for managing discussion threads and ensuring that only approved posts appear.

WSS 3.0 offers new features around e-mail enabling discussion boards, which can be a great way to handle a large amount of e-mail on a particular subject or project. Project managers who receive a lot of e-mails on a particular project can set up a discussion board to manage all of these communications.

Discussion boards are also a great place to capture knowledge management information within your organization. Capturing best practices, lessons learned, and other similar types of information can be quickly and easily accomplished in a SharePoint discussion board.

Creating a New Discussion Board

To create a new discussion board, a user with the appropriate permissions can perform the following steps:

1. On the site for which you would like to create the new discussion board, click View All Site Content and then click Create on the All Site Content page.

2. Under Communications, click Discussion Board.

Chapter 6

3. In the Name box, type a name for the discussion board, as shown in Figure 6-25. The name is required and will be displayed on the discussion board page. It will become part of the page's URL.

4. In the Description box, type a description of the discussion board.

5. In the Navigation section, specify whether you want the discussion board to appear on the Quick Launch bar.

6. To enable the discussion board to receive e-mail, under Allow This List To Receive E-Mail, select Yes. This option will not be available if your server is not set up to receive e-mail.

7. Under E-Mail Address, type a unique name to use as part of the e-mail address for the discussion board.

8. Click Create.

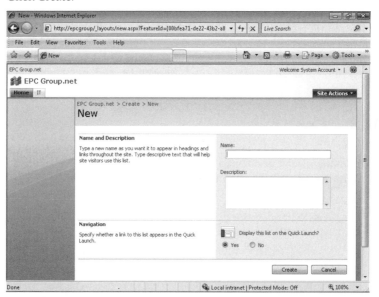

Figure 6-25 This is the New page used to name and describe a new discussion board.

Creating a New Discussion

You can easily start creating new discussions as soon as the discussion board has been created, or you can even use the out-of-the-box Team Discussions board that is created by the default team site template. To create a new discussion, do the following:

1. Open the discussion board for which you would like to create a new discussion.

2. On the New menu, click Discussion.

3. The rich-text editor opens, as shown in Figure 6-26. Type the text that you want for the subject and body of the message, and apply any formatting that you want.

4. Click OK.

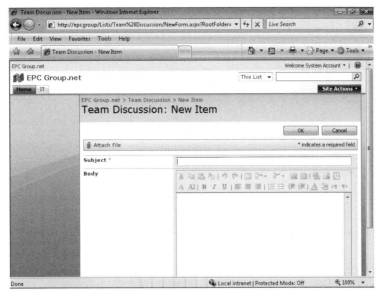

Figure 6-26   The rich text editor is used to create new discussion items.

Creating Surveys

A SharePoint survey list is a great way to capture feedback and information within your organization. A survey can capture things like employee feedback or even pose questions to the user base about how they like a new SharePoint site or how it could be improved.

Discussion boards can be configured so that users can only see responses to the surveys they created, and the user who created and owns the discussion board can use the out-of-the-box reporting that comes with all surveys.

Creating a New Survey

To create a survey, a user with the appropriate permissions can perform the following steps:

1. On the site for which you would like to create the new survey, click View All Site Content. Then click Create on the All Site Content Page.

2. Under Tracking, click Survey.

3. A New page will open, as shown in Figure 6-27. In the Name box, type a name for the survey. This name will appear at the top of the survey page and will become part of the page's URL.

4. In the Description box, type a description of the survey.

5. To add a link to this list on Quick Launch, click Yes in the Navigation section.

6. In the Survey Options section, specify whether you want people's names to appear with their responses and whether people can respond more than once to the survey.

7. Click Next.

8. On the New Question page in the Question And Type section, enter your question text and then select the type of answer that you would like for your first question.

9. In the Additional Question Settings section, specify additional settings for your question, such as whether an answer to the question is required. Depending on the question type, you may also display possible answers for the question. Then do one of the following:

   ○ To create additional questions, click Next Question and then enter information for the next question. Continue the process until you add all the questions you want.

   ○ If you are finished adding questions, click Finish.

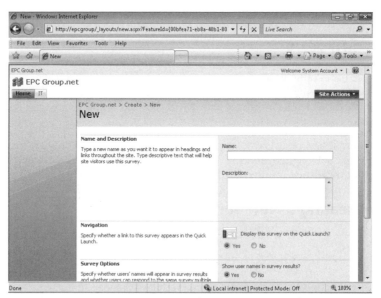

Figure 6-27 Start creating your survey on this New page.

In Summary...

This chapter explained how to create, modify, display, and delete lists and libraries. This includes the standard lists and libraries that come with Windows SharePoint Services as well as custom lists and libraries you design yourself. The next chapter begins Part 4, which explains how to use Microsoft SharePoint Designer 2007 to create and modify SharePoint. Using a Web design program like SharePoint Designer 2007 involves some extra complexity, but it also provides much more power and flexibility than you can possibly get with a browser interface.

Creating, Designing, and Managing Sites and Working with SharePoint Designer 2007

If the Microsoft Windows SharePoint Services 3.0 (WSS 3.0) facilities for using a browser to create and modify sites do not meet your needs, you may find Microsoft Office SharePoint Designer 2007 a much better match. Office SharePoint Designer 2007 can be purchased at major computer software retailers; it is not included with WSS 3.0 or bundled with any version of Microsoft Office. SharePoint Designer 2007 has powerful features for creating and designing SharePoint sites as well as built-in tools to automate business processes with Workflow Designer. As discussed in previous chapters, Windows SharePoint Services 2.0 and Microsoft FrontPage 2003 give users the ability to customize SharePoint sites, but in many cases, they cause them to become unghosted and also cause an assortment of other issues around performance, governance, and future upgradability. When a site becomes unghosted, a copy of the actual page is no longer generated dynamically from the site template.

With SharePoint Designer 2007, users can create SharePoint sites that meet the exact requirements of the organization while being monitored and controlled by site administrators to enforce governance policies and site standardization. The access model for SharePoint Designer 2007 enables administrators to set up contributor settings for each SharePoint user role within a site and control the specific actions each role is allowed to perform in SharePoint with SharePoint Designer 2007.

Using Out-of-the-Box Templates and SharePoint Designer 2007

WSS 3.0 comes right out of the box with five collaboration templates and five meeting templates. Microsoft has also developed at least 40 additional application templates to address the needs of different organizations and their initiatives. These templates can be downloaded from Microsoft.com and come ready to use, but they also work great with SharePoint Designer 2007 as a starting point for your SharePoint administrators and developers to build very sophisticated sites.

These application templates are separated into site Admin templates (*.stp files) for SharePoint administrators, and Server Admin templates (*.wsp files), which are site definitions.

> **For more information on the 40-plus application templates that are currently available, visit Microsoft TechNet (*www.microsoft.com/technet*). This link is available from the companion CD.**

Features of SharePoint Designer 2007

SharePoint Designer 2007 gives users a powerful and easy-to-use application tailored specifically for SharePoint. SharePoint Designer 2007 works with ASP.NET 2.0, cascading style sheets (CSS), and the Windows Workflow Foundation to give users the ability to create and design a dynamic site and even apply workflow to automate business processes.

With the new master page functionality, you can edit an entire SharePoint environment's look and feel by revising only the master pages and the cascading style sheets. If a user makes an editing mistake, they can simply revert to the previous template by using the Revert To Site Template Page function.

The uses of SharePoint Designer 2007 center around three main areas of functionality:

- Site development
- Site management
- Custom application development

Table 7-1 lists the site development–related functionality in SharePoint Designer 2007.

Table 7-1 SharePoint Designer 2007 Site Development Functionality

Feature	Description
SharePoint site customization	Enjoy deep editing support for the technologies underlying SharePoint products, including ASP.NET 2.0, cascading style sheets (CSS), and Windows Workflow Foundation.
ASP.NET master pages	Full support for ASP.NET master pages enables you to centralize changes to your site and help ensure a consistent look and feel across multiple pages.
Cascading style sheets	Make format and layout changes to entire SharePoint sites simply by editing the master page and modifying the SharePoint CSS. SharePoint Designer 2007 includes a CSS task pane for applying and editing CSS rules, a CSS Style Application Toolbar, and a CSS property grid.
Professional-grade design environment	Richly interact with a user interface (UI) that you can use to open, dock, and undock precisely the combination of task panes you want to use to design your site. Use task panes to identify and manipulate tag properties, CSS properties, and table and cell formats, and to insert SharePoint and ASP.NET 2.0 controls, among other capabilities.
Microsoft IntelliSense	IntelliSense technology helps eliminate errors in CSS, XSLT, ASP.NET, XHTML, and JScript. When you're in Code view, IntelliSense completes statements and shows available parameters for the work you're doing.

Table 7-2 lists the site management–related functionality in SharePoint Designer 2007.

Table 7-2 SharePoint Designer 2007 Site Management Functionality

Feature	Description
Site backup and restore	Save your site, including all of the pages and SharePoint list data, and restore it on another server.
Contributor settings	Exercise more control over your site. Use SharePoint permission levels to define the customization actions each user of SharePoint Designer 2007 can perform on your Web site.
Reset to site definition	Undo changes to the home page, master page, or other server-deployed pages in the site definition by using the Reset To Site Definition command.
Error checking	Check for broken links, unused pages, cascading style sheets usage, and master page usage.
Accessibility checking	Use the Accessibility Checker to select the guidelines (including U.S. Rehabilitation Act Section 508 guidelines) that you want to follow on your site. Get a list of suggestions to improve accessibility, and jump back and forth between that list and your site to address the issues.
Browser compatibility checking	Target the schemas supported by specific browsers. Simultaneously preview your site in multiple browsers.

Table 7-3 details functionality related to building custom applications in SharePoint Designer 2007.

Table 7-3 SharePoint Designer 2007 Building Custom Application Functionality

Feature	Description
Build sophisticated composite applications	Build interactive tracking, reporting, and data management applications rapidly using the "no code" features in SharePoint Designer 2007.
Access and aggregate multiple sources of data	Create Data Views and forms for working with a variety of data sources, including SharePoint lists and document libraries, XML files, SQL databases, Web services, and enterprise systems.
Format your data	Present data by using XSLT Data Views, Web Parts, Web Part connections, and ASP.NET controls. Use dynamic Data View tools such as calculated fields, conditional formatting, sorting, grouping, and filtering.
Interact with your data	Use custom form support to write information back to data sources, including SharePoint lists, SQL databases, and XML files.
Extend and customize prebuilt SharePoint applications	Download a range of prebuilt SharePoint applications from the TechNet Web site (*technet.microsoft.com*) and then use SharePoint Designer 2007 to refine them.

Table 7-3 SharePoint Designer 2007 Building Custom Application Functionality

Feature	Description
Support for interactive ASP.NET pages	SharePoint Designer 2007 provides the same level of support as Microsoft Visual Studio 2005 for ASP.NET control hosting, property grid editing, insertion from a toolbox palette, and Microsoft IntelliSense technology in Code view.
Add business logic to your Workflow Designer	Take advantage of the power of Workflow Designer. Set up custom workflow conditions and actions, link them to your SharePoint data, and deploy them with a single click, all without installing server code.

Creating a New Site

Users with the appropriate permissions can use SharePoint Designer 2007 to create new SharePoint sites. They can choose from two default categories of Web site templates: General and SharePoint. Here are some details about the categories:

- **General** The General category has two templates that both produce basic Web sites and are great for users who would like to build a site from the ground up. All elements must be added manually as the site is built.

- **SharePoint** These templates support all WSS 3.0 collaborative features and functionality as well as ASP.NET 2.0. They already contain SharePoint features such as lists and libraries and do not require all elements to be added manually.

Creating a SharePoint Site

To create a SharePoint site with SharePoint Designer 2007, a user must first be a member of a site group that has the Create Subsites permission level, which is included by default in the Full Control permission level. A user with the appropriate permissions can create a new site by doing the following:

1. Open SharePoint Designer 2007, and on the File menu, point to New and then click Web Site, as shown in Figure 7-1.

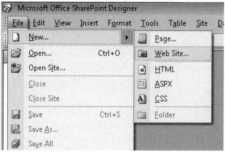

Figure 7-1 SharePoint Designer 2007 allows for easy creation of new SharePoint sites.

2. In the Specify The Location Of The New Web Site box, type the Web address (including the new path) on the SharePoint-enabled server where you want to create the new site and include a name for the site.

3. In the leftmost pane, click the category of template that you want to create. If you click SharePoint Templates, as shown in Figure 7-2, the list of available templates is retrieved from the server. Depending on the server you connect to, you may receive a different set of templates.

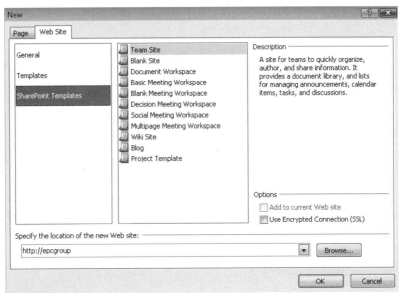

Figure 7-2 SharePoint Designer 2007 provides a list of available SharePoint templates to choose from when creating a new Web site.

4. In the center pane, click the template that you want to use to create your site.

5. If you want to add the new site to the current site—as folders in the current site, and not as a separate site—select the Add To Current Web Site check box. This check box is available only when you already have a site open.

> **Note**
> Because the Add To Current Web Site option applies the selected template to the current site, you can use the option only if no other template is already applied. For example, you cannot add a new site that you create from the Team Site template to a site that was created from the Blank Site template. In such a case, the only way to apply a new template is to delete the site and then re-create it based on another template.

6. If you want to use encrypted connections, select the Use Encrypted Connection (SSL) check box.

7. Click OK.

No-Code Solutions

One of the best things SharePoint Designer 2007 offers its users is the ability to produce no-code solutions. This means that the users creating the solutions do not have to be developers to:

- Build custom workflows.

- Integrate external data into the SharePoint site.

- Create custom list views and forms.

This is ideal for companies that do not have developers on staff or that are working toward a rapid development methodology. Although using Visual Studio 2005 and implementing custom .NET code is the most powerful way to get the exact solution you are looking for, it may be possible to develop that same solution in SharePoint Designer 2007 if the requirements are not too complex. Menus, task panes, and templates guide the user through the creation process.

Without any custom coding and with just SharePoint Designer and a browser, users can create a new SharePoint site with list and document libraries contained within it. They can also add several no-code Data Views/forms and workflows without a single ounce of development knowledge. They could then go in and add several Web Parts on the page and begin collaborating with their teams after having created their own robust SharePoint solution without even opening Visual Studio.

INSIDE OUT   Workflows for dummies!

No-code workflows based on rules are built on Windows Workflow Foundation hosting within SharePoint. They are composed of pre-existing building blocks and conditional logic based on events, actions, and conditions. They support rich data bindings to list items and are extensible via custom actions and conditions.

Opening a SharePoint Site

To open a SharePoint site, you must have at least the View permission for the site you would like to open in SharePoint Designer 2007. This permission is included by default in the Full Control, Design, Contribute, and Read permission levels. If you don't have the necessary permission, contact your server administrator. A user with the appropriate permissions can open a SharePoint site in SharePoint Designer 2007 by performing the following:

1. On the File menu, click Open Site. The Open Site dialog box will open.

2. In the Open Site dialog box, do one of the following:

    ○ In the main pane, click the site that you want to open and then click Open.

    ○ In the Site Name box, type the URL of the site that you want to open and then click Open.

3. If another site or file is currently open, the site opens in a new window.

Applying Styles

SharePoint Designer 2007 allows for the customization of a specific site's appearance by changing its default styles. This functionality enables SharePoint administrators to quickly apply a consistent organizational look and feel to new or existing SharePoint sites at any time.

Attaching a Site's Style Sheet to a Different Single SharePoint Site

A user with the appropriate permissions can apply a style sheet to another site by opening SharePoint Designer 2007 and performing the following actions:

1. Open the SharePoint site to which you would like to apply an existing customized style sheet.

2. In the site, open the default master page.

3. On the Format menu, point to CSS Styles and then click Attach Style Sheet.

4. In the Attach Style Sheet dialog box, click Browse to locate and select the customized style sheet that you want to apply.

5. In the Attach To section, click Current Page.

6. In the Attach As section, click Link and then click OK.

7. To save the master page with the new style sheet link, on the File menu, click Save.

Master Pages

With the master pages feature of ASP.NET 2.0, users can create a single page template that can then be used as the basis for many other new pages within an application. Master pages are a huge help for organizations that would like to govern the branding, or look and feel, of their SharePoint environment. On the flip side, though, master pages can also be a great way to allow specific departments to have their own branding and stand out from the rest of the organization. For example, in the past I have deployed SharePoint sites to departments that put a big emphasis on look and feel and making their site visually appealing. Departments such as marketing and their user base usually want to make the site more colorful and fun rather than bland and corporate. In previous versions of SharePoint, this was a challenge, but with WSS 3.0 and master pages, such creativity can be easily accomplished.

Master pages, which have the file name extension .master, contain two separate parts: the master page itself and a content page. Master pages define the layout, the navigational elements, and the common default content. The content page is a unique page that, when rendered in a browser, is supplied with common content by the master page while the content page supplies the page-specific content.

The default master page is stored in the Master Pages Gallery. A master page is created to enforce the site's look and feel, whereas the content page contains the unique content on each individual page. Those two pages merged together create the final product, which is the layout combined with the content.

Changing a Site's Default Master Page

All WSS 3.0 sites have a default master page named default.master, which is applied to all the pages within it. With the built-in tools provided by SharePoint Designer 2007, you can modify the default.master page for an entire site. The default.master page is located within the Master Page Gallery within a site. When a site is opened in SharePoint Designer 2007, the Master Page Gallery is the MasterPage folder, which is located in the _catalogs folder in the folder list.

Before you start to modify the existing master page, you can easily create a copy of it by viewing the folder list, right-clicking default.master, and then clicking Copy, as shown in Figure 7-3. You can then paste it to the same folder by right-clicking the folder and selecting Paste. This will create a default_copy(1).master backup copy of the default.master.

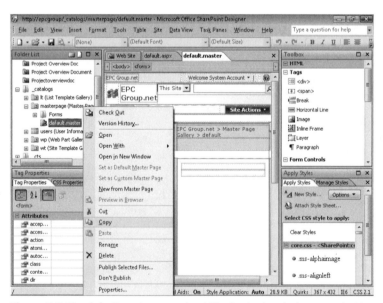

Figure 7-3 The default.master page should be backed up before you start to customize a master page.

Modifying the Styles of the Master Page

You can use the CSS tools in SharePoint Designer 2007 to identify the styles that are currently being used on the master page you would like to modify. Once you identify the styles and are ready to modify them, you first identify the styles for which the background color is defined and then change those styles to apply the new background color that you would like. To do so, follow these steps:

1. Double-click the default_copy(1).master file in which you want to modify the style. The page will be rendered in the center pane.

2. If the Apply Styles task pane is not visible, on the Task Panes menu, click Apply Styles.

3. In the Apply Styles task pane, click Options and then select Show Styles Used On Selection, as shown in Figure 7-4.

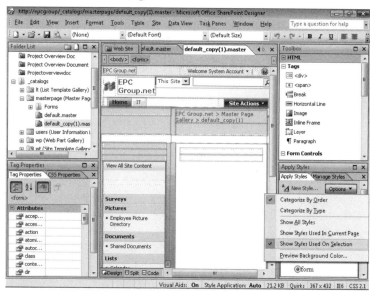

Figure 7-4 Choosing the Show Styles Used On Selection option.

4. Right-click the style that you want to modify and then click Select All X Instance(s), where X is the number of instances in which the style is applied on the page.

5. After you select all instances of the style, right-click the style again and then click Modify Style.

6. In the Modify Style dialog box, make the changes that you want and then click OK.

> **Note**
> When you modify a style on a site, a local copy of core.css is opened, and the changes are made to the local copy. If you make a mistake or are not satisfied with your changes, you can reset core.css to its former state.

Modifying the Content Placeholders

When a WSS 3.0 content page is requested, its content is retrieved from the server and rendered on the page. The text *Team Site*, which appears on most default.aspx pages, comes from the ASP.NET content placeholder controls that pull its content from the server. The *Team Site* text does not actually appear inside HTML tags in Code view, but you can use SharePoint Designer 2007 to replace this text with custom content.

Most of the default content placeholders on default.master are required by WSS 3.0 and should not be deleted. You can use SharePoint Designer 2007 to modify the default content placeholders to meet your organization's exact needs.

As discussed previously, to replace *Team Site,* a user with the appropriate permissions can perform the following:

1. Open SharePoint Designer 2007 and then open the SharePoint site that you would like to edit.

2. Open default.master.

3. To open the Master Page toolbar, on the View menu, point to Toolbars and then click Master Page, as shown in Figure 7-5.

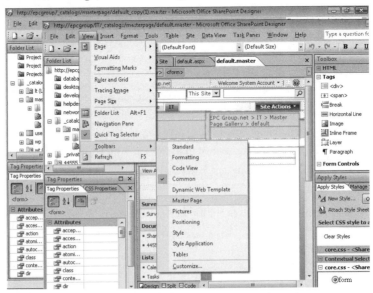

Figure 7-5 Open the Master Page toolbar to assist in editing the master page.

4. Use the Master Page toolbar to locate the content placeholder that you want to modify. To follow along with this example, on the Master Page toolbar, click the arrow to the right of the Regions drop-down menu (watch for the Regions tool tip when you hover over it) and then scroll down and select PlaceHolderSiteName.

5. Click the *Team Site* text to select the project property, as shown in Figure 7-6.

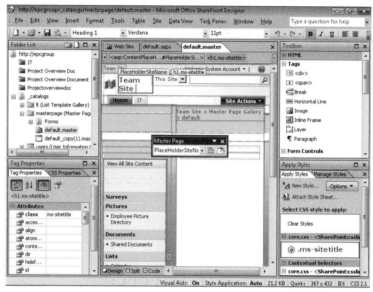

Figure 7-6 The PlaceHolderSiteName project property has been selected.

6. Type the new name for your site and then save your changes by clicking Save on the File menu. When you are prompted regarding saving the customizations, click Yes.

Adding a New Content Region

New content regions are added to a master page by adding a new content placeholder. These content placeholders cannot be inserted inside other content placeholders. If you have the appropriate permissions, you can add a new content region by following these steps:

1. Open the site to which you would like to add a new content region.

2. Select an available region for which you would like to add a new content region and then right-click the page in Design view and then click Manage Microsoft ASP.NET Content Regions on the context menu (see Figure 7-7). Note that you may be prompted to save the page as a new master page.

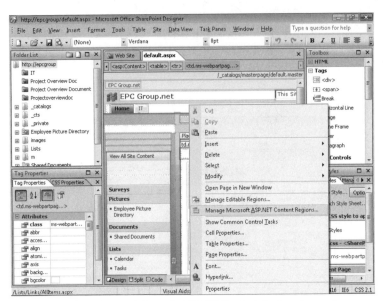

Figure 7-7 Select Manage Microsoft ASP.NET Content Regions to create a new content region.

3. In the Manage Content Regions dialog box, shown in Figure 7-8, in the Region Name box, type a name for your new content region and then click Add.

   To follow the example, type **ContentPlaceHolder1** in the Region Name box.

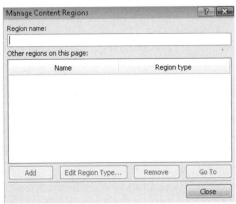

Figure 7-8 Use the Manage Content Regions dialog box to name and add the new content region.

4. Click Close, and a new content placeholder named ContentPlaceHolder1 will appear.

Applying the New Master Page

After you create the new master page, you can make it the default master page for the entire site. When a new master page is set as the default master page, all of the pages that are attached to the current version of default.master, including the pages that already exist on the site, will be attached to the new master page. In the MasterPage folder, right-click the page that you want to use as the new default master and then click Set As Default Master Page on the context menu.

> **Note**
>
> All future pages that are created will also be attached to default.master. If the master page is already the default master page for the site, the Set As Default Master Page command is unavailable.

For more information about master pages, refer to the section titled "Using Master Pages" in Chapter 9, "Creating and Modifying Basic Site Features."

Managing Access Control

Using SharePoint Designer 2007, organizations can use the application's out-of-the-box permission levels to manage access control. Permission levels cannot be created in SharePoint Designer 2007 and must first exist on a site before they can appear in the list of available permissions levels in SharePoint Designer 2007.

For more information about modifying permission levels on SharePoint sites, refer to the section titled "Changing Permissions for a List or Library" in Chapter 6, "Designing Lists, Libraries, and Pages."

Users can create Contributor groups—groups of users who are assigned to perform specific roles within the organization—with SharePoint Designer 2007. By default, you'll find three Contributor groups: Site Manager, Web Designer, and Content Author. You can assign specific Contributor groups sets of editing restrictions that tell SharePoint Designer 2007 what types of changes each group can make to a SharePoint site.

In summary, you can assign permission levels to users and groups, which are added via a browser to a SharePoint site. These permission levels are then linked to a Contributor group within SharePoint Designer 2007 to control the users and their specific abilities to edit SharePoint sites.

Creating a SharePoint Designer 2007 Contributor Group

A user with the appropriate permissions can create a SharePoint Designer 2007 Contributor group by performing the following actions:

1.   Open your site in SharePoint Designer 2007.

2. On the Site menu, click Contributor Settings, as shown in Figure 7-9.

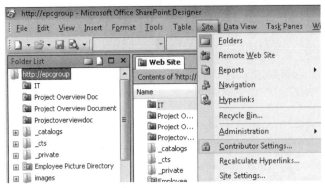

Figure 7-9 A user with sufficient permissions can create Contributor groups to govern the permission levels of SharePoint Designer 2007 users.

3. In the Contributor Settings dialog box, under Manage Contributor Groups, click Add.

4. In the Contributor Group Properties dialog box, under General, type a name in the Group Name box, as shown in Figure 7-10. As with most name dialog boxes, this information is required.

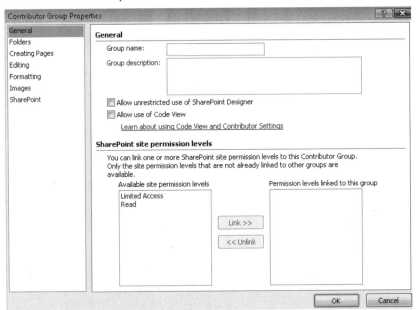

Figure 7-10 Use this dialog box to name the new Contributor group and apply other criteria to the properties of the group.

5. Under SharePoint Site Permission Levels, click each permission level that you want to link to the Contributor group. Then click Link.

6. In the Contributor Group Properties dialog box, you can click each category in the left column and then choose the settings for this Contributor group.

7. When you are done creating settings for the group, click OK.

Linking a Permission Level to a Contributor Group

A user with the appropriate permissions can link one or more permission levels to a Contributor group by performing the following actions:

1. Open your site in SharePoint Designer 2007.

2. On the site menu, click Contributor Settings, as shown in Figure 7-9.

3. Under Manage Contributor Groups, click the Contributor group to which you want to link a permission level and then click Modify.

4. In the Contributor Group Properties dialog box, under SharePoint Site Permission Levels, click each permission level that you want to link to the Contributor group and then click Link.

5. Click OK when done.

Setting a Contributor Group as the Default Group

A user with the appropriate permissions can set a SharePoint Designer 2007's Contributor group as the default group by performing the following actions:

1. Open your site in SharePoint Designer 2007.

2. On the site menu, click Contributor Settings.

3. Under Manage Contributor Groups, click the group that you want to set as the default and then click Set As Default.

Creating Data Views and Data Forms

SharePoint Designer 2007 contains functionality to assist your organization with tracking and reporting on its SharePoint sites. You can create customized views—called Data Views—of live data. With Data Views, you can view data from various sources including XML documents, database queries, Web services, lists, libraries, and server-side scripts. You can easily filter, sort, and group this data via Data Views.

You can insert a Data View within a page by dragging the data source from the folder list or data source library onto a site or by creating a Data View via the Insert Data View command. Once you have run Insert Data View, you can begin modifying the view by inserting the fields you would like to display from the Data Source Details task pane.

Creating an XML File to Be Used as a Data Source for a Data View

To create an XML file that will be used as a data source for a Data View, a user with the appropriate permissions can perform the following:

1. On the File menu, click Open Site.

2. In the Open Site dialog box, browse to and select your SharePoint site and then click Open.

3. If prompted, in the Connect To dialog box, type your user name and password and then click OK.

4. On the File menu, click New.

5. In the New dialog box, as shown in Figure 7-11, double-click Text File. A new text file will open in the center pane.

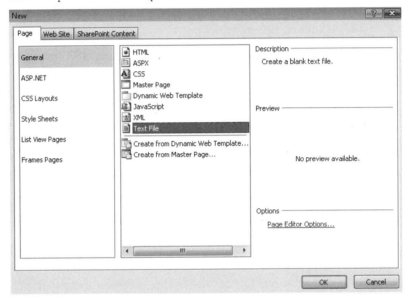

Figure 7-11 The New dialog box enables users to choose from a large selection of pages, Web sites, and SharePoint content.

6. Develop the appropriate XML to be used as a data source.

7. On the File menu, click Save As.

8. In the Save As dialog box, in the File Name box, type the name of the new XML file.

9. In the Save As Type list, click XML and then click Save.

Creating a Data View by Dragging the Data Source onto the Page

If you would like to use SharePoint Designer 2007 to drag the data source onto the page to create a Data View, you will first need to create a new ASP.NET page. A user with the appropriate permissions can accomplish this by performing the following:

1. On the File menu, click New.

2. In the New dialog box, shown in Figure 7-11, double-click ASPX. A new page with a FORM tag will open.

3. Then you will need to do one of the following:

   ○ In the Folder list, locate your data source and then drag it onto the page.

   ○ On the Task Panes menu, click Data Source Library. In the Data Source Library task pane, locate your data source and then drag it onto the page.

After one of the preceding two options has been completed, a Data View will display on the page, and the Data Source Details task pane will open.

Creating a Data View by Using the Data Source Details Task Pane

You can use the Data Source Details task pane to create a Data View. To do this, you will first need to insert a Data View onto the page and then select a data source in the Data Source Library. After a data source is selected, the Data Source Details task pane will open, and a user can choose the fields to display, and then simply insert them into the new Data View.

If you would like to create a Data View by using the data source task pane, first create a new ASP.NET page and then create a Data View by using the data source task pane, as detailed here:

1. On the File menu, click New.

2. In the New dialog box, double-click ASPX. A new page with a FORM tag will open.

3. On the Data View menu, click Insert Data View, as shown in Figure 7-12. An empty Data View will now display on the page, and the Data Source Library task pane will open. You are now ready to add data, as shown in Figure 7-13.

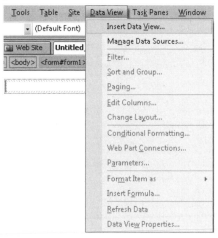

Figure 7-12 Select the Insert Data View command from the Data View menu.

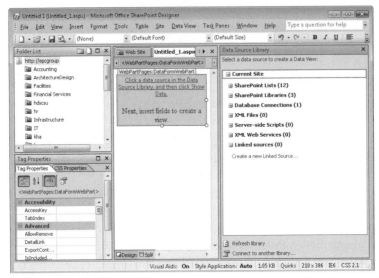

Figure 7-13 An empty Data View will be placed on the page with a link to enable the user to click a data source in the Data Source Library.

4. In the Data Source Library task pane, locate your data source, click it (as shown at right in Figure 7-14), and then click Show Data.

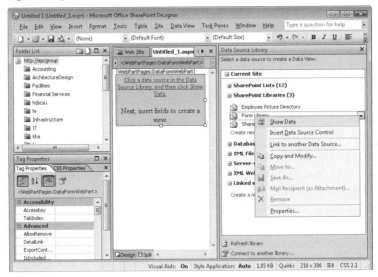

Figure 7-14 A SharePoint document library is one example of a data source.

5. In the Data Source Details task pane, click the fields that you want to insert in the Data View. You can select multiple fields by holding down Ctrl while you click them.

6. Click Insert Selected Fields As and then click Multiple Item View to insert the selected data into the Data View. When this is done, the fields that you selected in the Data Source Details task pane will appear in a table.

The Workflow Designer

As discussed previously, SharePoint Designer 2007 allows for the robust creation of workflows that add no-code application logic to your sites and applications. With the Workflow Designer, you can create rules that associate conditions and actions with SharePoint libraries and lists. The changes that occur in these lists and libraries trigger actions in the workflows that are created.

Designing a New Workflow by Using Workflow Designer

Once a workflow has been logically defined and is ready to be created, a user with the appropriate permissions can create a new workflow by performing the following:

1. On the File menu, click Open Site.

2. In the Open Site dialog box, browse to and select the SharePoint site where you want to create the workflow. Then click Open.

3. On the File menu, point to New and then click Workflow. The Workflow Designer will then load, as shown in Figure 7-15.

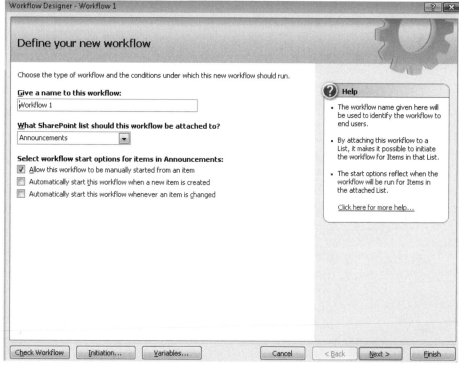

Figure 7-15 The Workflow Designer is a powerful no-code solution for creating workflows.

4. In the Give A Name To This Workflow box, type a name for this workflow. Users of the site will see this name when they view the workflow's status and other related pages in the browser.

5. Select an option in the What SharePoint List Should This Workflow Be Attached To list, as shown in Figure 7-16.

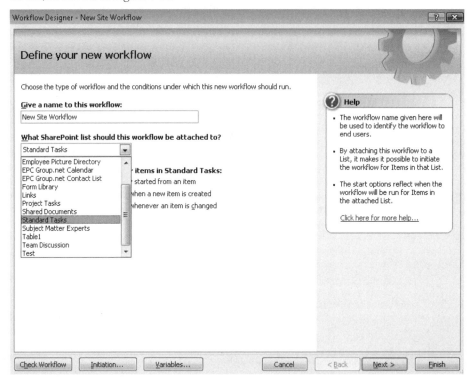

Figure 7-16 The user selects from a menu of SharePoint lists, designating which one the new workflow will attach to.

6. Under Select Workflow Start Options For Items In (*This List*), select one or more of the following check boxes:
   - ○ Allow This Workflow To Be Manually Started From An Item
   - ○ Automatically Start This Workflow When A New Item Is Created
   - ○ Automatically Start This Workflow Whenever An Item Is Changed

   After you have chosen your options, click Next.

7. In the Step Name box, shown in Figure 7-17, type a name for the first step of your workflow.

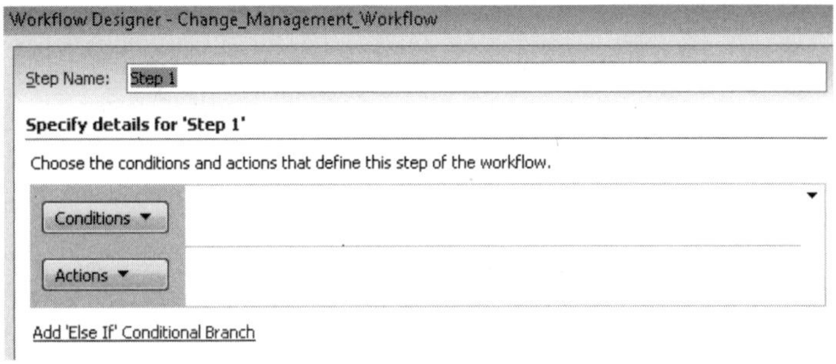

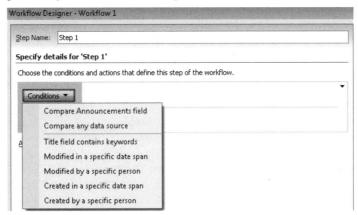

Figure 7-17 The new workflow should be given a name. Step 1 is displayed by default.

8. You will now create the workflow rules by choosing the actions that you want the workflow to perform. For each condition that you want to specify, click Conditions and then click that condition in the list. Repeat until you have specified all of the conditions that you want to include. SharePoint Designer 2007 provides you with a number of predefined conditions, as shown in Figure 7-18.

Figure 7-18 The Workflow Designer provides you with several predefined conditions and actions to choose from for the new workflow.

9. After you insert a condition, click each hyperlink and then choose a value for the required parameters.

10. For each action that you want to include, click Actions on the Workflow 1 page, and then click that action in the list. Repeat until you have specified all of the conditions that you want to include.

11. After you insert an action, click each hyperlink and then choose a value for the required parameters.

12. If you would like to add a conditional branch, click Add 'Else If' Conditional Branch and then repeat steps 7–11 to create another rule. When this step of the workflow is complete, click Next.

13. For each step in the workflow, repeat steps 7–12 to create additional sets of conditions and actions.

14. To check the workflow for errors before you exit the Workflow Designer, click Check Workflow. After you have checked the workflow for errors, click Finish. The workflow is saved and will be attached to the specified list.

Using Visual Studio 2005 to Customize Site Design

SharePoint Designer 2007 is a powerful application that gives users the ability to customize SharePoint sites and develop custom solutions. As a SharePoint consultant with a great deal of experience developing custom solutions for WSS 3.0 and Microsoft Office SharePoint Server 2007 (MOSS), I have seen the limitations that SharePoint Designer 2007 can have for more technical SharePoint solutions within an organization.

Microsoft Visual Studio 2005 can be the ultimate solution for these more advanced organizational requirements around custom workflows, custom Web Parts, external data source integration, and many other advanced development requirements.

Microsoft has released items such as the WSS 3.0 Tools: Visual Studio 2005 Extensions to give developers tools for developing custom SharePoint applications and solutions. This toolkit offers Visual Studio 2005 project templates for Web Parts, site definitions, and a standalone utility program called the SharePoint Solution Generator. In later chapters of this book, I will touch on advanced development techniques for developing custom solutions using these tools to assist you in developing the ultimate custom solutions for your organization in WSS 3.0.

For more information about customizing sites with Visual Studio 2005, refer to Chapter 18, "Advanced Design Techniques" and Chapter 19, "Beginning Web Part Development."

In Summary...

This chapter explained how SharePoint Designer 2007 can assist you in creating and designing sites as well as customizing SharePoint solutions to meet your organization's exact needs. The chapter also covered several powerful no-code solutions for organizations that are not heavily staffed with developers.

The next chapter will explain how to create and format Web Part pages in WSS 3.0.

Creating and Formatting Web Part Pages

Microsoft Windows SharePoint Services 3.0 (WSS 3.0) enables users to create and configure Web Part pages easily via a browser, but that experience lacks the flexibility and control that many SharePoint administrators and site designers demand. Usability and uniformity are key to the success of any Web site, and SharePoint's easy-to-use graphical user interface (GUI) promotes standardization and helps users to know where things are going to be when they open up a site.

Microsoft Office SharePoint Designer 2007 and Microsoft Visual Studio 2005 can create and configure Web Part pages with great flexibility, with or without the standard Share-Point menus, and format them in whatever way will meet the needs of the organization.

Working with Web Part Pages and Web Part Zones

As discussed in previous chapters, a Web Part is an ASP.NET server control that is designed to run in a browser and that enables users to modify it via a browser. Web Parts are a SharePoint component that pull information from various sources including, but not limited to, SharePoint lists, external databases, and XML sources. WSS 3.0 provides a Web Part infrastructure that is an extension of ASP.NET 2.0.

> **Note**
>
> Organizations that do not want to spend the licensing fees for Windows SharePoint Server 2007 but would still like to connect to external systems can do so via WSS 3.0, Office SharePoint Designer 2007 and/or Visual Studio 2005 custom development. Just because you don't have the Business Data Catalog (BDC) at your fingertips like those who have implemented Microsoft Office SharePoint Server 2007, doesn't mean your solution cannot connect to external data sources.

WSS 3.0 provides developers with a base class for creating Web Parts, namely *Microsoft .SharePoint.WebPartPages.WebPart.* This class provides the foundation upon which you can write any Web Part solution you would like. To *inherit* from this class (that is, to use it as a base), a developer uses a statement like the following in the source code for the Web Part:

```
public class WebPart1 : Microsoft.SharePoint.WebPartPages.WebPart
{
// Your custom code goes here.
}
```

Note the difference in ASP.NET, where your Web Part code is inherited from *System.Web.UI.WebControls.WebParts.* In addition, virtually all Web Parts override two methods in the *WebPart* class:

- **CreateChildControls**   The *WebPart* class calls this method to create child server controls that the Web Part will later convert to HTML.

- **RenderWebPart**   The *WebPart* class calls this method to render (that is, create) the HTML that the Web Part will display.

> **Note**
>
> Those of you who have developed ASP.NET custom controls that aren't Web Parts may be accustomed to overriding the *Render* method rather than the *RenderWebPart* method. In a Web Part, however, the *Render* method creates only the chrome of the Web Part (that is, the title bar and border). The *RenderWebPart* method creates the HTML that appears in the body of the Web Part.

A developer may override these methods because the versions in the *WebPart* class really do not do much of anything. Overriding these methods means that at the proper time, the *WebPart* class will call custom methods that you provide rather than its own methods. Adding these two overrides to the previous code gives the Web Part this structure:

```
public class WebPart1 : Microsoft.SharePoint.WebPartPages.WebPart
{
// Global declarations go here.
  protected override void CreateChildControls ()
  {
   // Code to create a list of Web or HTML server
   // controls goes here
  }
  protected override void RenderWebPart(HtmlTextWriter output)
  {
   //Code to render the list of Web or HTML server
   //controls goes here
  }
}
```

In practice, laying out page elements with a What You See Is What You Get (WYSIWYG) editor and writing program code that emits HTML aren't the grueling tasks you might expect. The reason is that the output of most Web Parts is fairly simple. Many page elements—such as the top navigation bar, the page banner, any toolbars, and any link areas—are part of the Web Part page or of other Web Parts. Any Web Parts you create inherit styles from the site's theme and need only display their specific data.

To make things easier, Microsoft has provided Windows SharePoint Services 3.0 Tools: Visual Studio 2005 Extensions, providing project templates that enable faster development in a WSS 3.0 environment. In addition, the extensions include a Web Part project template that streamlines the creation, deployment, and testing of Microsoft ASP.NET Web Parts in WSS 3.0.

To use the WSS Visual Studio 2005 Extensions to create a Web Part, you need to download it from Microsoft at the following URL: *http://www.microsoft.com/downloads/details. aspx?familyid=19f21e5e-b715-4f0c-b959-8c6dcbdc1057&displaylang=en.*

System requirements for installing the extensions package include:

- Windows Server 2003 or Windows Server 2008

- WSS 3.0

- Windows Visual Studio 2005

Once the extensions are installed on your SharePoint server, you can use the Web Part template in the extensions to create a Web Part by performing the following steps:

1. Open Visual Studio 2005.

2. Select New and then Project from the File menu.

3. In Project Types, select Visual C#, SharePoint. (The extension kit supports only C# development at this time.)

4. In the Templates area, select Web Part.

5. Type in the new solution name for your Web Part project and click OK.

In the Solution Explorer, you can see that the template has created a project containing the following:

- AssemblyInfo.cs

- The necessary references to various SharePoint DLLs

- Temporary.snk, the signature file to test your Web Part assembly

- C# code with a similar name to your Web Part, which includes code similar to the following, though probably with a different name and GUID:

    ```
    using System;
    using System.Runtime.InteropServices;
    ```

```
using System.Web.UI;
using System.Web.UI.WebControls.WebParts;
using System.Xml.Serialization;
using Microsoft.SharePoint;
using Microsoft.SharePoint.WebControls;
using Microsoft.SharePoint.WebPartPages;

namespace SampleWebPart
{
  [Guid("39e0f169-1ee9-4098-bbab-e49bff7ddd22")]
  public class SampleWebPart : System.Web.UI.WebControls.WebParts.WebPart
  {
    public SampleWebPart()
    {
      this.ExportMode = WebPartExportMode.All;
    }
    protected override void Render(HtmlTextWriter writer)
    {
      // TODO: add custom rendering code here.
      // writer.Write("Output HTML");
    }
  }
}
```

By default, your Web Part is inherited from *System.Web.UI.WebControls.WebParts.WebPart*. To build a more specific Web Part for WSS 3.0, change this to *Microsoft.SharePoint. WebPartPages.WebPart.*

Modify the default code so that it resembles the following code, which will print *Share-Point Version 3* as its output:

```
namespace SampleWebPart
{
  [Guid("39e0f169-1ee9-4098-bbab-e49bff7ddd22")]
  public class SampleWebPart : Microsoft.SharePoint.WebPartPages.WebPart
  {
    public SampleWebPart()
    {
      this.ExportMode = WebPartExportMode.All;
    }
protected override void RenderWebPart(HtmlTextWriter output)
    {
      output.Write("SharePoint Version 3");
      base.RenderWebPart(output);
    }
  }
}
```

> **Note**
>
> Programmers and Web designers create each Web Part independently, often without knowing which Web Part pages—or even how many Web Part pages—will display it. Web designers and in some cases even team members later decide what Web Part pages a site will contain, and which Web Parts those pages will display.

Creating Web Part Pages

In Chapter 5, "Creating SharePoint Sites, Workspaces, and Pages," I discussed how to use a browser to create a Web Part page. However, SharePoint Designer 2007 also enables you to create new Web Part pages. When you would like to add a new page to a SharePoint site, most of the time you will want to add an ASP.NET (.aspx) page because they support all of SharePoint's functionality. In SharePoint Designer, an .aspx page is the default for new pages in a SharePoint site when a user clicks the New Document icon on the common toolbar. Master pages also support all SharePoint functionality, so it is a best practice to use them whenever you would like to have several sites share the same look and feel or branding elements.

A user with the appropriate permissions can add a page of the default page type or use the New dialog box to choose any type of page available by performing the following steps:

1. Open SharePoint Designer 2007 and then open the site to which you would like to add a new page.

2. Click New Document icon on the common toolbar, or press Ctrl+N.

3. On the File menu, click Save, or press Ctrl+S.

4. In the Save As dialog box, type a name for the new page in the File Name box and then click Save.

5. You should be aware of the most commonly used page types you will want to add to a SharePoint site (see Table 8-1).

Table 8-1 Commonly Used Page Types

Page Type	Description
ASP.NET (.aspx)	This adds a blank .aspx page that is ready to be customized and to receive SharePoint elements.
Master Page	This adds an ASP.NET page with a file name extension of .master instead of .aspx. After this page is created, a user can use the Create From Master Page option to add multiple pages that are all based on that master page.

Table 8-1 Commonly Used Page Types

Page Type	Description
Page based on an existing master page	Adds an .aspx page that is based on a previously created master page and subsequently updated with any changes made to the appearance and behavior of that master page.
List View page	Adds an .aspx page that includes a new view of an existing list or document library. A List View page already includes page elements such as title bars, menus, and columns.
Web Part page	Adds an .aspx page with a predesigned layout that includes Web Part zones, into which you can insert Web Parts.

Creating, Configuring and Deleting Web Part Zones

Web Part zones can be easily inserted, configured, or deleted by an administrator using SharePoint Designer 2007.

Inserting and Configuring a Web Part Zone

A user with the aforementioned permissions can insert a Web Part zone by performing the following actions:

1. In Office SharePoint Designer 2007, open the page where you want to insert the Web Part zone.

2. If the Web Parts task pane is not already open, open it by clicking Web Parts on the Task Panes menu, as shown in Figure 8-1.

Figure 8-1 Select the Web Parts option from the Task Panes menu.

3. In Design view, click the location on the page where you want to insert the Web Part zone, as shown in Figure 8-2.

Figure 8-2 SharePoint Designer 2007 allows for the new Web Part zones to be inserted into a site to meet a team's exact needs.

4. At the bottom of the Web Parts task pane, click New Web Part Zone.

5. Right-click the new Web Part zone and then click Web Part Zone Properties on the shortcut menu.

6. In the Web Part Zone Properties dialog box, shown in Figure 8-3, do any of the following:

   ○ **Give the zone a title.** Under General Settings, in the Zone Title box, type a name for the new zone.

   ○ **Choose a frame style.** Under General Settings, in the Frame Style list, click the style that you want.

   ○ **Choose a layout for the zone.** Under Layout Of Web Parts Contained In The Zone, click either Top-To-Bottom (Vertical Layout) or Side-By-Side (Horizontal Layout).

   ○ **Control changes made in the browser.** Under Browser Settings For Web Parts Contained In The Zone, select check boxes to allow users to make the indicated changes while they view the page in a browser, or clear the check boxes to prevent users from making these changes.

Figure 8-3 A Web Part zone's properties can be easily modified in SharePoint Designer 2007.

7. When you finish, click OK.

Deleting a Web Part Zone

Use SharePoint Designer 2007 to delete an existing Web Part zone from a site. When a Web Part zone is deleted, SharePoint Designer 2007 will also delete any Web Parts located within the zone you are deleting. When deleting a Web Part zone, it is important to make sure you are selecting only the specific zone and not any other zone or object on the page. To prevent any mistaken deletions, it is helpful to use the Quick Tag Selector, shown in Figure 8-4 (at the top of the document window) to identify the specific object that is currently selected.

Figure 8-4 The Quick Tag Selector ensures users they are selecting the correct object.

A user with the appropriate permissions can delete a Web Part zone by performing the following actions:

1. In Office SharePoint Designer 2007, open the page from which you want to delete a Web Part zone.

2. In Design view, locate the Web Part zone that you want to delete and then click it to select it.

3. When you are sure that the Web Part zone is accurately selected, press the Delete key. The selected Web Part zone is deleted from the page, along with any Web Parts that are located in it.

INSIDE OUT   **Adding a Web Part zone via code in an .aspx page**

To add a new Web Part zone to an .aspx page, open the page in your favorite editor and add the following code inside <Form></Form> tags. Note: The ID should be a unique value for the given page.

```
<WebPartPages:WebPartZone id="MainZone" runat="server" title="Main Zone">
</WebPartPages:WebPartZone>
```

Adding Web Parts to the Zones

Once your page contains a Web Part zone, you'll no doubt want the zone to contain one or more Web Parts. In your browser, you can add Web Parts by entering edit mode and clicking Add A Web Part on the top of the Web Part zone. Then, the Add Web Part dialog box will appear. Select one or more Web Parts to add to the available zones.

For more information on adding Web Parts to Web Part zones, refer to the section titled "Adding Web Parts to a Page" in Chapter 5.

Controlling the Appearance of Web Parts

A user can modify the appearance of Web Parts by modifying their Web Part properties. All SharePoint Web Parts share a common set of properties that enable a user to set appearance, layout, and other advanced properties. If you have the appropriate permissions, you can modify the appearance of a Web Part from the browser by performing the following actions:

1. On the Site Actions menu, click Edit Page.

2. Click the Edit menu of the Web Part for which you want to change the properties, and do one of the following:

    ○ If you are in a shared view, click Modify Shared Web Part.

    ○ If you are in a personal view, click Modify My Web Part.

3. Change the properties that you want to change.

4. To save your changes and close the tool pane, click OK. To view your changes without closing the tool pane, click Apply.

The Appearance, Layout, and Advanced sections offer many configuration options. Expanding the Appearance section of a Web Part's properties dialog box, as shown in Figure 8-5, exposes the following settings:

- **Title**   Type the text that should appear in the Web Part's title bar.

INSIDE OUT Programmatic example of adding Web Parts to a zone

For reference purposes, these are the coding details behind adding a Web Part to a zone, in this case the Tasks Web Part:

```
//Open the SharePoint Web
SPWeb WssWeb = site.OpenWeb();
      //Get the Task list (Note: You can use any of the SharePoint lists
here)
  SPList taskList = WssWeb.Lists["Tasks"];
      //Set the update flag so that you can change
      //Web properties via code
WssWeb.AllowUnsafeUpdates = true;
      //Create dataview Web Part object
DataViewWebPart TaskView = new DataViewWebPart();
      //Set the properties of the Web Part
TaskView.ZoneID = "Main";
TaskView.Width = "400";
TaskView.Title = "Task List";
TaskView.FrameType = FrameType.None;
TaskView.ListName = taskList.ID.ToString("B").ToUpper();
TaskView.Description = taskList.ID.ToString("B").ToUpper();
      //Get the Web Part collection on the page mentioned
      //in the URL
SPWebPartCollection PageWebPartCollection = WssWeb.GetWebPartCollection(<<your
URL>>, Storage.Shared);
   if (WebPartCollection != null)
   {
   //Add TaskView Web Part to collection
PageWebPartCollection.Web.AllowUnsafeUpdates = true;
   PageWebPartCollection.Add(TaskView);
   }
   else
   {
   Response.Write("Error Occured ");
   }
```

- **Height** If you want the Web Part to always appear with the same height, select Yes, type a value, and select a unit of measure. Otherwise, select No. The height will automatically adjust to fit the zone.

- **Width** If you want the Web Part to have a constant width regardless of conditions, select Yes, type a value, and select a unit of measure. Otherwise, select No. The width will automatically adjust to fit the zone.

- **Chrome State** Select Minimized if only the title bar should be visible when the Web Part first appears. Otherwise, select Normal.

- **Chrome Type** Choose either Default, None, Title and Border, Title Only, or Border Only, as discussed in Table 8-2. Default inherits the frame style of the surrounding Web Part zone; the remaining self-explanatory values override it.

Figure 8-5 The Web Part's appearance properties enable you to modify the height, width, and other graphical aspects.

Table 8-2 **Chrome Type**

Frame Style	Description
Default	Web Parts in the zone default to the standard frame style. This is normally the title bar and border.
None	No visible frame will surround Web Parts in the zone.
Title And Border	A visible frame will surround the title bar and contents of each Web Part in the zone.
Title Only	A visible frame will surround the title bar of each Web Part in the zone.
Border Only	Only the border will appear for the Web Part in the zone.

Expanding the Layout section of a Web Part's properties dialog box, as shown in Figure 8-6, exposes the following settings:

- **Hidden** Select this check box if you want the Web Part to be hidden on the page.

- **Direction** Override the reading order of elements in the Web Part's text and frame. Choose None, Left To Right, or Right To Left.

- **Zone** Select the zone for which the Web Part should appear. Zones on the Web Part page are not listed in the list box when you do not have permission to modify the zone.

- **Zone Index** Specify the position of the Web Part in a zone when the zone contains more than one Web Part. To specify the order, type a positive integer in the text box.

Figure 8-6 The Web Part's layout properties enable a user to hide the Web Part or modify its zone or zone index.

Expanding the Advanced section of a Web Part's properties dialog box, as shown in Figure 8-7, exposes the following settings:

- **Allow Minimize** Select this check box if it's OK for team members to switch the Web Part display between minimized and normal.

- **Allow Close** Select this check box if it's OK for team members to close the Web Part display. This removes the Web Part completely from view.

- **Allow Hide** Select this check box if it's OK for team members to hide the Web Part. This removes the Web Part completely from view.

- **Allow Zone Change** Select this check box if it's OK for team members to move the Web Part to a different zone on the same page. They do this by changing the Web Part's Zone ID property, or by dragging the Web Part from zone to zone.

- **Allow Connections** Specify whether the Web Part can participate in connections with other Web Parts.

- **Allow Editing In Personal View** Specify whether the Web Part properties can be modified in a personal view.

- **Export Mode** Specify the level of data that is permitted to be exported for this Web Part. Depending on your configuration, this setting may not be available.

- **Title URL** Specify the URL of a file containing additional information about the Web Part. The file is displayed in a separate browser window when you click the Web Part title.

- **Description** Specify the ScreenTip that appears when you hover the mouse pointer over the Web Part title or Web Part icon. The value of this property is used when you search for Web Parts by using the Search command on the Find Web Parts menu of the tool pane in the following Web Part galleries: Site, Virtual Server, and Web Part Page.

- **Help URL** Specify the location of a file containing Help information about the Web Part. The Help information is displayed in a separate browser window when you click the Help command on the Web Part menu.

- **Help Mode** Specify how a browser will display Help content for a Web Part. Select one of the following Help Modes:

    - **Modal** Open a separate browser window, if the browser has this capability. A user must close the window before returning to the Web page.

    - **Modeless** Open a separate browser window, if the browser has this capability. A user does not have to close the window before returning to the Web page. This is the default value.

    - **Navigate** Open the Web page in the current browser window.

- **Catalog Icon Image URL** Specify the location of a file containing an image to be used as the Web Part icon in the Web Part List. The image size must be 16 × 16 pixels.

- **Title Icon Image URL** Specify the location of a file containing an image to be used in the Web Part title bar. The image size must be 16 × 16 pixels.

- **Import Error Message** Specify a message that appears if there is a problem importing the Web Part.

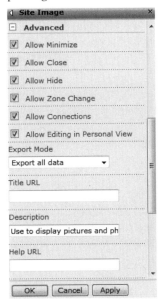

Figure 8-7 The Advanced section of the Web Part's properties dialog box contains a large number of properties that a user can modify.

In Summary...

This chapter explained how to create and format Web Part pages by using a browser, SharePoint Designer 2007, and Visual Studio 2005. In Chapter 18, "Advanced Design Techniques," and Chapter 19, "Beginning Web Part Development," we will go into a more in-depth look at code examples for custom WSS 3.0 development.

The next chapter will explain how to create and modify basic site features in WSS 3.0.

Creating and Modifying Basic Site Features

Once you have a Microsoft Windows SharePoint Services 3.0 (WSS 3.0) site and know how to create new pages, the next steps are to provide content, navigation, and a consistent look and feel. If your site consists entirely of SharePoint lists and libraries, and if the default page layouts are acceptable, you can use the collaboration and meetings templates that come right out of the box with WSS 3.0. If your organization has specific needs that are not met by these out-of-the-box templates, then what path should you take to meet those needs?

The new features and functionality in WSS 3.0 assist users in designing sites and workspaces that are tailored to their organizations' specific needs. Users can utilize either a compatible Web browser or an application such as Microsoft Office SharePoint Designer 2007 to modify a site or workspace template to meet each of their business or functional requirements.

Custom templates can be designed and saved so that others in the organization can use these templates when new sites need to be provisioned within the enterprise. Custom site templates also enhance SharePoint governance as well as standardization. Users can create master pages to allow for new pages to automatically inherit the navigational and branding elements of an existing site, which further enhances enterprise-wide SharePoint standardization.

The primary focus of this chapter is describing several ways of using the right template for the right job, creating organizationally specific templates, and customizing the look and feel of a SharePoint site via a master page with Office SharePoint Designer 2007.

Modifying Site Navigation

As discussed previously in Chapter 5, "Creating SharePoint Sites, Workspaces, and Pages," users can modify the Top Link bar as well as the Quick Launch by using a Web browser such as Microsoft Internet Explorer. SharePoint Designer 2007 also gives users the option of customizing these two navigation elements in a more visual manner by dragging pages onto the link bar.

Customizing the Built-in Navigation Features via SharePoint Designer 2007

To customize the Top Link bar, a user can add a link to a new or existing site as well as rename, remove, or change the order of the links. The Quick Launch will automatically display links to all lists and libraries on a site that is created in SharePoint Designer 2007 and, within the Sites section, will show all subsites of the site. You can customize the Quick Launch in much the same way, configuring the documents, lists, pictures, discussions, and surveys sections just how you want them. Read on to find out how to accomplish these customizations.

Customizing the Top Link Bar

With the appropriate permissions, you can use SharePoint Designer 2007 to customize the Top Link bar by performing the following actions:

1. Open the site that has the Top Link bar you want to modify.

2. On the Site menu, click Navigation, as shown in Figure 9-1. The Navigation view will open (see Figure 9-2), displaying a visual representation of the site. Link bars are represented by the boxes with the globe symbols.

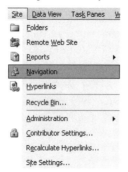

Figure 9-1 Select the Navigation option from the Site menu to inspect the link bars on a SharePoint site.

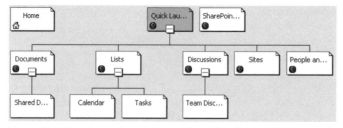

Figure 9-2 The Navigation view provides a visual representation of the site's link bars.

Adding a Link to an Existing Page on the Top Link Bar

With the appropriate permissions, you can enhance the Top Link bar by linking to an existing page on a site. To add a link, perform the following actions:

1. In the SharePoint Designer Folder List, click the page that you want to link to from the Top Link bar, as shown in Figure 9-3.

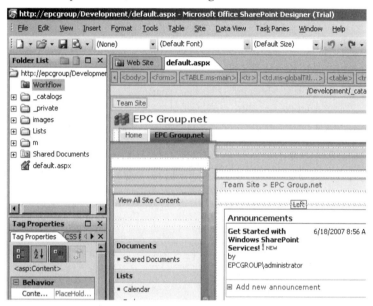

Figure 9-3 To add the Workflow team site to the Top Link bar, drag it from the Folders list to right below the SharePoint Top Navigation Bar box.

2. If the folder list is not visible, click Folder List on the Task Panes menu. If you cannot read the labels on the boxes in Navigation view because the text is cut off, hover the pointer over the box. The full name is displayed in a ScreenTip. If no pages are displayed under the SharePoint Top Navigation Bar box, you can click the plus sign at the bottom of the box to expand the list of pages.

3. Drag the selected file to a position just below the SharePoint Top Navigation Bar box.

4. On the View menu, click Page and then Design. When the modified page is displayed, you should see that a link to the selected page has been added to the Top Link bar.

> **Note**
> The main page for each list is named AllItems.aspx and is located in the Lists/*list name*/ directory on the site. Similarly, the main page for each library is named AllItems.aspx and is located in the *library name*/forms/ directory on the site.

Adding a Link to a New Page on the Top Link Bar

A user with the appropriate permissions can add a link to a new page on the Top Link bar by opening the site in Navigation view, right-clicking the SharePoint Top Navigation Bar, pointing to New, and clicking Page. A new page will be created. If you do not see the new page in the folder list, double-click the link in Navigation view to open the file for editing.

Renaming a Link on the Top Link Bar

With the appropriate permissions, you can rename a link on the Top Link bar by performing the following actions:

1. Under the SharePoint Top Navigation Bar box, right-click the page that you want to change and then click Rename.

2. Type the new name for the page. The link on the link bar is changed as soon as you click away from the page or press Enter.

Deleting a Link from the Top Link Bar

Deleting a link from the Top Link bar does not delete the page itself but rather just the link. To delete the link, in Navigation view, under the SharePoint Top Navigation Bar box, right-click the page that you want to delete and then click Delete as shown in Figure 9-4.

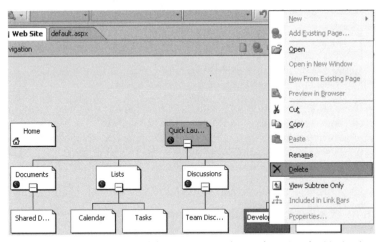

Figure 9-4 A user can easily delete navigational items by using the Navigation view in SharePoint Designer 2007.

Customizing the Quick Launch

With the appropriate permissions, you can use SharePoint Designer 2007 to customize the Quick Launch by performing the following actions:

1. In SharePoint Designer 2007, open the site on which you want to modify the Quick Launch.

2. On the Site menu, click Navigation. The Navigation view will open to display a visual representation of the site, with the link bars represented by boxes with globe symbols (refer to Figure 9-2).

Deleting a Section of the Quick Launch

With the appropriate permissions, you can use the Navigation view in SharePoint Designer 2007 to delete a section of the Quick Launch by right-clicking the box that represents the section you want to delete, such as Discussions, and then clicking Delete on the shortcut menu.

Adding a Link for a Site's Existing Page to the Quick Launch

With the appropriate permissions, you can use SharePoint Designer 2007 to add a link to a site's existing page on the Quick Launch. In the folder list, click the page that you want to link to from the Quick Launch and then drag the page to a location under the Quick Launch box.

INSIDE OUT   **How would you like the link to appear?**

If you would like the link that is being added to appear at the same level as the headings on the Quick Launch (for example, Documents or Pictures), make sure that you drag the page directly below the Quick Launch box. If you would like the link to appear below an existing heading, you will need to drag the page directly below the heading.

Adding a New Page Link to the Quick Launch

With the appropriate permissions, you can add a link to a new page on the Quick Launch by using SharePoint Designer 2007. With the Navigation view open, right-click the Quick Launch box, point to New on the shortcut menu, and then click Page. A new page and link will be created.

Renaming a Link on the Quick Launch

With the appropriate permissions, you can rename a link on the Quick Launch by using SharePoint Designer 2007 as follows:

1. In Navigation view under the Quick Launch box, right-click the page that you want to change and then click Rename.

2. Type the new name for the page. The link on the link bar is changed as soon as you click outside the page or press Enter.

Changing the Order of Links on the Quick Launch

With the appropriate permissions, you can change links on the Quick Launch by using SharePoint Designer 2007. In Navigation view, drag pages to reorder them and make sure that the link boxes remain under the Quick Launch box.

Selecting the Right Template

In Chapter 5, I discussed each of the available templates that come right out of the box with WSS 3.0. The two major categories of templates are collaboration templates and meetings templates.

For organizations that have already saved one of their existing sites as a site template, a third category of templates, called custom templates, is available (as shown in Figure 9-5).

Figure 9-5 Users can choose from three categories of site templates when creating a new site or workspace.

The following sections will go into detail about the different collaboration and meetings templates and discuss how you can use them within your organization.

Using Collaboration Templates

The collaboration templates available in WSS 3.0 are aimed at assisting teams or groups of users within an organization to better work together in a joint intellectual effort around topics, content, and documents. The collaboration templates are Team Site, Blank Site, Document Workspace, Wiki Site, and Blog.

These templates can be customized via a browser or a Web-design program that is compatible with WSS 3.0, such as SharePoint Designer 2007.

Team Site Template

The Team Site template, shown in Figure 9-6, is by far the most widely used template in WSS 3.0 and gives a team a great starting point for instant collaboration.

The team site includes a standard document library named Shared Documents. The team site also includes several lists, such as an Announcements list for communicating the latest news to the team and a Tasks list for tracking tasks. The Contacts and Links lists capture team contacts and frequently used links. The Announcements, Calendar, and Links list Web Parts are automatically added to the site along with an Image Web Part that by default displays the Microsoft WSS logo (though it can quickly be changed to display an image more specific to your organization).

Figure 9-6 This is the standard Team Site template, which is the most widely used template within SharePoint.

The team site contains a search box at the upper right corner of the site along with the Quick Launch on the left side of the page. You'll also find a Top Link bar and a Site Actions tab. These items are for searching, navigating, and customizing the site. The Team Site template should be used for most any new collaboration site within an organization, but as a best practice, on most occasions it should be customized and then saved as a new template. Such customization will be discussed in the section titled "Using Custom Templates" later in this chapter.

Blank Site Template

The Blank Site template, shown in Figure 9-7, allows for customization based on specific requirements. The Blank Site template does not contain any libraries or lists but does have an Image Web Part within the site that by default displays the Microsoft WSS logo.

The blank site contains a search box at the upper right corner of the site along with the Quick Launch on the left side of the page. You'll also find a Top Link bar and a Site Actions tab for the site's search, navigation, and customization. This template can be useful for sites that need to be created quickly for specific topics or for administrators who prefer to build a site from the ground up without any existing items residing on the site.

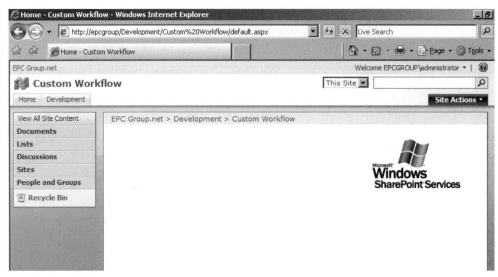

Figure 9-7 The Blank Site template enables users to customize a site from its inception.

Document Workspace Template

The Document Workspace template, shown in Figure 9-8, enables teams to work collaboratively on a document within a site that is dedicated to that primary document and its supporting files.

The Document Workspace template contains a document library called Shared Documents that is a standard out-of-the-box document library that a team can begin using to store the primary document and its supporting files. The Document Workspace template also includes several lists, such as an Announcements list for communicating the latest document-related news to the team, along with a Tasks list for tracking tasks. Calendar and Links lists capture events and related document links. The Announcements, Shared Documents, Tasks, Members, and Links list Web Parts are automatically added to the site.

The document workspace contains a search box at the upper right corner of the site along with the Quick Launch on the left side of the page. You'll also find a Top Link bar and a Site Actions tab for the site's search, navigation, and customization.

For additional information on document workspaces, refer to the section titled "Working with Document Workspaces" in Chapter 4, "Using SharePoint with Microsoft Office 2007."

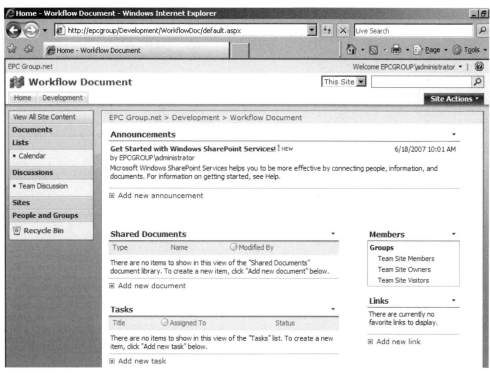

Figure 9-8 This Document Workspace template enables teams to work collaboratively on a document within a dedicated site.

Wiki Site Template

The Wiki Site template, shown in Figure 9-9, allows for a community to brainstorm and share ideas. It also provides Web pages that teams can quickly edit to record items of information and then link them together through keywords.

By using a Web browser, your team members can create and add explanatory notes on pages that link to each other without much effort or need for technical skills. These sites track changes as users add and otherwise change content, and they help your team put together an outline that you can create later in a word-processing program such as Microsoft Office Word 2007.

The Wiki Site template contains a wiki page library called Wiki Pages that is a standard out-of-the-box library to create content. The Wiki Site template does not include any other libraries or lists by default.

The Wiki Site template contains a search box at the upper right corner of the site along with the Quick Launch on the left side of the page. You'll also find a Top Link bar and a Site Actions tab for the site's search, navigation, and customization. You can use the Edit, History, and Incoming links on the Site Actions tab when you work with wiki content.

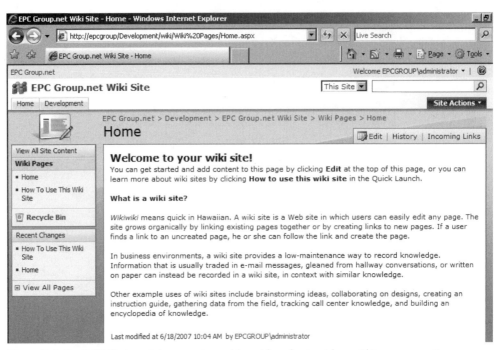

Figure 9-9 The Wiki Site template promotes quick and free-flowing ideas within a community.

For additional information on using wikis in WSS 3.0, refer to the sections titled "Wiki Page Library" and "Updating a Wiki Page Library," in Chapter 3, "Using the Built-In Features of Windows SharePoint Services 3.0."

Blog Template

The Blog template, shown in Figure 9-10, allows for a user or team to post ideas, best practices, lessons learned, observations, or other expertise that site visitors can view and comment on. On the site's creation, the Blog template contains a picture library named Photos as well as five SharePoint lists by default. The five lists are as follows:

- **Categories** Defines the categories available for the Posts list

- **Comments** Stores comments that have been made on the Posts list

- **Links** Stores links to Web pages that team members will find interesting or useful

- **Other Blogs** Stores links to other blogs

- **Posts** Stores blog posts on the site

The Blog template contains a search box at the upper right corner of the site along with the Quick Launch on the left side of the page. You'll also find a Top Link bar and a Site Actions tab for the site's search, navigation, and customization.

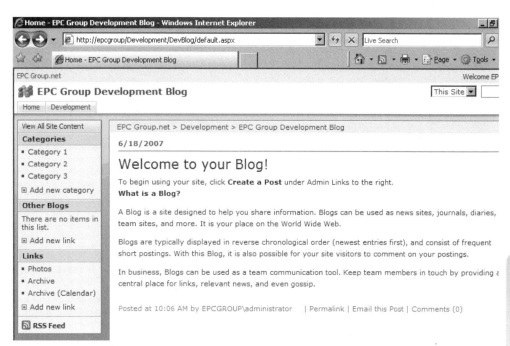

Figure 9-10 Use the Blog template to post ideas, best practices, lessons learned, and any other related observations.

You'll see an initial "Welcome To Your Blog!" post on the Posts list Web Part, which is loaded on the page by default. You'll also see an Admin Links Web Part. Use its six useful links—Create A Post, Manage Posts, Manage Comments, All Content, Set Blog Permissions, and Launch Blog Program To Post.

INSIDE OUT   Using a blog site within your organization

Blogs are more popular than ever before, and organizations are taking advantage of their users' personal blogging experience to reach their internal goals. These blog posts are easy for other users to access and read in a central location, and they are automatically managed by the Posts list included in the Blog Template. An organization's SharePoint governance model should address how to control the open flow of this information. Blogs should be used because they encourage employees to freely discuss issues. In addition, they bring together the collective intelligence of a specific team, group, or department almost instantaneously.

Blogs can lessen a user's load of daily e-mails or the need for ad hoc meetings, and they bring users together regardless of their locations, operational hours, or schedules. They can also increase knowledge-sharing within your organization by bringing together users who may not even know that the others have knowledge of a specific topic.

Chapter 9

Using Meetings Templates

Use WSS 3.0 Meetings workspace templates to gather information, content, and materials for meetings within an organization. These workspaces are ideal for capturing meeting agendas, related documents, objectives, and tasks in one central, secure location. They enable meeting attendees to stay up-to-date on meeting information and related documentation for as long as necessary regardless of a project's size or budget.

> **Note**
>
> Meeting workspace users cannot add items to announcement lists, document libraries, or discussion lists via e-mail, so users should be aware that they need a Web browser to add list items.

With a meeting workspace, a project manager can publish a meeting's agenda prior to the meeting along with the attendee list, the meeting location or call-in information, and any other documents or content that may be discussed. Once the meeting starts, a meeting facilitator can use lists from the workspace to record tasks and objectives, and to store and update related documents.

When the meeting adjourns, all the attendees will know the exact location of the workspace they will access to view all of this information as well as to provide updates on any deliverables or tasks to which they were assigned.

Meeting workspace sites can be created by adding an event to a WSS 3.0 calendar, by using a Microsoft Office 2007 application, or by simply creating a new meeting workspace site by clicking the Create link from the All Site Content page and then selecting Sites And Workspaces.

For additional information on creating document workspaces by using a Microsoft Office 2007 application, refer to the section titled "Working with Document Workspaces" in Chapter 4.

Basic Meeting Workspace Template

The Basic Meeting Workspace template, shown in Figure 9-11, is used to plan, organize, and capture results of an organization's meetings. It can be easily created and immediately used to capture meeting information.

The Basic Meeting Workspace template includes a standard out-of-the-box document library as well as three lists—Agenda, Attendees, and Objectives. Use the Agenda list to outline topics and a meetings timeline. Use the Attendees list to track the attendees of the meeting. Use the Objectives list to set the meeting's goals and objectives. The Objectives, Agenda, Attendees, and Document Library list Web Parts are automatically added to the site's available Web Part zones by default upon its creation.

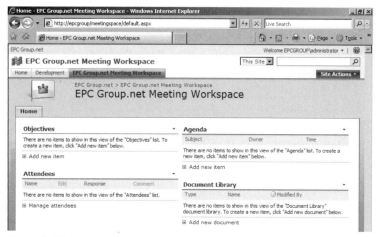

Figure 9-11 Use the Basic Meeting Workspace template to plan, organize, and capture results of an organization's meetings.

The basic meeting workspace site contains a search box at the upper right corner of the site as well as a Top Link bar and a Site Actions tab for the site's search, navigation, and customization. The Site Actions tab contains Add Pages and Manage Pages links to perform the actions for which they are named.

The Basic Meeting Workspace template, just like the Team Site template, should be customized and then saved as a new template so that participants at all future meetings can use a standardized and approved template. This will be discussed in the section titled "Using Custom Templates" later in this chapter.

TROUBLESHOOTING

Attendees may be receiving multiple notifications on a workspace site

On some occasions, meeting attendees may continue to receive multiple notifications about a meeting workspace site, which can quickly become annoying. If this issue occurs, it is possible that one of the following is the cause:

- Users were added from the Manage Users page within Meeting Workspace Site Settings, and the option to send an e-mail message to the user was selected. To resolve this issue and stop e-mail notifications to the user, go in and clear the Send The Following E-Mail To Let These Users Know They've Been Added check box.

- The SharePoint server that the meeting workspace was created on is configured to automatically send an e-mail message to users when they are added to a workspace site, and they may be receiving multiple notification e-mails. In this case, notify a SharePoint administrator of this issue.

Once you resolve this multiple notification e-mail issue, attendees will receive only meeting requests you send using a SharePoint calendar or compatible e-mail program such as Microsoft Office Outlook 2007.

Chapter 9

Blank Meeting Workspace Template

Users can customize the Blank Meeting Workspace template, shown in Figure 9-12, from its creation based on specific requirements. The Blank Meeting Workspace template does not contain any libraries but does contain one Attendees list to track the future attendees of the meeting. Upon creation, no Web Parts are added to any of the available Web Part zones.

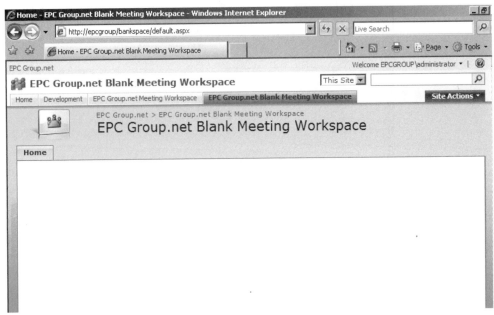

Figure 9-12 The Blank Meeting Workspace template enables users to customize the workspace template from its initial creation.

The Blank Meeting Workspace template contains a search box at the upper right corner of the site as well as a Top Link bar and a Site Actions tab for the site's search, navigation, and customization. The Site Actions tab contains Add Pages and Manage Pages links to perform the actions for which they are named.

Decision Meeting Workspace Template

Use the Decision Meeting Workspace template, shown in Figure 9-13, to track the status and decisions of meetings. The Decision Meeting Workspace template includes a standard out-of-the-box document library as well as five lists—Agenda, Attendees, Decisions, Objectives, and Tasks. Use the Agenda list to outline topics and a meeting's timeline. Use the Attendees list to track the attendees of the meeting. Use the Decisions list to update the meeting attendees about decisions that come out of the meeting. Use the Objectives list to set the meeting's goals and objectives, and the Tasks list to track tasks and deliverable requests that attendees are assigned within the related meetings.

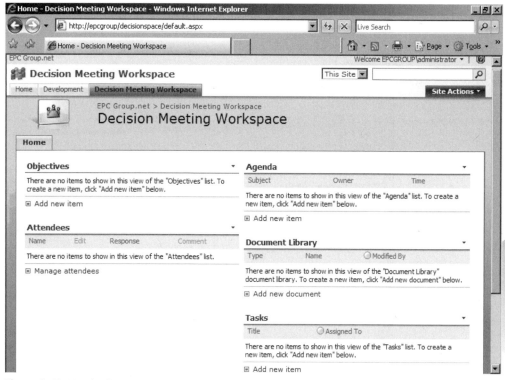

Figure 9-13 Use the Decision Meeting Workspace template to track the status and decisions of an organization's meetings.

The Objectives, Agenda, Attendees, Document Library, Tasks, and Decisions list Web Parts are automatically added to the site's available Web Part zones by default upon its creation.

The decision meeting workspace site contains a search box at the upper right corner of the site as well as a Top Link bar and a Site Actions tab for the site's search, navigation, and customization. The Site Actions tab contains Add Pages and Manage Pages links to perform the actions for which they are named.

Social Meeting Workspace Template

Use the Social Meeting Workspace template, shown in Figure 9-14, to plan social meeting occasions within an organization. The Social Meeting Workspace template does not include a document library but does include a picture library as well as three lists and a discussion board.

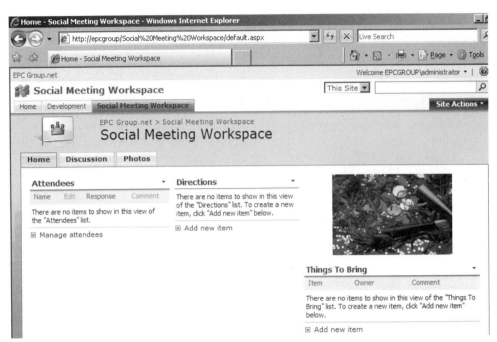

Figure 9-14 Use the Social Meeting Workspace template to plan social meetings.

The three lists are Attendees, Directions, and Things To Bring, and the discussion board is simply named Discussion Board. Use the Attendees list to track the attendees of the meeting and use the Directions list to assist users in finding the location of the organization's social meeting. You can use the Things To Bring list to notify and remind attendees about the items they should bring to the meeting.

The social meeting workspace site contains a search box at the upper right corner of the site as well as a Top Link bar with three default links to pages—Home, Discussion, and Photos. The Site Actions tab contains Add Pages and Manage Pages links to perform the actions for which they are named.

The home page contains the Attendees, Directions, and Things To Bring list Web Parts in the available Web Part zones by default upon its creation as well as an Image Web Part that displays a generic placeholder image that can quickly be changed to display an image more specific to your organization. The Discussion page within the Social Meeting Workspace template contains a Discussion Board Web Part by default, and the Photos page contains a Picture Library Web Part.

Multipage Meeting Workspace Template

Use the Multipage Meeting Workspace template, shown in Figure 9-15, to plan, organize, and capture the results of a meeting within the organization. The Multipage Meeting Workspace template does not include a document library but does contain three lists—Agenda, Attendees, and Objectives. Use the Agenda list to outline topics and a meeting timeline, and use the Attendees list to track the meeting's attendees. Use the Objectives list to set the meeting's goals and objectives.

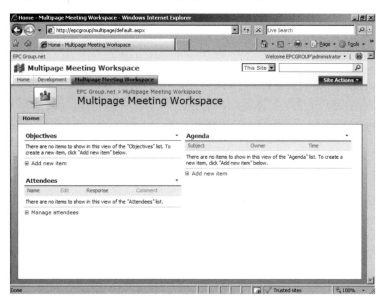

Figure 9-15 Use the Multipage Meeting Workspace template to plan meetings requiring more than one page of information.

The Multipage Meeting Workspace template contains a search box at the upper right corner of the site as well as a Top Link bar with three default links to pages—Home, Page 1, and Page 2. The Site Actions tab contains Add Pages and Manage Pages links to perform the actions for which they are named.

The home page contains the Objectives, Agenda, and Attendees Web Parts in the available Web Part zones by default upon its creation. The Page 1 and Page 2 pages within the Multipage Meeting Workspace template do not contain any Web Parts by default.

Using Custom Templates

Depending on the number of sites that will be created within your organization, it is a best practice for your organization to create custom team site and meeting workspace templates that contain specific libraries, lists, and Web Parts. This is helpful for promoting standardization and governance for any enterprise SharePoint deployment.

Templates also help promote the use of organizationally specific content types, custom columns, and other related metadata that enhance the organization's information management policies as well as improve SharePoint's search results.

INSIDE OUT   Creating a project landing area for your organization

If your organization would like to have a SharePoint site created for every project within the organization, you may want to consider creating a top-level project site and then creating all other project subsites within the top-level site. This would allow for what I sometimes refer to as a "landing area" for projects so that the navigational elements of the subsites can be inherited from the top-level parent project site. This is a great way to use the new navigational elements in WSS 3.0 to give your organization the functionality and feel of a genuine portal without having to implement Microsoft SharePoint Server 2007.

Having a SharePoint administrator create a new site from one of the existing templates and then customizing it to meet the organization's site standards is time-consuming and can allow room for unnecessary user error.

In addition, the SharePoint administrator who is forced to modify existing templates will also have a good answer for perspective SharePoint clients who ask why their department sites cannot be customized in a specific or unique way. These administrators can simply reply to the client by saying, "These are the approved templates for all SharePoint sites within the organization." Any SharePoint administrator should be prepared to answer this question because it will be asked by the current SharePoint user base as well as those who would like sites created for their departments or teams.

Custom templates save administrative support time, increase standardization, promote governance, and help ensure the success of your organization's SharePoint implementation.

Creating Custom Templates

Administrators can easily create custom templates by creating and customizing a site that they would like to use as an organizational site template. Regardless of whether sites are based on a team site, blank site, document workspace site, or any of the other available site templates, administrators can create custom site templates by using a Web browser or an application such as SharePoint Designer 2007, depending on the site's requirements.

You can save a site as a template by clicking the Site Actions menu within a site and selecting Site Settings. On the Site Settings page, in the Look And Feel section, click Save Site As Template to create the custom template. Make sure that if you would like to include the existing content in the template (for example, libraries or lists), you select the Include Content option before saving.

All of the custom templates in SharePoint are based on a site definition or feature definition that is stored on the SharePoint server. A user can access the custom site templates through the Site Template Gallery.

It is important to note that site templates are saved at the site collection level and will be made available to other users in the site collection in which the template resides. These templates can easily be imported by other site collections so that they do not have to be recreated, making the "one version of the truth" concept easier to adhere to within the organization.

For additional information on saving site templates, refer to the section titled "Save an Existing Site as a Template to Use During Site Creation" in Chapter 5.

Management of Custom Templates

As previously discussed, custom site templates are stored in the Site Template Gallery of a site collection. You can easily import these templates into the Site Template Gallery of another site collection. Simply save the template to a temporary storage location, such as a hard drive, and then upload it to another site collection's Site Template Gallery.

Adding a Site Template to the Site Template Gallery

Add a site template to the Site Template Gallery by opening the Site Settings page for the top-level Web site in a site collection and then doing the following:

1. On the top-level Web site, click the Site Actions menu and then click Site Settings.

2. On the Site Settings page, in the Galleries section, click Site Templates (see Figure 9-16).

Figure 9-16 The Galleries section on the Site Settings page contains links to several site and list galleries.

3. On the Site Template Gallery page, click Upload.

4. In the Name box, type the path to the template. Alternatively, click Browse.

5. When you are finished, click OK.

Modifying Settings or Deleting a Site Template from the Site Template Gallery

Delete site templates from the Site Template Gallery by going to the Site Settings page for the top-level Web site in a site collection and then doing the following:

1. On the top-level Web site, click the Site Actions menu and then Site Settings.

2. On the Site Settings page, in the Galleries section, click Site Templates (refer to Figure 9-16).

3. Find the site template you would like to modify (that is, change its settings or delete it) and then click the Edit icon next to the template's title.

4. When the Edit Item page loads, you can modify the site template's Name, Title, and Description boxes and then click OK to save the changes. Alternatively, to delete the site template, simply click Delete Item and then click OK.

Using Master Pages

As discussed earlier in Chapter 7, "What's New with Templates and Design," master pages are a feature of ASP.NET 2.0 that enables users to create a single page template that can then be used as the basis for many other new pages within an application. Master pages are a great mechanism for organizations to use to enforce SharePoint governance, look and feel, or branding standards. The popularity of custom master pages is amazing, and they are one of the top items that my organization develops for our clients besides custom workflows. In Chapter 7, I discussed how an organization can use SharePoint Designer 2007 to perform design tasks such as changing a site's default master page, modifying the styles of the master page, and modifying its content placeholders.

By default, WSS 3.0 sites have a few content pages that are automatically created upon the site's creation, for example:

- default.aspx

- Default content pages for lists such as AllItems.aspx, DispForm.aspx, NewForm.aspx, and EditForm.aspx

- Default content pages for document libraries such as Upload.aspx and WebFldr.aspx

These pages refer to the default master page of the site via their @ Page tag, for example:

```
<%@ Page MasterPageFile="~masterurl/default.master" %>
```

Content Pages

As discussed in Chapter 7, master pages contain two separate parts: the master page it-self and a content page. Master pages define the layout, navigational elements, common default content, and the content for the attached pages. The content page is a unique page that when rendered in a browser is supplied with common content by the master page. The content page supplies the page-specific content.

For more information about content pages, refer to the section titled "Master Pages" in Chapter 7.

Developing Master Pages

By default, WSS 3.0 stores master pages in the file system. However, if they are edited, SharePoint moves them to the content database. A content page that uses a master page is not affected when you edit that master page.

The compilation mode of master pages is similar to that of ASPX pages. You can change this at any time via a page directive or by changing values in Web.config, for example:

```
    </PageParserPaths>

<PageParserPaths >

    <PageParserPath VirtualPath="/*.master"

                    CompilationMode="Always"

                    AllowServerSideScript="true"

                    IncludeSubFolders="true">

    </PageParserPath>

</PageParserPaths>
```

However, compiled master pages can contain inline scripting that can sometimes cause a performance hit on an organization's SharePoint environment. Also be aware that if you edit the master page in SharePoint Desinger 2007 or a similar tool that does not support page compilation, your inline script will no longer run.

> Note
>
> As a best practice, I recommend that organizations not use inline scripts inside of Share-Point master pages.

TROUBLESHOOTING

Issues with locating a master page that multiple users edit

If you manage a site that multiple users edit and update, you may want an easy way to locate all of the master pages in the site. If the site contains master pages that have been customized, having an easy way to find all of the master pages may be important to you. The ability to find customized master pages in the site is useful if you want to identify and investigate all customized master pages before updating the default master page.

If you are the site owner, you may want to review all customized master pages that other members of your team have created so that you can decide either to reset those pages to the site definition before applying an update to the default master page, or to keep the customized master pages in their current unique forms.

When you are working with WSS 3.0, you can use SharePoint Designer 2007 to run site reports that collect a variety of information about your site's health, usage, and potential problems. To run a Customized Pages report, perform the following steps:

1. Open the site for which you want to run the report in Office SharePoint Designer 2007.

2. On the Site menu, point to Reports, point to Shared Content, and then click Customized Pages.

The report will open with all of the pages in the site listed, and the Customized column will indicate whether content has been customized for that page.

For WSS 3.0 and SharePoint Server 2007, data for the reports generated by SharePoint Designer is saved on the server on which the site is hosted. You can grant or deny access to these reports, but you must have at least Web Designer permissions on the server to open the site and run reports.

Content Placeholders

The default master page for WSS 3.0 contains a number of *ContentPlaceHolder* controls that enable administrators to customize an individual content page. The *ContentPlace-Holder* controls inside of the default.master page are listed in Table 9-1.

Table 9-1 WSS 3.0 Default Content Placeholders Inside the default.master Page

Placeholder Name	Placeholder Use
PlaceHolderFormDigest	The form digest security control
PlaceHolderBodyLeftBorder	The border element for the body
PlaceHolderBodyRightMargin	The right margin of the body
PlaceHolderCalendarNavigator	To show a date picker for the navigation in a calendar when it is visible on the page
PlaceHolderBodyAreaClass	Additional body styles in the page header

Table 9-1 WSS 3.0 Default Content Placeholders Inside the default.master Page

Placeholder Name	Placeholder Use
PlaceHolderAdditionalPageHead	Add additional content inside the page head tag
PlaceHolderGlobalNavigation	The global navigation breadcrumb for a page
PlaceHolderLeftActions	The bottom of the left navigation area for a page
PlaceHolderLeftNavBarTop	The top of the left navigation area for a page
PlaceHolderLeftNavBar	The left navigation area
PlaceHolderLeftNavBarBorder	The border element on the left navigation bar for a page
PlaceHolderLeftNavBarDataSource	The data source for the left navigation menu for a page
PlaceHolderHorizontalNav	The top navigation menu for a page
PlaceHolderMiniConsole	To show page-level commands for a location
PlaceHolderNavSpacer	The width of the left navigation area for a page
PlaceHolderPageDescription	The description of a page's contents
PlaceHolderPageImage	The page icon at the upper left corner of a page
WSSDesignConsole	A page's editing controls when a page is placed in editing mode
PlaceHolderSearchArea	A site's search box
PlaceHolderSiteName	A placeholder for a site's name
PlaceHolderTitleAreaClass	A placeholder for additional styles in the page header
PlaceHolderTitleAreaSeparator	To show shadows for the title area of a page
PlaceHolderTopNavBar	The top navigation area
PlaceHolderUtilityContent	Used for a placeholder for additional content that may need to reside at the bottom of a page
PlaceHolderPageTitleInTitleArea	The page title area shown underneath the breadcrumb
PlaceHolderMain	The main content of a page
PlaceHolderTitleLeftBorder	The left border of the title area for a page
PlaceHolderTitleRightMargin	The right margin of the title area for a page
PlaceHolderPageTitle	The page title that is shown within a Web browser's title bar
SPNavigation	Additional page controls if needed on a page

Although all of these content placeholders are not required to build a master page, you will need a number of tags to make your master page usable.

The Master Page Gallery

As discussed in Chapter 7, a master page in WSS 3.0 contains the page's design and layout elements that will need to be repeated on multiple pages in a site. Master pages allow for sites across the organization to have a consistent look and feel, which can boost an environment's usability so that users will always know the general location of key pieces of SharePoint functionality.

By default in WSS 3.0, every site has one master page that is stored in the Master Page Gallery, though that does not limit the total number of master pages an administrator can store in the Master Page Gallery. But do remember that only one master page can be used as the default master page for a particular site.

Using the Master Page Gallery to Edit a Master Page

To use the Maser Page Gallery to edit a master page, perform the following actions:

1. On the Site Actions menu from the top-level site, click Site Settings.

2. In the Galleries section, click Master Pages (refer to Figure 9-16).

3. Click the master page that you would like to edit.

4. Click Edit to edit a master page by using a Windows SharePoint Services–compatible Web-design program, such as SharePoint Designer 2007.

In Summary...

This chapter described a variety of options a user has available when creating a new collaboration or meeting workspace site by using out-of-the-box templates that ship with WSS 3.0.

I also discussed how an organization can and should create custom templates tailored specifically to their organization, not only to promote governance and standardization, but also to capture information management policies and metadata. Templates and master pages can make a huge difference in the success and supportability of most any SharePoint implementation.

The next chapter will explain how to create data sources and data views in WSS 3.0. These provide a powerful means for SharePoint to build on its already critical role within an organization and its functional capabilities to enable it to become a "one-stop shop" for a wealth of knowledge within any organization.

Creating Data Sources and Data Views

Chapter 6, "Designing Lists, Libraries, and Pages," described how you can design your own Microsoft Windows SharePoint Services 3.0 (WSS 3.0) lists and libraries, how you can create multiple views of any list or library, and how you can choose to display different views—all using only a Web browser. The capabilities offered here are robust, but like most any technique, they do have their limitations when it comes to certain customizations.

One way of gaining more flexibility is, of course, to write your own Web Parts in Microsoft Visual Studio 2005 or Microsoft Visual Studio 2008. Part 7, "Developing Web Parts in Visual Studio 2005, SharePoint Best Practices, and Maintaining Your Implementation," will explain the basics of writing and deploying such Web Parts, but the individual who would take on such tasks would need to have significant programming skills.

Users who need more power than Web-based design tools can provide and less complexity than developing custom code in Visual Studio 2005 or Visual Studio 2008 can find just the balance they require in Microsoft Office SharePoint Designer 2007. Office SharePoint Designer 2007 has some great new features for working with data in SharePoint lists, SharePoint libraries, external databases, and XML files and Web services accessible through WSS 3.0.

In Chapter 7, "What's New with Templates and Design," you learned how to use SharePoint Designer 2007 to create customized views of live data called Data views. In this chapter, you learn how to establish connections—called *data sources*—from a SharePoint site to SharePoint lists and libraries, non-SharePoint databases, XML files, server-side scripts, and XML Web services.

Best of all, none of this requires writing any program code at all. SharePoint Designer 2007 provides all the commands and configuration you need within its graphical interface.

> **Note**
> Throughout this chapter, unless otherwise stated, the term *library* means a SharePoint document library, form library, or picture library. The term *list* means a SharePoint list, survey, or discussion board.

Designing Lists and Libraries

With SharePoint Designer 2007, you can create and modify SharePoint lists and libraries with all the same capabilities that the browser interface provides. SharePoint lists and libraries appear in SharePoint Designer 2007 in the Folder List task pane with a special icon. The icon for a SharePoint list is the same in both the Folder List and the Data Source Library in the upper-right pane. The Folder List is useful because it will continue to populate as items within a site are created, or as you create or open other sites.

You can delete a list or library from the folder list just as if it were an ordinary file. For example, you can right-click it, select Delete, and then click Yes. Alternatively, select it and choose Delete from the Edit menu. The usual methods for renaming files and folders apply, as do the Copy and Cut commands.

Modifying SharePoint Lists and Libraries

With SharePoint Designer 2007, users can modify list and library settings at a granular level. This functionality enables a user to edit several different objects' permissions in much less time than would be required to open the objects in a browser and then edit their settings.

Configuring List and Library Settings

To modify a SharePoint list or library in SharePoint Designer 2007, a user can highlight the object in the Folder List, right-click it, and select Properties, as shown in Figure 10-1.

Figure 10-1 A user can open an object's properties by right-clicking it in the Folder List.

When the Properties dialog box loads, the General, Settings, Security, and Supporting Files category tabs will display, as shown in Figure 10-2. The following sections detail the property options available on the four tabs.

Figure 10-2 The General properties tab shows an overall summary of the object.

General

From the General tab, shown in Figure 10-2, a user can get a summary of the object, for example, its name, type, location, contents, and size. There are also check boxes that indicate whether to allow scripts or programs to be run, whether to allow an anonymous upload to this directory, and whether to allow uploaded files to overwrite existing filenames.

- **Name** Displays the object's name
- **Type** Displays the object's type
- **Location** Displays the location of the object
- **Contains** Displays the number of files and folders
- **Size** Displays the size of the object
- **Allow Scripts Or Programs To Be Run** Indicates whether scripts are allowed to be run
- **Allow Anonymous Upload To This Directory** Indicates whether anonymous uploads to the directory are allowed
- **Allow Uploaded Files To Overwrite Existing Filenames** Indicates whether uploaded files are allowed to overwrite existing files

Settings

The Settings tab, shown in Figure 10-3, allows a user to make changes to the name and description of the list or library as well as specify certain requirements such as whether to hide it from browsers, whether to require content approval for submitted items, and whether to require check out before editing items. Note that some of these properties may differ between lists and libraries as shown below.

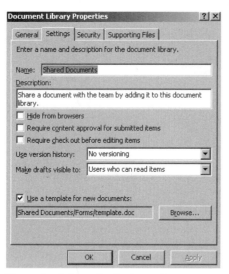

Figure 10-3 From the Settings tab, a user can modify the object's name and description, as well as determine several other options. The user can also choose to display additional properties for libraries.

- **Name** Edit an object's name

- **Description** Edit an object's description

- **Hide From Browsers** Select whether to hide the object from the browser or display the object

- **Require Content Approval For Submitted Items** Select whether to require content approval for submitted items

- **Require Check Out Before Editing Items** Select whether to require items to be checked out before they are edited

- **Use Version History** Select whether to use no versioning, major versions, or major and minor (draft) versions

- **Make Drafts Visible To** Select from three options concerning who will be able to view drafts—Users Who Can Read Items, Users Who Can Edit Items, and Approvers And Authors Only

- **Use A Template For New Documents** Browse for and specify a specific template for new documents as well their location

Security

SharePoint Designer 2007 makes it easy for users to configure the security of a list or library by using the security tab, shown in Figure 10-4, without having to browse to each individual list.

Figure 10-4 A user can modify an object's security settings via the Security properties tab.

- **Specify Which Items Users Can Read** Specify whether a user can view all items or only their own items; these permissions allow for the following:

  - **All Items** Any team member authorized to view the list can view all of its items.

  - **Only Their Own Items** Authorized team members can view only items they created.

- **Specify Which Items Users Can Edit** Specify whether a user can edit all items, only their own items, or no items; these permissions allow for the following:

  - **All Items** A team member authorized to edit the list can edit any and all items.

  - **Only Their Own Item** Authorized team members can edit only items they created.

  - **None** Only administrators and list managers can edit items.

  - **Manage Permission Using The Browser** Displays a hyperlink that will open users' browsers and take them to the item's Permissions page, on which they can then manage permissions.

Supporting Files

Normally, WSS 3.0 automatically maintains the URLs on the Supporting Files tab. However, you can override the following settings if necessary. The content of the Supporting Files tab varies between a list and a document library, as shown in Figure 10-5.

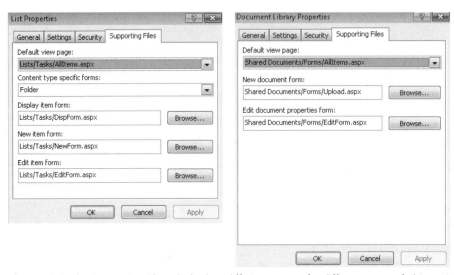

Figure 10-5 The Supporting Files tab displays differing content for different types of objects. It also enables a user to specify the object's default view page, content-type–specific form page, and several other object forms.

- **Default View Page** Specify the Web page that appears when team members initially choose to view the list or library

- **Content Type Specific Forms** Specify from two available options for this property: Folder or Task

- **Display Item Form** Specify the URL of the page that displays individual items in the list

- **New Item Form** Specify the URL of the page that adds new items to the list

- **Edit Item Form** Specify the URL of the page that modifies existing list items

- **New Document Form**   Specify the URL of the page that enables you to add a new document to a document library

- **Edit Document Properties Form** Specify the URL of the page that enables you to edit the properties of an existing document in a document library

Configuring a Custom Query for a List or Library

In SharePoint Designer 2007, SharePoint lists and library data sources, as they appear in the Data Source Library, are actually connections to the original data. This also means that on the object's creation, SharePoint automatically created the query that displays its results. That query cannot be modified, but it is possible to copy a connection to a SharePoint list or library and then create a custom query from it. This way you can apply a query that will display the data in the exact order you require.

When users create custom queries for SharePoint lists or libraries, they can specify the fields that will be available in a particular query as well as apply a custom filter to its results. Users also have the ability to apply sort criteria to the custom query as well as an item and folder scope. By using the item and folder scope, users can specify whether the current query should span folders and subfolders, which can be useful when working with libraries.

Copy a Data Source Connection and Create a New Query

To copy a data source connection, modify its properties, and then create a new data source query for a list or library, a user in SharePoint Designer 2007 can perform the following:

1. Open the specific site in SharePoint Designer 2007 that contains the objects with the data sources you want to copy.

2. If the Data Source Library isn't visible, on the Task Panes menu, click Data Source Library.

3. In the Data Source Library task pane, click the SharePoint list or library that you want to copy and modify, and then click Copy And Modify, as shown in Figure 10-6. The Data Source Properties dialog box will then open.

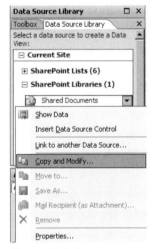

Figure 10-6 A user can copy and modify a data source connection and then create a new data source query for a list or library.

4. On the General tab, as shown in Figure 10-7, type a name in the Name box for your new data source. In the Description box, type a description for your new data source. In the Keywords box, type any keywords that you want to use. When you are finished entering the keywords, click the Source tab.

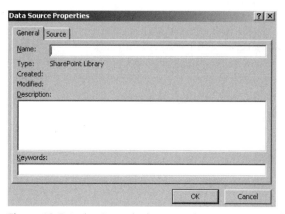

Figure 10-7 In the General tab's Name box, type a name for your new data source.

5. Figure 10-8 shows the Source tab of the Data Source Properties dialog box. In the Query section, click Fields. The Included Fields dialog box will open, as shown in Figure 10-9. You can then add, remove, or arrange the fields in the data source to meet your requirements. Here are your options:

    ○ To add a field to the data source, under Available Fields, click the field that you want and then click Add.

    ○ To remove a field from the data source, under Included Fields, click the field that you want and then click Remove.

    ○ To change the order of the fields in the data source, under Included Fields, click the field that you want to move and then click either Move Up or Move Down.

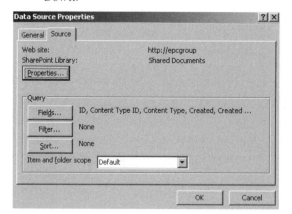

Figure 10-8 The Source tab of the Data Source Properties dialog box contains Properties, Fields, Filter, and Sort options as well as the Item And Folder Scope drop-down list.

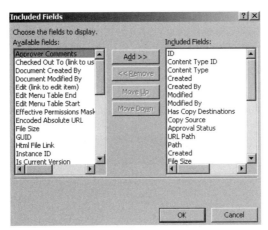

Figure 10-9 The Included Fields dialog box enables you to add, remove, or arrange the fields in the data source to meet your exact requirements.

6. After you are finished and have the correct fields in the Included Fields column, click OK.

    At this point, you can click OK once more to close the Data Source Properties dialog box and use the new custom data source query as it currently is, or you can continue on to step 7 to add a filter to the data source query.

7. To add a filter to the data source query, click Filter (refer to Figure 10-8). Filters are used to limit the display of data to what your filter criteria specify. The Filter Criteria dialog box will appear. Click on the phrase Click Here To Add A New Clause, as shown in Figure 10-10.

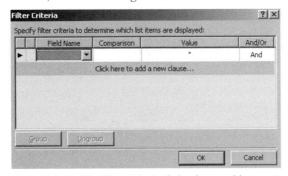

Figure 10-10 The Filter Criteria dialog box enables you to add a filter to the data source query to limit the data that is displayed to your specific criteria.

8. You will now need to specify the desired Field Name, Comparison, Value, and And/Or filter criteria. Once you have completed the first filter criteria item, you can either click OK to close the Filter Criteria dialog box or add another criteria item by clicking Click Here To Add A New Clause. Once you are finished entering criteria items, click OK.

Chapter 10

At this point, you can click OK once more to close the Data Source Properties dialog box and use the new custom data source query as it currently is, or you can continue on to step 9 to add a sort criterion to the custom data source query.

9. To sort the custom data source query, click Sort from the Data Source Properties dialog box (refer to Figure 10-8).

10. In the Sort dialog box, shown in Figure 10-11, under Available Fields click the field that you want to sort on. Then click Add.

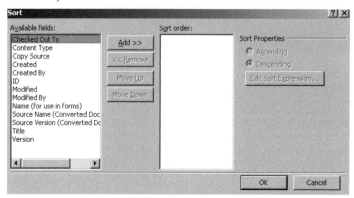

Figure 10-11 With the Sort dialog box, you can specify the field(s) that you would like the data source to sort on.

11. If no fields appear under Available Fields, double-click More Fields, click the field that you want to sort on, and then click OK.

12. Under Sort Properties, you will need to choose one of the following:
   ○ Select Ascending to sort a field from lowest to highest.
   ○ Select Descending to sort a field from highest to lowest.

13. To sort on multiple fields, add more fields to the Sort Order list. You can also change the order in which the fields are sorted. To change the order of the fields, click a field in the Sort Order list and then click Move Up or Move Down.

14. When you are finished adding sort criteria, click OK.

   At this point, you can click OK once more to close the Data Source Properties dialog box and use the new custom data source query as it currently is, or you can continue on to step 15 to specify the Item And Folder Scope criteria.

15. Specify one of options available in the Item And Folder Scope menu.
   ○ If you would like to apply the query to all of the files and all of the subfolders in the current folder, select Default.
   ○ If you would like to apply the query only to the files in the current folder and not to any of the subfolders, select FilesOnly.

○ If you would like to apply the query to all of the files in all of the folders and not to any of the subfolders in the entire site, select Recursive.

○ If you would like to apply the query to all of the files in all of the folders and all of the subfolders in the entire site, select RecursiveAll.

Creating a New List or Library

With SharePoint Designer 2007, you can easily create a new SharePoint list or library. When one is created, it will automatically be added to the Data Source Library. A user also has the option of selecting one of the available built-in SharePoint templates as a basis on which to create the new list or library.

Creating a List

To create a new SharePoint list, a user can either click Create New SharePoint List in the Data Source Library or click File, New. In this example, I will use the Create New Share-Point List option.

1. In the Data Source Library task pane, under SharePoint Lists, click Create New SharePoint List, as shown in Figure 10-12.

Figure 10-12 The Create New SharePoint List option in the Data Source Library task pane.

2. In the left pane, click Lists and then, in the middle pane, click the type of list that you want to add, as shown in Figure 10-13.

3. In the rightmost pane, under Options, type a name for the new list you are creating, and then click OK. This new list will appear in the SharePoint Lists section of the Data Source Library.

> **Note**
> You will also see a corresponding data source connection for the new list in the Folder List.

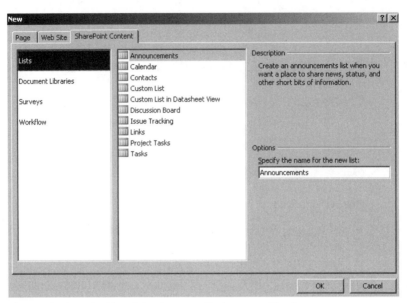

Figure 10-13 In the New dialog box, specify the type of list that you want to create.

Create the right kind of list or library

Certain SharePoint lists have "locked-in" attributes you can specify only by creating a new list. For example, you can't convert some other type of list into a Contacts list that can exchange data with Microsoft Office Outlook 2007. Similarly, you can't convert a list into a library, or one type of library into another. Therefore, when you create a list or library, be sure to create the type you really need.

Creating a Document Library

To create a new SharePoint library, a user can either click Create New Document Library in the Data Source Library task pane or click File, New. In this example, I will use the Create New Document Library option.

1. In the Data Source Library task pane, under SharePoint Libraries, click Create New Document Library.

2. In the left pane, click Document Libraries and then, in the middle pane, click the type of document library that you want to add.

3. In the rightmost pane, under Options, type a name for the new library and then click OK. The new document library will appear in the SharePoint Libraries section of the Data Source Library.

> **Note**
>
> You will also see a corresponding data source connection for the new library in the Folder List.

Managing the Data Sources

After opening a SharePoint site in SharePoint Designer 2007, you can easily view and maintain a list of the available data sources from which that site can retrieve data. SharePoint Designer 2007 calls this list the Data Source Library and it appears, logically enough, on the Data Source Library task pane. To display this task pane, click the Task Panes menu and then select Data Source Library.

SharePoint Designer 2007 also enables you to add a data source from another site to the current site so that data sources can be shared without the need for duplication. When another data source is added to the Data Source Library, it will be available to the site, but it does not automatically get applied to it.

When using a data source from another site, be aware that any modifications to or deletions of that data source on the other external site will also affect your site.

Adding a SharePoint Site

To add a new site to the Data Source Library, users must have permissions to view data from both the external site and the current site to which you are adding the data source. They also must have edit rights for the current site within SharePoint Designer 2007. To add a new site to the Data Source Library, perform the following:

1. At the bottom of the Data Source Library task pane, click Connect To Another Library, as shown in Figure 10-14.

Figure 10-14 Click Connect To Another Library to add a SharePoint site to the Data Source Library.

2. In the Manage Library dialog box, click Add.

Chapter 10

3. In the Collection Properties dialog box, in the Display Name box (shown in Figure 10-15), type a name for the site.

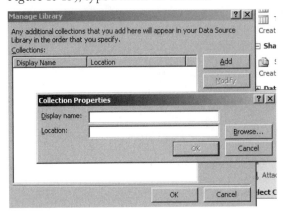

Figure 10-15 Specify the Display Name for the site that will be added to the Data Source Library.

4. Click Browse, Browse To, select the Web site that you want, and then click Open.

5. You will then need to click OK twice to complete the action.

Overview of Available Data Sources

In SharePoint Designer 2007, the Data Source Library task pane automatically displays SharePoint lists and libraries in their respective categories.

Besides SharePoint list and library data sources, SharePoint Designer 2007 offers additional data source connections such as the following:

- **XML Web services** Online services that use Simple Object Access Protocol (SOAP) to handle information requests.

- **Database connections** Database tables located outside the current SharePoint site. These can reside in SQL Server databases at any accessible network location, or in any other database accessible by the Object Linking and Embedding, Database (OLEDB) API.

- **Server-side scripts** Web locations that return data in XML format.

- **Linked data** Multiple data sources brought together into one single source.

- **XML files** Files that store data in XML format.

INSIDE OUT

Using an XML Web services or a server-side script in WSS 3.0

WSS 3.0 can configure XML Web services and server-side scripts as data sources, but the server administrator must first edit the Web.config file on the SharePoint server before this can be accomplished. Organizations with Microsoft Office SharePoint Server 2007 do not require this change, but it is a small price to pay to open up WSS 3.0 to this functionality.

The Web.config file must be edited to include the proxy server settings for the virtual server where your site resides. In a server farm environment, the server administrator must edit the Web.config file for each virtual server in every front-end Web server in the farm.

To configure the Web.config file in your WSS 3.0 environment, perform the following:

1. Start a text editor such as Notepad.

2. Locate and open the Web.config file for the virtual server where you want to allow users to create connections to XML Web service and server-side script data sources. The folder that contains the Web.config file is located in the content area of your server, for example, the default path could be \Inetpub\wwwroot\wss\ VirtualDirectories\80.

3. Do one of the following:

   ○ If you are running WSS 3.0, copy and paste the following lines into the Web.config file anywhere at the level directly below the <configuration> node.

```
<system.net>
 <defaultProxy>
  <proxy autoDetect="true" />
 </defaultProxy>
</system.net>
```

   ○ If you are running WSS 2.0, copy and paste the following lines into the Web.config file anywhere at the level directly below the <configuration> node. Change *<ProxyServer>* to the name of your proxy server and *<Port>* to the port that you are using.

```
<system.net>
 <defaultProxy>
  <proxy proxyaddress="http://<ProxyServer>:<Port>" bypassonlocal = "true"/>
 </defaultProxy>
</system.net>
```

4. Save the Web.config file and then exit the text editor.

5. Reset Internet Information Services (IIS) to apply your changes. Alternatively, you can reset after the next step to apply your changes to multiple virtual servers at one time. To reset IIS, open a command line window and type **iisreset** at the command prompt.

6. Repeat steps 1–5 for each virtual server where you want to allow users to create connections to XML Web service and server-side script data sources.

Chapter 10

Configuring an XML Web Service as a Data Source

An XML Web service is a specialized program on a Web server that both receives requests and transmits responses in XML format.

SharePoint Designer 2007 can interact with existing Web services when a user includes an XML Web service data source control on the Web pages. This is usually done by configuring an XML Web service as a data source and then creating data views of that data, as discussed previously in Chapter 5, "Creating SharePoint Sites, Workspaces, and Pages."

Every installation of WSS 3.0 provides Web services that can interact with almost any aspect of a SharePoint server, site, list, library, survey, or Web page.

> **Note**
>
> Data views will help your administrator manage the SharePoint sites within the organization. They can create a data view that will display the names and URLs of all subsites in the current site collection, which can be a valuable management tool.

To add an XML Web service as a data source, perform the following:

1. If the Data Source Library is not visible, on the Task Panes menu, click Data Source Library.

2. In the Data Source Library task pane, under XML Web Services, click Connect To A Web Service.

3. In the Data Source Properties dialog box, shown in Figure 10-16, in the Service Description Location box on the Source tab, type the URL for the Web service or click Browse to locate and select the Web Service Definition Language (WSDL) file. For example, *http://your server name/_vti_bin/Webs.asmx?WSDL*.

4. Click Connect Now.

5. The Select Which Data Command To Configure list has several options:
   - The Select command retrieves information from the Web service. You can then display the information on your site by creating a data view.
   - The Insert, Update, and Delete commands also retrieve information from the Web service. However, you cannot create a data view that displays or modifies information that is retrieved using these commands. You can only use a data view to display information that is retrieved by using the Select command.

6. In the Port list, click the application protocol that you want to use for accessing the Web service.

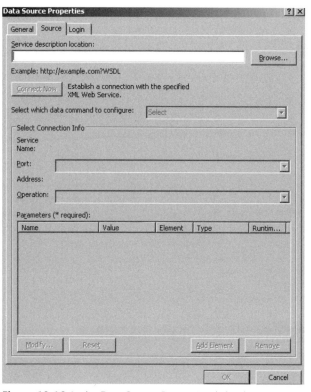

Figure 10-16 In the Data Source Properties dialog box, you can specify information about the new XML Web service.

7. In the Operation list, click the operation that you want the Web service to perform.

8. The Parameters list displays the names of any parameters that the Web service requires or accepts. To configure the permanent or default value of any parameter, click it and then click Modify.

9. Click OK, and the XML Web service will be listed in the Data Source Library.

For more information about WSS Web services, browse *http://msdn2.microsoft.com/en-us/library/ms479390.aspx.*

Adding a Database as a Data Source

SharePoint Designer 2007 can connect to a wide variety of databases including Microsoft SQL Server, Oracle, and databases accessible via the Open Database Connectivity (ODBC) specification. WSS 3.0 does not activate any database connections by default.

Before establishing the connection, the user should have answers to the following questions:

- What is the location of the site in SharePoint on which I am working?
- What is the name of the database server and its location?
- What data provider should I use to access the database?
- What type of authentication should I use to connect to the database?

> **Note**
> A best practices approach for connecting to a database within a WSS 3.0 environment is to do so by using the *Connect to a database by saving the user name and password* method. When you apply this method, SharePoint Designer 2007 generates a SQL-based connection string that stores the user name and password in the data source connection. For more information, see *http://office.microsoft.com/en-us/sharepointdesigner/HA101009081033.aspx#2.*

To add a database as a data source, the user can perform the following:

1. If the Data Source Library task pane is not visible, on the Task Panes menu, click Data Source Library. In the Data Source Library task pane, under Database Connections, click Connect To A Database.

2. In the Data Source Properties dialog box, on the Source tab, click Configure Database Connection.

3. In the Configure Database Connection dialog box, shown in Figure 10-17, under Server Information, in the Server Name box, type the name of the server where your database resides.

4. In the Provider Name box, do one of the following:
   - If you are connecting to an external Microsoft SQL Server 2000 database or an external Microsoft SQL Server 2005 database, select Microsoft .NET Framework Data Provider For SQL Server.
   - If you are connecting to an external database that is OLE DB compatible, including versions of SQL other than Microsoft SQL such as MySQL, select Microsoft .NET Framework Data Provider For OLE DB.

5. Under Authentication, select Save This Username And Password In The Data Connection, because this is the recommended method with WSS 3.0.

6. In the User Name box, type your user name.

7. In the Password box, type your password. Click Next.

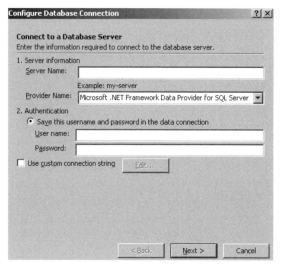

Figure 10-17 Use the Configure Database Connection dialog box to specify the information required to connect a database as a data source.

> **Note**
>
> Because SQL authentication saves the user name and password as text in the data connection, any user with permission to open the site in SharePoint Designer 2007 can view these credentials. A security warning informs you that the user name and password are saved as clear text in the data connection and that other site members can access this data source. If you want other site members to access the database by using the same user name and password, click OK. If you do not want other site members to access the database by using the same user name and password, click Cancel.

8. In the Database list, click the database that you want to use as a data source and then do one of the following:

- Click Select A Table Or View, click the table or saved view that you want from the list, and then click Finish.

- Click Specify Custom Select, Update, Insert, And Delete Commands Using SQL Or Stored Procedures, and then click Finish.

9. In the Data Source Properties dialog box, click the General tab, type a name for the data source, and then click OK. The new database connection will appear in the Data Source Library task pane.

Chapter 10

TROUBLESHOOTING

Single Sign-On (SSO) data connections

Sometimes it can be very difficult to troubleshoot error messages in SharePoint Designer. Single Sign-On does, however, give you helpful information in the SharePoint server's Event Viewer. To find errors, you can search for the app def name in the Description field of Error Events.

Configuring a Server-Side Script Data Source

A server-side script is a small program that sits on the server and runs in response to specific actions of the Web browser, and it can be written in a variety of languages. Unlike a client-side script written in JavaScript, server-side scripts are run on the server in response to user action before the Web page appears in the browser.

To configure a server-side script as a data source, the server administrator must modify the Web.config file of the WSS 3.0 implementation as described in the previous Inside Out sidebar titled "Using an XML Web Services or a Server-Side Script in WSS 3.0."

To add a server-side script as a data source, a user can do the following:

1. If the Data Source Library is not visible, on the Task Panes menu, click Data Source Library.

2. In the Data Source Library, under Server-Side Scripts, click Connect To A Script Or RSS Feed.

3. On the Source tab of the Data Source Properties dialog box, shown in Figure 10-18, in the HTTP method list, select either HTTP Get or HTTP Post.

   o The HTTP Get method appends any parameter names and values to the URL.

   o The HTTP Post method sends any parameter names and values to the URL in the body of the request.

4. The menu Select Which Data Command To Configure contains several options:

   o The Select command retrieves information by using the server-side script. You can then display the information on your site by creating a data view.

   o The Insert, Update, and Delete commands also retrieve information by using the server-side script. However, you cannot create a data view that displays or modifies information that is retrieved by using these commands. You can only use a data view to display information that is retrieved by using the Select command.

5. Under Select Connection Info, in the box Enter The URL To A Server-Side Script, type the URL for the script or RSS feed to which you want to connect.

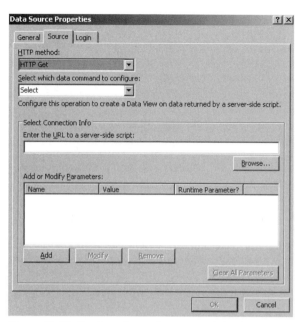

Figure 10-18 The Data Source Properties dialog box enables you to specify information regarding the server-side script that you would like to add to the Data Source Library.

6. Some server-side scripts require additional information that is passed from the browser to the server in the form of parameters. The example I'm providing here does not require parameters. If your server-side script requires parameters, do any of the following as needed:

 ○ To add a parameter, click Add. Then, in the Parameter dialog box, type a name and default value for the parameter.

 ○ To modify an existing parameter, click the parameter in the list and click Modify. Then, in the Parameter dialog box, modify the name or default value for the parameter.

 ○ To remove an existing parameter, click the parameter in the list and then click Remove.

7. Click OK, and the server-side script appears in the Data Source Library.

Configuring a Linked Data Source

SharePoint Designer 2007 enables users to bring together their organization's data when it is stored in multiple locations. You can link data sources that contain interrelated data to one another through a linked data source.

Chapter 10

Creating a Linked Data Source by Merging Multiple Data Sources

If you would like to merge more than two data sources, you can follow the merge data source path for creating a linked data source. Before you can do this, all of the data sources must contain exactly the same fields so that you can merge them into a single source. To merge multiple data sources and create a linked data source, a user can perform the following:

1. If the Data Source Library is not visible, on the Task Panes menu, click Data Source Library.

2. In the Data Source Library task pane, under Linked Sources, click Create A New Linked Source.

3. In the Data Source Properties dialog box, on the Source tab, click Configure Linked Source.

4. In the Link Data Sources Wizard, shown in Figure 10-19, under Available Data Sources, click your first data source and then click Add. Next, click the data source that you want to link with the first data source and then click Add.

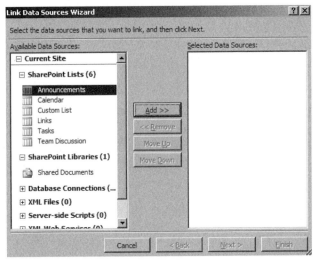

Figure 10-19 The Link Data Sources Wizard is useful in creating linked data sources for the Data Source Library.

5. Click Next.

6. Under the heading Select The Link Type That Best Represents The Relationship Between The Selected Sources, shown in Figure 10-20, select Merge The Contents Of The Data Sources. (The other option, Join The Contents Of The Data Sources, will be discussed in the next procedure.)

7. Click Finish. In the Data Source Properties dialog box, click the General tab.

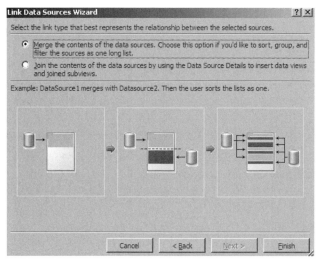

Figure 10-20 The Linked Data Source Wizard assists you in selecting the best representation of the relationship between data sources.

8. In the Name box, type a new name for your data source and then click OK.

9. Click OK, and the new data source will appear in the Data Source Library under Linked Sources.

Creating a Linked Data Source by Merging Two Sources

A user who would like to merge two separate data sources together that have a common field association can perform the following:

1. On the Task Panes menu, click Data Source Library.

2. In the Data Source Library task pane, under Linked sources, click Create A New Linked Source. In the Data Source Properties dialog box, click Configure Linked Source.

3. In the Link Data Sources Wizard under Available Data Sources (refer to Figure 10-19), click your data source and then click Add. Next, click the data source that you want to link with the first data source and then click Add. Click Next.

4. Under Select The Link Type That Best Represents The Relationship Between The Selected Sources (refer to Figure 10-20), select Join The Contents Of The Data Sources By Using The Data Source Details To Insert Data Views And Joined Subviews.

5. If you are joining data sources that are not all database tables, click Finish. If you are joining database tables such as two SQL data tables, click Next.

   If you are linking two tables that both reside in the same database, you will be prompted to choose the field that contains the matching data from each table. If you are linking more than two tables from the same database, two tables from separate databases, or two data sources that are not database tables, skip to step 6.

If you are linking two tables from the same database, then in the Link Data Sources Wizard, choose the field from each column that contains the matching field. In this example, the matching field is *CategoryID*.

6. Click Next. All the fields in both data sources are displayed by default. You can either:

   ○ Remove a field from the data source display by clicking the field in the Display Fields list and clicking Remove.

   ○ Add a field to the data source display, click the field in the Available Fields list, and then click Add.

7. Click Finish. Both data sources, as well as the link type that you chose, appear in the Data Source Properties dialog box. In the Data Source Properties dialog box, click the General tab.

8. In the Name box, type a new name for your data source.

9. Click OK, and the Linked Data Source will display in the Data Source Library under Linked Sources.

Configuring an XML File as a Data Source

SharePoint Designer 2007 enables you to create an XML file as a data source in several different ways. You can:

- Create an XML file in SharePoint Designer 2007 and save it as part of your Web site.

- Import an XML file from a file or folder on your computer or network.

- Connect to an XML file that resides on an external server.

When a user creates or imports a new XML file, a corresponding connection automatically appears within the Data Source Library.

Creating an XML File

When you create an XML file in SharePoint Designer 2007 and save it as part of your Web site, a corresponding data source connection automatically appears in the Data Source Library.

To create an XML file in SharePoint Designer 2007 and save it as part of a Web site, a user can perform the following:

1. On the File menu, click New.

2. In the New dialog box, on the Page tab, click General and then click XML.

3. Click OK. A new XML file with an *XML DOCTYPE* declaration (`<?xml version="1.0" encoding="utf-8">`) opens in your Web site.

4. In SharePoint Designer 2007, position the insertion point after the *XML DOCTYPE* declaration and then press Enter to begin your XML file. After you create your XML file, make sure that the </xml> closing tag is included.

5. On the File menu, click Save As.

6. In the File Name box, type a name for your XML file and then click Save.

Importing an XML File

When you import an XML file into a site, a corresponding connection automatically appears in the Data Source Library.

To import an XML file into a site, a user can perform the following:

1. On the Task Panes menu, click Data Source Library.

2. In the Data Source Library task pane, under XML Files, click Add An XML File. If the XML Files heading is collapsed, click the plus sign (+) to expand it.

3. In the Data Source Properties dialog box, shown in Figure 10-21, in the Location box on the Source tab, type the path to the XML file that you want, or click Browse to locate and select it.

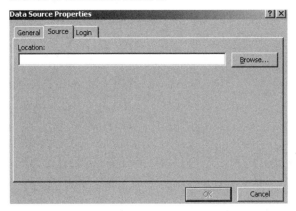

Figure 10-21 An XML file can easily be added to the Data Source Library.

4. When you are prompted to import the file, click OK. Click OK again.

Connecting to an External XML File

When you connect to an XML file located on an external server (unlike when you import an XML file on your own computer or network), you do not import the file to your site. Instead, you link to it directly by using the URL of the external XML file.

1. On the Task Panes menu, click Data Source Library.

2. In the Data Source Library task pane, under XML Files, click Add An XML File. If the XML Files heading is collapsed, click the plus sign (+) to expand it.

Chapter 10

3. In the Data Source Properties dialog box (refer to Figure 10-21), in the Location box on the Source tab, type the URL for the XML file that you want, or click Browse to locate and select it.

4. Click OK. If the XML file resides in a site that requires a user name and password, you are prompted to provide these credentials.

5. The XML file may also require logon credentials beyond those for the current SharePoint site. You might need a user name and password to change the properties or to access the data, for example. If you know that you need additional credentials, click the Login tab, as shown in Figure 10-22, and then select one of the following options:

- **Don't Attempt To Authenticate** This option either attempts an anonymous connection or supplies the current team member's credentials. Select this option if the XML file is not password-protected, or if you want to require team members to use their user names and passwords to access any protected files.

- **Save This User Name And Password In The Data Connection** This option stores the provided user name and password so that anyone can access the file. Use this option if you want to bypass any existing password protection by typing the user name and password in the corresponding boxes.

- **Use Windows Authentication** This option uses the current team member's user name and password. This option works only when WSS 3.0 and the XML file are located on the same server.

- **Use Single Sign-On Authentication** (requires Microsoft Office SharePoint Server 2007) This option can be used when your site is part of a portal site created by using Office SharePoint Server 2007, and when the administrator has enabled and configured Single Sign-On authentication. If you want to use Single Sign-On authentication, select this option and then click Settings. In the Single Sign-On Settings dialog box, do the following:

  - In the Application Name box, type the application name for your database.

  - In the Application Field To Use As The User Name box, type the name of the field in which your user name is stored.

  - In the Application Field To Use As The Password box, type the name of the field in which your password is stored.

  - If you do not have the necessary information, contact your server administrator.

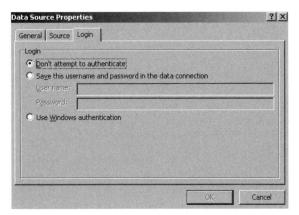

Figure 10-22 A user can specify the logon method of the XML file that is being added to the Data Source Library.

In Summary...

This chapter explained how to create data sources and data views in WSS 3.0. These can be SharePoint lists, SharePoint libraries, external databases, XML files, server-side scripts, and Web services.

The next chapter will explain how to use WSS 3.0 Web Parts and will go into detail regarding their capabilities and how you can get the most out of them in your site or workspace.

Using WSS 3.0 Web Parts

Creating lists, libraries, and data sources that make up a Microsoft Office SharePoint Server 2007 (MOSS) site is satisfying and necessary work, but the real payback usually comes on output. The Web Parts that are loaded within a site's Web Part zones usually determine how popular a site truly will become. Fortunately, Microsoft Windows SharePoint Services 3.0 (WSS 3.0) provides not only the List View Web Parts we have briefly discussed in previous chapters, but it also provides several additional out-of-the-box Web Parts that offer your site a treasure trove of other functionality to meet your exact needs.

This chapter will present the additional set of Web Parts that comes right out of the box with WSS 3.0 and their available functionality.

Introducing Out-of-the-Box Web Parts for WSS 3.0

The next two sections will discuss the List View Web Parts as well as the Miscellaneous category of Web Parts, respectively.

> **Note**
> Generally, the term *List View* is synonymous with *List View Web Part*.

List View Web Parts

If you look for a Web Part called List View, you will not find it. WSS 3.0 creates a List View Web Part whenever you create a list or library. These Web Parts are also automatically added to the home page of a new site after it is created from a site template. For example, when a new team site is created, it automatically contains the Announcements, Calendar, and Links List View Web Parts.

The List View Web Parts are used to display and edit the data within lists or libraries that exist within a site and allow for quick access to these objects. The main component is the List View page. This is the same page that will be displayed if you select a list or library from the View All Site Content page in a SharePoint site.

Add a List View Web Part to a page by using the Add A Web Part command after you click Edit Page from the Site Actions menu. Adding Web Parts to a page is discussed in detail in the section titled "Creating and Configuring Basic and Web Part Pages" in Chapter 5, "Creating SharePoint Sites, Workspaces, and Pages."

Figure 11-1 shows a typical Tasks List View page, and Figure 11-2 shows that same Tasks list displayed as a Tasks List View Web Part within a site. List View Web Parts are displayed in one of two tabular views: the Standard view or the Datasheet view.

> **Note**
> To use the Datasheet view, a user must have a program or control that is compatible with Windows SharePoint Services, such as Microsoft Office Access 2007, as well as Microsoft ActiveX control support.

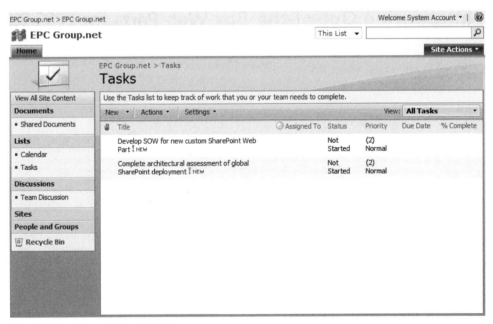

Figure 11-1 A standard Tasks list view page.

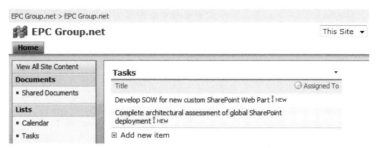

Figure 11-2 A Tasks List View Web Part that has been added to a standard SharePoint team site.

The preconfigured List View Web Parts are as follows:

- **Announcements** This Web Part is great for posting news and other short pieces of information within a site.

- **Calendar** This Web Part is great for tracking events and team members' schedules.

- **Links** Use this Web Part to post hyperlinks to Web pages that interest your team.

- **Shared Documents** Use this Web Part to share files from the default document library with site users. This can be helpful if you want to save users from browsing for content by posting frequently used documents right out on the site for users to download.

- **Tasks** Use this Web Part to assign a task to a member of your team, specify its due date and priority, and indicate its status and progress.

- **Team Discussions** Use this Web Part to provide a forum for talking about topics that interest your team. This Web Part is great for promoting knowledge management within your team and for capturing best practices and lessons learned.

For more information about modifying lists by using a browser, refer to the section titled "Modifying Lists and Libraries" in Chapter 6, "Designing Lists, Libraries, and Pages."

Miscellaneous Web Parts in WSS 3.0

WSS 3.0 also contains another powerful group of Web Parts to use within SharePoint sites. These are in the Miscellaneous category, as shown in Figure 11-3. Access them by clicking All Web Parts in the Add Web Parts dialog box. Alternatively, find them within the Web Part list of the current site's Web Part Gallery, as shown in Figure 11-4.

Chapter 11

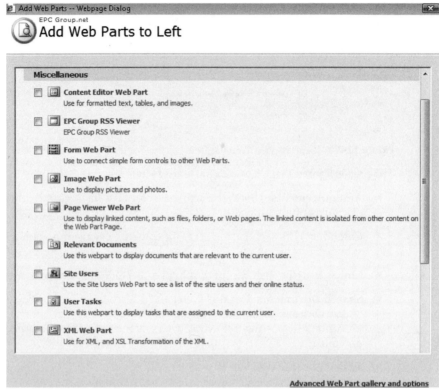

Figure 11-3 The Miscellaneous category of Web Parts in the Add Web Parts dialog box.

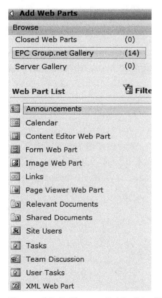

Figure 11-4 The available list of Web Parts in the current site's Web Part Gallery.

The Miscellaneous Web Parts are introduced in Table 11-1.

Table 11-1 **Miscellaneous Web Parts**

Web Part	What It's Used For
Content Editor Web Part	This Web Part can be one of the most useful default Web Parts. It can store formatted text, hyperlinks, images, and tables to a Web Part page. It can render HTML content as well.
Form Web Part	Use this Web Part to connect to and filter a column of data in another Web Part. Both Web Parts must run on the same server.
Image Web Part	Use this Web Part to add a picture or graphic to a Web Part page. To more easily coordinate the image with other Web Parts on the page, you can control the vertical alignment, horizontal alignment, and background color of the image inside the Image Web Part by editing its custom properties in a shared view.
Page Viewer Web Part	Use this Web Part to display a Web page, file, or folder on a Web Part page.
Relevant Documents Web Part	Use this Web Part to display documents that are relevant to the user who is viewing a particular SharePoint site.
Site Users Web Part	Use this Web Part to display or add a list of users and groups who have permission to use a site. The Site Users Web Part automatically appears on the home page of a Document Workspace site.
User Tasks Web Part	Use this Web Part to display tasks that are assigned to the current user of the SharePoint site. The Web Part displays tasks that have been assigned to the user within that particular SharePoint site.
XML Web Part	Use this Web Part to display Extensible Markup Language (XML) and apply Extensible Style Sheet Language Transformations (XSLT) to the XML before the content is displayed.

Each of these Web Parts is discussed in more detail below.

The Content Editor Web Part

The Content Editor Web Part enables users to add HTML content within a Web Part page. You can also use this Web Part to link to different sites and content, because it contains a rich text editor for users who do not have knowledge of HTML and a source editor for those who would like to use HTML code to display content.

It's also great for adding an introduction about the site's department or team or inserting a table on the page to show multiple columns of information.

Chapter 11

Adding Content to the Content Editor Web Part

You can add content to the Content Editor Web Part in three main ways:

- You don't need any knowledge of HTML syntax to use the rich text editor, shown in Figure 11-5, to add formatted content. The Standard and Formatting toolbars at the top of the window have a collection of buttons to help you enter and format the content.

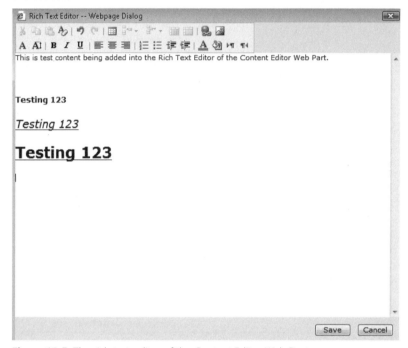

Figure 11-5 The rich text editor of the Content Editor Web Part.

- Use the source editor, shown in Figure 11-6, to enter or modify HTML source code. The source editor is a plain text editor that requires familiarity with HTML syntax.

- Rather than editing content, use the Content link by placing a hyperlink to existing content such as a text file that contains HTML source code. The two valid hyperlink protocols that you can use are:
    - Hypertext Transfer Protocol (with the URL prefix *http://*).
    - Hypertext Transfer Protocol with privacy, which uses Secure Sockets Layer (SSL) encryption (with the URL prefix *https://*).

When working with these hyperlink protocols, you can use an absolute URL or a relative URL. You should not use a file path within the Content link because users on the network will not be able to view this content, and it will cause an error within the Web Part. The content to which the hyperlink points should also allow for anonymous access, or the link may not work properly.

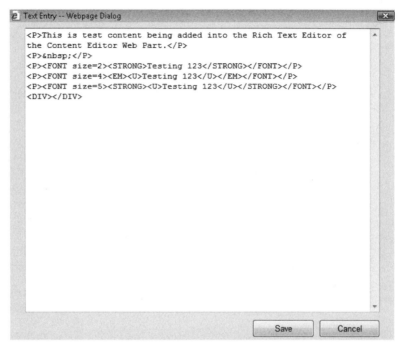

```
Text Entry -- Webpage Dialog                                          [X]

<P>This is test content being added into the Rich Text Editor of
the Content Editor Web Part.</P>
<P> </P>
<P><FONT size=2><STRONG>Testing 123</STRONG></FONT></P>
<P><FONT size=4><EM><U>Testing 123</U></EM></FONT></P>
<P><FONT size=5><STRONG><U>Testing 123</U></STRONG></FONT></P>
<DIV></DIV>




                                            [  Save  ]  [ Cancel ]
```

Figure 11-6 The source editor of the Content Editor Web Part.

Note

The HTML *Form* element is not supported in the Content Editor Web Part. If you need to add a Web Part that uses the *Form* element, you should use the Page Viewer Web Part or the Form Web Part.

TROUBLESHOOTING

Make sure to add valid characters to the Content Editor Web Part

If you are working with the Content Editor Web Part on your WSS 3.0 site, there are times when you may enter invalid characters. This could happen if you edit the Content Editor Web Part by clicking Source Editor and then add invalid characters. If invalid characters are entered, you may receive the following error message: "An unexpected error has occurred." Also, when you visit the SharePoint site, some of the Web Parts may not be properly displayed.

To resolve this issue, you can perform one of the following actions:

- Access the Web Part Page Maintenance Web page by adding the *?contents=1* query parameter to the Windows SharePoint Services site URL. Verify the Web Part, and then click Delete or Close to remove the Web Part.

- Visit the page library for the Windows SharePoint Services site. Typically, the URL for the page library is as follows: *http://SiteName/pages/forms/allitems.aspx*. On the menu of the affected Web page, click Discard Check Out Item, and then click Delete or Close.

- Open the Windows SharePoint Services Web site by using SharePoint Designer. On the menu of the affected Web page, select the Web Part, click Discard Check Out Item, and then click Delete or Close.

The Form Web Part

With the Form Web Part, shown in Figure 11-7, you connect to and filter a column of data in another SharePoint Web Part. For the Form Web Part to function properly, the Web Parts must both be installed on the server running WSS 3.0.

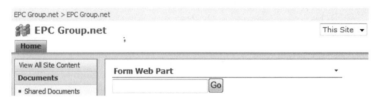

Figure 11-7 The Form Web Part within a SharePoint team site.

This Web Part is great for performing functions like filtering tasks for specific resources in a List View Web Part that contains task information. This Web Part can be customized by adding check boxes, option buttons, and text boxes with default values to be filtered by a List View Web Part that contains specific information that you are looking for, such as project or product information.

Connecting the Form Web Part to Another Web Part

You can connect the Form Web Part to another Web Part by selecting from the Connections submenu in the Web Parts menu (as shown in Figure 11-8). This Web Part can connect to one or more Web Parts within a Web Part page. To perform this action, do the following:

1. If you are not already in Edit mode, on the Site Actions menu, click Edit Page.

2. Click the Edit menu for the Web Part and then point to Connections.

3. Point to Provide Form Values To and then click the name of the Web Part to which you want to link.

After the connection is made to the other Web Part, you can type text in the text box and then click Go. Alternatively, press Enter, and the Web Part displays the data that matches the text you typed. If you would like to perform a new search, you can clear the text box to type in new text by simply deleting the current text in the text box.

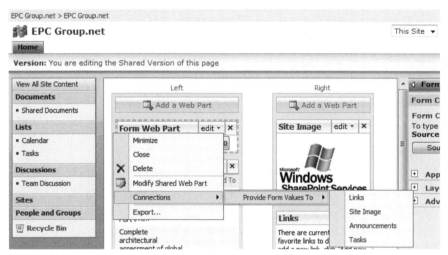

Figure 11-8 The Connections submenu of the Form Web Part.

Customizing the Form Web Part

The Form Web Part can be customized by using either the source editor, as shown in Figure 11-9, or a program such as Microsoft Office SharePoint Designer 2007. You can continue to enhance the Web Part by adding additional Form elements such as check boxes, list boxes, and option buttons. Multiple Form element fields can be created so that a more complex set of filter criteria is passed to the connected Web Part. In addition, each page can have more than one instance of a Form Web Part.

Unlike the Content Editor Web Part, the Form Web Part does use the HTML Form element.

For the Web Part to functional properly, all form field names must be unique because each name value is used to connect to a corresponding column name in the Web Part to which you are connecting.

Table 11-2 provides a list of HTML *Form* element controls that you can use with the Form Web Part. In addition, it shows the values they pass to the other Web Part.

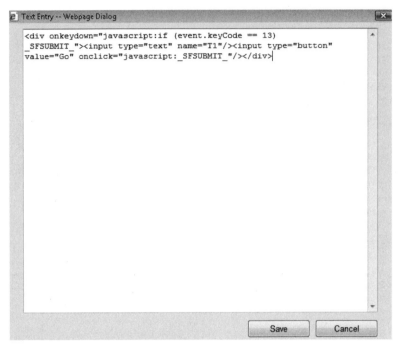

Figure 11-9 The source editor of the Form Web Part can accept HTML Form element controls.

Table 11-2 Available HTML *Form* Element Controls and the Values Passed

Control	HTML Element	Value Passed
Text Box	*<INPUT TYPE="text">*	The Value attribute
Text Area	*<TEXTAREA>*	The Value attribute
Check Box	*<INPUT TYPE="checkbox">*	The Value attribute if selected; the string "off" if not selected
Option Button	*<INPUT TYPE="radio">*	The Value attribute if selected; the string "off" if not selected
Drop-down List Box	*<SELECT>*	A comma-delimited string of the Value attributes of the selected options; the string "off" if no selection (for example, if chairs and tables are selected, the Value attribute is chairs, tables)

> **Note**
>
> The Form Web Part provides data only *to* another connectable Web Part. It cannot get data *from* another Web Part.

The Image Web Part

Use the Image Web Part, shown in Figure 11-10, to add a picture or graphic to a Web Part page. By selecting Modify Share Web Part in the Edit menu, you can control the image's properties—for example, horizontal alignment, vertical alignment, and background color.

Figure 11-10 The Image Web Part displaying the default WSS logo.

This Web Part is great for displaying the logo of your organization or specific department, or possibly a photo of a specific product or employee. This can add a little fun to the site, make it more visually appealing, and help draw users.

Choose one of two ways to display an image within this Web Part:

- In the Image Link property text box, display an image by entering a file path or hyperlink to the image file.

> **Note**
>
> It is important to keep in mind that the file path should not point to a location on a specific user's computer. The permissions at that location should allow for anonymous viewing of the image because the image may not display properly if any security restrictions are in place.

- Display an image by connecting the Image Web Part to another Web Part that provides a file path or hyperlink to an image. This would allow for the image to be dynamic and change as a result of an action that takes place in the other Web Part.

Connecting the Image Web Part to Another Web Part

To connect the Image Web Part to another Web Part, perform the following actions:

1. On the Site Actions menu, click Edit Page.

2. Click the Web Part menu and then point to Connections.

3. Point to Get An Image From and then select the name of the Web Part to which you want to link.

The Page Viewer Web Part

Use the Page Viewer Web Part, shown in Figure 11-11, to display a Web page, file, or folder on a Web Part page. The Page Viewer Web Part must be used in a browser that supports HTML IFrames—for example, Microsoft Internet Explorer—because this Web Part uses an IFrame element to completely isolate the included content from the rest of the Web Part page.

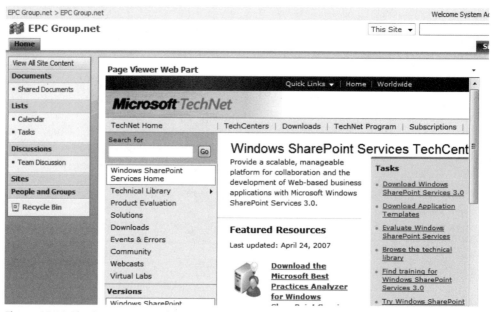

Figure 11-11 The Page Viewer Web Part is displaying content from Microsoft.com within a SharePoint site.

Content is displayed asynchronously from the rest of the page's content, which will lessen the performance risks to the Page Viewer Web Part if the linked content is sometimes slow to load. Use the Page Viewer Web Part to display items such as:

- A Web site or Internet news source that the members of the site frequent.

- A document or spreadsheet that is commonly used on the site.

- A list of workgroup files that are stored on a network server and are used on a regular basis.

The Relevant Documents Web Part

Use the Relevant Documents Web Part, shown in Figure 11-12, to display documents that are relevant to the current user. By default, the Web Part shows items such as the document's name, type, last modified date, and location. It also shows a Properties icon to allow for quick editing.

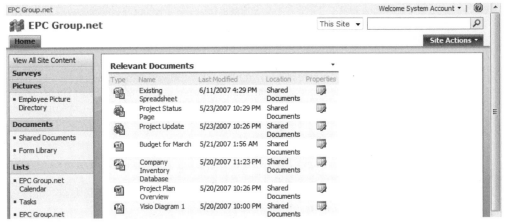

Figure 11-12 How the Relevant Documents Web Part displays a list of a user's documents when they are stored within a SharePoint site.

Within the Data section of the Relevant Documents Web Part's shared view custom properties, specify items such as:

- Whether the Web Part should list documents last modified by the user.

- Whether the Web Part should list documents created by the user.

- If a link to the containing folder or list should be displayed.

- The maximum number of items, from 1 through 10,000, that the Web Part should display.

The Site Users Web Part

Use the Site Users Web Part, shown in Figure 11-13, to display a list of users and groups who have permission to use a SharePoint site. The Site Users Web Part also helps you see information about other users of your site and enables you to click site users' names and view a page that provides information about them. This Web Part is automatically added to a document workspace page, but it can also be added to any other Web Part page.

Chapter 11

Figure 11-13 The Site Users Web Part displays a list of groups that have access to a particular SharePoint site.

A presence indicator will also be displayed next to a user's name if your organization is using an instant messaging service such as Windows Messenger or Office Communicator. By clicking a user's presence indicator, you can send an e-mail message, schedule a meeting, make a phone call, send an instant message, or add the user to your address book in Microsoft Office Outlook or another compatible e-mail program.

The User Tasks Web Part

Use the User Tasks Web Part to display tasks that are assigned to you from within the current SharePoint site. The Web Part displays tasks that have been assigned to you within that particular SharePoint site and does not include tasks that you may have in Office Outlook or Microsoft Exchange Server.

INSIDE OUT   Proper management of tasks

As a best practice, if you would like to manage a task list from both SharePoint and Outlook, you should first start from a SharePoint task list and then connect it to Outlook via the Actions, Connect To Outlook option within a task list.

The XML Web Part

Use the XML Web Part to display XML and apply XSLT to the XML before the content is displayed on a page. The content that is displayed in the Web Part cannot contain the HTML *Form* element. If you need to use the *Form* element, use the Page Viewer Web Part discussed earlier in this chapter.

Use the XML Web Part to display:

- Structured data from database tables or queries.

- XML-based documents.

- XML forms that combine structured and unstructured data, such as weekly status reports or travel expense reports.

Adding Content to the XML Web Part

Add content to an XML Web Part by:

- Using an XML or XSL editor to enter or modify XML and XSLT source code. These editors are plain text editors that are intended for users who have knowledge of XML and XSLT syntax. You can open either of the editors by clicking its button on the XML Web Part tool pane, as shown in Figure 11-14.

- Using XML and XSL links, shown in Figure 11-14, to a text file that contains XML and XSLT source code. The two valid hyperlink protocols that you can use are:
    - Hypertext Transfer Protocol (with the URL prefix *http://*).
    - Hypertext Transfer Protocol with privacy, which uses Secure Sockets Layer (SSL) encryption (with the URL prefix *https://*).

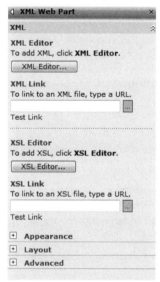

Figure 11-14 The XML Web Part's tool pane provides buttons to open either the XML editor or the XSL editor. A user can also specify a link to an XSL file.

Connecting Web Parts

You can use Web Part connections to enhance your page and enhance the overall user experience. By using menus and dialog boxes, you can connect Web Parts, pass data between them, and synchronize their behavior.

Creating a New Web Part Connection

Connect two Web Parts by performing the following actions:

1. Open the Web Part page.

2. On the Site Actions menu, click Edit Page.

3. Decide which two Web Parts you want to connect. A connection can be created or changed by starting from either Web Part.

4. From either one of the Web Parts, click the Web Part Edit menu, point to Connections (as shown previously in Figure 11-8), and then point to the type of connection that you want to create or change, such as Provide Row To or Get Sort/Filter From. Then select the name of the Web Part for which you want to create or change a connection.

> **Note**
>
> Depending on the complexity of your Web Part connection, you may need to select additional information in the Configure Connection dialog box. The Connection submenu will also vary from Web Part page to Web Part page and from Web Part to Web Part. Only Web Parts available on the Web Parts submenu can be connected.

> **Note**
>
> It is possible to hide a Web Part on the page if you would like to use it to provide data to another Web Part through a connection but not actually display it to other users. You can hide a Web Part by checking the Hidden option on the Layout section of a Web Part's custom shared properties.

Removing a Connection Between Web Parts

Remove an existing connection between two Web Parts by performing the following actions:

1. Open the Web Part page.

2. On the Site Actions menu, click Edit Page.

3. From either one of the Web Parts from which you want to remove the connection, click the Web Part Edit menu, point to Connections, and then select the type of connection that you want to remove.

> **Note**
>
> There will be a check mark on the connections submenu for each selection that has a connection enabled. If a check mark is not displayed, no connection is enabled.

4. In the Configure Connection dialog box, click Remove Connection.

5. When you are prompted to confirm that you want to remove the connection between Web Parts, click OK.

Web Part Gallery Management

SharePoint Web Parts are stored within a repository called the Web Part Gallery. A Web Part Gallery contains all of the Web Parts available to the site. There may be up to four available galleries, including:

- **Closed Web Parts** A collection of Web Parts that is available to a specific Web Part page, but which is not visible on the page, whether you are browsing through or designing the page. Each Web Part page has its own Closed Web Parts gallery.

- *Site Name* **Gallery** The *Site Name* Gallery is often the central Web Part gallery for your work group. This Web Part gallery is typically managed by your server administrator, who decides which Web Parts are available and safe for your site. The name of this gallery is based on the title of your site.

- **Server Gallery** Organizations that have a large number of SharePoint sites and have decided to install the same set of Web Parts on many sites may store Web Parts in the Server gallery. Web Parts can be deployed in a Server gallery by developing a Web Part Package file (.cab).

- **Manage The Web Part Gallery** You can use a gallery of Web Parts to manage the Web Parts that are available to your site and all sites under it. You can add and upload new Web Parts and change certain Web Part properties in the Web Part Gallery. Web Parts added to the gallery are listed under the *Site Name* Gallery on the tool pane.

> **Note**
>
> For more information about deploying Web Parts on servers within your organization, see the Microsoft Windows SharePoint Services 3.0 SDK, which is available for download from the Windows SharePoint Services Development Center on MSDN at *http://www.msdn.microsoft.com/sharepoint*.

Managing the Web Part Gallery

If you have a Full Control permission level, you can manage the Web Part Gallery at the root site of the site collection by performing the following actions:

1. On the Site Actions menu, click Site Settings.

2. In the Galleries column, click Web Parts. The Web Part Gallery page will then load, as shown in Figure 11-15.

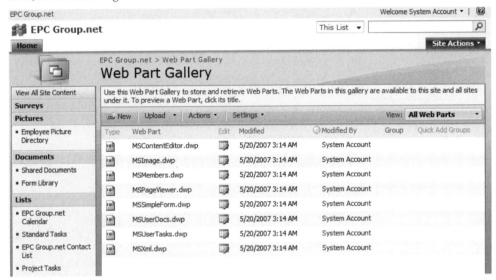

Figure 11-15 The Web Part Gallery from the root site of the site collection.

3. You can now perform any of the following actions:
   - To add a new Web Part to the gallery, click New.
   - To upload a Web Part by using a .dwp or .webpart file, click Upload.
   - To edit the properties for a specific Web Part, click the Edit button next to the name of the Web Part.

INSIDE OUT   Importing and exporting Web Parts within your organization

WSS 3.0 makes it easy for you to import and export proven and customized Web Parts throughout your organization. You can share these Web Parts with other users at your site or even another site. You can export the Web Part from a Web Part page and share the Web Part description file (.dwp or .webpart) with other SharePoint users, who can then import the Web Part to a Web Part page.

Exporting a Web Part

Export a Web Part and share it with other users by performing the following actions:

1. On the Site Actions menu, click Edit Page.

2. Click the Edit menu of the Web Part that you want to edit and then select Export, as shown in Figure 11-16.

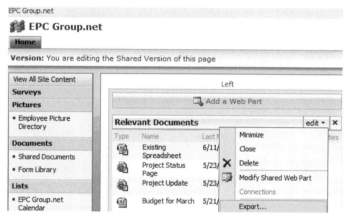

Figure 11-16 Select the Export option within a Web Part's menu.

3. In the File Download dialog box, click Save.

4. Select the location to which you want to save the Web Part file.

5. If you want the file to have a different name, type the name in the File Name box.

6. Click Save.

> **Note**
> You cannot export List View Web Parts.

Importing a Web Part

Import a Web Part by performing the following actions:

1. On the Site Actions menu, click Edit Page.

2. In the Web Part zone that you want to add the Web Part to, click Add A Web Part.

3. Click Advanced Web Part gallery and options to display the tool pane.

4. At the top of the tool pane, click the arrow and then select Import, as shown in Figure 11-17.

Figure 11-17 Select the Import option within the Advanced Web Part gallery to import a Web Part.

5. Click Browse.

6. Locate the Web Part file that you want to import and then click Open.

7. Click Upload.

8. Select the Web Part zone that you want to add the Web Part to and then click Add.

> **Note**
>
> When importing a Web Part, it is important to keep in mind that it will be available only to the Web Part page to which it is imported and not the other pages on the site.

In Summary...

This chapter explained how to use out-of-the-box Web Parts for WSS 3.0. It also covered such topics as connecting Web Parts to one another to increase the overall user experience and Web Part management within your organization's environment. The next chapter will address how to manage the content within your WSS 3.0 sites.

An organization's Microsoft Office SharePoint Server 2007 (MOSS) sites should contain content that will draw users to them and become an integral part of users' daily activities. For this to happen, the content must stay up to date and relevant. It takes only a handful of visits for a user to lose interest in a site or start to feel that it is not relevant if its content is old and out of date.

With Windows SharePoint Services 3.0 (WSS 3.0), images, documents, spreadsheets, presentations, video, multimedia, drawings, and even e-mail may be contained within a site. This content may be structured or unstructured depending on how and where it was stored. In previous chapters, I discussed how important it is to implement a Share-Point governance model within your organization from day one and make sure that it is followed and continues to evolve with your SharePoint enterprise solution. WSS 3.0 champions collaboration and the creation of content within your organization at an explosive pace. That is why it is key to keep the most current and relevant content at the fingertips of the sites' users.

WSS 3.0 gives organizations the advantage of enabling users to perform content up-dates within its interface, which contains easy-to-use authoring tools for creating content as well as the ability to automate some of the publishing processes if necessary.

Prior to SharePoint, many organizations were forced to deal with customized anarchy-style intranet Web sites that contained a mixture of fonts, color schemes, and content that in many cases required the sites' creators to update content. At first, the content on a majority of these old intranet sites is kept up to date, but then after a short time the content begins to grow stale, and the user base begins to fade. WSS 3.0 enables organizations to use internal tools so that sites are not neglected but will actually grow and prosper as the hubs for information sharing that they were meant to be.

Organizations and departments benefit when they are in charge of their own site content and don't have to approach IT every time they want to try out a new initiative or make a change. This empowers your user base to be self-reliant while minimizing IT support calls.

This chapter will discuss best practices around managing a SharePoint site's content so that the site will stay on the minds of its user base, and collaboration levels within your department or organization will remain high.

Keeping Content Up to Date and Relevant

To ensure that content on your SharePoint site is kept up to date, you first need to identify the personnel responsible for performing this task. Will you be the primary resource for updating your site, or will this task be delegated to others? In large organizations, one individual cannot possibly be responsible for ensuring all SharePoint sites are up to date at all times, so power users or content owners must be identified to perform these tasks.

In past SharePoint implementations, I have personally referred to these other individuals in several different ways depending on the organization or type of business. In some organizations, this person is called a power user. In others, the title could be a content owner or even a mall manager or store owner depending on the organization's needs. For example, a store owner might own one subsite within the information technology department's SharePoint site, but the mall manager may ultimately be responsible for the entire top-level information technology site and the content on all of its subsites.

In this chapter, I will use the term *power user* to refer to the person who is in charge of a site or subsite's content and its day-to-day activities and design.

Adding the Right Web Parts to Your Page

In previous chapters, I discussed the available out-of-the-box Web Parts that WSS 3.0 makes available to its users. Most sites will contain at least one list or library; probably they will contain several of each. For example, the Team Site template automatically installs a Shared Documents library as well as Announcements, Calendar, Links, and Tasks lists. The site also contains a Team Discussion board. If you open the All Site Content page, shown in Figure 12-1, for a newly created team site, you see these six securable objects. If you open just the team site, you see the Announcements, Calendar, and Lists View Web Parts loaded on the page along with an Image Web Part, as shown in Figure 12-2.

Will your current site's design meet the needs of your organization or department? You should ask yourself these questions:

- What Web Parts would my users like to see on the page?

- How would my users like to see them on the page?

- Which Web Part zones should specific Web Parts go into?

- What should the names of these Web Parts be?

- Which of the non–List View Web Parts would help present the content I want my users to view?

- Which Web Parts would encourage collaboration on my site?

- Which Web Parts would lessen the load on my user base or help them to finish some of their day-to-day tasks and activities?

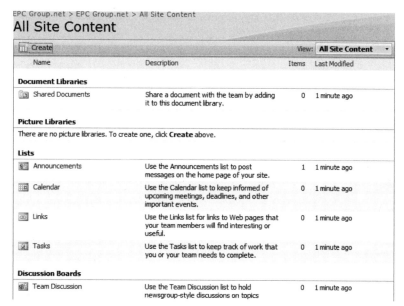

Figure 12-1 The All Site Content page shows the objects that reside in a site.

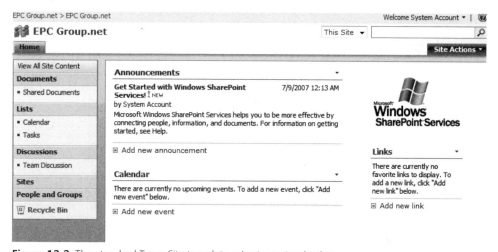

Figure 12-2 The standard Team Site template prior to customization.

- Should I use the Content Editor Web Part to show any formatted text, images, or tables that I want to create quickly?
  - How can I use the rich text editor in the Content Editor Web Part?
  - How can I use the source editor in the Content Editor Web Part to get my content "just right"?
- What type of toolbar should I use for the Web Parts on the page?

For example, if you choose the Summary Toolbar in a Web Parts tool pane, as shown in Figure 12-3, a user would be able to perform actions such as adding a new announcement on the Announcements List View Web Part right on the page, as shown in Figure 12-4, without having to actually open up the list.

Figure 12-3 By selecting the Summary Toolbar on the Announcement List View Web Part, you allow users to quickly add new items to the list.

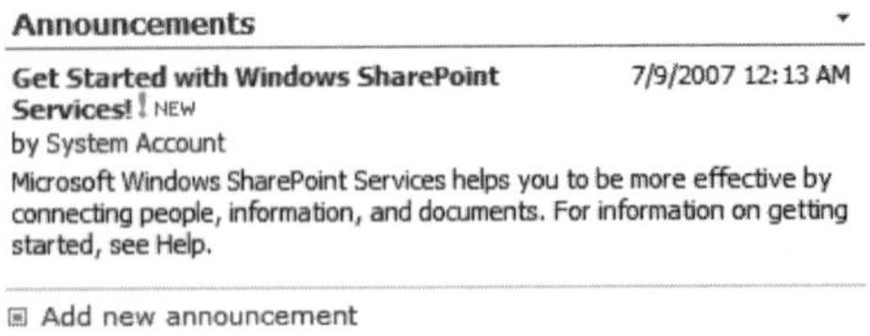

Figure 12-4 With the Summary Toolbar selected, the Announcements List View Web Part makes an Add New Item link available to the user.

You want to avoid cluttering the page with too many Web Parts or too many "bells and whistles" while still trying to keep the sites that you own or manage as consistent in nature as possible. Less can in fact be more in some cases, and a streamlined page can help prevent users from viewing nonpertinent information. Figure 12-5 shows a site with so many Web Parts that a user has to scroll down the page to view all of them. This could be considered a site usability issue.

Gathering your site's design and functional requirements prior to its actual design will assist you in making sure you take all aspects of your users' requirements into account prior to rolling it out to the user base and going into production. You will also want to ask yourself design questions such as:

- How will the site be structured and divided into a set of subsites?

- How will site users navigate through the site?

- How will the site's information be targeted at specific audiences?

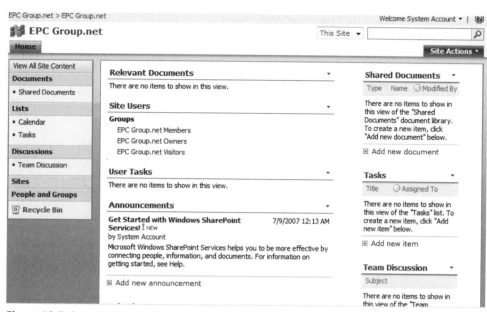

Figure 12-5 Sometimes less is more when too many Web Parts force the user to scroll down the page.

> ## Note
>
> Surveys are a great tool for users to provide constructive criticism and design recommendations to you and the other SharePoint administrators or power users so that improvements can continually be made to the SharePoint environment. See Figure 12-6, which shows an image that is located in a Content Editor Web Part that users can click to open a survey so that they can provide site feedback.

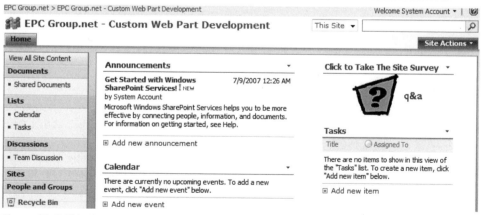

Figure 12-6 This site contains an image located in a Content Editor Web Part that users can click to open a site survey.

Possible Uses for Web Parts

Table 12-1 lists the out-of-the-box List View Web Parts in WSS 3.0 and their possible uses.

Table 12-1 WSS 3.0 List View Web Parts and Possible Uses

Web Part	Possible Uses
Announcements	<ul><li>To let your department or team know about an upcoming event</li><li>To post important breaking news</li><li>To post change management topics about the site, which is great for letting users know if the site will be down for a specific period of time for maintenance or if there are new features being added to the site</li><li>To give accolades to team members for great work they have done</li><li>To announce a management or organizational change within the organization</li><li>To discuss a facilities issue such as new construction or parking updates</li></ul>
Calendar	<ul><li>To post information about an upcoming meeting</li><li>To list your organization's holiday schedule</li><li>To list who is out of the office today</li><li>To track upcoming vacation schedules</li><li>To track paydays for the organization</li><li>To track your organization's training events</li><li>To list offsite team building sessions, town hall meetings, and so on</li></ul>
Links	<ul><li>To track frequently used links that everyone in your department may visit, for example:<ul><li>News sites</li><li>Stock sites</li><li>Partner sites</li><li>Distributors' sites</li><li>Links to internal reports such as SQL Reporting Services reports</li><li>Links to other SharePoint sites, libraries, or lists that are not linked on the Quick Launch or Top Link bar</li><li>Links to file shares within your organization</li><li>Links to other intranet sites</li></ul></li></ul>

Table 12-1 WSS 3.0 List View Web Parts and Possible Uses

Web Part	Possible Uses

Shared Documents	• To place a document library right on the page in a Web Part zone to allow users to quickly view and access specific documents; works great for documents such as:
	  ○ Policies and procedures
	  ○ Human resource documents
	  ○ Document templates
	  ○ Frequently used forms
	  ○ Meeting agendas
	  ○ Popular reports
	  ○ Time off or vacation requests

Tasks	• To place a Tasks list right on the page in a Web Part zone to allow users to quickly view and access task information (doing this can sometimes assist users in getting to tasks more quickly if they realize that the entire department or team knows that a specific task is assigned to them); this also enables project managers to quickly scan a site to see a list of current tasks
Team Discussions	• To place a Team Discussions list right on the page to help promote discussions • To entice users to visit the page so that they see what the latest discussion topic is within their team or department site (users sometimes like to be the most responsive in their group, so this usage can spark competition within a department as users race to see who will be the first to respond to a certain topic) • To have a Team Discussion List View Web Part on the page for sites that are dedicated to knowledge sharing (knowledge sharing discussion boards should be prevalent on the page so that users are not forced to do extra clicking and so that usability best practices are followed)

Table 12-2 lists the available miscellaneous Web Parts in WSS 3.0 and their possible uses.

Table 12-2 WSS 3.0 Miscellaneous Web Parts and Possible Uses

Web Part	Possible Uses
Form	• To filter all employees with the same last name in a List View Web Part that contains employee data • To create custom option buttons, check boxes, and text boxes to filter a List View Web Part that contains product information related to your department or team

Image	• To place any of the following on the page:
	  ○ A company logo
	  ○ A departmental- or team-specific image
	  ○ Pictures of team members or possibly the department or team's manager
	  ○ A picture of products or services that the team offers
	  ○ A fun image to make the page a little less corporate and a little more aesthetically pleasing to the user base

Content Editor	• To create a table right on the page, containing multiple columns of information that users would be interested in viewing each time they visit the page • To place an image on the page with text around it or in a specific format • To render custom HTML content right on the page in a prominent Web Part zone • To give a quick description about the department or team site
Page Viewer	• To have an external Web site load right on the page along with the department or team's other content • To display a specific file right on the page in a Web Part zone • To display a folder on a page that the team members frequent • To display another SharePoint site right on the page
Relevant Documents	• To enable users to always find relevant documents on a page without having to navigate or search within a site • To increase the usability of a site by minimizing clicks that a user must follow to find correct content
Sites Users	• To display the users or groups that have permissions to the site you are viewing • To assist you in quickly adding users or groups to a site by minimizing the clicks necessary for a user to go to the Site Settings page

Table 12-2 WSS 3.0 Miscellaneous Web Parts and Possible Uses

Web Part	Possible Uses
XML Web Part	• To display Extensible Markup Language (XML) and apply Extensible Stylesheet Language Transformations (XSLT) to the XML before the content is displayed on a page
	• To display structured data from database tables or queries, XML-based documents, or XML forms that combine structured and unstructured data
	• To display reports such as weekly status reports or travel expense reports

WSS 3.0 allows for rich, Web-based WYSIWYG (what you see is what you get) editing with support for tables, as well as tools for checking spelling and choosing images. Figure 12-7 shows the Content Editor Web Part's rich text editor's WYSIWYG editing capabilities. Power users can link to important, reusable HTML fragments that serve as building blocks for users who are not that familiar with Web design. Placing the right Web Parts on the page allows users to author their content within the context of the Web page and to view the content layout as they edit it.

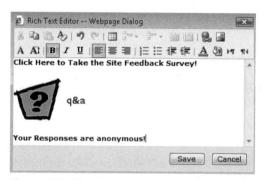

Figure 12-7 The rich text editor of the Content Editor Web Part is a great WYSIWYG editing tool.

Delegating Site Management to Power Users

Power users are key to the success of your organization's SharePoint implementation. Site update tasks must be assigned to a specific power user or users so that site content stays up to date and relevant. A power user should be very familiar with how WSS 3.0 works and have either Full Control or Design permissions (or their equivalent), as shown in Figure 12-8, for the site they will manage. In addition, they should belong to a power users SharePoint group.

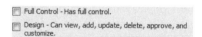

Figure 12-8 The Full Control or Design permissions that power users need.

INSIDE OUT

A few best practices for power users in your organization

As a best practice, your organization should create a dedicated power users security group. It is also a good idea to have a power users SharePoint site so that all the power users can share best practices and lessons learned with one another. This can also allow them to support each other if a specific power user is going to be out of the office or unavailable.

You may also want to empower your power users to train new SharePoint users to use their sites. Giving them the proper training materials, videos, or similar training vehicles to hand off to new users will also lower the costs involved with having IT train new users.

You want to delegate the right type of site management tasks to power users so that you can get the most out of their efforts. Tasks that should be delegated to power users include:

- Managing Web Parts within a site
- Updating the List View Web Parts on the page to make sure the content that is displayed within them—which is what is most visible to the user base—is updated and accurate
- Managing all existing lists and libraries and their content within the site
- Creating new lists or libraries based on new requirements or user requests

When developing your overall SharePoint support processes and model, you will want to determine how much control of the SharePoint environment or specific sites you want to turn over to power users. The preceding bulleted tasks are standard and should be managed by power users. You can also delegate other support process tasks if you feel confident in your power users' SharePoint abilities and that they will follow the organization's SharePoint governance policies. These additional tasks could include:

- Creating subsites within their site or sites
- Managing the user base of the SharePoint site
- Customizing the navigation (that is, the Quick Launch and the Top Link bar) of a site
- Creating new workflows
- Managing Content Types within their sites
- Creating and managing site and list templates
- Managing master pages

It is also possible to allow power users to modify their sites with Microsoft Office SharePoint Designer. This can be a risky endeavor if the power user is not an extremely technical SharePoint user or subject matter expert, and it may be best to reserve Office SharePoint Designer access for SharePoint administrators.

Power users will interface daily with the user population and may receive requests about customization or the possibility of introducing third-party Web Parts or SharePoint solutions into the environment. The organization's overall SharePoint support and governance model should have policies and procedures so that power users can give accurate answers to users inquiring about these types of actions.

Managing Your Site Content

The key to managing your site content is to make sure that you always have your users' experience in mind at all times. You want your users to have a great experience with the site each and every time they visit it. You need to make sure that you do not inundate your users with too many Web Parts on the page while still making sure you have the right ones there for them. Make sure that the content on your site has a clear and specific purpose. It may be useful to have a short introduction or description of the site's purpose in a Content Editor Web Part at the top of the page.

The content on your site should enable users to get their jobs done in an efficient manner and make that work easily accessible to those who need it. Navigation to the content should be concise. If specific content on a site is frequently accessed, it should be right there on the page in clear sight. In some cases, though, less can in fact be more, and it is OK to have a comprehensive list of links on the Quick Launch to specific content so that the main page is not cluttered, as shown in Figure 12-9.

Figure 12-9 This site has a comprehensive list of links on the Quick Launch to all of the lists and libraries on the site.

Graphics on the site should be used appropriately but can be a powerful tool to communicate with your user audience. Graphics should always be relevant to the site's purpose.

Planning Content Administration

Your organization's power users should be empowered and proactive about a site's content administration. Proper content administration planning can drastically reduce the time and cost involved in site content administration. If you can count on your power users to manage the majority of user requests and keep site content up to date, you will have a much more efficient and successful SharePoint environment within your organization. Power users will also decrease the number of requests to an organization's help desk, allowing IT to focus on supporting other systems within your organization.

SharePoint administrators should give the power users a clear set of objectives regarding content administration and overall site support. One of the main goals for power users should be to not only manage and update a site's content, but also to make sure the power users handle as many of the administrative requests for their site as possible without having to get IT involved.

If at all possible, administration tasks for a site's content should be performed on a daily basis. A dedicated power user should be assigned to every site, and this user should be tasked with performing content administration tasks each day alongside other assigned duties.

If a power user is going to be out of the office or unavailable, a backup power user should be assigned to each SharePoint site. Figure 12-10 shows a custom SharePoint list that was created to track an organization's power users, the sites they own, and their backup power user resources.

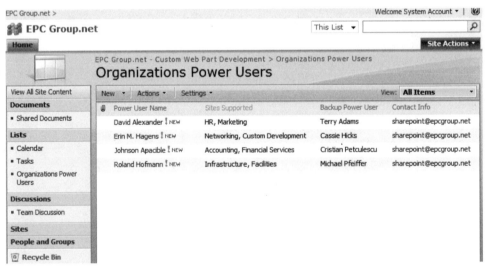

Figure 12-10 A custom SharePoint list created to track the organization's SharePoint power users.

The following tasks should be performed either daily or as frequently as possible for each and every SharePoint site within your organization:

- Review the content in the Web Parts that are within your site's Web Part zones.

- Review the documents in each library to make sure they are relevant to the site.

- Review the items in each list on the site.

- Make sure that all old or expired content no longer displays on your site.

- Review the users and groups on the site and their associated permissions levels.

- Review any open requests that users have submitted about the site.

- To give the site an updated look, update any graphics on the site that may be old or no longer appropriate.

TROUBLESHOOTING

Find out which users have access to specific sites

With SQL Server 2005 SP2 Reporting Services, you can tightly integrate Reporting Services and WSS 3.0. You can develop custom reports to provide a holistic view of your SharePoint environment. This includes custom reports that allow you to troubleshoot many different types of issues such as a SharePoint security auditing report to show you which users have access to specific sites.

Keeping Your Site Relevant

SharePoint is often so popular within organizations that it is important to keep your site relevant, because there will likely be a large number of SharePoint sites competing with it for attention. Some users will use their team or department's site because it is dedicated to their work and daily duties, but you'll still want to keep all users interested in your site's content—even those who *must* use the site. To promote collaboration, you need to keep your site relevant, current, and as interesting as you possibly can.

Site users should easily understand your site's architecture. Users who must search through multiple pages or click multiple links to find the information they're looking for won't be site visitors much longer. A clear idea of what your site is about should be apparent immediately. To keep your site relevant, you should:

- Update the site frequently.

- Make sure that it is easy to use.

- Test the site's search to make sure it is giving users the results they are looking for.

- Review the site's usage to make sure it is being accessed frequently.

- Make sure that site navigation is the best that it possibly can be.

- Ask your users to complete periodic feedback surveys about the site.

- Add content that could be useful to your users.

- Make sure the contact information for power users or SharePoint administrators that support the site is readily available on the site.

- Test all links on the site as frequently as possible.

- Review what other sites within your organization are doing so that you can get new ideas.

- Keep your users informed about what is going on within your team, department, or organization.

- Provide a possible anchor application for your site to draw users to the site every day. This could be a list of today's birthdays, today's employee hire–date anniversaries, or a department contact list.

Managing Subsites

In WSS 3.0, you will have top-level Web sites and subsites to help you divide site content into distinct and separately manageable sites. Your top-level Web sites can have multiple subsites, and subsites themselves can have multiple subsites down as many levels as your users need. For example, an IT department's site may have several subsites such as Help Desk, Development, Database, Network Security, Active Directory, and Hardware Support.

> **Note**
>
> The entire structure of a top-level Web site and all of its subsites is called a site collection.

This type of site hierarchy allows for a main site for the entire team, and individual sites and shared sites for projects or specific initiatives. When you create a subsite, you can determine whether the site is displayed on the Quick Launch of the parent site and whether the site should inherit the Top Link bar of the parent, as shown in Figure 12-11. If you choose not to inherit the Top Link bar of the parent, the subsite will be named Home on the Top Link bar.

Figure 12-11 When creating a subsite, you can choose whether to inherit the navigation elements of the parent site.

Permissions for a Subsite

In WSS 3.0, you can configure a subsite either to inherit permissions from a parent site or to break the inheritance and create unique permissions for the site, as shown in Figure 12-12. In most cases, you will want to inherit permissions for a subsite because that is the easiest way to manage a group of SharePoint sites. The site owners of subsites that inherit permissions from a parent site can edit the permissions of the parent site. Therefore, you must ensure that any changes you make to the permissions on the parent site are appropriate for the parent site and all subsites that inherit those security permissions. subsites will have lists and libraries that can be individually securable objects. By default, these securable objects automatically inherit permissions from their parent. For example, a list or library inherits permissions from the site, and list items and documents inherit permissions from the list, library, or folder that contains them.

Figure 12-12 A site can use the same permissions as the parent site, or it can have unique permissions.

WSS 3.0 enables you to break this inheritance at any point in the hierarchy and assign unique permissions to any of these securable objects, as shown in Figure 12-13. When you break the inheritance from the parent, the securable object from which you broke the inheritance receives a copy of the parent site's permissions. You can then edit those permissions to be unique for the securable object, and they will not affect the parent site.

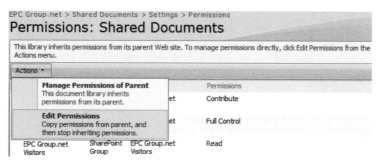

Figure 12-13 Permissions can be broken so that a securable object no longer inherits permissions from its parent.

In most cases, it is best to manage permissions at the site level and design your organization's site hierarchy in a way that allows you to assign site permissions that are appropriate to all securable objects. When you decide to give unique permissions to securable objects in your site hierarchy, you must document and track these unique objects so that they do not cause security loopholes in your overall SharePoint security model.

Chapter 12

In Summary...

This chapter explained how your organization can manage the content within your SharePoint environment so that it is kept up to date and relevant to your user base.

It also discussed how your organization can utilize power users to lessen the burden on the IT department. Power users can also champion their SharePoint sites' content and keep users coming back to their sites frequently. It also discussed subsite management and how permissions and navigational elements can be either inherited from the parent or uniquely managed.

The next chapter will discuss how to install WSS 3.0 and the preparation that must be undertaken for that task.

PART 5

Installing Windows SharePoint Services 3.0

Planning and Installing Windows SharePoint Services 3.0

M ost people who use Microsoft Windows SharePoint Services 3.0 (WSS 3.0) will never actually install the application. They will simply connect as clients, using either a browser or a Microsoft Office program.

If you're a server administrator, however, then installation and system configuration will be something that you must undertake and perfect. You may also be tasked with the technical requirements of assessing needs and architecting the solution. This is just as true for part-time administrators in small organizations as it is for enterprise administrators in large organizations.

If your needs are simple, so is the task of installing WSS 3.0. You make sure Internet Information Services (IIS) is running on a copy of Windows Server 2003 or Windows Server 2008. Then download WSS 3.0 and the .NET 3.0 Framework, install and configure them, and after just a few clicks WSS 3.0 should be up and running at your organization.

If your needs are more complex, the task of installation will be more complex as well. This should come as no surprise. Fortunately, however, none of the additional tasks are onerous. You may need to configure settings in Microsoft SQL Server, create some domain user accounts, create a Microsoft Active Directory directory service organization unit, or run a few command-line programs. Individually, none of these tasks is difficult, and this chapter will provide information about and step-by-step instructions to perform each one.

Planning Your Installation

WSS 3.0 supports a wide variety of system configurations. If you want, you can run all the required components on a single computer, as shown in Figure 13-1. But if you need more capacity or performance, you can distribute these components across several computers, or even dedicate multiple computers to share the load of a single function. If you need more reliability, you can run redundant Web servers or clusters of SQL servers.

User Requests

Web Server
Search Server
Database

Figure 13-1 The architecture diagram of a single-server WSS 3.0 environment.

Even if you don't need these advanced configurations immediately, it's good to plan for them. Your needs, after all, are likely to increase over time. In addition, WSS 3.0 has numerous configuration options, some of which you must choose at installation. You can modify these options down the road if you need to scale WSS 3.0 to your growing organization.

The topics in this section, therefore, provide information and guidance on the major choices you'll need to make during installation.

Requirements Gathering and Planning

For information on requirements gathering and planning, refer to the sections titled "Overview of a SharePoint Enterprise Deployment" in Chapter 2, "Introducing Microsoft Office SharePoint Server 2007," and "Planning a Best-Practices Approach" in Chapter 5, "Creating SharePoint Sites, Workspaces, and Pages."

WSS 3.0 System Requirements

Table 13-1 shows the system requirements for WSS 3.0.

Table 13-1 System Requirements for WSS 3.0

Component	Requirements
Software	Windows Server 2003 Service Pack 1 (SP1) or Windows Server 2003 x64 or Windows Small Business Server 2003 or Windows Server 2008; .NET Framework 3.0; Internet Information Services (IIS) 6.0 with common files, Simple Mail Transfer Protocol (SMTP) service, and Internet service
Hardware	**Single-server installation** Server with a processor speed of at least 2.5 gigahertz (GHz); random access memory (RAM) capacity of 1 gigabyte (GB) minimum, 2 GB recommended; disk space up to 2 GB for installation minimum, 5 GB or more minimum for data **Farm deployment** Server with a processor speed of at least 2.5 GHz and RAM capacity of 1 GB minimum, 2 GB recommended; SQL Server 2000 SP3 (or later) or SQL 2005 system with dual processors of 2.5 GHz and 2 GB RAM minimum; disk space up to 2 GB for installation minimum, 5 GB or more minimum for data
Network	Broadband Internet connection, 128 kilobits per second (Kbps) or greater, for download and activation of products

SQL Server 2005 Enterprise System Requirements

Table 13-2 covers the system requirements for the SQL Server 2005 Enterprise Edition on 32-bit and x64 platforms.

Table 13-2 SQL Server 2005 Platform-Specific Requirements

	32-bit	x64
Processor	600 MHz Pentium III–compatible or faster processor, 1 GHz or faster processor recommended	1 GHz AMD Opteron, AMD Athlon 64, Intel Xeon with Intel EM64T support, Intel Pentium IV with EM64T support processor or faster
Operating system	Windows 2000 Server with SP4 or later; Windows Server 2003 Standard Edition, Enterprise Edition, or Datacenter Edition with SP1 or later; Windows Small Business Server 2003 with SP1 or later	Windows Server 2003 Standard x64 Edition, Enterprise x64 Edition, or Datacenter x64 Edition with SP1 or later

Both the 32-bit and x64 platforms have the following requirements for memory, hard disk, and display:

- Memory should be 512 MB of RAM minimum, but 1 GB or more is recommended.

- Hard disk should be approximately 350 MB of available space for the recommended installation. There should be approximately 425 MB of additional available hard disk space for SQL Server Books Online, SQL Server Mobile Books Online, and sample databases.

- Display should be Super VGA (1,024 × 768) or higher resolution video adapter and monitor.

Choosing the Proper Server Farm Configuration

As mentioned previously, the installation scenarios for WSS 3.0 can range from a stand-alone installation to an installation on several computers in a server farm. A server farm is a group of one or more servers working together to provide unified WSS 3.0 functionality, with each server having one or more roles.

Availability is a measure of how often the application is ready to handle service requests as compared to the total planned run time. WSS 3.0 supports building scalable server farms to increase availability and performance output. Depending on the number of concurrent user requests, an organization's size, and the organization's acceptable service level agreements for downtime, you can determine a level of availability.

An organization should carefully compare the cost of downtime (for example, the loss of productivity, the impact on different teams and departments, and so on) against the cost of additional servers (for example, hardware, licensing costs, administration, and required maintenance). After these calculations are made based on the organization's requirements (for example, high availability and little or no downtime), you might decide that a server farm solution is required.

Two-Server Example

Unless your organization is very small or you want to test WSS 3.0 and implement a proof-of-concept environment, I recommended your organization's WSS 3.0 deployment be at least two computers, as shown in Figure 13-2. Server 1 is the front-end Web server and search server, and Server 2 should be the SQL 2005 server.

User Requests

Web Server
Search Server

Database

Figure 13-2 The architecture diagram of a two-server WSS 3.0 environment.

Four-Server Example

Server farms such as a medium farm or a large farm enable Web and search components to run on separate servers. Medium server farms become large server farms by adding Web/search front-end servers.

Larger organizations can implement server farms such as the following that has four servers (see Figure 13-3):

- **Server 1** Front-end Web server
- **Server 2** Front-end Web server and search server
- **Server 3** SQL 2005 Server (clustered or mirrored)
- **Server 4** SQL 2005 Server (clustered or mirrored)

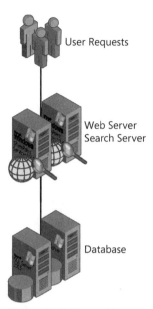

User Requests

Web Server
Search Server

Database

Figure 13-3 The architecture diagram of a four-server WSS 3.0 environment.

Five-Server Example

Larger organizations can implement larger server farms such as the following, which contains five servers (see Figure 13-4).

- **Server 1** Front-end Web server

- **Server 2** Front-end Web server

- **Server 3** Search server

- **Server 4** SQL 2005 Server (clustered or mirrored)

- **Server 5** SQL 2005 Server (clustered or mirrored)

In this topology, the search server is installed on a separate computer. This is the most common topology for high availability.

You can increase the reliability of each server role. The front-end Web servers can use the network load balancing (NLB) services in Windows 2003.

In WSS 3.0, the search-server role includes both the search and index modules. If your organization has a large amount of content (that is, several gigabytes of electronic documents, or other large amounts of content), SharePoint's search performance can be increased by deploying search on multiples servers and configuring each one to crawl and index a different content database.

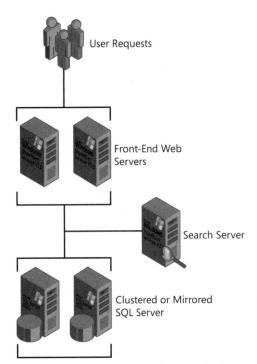

Figure 13-4 The architecture diagram of a five-server WSS 3.0 environment.

Configuring Security

WSS 3.0 security is best managed via a central component of the Windows platform called Active Directory. This service provides organizations with a robust and cost-effective means to manage users' identities and their relationships along with other securable objects that make up WSS 3.0. Active Directory provides single sign-on (SSO) capabilities and a central repository for security information.

Active Directory works with WSS 3.0's new security model and SharePoint groups that control membership, item, and document-level permissions. The following sections detail procedures that you can undertake as you work with Active Directory within your organization.

An administrator can perform the following procedures on a domain controller that runs at least Windows Server 2003 SP1 (with DNS Manager) and Microsoft Exchange Server 2003 SP1. The administrator must also have membership in the Domain Administrators group or delegated authority for domain administration.

Creating an Organizational Unit in Active Directory

An administrator with the appropriate permissions can perform the following procedure to create an organizational unit in Active Directory:

1. Click Start, point to Control Panel, point to Administrative Tools, and then click Active Directory Users And Computers.

2. In Active Directory Users And Computers, select the folder for the second-level domain that contains your server farm.

3. Right-click the folder, point to New, and then click Organizational Unit.

4. Type the name of the organizational unit and then click OK.

Adding Permissions for the Application Pool Account

It is also possible to directly add permissions for the Central Administration application pool account by performing the following steps:

1. In Active Directory Users And Computers, click the View menu and then click Advanced Features.

2. Right-click the organizational unit that you just created and then click Properties.

3. In the Properties dialog box, click the Security tab and then click Advanced.

4. Click Add and then type the name of the application pool account.

5. Click OK.

Planning for Authentication

Authentication validates a user's identity, and WSS 3.0 has built-in support for the following authentication methods:

- Windows (Basic/Digest/Kerberos/NTLM/Certificates/Anonymous)
- ASP .NET Forms (SQL Database/LDAP/Other)
- Web single sign-on (Active Directory Federation Services/Other)

The authentication module in WSS 3.0 is extensible, and you can very easily build your organization's own membership provider to authenticate users against a WSS 3.0 list, for example.

> **Note**
> When WSS 3.0 is installed, only NTLM (NT LAN Manager), Kerberos, and Anonymous are listed as authentication methods. Other methods can be enabled within SharePoint Central Administration.

For Kerberos, Forms, and Web SSO, additional configuration methods are required. For example, the *Forms Authentication* method requires a membership provider and a role manager to be recorded in the Web application's Web.config file and also requires registration of the membership provider in the WSS central administration site. Web SSO requires registering an HTTP module.

A single site collection can use different authentication methods, and this configuration can be accomplished by using zones. Zones represent different logical paths of gaining access to the same physical application. Figure 13-5 shows the different configuration options available in SharePoint Central Administration for a zone.

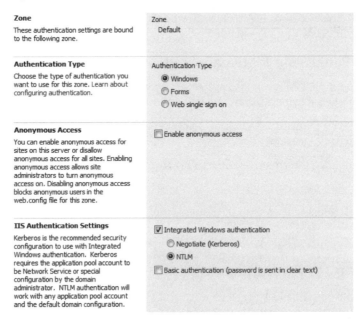

Figure 13-5 An administrator can enable additional authentication methods within SharePoint Central Administration. The zones have multiple configuration options.

Consider a typical zone scenario in which the employees of an organization need access to a department's SharePoint sites both from inside the company network and also from the Internet. Up to five zones, each with its own authentication mechanism, can be configured for a site collection. The built-in zones are:

- Default
- Intranet
- Internet
- Custom
- Extranet

> **Note**
>
> When you create zones, it is important to keep in mind that the SharePoint crawler users NTLM authentication. Make sure you have zones that can be accessed using this authentication method.

Table 13-3 provides a list of the available authentication methods and recommendations for their use.

Table 13-3 SharePoint Authentication Methods

Authentication Method	Recommended Use
NTLM	For internal departments or teams within your organization
Kerberos	For internal departments or teams within your organization with high security requirements (for example, the human resources department)
ASP .NET Forms	For partner companies to access extranet sites
Web SSO	For federated identity management
Anonymous	For Internet-facing portals where content is public

Active Directory Federation Services

Another aspect of Active Directory is the Active Directory Federation Services (ADFS), which enables the secure sharing of users' identity information between different organizations. ADFS provides Web single sign-on technologies to authenticate users to multiple Web applications during a single online session. Two membership and role provider classes are included with ADFS:

- **SingleSignOnMembershipProvider/SingleSignOnRoleProvider** Included with Windows Server 2003 R2; the standard role and membership provider

- **SingleSignOnMembershipProvider2/SingleSignOnRoleProvider2** Can operate in partial trust environments

Planning Users and Roles

A new feature of WSS 3.0 differentiates administrative roles into two tiers:

- **Tier 1** Farm-level administrators
- **Tier 2** Site collection administrators

The farm administrators have control over all the servers in the farm. The following is a summary of aspects of farm-level account planning:

- **SQL Server service account** Use as a service account for MSSQLSERVER and SQLSERVERAGENT

- **Setup user account**   Run the setup on each server, the SharePoint configuration wizard, and the Psconfig.exe and Stsadm.exe command-line tools
- **Server farm account**   Run the application pool for SharePoint Central Administration and the Windows SharePoint Services Timer service; the user on this account will need access to the SQL Server content database

For WSS Search, you should have at least two accounts:

- **WSS search service account**   Run the search service with this account user's credentials
- **WSS search content access account**   Use for crawling content across sites

Table 13-4 provides recommendations for application pool accounts in a single server deployment.

Table 13-4 Recommendations for Application Pool Accounts for a Single Server Deployment

Account	Configuration
SQL Server service	Local system account
Setup user	Member of the local Administrators group
Server farm	<ul><li>Network Service (default)</li><li>No manual configuration is necessary</li></ul>
Windows SharePoint Services search service	<ul><li>By default, this account runs as the local service account</li><li>A domain account can be used if remote content needs to be crawled</li><li>If this account is not changed to a domain account, then the default content access account can also not be changed to a domain account, which prevents elevation of privilege for any other process running as the local service account</li></ul>
Windows SharePoint Services search content access	<ul><li>Member of the Farm Administrators group</li><li>Read access to Web applications</li></ul>
Application pool process	No manual configuration is necessary

Table 13-5 provides recommendations for application pool accounts in a server farm deployment.

Table 13-5 Recommendations for Application Pool Accounts in a Server Farm Deployment

Account	Configuration
SQL Server service	• Database system administrator • A domain account is recommended over a SQL Server account or a local account • No special domain permissions are required • Do not use the server farm account for this account

Setup user	• Domain user account
	
	• Member of the Administrators group on each server where the setup is run
	
	• Member of the following SQL Server security roles:
	  ○ Logins
	  ○ Securityadmin
	  ○ Dbcreator

Server farm	• Domain user account
	
	• When WSS 3.0 is installed, additional permissions are automatically granted to this account
	
	• This account is automatically added to the following SQL Server security roles:
	  ○ Logins
	  ○ Dbcreator
	  ○ Securityadmin
	  ○ Database owner (db_owner) for all databases in the server farm

Windows SharePoint Services search service	• Must be a domain account
	
	• Must not be a member of the Farm Administrators group
	
	• Additional permissions are automatically granted when WSS 3.0 is installed:
	  ○ Read/write to content databases for Web applications
	  ○ Read from the configuration database
	  ○ Read/write to the Windows SharePoint Services search database
	
	• The local service account is used by default; after completing setup, change this account to a domain account

Table 13-5 Recommendations for Application Pool Accounts in a Server Farm Deployment

Account	Configuration
Windows SharePoint Services search content access	• The same requirements as for the search service account
	• Read access to Web applications
	• Permissions are automatically granted for this account when WSS 3.0 is installed
	• Added to the Web application Full Read policy for your farm
	• The local service account is used by default
	• After completing setup, change the local service account to a domain account
	• You can use the same account used by the Windows SharePoint Services search service
	• If you implement multiple search servers for isolation, use a separate account for each
	• I would recommend that you select a unique user account that cannot modify content and is not a member of the Administrators group on your front-end Web servers or on your database servers
Application Pool Process	• No manual configuration is necessary
	• The following SQL Server roles and permissions are automatically assigned to this account:
	○ Database owner role for content databases associated with the Web application
	○ Read from the configuration database
	○ Additional permissions for this account on front-end Web servers and search servers are automatically granted by WSS 3.0 and Office Project Server 2007
	Plan a unique domain account for each application pool (it is recommended that you select a unique user account that does not have administrative rights on your Web servers or on your database servers)

Depending on how your organization's server farm is configured, domain trust relationships could be necessary. There are scenarios in which the perimeter network has its own Active Directory service infrastructure and domain. To authenticate remote users who are using domain credentials (Windows Authentication), you will have to configure a one-way trust relationship in which the perimeter domain trusts the corporate domain. If you are using Forms authentication or Web SSO, this configuration is not necessary.

When the farm has servers installed in both perimeters, if Windows accounts are used, a domain trust relationship is required. The perimeter network will have to trust the corporate network.

Choosing a Database Type and Location

For your WSS 3.0 implementation, the database type is quite simple to determine. Are you using a single server deployment or a server farm? If you are using a single server deployment, then you can either go with the Windows Internal Database or install SQL Server on the stand-alone machine along with the other components.

If you are going with a server farm deployment, then you should choose SQL Server 2005. The question will then be whether you are going to go with just a single SQL Server 2005 server or if you are going to have clustered or mirrored SQL Server 2005 database servers. These answers to these questions can be found in the sections titled "Requirements Gathering and Planning" and "Choosing the Proper Server Farm Configuration" earlier in this chapter.

The database location question can be answered by taking into consideration questions such as these:

- Do you have any high latency and low bandwidth locations that may have problems accessing a data center housing a database server?

- Do you have any disaster recovery policies and procedures that must be followed?

- Are there any backup constraints that should be taken into consideration regarding a specific database location?

As a best practice, your organization should plan disaster recovery scenarios for at least one to two SQL Server database servers to ensure your SharePoint content is safe and secure.

The actual storage location of the SQL Server database files is a completely separate issue that should be managed by your database administrators. Based on your storage requirements, the files should more than likely be stored on a scalable storage network such as a SAN (Storage Area Network).

Configuring SQL Server

Your new database server computer must be running Microsoft SQL Server 2005 or Microsoft SQL Server 2000 with SP3a or later, although I would recommend deploying SQL Server 2005.

The WSS 3.0 setup program automatically creates the necessary databases when you install and configure WSS 3.0, so you don't have to individually create a database. You may need to configure your surface area settings in SQL Server 2005.

For more information on configuring SQL Server 2005, refer to "Configuring a SQL Server Installation" at *http://msdn2.microsoft.com/en-us/library/ms143693.aspx*.

Planning the Content Databases

WSS 3.0 enables you to store extremely large amounts of content within your organization. Several factors are involved in determining how large your content databases should be:

- Disaster recovery requirements

- High latency/low bandwidth locations

- Your organization's current storage solution and its current capacity and limitations (that is, SAN)

An interesting item to keep in mind is WSS 3.0's document file size recommended limit and the system programmed limit. The default maximum file size is 50 MB, and the system limitation file size is 2 GB.

Whenever possible, organizations should try to reduce the number of content databases that support a Web application. It is possible to leverage SQL Server 2005 database mirroring and log shipping to assist with managing a high volume of content databases.

Reducing the number of content databases will more than likely result in larger content databases that host more site collections. With WSS 3.0, you are able to create content databases through the Central Administration user interface or by using the SharePoint Administration Tool (that is, STSADM).

You can also repartition SharePoint content databases as they grow and it becomes necessary to introduce additional data files to support the content's growth and SharePoint's performance. By adding data files, your content database can grow to support additional content through the introduction of new site collections. This can also be done by repartitioning your existing content databases.

If your organization uses multiple data files, your SharePoint databases will have improved performance because your databases can be created across multiple disks, controls, or Redundant Array of Inexpensive Drives (RAID) systems. You can stripe a content database across multiple disks, which will allow more read/write heads to access the data in parallel.

It is better for your organization to go with small content databases around 100 GB or 200 GB and use the manual file growth option in SQL Server. The maximum content database size I would recommend for almost any organization is 250 GB. This will allow for good performance and is quickly disaster recoverable because it will have a single data file and a single transaction log file.

Planning Your Storage Requirements

WSS 3.0 can quickly become one of the most popular places to store content within an organization. Your organization's initial storage needs may vary depending on your requirements, but it is important to keep in mind both your current data volume and an allowance for data and site growth over time. If you plan your server farm only for the initial data volume, it can quickly be outgrown.

If you are upgrading from WSS 2.0 or SharePoint Portal Server 2003, you may have a good idea of what your storage requirements will be for WSS 3.0. If this is a new implementation, you can utilize your existing storage statistics to calculate your new storage requirements. Doing it this way, though, will prove slightly less accurate.

Table 13-6 provides recommendations for planning your organization's storage requirements.

Table 13-6 Planning Storage Requirements

Storage Role/Type	Calculation for Near-Term Future Growth
Current file share or content database	200% of the total size of all documents stored in this location
Index	50% of the total size of all documents included in the current indexes on that computer
Search	100% of the total size of all documents indexed

If your organization's current portal stores 1 million documents with an average document size of 100 kilobytes (KB) for a total of 100 GB of document data, you'll need 200 GB of storage space in the near-term future.

Another way to look at this same issue would be from the perspective of an organization that is not currently using SharePoint and would like to move off of their current file share or storage solution. If your current file share has 100 GB of content, and you plan on migrating that content to SharePoint, you must plan for the 100 GB of space that content will require and the space needed to build the files that WSS 3.0's search builds when it performs its crawls.

Planning Site Collections

WSS 3.0 enables you to store extremely large amounts of content within Site Collections.

It is a good idea to also keep in mind WSS 3.0's recommendations for acceptable performance when planning sites and site collections. For example:

- **Number of site collections** 50,000 per content database

- **Web sites** If sites are nested, then you can reach a lot of sites; the maximum recommended number of sites and subsites is 125 sites with 2,000 subsites each, for a total of 250,000 sites per site collection

- **Subsites** 2,000 per Web site

- **Documents** 5 million per library

- **Library** 2,000 items; indexes should be used to improve performance for large numbers of list items

- **Document file size in your site or site collection** 50 MB is the default maximum, but the system allows the maximum to be set as high as 2 GB

- **List** 2,000 per Web site

- **Columns** 2,000 per document library and 4,096 per list

- **Web Parts** 50 per page; this is an approximate number and depends a lot on the complexity of the Web Parts and on how intensive the operations they made are

When determining how many site collection your organization will require, you should gather specific information:

- How many users within your organization will use SharePoint sites?

- How are the users related to each other in specific departments, teams, or projects?

- What type of content will these sites contain?

- How complex is the content and information you are trying to store and organize?

Based on the answers to these questions and the information you gained when you worked through the section titled "Planning Site Collections, Top-Level Sites, and Containers" in Chapter 5, you can decide how many individual SharePoint sites your organization will require.

SharePoint Central Administration enables users to set site quota limits to determine a site's storage size. Another feature will send e-mail alerts when a site's storage reaches a certain size. See Figure 13-6.

Working with Kerberos Authentication

Integrated Windows Authentication can be implemented using NTLM or Kerberos. NTLM is a challenge/response protocol. When the client tries to connect to the secured application, a challenge is sent by the server to the client. The client will send back a hashed value, which the server will use to authenticate the user.

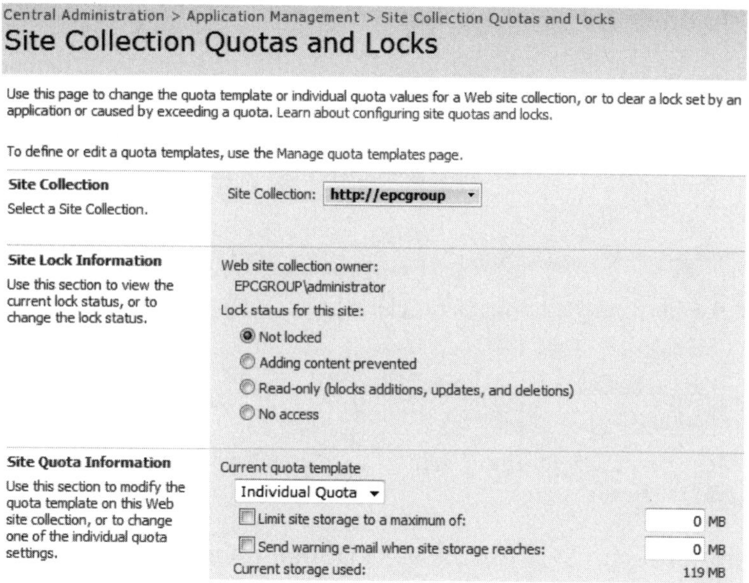

Central Administration > Application Management > Site Collection Quotas and Locks

Site Collection Quotas and Locks

Use this page to change the quota template or individual quota values for a Web site collection, or to clear a lock set by an application or caused by exceeding a quota. Learn about configuring site quotas and locks.

To define or edit a quota templates, use the Manage quota templates page.

Site Collection

Select a Site Collection.

Site Collection: **http://epcgroup** ▾

Site Lock Information

Use this section to view the current lock status, or to change the lock status.

Web site collection owner:

   EPCGROUP\administrator

Lock status for this site:

   ◉ Not locked

   ◯ Adding content prevented

   ◯ Read-only (blocks additions, updates, and deletions)

   ◯ No access

Site Quota Information

Use this section to modify the quota template on this Web site collection, or to change one of the individual quota settings.

Current quota template

Individual Quota ▾

☐ Limit site storage to a maximum of: 0 MB

☐ Send warning e-mail when site storage reaches: 0 MB

Current storage used: 119 MB

Figure 13-6 Set site storage limits and configure e-mail alerts in SharePoint Central Administration.

Kerberos is a ticket-based authentication protocol. Named after the three-headed dog that guards the entrance to the underworld in Greek mythology, it is the favored Windows authentication method for guarding the gates of WSS 3.0. When the client wants to access a secured system or application, Kerberos requires a ticket from the KDC (Key Distribution Center), which can be used only if the client has the correct password. The ticket is then cached and can be used multiple times for authentication against other applications. Kerberos has several advantages over NTLM:

- Faster authentication due to the unique ticketing system (the client can use the same authentication ticket to connect to different applications/systems)

- Mutual authentication because both the client and the service authenticate against each over

- Open standard (Kerberos 5 – RFC 1510) so that Windows clients can be authenticated against other systems that implement the standard

- Support for authentication delegation (also known as authentication forwarding), which is useful when a Web Part solution needs to use the current user credentials to connect to a different line-of-business application or database

- Support for the smart-card logon feature

Kerberos requires additional configuration steps. You need to configure a service principal name (SPN) for the domain user account. In addition, to configure Kerberos, a server administrator must be a member of the Domain Admins group and perform the actions detailed in the following procedures.

Configuring Trust Delegation

To configure the IIS installation where the WSS Front End is located, follow these steps:

1. Connect to the Active Directory as a domain administrator.

2. Start Active Directory Users And Computers.

3. Click Computers.

4. Right-click the computer. Then click Properties.

5. On the General tab, click to select the Trust For Delegation check box. Then click OK.

6. Go to the Users folder. For WSS Application Pool User, check Properties, Account, Account Is Trusted For Delegation.

7. Create an SPN for the accounts modified in step 6 (use the instructions provided in the next section).

Configuring an SPN for the WSS Domain Account

A server administrator will need to configure a service principal name for the application pool user identity under which WSS is running.

> **Note**
>
> If a built-in security principal is used, such as NT Authority/Network Service or NT Authority/Local System, you do not have to perform this procedure.

To configure an SPN, a server administrator will need to perform the following:

1. Download the SPN command line tool from *http://www.microsoft.com/downloads/details.aspx?FamilyId=6EC50B78-8BE1-4E81-B3BE-4E7AC4F0912D&displaylang=en*.

2. Create the SPN for the domain account by opening the command prompt and typing the appropriate setspn.exe command.

Configuring an Existing Web Application

In case you need to enable Kerberos on an existing Web application, you must configure an SPN for the application pool user and after that, enable Kerberos for your Web application. To enable Kerberos for a Web application, a server administrator with the appropriate permissions must open the command prompt and type:

```
cscript c:\inetpub\adminscripts\adsutil.vbs set w3svc/1/root/

NTAuthenticationProviders "Negotiate,NTLM"
```

> **Note**
>
> Between *w3svc/* and */root/*, you must fill in the IIS virtual server ID (that is, your Web application). In this case, it is 1. You can find the ID for your Web application by opening the Web Sites folder in IIS Manager and looking in the Identifier column.

Enabling Kerberos for a Web application will allow IIS to authenticate users with Kerberos or NTLM authentication. If you remove NTLM, users who cannot see the KDC or who have unsynchronized clocks will not be able to authenticate.

Installing WSS 3.0 on a Stand-Alone (Single) Server

WSS 3.0 can be quickly and easily installed on a single server computer so that you and your organization can start to publish SharePoint sites in a very short amount of time. Before you start installing SharePoint on a single server, you should know that a direct upgrade from a stand-alone installation to a farm installation is not available. But if upgrading is never going to be on your horizon and will never become an issue, then the installation process can be quite painless.

A stand-alone configuration can be useful for organizations that want a proof-of-concept of WSS 3.0's features and capabilities around collaboration, document management, and search. Also, if this implementation is going to be for a small organization that doesn't have a large budget and that has a small number of sites, a stand-alone configuration can work well.

When you deploy WSS 3.0 on a single server using the default settings, the setup program automatically installs the Windows Internal Database and uses it to create the configuration database and content database for your SharePoint sites. Windows Internal Database uses SQL Server technology as a relational data store for Windows roles and features only, such as Windows SharePoint Services; Active Directory Rights Management Services; Universal Description, Discovery, and Integration (UDDI) Services; Windows Server Update Services; and Windows System Resources Manager. In addition, setup installs the SharePoint Central Administration Web site and creates your first SharePoint site collection and site.

Installing the Stand-Alone Prerequisites

To install and configure WSS 3.0, you must first install or enable the required software. This includes the installation and configuration of IIS so that your computer acts as a Web server, the installation of Microsoft .NET Framework version 3.0, and enabling ASP.NET 2.0.

Note

Internet Information Services (IIS) is not installed or enabled by default in the Windows Server 2003 operating system. For users who are running Microsoft Windows Server 2008, please go to *http://www.microsoft.com* to download the installation and configuration instructions.

Installing and Configuring IIS for Windows Server 2003 in a Stand-Alone Deployment

Windows Server 2003 server administrators can easily install and configure IIS by performing the following steps:

1. Click Start, point to All Programs, point to Administrative Tools, and then click Configure Your Server Wizard.

2. On the Welcome To The Configure Your Server Wizard page, click Next.

3. On the Preliminary Steps page, click Next.

4. On the Server Role page, click Application Server (IIS, ASP.NET) and then click Next.

5. On the Application Server Options page, click Next.

6. On the Summary Of Selections page, click Next.

7. Click Finish.

Now that IIS is installed, you need to tweak its configuration.

1. Click Start, point to All Programs, point to Administrative Tools, and then click Internet Information Services (IIS) Manager.

2. In the IIS Manager tree, click the plus sign (+) next to the server name, right-click the Web Sites folder, and then click Properties.

3. In the Web Sites Properties dialog box, click the Service tab.

4. In the Isolation mode section, clear the Run WWW Service In IIS 5.0 Isolation Mode check box and then click OK.

This completes the installation and configuration of IIS. You will now need to install the Microsoft .NET 3.0 Framework as detailed in the following section.

Installing the Microsoft .NET Framework Version 3.0 in a Stand-Alone Deployment

Windows Server 2003 does not have the Microsoft .NET 3.0 Framework installed by default, so the following procedure must be completed prior to installing WSS 3.0.

Windows Server 2003 server administrators can easily install and configure the Microsoft .NET 3.0 Framework by performing the following steps:

1. Open a Web browser and go to the Microsoft Download Center Web site, which is located at *http://go.microsoft.com/fwlink/?LinkID=72322&clcid=0x409*.

2. On the Microsoft .NET Framework 3.0 Redistributable Package page, click the Download button to start the download bootstrapper. The bootstrapper will save the correct package to your computer.

> **Note**
>
> Microsoft provides separate packages for x86-based computers and x64-based computers. The download bootstrapper should automatically download the correct version for your system. If it does not, you can use the provided links to directly download the correct redistributable package.

3. Open the downloaded package by double-clicking it. You may be shown the Welcome To Setup screen, which will ask you to accept the terms of the license agreement. After you accept the license agreement, click Install to complete the installation.

> **Note**
>
> The .NET Framework version 3.0 download also contains the Windows Workflow Foundation technology, which is required by workflow features.

Enabling ASP.NET 2.0 in a Stand-Alone Deployment

A Windows Server 2003 server administrator will now need to enable ASP.NET 2.0, which is required for proper functioning of Web content, of the Central Administration Web site, and of many other features and functions of WSS 3.0. A Windows Server 2003 server administrator can enable ASP.NET 3.0 by performing the following actions:

1. Click Start, point to All Programs, point to Administrative Tools, and then click Internet Information Services (IIS) Manager.

2. In the Internet Information Services tree, click the plus sign (+) next to the server name and then click the Web Service Extensions folder.

3. In the details pane, right-click ASP.NET v2.0.50727 and then click Allow.

Configuring WSS 3.0 for a Stand-Alone Deployment by Using Windows Internal Database

You will now need to run the WSS 3.0 setup program using the Basic option. This option uses the setup program's default parameters to install WSS 3.0 and the Windows Internal Database on a single server.

INSIDE OUT   **Reinstallation woes: Uninstalling WSS 3.0 and reinstalling it later on the same computer**

If you uninstall WSS 3.0 and then later install WSS 3.0 on the same computer, the setup program could fail when creating the configuration database. This could cause the entire installation process to fail. You can prevent this failure by either deleting all the existing WSS 3.0 databases on the computer or by creating a new configuration database. You can create this new configuration database by running the following command from a command prompt: **psconfig -cmd configdb -create -database <uniquename>**.

A server administrator can install and configure WSS 3.0 by performing the following actions:

1. Open a Web browser and go to *http://www.microsoft.com/technet/windowsserver/ sharepoint/download.mspx*.

2. On the Download Windows SharePoint Services 3.0 page, download the appropriate WSS 3.0 installation file from the box of links at the right.

3. To run the setup program, open the WSS 3.0 file that you downloaded by double-clicking it.

4. On the Read The Microsoft License Terms page, review the terms, select the I Accept The Terms Of This Agreement check box, and then click Continue.

5. On the Choose The Installation You Want page, click Basic to install to the default location. To install to a different location, click Advanced and then on the Data Location tab, specify the location you want to install to and finish the installation.

6. When setup finishes, a dialog box prompts you to complete the configuration of your server. Be sure that the Run The SharePoint Products And Technologies Configuration Wizard Now check box is selected.

7. Click Close to start the configuration wizard.

The Configuration Wizard in a Stand-Alone Deployment

When the configuration wizard loads, perform the following actions:

1. On the Welcome To SharePoint Products And Technologies page, click Next.

2. In the dialog box that notifies you that some services might need to be restarted or reset during configuration, click Yes.

3. On the Configuration Successful page, click Finish. Your new SharePoint site opens.

> **Note**
>
> If you are prompted for your user name and password, you might need to add the SharePoint site to the list of trusted sites and configure user authentication settings in Microsoft Internet Explorer. Instructions for configuring these settings are provided in the following procedure.

> **Note**
>
> If you see a proxy server error message, you might need to configure your proxy server settings so that local addresses bypass the proxy server. Instructions for configuring proxy server settings are provided later in this section.

Adding a Site to Trusted Sites

You should add the new SharePoint site to the list of trusted sites in Internet Explorer versions 6 and 7. You can do so by performing the following actions:

1. In Internet Explorer, on the Tools menu, click Internet Options.

2. On the Security tab, in the Select A Zone To View Or Change Security Settings box, click Trusted Sites and then click Sites.

3. Clear the Require Server Verification (Https:) For All Sites In This Zone check box.

4. In the Add This Website To The Zone box, type the URL to your site and then click Add.

5. Click Close to close the Trusted Sites dialog box.

6. Click OK to close the Internet Options dialog box.

> **Note**
>
> If you are using a proxy server, follow the steps in the next section to configure Internet Explorer to bypass the proxy server for local addresses.

Bypassing the Proxy Server for Local Addresses

You should now configure Internet Explorer to bypass the proxy server for local Web addresses. This can be accomplished by performing the following actions:

1. In Internet Explorer versions 6 or 7, on the Tools menu, click Internet Options.

2. On the Connections tab, in the Local Area Network (LAN) settings area, click LAN Settings.

3. In the Automatic Configuration section, clear the Automatically Detect Settings check box.

4. In the Proxy Server section, select the Use A Proxy Server For Your LAN check box.

5. In the Address box, type the address of the proxy server.

6. In the Port box, type the port number of the proxy server.

7. Select the Bypass Proxy Server For Local Addresses check box.

8. Click OK to close the Local Area Network (LAN) Settings dialog box.

9. Click OK to close the Internet Options dialog box.

WSS 3.0 Postinstallation Tasks in a Stand-Alone Deployment

After you have finished running WSS 3.0's setup, your browser window will open the home page of your new SharePoint site. It is possible to start adding content right away, but it is best to perform the following administrative tasks before you start to use Share-Point. Use the SharePoint Central Administration Web site to perform the following tasks:

- **Configure incoming e-mail settings** Configure incoming e-mail settings so that SharePoint sites accept and archive incoming e-mail.

- **Configure outgoing e-mail settings** Configure outgoing e-mail settings so that your Simple Mail Transfer Protocol (SMTP) server will send e-mail alerts to Share-Point site users and notifications to site administrators.

- **Configure diagnostic logging settings** Configure several diagnostic logging settings to help with troubleshooting SharePoint.

- **Configure antivirus protection settings** Configure antivirus settings if you have an antivirus program that is designed for WSS 3.0. Antivirus settings enable you to control whether documents are scanned on upload or download, and whether users can download infected documents.

After WSS 3.0 setup finishes, one Web application that was created will contain a single SharePoint site collection. This Web application will host a SharePoint site, and you have the option of creating more SharePoint site collections, sites, and Web applications to meet your organization's requirements.

Installing WSS 3.0 for a Server Farm Deployment

Before installing WSS 3.0 on a server, you should verify that:

- The computer is running Microsoft Windows Server 2003 or Microsoft Windows Server 2008. Standard, Enterprise, Datacenter, and Web editions are all acceptable.

- The computer is running Internet Information Services (IIS) in IIS 6.0 Worker Process Isolation mode.

- The computer is running ASP.NET 1.1 or later.

- The computer is using the NTFS file system.

The client computers must be running Internet Explorer 5.01 or later or Netscape Navigator 6.2 or later to use WSS 3.0 features. Of course, the most recent release available of Internet Explorer will get the best results.

> **Note**
>
> Windows Server 2003 includes a utility named convert.exe that converts an existing file allocation table (FAT) volume to NTFS without loss of data.

Installing and Configuring IIS for Windows Server 2003 in a Farm Deployment

Windows Server 2003 server administrators can easily install and configure IIS by performing the following steps:

1. Click Start, point to All Programs, point to Administrative Tools, and then click Configure Your Server Wizard.

2. On the Welcome To The Configure Your Server Wizard page, click Next.

3. On the Preliminary Steps page, click Next.

4. On the Server Role page, click Application Server (IIS, ASP.NET) and then click Next.

5. On the Application Server Options page, click Next.

6. On the Summary Of Selections page, click Next.

7. Click Finish.

Now that IIS is installed, you need to tweak its configuration.

1. Click Start, point to All Programs, point to Administrative Tools, and then click Internet Information Services (IIS) Manager.

2. In the IIS Manager tree, click the plus sign (+) next to the server name, right-click the Web Sites folder, and then click Properties.

3. In the Web Sites Properties dialog box, click the Service tab.

4. In the Isolation mode section, clear the Run WWW Service In IIS 5.0 Isolation Mode check box and then click OK.

This completes the installation and configuration of IIS. You will now need to install the Microsoft .NET 3.0 Framework, as detailed in the following section.

> **Note**
>
> IIS is not installed or enabled by default in the Windows Server 2003 operating system. For users who are running Windows Server 2008, please go to *http://www.microsoft.com* to download the installation and configuration instructions.

.NET 3.0 Framework and ASP.NET 2.0

The Microsoft .NET Framework 3.0 is the new managed-code programming model for Windows. It combines the power of the .NET Framework version 2.0 with new technologies for building applications that have visually compelling user experiences, seamless communication across technology boundaries, and the ability to support a wide range of business processes. These new technologies are Windows Presentation Foundation, Windows Communication Foundation, Windows Workflow Foundation, and Windows CardSpace.

Installing the Microsoft .NET Framework Version 3.0 in a Farm Deployment

Windows Server 2003 does not have the Microsoft .NET 3.0 Framework installed by default, so you must complete installation of .NET Framework prior to installing WSS 3.0. Windows Server 2003 server administrators can easily install and configure the Microsoft .NET 3.0 Framework by performing the following steps:

1. Open a Web browser and go to the Microsoft Download Center Web site, which is located at *http://go.microsoft.com/fwlink/?LinkID=72322&clcid=0x409*.

2. On the Microsoft .NET Framework 3.0 Redistributable Package page, click the Download button to start the download bootstrapper. The bootstrapper will save the correct package to your computer.

> **Note**
>
> Microsoft provides separate packages for x86-based computers and x64-based computers. The download bootstrapper should automatically download the correct version for your system. If it does not, you can use the provided links to directly download the correct redistributable package.

3. Open the downloaded package by double-clicking it. You may be shown the Welcome To Setup screen, which will ask you to accept the terms of the license agreement. After you accept the license agreement, click Install to complete the installation.

> **Note**
>
> The .NET Framework version 3.0 download also contains the Windows Workflow Foundation technology, which is required by workflow features.

Enabling ASP.NET 2.0 in a Farm Deployment

A Windows Server 2003 server administrator will now need to enable ASP.NET 2.0, which is required for proper functioning of Web content, of the Central Administration Web site, and of many other features and functions of WSS 3.0. To enable ASP.NET 3.0, a Windows Server 2003 server administrator can perform the following actions:

1. Click Start, point to All Programs, point to Administrative Tools, and then click Internet Information Services (IIS) Manager.

2. In the Internet Information Services tree, click the plus sign (+) next to the server name and then click the Web Service Extensions folder.

3. In the details pane, right-click ASP.NET v2.0.50727 and then click Allow.

Configuring WSS 3.0 for Use with SQL Server 2005 in a Farm

Once you have prepared the servers you are going to use for your WSS 3.0 implementation, you can run WSS 3.0's setup program and then run the SharePoint Products And Technologies Configuration Wizard on all your farm servers. WSS 3.0 is very scalable, and it enables you to add redundancy by adding servers to the farm at any time—for example, additional load-balanced Web servers.

As a best practice, you should install and configure WSS 3.0 on all of your farm servers before you configure WSS 3.0 services and start to create sites. Also, the SQL Server 2005 database must be up and running on at least one back-end database server before you install WSS 3.0 on your farm servers. A server administrator can configure WSS 3.0 for use with SQL Server 2005 in a farm by performing the following actions:

1. Open a Web browser and go to *http://www.microsoft.com/technet/windowsserver/sharepoint/download.mspx*.

2. On the Download Windows SharePoint Services 3.0 page, download the appropriate WSS 3.0 installation file from the box of links at the right.

3. To run the setup program, double-click the WSS 3.0 file that you downloaded.

4. On the Read The Microsoft Software License Terms page, review the terms, select the I Accept The Terms Of This Agreement check box, and then click Continue.

5. On the Choose The Installation You Want page, click Advanced.

6. On the Server Type tab, click Web Front End. The Stand-Alone option is for stand-alone installations.

7. Optionally, to install Windows SharePoint Services 3.0 at a custom location, select the Data Location tab and then type the location name or browse to the location.

8. Optionally, to participate in the Customer Experience Improvement Program, select the Feedback tab and select the option you want. To learn more about the program, click the link. You must have an Internet connection to view the program information.

9. When you have chosen the correct options, click Install Now.

10. When setup finishes, a dialog box appears that prompts you to complete the configuration of your server. Be sure that the Run The SharePoint Products And Technologies Configuration Wizard Now check box is selected.

11. Click Close to start the configuration wizard. Instructions for completing this wizard are provided in the following procedure.

The Configuration Wizard in a Farm Deployment

Once setup is complete, the SharePoint Products And Technologies Configuration Wizard will load to assist you in configuring WSS 3.0. The wizard automates several configuration tasks including installing and configuring the configuration database, installing WSS 3.0 services, and creating the Central Administration Web site. When the configuration wizard loads, perform the following actions:

1. On the Welcome To SharePoint Products And Technologies page, click Next.

2. In the dialog box that notifies you that some services might need to be restarted during configuration, click Yes.

3. On the Connect To A Server Farm page, click No, I Want To Create A New Server Farm and then click Next. In the Specify Configuration Database Settings dialog box, in the Database Server box, type the name of the computer that is running SQL Server.

4. Type a name for your configuration database in the Database Name box, or use the default database name. The default name is SharePoint_Config.

5. In the User Name box, type the user name of the server-farm account. (Be sure to type the user name in the format DOMAIN\username.) In the Password box, type the user's password and then click Next.

6. On the Configure SharePoint Central Administration Web Application page, select the Specify Port Number check box. Type a port number if you want the SharePoint Central Administration Web application to use a specific port. If you do not care which port number the SharePoint Central Administration Web application uses, you can leave the Specify Port Number check box cleared.

7. In the Configure SharePoint Central Administration Web Application dialog box, do one of the following:

   ○ If you want to use NTLM authentication (the default), click Next.

   ○ If you want to use Kerberos authentication, click Negotiate (Kerberos) and then click Next.

8. On the Completing The SharePoint Products And Technologies Configuration Wizard page, click Next.

9. On the Configuration Successful page, click Finish.

Adding a Site to Trusted Sites for a Farm Deployment

You should add the new SharePoint site to the list of Trusted Sites in Internet Explorer. This can be accomplished by performing the following:

1. In Internet Explorer, on the Tools menu, click Internet Options.

2. On the Security tab, in the Select A Web Content Zone To Specify Its Security Settings box, click Trusted Sites and then click Sites.

3. Clear the Require Server Verification (Https:) For All Sites In This Zone check box.

4. In the Add This Website To The Zone box, type the URL to your site and then click Add.

5. Click Close to close the Trusted Sites dialog box.

6. Click OK to close the Internet Options dialog box.

Bypassing the Proxy Server for Local Addresses for a Farm Deployment

You should now configure Internet Explorer to bypass the proxy server for local Web addresses. This can be accomplished by performing the following actions:

1. In Internet Explorer, on the Tools menu, click Internet Options.

2. On the Connections tab, in the Local Area Network (LAN) settings area, click LAN Settings.

3. In the Automatic Configuration section, clear the Automatically Detect Settings check box.

4. In the Proxy Server section, select the Use A Proxy Server For Your LAN check box.

5. In the Address box, type the address of the proxy server.

6. In the Port box, type the port number of the proxy server.

7. Select the Bypass Proxy Server For Local Addresses check box.

8. Click OK to close the Local Area Network (LAN) Settings dialog box.

9. Click OK to close the Internet Options dialog box.

Adding New Servers to the Farm

If your organization's WSS 3.0 implementation's requirements have expanded, you may need to add additional servers to your existing farm. This can be easily accomplished by running the same setup program that was run when you first configured WSS 3.0. An administrator can add a new server to the farm by performing the following actions:

1. Run the setup program.

2. On the Read The Microsoft Software License Terms page, review the terms, select the I Accept The Terms Of This Agreement check box, and then click Continue.

3. On the Choose The Installation You Want page, click Advanced. The Basic option is for stand-alone installations.

4. On the Server Type tab, click Web Front End. The Stand-Alone option is for stand-alone installations.

5. Optionally, to install WSS 3.0 at a custom location, select the Data Location tab and then type the location name or browse to the location.

6. Optionally, to participate in the Customer Experience Improvement Program, select the Feedback tab and select the option you want. To learn more about the program, click the link. You must have an Internet connection to view the program information.

7. When you have chosen the correct options, click Install Now.

8. When setup finishes, a dialog box appears that prompts you to complete the configuration of your server. Be sure that the Run The SharePoint Products And Technologies Configuration Wizard is not checked if you are finished adding additional servers.

Preparing Search Servers

An administrator must start the WSS Search service on every computer that you want to search content. You must start it on at least one of your servers.

Starting the Windows SharePoint Services Search Service

To start the WSS 3.0 search service, an administrator can perform the following actions:

1. On the SharePoint Central Administration home page, click the Operations tab on the Top Link bar.

2. On the Operations page, in the Topology And Services section, click Servers In Farm.

3. On the Servers In Farm page, click the server on which you want to start the Windows SharePoint Services Search service.

4. Next to Windows SharePoint Services Search, click Start.

5. On the Configure Windows SharePoint Services Search Service Settings page, in the Service Account section, specify the user name and password for the user account under which the Search service will run.

6. In the Content Access Account section, specify the user name and password for the user account that the Search service will use to search over content. This account must have read access to all the content you want it to index. If you do not enter credentials, the same account used for the Search service will be used.

7. In the Indexing Schedule section, either accept the default settings or specify the schedule that you want the Search service to use when searching over content.

8. After you have configured all the settings, click Start.

INSIDE OUT   **Making use of a great tool: The Microsoft Best Practices Analyzer For Windows SharePoint Services 3.0**

Microsoft offers the Microsoft Best Practices Analyzer For Windows SharePoint Services 3.0 and The 2007 Microsoft Office System for you to check for common issues and best security practices. The tool generates a report that can help you optimize the configuration of your system. The tool can be run locally or from a server that is not attached to the server farm. This tool is available for download at *http://www.microsoft.com/downloads/details.aspx?FamilyID=cb944b27-9d6b-4a1f-b3e1-778efda07df8&DisplayLang=en*.

Installing WSS 3.0 from the Command Line

WSS 3.0 can be installed from the command line as described in the following sections.

How to Use a Setup.exe Command-Line Switch

When you run setup.exe, you can include a space after the command, followed by a slash (/) and the name of the switch, and sometimes followed by another space and one or more parameters, which are specific instructions that give the program more information about how to execute the command.

Table 13-7 summarizes all the command-line switches for setup.exe, the WSS 3.0 setup program.

Table 13-7 **Setup.exe Command-Line Options**

Switch	Description
/config [*path and file name*]	Specifies the configuration file that setup uses during the installation. By default, the config.xml file stored in the core product folder directs setup to install that product. You can edit the config.xml file to make additional customizations to the installation, or you can point to a different configuration file. Use /config on the setup command line to point to the location of the default config.xml file for a particular product or to point to a custom configuration file. For example, to point to a customized config.xml file, you can type **\\\<*server*>\\\<*share*>\setup.exe /config \\\<*server*>\\\<*share*>\\\<folder>\config.xml,** where *<folder>* is the folder that contains the config.xml file. Or, to point to a different configuration file: **\\\<*server*>\\\<*share*>\setup.exe /config \\\<*server*>\\\<*share*>\configfiles\wss-quiet.xml**. You must use a fully qualified path.
/modify [*productID*]	Used with a modified config.xml file to run setup in Maintenance mode and make changes to an existing Microsoft Office installation, such as adding or removing features. Look up the value of [*productID*] in the setup.xml file for the product you want to modify. The setup.xml file is located in the core product folder. In setup.xml, [*ProductID*] is equal to the value of the Id attribute of the Setup element. For example: • <Setup Id="Wss" Type="Product" Product-Code="{40120000-1110-0000-0000-0000000FF1CE}"> • \\<server>\<share>\setup.exe /modify Wss /config \\<server>\<share>\<folder>AddConfig.xml
/repair [*productID*]	Runs setup to repair the files needed for the specified product. Look up the value of [*productID*] in the setup.xml file for the product you want to modify. Running setup in repair mode affects only the program files and does not repair your server configuration or any sites. You should also run the SharePoint Products And Technologies Configuration Wizard after you run setup.exe /repair to complete the repair of the configuration. If you are using a stand-alone configuration, you can run psconfig.exe -setup from the command line to repair the configuration instead of using the wizard. If you are in a server-farm configuration, you should use the full wizard interface. For more information, see the Help for the SharePoint Products And Technologies Configuration Wizard.
/uninstall [*productID*]	Removes the specified product from the user's computer. Look up the value of [*productID*] in the setup.xml file for the product you want to modify. For example, \\<server>\<share>\setup.exe /uninstall wss.

> **Note**
>
> For information about the use of psconfig.exe commands in conjunction with the Share-Point Products and Technologies Configuration Wizard (Windows SharePoint Services), go to TechNet at *http://technet2.microsoft.com/Office/en-us/library/a59c4e8f-9b7f-4127-8199-1b9ab76991501033.mspx?mfr=true*.

TROUBLESHOOTING

Application errors may be sent to Microsoft without notice

Microsoft has released an update for WSS 3.0 that fixes the issue of Microsoft Application Error Reporting sending application errors to Microsoft without notifying you.

This update for WSS 3.0 fixes the following issue that was not previously documented in the Microsoft Knowledge Base: Some Microsoft Office 2007 program files that are opened or saved on a WSS 3.0 Web site use Microsoft Application Error Reporting (DW 2.0) to report problems to Microsoft. If an unsafe COM control is detected, a problem report may be sent to Microsoft without first verifying that you have granted permission for this reporting operation. The problem reports that may be sent do not contain personal information.

This update (Update 932091) makes a change to Microsoft Application Error Reporting (DW 2.0) to help ensure that DW 2.0 problem reports are sent only after you grant permission.

The update is located at the Microsoft Download Center. To obtain this update and to obtain installation instructions and deployment strategies, visit the following Microsoft Web site: *http://www.microsoft.com/downloads/details.aspx?FamilyId=A49472F9-93EF-4423-BD0B-06B1B331C7AC*.

After you run the installation process for the update, you are prompted to run the Share-Point Products and Technologies Configuration Wizard to complete the installation of the update.

Extranet Capabilities in WSS 3.0

Microsoft TechNet defines an extranet environment as a private network that is securely extended to share part of an organization's information processes with remote employees, external partners, or customers. The remote employees may need to be able to access internal networks by using mobile devices. They may also need to access dashboards to provide information necessary to make a fast sales decision, and they may even be geographically dispersed.

The partners will have their own special requirements and will need to participate in common business processes. They may also need to have access to real time reports. This type of integration with external partners comes with some security concerns that must be addressed. Partners should be compartmentalized from one another without the possibility of seeing or modifying their colleagues' information. This will require a carefully designed security model for site lists and document libraries. External partners will also need to have communication channels with some company employees.

In a past WSS 3.0 extranet implementation, I met with a client who was trying to be helpful to new potential clients, granting them access to the organization's external facing SharePoint site along with a few internal discussion boards so that they could participate in discussions to see how the firm really worked. This ended up being a big mistake that cost my client a large sum of money and ended in an expensive legal battle because some sensitive information was shared and then reshared. Obviously, not all situations will end in this manner, but you must think through these types of issues when crafting your internal and external security models.

Using automated business processes (implemented in WSS 3.0 with Windows Workflow Foundation) with an application programming interface (API) for external customers to access has become common in today's increasingly agile business world. You may even have requirements for the extranet to support anonymous authentication. All of these considerations must be carefully thought through when you are developing an extranet environment. The extranet environment is the result of several steps:

- Availability planning
- Extranet farm topology planning
- Authentication planning
- Environment security hardening planning

Availability Planning

For information on availability planning, refer to the section titled "Choosing the Proper Server Farm Configuration" earlier in this chapter.

Extranet Farm Topology Planning

In addition to availability, security is a major factor to consider when choosing the extranet topology.

Your organization's employees will need secure access to corporate information, but may not always be able to use VPN (Virtual Private Network) to accomplish this. If they plan on using internal domain credentials for authentication, then the authentication process must be secured.

As mentioned previously, external partners should not have access to other partners' information for a variety of reasons, and each partner should be isolated.

The WSS 3.0 extranet topologies most commonly used are the following:

- Edge firewall topology
- Tri-homed perimeter
- Back-to-back perimeter topology
- Split back-to-back topology

Before choosing and implementing a topology, you first need to plan availability, authentication, and security hardening. Once these items are covered, and you have gathered your requirements, you will begin to get a clearer picture of which extranet topology will best suit the needs of your organization.

Edge Firewall Topology (Perimeter in Proxy)

In an edge firewall scenario, the server farm is located in the corporate network. A reverse proxy server is placed on the border of the network and intercepts requests to the Web front end. If these requests are for the extranet, then the requested URLs are translated into internal URLs and forwarded to the extranet Web server. Figure 13-7 shows the edge firewall topology.

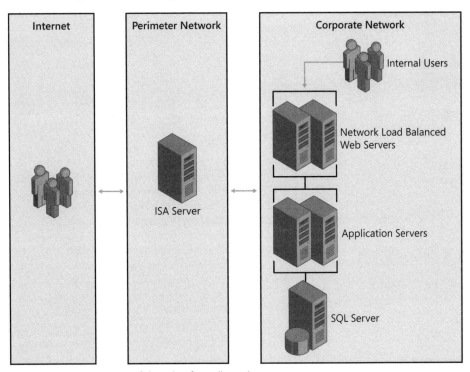

Figure 13-7 Architecture of the edge firewall topology.

Pros of the edge firewall topology:

- Simplest solution that requires the minimum amount of hardware and configuration
- All the data is in one place
- Data is located/persisted in the trusted network
- All the maintenance is done in a single place
- Allows for fine-grained security rules for authentication and requested URLs
- Flexible Secure Socket Layer (SSL) usage—use either SSL bridging or SSL-to-HTTP bridging
- Internal user requests are not passed through a proxy server

Con of the edge firewall topology:

- Single firewall. This will be the single obstacle for intruders—if they defeat this firewall, they will have access to the entire corporate network.

Tri-Homed Perimeter

The tri-homed perimeter is similar to perimeter in proxy. As in the first topology, there's a single firewall, but this time, the WSS farm is in the perimeter network. The computer on which the firewall will be installed has three network adapters, each connected to a separate network: Internet, perimeter, and corporate.

Pros of the tri-homed perimeter: A single firewall, easy setup.

Con of the tri-homed perimeter: A single point of failure.

Back-to-Back Perimeter Topology

In a back-to-back perimeter topology, as shown in Figure 13-8, the WSS 3.0 farm is isolated in a separate perimeter network. External (Internet) user requests are routed to the WSS 3.0 Web servers through the Internet Security and Acceleration (ISA) Server A. The Microsoft Internet Security and Acceleration (ISA) Server 2006 is the integrated edge-security gateway that helps protect IT environments from Internet-based threats while providing users with fast and secure remote access to applications and data. The corporate network users can access WSS via a firewall (ISA Server B) between the perimeter network and the corporate network. It is also possible to design the topology so that corporate users would access the WSS farm through ISA Server A.

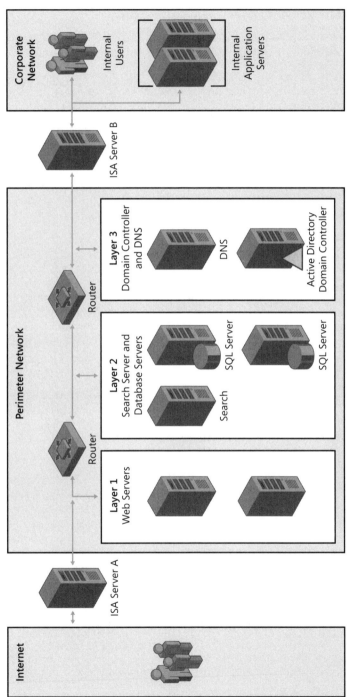

Figure 13-8 Architecture of the back-to-back perimeter topology.

Pros of the back-to-back perimeter topology:

- External users' access is isolated to the perimeter network so that if this network is compromised, they will not have access to the corporate network.

- With use of separate Active Directory services for the perimeter network to manage external user accounts, this topology will be safer than one that adds those accounts to the corporate network AD server.

- The WSS farm can easily be scaled, without depending in any way on the corporate hardware resources.

- All the WSS 3.0 servers are in one place, making for easier maintenance.

Cons of the back-to-back perimeter topology:

- Additional hardware needs to be purchased and configured.

- If the perimeter network has its own Active Directory, a trust relationship will need to be configured with the corporate network.

Split Back-to-Back Topology

This topology splits the farm between the perimeter and the corporate networks. The WSS Web server is placed in the perimeter network and the database server in the corporate network. The Search server can be placed in either network, but to increase the WSS 3.0 Search performance, the Search server should be placed on the same network as the database.

If the Search server is placed in the corporate network, a trust relationship will have to be created, whether you use Windows or SQL Server Authentication for the database.

Pros of the split back-to-back topology:

- Database servers are located in the corporate network and can also be used by corporate applications.

- The perimeter network Active Directory provides easier management of external users.

Cons of the split back-to-back topology:

- Higher degree of complexity.

- If intruders compromise the perimeter network, they can gain access to the corporate network content by using the SQL Server or the Search server accounts.

Environment Security Hardening Planning

The topic of security hardening can be split across two separate areas: securing the extranet environment's servers and securing the WSS 3.0 environment's servers.

Securing the Extranet Environment

Depending on what network topology you choose to implement, domain trust relationships might need to be created. If the server farm resides in the perimeter network, you will usually create a separate Active Directory infrastructure for it. Don't create trust relationships unless employees will need to authenticate using their corporate domain credentials.

Securing Windows 2003

Before installing WSS 3.0, you'll need to harden the operating system and the database servers. Windows Server 2003 SP1 comes with a Security Configuration Wizard. With this tool, shown in Figure 13-9, you can build or load security templates. Once a template is loaded, everything except the specified configuration file is locked down. This tool is not installed by default, but it can be installed via Control Panel by selecting Add Or Remove Programs and then Add/Remove Windows Components. The security templates can be applied directly to an Active Directory group.

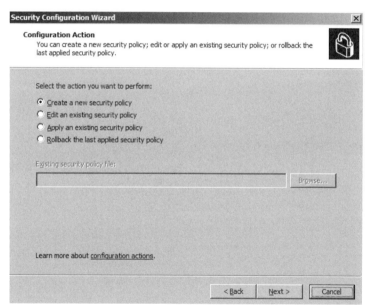

Figure 13-9 The Security Configuration Wizard.

MBSA

Microsoft Baseline Security Analyzer (MBSA) is a free, easy-to-use tool designed for the IT professional. It helps small- and medium-sized businesses determine their security state in accordance with Microsoft security recommendations and offers specific remediation guidance. It can be downloaded from *http://www.microsoft.com/technet/security/tools/mbsahome.mspx*.

The MBSA tool creates a report that warns you about security packs that aren't installed, security misconfigurations, and other vulnerabilities. With MBSA, you can scan for vulnerabilities on a single computer or more (by choosing an IP range or computers from a specific domain).

Securing the SQL Server

Unless you have opted to store your content in the Windows Internal Database, WSS 3.0's content and its configurations are stored in SQL Server. The most recent version of SQL Server, SQL Server 2005, brings improvements in this area by providing more granular permissions, surface area reduction, and security policies.

When you install SQL Server, you can choose between two types of authentication: Windows Authentication Mode and SQL Server Authentication Mode. Windows Authentication Mode authenticates users against an Active Directory service or by using the machine local accounts. SQL Server Authentication enables both Windows Authentication and SQL Server accounts.

Of these two options, Windows Authentication is recommended if the WSS front-end server and the SQL database are in the same domain or in domains with trust relationships between them. The reasons for this are:

- Windows Authentication, using the Active Directory infrastructure, provides a way to more easily manage the users who already have accounts on the domain server.

- SQL Server 2005 now comes with support for security policies, password expiration, password strength, and so on.

Securing the WSS Front-End Server

Security is one of the major areas of improvement in WSS 3.0. These security improvements include:

- Item-level and document-level security

- Security trimming

- .NET code access security

Securing a WSS 3.0 site can be split in three main areas:

- Server security (physical security)

- Operations security (how the WSS 3.0 administrator should connect to the server, password policies, and so on)

- Solutions security (assigning user rights in a correct manner, security trimming, and so on)

Installing Language Template Packs

WSS 3.0 language packs enable site owners and site collection administrators to create SharePoint sites and site collections in multiple languages without requiring separate installations. Language packs are installed on your front-end Web servers. When your organization's administrator creates a site or a site collection based on a language-specific site template, the text that appears on the site or the site collection is displayed in the site template's language.

Language packs are typically used within organizations that require multinational deployments where a single server farm supports people in different locations or in situations where sites and Web pages must be duplicated in one or more languages. These language packs are being used more and more now that WSS 3.0 has robust and updated features in Internet facing sites.

> **Note**
> You cannot change an existing site, site collection, or Web page from one language to another by applying different language-specific site templates. Once you choose a language-specific site template for a site or a site collection, the site or site collection will always display content in the language of the original site template.

Your organization can also use word breakers and stemmers, which linguistically analyze stored full-text data to determine appropriate word breaks and verb stems in order to facilitate searching. Word breakers and stemmers enable you to efficiently and effectively search across content on SharePoint sites and site collections in multiple languages without requiring separate installations of WSS 3.0. These word breakers and stemmers are automatically installed on your front-end Web servers after the initial setup is completed.

For more information on word breakers and stemmers, go to *http://technet.microsoft.com/ en-us/library/ms142509.aspx*.

Table 13-8 lists the language packs that are available for Windows SharePoint Services 3.0.

Table 13-8 Available WSS 3.0 Language Packs

Language	Country/Region	Language ID
German	Germany	1031
English	United States	1033
Japanese	Japan	1041

Preparing Front-End Web Servers for Language Packs

Before your organization installs language packs on its front-end Web servers, the following steps must be completed:

- Install the necessary language files on your front-end Web servers.
- Install WSS 3.0 on each of your front-end Web servers.
- Run the SharePoint Products And Technologies Configuration Wizard on each of your front-end Web servers.

Language files are used by the operating system and provide support for displaying and entering text in multiple languages. Language files include:

- Keyboard files
- Input Method Editors (IMEs)
- TrueType font files
- Bitmap font files
- Code page conversion tables
- National Language Support (.nls) files
- Script engines for rendering complex scripts

Most language files are installed by default on the Windows Server 2003 operating system. You must install supplemental language files for East Asian languages and languages that use complex script or require right-to-left orientations. The East Asian languages include Chinese, Japanese, and Korean; the complex script and right-to-left oriented languages include Arabic, Armenian, Georgian, Hebrew, the Indic languages, Thai, and Vietnamese. Instructions for installing these supplemental language files are provided in the following procedure.

Because they take a lot of space, you should install the East Asian language files only if you have to. You will first need to install the language files, and then you can install the language packs.

Installing the Language Files

An administrator can install the language files by performing the following actions:

1. On your front-end Web server, click Start, point to Settings and then Control Panel, and then click Regional And Language Options.

2. In the Regional And Language Options dialog box, on the Languages tab, in the Supplemental Language Support section, select one or both of the following check boxes:

   ❍ Install Files For Complex Script And Right-To-Left Languages

   ❍ Install Files For East Asian Languages

3. Click OK in the dialog box that alerts you that additional disk space is required for the files.

4. Click OK to install the additional language files.

5. When prompted, insert your Windows Server 2003 product disc or provide the location of your Windows Server 2003 installation files.

6. When prompted to restart your computer, click Yes.

Installing the Language Packs

An administrator can install language packs by performing the following actions:

1. Run setup.exe.

2. On the Read The Microsoft Software License Terms page, review the terms, select the I Accept The Terms Of This Agreement check box, and then click Continue.

3. On the Installation Types page, click Basic.

4. The setup wizard runs and installs the language pack.

Rerunning the SharePoint Products and Technologies Configuration Wizard

An administrator will need to rerun the SharePoint Products And Technologies Configuration Wizard after the installation of the language pack, or it will not be installed properly. Do so by performing the following steps:

1. Click Start, point to All Programs, point to Administrative Tools, and then click SharePoint Products And Technologies Configuration Wizard.

2. On the Welcome To SharePoint Products And Technologies page, click Next.

3. Click Yes in the dialog box that alerts you that some services might need to be restarted during configuration.

4. On the Modify Server Farm Settings page, click Do Not Disconnect From This Server Farm and then click Next.

5. If the Modify SharePoint Central Administration Web Administration Settings page appears, do not modify any of the default settings. Then click Next.

6. On the Completing The SharePoint Products And Technologies Configuration Wizard page, click Next.

7. On the Configuration Successful page, click Finish.

When you install language packs, the language-specific site templates are installed in the \Program Files\Common Files\Microsoft Shared\web server extensions\12\ template*number* directory, where *number* is the Language ID for the language that you are installing. For example, the US English language pack installs to the \Program Files\ Common Files\Microsoft Shared\web server extensions\12\template\1033 directory.

> **Note**
>
> After you install a language pack, site owners and site collection administrators can create sites and site collections based on the language-specific site templates by specifying a language when they are creating a new SharePoint site or site collection.

Uninstalling Language Packs

If your organization no longer needs to support a language for which you have installed a language pack, it can be removed via Add Or Remove Programs in Control Panel. Once you remove a language pack, the language-specific site templates from your computer are also removed. All of the SharePoint sites that were created with those language-specific site templates will no longer work, and you will receive an HTTP 500 (Internal Server Error) page. This error will go away only if you reinstall the language pack you removed.

> **Note**
>
> You cannot remove the language pack for the version of WSS 3.0 that you have installed on your server. For example, if you are running the Japanese version of WSS 3.0, you cannot uninstall the Japanese language support for WSS 3.0.

In Summary...

This chapter explained the system requirements and server topology options for WSS 3.0. It explained how to install the product in the most common and likely scenarios. It also covered WSS 3.0's extranet and multiple language capabilities.

The next chapter will explain how to back up and restore SharePoint sites, and how to migrate and update sites.

Backing Up, Restoring, and Migrating Sites

In most organizations, little surprises may occur from time to time. A file that is supposed to be saved is accidentally deleted. A sales representative in marketing overwrites a critical document version. An engineer in product development needs a document from someone who left the company. The five new SharePoint servers that were sitting out on the loading dock were accidentally placed in the trash compactor (true story).

The lesson of each of these little surprises is that it is always a best practice to back up your files. For those in areas prone to bad weather such as hurricanes, where power may be out for days on end, a disaster recovery plan must be in place, and it must be tested and proven. This chapter describes the ways your organization can back up Microsoft Windows SharePoint Services 3.0 (WSS 3.0) as well as restore it. This chapter also covers the methods for moving sites from one server to another and for upgrading from Windows SharePoint Services 2.0 (WSS 2.0).

Choosing a Backup Option for WSS 3.0

Your organization can choose from several different options when deciding how to back up WSS 3.0 content and then restore it. This latest version of WSS has drastically improved methods for performing these tasks. These methods are as follows:

- **Central Administration backup** The new features of Central Administration in WSS 3.0 have made backing up and restoring SharePoint easier than ever. This is the simplest method for performing these tasks.

  You can specify the items that you'd like to back up or restore. For example, you could choose to back up a single content database, or you can select the entire WSS 3.0 farm.

- **The Stsadm command-line tool** This program has backup and restore options that can back up and restore one site collection at a time. The main advantages of this approach are that you get a complete backup or restore of an entire site collection, and because this is a command-line program, you can use it in batch files. Furthermore, you can run the program itself or the batch files from Windows Scheduler. The disadvantage is that you must have a local administrator account on the database server.

- **SharePoint Designer**   With Microsoft Office SharePoint Designer 2007, you can both back up and restore SharePoint sites. Using Office SharePoint Designer 2007 for backup/restore offers several advantages. The SharePoint Designer graphical user interface (GUI) is more intuitive than a command-line tool for team members more familiar with graphical interfaces. It prompts you to supply missing or incorrect additional logon credentials when there's a problem with the network connection.

- **Microsoft SQL Server 2005 tools** If WSS 3.0 is using a SQL Server database, you can use the backup tools that come with SQL Server 2005 to get a complete backup of your SharePoint databases. Among the merits of this approach are that this option can be the most secure of the available backup and restore options. However, to use this method, you must have a local administrator account on the server computer that is running SQL Server. Also, this option isn't very granular. The smallest unit you can back up and restore is one configuration database, along with all the content databases from sites using that configuration database. In other words, you have to back up or restore a whole server or server farm at once.

Backups are more difficult and expensive to run than you might suspect. Here are some of the reasons:

- In many cases, backups are the most resource-intensive processes that run on your server. Nothing else is likely to exercise your file system, your database, your CPU, and your network connection as hard as a backup program striving to access 100 percent of your data in minimum time.

- Secondary storage systems are expensive and labor-intensive. Because they are exposed to air and dust, tapes and tape drives are prone to physical error. In addition, tapes require operator handling, at least for off-site storage. Secondary disk systems require monitoring, management, and maintenance.

- Unless you back up directly to tape, each backup will probably require more physical disk space than the original data. If, for example, you have 4 gigabytes (GB) of data, each full backup you keep online will probably consume 5 GB of space.

To balance these factors, you must consider the time importance of your data. For example:

- If you only back up once a week—on Saturday night, perhaps—how much would it cost your company if a failure or error occurred on Thursday, and your restoration lacked three or four days of activity?

- If the server became unusable and you had to rebuild it from scratch, what would be the cost per hour or cost per day of having the server unavailable?

The answers to these types of questions will, of course, vary from one organization to the next. Even within a single organization, they'll vary over time. As a result, no one backup schedule can possibly be right for every case. For starters, however, consider this approach:

- Make SQL Server backups every week, primarily for disaster recovery.

- Once a week, probably over the weekend or during some other period of minimal use, run a Stsadm backup or use the Central Administration backup for every site collection.

- Once a day, run a Stsadm backup or Central Administration backup for site collections that have changed.

Developing a Robust Disaster Recovery Plan for Your SharePoint Environment

With SharePoint's growing popularity, it is quickly becoming the primary collaboration and content management solution for many organizations.

It is important that you put a disaster recovery plan in place and test it thoroughly. Do not store disaster recovery policies and procedures for all your other systems in SharePoint without having printed out a hard copy in case SharePoint goes down. Also, what happens if a user is accidentally given administrator rights or full control over a site, and he or she accidentally deletes it?

You can go to the Recycle Bin to recover an item that a user has deleted, but this feature does not enable the recovery of entire sites. If you needed to recover an entire site, you would have to perform a restore operation from a previously successful backup of the content database. If a particular site was deleted at 4 P.M. and the last backup was made at midnight the night before, then your department or team may be out of luck regarding the work that they completed that day.

Your organization would need to investigate the third-party utilities available, for example, AvePoint's solution to restore more granular aspects of WSS 3.0, which is discussed later in this chapter.

Backing Up and Restoring Sites by Using the Operations Page in SharePoint Central Administration

Using the Central Administration Web page is the easiest way to back up WSS 3.0 sites. System administrators usually make this type of backup. Within Central Administration, the Operations page provides an entire category of features called Backup And Restore, as shown in Figure 14-1.

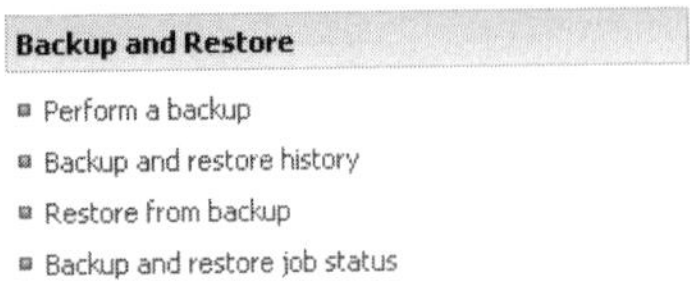

Backup and Restore

- Perform a backup
- Backup and restore history
- Restore from backup
- Backup and restore job status

Figure 14-1 Backup And Restore options available on the Central Administration Operations page.

At this point, you are really just a few simple clicks away from being able to perform a backup, view the backup and restore history, restore from a previous backup, or view the backup and restore job status.

Performing a Backup in Central Administration

Site administrators can easily perform a new SharePoint backup within Central Administration by performing the following:

1. On the Web server, navigate to the Central Administration by clicking Start, Administrative Tools, and then SharePoint 3.0 Central Administration.

2. Click Operations on the top navigation bar.

3. In the Backup And Restore section of the Operations page, click Perform A Backup.

4. On the Select Component To Backup page, shown in Figure 14-2, choose the components you want to back up, such as a Web application, a content database, or an entire farm. You can select any one component and all components under it.

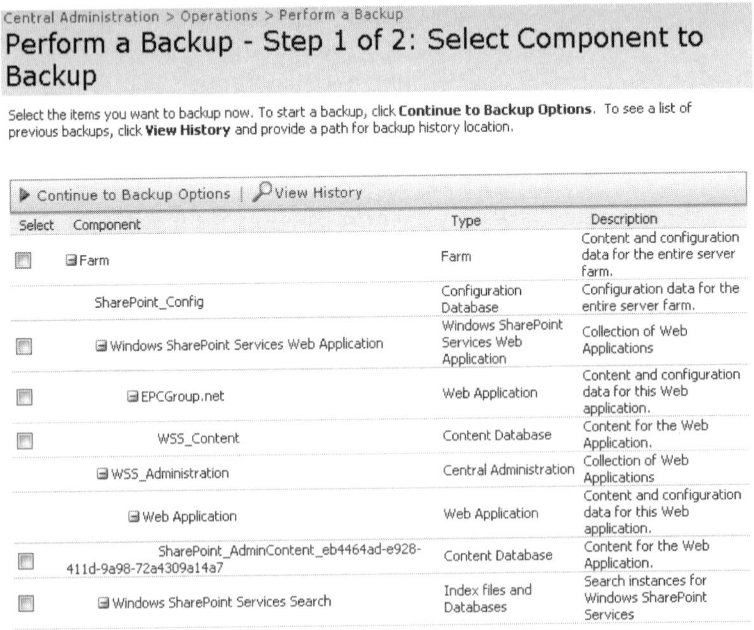

Central Administration > Operations > Perform a Backup

Perform a Backup - Step 1 of 2: Select Component to Backup

Select the items you want to backup now. To start a backup, click **Continue to Backup Options**. To see a list of previous backups, click **View History** and provide a path for backup history location.

▶ Continue to Backup Options | 🔍 View History

Select	Component	Type	Description
☐	⊟ Farm	Farm	Content and configuration data for the entire server farm.
	SharePoint_Config	Configuration Database	Configuration data for the entire server farm.
☐	⊟ Windows SharePoint Services Web Application	Windows SharePoint Services Web Application	Collection of Web Applications
☐	⊟ EPCGroup.net	Web Application	Content and configuration data for this Web application.
☐	WSS_Content	Content Database	Content for the Web Application.
	⊟ WSS_Administration	Central Administration	Collection of Web Applications
	⊟ Web Application	Web Application	Content and configuration data for this Web application.
☐	SharePoint_AdminContent_eb4464ad-e928-411d-9a98-72a4309a14a7	Content Database	Content for the Web Application.
☐	⊟ Windows SharePoint Services Search	Index files and Databases	Search instances for Windows SharePoint Services

Figure 14-2 Step 1 of the Perform A Backup procedure is selecting the component to back up.

5. When you have selected all the components you want to back up, click Continue To Backup Options.

6. On the Select Backup Options page, select the type of backup you would like. The backup can be either full or differential, as shown in Figure 14-3.

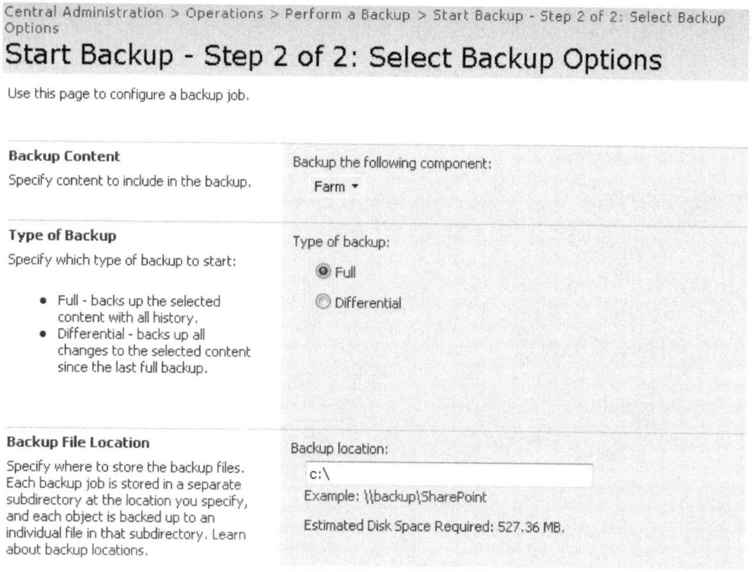

Central Administration > Operations > Perform a Backup > Start Backup - Step 2 of 2: Select Backup Options

Start Backup - Step 2 of 2: Select Backup Options

Use this page to configure a backup job.

Backup Content
Specify content to include in the backup.

Backup the following component:
Farm ▾

Type of Backup
Specify which type of backup to start:

- Full - backs up the selected content with all history.
- Differential - backs up all changes to the selected content since the last full backup.

Type of backup:
◉ Full
○ Differential

Backup File Location
Specify where to store the backup files. Each backup job is stored in a separate subdirectory at the location you specify, and each object is backed up to an individual file in that subdirectory. Learn about backup locations.

Backup location:
c:\
Example: \\backup\SharePoint
Estimated Disk Space Required: 527.36 MB.

Figure 14-3 Step 2 of the Perform A Backup procedure is selecting the type of backup you would like to perform and indicate where you'd like to store the backup files.

7. While still on the Select Backup Options page, in the Backup File Location section, enter the Universal Naming Convention (UNC) path to the backup folder.

8. Click OK.

You can view the backup job status on the backup status page by clicking Refresh. The page also refreshes every 30 seconds automatically. Backup and recovery is a Timer service job, so it may take about a minute for the backup to start.

If you receive any errors, you can find more information by looking in the spbackup. log file at the UNC path you specified previously. Most errors are caused by permission-related issues.

When you clicked OK, a job was created, and it will be run by the WSS Timer service. The result will consist of an XML manifest and some BAK files that will appear in the backup location you set up.

Restoring from a Backup in Central Administration

Site administrators can easily restore a SharePoint backup to the original server farm. This can be accomplished by performing the following:

1. On the Web server, navigate to Central Administration by clicking Start, Administrative Tools, and then SharePoint 3.0 Central Administration.

2. Click Operations on the top navigation bar.

3. In the Backup And Restore section of the Operations page, click Restore From Backup.

4. On the Restore From Backup: Step 1: Select Backup Location page, in the Backup File Location section, enter the UNC path to the backup folder and click OK.

5. On the Restore From Backup: Step 2: Select Backup Package To Restore page, choose the target backup package, as shown in Figure 14-4, and click Continue Restore Process.

Central Administration > Operations > Backup and Restore History

Restore from Backup - Step 2 of 4: Select Backup to Restore

Use this page to manage the history logs for backup and restore operations.

Results 1-2 of 2 jobs.

▶ Continue Restore Process | 📁 Change Directory

Select	Type	Method	Top Component	Start Time	Finish Time	Failure Message	Requested By	Backup ID
⊙	Backup	Full	Farm	7/12/2007 11:01 PM	7/12/2007 11:02 PM		EPCGROUP\Administrator	a6e18952-db06-49(
⊙	Backup	Full	Farm	7/6/2007 2:24 PM	7/6/2007 2:26 PM		EPCGROUP\Administrator	2cb4db5a-98b8-4f8

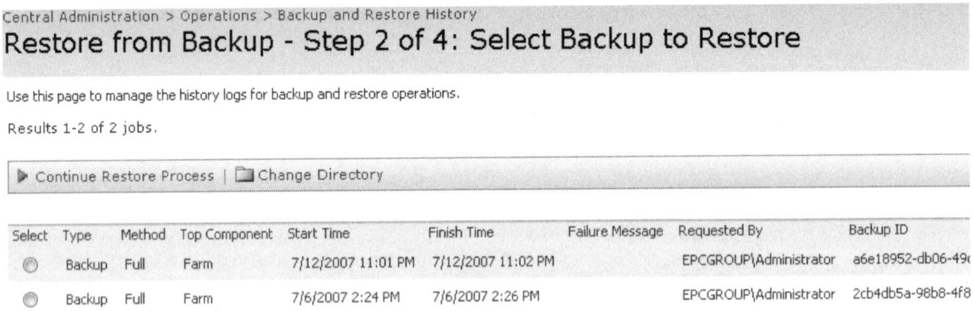

Figure 14-4 Step 2 of the Restore From Backup procedure is choosing the target backup package.

6. On the Restore From Backup: Step 3: Select Component To Restore page, choose the restore level (Farm, Service, Database, or SSP) and then click Continue Restore Process.

7. On the Restore From Backup: Step 4: Select Restore Options page, select Same Configuration (rather than the default value, New Configuration) and then click OK in the dialog box that appears.

8. In the Login Names And Passwords section, enter the user name and password for the Web applications listed on the page.

9. Click OK.

TROUBLESHOOTING

One-time timer jobs in WSS 3.0 are delayed when the jobs are scheduled to occur during Daylight Saving Time (DST)

When you use SharePoint 3.0 Central Administration to schedule a one-time timer job in WSS 3.0 during Daylight Saving Time (DST), the job may be delayed by at least one hour. You may experience the following symptoms:

- You click Perform A Backup to set up a backup operation. However, the backup job is delayed. It takes at least one hour before the backup job starts. If you include indexes in the backup, it may take two hours before the backup job starts.

- You click Restore From Backup to set up a restore operation from a backup. However, the restore job is delayed. It takes at least one hour before the restore job starts.

In addition to backup jobs and restore jobs, examples of one-time timer jobs include the following:

- Migration
- Content deployment
- Provision Web application
- Publishing

To fix this problem, you can obtain the hotfix package dated June 11, 2007 by going to *http://support.microsoft.com/kb/938535*.

You will not experience this delay when you use SharePoint 3.0 Central Administration to schedule one-time timer jobs during standard time.

Using Stsadm to Back Up and Restore a Site, Server Farm, Database, or Web Application

WSS 3.0 comes with Stsadm.exe, a command-line program that can back up and restore SharePoint sites. You can also use it to perform actions such as restoring a server farm, database, or Web application.

INSIDE OUT   Advantages of using Stsadm

There are several advantages to using the Stsadm program:

- It works with most any kind of database.
- Each backup creates a single file in the server's file system. This file retains all the sites in the collection including all Web pages; all files in document libraries; all lists; and all security, permission, and feature settings.

- A restored backup can replace the original collection, or it can create a new one.
- Replacing a collection is more appropriate if someone accidentally deleted it, or if the collection became hopelessly corrupted.
- Restoring to a new location is more appropriate if you only want to recover selected content. Team members will be able to access both the original and restored sites, and therefore recover just the information they need.
- Because Stsadm.exe is a command-line program, you can run it in batch files or scripts. In addition, you can run the program itself, batch files that call it, or scripts that call it from Windows Scheduler.

Using Stsadm to Back Up a Site

Site administrators can easily back up a site by using the Stsadm command-line tool as follows:

1. For 32-bit versions of Windows Server 2003, open a command prompt window and change the directory to where the Stsadm command-line tool is located, usually at the following path: %*drive*%\%*ProgramFiles*%\common files\Microsoft shared\web server extensions\12\bin.

    Or:

    For 64-bit versions of Windows Server 2003, open a command prompt window and change the directory to where the Stsadm command-line tool is located, usually at the following path: %*drive*%\%*ProgramFiles*%\common files\Microsoft shared\web server extensions\12\bin.

2. To back up a site, use the command Stsadm.exe with the appropriate switches. For example:

    Stsadm.exe -o backup -url http://servername/sites/sitename -filename c:\wssbackup\sitename.bak

3. When you receive a warning that all selected items will be overwritten, type **y** and press Enter.

Using Stsadm to Restore a Site

Site administrators can easily restore a site by using the Stsadm command-line tool as follows:

1. For 32-bit versions of Windows Server 2003, open a command prompt window and change the directory to where the Stsadm command-line tool is located, usually at the following path: %*drive*%\%*ProgramFiles*%\common files\Microsoft shared\web server extensions\12\bin.

    Or:

For 64-bit versions of Windows Server 2003, open a command prompt window and change the directory to where the Stsadm command-line tool is located, usually at the following path: *%drive%\%ProgramFiles%*\common files\Microsoft shared\Web server extensions\12\bin.

2. To back up a site, use the command Stsadm.exe with the appropriate switches. For example:

   Stsadm.exe -o restore -url http://servername/sites/sitename

3. When you receive a warning that all selected items will be overwritten, type **y** and press Enter.

Using Stsadm to Restore a Server Farm

You can use the procedures in this section to restore a server farm. These procedures assume that you are restoring to the server that produced the backup. In other words, you are not migrating to a new or different server.

1. For 32-bit versions of Windows Server 2003, open a command prompt window and change the directory to where the Stsadm command-line tool is located, usually at the following path: *%drive%\%ProgramFiles%*\common files\Microsoft shared\web server extensions\12\bin.

   Or:

   For 64-bit versions of Windows Server 2003, open a command prompt window and change the directory to where the Stsadm command-line tool is located, usually at the following path: *%drive%\%ProgramFiles%*\common files\Microsoft shared\web server extensions\12\bin.

2. To obtain the backup globally unique identifier (GUID) for the specific backup that you want to restore, type the command **Stsadm.exe -o \\backuphistory** *server\share*, where *server\share* is the UNC path to the shared folder that contains the backup.

3. To restore a server farm, type the command **Stsadm.exe -o restore -directory ** *server\share* **-backupid** *12345678-90ab-cdef-1234-567890abcdef* **-restoremethod overwrite**, where *server\share* is the UNC path to the backup shared folder, and where *12345678-90ab-cdef-1234-567890abcdef* is a valid GUID.

4. When you receive a warning that all selected items will be overwritten, type **y** and press Enter.

5. When prompted, enter the user name and password for the Web application and content databases.

Using Stsadm to Restore a Web Application

You can use the procedures in this section to restore a Web application. These procedures assume that you are restoring to the server that produced the backup. In other words, you are not migrating to a new or different server.

1. For 32-bit versions of Windows Server 2003, open a command prompt window and change the directory to where the Stsadm command-line tool is located, usually at the following path: *%drive%\%ProgramFiles%*\common files\Microsoft shared\web server extensions\12\bin.

    Or:

    For 64-bit versions of Windows Server 2003, open a command prompt window and change the directory to where the Stsadm command-line tool is located, usually at the following path: *%drive%\%ProgramFiles%*\common files\Microsoft shared\web server extensions\12\bin.

2. To obtain the backup GUID for the specific backup that you want to restore, type the command **Stsadm.exe -o backuphistory *server**share***, where *server**share* is the UNC path to the shared folder that contains the backup.

3. If you do not already know the name of the Web application that you want to back up, type the command **Stsadm.exe -o restore -showtree -directory *server*\\ *share* -backupid *12345678-90ab-cdef-1234-567890abcdef***, where *server**share* is the UNC path to the shared folder that contains the backup and where *12345678-90ab-cdef-1234-567890abcdef* is a valid GUID.

4. To restore a Web application, type the command **Stsadm.exe -o restore -directory *server**share* -backupid *12345678-90ab-cdef-1234-567890abcdef* -item "*Windows SharePoint Services Web Application*" -restoremethod overwrite** where *server**share* is the UNC path to the backup shared folder, where *12345678-90ab-cdef-1234-567890abcdef* is a valid GUID, and where "*Windows SharePoint Services Web Application*" is the name of the Web application that you want to restore.

5. When you receive a warning that all selected items will be overwritten, type **y** and press Enter.

6. When prompted, enter the user name and password for the Web application.

Using Stsadm to Restore a Database

You can use the procedures in this section to restore a database. These procedures assume that you are restoring to the server that produced the backup. In other words, you are not migrating to a new or different server.

1. For 32-bit versions of Windows Server 2003, open a command prompt window and change the directory to where the Stsadm command-line tool is located, usually at the following path: *%drive%\%ProgramFiles%*\common files\Microsoft shared\web server extensions\12\bin.

    Or:

    For 64-bit versions of Windows Server 2003, open a command prompt window and change the directory to where the Stsadm command-line tool is located, usually at the following path: *%drive%\%ProgramFiles%*\common files\Microsoft shared\Web server extensions\12\bin.

2. To obtain the backup GUID for the specific backup that you want to restore, type the command **Stsadm.exe -o backuphistory** *server**share*, where *server*\ *share* is the UNC path to the shared folder that contains the backup.

3. If you do not already know the name of the database you want to back up, type the command **Stsadm -o restore -showtree -directory** *server**share* **-backupid** *12345678-90ab-cdef-1234-567890abcdef*, where *server**share* is the UNC path to the shared folder that contains the backup, and where *12345678-90ab-cdef-1234-567890abcdef* is a valid GUID.

4. To restore a database, type the command Stsadm.exe **-o backup -directory** \\ *server**share* **-backupid** *12345678-90ab-cdef-1234-567890abcdef* **-item "WSS_ Content"**, where *server**share* is the UNC path to the backup share, where *12345678-90ab-cdef-1234-567890abcdef* is a valid GUID, and where *"WSS_Content"* is the name of the database that you want to back up.

5. When you receive a warning that all selected items will be overwritten, type **y** and press Enter.

Using Stsadm to Restore a Site Collection

You can use the procedures in this section to restore a site collection. These procedures assume that you are restoring to the server that produced the backup. In other words, you are not migrating to a new or different server.

1. For 32-bit versions of Windows Server 2003, open a command prompt window and change the directory to where the Stsadm command-line tool is located, usually at the following path: %*drive*%\%*ProgramFiles*%\common files\Microsoft shared\web server extensions\12\bin.

   Or:

   For 64-bit versions of Windows Server 2003, open a command prompt window and change the directory to where the Stsadm command-line tool is located, usually at the following path: %*drive*%\%*ProgramFiles*%\common files\Microsoft shared\web server extensions\12\bin.

2. To restore a site collection, type the command Stsadm.exe **-o restore -url** *http://servername* **-directory** *server**share* **-restoremethod overwrite**, where *http://servername* is the URL of the site collection that you want to restore, and where *server**share* is the UNC path to the backup share.

3. When you receive a warning that all selected items will be overwritten, type **y** and press Enter.

4. When prompted, enter the user name and password for the Web application and content databases.

Using Stsadm to Import Sites and Subsites

When you use the *import* operation, you are restoring a site or subsite that can be exported from the same or another WSS 3.0 server. Though using import restores data for you, it is not the same as using the restore operation within the SharePoint Central Administration.

1. For 32-bit versions of Windows Server 2003, open a command prompt window and change the directory to where the Stsadm command-line tool is located, usually at the following path: *%drive%\%ProgramFiles%*\common files\Microsoft shared\web server extensions\12\bin.

   Or:

   For 64-bit versions of Windows Server 2003, open a command prompt window and change the directory to where the Stsadm command-line tool is located, usually at the following path: *%drive%\%ProgramFiles%*\common files\Microsoft shared\web server extensions\12\bin.

2. To import a site collection, type the command **Stsadm.exe -o import -url** *http://servername/sites/sitename* **-filename** *server**share***import.bak**, where *http://servername/sites/sitename* is the URL of the site or subsite that you want to back up, and where *server**share**import.bak* is the UNC path and file name of the file you want to import.

   If your import finishes successfully, in the command prompt window, you will see Operation Completed Successfully.

Backing Up and Restoring Databases by Using the SQL Server 2005 Tools

Besides the content and configurations databases, WSS 3.0 also has databases in SQL Server for search and indexing. These databases can be backed up with SharePoint Central Administration.

However, you should also have a backup plan for SQL Server in case a disaster occurs, or if the SharePoint backups fail. This plan should back up all the databases, not only the WSS 3.0 databases. No matter what option you choose (full, differential, transaction logs backup), the backups should be tested after they are created.

To reduce the time dedicated to verifying the backups, create a script that copies the backup and restores it on a test server or server farm on which you have a copy of the live WSS 3.0 environment.

Backing Up a Database in SQL Server 2005

Microsoft SQL Server 2005 provides high-performance backup capabilities as an essential safeguard for protecting critical data stored in SQL Server databases. An administrator can back up a SQL Server 2005 database by performing the following:

1. From the Start menu, navigate to All Programs and then Microsoft SQL Server 2005. Open Microsoft SQL Server Management Studio and connect to the

appropriate instance of the Microsoft SQL Server Database Engine. In Object Explorer, click the server name to expand the server tree.

2. Expand Databases, and, depending on the database, either select a user database or expand System Databases and select a system database. Right-click the database, point to Tasks, and then click Back Up. The Back Up Database dialog box appears.

3. In the Database drop-down menu, verify the database name. You can optionally select a different database from the menu.

4. You can perform a database backup for any recovery model (Full, Bulk_Logged, or Simple). In the Backup Type list box, select Full.

> **Note**
>
> After a successful full database backup is created, you will be able to create differential backups in the future.

5. For Backup Component, click Database.

6. In the Backup Set section, accept the default name suggested in the Name text box or enter a different name for the backup set. Optionally, in the Description text box, enter a description of the backup set.

7. Specify when the backup set will expire and can be overwritten without explicitly skipping verification of the expiration data.

8. Choose the type of backup destination by clicking Disk or Tape. To select the paths of up to 64 disk or tape drives containing a single media set, click Add. The selected paths are displayed in the Back Up To list box. To remove a backup destination, select it and click Remove. To view the contents of a backup destination, select it and click Contents.

9. To view or select the advanced options, click Options in the Select A Page pane.

10. Select an overwrite media option by clicking one of the following:

    - **Back Up To The Existing Media Set** For this option, click either Append To The Existing Backup Set or Overwrite All Existing Backup Sets. Optionally, check the Check Media Set Name And Backup Set Expiration check box and, optionally, enter a name in the Media Set Name text box. If no name is specified, a media set with a blank name is created. If you specify a media set name, the media (tape or disk) is checked to see whether the actual name matches the name you enter here.

    - **Back Up To A New Media Set, And Erase All Existing Backup Sets** For this option, enter a name in the New Media Set Name text box, and, optionally, describe the media set in the New Media Set Description text box.

11. In the Reliability section, optionally check Verify Backup When Finished. Then check Perform Checksum Before Writing To Media, and, optionally, Continue On Error.

12. If you are backing up to a tape drive (as specified in the Destination section of the General page), the Unload The Tape After Backup option is active. Clicking this option activates the Rewind The Tape Before Unloading option.

Restoring a Database in SQL Server 2005

Just as Microsoft SQL Server 2005 provides high-performance backup capabilities, it also provides corresponding restore capabilities. An administrator can restore a SQL Server 2005 database by performing the following:

1. From the Start menu, navigate to All Programs and then to Microsoft SQL Server 2005. Open Microsoft SQL Server Management Studio and connect to the appropriate instance of the Microsoft SQL Server Database Engine. In Object Explorer, click the server name to expand the server tree.

2. Expand Databases, and, depending on the database, either select a user database or expand System Databases and select a system database.

3. Right-click the database, point to Tasks, and then click Restore.

4. Click Database, which opens the Restore Database dialog box.

5. On the General page, the name of the database being restored appears in the To Database list box. To create a new database, enter its name in the list box.

6. In the To A Point In Time text box, either retain the default (Most Recent Possible) or select a specific date and time by clicking the browse button, which opens the Point In Time Restore dialog box.

7. To specify the source and location of the backup sets to restore, click one of the following options:

   ○ **From Database** Enter a database name in the list box.

   ○ **From Device** Click the browse button, which opens the Specify Backup dialog box. In the Backup Media list box, select one of the listed device types. To select one or more devices for the Backup Location list box, click Add.

   After adding the device(s) you want to the Backup Location list box, click OK to return to the General page.

8. In the Select The Backup Sets To Restore grid, select the backups to restore. This grid displays the backups available for the specified location. By default, a recovery plan is suggested. To override the suggested recovery plan, you can change the selections in the grid. Backups that depend on the restoration of an earlier backup are automatically deselected when the earlier backup is deselected.

9. To view or select the advanced options, click Options in the Select A Page pane.

10. In the Restore Options section, you can select any of the following options: Overwrite The Existing Database, Preserve The Replication Settings, Prompt Before Restoring Each Backup, and Restrict Access To The Restored Database. You can then choose a name for the restored database files under Restore The Database Files As.

11. In the Recovery State section, specify the state of the database after the restore operation by selecting one of these options:

   ○ Leave The Database Ready To Use By Rolling Back The Uncommitted Transactions. Additional Transaction Logs Cannot Be Restored.

   ○ Leave The Database Non-Operational, And Do Not Roll Back Uncommitted Transactions. Additional Transaction Logs Can Be Restored.

   ○ Leave The Database In An Unrecovered State. Undo Committed Transactions, But Save The Undo Actions In A Standby File So That Recovery Effects Can Be Reversed. (This option is equivalent to using the NoRecovery option in a Transact-SQL RESTORE statement.)

12. Optionally, specify a standby filename in the Standby File text box. This option is required if you leave the database in read-only mode. You can browse for the standby file or type its path name in the text box.

Backing Up and Restoring with Office SharePoint Designer 2007

I have discussed the backup and restore options for SharePoint using both the SharePoint Central Administration and SQL Server 2005's built-in tools. SharePoint Designer 2007 also enables you to back up and restore SharePoint sites. The following sections explain how you can use SharePoint Designer 2007 to perform these backup and restore functions.

Backing Up a Site with SharePoint Designer

A user can backup a site with SharePoint Designer by performing the following:

1. In SharePoint Designer, open the site you'd like to back up.

2. Go to Site menu and choose Administration, Backup Web Site, as shown in Figure 14-5.

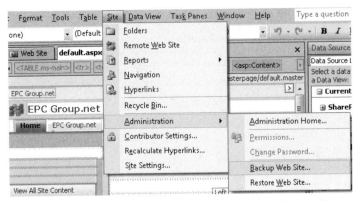

Figure 14-5 SharePoint Designer enables you to easily back up a site.

3. On the next screen, click Advanced, which will allow you to set up a location for the temporary backup file.

4. Click OK, which will allow you to set a location for the Content Migration Package (that is, the backup file). The backup process will begin.

Restoring a Site with SharePoint Designer

SharePoint Designer also enables you to restore a site. Before you can restore a site, you first need to delete any existing site. Follow these steps to restore a site:

1. You can delete an existing site from within SharePoint Designer or from your Web browser.

2. You will then need to recreate the site with an identical name and location. You should select the Blank Site template for this site recreation.

3. You now need to restore the site. Go to the Site menu and select Administration, Restore Website.

4. Select the appropriate *.cmp package to restore the site.

> **Note:**
> SharePoint Designer does not restore the permissions or users of a site after a site is restored.

Migrating and Upgrading Web Sites

Server administrators or members of the Farm Administrators group in Central Administration can upgrade sites from WSS 2.0 to WSS 3.0. The structure and data of a site are preserved, and WSS 3.0 will make the following changes:

- Upgrade the WSS technology

- Upgrade the data to the WSS 3.0 database schema

- Update the user rights, site groups, and cross-site groups to WSS 3.0 user permissions, permission levels, and SharePoint groups

- Upgrade any Web Part customizations your organization may have implemented

- Upgrade any site customizations that may have been made with a Web design program

> **Note**
>
> There is no direct upgrade from SharePoint Team Services (STS) to WSS 3.0. To upgrade from STS, you must first upgrade to WSS 2.0 and then to WSS 3.0.

The WSS 3.0 Setup Wizard provides two types of upgrades: the in-place and gradual upgrades. Use an in-place upgrade to upgrade all sites at one time. This is tailored more toward single-server or small-volume deployments. This type of upgrade allows for more granular control of the upgrade process by enabling one or more site collections to be upgraded to WSS 3.0 at one time. A gradual upgrade is great for large deployments of WSS.

For larger organizations with many SharePoint Sites, the gradual upgrade is the best option because it enables the administrator to control the number of site collections that should be upgraded at one time. With the communication involved in contacting the users currently running WSS 2.0 to notify them of the 3.0 upgrade, the gradual upgrade enables your organization to spread the upgrade over several weekends while you continue to host the previous version sites. This process also enables you to host the sites that have not yet been upgraded on the same server as the WSS 3.0 upgraded sites.

The following is a high-level timeline of how site administrators and site owners can work together to accomplish an upgrade:

1. The server administrator prescans all Web servers, checks logs, and either fixes the issues described in the logs or forwards the issues that might need attention before the upgrade to the appropriate site owner or designer.

Chapter 14

2. Site owners verify whether any customizations exist on their sites (including site templates and changes to core ASPX files) and then note the results.

3. Site owners note what theme is currently associated with each site so that a similar theme can be reapplied after the upgrade.

4. Site owners communicate downtime expectations to site visitors.

5. The server administrator alerts the appropriate site owner and designer after each site collection has been upgraded and reports on whether their site or sites have been upgraded successfully in addition to whether any issues need their attention.

6. If a gradual upgrade was performed, the server administrator notifies the site owners of how long the WSS 2.0 sites will be maintained before they are deleted.

7. The site owner should verify site functionality and reapply any necessary customizations. For sites that were customized in WSS 2.0 with a design program such as Microsoft Office FrontPage, the site's home page will still have the WSS 2.0 look and feel. Site owners should consider removing those customizations by using the Reset To Site Definition link within Site Settings on pages that retain the WSS 2.0 look and feel. They can then upgrade the pages to WSS 3.0's look and feel.

8. Site owners and designers resolve any issues found in step 7. If the issues cannot be resolved, the server administrator can be asked to roll back the upgraded site to the WSS 2.0 version, if a gradual upgrade was performed. Otherwise, all issues must be fixed.

9. After the upgraded sites are verified and the necessary fixes are performed, the upgrade team notifies the site members and visitors of the status of their sites. After all sites have been successfully upgraded, the server administrator can uninstall WSS 2.0.

> **Note**
> If your organization has upgraded from WSS 2.0 to WSS 3.0 by using the gradual upgrade option, you should consider keeping your WSS 2.0 sites online for a period of time so that you can correct issues that may occur if any components were missed.

Once the upgrade is completed, you should verify all navigational hyperlinks within a site, internal as well as external. It is also a good idea for your users to test all Web Part functionality within a site and to confirm that all previous components are present in the new site.

Migration Considerations

There are several different ways to migrate from WSS 2.0 to WSS 3.0. Your organization can use the following options for your upgrade:

- **The Stsadm command-line tool** Use the -o backup and -o restore operations of the Stsadm.exe command-line tool. This is the best option for migrating an entire site collection, because it is the only method that migrates workflows, alerts, and metadata at the site collection level. To use this tool, you must be a member of the local Administrators group or a member of the Farm Administrators group at the Central Administration level.

- **Central Administration** Use the Perform A Backup and Restore From Backup links on the Operations page in Central Administration. This is the easiest way to migrate individual sites. To perform these operations, you must be a member of the Farm Administrators group at the Central Administration level.

- **The Windows SharePoint Services object model** This is a new method in WSS 3.0 and the most flexible way to migrate from WSS 2.0. The migration-related application programming interfaces (APIs) in the object model can be used to migrate sites and any combination of objects below the site level. To use the API, you must be a member of the Farm Administrators group at the Central Administration level. You must also be a site collection administrator with permissions to read the objects that are being migrated and have permissions to change objects in the site you are migrating.

- **SharePoint Designer** SharePoint Designer enables you to perform migrations, but only of entire Web sites. The globally unique identifiers (GUIDs) are not migrated for any object, which means that all migrated objects will not be globally unique. You must be a site collection administrator and have permissions to read objects being migrated and permissions to change objects in the site you are migrating.

Migrating Sites Using Stsadm

In previous sections of this chapter, I discussed how the Stsadm command-line tool can be used to back up and restore SharePoint. It also provides methods for migrating sites. A new import/export feature is based on the Content Migration APIs. With this feature, you can migrate either subsites or entire site collections, and you can import a subsite into an existing site collection. It is important to note that import/export requires that the site you import to must already exist.

Importing/Exporting

Use the following command syntax to import the subsite or site collection:

Stsadm.exe -o import -url <URL> -includeusersecurity

The *includeusersecurity* parameter specifies that you want to import the security settings for the subsite or site collection. If you do not need the security settings, you can omit this parameter.

Export the subsite or site collection by following these steps:

1. From the command line, run Stsadm.exe -o export -url *<URL of the site>* -includeusersecurity.

2. In Central Administration, on the Manage Content Databases page, set all databases to offline except the one that currently contains the subsite or site collection.

3. Create a blank site or site collection to contain the content you are exporting.

Migrating a Site Collection by Using Backup/Restore

You can migrate an entire site collection by using the backup and restore operations with Stsadm. You first need to back up the site collection that you want to move and then delete it from the current database as well as take the database offline. After that, you can restore the site collection to a new URL.

Backing Up/Restoring

To use backup/restore to migrate a site collection, first use the following process to back up the site collection:

1. From the command line, run Stsadm.exe -o backup -url *<URL of the site>*.

2. In Central Administration, on the Manage Content Databases page, set to offline the database that currently contains the site collection.

To restore the site collection, use following process:

1. From the command line, run stsadm.exe -o restore -url *<URL of the site>*.

2. In Central Administration, on the Manage Content Databases page, set to online the database that originally contained the site collection.

Migrating by Using the WSS Object Model

You can use the WSS object model to migrate objects within your organization on the same Web server, across Web servers in same server farm, or across server farms. The user running the WSS object model must be a server administrator on both the staging server and the production server.

For more information on the Content Migration object model, go to *http://msdn2.microsoft.com/en-us/library/ms439864.aspx*.

Migrating WSS 3.0 by Using Central Administration

SharePoint Central Administration is a great tool for migrating SharePoint sites. Users can migrate data to a new or completely different server farm by using the Central

Administration GUI even if they lack in-depth knowledge of the Stsadm command-line tool or the SharePoint Services object model.

Migrating to a New Server Farm by Using Central Administration

A user with membership in the Farm Administrators group can migrate sites to a new server farm by using Central Administration. This can be done by performing the following:

1. On the Web server, navigate to Central Administration by clicking Start, Administrative Tools, and then SharePoint 3.0 Central Administration.

2. Click Operations on the top navigation bar.

3. In the Backup And Restore section of the Operations page, click Restore From Backup.

4. On the Restore From Backup: Step 1: Select Backup File page, under Backup File Location, enter the UNC path to the backup folder and then click OK.

5. On the Restore From Backup: Step 2: Select Backup Package To Restore page, choose the target backup package and then click Continue Restore Process.

6. On the Restore From Backup: Step 3: Select Component To Restore page, choose the restore level and then click Continue Restore Process.

7. On the Restore From Backup: Step 4: Select Restore Options page, select New Configuration and then click OK in the dialog box that appears.

8. In the Login Names And Passwords section, enter the user name and password for the Web applications listed on the page. In the New Names section, to create copies of the restored content, specify the Web application URL and name, the database server name, the file location on the server, and the new name for the new databases. Click OK.

9. You can view the recovery job status on the recovery status page by clicking Refresh. Backup and recovery is a Timer service job, so it may take a few seconds for the recovery to start. When the recovery has finished, restart Internet Information Services (IIS) to make sure that the settings are propagated to the IIS metabase. If you receive any errors, you can find more information by looking in the sprestore.log file located at the UNC path you specified previously.

Migrating to an Existing Server Farm by Using Central Administration

You can migrate a SharePoint site to an existing server farm by using Central Administration. The steps are the same as in the section titled "Migrating to a New Server Farm by Using Central Administration" earlier in this chapter, but when you migrate to an existing server farm, you need to determine if you would like to add your content database to an existing Web application or create a new Web application. The main reason for creating a new Web application would be for authentication requirements regarding the content you are migrating.

Creating a New Web Application

If you determine that you need to create a new Web application to add a content database to, perform the following:

1. In Central Administration, on the Application Management page, in the SharePoint Web Application Management section, click Create Or Extend Web Application.

2. On the Create Or Extend Web Application page, in the Adding A SharePoint Web Application section, click Create A New Web Application.

3. On the Create New Web Application page, in the IIS Web Site section, configure the settings for your new Web application:

   - To choose to create a new Web site, select Create A New IIS Web Site and type the name of the Web site in the Description box.

   - In the Port box, type the port number you want to use to access the Web application. If you are creating a new Web site, this field is filled with a suggested port number. If you are using an existing Web site, this field is filled with the current port number.

   - In the Host Header box, type the URL you want to use to access the Web application. This is an optional field.

   - In the Path box, type the path to the site directory on the server. If you are creating a new Web site, this field is filled with a suggested path. If you are using an existing Web site, this field contains the current path.

4. In the Security Configuration section, configure authentication and encryption for your Web application.

   - In the Authentication Provider section, choose either Negotiate (Kerberos) or NTLM.

   - In the Allow Anonymous section, choose Yes or No. If you choose to allow anonymous access, this enables anonymous access to the Web site by using the computer-specific anonymous access account (that is, IUSR_<computername>).

   - In the Use Secure Sockets Layer (SSL) section, select Yes or No. If you choose to enable SSL for the Web site, you must configure SSL by requesting and installing an SSL certificate.

5. In the Load Balanced URL section, type the URL for the domain name for all sites that users will access in this Web application. This URL domain will be used in all links shown on pages within the Web application. By default, the box is filled with the current server name and port. The Zone box is automatically set to Default for a new Web application, and it cannot be changed from this page.

To change the zone for a Web application, see the section titled "Extending an Existing Web Application" later in this chapter.

6. In the Application Pool section, choose to create a new application pool for this Web application by selecting Create A New Application Pool.

   ○ In the Application Pool Name box, type the name of the new application pool, or keep the default name.

   ○ In the Select A Security Account For This Application Pool section, select Predefined to use an existing application pool security account and then select the security account from the drop-down menu.

   ○ Select Configurable to use an account that is not currently being used as a security account for an existing application pool. In the User Name box, type the user name of the account you want to use and type the password for the account in the Password box.

7. In the Reset Internet Information Services section, choose whether to allow WSS 3.0 to restart IIS on other farm servers. The local server must be restarted manually for the process to finish. If this option is not selected and you have more than one server in the farm, you must wait until the IIS Web site is created on all servers and then run iisreset /noforce on each Web server. The new IIS site is not usable until that action is completed. The choices are unavailable if your farm contains only a single server.

8. In the Database Name And Authentication section, choose the database server, database name, and authentication method for your new Web application. This will be the content database that you restore when migrating your content.

9. Click OK to create the new Web application or click Cancel to cancel the process and return to the Application Management page.

Extending an Existing Web Application

If you determine that you need to extend a Web application to add a content database, perform the following:

1. In Central Administration, on the Application Management page, in the SharePoint Web Application Management section, click Create Or Extend Web Application.

2. On the Create Or Extend Web Application page, in the Adding A SharePoint Web Application section, click Extend An Existing Web Application.

3. On the Extend Web Application To Another IIS Web Site page, shown in Figure 14-6, in the Web Application section, click the Web Application menu and then click Change Web Application.

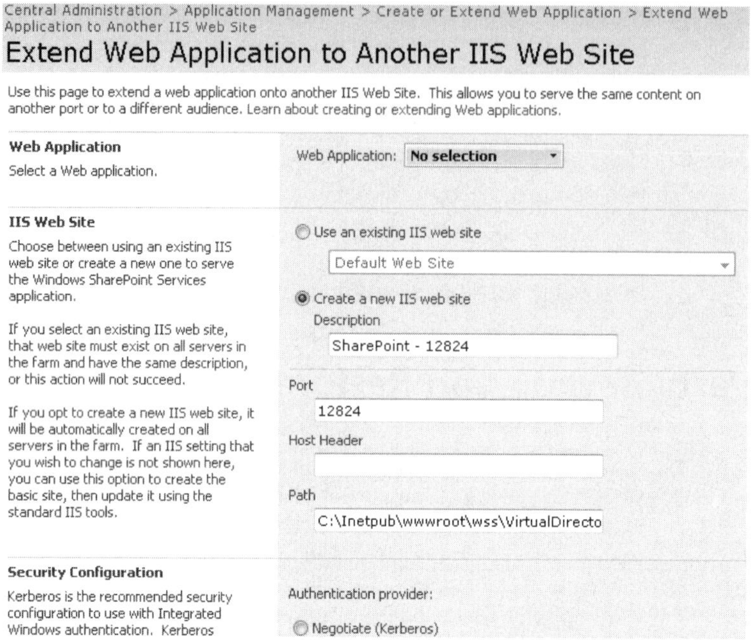

Central Administration > Application Management > Create or Extend Web Application > Extend Web Application to Another IIS Web Site

Extend Web Application to Another IIS Web Site

Use this page to extend a web application onto another IIS Web Site. This allows you to serve the same content on another port or to a different audience. Learn about creating or extending Web applications.

Web Application
Select a Web application.

Web Application: | No selection ▼ |

IIS Web Site
Choose between using an existing IIS web site or create a new one to serve the Windows SharePoint Services application.

If you select an existing IIS web site, that web site must exist on all servers in the farm and have the same description, or this action will not succeed.

If you opt to create a new IIS web site, it will be automatically created on all servers in the farm. If an IIS setting that you wish to change is not shown here, you can use this option to create the basic site, then update it using the standard IIS tools.

○ Use an existing IIS web site

| Default Web Site ▼ |

◉ Create a new IIS web site
Description

| SharePoint - 12824 |

Port

| 12824 |

Host Header

| |

Path

| C:\Inetpub\wwwroot\wss\VirtualDirecto |

Security Configuration
Kerberos is the recommended security configuration to use with Integrated Windows authentication. Kerberos

Authentication provider:

○ Negotiate (Kerberos)

Figure 14-6 Within Central Administration, you can easily perform actions such as extending a Web application to another IIS Web site.

4. On the Select Web Application page, click the Web application you want to extend.

5. Back on the Extend Web Application To Another IIS Web Site page, in the IIS Web Site section, you can select Use An Existing IIS Web Site to use a Web site that has already been created, or you can choose to leave Create A New IIS Web Site selected. The Description, Port, and Path boxes are filled for either choice. You can choose to use the default entries or type the information you want in the boxes.

6. In the Security Configuration section, configure authentication and encryption for the extended Web application.

   ○ In the Authentication Provider section, choose either Negotiate (Kerberos) or NTLM.

   ○ In the Allow Anonymous section, choose Yes or No. If you choose to allow anonymous access, this enables anonymous access to the Web site by using the computer-specific anonymous access account (that is, IUSR_<*computername*>).

   ○ In the Use Secure Sockets Layer (SSL) section, select Yes or No. If you choose to enable SSL for the Web site, you must configure SSL by requesting and installing an SSL certificate.

7. In the Load Balanced URL section, type the URL for the domain name for all sites that users will access in this Web application. This URL domain is used in all links shown on pages within the Web application. By default, the text box is filled with the current server name and port.

8. In the Load Balanced URL section, under Zone, select the zone for the extended Web application from the drop-down menu. You can choose Intranet, Internet, Custom, or Extranet.

9. Click OK to extend the Web application or click Cancel to cancel the process and return to the Application Management page.

Third-Party Backup and Restore Tools

Third-party backup and restore tools can assist your organization in its SharePoint disaster recovery and backup and restore operations. Two popular third-party tools are from AvePoint (*www.avepoint.com*) and CommVault (*www.commvault.com*). These tools can save your organization both time and money by providing a supercharged solution for quick, secure, and granular disaster recovery.

For more information about either one of these solutions, please visit these companies' respective Web sites to download product information.

In Summary...

This chapter explained how your organization should plan for disaster recovery scenarios for your WSS 3.0 implementation. It explained the ways you can back up and restore sites and other objects by using a variety of methods. It also explained how to migrate sites from WSS 2.0 to WSS 3.0.

The next chapter begins Part 6, "Administering SharePoint Services," which explains how to administer WSS 3.0.

Administering SharePoint Services

Administering a SharePoint Server

Once you've installed Microsoft Windows SharePoint Services 3.0 (WSS 3.0), you will want to monitor its performance, be notified when the server is possibly experiencing issues, and receive specific matrices and other reports. You will also undoubtedly want to change settings to suit your environment, create sites, assign permissions, and perform a myriad of other tasks, all in the context of site administration. That's what the chapters in this part explain how to do.

The servers that run WSS 3.0 will more than likely become some of the most valuable servers you have running in your organization. This chapter explains how to monitor your server by using built-in tools in Windows Server as well as how to use other tools such as the Microsoft Operations Manager 2005 (MOM) or System Center Operations Manager 2007 and SQL Reporting Services to receive additional matrices and reports.

Chapter 16, "Managing Site Settings," and Chapter 17, "SharePoint Central Administration," will explain how to administer individual sites as well as use SharePoint Central Administration's Operations and Applications Management pages to manage the overall environment. In short, Chapters 15 and 17 are for server administrators, and Chapter 16 is for the owners of individual sites.

Administering an Entire Server

This section will explain how to configure Windows Server to monitor system performance, and it describes the variety of logs available on a server running WSS 3.0.

WSS 3.0 Monitoring

To get the most out of your WSS 3.0 implementation, you will need to monitor the performance and health of your servers. Verifying specific performance indicators and checking the logs for errors should be part of your job as administrator and should be done on a daily basis. This proactive and continuous systems monitoring will help you detect and mitigate performance, hardware, and high memory-consumption issues.

For these purposes, you should use three tools: WSS Logging and Reporting, Performance Tool (System Monitor), and Microsoft Operations Manager 2005 (or System Center Operations Manager 2007).

WSS Logging and Reporting

The SharePoint Central Administration's Operations page has a section for logging and reporting. Diagnostic logging configurations can be set for:

- **Customer Experience Improvement Program** Specify whether you would like to sign up for the Customer Experience Improvement Program (CEIP). CEIP collects information about how you use Microsoft programs and about some of the problems you encounter. Microsoft uses this information to improve the products and features you use most often and to help solve problems. Participation in the program is strictly voluntary, and the end result is software improvements that better meet your needs.

- **Error reports** Specify whether you would like WSS 3.0 to create error reports when your system encounters hardware or software problems. You can also specify whether you would like to periodically download files that can help identify system problems or change the computer's error collection policy to silently send all reports to you.

- **Event throttling** Control the severity of the events captured in the Windows event log and trace log. You can also change the settings for any single category of events, or for all categories.

- **Trace log** Set up the location for the log files and the number of log files as well as the number of minutes to use a log file.

Usage Analysis Processing configurations can be set for:

- **Logging settings** Configure special log files that are used to run usage analysis processing. These settings will enable logging, identify the location to store log files, and set the number of log files per Web application.

- **Processing settings** Specify whether to enable usage processing on Web server computers and set the time of day to run usage processing.

WSS logging and reporting is discussed in detail in the section titled "Operations Page of Central Administration" in Chapter 17.

Performance Tool (System Monitor)

The Performance tool, shown in Figure 15-1, enables you to monitor system health and track usage demands. This tool comes out of the box with Windows Server 2003 and is great for monitoring WSS 3.0. You can use it to monitor performance counters that you think could identify performance bottlenecks or performance counters that can give you an overview of the server's health. This tool has four components: System Monitor, Counter Logs, Trace Logs, and Alerts. The configuration of these components is detailed in the following sections.

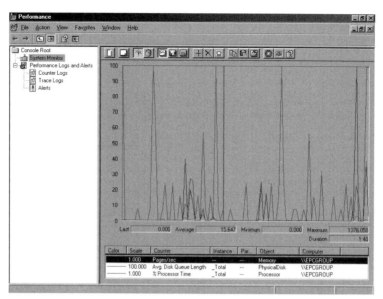

Figure 15-1 This tool comes out of the box with Windows Server 2003 and is great for monitoring the performance of WSS 3.0.

System Monitor

With this tool, you can collect and view data about the usage of hardware resources and the activity of system services on computers you administer. You can define the data that the System Monitor collects by:

- **The type of data** To select the data to be collected, you specify performance objects, performance counters, and performance object instances.

- **The source of data** System Monitor can collect data from your local computer or from other computers on the network for which you have administrative credentials. By default, administrative credentials are required. In addition, you can include real-time data or data collected previously using counter logs. With the Windows Server 2003 family, you can now view performance data that was previously collected and stored in an SQL database by the Performance Logs and Alerts service.

- **Sampling parameters** System Monitor supports manual, on-demand sampling or automatic sampling based on a time interval you specify. This functionality applies to real-time data only. When viewing logged data, you can also choose starting and stopping times so that you can view data spanning a specific time range.

You can also change the appearance of your System Monitoring views by:

- **Type of display** This supports Graph, Histogram, and Report views.

- **Display characteristics** For the three views, you can define the fonts and colors for the display.

Counter Logs

The counter logs can be set to observe performance counters over a period of time. The following is an example of how you can configure a counter log in Windows Server 2003 to monitor unauthorized file access and logon attempts:

1. Click Start, point to Programs, point to Administrative Tools, and then click Performance.

2. Expand Performance Logs and Alerts and then click Counter Logs.

3. Right-click an empty area of the right pane and then click New Log Settings.

4. In the Name box, type a name for the log and then click OK.

5. On the General tab, click Add Objects and then select Use Local Computer Counter Objects.

6. In the Performance Objects box, select Server, click Add, and then click Close.

7. Click the Log Files tab and then do the following:

    ○ Click Configure and then specify the location where you want to store the log files, for example, C:\PerfLogs.

    ○ In the File Name box, type the name that you want for the log file.

    ○ Within Log File Size, select Maximum Limit or click Limit Of and specify a limit. Then click OK.

8. Click the Schedule tab. Then specify the start and stop times for the start log.

9. Under Stop Log, specify your desired selection.

10. Under When A Log File Closes, select either Start A New Log File or Run This Command. Alternatively, leave the selection blank.

11. Click OK.

Trace Logs

Your organization's developers can program applications to write custom operations messages directly to the trace logs. The trace logs, shown in Figure 15-2, are the same logs that WSS 3.0 uses to log developer-oriented information and events. By writing to the same trace log that is used by WSS 3.0, developers of all types of applications can view their custom application's traces in the larger overall content of WSS 3.0's operations.

> **Note**
> Keep in mind that trace logs may be uploaded to Microsoft as part of customer technical service and support, so you should not include any personal or proprietary information with the trace log.

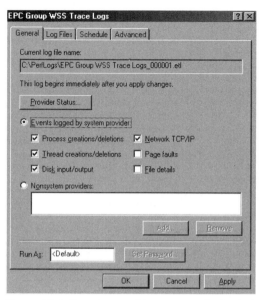

Figure 15-2 Trace logs enable your organization's developers to program applications to write custom operations messages to log.

WSS 3.0 also provides you with an interface to define and expose the categories to use for trace logging messages generated by your application within SharePoint Central Administration.

Alerts

Alerts, shown in Figure 15-3, enable you to manage multiple counters and set rules for each one of the alerts to trigger it when a threshold is reached. Add new alerts in the same manner as you do new counter logs and trace logs. You can easily specify the Alerts schedule, shown in Figure 15-4, to meet the needs of the organization. When an alert is triggered, it can:

- Log an entry in the application log.
- Send a network message.
- Start a performance data log (counter log).
- Run a program.

The most important performance counters that should be monitored can be grouped in four categories:

- Processor
- Memory
- Disk
- Network

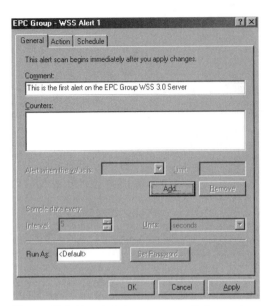

Figure 15-3 Use alerts to manage multiple counters and set rules.

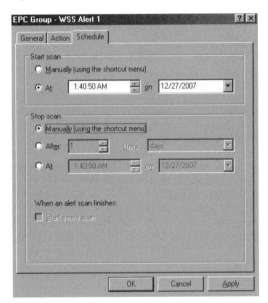

Figure 15-4 With alerts, your organization can specify items such as Start Scan and Stop Scan and whether to send an alert when the scan finishes.

Microsoft Operations Manager 2005 (MOM) or System Center Operations Manager 2007

With Microsoft Operations Manager 2005 (MOM) (or the latest version, System Center Operations Manager 2007) you can monitor and manage your Windows infrastructure by receiving real-time reports about the status and performance of your servers and the individual applications installed on them. This software does not come with Windows Server or WSS 3.0 and must be purchased separately at a retail outlet.

More information about Microsoft Operations Manager 2005 pricing can be found at *www. microsoft.com/mom/howtobuy/default.mspx* **and more information on System Center Operations Manager 2007 can be found at** *www.microsoft.com/systemcenter/default.aspx.*

Each version of Microsoft Operations Manager has the same core components:

- **Management server** The central location where data from all monitored resources is gathered and analyzed. This collected data can be Windows events logs, performance counters, trace logs, and WMI (Windows Management Instrumentation).

- **Managed computers and agents** For your computers to be monitored or managed by MOM, they must be added in the computer's group on the MOM server. The two types of managed computers are agent-managed and agent-less.

- **User interfaces** The separate user interfaces that are used by administrators and operators.

- **Management packs** Management packs dedicated to a specific product such as Microsoft Active Directory directory service, SQL Server, and WSS. The packs contain items such as tasks that can be run from the server, alert definitions, views, and rule sets that determine which events will be monitored.

When you install MOM within your organization, it is recommended that you divide your deployment tasks into phases to ensure that each MOM component is installed in the correct order. The recommended phases for implementing MOM are as follows:

1. Install the MOM 2005 server components.

2. Discover computers and deploy agents.

3. Install MOM 2005 Reporting (optional).

4. Import management packs.

Setup installs the MOM 2005 management pack automatically when you install the MOM Server components. You can import additional management packs from the MOM 2005 product CD after you have installed the management servers, deployed agents, and (optional) MOM Reporting.

> **Note**
>
> The WSS 3.0 Management Pack for MOM 2005 can be downloaded at *www.microsoft. com/downloads/details.aspx?FamilyId=DB1CADF7-1A12-40F5-8EB5-820C343E48CA&displaylang=en.*

Chapter 15

After you install the management pack on the server where MOM is installed, the pack must be imported into MOM. This can be accomplished by performing the following:

1. Open the MOM Administration Console.

2. Go to the Management Packs node.

3. Click Import/Export Management Packs.

4. Click Next on the first screen and then click Import Management Packs.

5. Choose the WSS management pack from the list and click Next. The import operation will start.

> **Note**
>
> For guidance and recommended best practices for backing up, restoring, maintaining, optimizing, and monitoring Microsoft Operations Manager 2005 in your existing IT infrastructure, you can download the Microsoft Operations Manager 2005 Operations Guide at *http://www.microsoft.com/downloads/details.aspx?FamilyID=a0e40758-cab8-4588-b0f2-1508d84906cc&displaylang=en*.

Each server from the WSS 3.0 farm will have to be monitored. You can manually install agents on each server or configure MOM to do that for you. After the management pack and the agents are installed and configured, you can start monitoring WSS 3.0 performance counters, set alerts, and take advantage of the rest of MOM's functionality.

Reporting: Using SQL Reporting Services

Use SQL Reporting Services to configure a report server to run within a deployment of a SharePoint regardless of whether it's WSS 3.0 or SharePoint Server. Integrating a report server in conjunction with your SharePoint deployment provides several advantages for your organization. You can use the same site access for all documents, reports, report models, and external or third-party data sources.

When report server is implemented, the items and properties are stored in the SharePoint content databases. This way, you can use your existing backup-and-restore strategy for SQL Reporting Services. You will also be able to use the collaboration and document management features of WSS 3.0 to check reports in and out for modification, use alerts for item changes, and use the Report Viewer Web Part on Web Part pages and sites.

Users with appropriate permissions can generate reports from any shared data sources and use Report Builder to create new reports. The report server synchronizes with WSS 3.0, and when any properties or settings are modified for any report server items, the changes are stored within the SharePoint database and then copied to a report server database that provides internal storage to the report server.

Integrating WSS 3.0 and SQL Reporting Services

WSS 3.0 and SQL Reporting Services can easily be integrated via an installation of WSS 3.0, SQL Server 2005 with Service Pack 2 (SP2), and the Reporting Services Add-in for SharePoint Technologies. The Reporting Services Add-in is a freely distributable component that you can download from *http://www.microsoft.com/downloads/details. aspx?displaylang=en&FamilyID=1e53f882-0c16-4847-b331-132274ae8c84* (see Figure 15-5).

Figure 15-5 The Reporting Services Add-in for SharePoint can be downloaded from the Microsoft Web site.

In a single server deployment, the component will need to be installed on the server that is running WSS 3.0. In a server-farm deployment, install the WSS 3.0 front end on the report server computer. By installing the Web front end, you join the report server computer to a SharePoint farm.

> **Note**
> Only one report server can be added to a SharePoint farm. The report server can be a stand-alone report server installation, or it can be a scale-out deployment that is accessed through a single URL.

The Reporting Services Add-in provides a URL proxy endpoint, a Report Viewer Web Part, and application pages so that you can view, store, and manage report server content on a SharePoint site or farm. With SQL Server SP2 loaded on the report server, you will be able to work with updated program files, a new SOAP endpoint, custom security and delivery extensions, a revised Reporting Services configuration tool, scripts for granting access to SharePoint configuration and content databases, and a script for creating a report server database that supports SharePoint integrated mode. The report server must be configured to run in SharePoint integrated mode and dedicated exclusively to supporting report access and delivery through your SharePoint site.

> **Note**
>
> The Microsoft SQL Server 2005 Reporting Services Add-in for Microsoft Share-Point Technologies can be downloaded at *www.microsoft.com/downloads/details. aspx?familyid=1E53F882-0C16-4847-B331-132274AE8C84&displaylang=en.*

The report server is implemented as a Web service and as a Windows service that runs under built-in accounts or Windows user accounts. In SharePoint integrated mode, both services connect to the SharePoint configuration and content databases with write and execute permissions. Because the services must connect to the SharePoint databases, the accounts that you can use to run the services will have different requirements depending on whether remote connections are used and whether the proxy endpoint connection uses Windows integrated security or Trusted Account mode.

INSIDE OUT   Proper planning for SQL Reporting Services

With SQL Reporting Services, the contents in the database are mode-specific and are not interchangeable across server modes. If you create a report server database to support SharePoint integrated mode, you cannot later automatically convert or migrate the database to run with a native mode report server instance.

In Summary...

This chapter explained how server administrators and SharePoint administrators can configure the server to monitor system performance, enable and track logs, implement monitoring applications, and work with SQL Reporting Services within your WSS 3.0 environment.

The next two chapters will explain how site owners and site administrators can maintain their own SharePoint sites as well as control the settings for the overall WSS 3.0 enterprise.

This chapter explains how to administer and control existing Microsoft Windows SharePoint sites. Much of this involves security settings, such as who can access the site and what functions they can perform, but other aspects control the site's overall appearance and navigation, as well as a site's features and the settings that oversee its content. In a default installation, you will need to be a site collection administrator or site owner of the SharePoint site you want to modify to perform the actions in this chapter.

This chapter explains the pages that appear on the Site Settings menu of most sites. Chapter 17, "SharePoint Central Administration," will explain the SharePoint Central Administration's Operations page and Application Management page, which are geared more directly toward site collection and server administrators.

Displaying the Site Settings Page

To manage settings and team member information for a site, click the Site Actions link and then the Site Settings link, which by default is located at the upper-right corner of a site. This displays the Site Settings page, shown in Figure 16-1.

The remaining sections in this chapter will explain how to use all of the links on this page. If you are in a subsite when you click Site Settings, you will not see all of the options that would be available for someone who performs this action on the top-level site settings page. You will instead have a list under the Site Collection Administration section called Go To Top Level Site Settings. The Site Collection Administration options will be covered in the "Site Collection Administration" section of this chapter.

Each of the functions in this chapter requires access to one of these roles:

- **Site Collection Administrators** Site Collection Administrators have the Full Control permission level on all Web sites and content within a site collection. From the site collection level, site collection administrators manage settings (such as site collection features, site collection audit settings, and site collection policies) from the Site Settings page for the top-level site.

- **Site Owners** Site Owners are those who have been specifically granted the Full Control permission level on the site, either directly or by being a member of a SharePoint group.

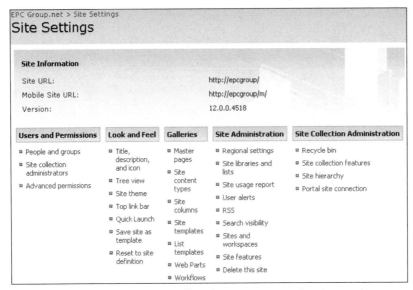

Figure 16-1 The Site Settings page allows for management of settings and team members for the current site.

The Site Settings Page displays a site's URL, a mobile site URL, and version information at the top of the page.

Users and Permissions

Depending on your organization's needs, SharePoint site access can widely vary. Some organizations may leave all sites open to all users, some may restrict content to specific sites, or some may permit access to sites only by team members. The Site Collection Administrators role should be limited to very experienced SharePoint administrators because the role can perform any available action within a site collection.

The following permission levels are provided by default in WSS 3.0: Full Control, Design, Contribute, Read, and Limited Access. For example, you may give Site Owners of a site the Full Control permissions level, power users to a site the Design permissions level, and users who are in a different department and just guests to your site the Read permissions level. Note that this is not a recommendation but rather a simple example.

People and Groups

The People And Groups page, shown in Figure 16-2, has the following options available:

- **New** The New link contains the following:
  - **Add Users** Add a user to a group or site.

- ○ **New Group** Create a new group.

- **Actions** The Actions link contains the following:
  - ○ **E-Mail Users** Allow a selected user to be sent a new e-mail. This option will open up the computer's default e-mail program such as Microsoft Office Outlook.
  - ○ **Call/Message Selected Users** Place a call or send a message to the selected user.
  - ○ **Remove Users From Group** Remove selected users from the SharePoint group.

- **Settings** This area provides the following commands to create a new column or view for the list as well as access to the list settings:
  - ○ **Group Settings** Manage group settings. This option will open up the group's Change Group Setting page.
  - ○ **View Group Permissions** View the permission assignments that the selected SharePoint group has in the site collection.
  - ○ **Edit Group Quick Launch** Modify the SharePoint groups that appear in the Quick Launch on the People And Groups page.
  - ○ **Set Up Groups** Specify who can access your site. You can choose from three selections: Visitors To This Site, Members Of This Site, or Owners Of This Site.
  - ○ **List Settings** Customize the User Information list.

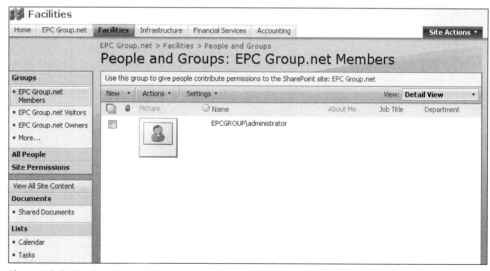

Figure 16-2 The People And Groups page enables you to modify the team members and groups associated with a site.

Adding Users or Groups to a Site

To add a user or group to a site, you can perform the following steps:

1. Click Site Actions, and then Site Settings, and then People And Groups in the site to which you would like to add a new user or group.

2. On the New menu, click Add Users.

3. In the Add Users section, specify the users and groups you would like to add to the site.

4. In the Give Permission section, you can add users to an existing SharePoint group or give them permission directly, if allowed by the site.

5. When you have finished selecting the appropriate permissions, click OK.

Removing Users or Groups from a Site

To remove a user from a site, you can perform the following steps:

1. Click Site Actions, and then Site Settings, and then People And Groups on the site to which you would like to remove a user or group.

2. Select the check boxes for the users and groups you would like to remove from the site.

3. On the Actions menu, click Remove User From Group and then click OK to remove the selected users.

Site Collection Administrators

The Site Collection Administrators page enables you to add site collection administrators to the current site collection, as shown in Figure 16-3. These users will also receive site user confirmation e-mails.

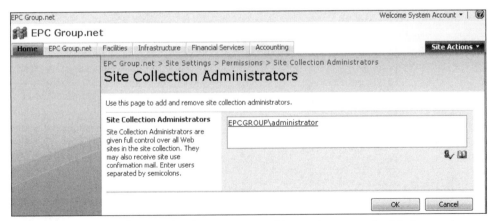

Figure 16-3 The Site Collection Administrators page enables you to manage the list of users who have this very powerful permission level.

If you do not know a user's name, you can click the Browse icon to use the Select People dialog box to search for the appropriate site collection administrators.

Advanced Permissions

The Permissions page, shown in Figure 16-4, has the following options available:

- **New** The New link drop-down contains the following:
  - **Add Users** Add a user to a group or site.
  - **New Group** Create a new SharePoint group.
- **Actions** This area provides the following commands to help create a new column or view for the list as well as access to the list settings:
  - **Manage Permissions Of Parent** Manage the permissions from parent.
  - **Edit Permissions** Copy permissions from the parent site and then stop inheriting permissions.

  If you are opening the Permissions page from the top-level site, you will also receive this option:

- **Settings** This area provides the following commands to help create a new column or view for the list as well as access to the list settings:
  - **Site Collection Administrators** Add and remove site collection administrators.
  - **Access Requests** Enable or disable access requests for the site.
  - **Permission Levels** Configure the available permission levels on the site.

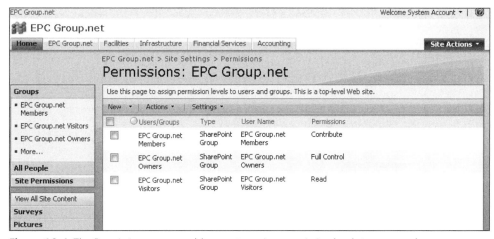

Figure 16-4 The Permissions page enables you to assign permission levels to users and groups on a site.

Look and Feel

The Look And Feel section contains links that enable you to modify a site's appearance and navigational elements, as well as to save the site as a template or reset the site's site definition.

Title, Description, and Icon

The Title, Description, And Icon page, shown in Figure 16-5, has the following options available:

Title and Description:

- **Title** Specify a title for the site. It will be displayed on each page in the site.

- **Description** Specify a description for a site. It will be displayed on the home page.

Logo URL and Description:

- **URL** Associate a logo with the site by specifying the URL of an image file. Click Here To Test enables you to test your link prior to clicking OK.

- **Enter A Description** Add an optional description for the image.

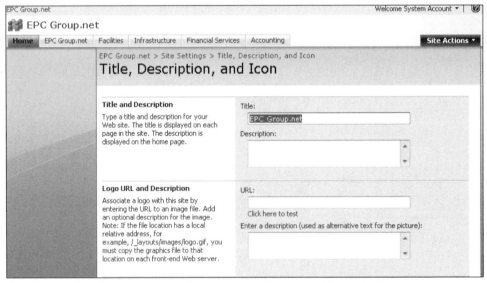

Figure 16-5 The Title, Description, And Icon page enables you modify a site's title, description, logo URL, and logo description.

Tree View

The Tree View page has the following options available to assist you in managing the site's left navigation panel:

- **Enable Quick Launch** Specify whether the Quick Launch should be displayed to assist users with navigation.

- **Enable Tree View** Specify whether a tree view should be displayed to assist users with navigation.

Site Theme

The site's theme is a set of colors, fonts, and decorative elements that gives your site a consistent appearance. A site comes with a set of themes that enables you to quickly change the appearance based on your organization's needs. Select A Theme is the only option available on the Site Theme page, shown in Figure 16-6. With this option, you can select an available theme for your site and then click Apply.

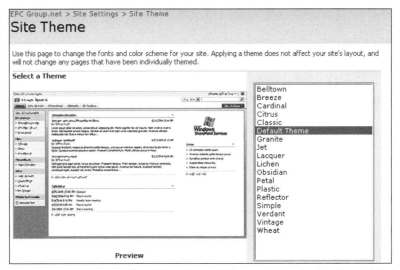

Figure 16-6 On the Site Theme page, you can browse through a list of available themes and then apply a theme to your site.

Changing a Site's Theme

To change the theme of a site, you can perform the following steps:

1. On the Site Actions menu, click Site Settings. (On a site for which the Site Actions menu is customized, point to Site Settings and then click the settings that you want to view.)

2. Under Look And Feel, click Site Theme.

3. Select the theme that you want.

4. Click Apply.

Top Link Bar

The Top Link bar page, shown in Figure 16-7, displays a row of tabs at the top of every page to give users of a site a way to get to other areas of the site. The Top Link bar page offers the following options:

- **New Link** Add new links that appear on the Top Link bar for the site. You can also include links to other sites outside of your site collection.

- **Change Order** Change the order in which the tabs are displayed on the Top Link bar. Any changes that you make to the order of items on the Top Link bar are reflected on any sites that inherit Top Link bar navigation from your site.

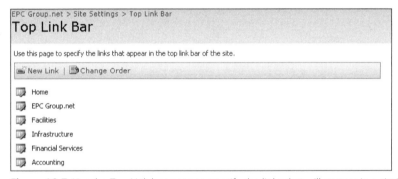

Figure 16-7 Use the Top Link bar page to specify the links that will appear in a site's Top Link bar.

For more information regarding editing the Top Link bar, refer to the section titled "Editing the Top Link Bar" in Chapter 5, "Creating SharePoint Sites, Workspaces, and Pages."

Quick Launch

The Quick Launch is displayed on the home page of a Microsoft Windows SharePoint Services 3.0 (WSS 3.0) site and contains links to featured lists and libraries on the site, subsites of the current site, and People And Groups.

The Quick Launch page, shown in Figure 16-8, has the following options available:

- **New Link** Add new links to the Quick Launch for any lists, links, or sites regardless of their location. You can also use this option to add external URLs to the Quick Launch.

- **New Heading** Add a new heading to the Quick Launch. You can easily manage groups of links by grouping them under specific headings.

- **Change Order** Change the order of both headings and their related links.

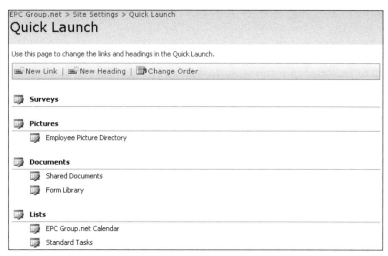

Figure 16-8 The Quick Launch page enables you to change the links and headings in the Quick Launch.

For more information regarding editing the Quick Launch, refer to the section titled "Editing the Quick Launch" in Chapter 5.

Save Site As Template

If you would like to save an existing site as a template so that you can quickly re-create the design, structure, or content of the site, you can save the site as a site template. Once a site is saved as a template, users can select the template when creating a new site.

The Save Site As Template page, shown in Figure 16-9, has the following options available:

- **File Name** Specify the file name for the template you are saving. This file name will be displayed in the Site Template gallery.

- **Name And Description** Specify the name and description of the template you are saving.

- **Include Content** Save the template and include the content of the site within the template. When a new site is created from this template, the content that exists in the template will automatically reside in the new site.

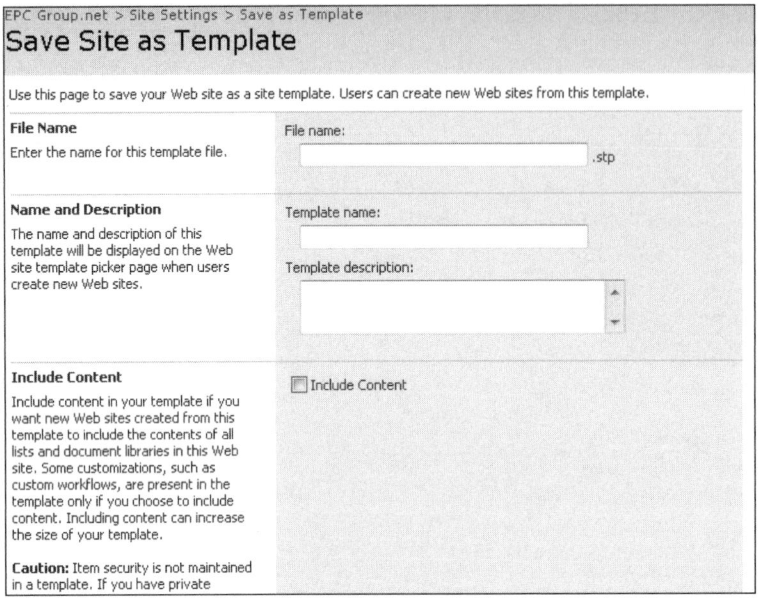

EPC Group.net > Site Settings > Save as Template

Save Site as Template

Use this page to save your Web site as a site template. Users can create new Web sites from this template.

File Name

Enter the name for this template file.

File name:

[   ] .stp

Name and Description

The name and description of this template will be displayed on the Web site template picker page when users create new Web sites.

Template name:

[   ]

Template description:

[   ]

Include Content

Include content in your template if you want new Web sites created from this template to include the contents of all lists and document libraries in this Web site. Some customizations, such as custom workflows, are present in the template only if you choose to include content. Including content can increase the size of your template.

Caution: Item security is not maintained in a template. If you have private

☐ Include Content

Figure 16-9 Save your Web site as a site template that can be used during future site creation.

Saving an Existing Site as a Template

To save a site as a template, perform the following actions:

1. On the Site Actions menu, click Site Settings.

2. On the Site Settings page, in the Look And Feel section, click Save Site As Template.

3. On the Save Site As Template page, in the File Name section, type a name for the template file.

4. In the Name And Description section, type a name and optionally a description.

5. In the Include Content section, select Include Content if you want new Web sites created from this template to include the contents of all lists and document libraries on the Web site.

6. Click OK.

The next time you create a site, the site template will appear in the list of available site templates.

TROUBLESHOOTING

Avoiding an "invalid template" error when you create a site collection

In one of the following scenarios, you may receive the following error message: "The template you have selected is invalid or cannot be found."

- You use an existing site template to create a new site collection in WSS 3.0.

- The site template is associated with a workflow.

- You move the site template to the top-level site template gallery.

- You try to create a new site collection by using the site template in the top-level site template gallery.

- The user account that you use when you try create the second new site collection is not the same account that is used by the application pool identity.

To resolve this problem, you can create a policy that grants Full Control permissions to the user account that you want to use to create the second new site collection. To do this, perform the following:

1. Click Start, point to Administrative Tools, and then click SharePoint 3.0 Central Administration.

2. On the Central Administration page, click Site Actions, and then click Site Settings.

3. Under Galleries on the Site Settings page, click Site templates.

4. On the Site Template Gallery page, click Settings, and then click Gallery Settings.

5. Under Permissions And Management on the Customize Site Template Gallery page, click Permissions For This Gallery.

6. On the Permissions: Site Template Gallery page, click New, and then click Add Users.

7. In the Users/Groups box on the Add Users: Site Template Gallery page, type the name of the user you want to add. In the Give Permission section, click to select the Full Control check box, select any additional options that you want, and then click OK.

Reset To Site Definition

The Reset To Site Definition page enables you to reset the current site definition, which will remove all customizations from a page.

- **Reset Specific Page To Site Definition Version** Specify a specific URL for which the current page should reset its site definition.

- **Reset All Pages In This Site To Site Definition Version** Reset all pages in this site to a site definition version.

Galleries

WSS 3.0 galleries provide a central location to store objects such as master pages, site templates, list templates, Web Parts, workflows, site columns, and site templates.

Master Page Gallery

The Master Page Gallery page, shown in Figure 16-10, has the following options available:

- **New** Add a new folder to the Master Page Gallery.

- **Upload** This area provides the following commands for working with the gallery:
  - **Upload Document** Upload a document from your computer into the Master Page Gallery.
  - **Upload Multiple Documents** Upload multiple documents at once from your computer into the Master Page Gallery.

- **Actions** This area provides the following commands for working with the Gallery:
  - **Edit In Datasheet** Bulk edit items by using a datasheet format.
  - **Open With Window Explorer** Open the document library in a separate Windows Explorer window to allow for dragging and dropping files into this Gallery.
  - **Connect To Outlook** Synchronize items within Office Outlook 2007 so that they are available offline.
  - **Export To Spreadsheet** Download a Microsoft Excel Web Query file. Such files have an .iqy file extension that, by default, causes Microsoft Office Excel to start. Office Excel then connects to the Team Site database and downloads the data for the list you requested.
  - **View RSS Feed** Track information via Really Simple Syndication (RSS) feeds. You can use RSS feeds to receive periodic updates about the gallery.
  - **Alert Me** Specify alerts' titles on a New Alert page. In addition, you can specify the list of users to whom an alert's e-mail notification should be sent when there are changes to a specific item, document, list, or library.

- **Settings** This area provides the following commands for working with the Master Page Gallery:
  - **Create Column** Add a column to store additional information about each item in the gallery.
  - **Create View** Create a view to select columns, filters, and other display settings in the gallery.
  - **Document Library Settings** Access a page with options to manage document library settings such as version settings, permissions, columns, views, workflow, and policy.

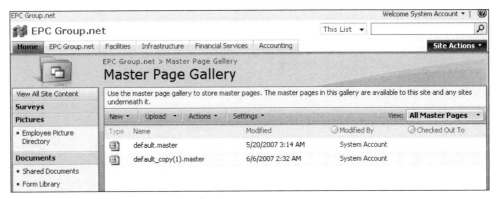

Figure 16-10 Use this page to store and manage master pages.

For more information regarding the Master Page Gallery, refer to the section titled "Using Master Pages" in Chapter 9, "Creating and Modifying Basic Site Features."

Site Content Type Gallery

WSS 3.0 enables your organization to define site content types, which are groups of reusable settings that describe the shared behaviors for a specific type of content. Site content types are available for use in any subsites of the site for which they have been defined. The Site Content Type Gallery page is shown in Figure 16-11.

EPC Group.net > Site Settings > Site Content Type Gallery

Site Content Type Gallery

Use this page to create and manage content types declared on this site and all parent sites. Content types visible on this page are available for use on this site and its subsites.

Create   Show Group: All Groups

Site Content Type	Parent	Source
Document Content Types		
Basic Page	Document	EPC Group.net
Document	Item	EPC Group.net
Dublin Core Columns	Document	EPC Group.net
Form	Document	EPC Group.net
Link to a Document	Document	EPC Group.net
Master Page	Document	EPC Group.net
Picture	Document	EPC Group.net
Web Part Page	Basic Page	EPC Group.net
Folder Content Types		
Discussion	Folder	EPC Group.net
Folder	Item	EPC Group.net
List Content Types		
Announcement	Item	EPC Group.net

Figure 16-11 This page is used to create and manage content types declared on this site and all parent sites.

Chapter 16

When you click Create on the Site Content Type Gallery page, the New Site Content Type page appears, providing the following options:

- **Name and Description** Specify a name and description for the new site content type.
- **Parent Content Type** Specify information regarding the parent content type:
  - **Select Parent Content Type From** Select a location from which the parent content type will be derived.
  - **Parent Content Type** Select the parent content type.
- **Group** Specify a site content type group:
  - **Existing Group** Select from an existing group.
  - **New Group** Specify a new group.

Creating a Site Content Type

To create a site content type, you can perform the following steps:

1. On the Site Content Type Gallery page, click Create. The New Site Content Type page appears.

2. In the Name and Description section, type a name and optionally a description for the new site content type.

3. In the Select Parent Content Type From list, select the group on which you want to base this new content type.

   In the Parent Content Type list, select the parent content type that you want to base your content type on. Note that the list of parent content types differs depending on the option that you selected in the previous step.

4. In the Group section, choose whether to store this new site content type in an existing group or create a new group.

5. Click OK.

   The Site Content Type: *Your New Content Type* name page appears. You can choose options on this page to further define your new content type.

Site Columns

The Site Column Gallery page is shown in Figure 16-12.

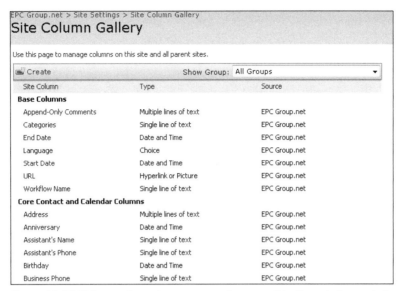

Figure 16-12 This page is used to manage columns on this site and all parent sites.

When you click Create on the Site Column Gallery page, the New Site Column page appears, providing the following options:

- **Name and Type** Add a new site column in the gallery by selecting from the following options:
    - **Column Name** Specify a name for the new column.
    - **The Type Of Information In This Column Is** Select the type of information that will be stored in the column.
- **Group** Specify a site group column:
    - **Existing Group** Select from a drop-down of existing groups.
    - **New Group** Specify a new group.
- **Additional Column Settings** Specify additional information about the column settings.
    - **Description** Specify a description for the new site column.
    - **Require That This Column Contains Information** Specify whether a particular column must have information.
    - **Maximum Number Of Characters** Specify the number of characters for the new site column type.
    - **Default Value** Specify a default value.

Chapter 16

Creating a Site Column

To create a site column, you can perform the following steps:

1. On the Site Column Gallery page, click Create.

2. In the Name And Type section, in the Column Name box, type the name that you want for the new site column.

3. Select the type of information you want to store in the column.

4. In the Group section, select the existing group in which to store the new site column. Alternatively, create a new group to store the column.

5. In the Additional Column Settings section, select the additional column settings you want. The options available in this section differ depending on the type of column that you select in the Name And Type section.

6. Click OK.

Site Templates

The Site Template Gallery page, shown in Figure 16-13, has the following options available:

- **Upload** This area provides the following commands for working with the Site Templates Gallery:
  - **Upload Document** Upload a single document from your computer into the Site Template gallery.
  - **Upload Multiple Documents** Upload multiple documents from your computer at one time into the Site Template gallery.

- **Actions** This area provides the following commands for working with the Site Templates Gallery:
  - **Open With Window Explorer** Open the document library in a separate Windows Explorer window to allow for dragging and dropping of files into this gallery.
  - **Export To Spreadsheet** Download a Microsoft Office Excel Web Query file. Such files have an .iqy file extension that, by default, causes Excel to start. Excel then connects to the Team Site database and downloads the data for the list you requested.
  - **Alert Me** Display a New Alert page where you can specify an alert's title as well as specify the list of users to whom an alert's e-mail notification should be sent when there are changes to a specific item, document, list, or library.

- **Settings** This area provides the following commands for working with the list:
  - **Create Column** Add a column to store additional information about each item in the gallery.

○ **Create View** Create a view to select columns, filters, and other display settings in the gallery.

○ **Gallery Settings** Manage settings for the gallery such as permissions, columns, views, and policy.

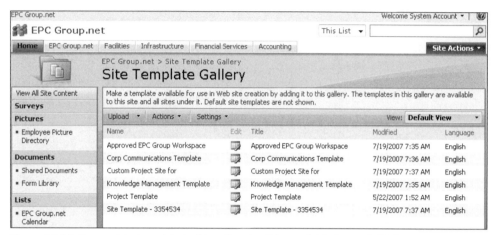

Figure 16-13 If you add a template to this gallery, it will be available for use in Web site creation.

Saving a Site as a Template

To save a site as a template, you can perform the following steps:

1. On the Site Actions menu, click Site Settings. On a site with a customized Site Actions menu, point to Site Settings and then click the settings that you want to view.

2. On the Site Settings page, in the Look And Feel section, click Save Site As Template.

3. On the Save Site As Template page, in the File Name section, type a name for the template file.

4. In the Name and Description section, type a name and optionally a description.

5. In the Include Content section, select the Include Content check box if you want new Web sites created from this template to include contents from all lists and document libraries on the Web site.

   Note that some customizations, such as custom workflows, are present in the template only if you choose to include content. Including content can increase the size of your template. The size limit for Include Content is 10 megabytes (MB).

6. Click OK.

The next time you create a site, the site template will appear in the list of available site templates.

List Templates

The List Template Gallery page, shown in Figure 16-14, has the following options available:

- **Upload** This area provides the following command for working with the list:
  - **Upload Document** Upload a single document from your computer into the List Template gallery.

- **Actions** This area provides the following commands for working with a list:
  - **Export To Spreadsheet** Download a Microsoft Excel Web Query file. Such files have an .iqy file extension that, by default, causes Microsoft Office Excel to start. Office Excel then connects to the Team Site database and downloads the data for the list you requested.
  - **Alert Me** Display a New Alert page where you can specify an alert's title as well as specify the list of users to whom the alert's e-mail notification should be sent when there are changes to a specific item, document, list, or library.

- **Settings** This area provides the following commands for working with a list:
  - **Create Column** Add a column to store additional information about each item in the gallery.
  - **Create View** Create a view to select columns, filters, and other display settings in the gallery.
  - **Gallery Settings** Manage settings for the gallery such as permissions, columns, views, and policy.

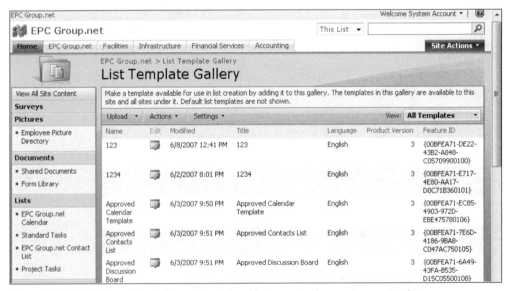

Figure 16-14 Add a template to this gallery to be able to use it when you're creating lists.

Web Parts

The Web Part Gallery page, shown in Figure 16-15, has the following options available:

- **New** This area allows you to add a new item to the list:
  - **New Web Parts** Display all available Web Parts for this gallery. Select Web Parts that you want to add and then click Populate Gallery.
- **Upload** This area provides the following commands for working with the Web Part Gallery:
  - **Upload Document** Allow for the upload of a single document into the Web Part Gallery from your computer.
- **Actions** This area provides the following commands for working with the Web Part Gallery:
  - **Export To Spreadsheet** Download a Microsoft Excel Web Query file. Such files have an .iqy file extension that, by default, causes Microsoft Office Excel to start. Office Excel then connects to the Team Site database and downloads the data for the list you requested.
  - **Alert Me** Display a New Alert page where you can specify an alert's title as well as specify the list of users to whom the alert's e-mail notification should be sent when there are changes to a specific item, document, list, or library.
- **Settings** This area provides the following commands for working with the Web Part Gallery:
  - **Create Column** Add a column to store additional information about each item in the gallery.
  - **Create View** Create a view to select columns, filters, and other display settings in the gallery.
  - **Gallery Settings** Manage settings for the gallery such as permissions, columns, views, and policy.

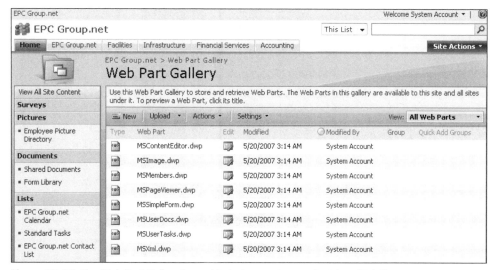

Figure 16-15 The Web Part Gallery is used to help you store and retrieve Web Parts.

Chapter 16

Workflows

The Site Collection Workflows page lists the available workflows in the current site collection, as shown in Figure 16-16.

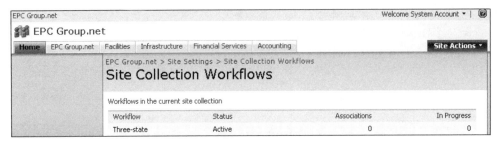

Figure 16-16 Site Collection Workflows displays the workflows that are in the current site collection.

Site Administration

The Site Administration section enables you to modify regional settings, change the design of objects, view site usage, update user alerts, and perform other related administrative tasks.

Regional Settings

The Regional Settings page, shown in Figure 16-17, provides the following options:

- **Locale** Specify the world region that you would like the site dates, numbers, and sort order to be based on.

- **Sort Order** Specify the sort order.

- **Time Zone** Specify the standard time zone.

- **Set Your Calendar** This area provides for calendar settings:
  - **Calendar** Specify the type of calendar.
  - **Show Week Numbers In The Date Navigator** Specify whether to show week numbers in the date navigator.
  - **Enable An Alternate Calendar** Specify a secondary calendar that provides extra information on the calendar features.
  - **Define Your Work Week** Select which days comprise your work week.
  - **(Select Days)** Sun, Mon, Tue, Wed, Thu, Fri, Sat.
  - **First Day of Week** Select the day that begins your week.
  - **Start Time** Select the start time of your week.
  - **First Day of Year** Select the first week of the year for your organization.

○ **End Time** Select the end time of your week.

○ **Time Format** Specify whether you want to use the 12-hour time format or the 24-hour format.

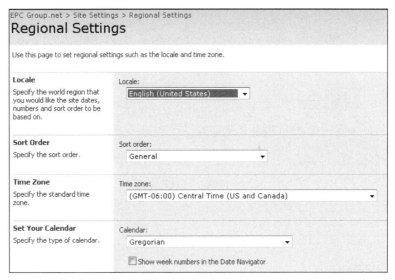

Figure 16-17 Set regional settings such as the locale and time zone.

Site Libraries and Lists

The Site Libraries And Lists page enables you to change the design of a list, document library, discussion board, or survey by selecting a customize link for an object.

Site Usage Report

Use the Site Usage Report page to view a detailed usage report for a particular Web site. The report does not include data for subsites. To see detailed data for these sites, look at their corresponding usage reports. For usage information on all sites in a particular site collection, see the Web site collection usage summary.

If you go to the Site Usage Report page and you do not have a report available, you will receive the following error message: "A usage report is not available for this site. Usage processing may be disabled on this server or the usage data for the site has not been processed yet."

To resolve this, you must turn on logging and usage processing. Contact your site administrator to verify that logging and usage processing are turned on in WSS 3.0. Also, if the site is new or has not been used before the day you are checking the report, no data will appear until the usage log processing is completed. The typical log processing time is approximately 24 hours. If there has been no activity on the site for the past 31 days, you will see the "no data" message.

Chapter 16

User Alerts

Go to the User Alerts page, shown in Figure 16-18, to manage alerts for users. You can select a name in the drop-down list and then click Update to view that user's alert settings. You can then delete alerts by selecting the alerts and clicking Delete Selected Alerts.

Figure 16-18 The User Alerts page enables you to manage alerts for users.

Search Visibility

The Search Visibility page, shown in Figure 16-19, controls a site's search visibility settings and provides the following options:

- **Indexing Site Content** Specify whether to allow this Web site to appear in Share-Point's search results.

- **Indexing ASPX Page Content** Specify whether you want to index ASPX page Content.

Sites and Workspaces

The Sites And Workspaces page has the following options available:

- **Create** Open the New SharePoint Site page, which will enable you to create a new site or workspace.

- **Site Creation Permissions** Enable workspace creation for individual permission levels. You can select which permission levels are allowed to create sites and workspaces.

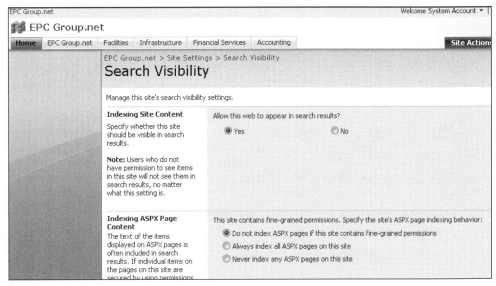

Figure 16-19 Manage a site's search visibility settings.

Site Features

The Site Features page lists all of the features available to the site. Depending on the current status of a feature, you will see either an Activate or a Deactivate button next to the feature along with its current status, as shown in Figure 16-20. These self-explanatory commands do the following:

- **Activate** Activate a feature that is currently not active.

- **Deactivate** Deactivate a feature that is currently active.

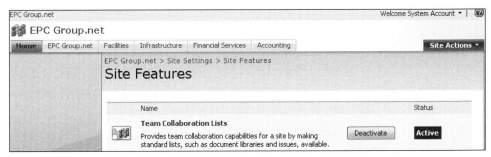

Figure 16-20 This page lists the available features along with a command button to either activate or deactivate the feature along with its current status.

Your organization can implement features to reduce the complexity involved in making simple site customizations and can be extremely powerful and timesaving when upgrades are applied to a deployment. Features eliminate the need to copy large amounts of code to change simple site functionality. They also reduce versioning and inconsistency issues that may arise among front-end Web servers.

Features make it easier to activate or deactivate functionality in the course of a deployment, and administrators can easily transform the template or definition of a site by simply toggling a particular feature on or off in the user interface.

INSIDE OUT **Administrators love features—features are definitely the way to go!**

My organization, EPCGroup.net, develops a large number of custom workflows for our clients. I can tell you from firsthand experience, SharePoint administrators and those supporting a WSS 3.0 implementation absolutely love working with features to activate or deactivate a custom solution. You should definitely become familiar with how features work and plan on managing your WSS 3.0 functionality in this manner.

Feature Implementation

To implement a feature, add a subfolder containing a feature definition within the Features setup directory (*Local_Drive:\Program Files\Common Files\Microsoft Shared\ web server extensions\12\TEMPLATE\FEATURES*). The Feature subfolder includes a Feature.xml file that defines the base properties of the feature and lists elements bound to it, such as XML files containing element manifests and any other supporting files. A Feature folder may contain only a Feature.xml file, or it may contain a Feature.xml file and any number of supporting element files, including XML files and also ASPX, HTM, XSN, RESX, DLL, and other file types.

After creating the Feature folder, you can install and activate the feature through command-line operations of Stsadm.exe, or through the object model. You can also activate a feature through the user interface. Installing a feature makes its definition and elements known throughout a server farm, and activating the feature makes it available at a particular scope.

Delete This Site

Use the Delete This Site page to delete the site on which the Delete This Site link was selected. The specific site will be shown on the page to ensure you are deleting the correct URL. If you wish to delete the site, click Delete. If you do not wish to delete the site, click Cancel.

Site Collection Administration

Use the Site Collection Administration section of links to access and configure site collection settings such as the Site Collection Recycle Bin, the Site Collection Usage Summary, Storage Space Allocation, Site Collection Features, Site Hierarchy, and Portal Site Connection.

Chapter 16

Recycle Bin

When your organization's users clean out their Recycle Bins, the files are sent to the Site Collection Recycle Bin. From this point, SharePoint site collection administrators can then manage the deletion of the items. Items that were deleted more than 30 day(s) ago will be automatically emptied.

The Site Collection Recycle Bin page, shown in Figure 16-21, provides the following options:

- **Restore Selection** Restore the items that you have selected on the page.

- **Delete Selection** Delete the items that you have selected on the page.

- **Empty Recycle Bin** Empty the entire Site Collection Recycle Bin.

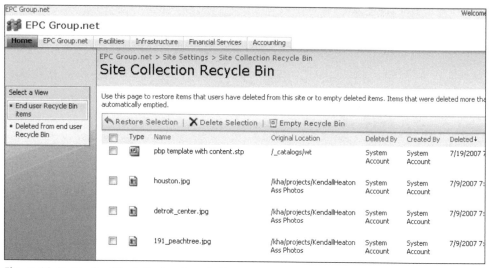

Figure 16-21 Use the Site Collection Recycle Bin page to restore items that have been deleted from a particular site or to empty deleted items.

Site Collection Features

The Site Collection Features page lists all the features that are available to the site collection. Depending on the current status of a feature, you will see either an Activate or a Deactivate button next to the feature along with its current status. These self-explanatory commands do the following:

- **Activate** Activate a features that is currently not active.

- **Deactivate** Deactivate a feature that is currently active.

Chapter 16

Site Hierarchy

The Site Hierarchy page, shown in Figure 16-22, shows all of the Web sites that have been created under the current site collection. The URL of the site collection will be displayed to ensure that—if you have several site collections—you are looking into the correct site collection. The site's URL and title are displayed along with a Manage link, which will take you to the Site Settings page of the selected site.

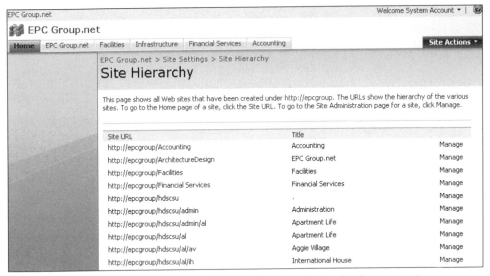

Figure 16-22 This page shows all Web sites that have been created under the current site.

Portal Site Connection

The Portal Site Connection page, shown in Figure 16-23, has the Portal Configuration option available. This option enables you to specify whether to connect to a portal site. If you are connecting to a portal site, you will need to enter the portal's Web address and specify the portal name.

Updating Your Personal Information

With WSS 3.0, you can update user information, regional settings, and alerts by clicking on your user name at the upper right of a page and selecting My Settings. This will take you to the User Information page. The User Information page has the following options available:

- **Edit Item** Edit your user information settings.

- **My Regional Settings** Configure your regional settings.

- **My Alerts** Manage the list of libraries, files, lists, and items for which you receive alerts.

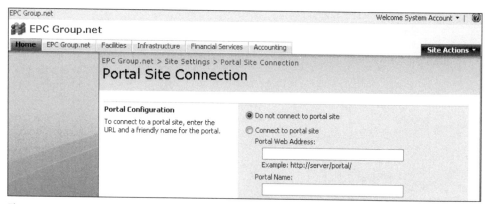

Figure 16-23 Specify whether to connect to a portal site.

In Summary...

This chapter explained how to use the most common commands for managing team members, access, appearance, and capabilities of a SharePoint site.

The next chapter will explain additional configuration options that are mostly of interest to administrators.

This chapter explains how to administer the Operations and Applications Management pages of Microsoft SharePoint Central Administration. You will undoubtedly need to modify the settings in these areas from time to time to keep your environment up to date and running smoothly.

This chapter is geared directly toward site collection and server administrators because these pages control almost every aspect of your organization's Microsoft Windows SharePoint Services 3.0 (WSS 3.0) implementation.

Operations Page of Central Administration

The Operations page of the SharePoint Central Administration contains links to pages that help you manage your server or server farm, for example, changing the server farm topology, specifying which services are running on each server, and changing settings that affect multiple servers or applications.

As you can see in Figure 17-1, the Operations page has six sections: Topology And Services, Security Configuration, Logging And Reporting, Global Configuration, Backup And Restore, and Data Configuration.

Topology And Services

The Topology And Services section enables you to configure the servers and services within your SharePoint environment. This section also controls your organization's incoming and outgoing e-mail configurations for SharePoint.

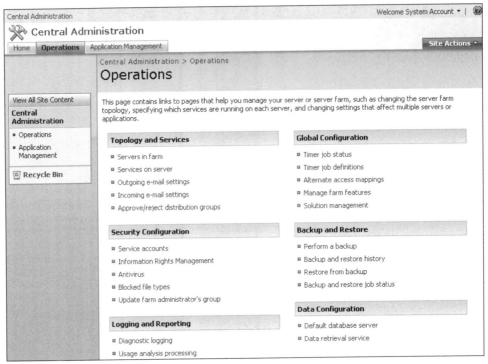

Figure 17-1 The Operations page of SharePoint Central Administration.

Servers In Farm

The Servers In Farm page, shown in Figure 17-2, has the following information and options available:

- **Farm Information** This section provides the following:
    - **Version** Displays the version number of your WSS 3.0 implementation.
    - **Configuration Database Server** Displays the name of your configuration database server.
    - **Configuration Database Name** Displays the name of your configuration database.

- **Servers In Farm Information** This section displays detailed information on the available servers in the farm. The following information is displayed:
    - **Server** Displays the name of a server in your deployment. The server's name contains a link that when clicked will take you to the Services On Server page, which displays the services for the selected server.
    - **Services Running** Displays the services that are running for the server.
    - **Version** Displays the WSS 3.0 version number on the server.

o **Remove Server** Clicking this link removes the server from the Servers In Farm page. When you click this link, you receive a warning message notifying you that the recommended method for removing a server is to uninstall SharePoint Products and Technologies from the server rather than using this method.

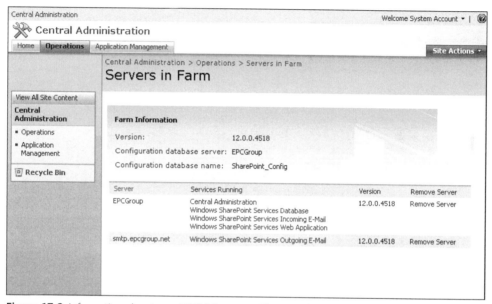

Figure 17-2 Information about your WSS 3.0 servers. The page has two links to perform additional actions.

Note

The original release version of WSS 3.0 is 12.0.0.4518.

The Servers In Farm page should be used to manage the servers in your WSS 3.0 implementation.

Services On Server

The Services On Server page, shown in Figure 17-3, has the following information and options available:

- **Server** In a drop-down box, displays the name of a server in your implementation. You can select Change Server, which will load a Select Server dialog box of your other available servers.

- **Services On Server** Displays detailed information on the available servers in the farm. The following information is displayed:

  - **Service** Displays a list of WSS 3.0 services.

  - **Comment** Displays any comments for the service.

  - **Status** Displays whether the service is started or stopped.

  - **Action** Contains a link to either start or stop the service depending on its current status.

  - **When Finished, Return To The Central Administration Home Page** Contains a Central Administration link that will take you back to the home page.

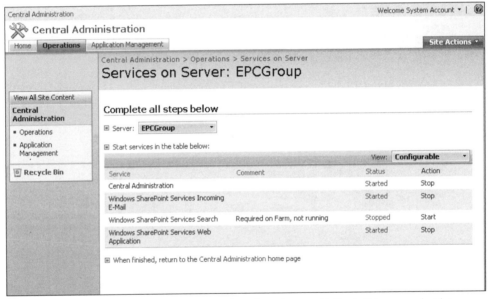

Figure 17-3 This page displays the services on the selected server. Notice in this screen shot how one of the services is stopped. You could start this service by clicking the Start link.

This page is useful for administrators to find out which services are started for a specific server. You can use one of two available views to show either all the services or just the configurable ones.

Outgoing E-Mail Settings

The Outgoing E-Mail Settings page, shown in Figure 17-4, has the following options available:

- **Outbound SMTP Server** Specify your organization's outbound Simple Mail Transfer Protocol (SMTP) server to be used for e-mail–based notifications for alerts, invitations, and administrator notifications.

- **From Address** Specify the From address for e-mail-based notifications.

- **Reply-To Address** Specify the Reply-to address for e-mail–based notifications.

- **Character Set** Specify the character set for e-mail–based notifications.

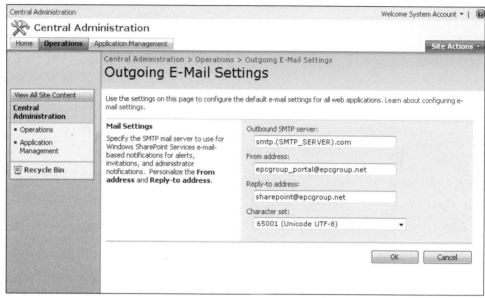

Figure 17-4 Specify the settings for your organization's WSS 3.0 e-mail–based notifications.

The Outgoing E-Mail Settings page is used to specify your organization's e-mail settings for WSS 3.0. You should use e-mail addresses that make sense for your organization and an SMTP server that is highly available.

Incoming E-Mail Settings

The Configure Incoming E-Mail Settings page, shown in Figure 17-5, has the following options available:

- **Enable Incoming E-Mail** This section contains the following:
  - ○ **Enable Sites On This Server To Receive E-Mail** Select whether sites will have the ability to receive e-mail.
  - ○ **Settings Mode** Select either Automatic or Advanced mode.

- **Directory Management Service** Specify whether to use the SharePoint Directory Management Service to create distribution groups and contacts, or select Use Remote.

- **Incoming E-Mail Server Display Address** The address used here will be the e-mail address that is displayed on Web pages when a user creates an incoming e-mail address for a site.

- **E-Mail Drop Folder** Specify the folder in which to look for e-mail messages.

Chapter 17

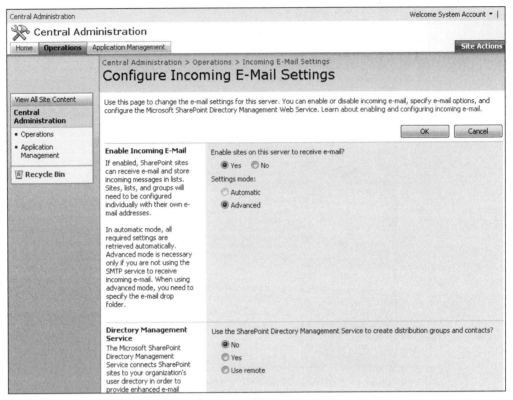

Figure 17-5 Change the e-mail settings for a particular server.

Use the Configure Incoming E-Mail Settings page to manage e-mail settings for your environment. If you want to enable sites on this server to receive e-mail, then this is where you should configure the environment to do so.

For example, someone such as a project manager may find it extremely useful to have an e-mail enabled discussion board in existence to receive the hundreds of similar e-mails that they might receive on a weekly basis. This way, they can have all the e-mails reside in one location where project team members can review them and stay up to date. Even if this is something you are weary of enabling, I would recommend e-mail enabling a few objects in SharePoint and testing out this powerful functionality.

Approve/Reject Distribution Groups

WSS 3.0 gives you the ability to assign an e-mail address to a Site Group when you create a site. When you e-mail–enable a group in SharePoint, it creates a Distribution Group in the Microsoft Active Directory directory service for you. The Approve/Reject Distribution Groups page is the approval method for administrators to first evaluate a new group before it is actually created in Active Directory. If you turn on approval, then the Distribution Group is automatically created in Active Directory if the Central Administration application pool has the create object rights in Active Directory.

The Approve/Reject Distribution Groups page has the following options available: New, Actions, and Settings:

New

This area provides the following commands for working with the Approve/Reject Distribution Groups list.

- **New Item** Load the New Item page and add a new item to the list. The New Item page contains the following:
  - ○ **Title** The title of the new item
  - ○ **Alias** The alias of the new item
  - ○ **Description** The description of the new item
  - ○ **Justification** The justification of the new item
  - ○ **Owner Email** The owner e-mail address of the new item
  - ○ **New Alias** The new alias of the new item

- **New Folder** Load the New Folder page and add a new folder to the list. The New Folder page contains the following:
  - ○ **Title** The title of the new folder
  - ○ **Alias** The alias of the new folder
  - ○ **Description** The description of the new folder
  - ○ **Justification** The justification of the new folder
  - ○ **Owner Email** The owner e-mail address of the new folder
  - ○ **New Alias** The new alias of the new folder

Actions

This area provides the following commands for working with the list:

- **Edit In Datasheet** Bulk-edit items by using a datasheet format.

- **Export To Spreadsheet** Download a Microsoft Excel Web Query file. Such files have an .iqy file extension that, by default, causes Microsoft Office Excel to start. Office Excel then connects to the Team Site database and downloads the data for the list you requested.

- **Open With Access** Work with items in a Microsoft Access database.

- **View RSS Feed** Track information via Really Simple Syndication (RSS) feeds. You can use RSS feeds to receive periodic updates about the list.

- **Alert Me** Display a New Alert page where you can specify an alert's title as well as specify the list of users to whom the alert's e-mail notification should be sent when there are changes to a specific item, document, list, or library.

Chapter 17

Settings

This area provides the following commands for working with the list:

- **Create Column** Add a column to store additional information about each item in the list.

- **Create View** Create a view to select columns, filters, and other display settings in the list.

- **List Settings** Manage settings for the list such as permissions, columns, views, and policy.

Security Configuration

This section contains links to pages that enable you to configure service accounts as well as information rights management settings. There are also pages around configuring antivirus settings, configuring blocked file types, and updating the farm administrator's group.

Service Accounts

The Credential Management section of the Service Accounts page has the following options available:

- **Windows Service** Select a Windows service to update.

- **Web Application Pool** Select a Web application pool to update. Then select the following:
  - **Web Service** Select a Web server to update.
  - **Application Pool** Once the Web service is selected, you can select an application pool to update.

- **Select An Account For This Component** Select an account for this component and then select the following:
  - **Predefined** Select a predefined account for this component.
  - **Configurable** Specify a configurable account for this component by assigning a user name for this component (that is, DOMAIN*User name*) and a password for this account.

Use the Service Accounts page to configure service accounts in the farm. It is extremely useful to be able to use drop-down boxes to select a specific Windows service or Web application pool and the corresponding account information.

Information Rights Management

The Information Rights Management page allows you to indicate the location of the Windows Rights Management Services (RMS) and then specify the following:

- **Do Not Use The IRM On This Server** Choose to not use IRM on this server.

- **Use The Default RMS Server Specified In Active Directory** Choose to use the default RMS server that is specified in Active Directory.

- **User This RMS Server** Specify the RMS server that should be used.

The Information Rights Management page enables you to configure your WSS 3.0 environment to integrate with your Information Rights Management server.

For more information on Information Rights Management, refer to "Information Rights Management in Windows SharePoint Services: Overview," which can be found at *http://msdn2.microsoft.com/en-us/library/ms458245.aspx*.

Antivirus

The Antivirus page, shown in Figure 17-6, has the following options available:

- **Antivirus Settings** Specify when documents that are stored in libraries and lists should be scanned, and whether the virus scanner should attempt to clean infected documents. Choose from among the following options:
  - **Scan Documents On Upload** Enable scanning documents when they are being uploaded.
  - **Scan Documents On Download** Enable scanning documents when they are being downloaded.
  - **Allow Users To Download Infected Documents** Download infected documents.
  - **Attempt To Clean Infected Documents** Enable attempt to clean infected documents.

- **Antivirus Time Out** Specify the time out duration (in seconds) for the virus scanner.

- **Antivirus Threads** Specify the number of execution threads on the server that the virus scanner may use.

INSIDE OUT   **Do I need an antivirus solution for SharePoint?**

Even though your organization may have an antivirus program on your users' desktops as well as on the SharePoint servers, SharePoint antivirus solutions can save your organization from possible threats. If you have an Internet-facing WSS 3.0 site, then you need to seriously consider purchasing an antivirus solution. Microsoft's Forefront Security for SharePoint manages and integrates solutions that provide protection against threats, inappropriate content, and disclosure of confidential information. This is something you definitely need to investigate even if you are not ready to purchase a solution. Having this on your radar screen for the future is important!

Chapter 17

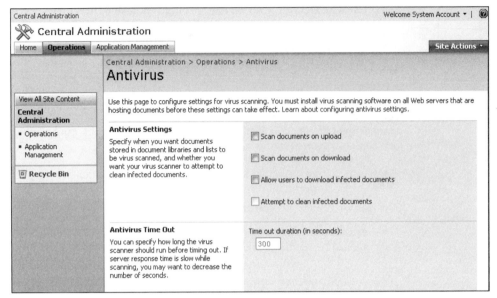

Figure 17-6 Configure settings for virus scanning.

For more information on a powerful SharePoint antivirus solution, research Microsoft Forefront Security for SharePoint at *http://microsoft.com/forefront/serversecurity/sharepoint/default. mspx.*

Blocked File Types

Blocking specific file types that should not be allowed in your environment is a good way to enforce additional site governance. The Blocked File Types page has the following options available:

- **Web Application** View the Web application to which the blocked file types will apply. Select Change Web Application to select another Web application.

- **Specify File Extensions** Specify which file types will be blocked in the selected Web application. Each specified file type extension should be on a separate line.

Use the Blocked File Types page to enforce blocked file types so that you do not incur the risk inherent in allowing certain file types to be saved within your enterprise. This is a good way to enforce governance in WSS 3.0. File types such as MP3s or MP4s are just two examples of file types you may want to exclude.

For more information regarding governing your WSS 3.0 environment, refer to the section titled "Site Governance Best Practices" in Chapter 5, "Creating SharePoint Sites, Workspaces, and Pages."

Update Farm Administrator's Group

The People And Groups page, which opens when you select Update Farm Administrator's Group, has the following options available:

New

This area provides the following commands for working with the list:

- **Add Users** This will load the Add Users page, which provides the following configuration options:
  - ○ **Add Users** Enter user names, group names, or e-mail addresses of users you would like add.
  - ○ **Give Permissions** Choose the permissions you want these new users to have.
  - ○ **Send E-Mail** Send e-mail to your new users.
- **New Group** This will load the New Group page, which provides the following configuration options:
  - ○ **Name And About Me Description** Specify a name and description for the new group.
  - ○ **Owner** Specify an owner of the new group.
  - ○ **Group Settings** Specify who can view the membership of the group (either Group Members or Everyone) and specify who can edit the membership of the group (either Group Owner or Everyone).
  - ○ **Membership Requests** Specify how to handle membership requests. The available options are Allow Requests To Join/Leave This Group, Auto-Accept Requests, and Send Membership Requests To The Following E-Mail Address.
  - ○ **Give Group Permission To This Site** Specify the permission level group members will get on this site. The available options are Full Control, Designer, Contributor, or Read.
- **Actions** This area provides the following commands for working with the list:
  - ○ **E-Mail Users** Allow for the selected user to be sent a new e-mail. This option will open up the computer's default e-mail program such as Microsoft Office Outlook.
  - ○ **Call/Message Selected Users** Place a call to the selected user.
  - ○ **Remove Users From Group** Remove selected users from the SharePoint group.
- **Settings** This area provides the following configuration options:
  - ○ **Group Settings** Manage group settings. This option will open up the group's Change Group Setting page.
  - ○ **View Group Permissions** View permission assignments that the selected SharePoint group has in the site collection.
  - ○ **Edit Group Quick Launch** Modify the SharePoint groups that appear in the Quick Launch on the People And Groups page.
  - ○ **Set Up Groups** Specify who can access your site. You can select from three selections: Visitors To This Site, Members Of This Site, and Owners Of This Site.
  - ○ **List Settings** Customize the User Information List.

The People And Groups page can help you to manage the members of the Farm Administrators group. The members of this group have full access to all settings in the farm and can take ownership of any content site.

Logging And Reporting

This section enables you to configure diagnostic logging for your environment so that error reports are created when your system encounters hardware or software issues. You also have configuration options around event throttling to control the severity of events that are captured in the event log and trace logs. Usage analysis processing configuration options in this section enable you to configure your WSS 3.0 logging settings.

Diagnostic Logging

The Diagnostic Logging page, shown in Figure 17-7, has the following options available:

- **Customer Experience Improvement Program** Specify whether you would like to sign up for the customer experience improvement program. The Customer Experience Improvement Program (CEIP) is designed to improve the quality, reliability, and performance of Microsoft products and technologies. With your permission, anonymous information about your server will be sent to Microsoft to help them improve SharePoint products and technologies.

- **Error Reporting** Error reports are created when your system encounters hardware or software problems. This area provides the following configuration options:

    o **Collect Error Reports** Collect error reports and specify one of the following options: Periodically Download A File That Can Help Identify System Problems or Change This Computer's Error Collection Policy To Silently Send All Reports.

    o **Ignore Errors And Don't Collection Information** Ignore errors and don't collect any information about the errors.

- **Event Throttling** Control the severity of events captured in the Windows event log and the trace logs. This area provides for the following configuration options:

    o **Select A Category** Select a category for which event throttling will be configured.

    o **Least Critical Event To Report To The Event Log** Select the least critical event to report to the event log.

    o **Least Critical Event To Report To The Trace Log** Select the least critical event to report to the trace log.

- **Trace Log** If tracing has been enabled, this area provides the following configuration options:

    o **Path** Specify the location of the trace log.

    o **Number Of Log Files** Specify the number of log files.

○ **Number Of Minutes To Use A Log File** Specify the number of minutes to use a log file.

The Diagnostic Logging page enables you to configure diagnostic logging for your environment. Items like error reports, event throttling, and trace logs are critical to the efficient management of your WSS 3.0 environment.

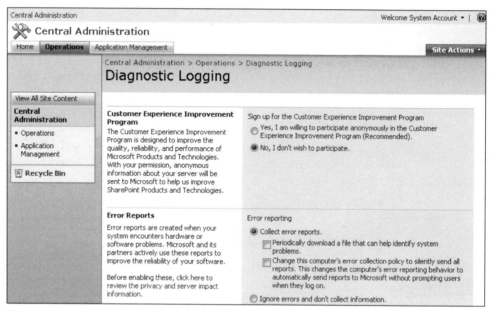

Figure 17-7 Configure diagnostic logging in your environment.

Usage Analysis Processing

The Usage Analysis Processing page provides the following options:

- **Logging Settings** Use the special log files to efficiently run usage analysis processing. Use these settings to enable logging, identify the location to store log files, and set the number of log files per Web application. This area provides the following configuration options:
    - ○ **Enable Logging** Specify whether to enable logging.
    - ○ **Log File Location** Specify the location where the log file should be stored.
    - ○ **Number Of Log Files To Create** Specify the number of log files to create.
- **Processing Settings** Specify whether to enable usage processing on Web server computers, and set the time of day to run usage processing. This section provides the following configuration options:
    - ○ **Enable Usage Analysis Processing** Specify whether to enable usage analysis processing.

    ○ **Run Processing Between These Times Daily** Specify whether to enable usage processing on Web server computers, and set the time of day to run usage.

Site administrators use this technology when they want to review their Site Usage Reports because usage processing must be enabled for those to work properly. It is also a good idea for you to run usage processing during nonbusiness hours.

Global Configuration

Go to the Global Configuration section to configure the timer job status and the timer job definitions. You also have configuration options related to alternate access mappings, managing farm features, and solution management.

Timer Job Status

On the Timer Job Status page, the Timer Job Status Information section displays detailed information on the status of timer jobs in the farm. The following information is displayed:

- Job title
- Server
- Status
- Progress
- Started

Use this page to view the status of the timer jobs that exist within your environment. You can view the status or progress of jobs as well as information regarding when they were started. The Timer Job Status Page has three available views: All, Services, and Web Application.

Timer Job Definitions

The Timer Job Definitions Information section of the Timer Job Definitions page, shown in Figure 17-8, displays detailed information on the timer jobs definitions in the farm. The following information is displayed:

- **Job Title**
- **Web Application**
- **Schedule Type**

The Timer Job Definitions page has three available views: All, Service, and Web Application.

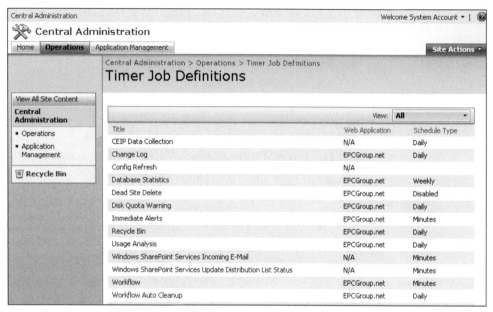

Figure 17-8 The timer job definitions. You can view which Web application they are associated with as well as their schedule type.

Alternate Access Mappings

The Alternate Access Mappings page contains the following options:

- **Edit Public URLs** Go to the Edit Public Zone URLs page, which has the following options:
  - **Alternate Access Mapping Collection** Select an alternate access mapping collection from an available drop-down list.
  - **Public URLs** Enter the public URL protocol, host, and port to use for this resource in any or all of the zones listed. The available zones are Default, Intranet, Internet, Custom, and Extranet.
- **Add Internal URLs** Go to the Add Internal URLs page, which has the following options:
  - **Alternate Access Mapping Collection** Select an alternate access mapping collection from an available drop-down list.
  - **Add Internal URL** Enter the protocol, host, and port portion of any URL that should be associated with this resource. Also select the proper zone— the available zones are Default, Intranet, Internet, Custom, and Extranet.

- **Map to External Resources** Go to the Create External Resource Mapping page, which enables you to define a URL mapping for a resource outside of SharePoint. This provides for the following configuration options:
  - **Resource Name** Supply a unique resource name.
  - **URL Protocol, Host And Port** Supply a unique URL in the farm for this resource.
- **Internal URL** Displays the Internal URL address. Click the URL to go to the Edit Internal URLs page, which has the following options:
  - **Edit Internal URL** Change the zone this URL is associated with, which provides for the following configuration options:
    - **URL Protocol, Host And Port** Supply a URL along with a host and port.
    - **Zone** Specify the zone that should be associated with this internal URL. The available zones are Default, Intranet, Internet, Custom, and Extranet.
- **Zone** Displays the zone for which the internal URL is assigned.
- **Public URL for Zone** Displays the public URL for the zone.

Use the Alternate Access Mapping page to manage alternate access mappings and direct users to the correct URLs during their interaction with WSS 3.0. Alternate access mappings enable WSS 3.0 to map Web requests to the correct Web applications and sites, and they enable WSS 3.0 to serve the correct content back to the user.

Alternate access mappings have been implemented because there are common Internet deployment scenarios in which the URL of a Web request received by Internet Information Services (IIS) is not the same as the URL that was typed by the user accessing the page. This most often occurs in deployment scenarios that include reverse proxy publishing and load balancing.

The Show All Alternate Access Mapping Collection view is displayed by default. You also have the option to click the drop-down box and select Change Alternate Access Mapping Collection.

Manage Farm Features

Go to the Manage Farm Features page to manage SharePoint-wide features. This page lists the name and status of all farm features. Your organization can implement features to reduce the complexity involved in making simple site customizations, and these features are robust when upgrades are applied to a deployment. They eliminate the need to copy large amounts of code to change simple site functionality. They also reduce versioning and inconsistency issues that may arise among front-end Web servers.

Features make it easier to activate or deactivate functionality in the course of a deployment, and administrators can easily transform the template or definition of a site by simply toggling a particular feature on or off in the user interface.

How to Implement a Farm Feature

Your organization can implement a feature by adding a subfolder containing a feature definition within the Features setup directory (*Local_Drive*:\Program Files\Common Files\Microsoft Shared\web server extensions\12\TEMPLATE\FEATURES). The Feature subfolder includes a Feature.xml file that defines the base properties of the feature and lists elements bound to it, such as XML files containing element manifests and any other supporting files. A Feature folder may contain only a Feature.xml file, or it may contain a Feature.xml file and any number of supporting element files, including XML files, but also ASPX, HTM, XSN, RESX, DLL, and other file types.

After you create the Feature folder, you can then install and activate the feature through Stsadm.exe, or through the object model. It is also possible to activate a feature through the SharePoint user interface. Installing a feature makes its definition and elements known throughout a server farm, and activating the feature makes the feature available at a particular scope.

Solution Management

The Solution Management page lists all of the solutions in the farm. The page lists the solution's name, status, and deployed to URL location. If you have a solution that resides in your farm, you can click its name, which contains a link that will take you to the Solution Properties page, shown in Figure 17-9. If you do not have a solution deployed within your environment, you will receive a notification message stating that there are no solutions in the solution store.

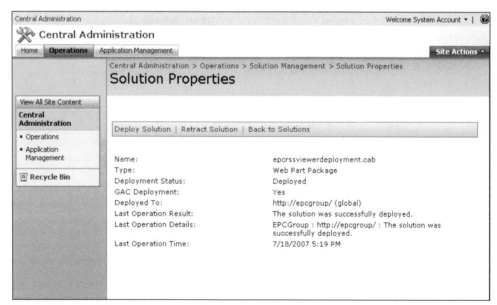

Figure 17-9 Use Solution Properties to deploy or retract a solution.

The Solution Properties page contains the following options and information:

- **Deploy Solution**   Click to go to the Deploy Solution page, where you can specify when you would like to deploy the solution as well as the Web application for which it should be displayed and where the assemblies should be installed.

- **Retract Solution**   Click to go to the Retract Solution page, which lists the solutions information along with a choice of when you would like the solution to be retracted. There is also an option to specify the Web application for which to retract the solution.

- **Back To Solutions**   Go back to the Solution Management page.

- **Solutions Information**   The following Solutions Properties are displayed on the Solution Management Page:
  - Name
  - Type
  - Deployment Status
  - GAC Deployment
  - Deployed To
  - Last Operation Result
  - Last Operation Details
  - Last Operation Time

The Solution Management page enables you to view the solutions that exist within the farm. For more information on solutions, refer to the section titled "Creating a New Web Part Solution" in Chapter 19, "Beginning Web Part Development."

Backup And Restore

The Backup And Restore section on the Operations page enables you to perform backup and restore operations for your WSS 3.0 environment. The four available links are Perform A Backup, Backup And Restore History, Restore From Backup, and Backup And Restore Job Status.

Perform A Backup

For information on the Perform A Backup page, refer to the section titled "Backing Up and Restoring Sites by Using the Operations Page in SharePoint Central Administration" in Chapter 14, "Backing Up, Restoring, and Migrating WSS 3.0 Sites."

Backup And Restore History

The Backup And Restore History page provides the following options:

- **Continue Restore Progress**   Restore from an available backup you select on the page. Once you select the Continue Restore Progress option, you will be taken to a screen where you can select the components of the backup you want to restore.

- **Change Directory** Specify a location of available backup files.

Restore From Backup

For information on the Restore From Backup page, refer to the section titled "Backing Up and Restoring Sites by Using the Operations Page in SharePoint Central Administration" in Chapter 14.

Backup And Restore Job Status

The Backup And Restore Job Status page provides the following options:

- **Refresh** Refresh the page to return the most updated information.
- **View History** Go to the Backup And Restore History page.
- **Backup Information** Display detailed information on the backup or restore job status. The following information regarding the backup is displayed:
  - Requested by
  - Phase
  - Start time
  - Finish time
  - Top component
  - Backup ID
  - Directory
  - Backup method
  - Warnings
  - Errors
- **Backup Components** The Backup And Restore Job Status page also displays detailed information regarding the backup's components along with the progress of each component and the Last Updated date and time information. The page also shows a failure message (if one exists) for any of the components.

Data Configuration

The Data Configuration section enables you to configure the default database server as well as the data retrieval service for your WSS 3.0 implementation.

Default Database Server

The Default Database Server page, shown in Figure 17-10, has the following options available:

- **Content Database Server** Specify the content database server for your implementation.

- **Database Username and Password** Use this section only if you are using SQL Server authentication to connect to SQL Server. It is strongly recommended that you use Windows authentication instead, in which case you should leave these fields blank:
    - **Account** The account name for the database.
    - **Password** The password for the account name being used for the database.

Use the Default Database Server page to set the default content database server. When you extend a new Web application, the content database for the Web application is created on the default content database server unless you specify a different server.

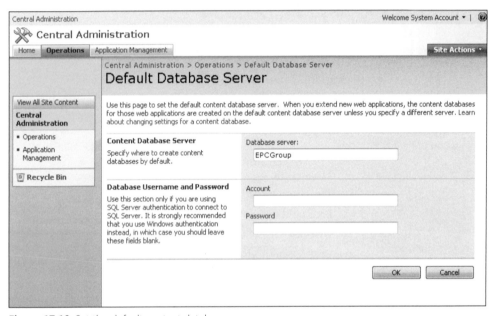

Figure 17-10 Set the default content database server.

Data Retrieval Service

The Data Retrieval Service page has the following options available:

- **Web Application** Select a Web application for the data retrieval service.
- **Enable Data Retrieval Services** Specify whether to enable the data retrieval services.
- **Limit Response Size** Specify the size of the Simple Object Access Protocol (SOAP) response that the data source returns to the data retrieval service.
- **Update Support** Specify whether to enable update query support.

- **Data Source Time-Out** The data retrieval service will time out if the data source does not respond within the amount of time you specify in this setting.

- **Enable Data Source Controls** Specify whether to enable data source controls. They can be disabled so that no query requests will be processed.

Use the Data Retrieval Service page to configure the settings for the data retrieval services. The set of data retrieval services on the server can be disabled so that no query requests will be processed. Data retrieval services include the following: Windows SharePoint Services, OLEDB, SOAP Passthrough, and XML-URL.

Application Management Page of Central Administration

The Application Management page of Central Administration contains links to pages that will help configure your organization's settings for applications and components that are installed on the WSS 3.0 server. The Application Management page has five sections, as shown in Figure 17-11: SharePoint Web Application Management, Application Security, Workflow Management, SharePoint Site Management, and External Service Connections.

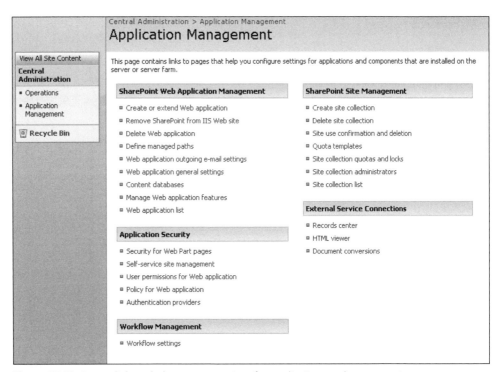

Figure 17-11 Access links to help manage settings for applications and components on your WSS 3.0 server.

SharePoint Web Application Management

The SharePoint Web Application Management section enables you to manage your organization's SharePoint Web applications and perform actions such as creating or extending a Web application or even deleting an existing Web application. You can manage your Web applications' general settings, which can control things like maximum file upload size and quota limits.

The nine available pages in this section are Create Or Extend Web Application, Remove SharePoint From IIS Web Site, Delete Web Application, Define Managed Paths, Web Application Outgoing E-Mail Settings, Web Application General Settings, Content Databases, Manage Web Application Features, and Web Application List.

Create Or Extend Web Application

On the Create Or Extend Web Application page, you can choose the Adding a SharePoint Web Application option. With this, you can select Create A New Web Application, which takes you to the Create New Web Application page, as shown in Figure 17-12. You can also select Extend An Existing Web Application, which takes you to the Extend Web Application To Another IIS Web Site page. This page enables you to create a new Web application or extend an existing Web application.

Figure 17-12 Create a new Web application.

Creating a New Web Application

To create a new Web application, perform the following steps:

1. On the Application Management page, in the SharePoint Web Application Management section, click Create Or Extend Web Application.

2. On the Create Or Extend Web Application page, in the Adding A SharePoint Web Application section, click Create A New Web Application.

3. On the Create New Web Application page, in the IIS Web Site section, you can configure the settings for your new Web application as follows:

   a. *To use an existing Web site,* select Use An Existing Web Site and specify the Web site on which you want to install your new Web application by selecting it from the drop-down menu.

      To create a new Web site, select Create A New IIS Web Site and type the name of the Web site in the Description box.

   b. In the Port box, type the port number you want to use to access the Web application. If you are creating a new Web site, this field is populated with a suggested port number. If you are using an existing Web site, this field is populated with the current port number.

   c. In the Host Header box, type the URL you want to use to access the Web application. This is an optional field.

   d. In the Path box, type the path to the site directory on the server. If you are creating a new Web site, this field is populated with a suggested path. If you are using an existing Web site, this field is populated with the current path.

4. In the Security Configuration section, configure authentication and encryption for your Web application:

   a. In the Authentication Provider section, choose either Negotiate (Kerberos) or NTLM.

   b. In the Allow Anonymous section, choose Yes or No. If you choose to allow anonymous access, the Web site can be anonymously accessed by using the computer-specific anonymous access account (that is, IUSR_ *<computername>*).

   c. In the Use Secure Sockets Layer (SSL) section, select Yes or No. If you choose to enable SSL for the Web site, you must configure SSL by requesting and installing an SSL certificate.

5. In the Load Balanced URL section, type the URL for the domain name for all sites that users will access in this Web application. This URL domain will be used in all links shown on pages within the Web application.

6. In the Application Pool section, choose whether to use an existing application pool or create a new application pool for this Web application.

   a. *To use an existing application pool,* select Use Existing Application Pool. Then, from the drop-down menu, select the application pool you want to use.

Chapter 17

To create a new application pool, select Create A New Application Pool.

   b. In the Application Pool Name box, type the name of the new application pool, or keep the default name.

   c. In the Select A Security Account For This Application Pool section, select Predefined to use an existing application pool security account. Then select the security account from the drop-down menu.

   d. Select Configurable to use an account that is not currently being used as a security account for an existing application pool. In the User Name box, type the user name of the account you want to use and then–in the Password box–type the password for the account.

7. In the Reset Internet Information Services section, choose whether to allow WSS 3.0 to restart IIS on other farm servers. The local server must be restarted manually for the process to finish. If this option is not selected and you have more than one server in the farm, you must wait until the IIS Web site is created on all servers and then run iisreset /noforce on each Web server. The new IIS site is not usable until that action is completed. The choices are unavailable if your farm contains only a single server.

8. In the Database Name And Authentication section, choose the database server, database name, and authentication method for your new Web application.

9. Click OK to create the new Web application, or click Cancel to cancel the process and return to the Application Management page.

Extending an Existing Web Application

To extend an existing Web application, perform the following steps:

1. On the SharePoint Central Administration Web site, on the Application Management page, in the SharePoint Web Application Management section, click Create Or Extend Web Application.

2. On the Create Or Extend Web Application page, in the Adding A SharePoint Web Application section, click Extend An Existing Web Application.

3. On the Extend Web Application To Another IIS Web Site page, in the Web Application section, click the Web Application link and then click Change Web Application.

4. On the Select Web Application page, click the Web application you want to extend.

5. On the Extend Web Application To Another IIS Web Site page, in the IIS Web Site section, you can select Use An Existing IIS Web Site to use a Web site that has already been created, or you can choose to leave Create A New IIS Web Site selected. The Description, Port, and Path boxes are populated for either choice. You can choose to use the default entries or type the information you want in the boxes.

6. In the Security Configuration section, configure authentication and encryption for the extended Web application:

   a. In the Authentication Provider section, choose either Negotiate (Kerberos) or NTLM.

   b. In the Allow Anonymous section, choose Yes or No. If you choose to allow anonymous access, the Web site can be anonymously accessed by using the computer-specific anonymous access account (that is, IUSR_ *<computername>*).

   c. In the Use Secure Sockets Layer (SSL) section, select Yes or No. If you choose to enable SSL for the Web site, you must configure SSL by requesting and installing an SSL certificate.

7. In the Load Balanced URL section, type the URL for the domain name for all sites that users will access in this Web application. This URL domain will be used in all links shown on pages within the Web application. By default, the text box is populated with the current server name and port.

8. In the Load Balanced URL section, under Zone, select the zone for the extended Web application. You can choose Intranet, Internet, Custom, or Extranet.

9. Click OK to extend the Web application, or click Cancel to cancel the process and return to the Application Management page.

TROUBLESHOOTING

Issue: "The IIS Web Site you have selected is in use by SharePoint."

You may receive an error message when you are in SharePoint 3.0 Central Administration and try to create a WSS 3.0 Web application and then extend the Web application to a Microsoft Internet Information Services (IIS) Web site. When you configure the settings for the Web site, you do not assign a host header name to the Web site. However, when you click OK on the Create New Web Application page, you receive the following error message: "The IIS Web Site you have selected is in use by SharePoint. You must select another port or hostname."

This issue can occur if the following conditions are true:

- A Web site already exists on the same port.
- The existing Web site is not assigned a host header name.
- The existing Web site has an IP address assigned to it.

To work around this issue, follow these steps:

1. In SharePoint 3.0 Central Administration, assign a host header name to each Web application that you create that uses the same port. The host header name differentiates each Web site on the port. To assign a host header name when you create a Web application, follow these steps:

   a. Start SharePoint 3.0 Central Administration.

b. Click Application Management and then click Create or Extend Web Application Under SharePoint Web Application Management.

c. On the Create or Extend Web Application page, click Create A Web Application.

d. On the Create A New Web Application page, specify the settings that you want for the Web application. In the IIS Web Site area, make sure that you specify the host header name in the Host Header box.

e. Click OK.

2. After the Web site is created in IIS, use Internet Information Services (IIS) Manager to remove the host header name. Then, assign an IP address to the Web site. To do this, follow these steps:

a. Start Internet Information Services (IIS) Manager.

b. Expand *ServerName* and then expand Web Sites.

c. Right-click the Web site that you want to configure and then click Properties.

d. Click the Web Site tab and then click Advanced.

e. In the Advanced Web Site Identification dialog box, click the entry for the Web site and then click Edit.

f. Remove the host header name that appears in the Host header value box and then assign the IP address that you want in the IP address box.

g. Click OK three times.

Remove SharePoint From IIS Web Site

The Remove SharePoint From IIS Web Site page enables you to remove WSS 3.0 from an IIS Web site and has the following options available:

- **Web Application** Select the Web Application you would like to remove.

- **Deletion Option** With this option, you can choose:
  - **Select IIS Web Site And Zone To Remove** Select the site and zone you would like to remove.
  - **Delete IIS Web Site** Specify whether to delete the associated IIS Web sites.

Delete Web Application

The Delete Web Application page enables you to delete a Web application and has the following options available:

- **Web Application** Select the Web application you would like to delete.

- **Deletion Option** With this option, you can choose:
  - **Delete Content Databases** Select whether to delete the associated content databases.
  - **Delete IIS Web Site** Specify whether to delete the associated IIS Web sites.

Define Managed Paths

The Define Managed Paths page, shown in Figure 17-13, has the following options available:

- **Web Application** Select the Web application you would like to configure.

- **Included Paths** Specifies which paths within the URL namespace are managed by WSS 3.0 You also have the option to select one of these paths and click Delete Selected Paths for any of the paths you would like to remove.

- **Add A New Path** With this option, you can choose:
  - **Path** Specify the new managed path.
  - **Check URL** Double-check the managed path you specified.
  - **Type** Select from the available drop-down Type selections: Explicit Inclusion and Wildcard Inclusion.

This page enables you to define managed paths. With managed paths, you can specify which paths in the URL namespace of a Web application are used for site collections. You are able to specify that one or more site collections exist at a specified path.

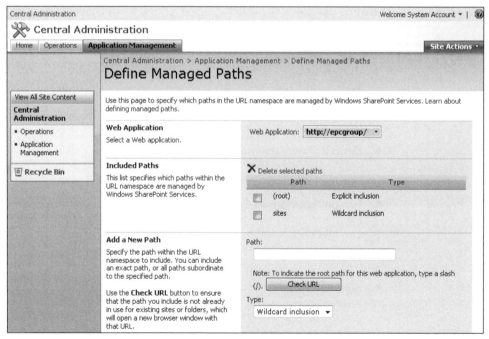

Figure 17-13 Define managed paths.

Web Application Outgoing E-Mail Settings

The Web Application Outgoing E-Mail Settings page has the following options available:

- **Web Application** Select the Web application you would like to configure.

- **Mail Settings** Specify the related mail settings:
    - **Outgoing SMTP Server** Specify the SMTP mail server to use for WSS 3.0.
    - **From Address** Specify the From address that will be displayed from WSS 3.0 e-mail–based notifications.
    - **Reply-To Address** Specify the Reply-to address for WSS 3.0 e-mail–based notifications.
    - **Character Set** Specify the character set for outgoing WSS 3.0 e-mail–based notifications.

The Web Application Outgoing E-Mail Settings page is similar to the Operations page on Outgoing e-mail settings. The Web Application Outgoing E-Mail Settings page allows you to configure the e-mail settings for this Web application.

Web Application General Settings

The Web Application General Settings page, shown in Figure 17-14, lets you configure the Web application's general settings such as those around quotas, file upload sizes, alerts, RSS settings, and other critical functionality settings.

The Web Application General Settings page has the following options available:

- **Web Application** Select the Web application you would like to configure.

- **Default Time Zone** Specify the default time zone for sites that get created on the Web application you selected previously.

- **Default Quota Template** Select the quota template that is used by default for all sites' collections. The No Quota option is selected by default. These options also specify the storage limit that is currently specified.

- **Person Name Smart Tag And Presence Settings** Specify whether to enable Person Name smart tag and Online Status for members. If you select Yes, online present information will be displayed next to member names, and the Person Name smart tag will appear when users hover over a member name anywhere on this site.

- **Maximum Upload Size** Specify the maximum upload file size for a single upload to any site. No single file, group of files, or content can be uploaded if the combined size is greater than this setting.

- **Alerts** With this option, you can choose:
    - **Alerts On This Server Are** Specify whether the e-mail alerts are enabled for this Web application.

- **Maximum Number Of Alerts That A User Can Create** Specify the maximum number of alerts that a user can create. You can specify a maximum number or select Unlimited.
- **RSS Settings** Specify whether RSS feeds are enabled for this Web application.

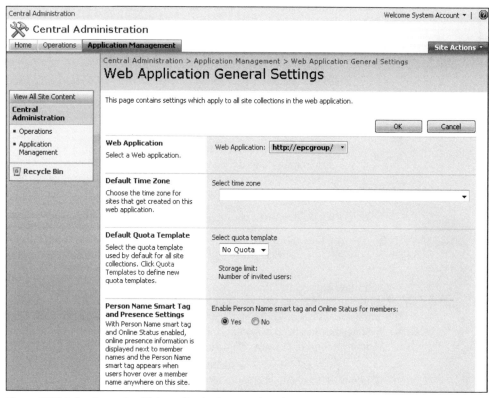

Figure 17-14 Configure the Web application's general settings.

- **Blog API Settings** With this option, you can choose:
  - **Enable Blog API** Specify whether to enable the MetaWeblog application programming interface (API) for this Web application.
  - **Accept User Name And Password From The API** Specify whether a user name and password will be accepted from the MetaWeblog API.

- **Web Page Security Validation** With this option, you can choose:
  - **Security Validation Is** Specify whether security validation is turned on.
  - **Security Validation Expires** Specify whether security validations expire after a specified number of minutes or they never expire.
  - **Send User Name And Password In E-Mail** Specify whether to send users their user names and passwords by e-mail. If this option is turned off, a new

> user cannot bind document libraries to backward-compatible event handlers.

○ **Backward-Compatible Event Handlers** Specify whether to turn on Backward-Compatible Event Handles.

○ **Change Log** Specify how long entries are kept in the change log. You can specify a number of days or specify that they should never be kept.

● **Recycle Bin** With this option, you can choose:

○ **Recycle Bin Status** Specify whether the Recycle Bins of all sites in this Web application are turned on. If you set the Recycle Bin Status to off, all Recycle Bins within the Web application will be emptied.

○ **Delete Items In The Recycle Bin** Specify how long items should reside in the Recycle Bin after they are deleted. You can specify a specific number of days or never.

○ **Second Stage Recycle Bin** Configure the second stage Recycle Bin. This stores items that users have deleted from their Recycle Bins for easier restore if needed. You can specify to add a certain percentage of the live site quota for second stage deleted items or simply turn off the second stage Recycle Bin.

INSIDE OUT Don't forget! The Recycle Bin does not enable the recovery of entire sites!

If a site is deleted by accident, you will have to perform a restore operation from a previously successful backup of the content database unless you have invested in a third-party application such as AvePoint's DocAve. With no third-party backup and restore solution, you need to use Backup And Restore from the Operations page of the SharePoint Central Administration to perform the restore operation.

AvePoint's DocAve was discussed in "Third-Party Backup and Restore Tools" in Chapter 14. I have no allegiance to any one tool, but I have had success in the past with AvePoint's solution. It is important to decide whether your organization can afford to lose the work and content that may have been completed after the last successful backup was made versus investing money in a third-party solution that can save such work via an item-level restore.

Content Databases

The Content Databases page enables you to manage content databases for this Web application. This page has the following options available:

● **Add A Content Database** Go to the Add Content Database page. For more information on adding a new content database, refer to the following section titled "Adding a Content Database to a Web Application."

- **Content Databases** Display detailed information on the existing content databases for this Web application. The following information regarding the content databases is displayed:
  - ○ Database name
  - ○ Database status
  - ○ Current number of sites
  - ○ Site level warning
  - ○ Maximum number of sites

Adding a Content Database to a Web Application

To add a Content Database to a Web application, perform the following steps:

1. On the SharePoint Central Administration Web site, on the Application Management page, in the SharePoint Web Application Management section, click Content Databases.

2. On the Manage Content Databases page, click Add A Content Database.

3. In the Web Application area, click the name of the Web application to which you want to add the content database.

4. In the Database Name And Authentication area, specify the name of the database server, the name of the database, and the database authentication method.

5. In the Search Sever area, you may have the option to choose to associate a content database with a specific server that is running the WSS 3.0 search service. If this option is available, you can select one of available WSS 3.0 search servers.

6. In the Database Capacity Settings area, type the number that you want in the Number Of Sites Before A Warning Event Is Generated box and in the Maximum Number Of Sites That Can Be Created In This Database box and then click OK.

> **Note**
>
> If you configured permissions for the database with the NT Authority\Network Service account, you have to add the Network Service account to the System Administrators role in SQL Server before you can follow step 6. You cannot make the Network Service account the database owner (dbo) of the database. You have to add the Network Service account to the System Administrators role before you can add the database to the virtual server. After you add the database to the virtual server, remove the Network Service account from the System Administrators role in SQL Server.

Chapter 17

Managing Web Application Features

The Manage Web Application Features page enables you to manage Web application features. This page has the following options available:

- **Web Application** Select the Web Application you would like to configure.
- **Web Application Features** Display detailed information about the Web application features that exist for this Web application. The following information is displayed:
  - Name
  - Status

For more information on features, refer to Chapter 19.

Web Application List

The Web Application List page displays detailed information about your Web applications and enables you to manage your Web applications. This page has the following options available:

- **Name** Display the name of the Web application, which contains a link that will take you to that specific Web application.
- **URL** Display the URL of the Web application.

Application Security

This section enables you to manage your WSS 3.0 application security. You can manage your Web Part pages, policies, and authentication providers. This section has five pages: Security For Web Part Pages, Self-Service Site Management, User Permissions For Web Application, Policy For Web Application, and Authentication Providers.

Security For Web Part Pages

The Security For Web Part Pages page, shown in Figure 17-15, has the following options available:

- **Web Application** Select the Web application you would like to configure.
- **Web Page Connections** Specify whether you will allow Web Part connections by passing data or values from a source Web Part to a target Web Part.
- **Online Web Part Gallery** Specify whether to allow users to access the online Web Part gallery.
- **Restore Defaults** Restore the default options to this page.

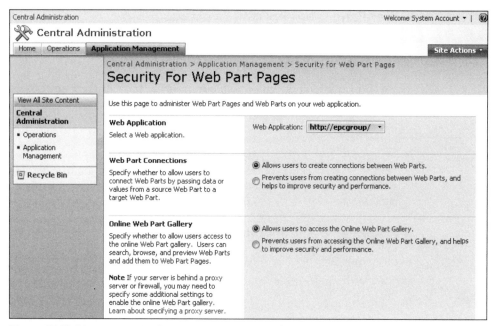

Figure 17-15 Manage security for your organization's Web Part pages.

Use the Security For Web Part Pages page to specify security settings for Web Part pages. This page's settings configure items such as whether users will be able to create connections between Web Parts or if users will be able to access the online Web Part gallery.

Self-Service Site Management

The Self-Service Site Management page has the following options available:

- **Web Application** Select the Web application you would like to configure.

- **Enable Self-Service Site Creation** Specify whether to allow self-service site creation. You also have the option to require a secondary contact name on the sign-up page. If this option is allowed, an announcement will be added to the Announcement list on the home page of the top-level Web site. The announcement will provide a link to the site creation page.

The Self-Service Site Management page enables you to configure self-service site management for the Web application. Self-service site management enables users to create site collections under the /sites path (or other path you specify) within a particular Web application. This method is best used when you want to allow groups or communities to create sites. This method also works well if you are hosting sites and want to allow users to create sites without waiting for a complicated process. The sign-up page for Self-Service Site Management can be customized or replaced with a page that includes all of the information you might need to integrate with a billing system or to track custom metadata about the site at creation time.

Chapter 17

User Permissions For Web Application

The User Permissions For Web Application page has the following options available:

- **Web Application** Select the Web application you would like to configure.

- **Permissions** Specify which permissions can be used in permission levels within this Web application. If you would like to disable permission, clear the check box next to the permission name. To enable permission, select the check box next to the permission name. Use the Select All check box to select or clear all permissions.

The User Permissions For Web Application page enables you to specify user permissions for the Web application. You can choose from more than 30 different permission options.

Policy For Web Application

The Policy For Web Application page has the following options available:

- **Web Application** Select the Web application you would like to configure.

- **Add Users** Adds Users to the Web application and zone that you select. The security policy will apply to requests made through the specified zone.

- **Delete Selected Users** Delete the users you select on the page.

- **Edit Permissions Of Selected Users** Go to the Edit Users page. This page enables you to edit the permissions of the users you selected on the Policy For Web Application page. The Edit Users page enables you to set the permission policy levels for the selected users. There is also an option to choose system settings for the selected users, because they will not be recorded in the User Information lists.

This page enables you to specify a Web application and then manage the users, set permission policy levels, and select the zone for which the policy will apply.

Authentication Providers

The Authentication Providers page has the following options available:

- **Web Application** Select the Web application you would like to configure.

- **Authentication Providers** Display detailed information on the authentication providers, including the following:
    - ○ **Zone** Display the name of the authentication provider, which contains a link that will take you to the Edit Authentication page (shown in Figure 17-16).
    - ○ **Membership Provider Name** Display the membership provider name for the authentication provider.

The Edit Authentication page, shown in Figure 17-16, contains the following options and information:

- **Web Application** Select the Web application you would like to configure.

- **Zone** Display the zone for which the authentication settings are bound.

- **Authentication Type** Specify the authentication type for the authentication provider.

- **Anonymous Access** Enable anonymous access for sites on this server.

- **IIS Authentication Settings** Specify Integrated Windows Authentication, Negotiate (Kerberos) or NTML, or Basic authentication.

- **Client Integration** Specify whether to enable client integration. By disabling client integration, you will remove features that will launch client applications.

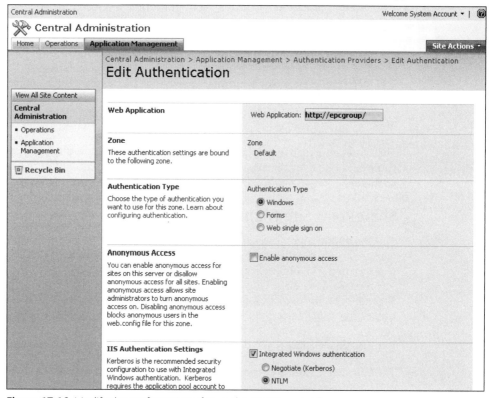

Figure 17-16 Modify the configuration of an authentication provider.

The Edit Authentication page enables you to view and edit the authentication providers that are available for the Web application. If you click an authentication provider, it will take you to the Edit Authentication page, which allows for easy editing of its settings.

For more information on Authentication Providers, refer to "Plan Authentication Settings for Web Applications (Windows SharePoint Services)," which can be found at *http://technet2. microsoft.com/windowsserver/WSS/en/library/cb8409f9-cd8a-4651-b644-250ff6b86c761033. mspx?mfr=true.*

Workflow Management

The Workflow Management section enables you to manage workflow for your organization's WSS 3.0 environment. The section has one page—Workflow Settings—to manage these settings.

Workflow Settings

The Workflow Settings page has the following options available:

- **Web Application** Select the Web application you would like to configure.
- **User-Defined Workflows** Specify whether to enable user-defined workflows for this site. These workflows cannot add code, and users can only reuse code that is already deployed by the administrator.
- **Workflow Task Notifications** Specify whether to alert internal users who do not have site access when they are assigned a workflow task. You also have the option here to specify whether to allow external users to participate in workflows by sending them a copy of the document related to the workflow.

The Workflow Settings page enables you to select a Web application and specify whether you would like to enable user-defined workflows for sites as configure notification settings.

SharePoint Site Management

The SharePoint Site Management section is critical to WSS 3.0 administration. You can manage your site collections and their related quotas and locks, as well as the users who can perform administration actions within the site collections. This section has seven pages: Create Site Collection, Delete Site Collection, Site Use Confirmation And Deletion, Quota Templates, Site Collection Quotas And Locks, Site Collection Administrators, and Site Collection List.

Create Site Collection

The Create Site Collection page has the following options available:

- **Web Application** Select the Web application for which you would like to create the new site collection.
- **Title and Description** Specify a title and description for the new site collection.
- **Web Site Address** Specify the path for which the new site should be created for the new site collection.

- **Template Selection** Select a template for the new top-level site.

- **Primary Site Collection Administrator** Specify the primary administrator for this Web site collection.

- **Secondary Site Collection Administrator** Specify a secondary administrator for this Web site collection.

- **Quota Template** Select a quota template for the new site collection. This option also displays the site's storage limit.

When you create a site collection, you also create the top-level site within that site collection. This page enables you to create a new site collection for a specified Web application.

Creating a New Site Collection

To create a new site collection, perform the following steps:

1. In the SharePoint Central Administration Web site, on the Application Management page, in the SharePoint Site Management section, click Create Site Collection.

2. On the Create Site Collection page, in the Web Application section, if the Web application in which you want to create the site collection is not selected, click Change Web Application on the Web Application menu. Then on the Select Web Application page, click the Web application in which you want to create the site collection.

3. In the Title And Description section, type the title and description for the site collection.

4. In the Web Site Address section, under URL, select the path to use for your URL (such as an included path like /sites/ or the root directory, /).

5. In the Template Selection section, in the Select A Template list, select the template that you want to use for the top-level site in the site collection.

6. In the Primary Site Collection Administrator section, enter the user name (in the form *DOMAIN\username*) for the user who will be the site collection administrator.

7. If you want to identify a user as the secondary owner of the new top-level Web site (recommended), in the Secondary Site Collection Administrator section, enter the user name for the secondary administrator of the site collection.

8. If you are using quotas to limit resource use for site collections, in the Quota Template section, click a template in the Select A Quota Template list and then Click OK.

Delete Site Collection

The Delete Site Collection page has the following options available:

- **Site Collection** Select the site collection you would like to delete.

Chapter 17

- **Warning** This section offers a warning message and displays the URL, title, and description of the site collection that you are about to delete.

- **Delete** Perform the delete for the site collection you selected in the previous options.

Site Use Confirmation And Deletion

The Site Use Confirmation And Deletion page has the following options available:

- **Web Application** Select the Web application for which you would like to require site owners to confirm the use of their site collections.

- **Confirmation And Automatic Deletion Settings** Specify whether to send e-mail notifications to owners of unused site collections as well as the number of days the notifications should be sent after a site has not been used. This option enables you to specify the frequency of these notifications, and you have the option to automatically delete the site after a user has not confirmed a site's use in a specified number of notices.

The Site Use Confirmation And Deletion page enables you to require site owners to confirm that their Web site collections are in use. You can also configure automatic deletion for unused Web site collections.

Quota Templates

The Quota Templates page has the following options available:

- **Template Name** Create a new quota template from either a blank template or one of the available existing quota templates. You can also specify the new template's name.

- **Storage Limit Values** Specify whether to limit the amount of storage available on a site and to set the maximum amount of storage. You can also specify whether to send warning e-mails when a site's storage reaches a certain storage capacity.

The Quota Templates page enables you to create or modify a quota template. You can also specify whether to limit the amount of storage on a site as well as set the maximum amount of storage and a warning level for the templates.

Site Collection Quotas And Locks

The Site Collection Quotas And Locks page, shown in Figure 17-17, has the following options available:

- **Site Collection** Select the site collection for which you would like to define or edit quota templates.

- **Site Lock Information** Specify the lock status for the site. You can select from Not Locked, Adding Content Prevented, Read-Only, or No Access.

- **Site Quota Information** Modify the quota template on this site collection or change one of the individual quota settings. You can specify the current quota template as well as a site storage limit and e-mail warning site storage notification limit.

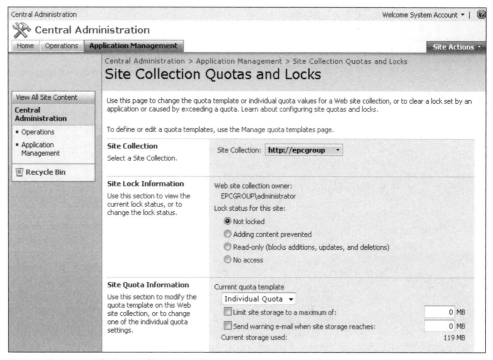

Figure 17-17 Modify the configuration of an authentication provider.

The Site Collection Quotas And Locks page enables you to change the quota template or individual quota values for a Web site collection, or to clear a lock set by an application or caused by exceeding a quota.

Site Collection Administrators

The Site Collection Administrators page has the following options available:

- **Site Collection** Select the site collection for which you would like to manage the administrators.

- **Primary Site Collection Administrator** Specify the primary site collection administrator.

- **Secondary Site Collection Administrator** Specify the secondary site collection administrator.

This Site Collection Administrators page enables you to view and change the primary and secondary site collection administrators for a site collection. Site collection administrators have the Full Control permission level on all Web sites and content within a site collection. From the site collection level, site collection administrators manage settings (such as site collection features, site collection audit settings, and site collection policies) from the Site Settings page for the top-level site.

Site Collection List

The Site Collection List page displays the list of available site collections along with detailed information about each site collection. This page has the following options available:

- **URL Search** Perform a URL search for a specific site collection.

- **Web Application** Select a specific Web application. The page will then update the site collection list based on the selected Web application.

- **Site Collection Information** Displays detailed information on the available site collections. The following information is displayed:
    - URL
    - Title
    - Description
    - Primary administrator
    - E-mail address
    - Database name

The Site Collection List page displays the list of available site collections along with detailed information about each site collection.

External Service Connections

This section enables you to manage external service connections for your organization's WSS 3.0 environment. If your organization has implemented SharePoint Server 2007 and has Records Center enabled, you can connect your WSS 3.0 implementation to the available Records Center. You can also specify information around the HTML viewer and the configuration of document conversations. This section has three available pages: Records Center, HTML Viewer, and Document Conversions.

Records Center

The Configure Connection To Records Center page has the Records Center Connection option, where you can specify whether to connect to a Records Center. If you choose to connect to a Records Center, you are able to specify its URL and display name.

The Records Center site template in SharePoint Server 2007 is designed to help organizations implement their records management and retention programs.

The Records Center is intended to serve as a central repository in which an organization can store and manage all of its records. The Records Center supports the entire records management process, from records collection through records management to records disposition. Records Center is only available in SharePoint Server 2007.

HTML Viewer

The HTML Viewer page has the following options available:

- **Turn On HTML Viewer** Specify whether to allow HTML viewing.

- **Server Location** Specify the path to the HTML Viewer service.

- **Maximum Cache Size** Specify the maximum cache size for the HTML Viewer cache. This cache counts against the size of the content database.

- **Maximum File Size** Specify the maximum file size of the largest file the service will view in HTML.

- **Timeout Length** Specify the integer number of seconds the service will wait for HTML viewing to complete.

The HTML Viewer page enables you to view, change, and configure the HTML Viewer service.

Document Conversions

The Configure Document Conversions page has the following options available:

- **Web Application** Select the Web application for which you would like to configure document conversions.

- **Enable Document Conversion** Specify whether to enable document conversions for this site.

- **Load Balancer Server** Specify the load balancer with which to associate this Web application.

- **Conversion Schedule** Specify which schedule to use to process blocks of conversions.

- **Converter Settings** Display information regarding any custom converters that are currently installed within the Web application.

WSS 3.0 provides interfaces for implementing the two WSS services that are needed to enable document converters. These two WSS services are as follows:

- **Document Conversion Load Balancer Service** This service balances the document conversion requests from across the server farm. When it receives a converter request from WSS 3.0, the document conversion load balancer service must return a URI to the appropriate document conversion launcher service. WSS 3.0 connects to the specified launcher via .NET Remoting and requests that it convert the specified document.

Chapter 17

- **Document Conversion Launcher Service** This service schedules and initiates the document conversions. When WSS 3.0 passes a document conversion request to the document conversion launcher service, the service must call the appropriate document converter.

The Configure Document Conversions page enables you to configure the document conversions.

In Summary...

This chapter explained how to administer SharePoint Central Administration for your WSS 3.0 environment. These settings control almost every aspect of your deployment.

The next part will discuss a number of advanced techniques that are useful when designing SharePoint sites and that will require administrative privileges for the environment.

PART 7

Developing Web Parts in Visual Studio 2005, SharePoint Best Practices, and Maintaining Your Implementation

Advanced Design Techniques

This chapter details a number of techniques that are useful when designing Microsoft Windows SharePoint Services 3.0 (WSS 3.0) sites. These techniques require you to have administrative privileges to install, enable, or deploy the solutions.

Delegate Controls

Delegate controls is a new WSS 3.0 feature that enables you to declare candidate controls for functionality and provides a mechanism for choosing a single functionality provider. The candidate controls are identified using Features.

Let's look at an example taken from the WSS 3.0 master page:

```
<SharePoint:DelegateControl runat="server" ControlId="SmallSearchInputBox"/>
```

This is where the search control will be loaded in the page.

This delegate control has no default content. When the page is loaded, WSS 3.0 looks through the features list for one that has the id "SmallSearchInputBox." For WSS 3.0, the *ContentLightup* feature will be found.

```
<?xml version="1.0" encoding="utf-8"?>
<Elements xmlns="http://schemas.microsoft.com/sharepoint/">
    <Control
        Id="SmallSearchInputBox"  Sequence="100"
        ControlSrc="~/_controltemplates/searcharea.ascx">
    </Control>
    <CustomAction>…
</Elements>
```

The feature's SearchArea.xml file tells WSS 3.0 to load the *searcharea.ascx* control and also that the control has the sequence number 100 (which is the WSS default).

If I want to replace the WSS 3.0 search control with a custom control of my own, all I need to do is add to a feature a Control element with a sequence number smaller than 100.

```
<Control
    Id="FancierSearchInputBox" Sequence="10"
    ControlSrc="~/_controltemplates/fancysearcharea.ascx">
</Control>
```

> **Note**
> Microsoft Office SharePoint Server 2007 (MOSS) has two additional versions of the search area control, one for the standard edition (Sequence=50) and one for enterprise (Sequence=25).

The default.master page also uses the delegate control for other controls such as *TopNavigationDataSource*, *PublishingConsole*, *QuickLaunchDataSource*, *AdditionalPageHead*, and *GlobalSiteLink*. Customizing one of these controls, such as providing a custom data source for the Quick Launch, is a straightforward task.

> **Note**
> Delegate controls marked as *"AllowMultiple"* = *true* can host more than one child control. If there are multiple delegate control registrations, they are all added as children. This is used in some cases, for example, the *AdditionalHeader* delegate control, which enables you to add multiple delegate controls to a page.

In WSS 2.0, the user controls and server controls are added directly to an ASPX page (similar to the search controls). In WSS 3.0, the delegate control should also be used rather than user controls and server controls being added directly, as in WSS 2.0.

Using the delegate control is an elegant and extensible approach when you have to substitute controls in the layout of a WSS 3.0 page.

Additional information on the delegate control can be found at *http://msdn2.microsoft.com/en-us/library/ms470880.aspx*.

Advanced Web Parts Development Topics

Having .NET development experience will definitely give you a head start in your quest to develop custom solutions for WSS 3.0. SharePoint development requires mastering several development techniques centered around WSS 3.0. They are covered in the next section.

Building Connected Web Parts

Collaboration is one of the key drivers behind WSS 3.0. How can we apply this to Web Parts and make them programmatically speak or communicate with one another? WSS 3.0 enables us to do this by using an interface. Two options are available: define our own interfaces or use the standard WSS interfaces.

Defining Our Own Interface

When we define our own interface, we begin by deciding which will be the provider Web Part, which will be the consumer Web Part, and the type of data that we will need to pass between them. For example:

```
public interface IIntSales
{
    int SalesReportID {get;}
}
```

The provider Web Part is offering specific information, in this case the id of a report, which implements this interface. It also exposes a property, decorated with the *ConnectionProvider* attribute, which returns a reference to the interface.

The consumer Web Part contains a method, decorated with *Connection Consumer*, where the data will be received.

```
//The provider
public class SalesReportProvider : WebPart, IIntSales
{
    private int reportID = 1;
    [ConnectionProvider("Report ID Provider")]
    public IIntSales SalesReportIDInterface()
    {
        return this;
    }
    public int SalesReportID
    {
        get { return reportID; }
    }
}
//The consumer
public class SalesReportConsumer : WebPart
{
    IIntSales provider = null;
    [ConnectionConsumer("Report ID Consumer")]
    public void GetReportId(IIntSales _provider)
    {
        provider = _provider;
    }
    protected override void RenderContens(HtmlTextWriter writer)
    {
        try
        { writer.Write(provider.SalesReportID); }
        catch
        {
            // an error occurred or no connection
        }
    }
}
```

After the Web Parts are deployed and added on a page in a site, they can be connected using the Connections option from the Web Parts menu. WSS 3.0 detects if two Web Parts from the same page can share data between them (that is, the interfaces are compatible) and automatically populates the Connections menu of the Web Part.

Using the WSS Interfaces

When we want to communicate with a Web Part, we need to implement one of the interfaces offered by WSS 3.0, which are as follows: *IWebPartField*, *IWebPartRow*, *IWebPartTable*, and *IWebPartParameters*.

Table 18-1 lists interfaces offered by WSS 3.0 along with a brief description of each of them.

Table 18-1 Interfaces Offered by WSS 3.0

Name	Description
IWebPartField	Defines a provider interface for connecting two server controls using a single field of data
IWebPartRow	Defines a provider interface for connecting two server controls using a row of data
IWebPartTable	Defines a provider interface for connecting two server controls using an entire table of data
IWebPartParameters	Defines the contract a Web Parts control implements to pass a parameter value in a Web Parts connection

This is a simple skeleton for an *IWebPartField* implementation.

```
public sealed class FieldProviderWebPart : WebPart, IWebPartField
{
    private DataTable _table;
    public FieldProviderWebPart()
    {
        _table = new DataTable();
    }
    [ConnectionProvider("FieldProvider")]
    public IWebPartField GetConnectionInterface()
    {
        return new FieldProviderWebPart();
    }
    public PropertyDescriptor Schema
    {
        get
        {
            return TypeDescriptor.GetProperties(_table.DefaultView[0])[2];
        }
    }
    void IWebPartField.GetFieldValue(FieldCallback callback)
    {
        callback(Schema.GetValue(_table.DefaultView[0]));
    }
}
```

```
public class FieldConsumerWebPart : WebPart
{
    private IWebPartField _provider;
    private object _fieldValue;
    private void GetFieldValue(object fieldValue)
    {
        _fieldValue = fieldValue;
    }
    [ConnectionConsumer("FieldConsumer")]
    public void SetConnectionInterface(IWebPartField provider)
    {
    }
}
```

For more information about and examples of connecting Web Parts, refer to the articles titled "Web Parts Connections Overview" at *http://msdn2.microsoft.com/en-us/library/ms178187. aspx* and "IWebPartField Interface" at *http://msdn2.microsoft.com/en-us/library/system.web. ui.webcontrols.webparts.iwebpartfield(VS.80).aspx*.

Building AJAX Web Parts

ASP.NET AJAX enables you to quickly create Web pages that include a rich user experience with responsive and familiar user interface (UI) elements.

The processing time will be shorter, because you will not send the whole page back to the server to be processed. Instead, the browser will make a call by using the *XmlHttpRequest* object, requesting only the information that it needs.

Using AJAX in your Web Parts requires a JavaScript component on the client, which will implement the appearance of the Web Part and a library of XML API on the server. The client-server communication can be done using XML request and Web service calls.

You can use several AJAX toolkits on the market today. One good tool, designed for SharePoint, is the SharePoint AJAX Toolkit, which extends the Microsoft ASP.NET AJAX library. You can download it at *www.codeplex.com/sharepointajax*.

> **Note**
> CodePlex is Microsoft's open source project hosting site.

This SharePoint AJAX Toolkit includes a base Web Part class with AJAX support (80 percent of your work is done if you use it), a script library for client size data processing, and a Solution package installer.

For displaying data in the provided Web Part, called *XMLWebPart*, use XSLT (the *XMLTransformation* method from the toolkit will assist you). Other methods are also available to help you communicate with the server endpoints.

Chapter 18

Creating Editor Web Parts

When a page is placed in Edit Mode, a user can select to edit a Web Part's control properties. An *EditorPart* control enables a user to edit an associated Web Part control to modify its layout, appearance, properties, behavior, or other related characteristics.

Sometimes the default functionality will not be enough for your needs. For example, a Web Part could have a string property with complicated validation logic behind it, or you may want a Web Part property to be a filter field. You may also want a Web Part to be rendered like a drop-down list, which will contain dynamically loaded information.

To create an *EditorPart* control, you need to implement a control that derives from the *EditorPart* class. Next, you will have to override the *ApplyChanges* and the *SyncChanges* methods. *ApplyChanges* applies changes made in the editor control to the Web Part control being edited when the user clicks OK or Apply. The *SyncChanges* method gets the current values of the Web Part control being edited and passes them to the editor so that the editor control can edit them (this also avoids synchronization problems between the Web Part and the editor).

Next, to render your custom HTML, you need to override the *CreateChildControls* and the *RenderContents* functions.

Here is an example of a skeleton for a ZIP Code editor part, which provides a text box where you can enter a ZIP Code as well as validate it.

```
public class ZipCodeEditor : EditorPart
{
    TextBox input = null;
    Label displaymessage = null;
    Literal lineBreak;
    protected override void CreateChildControls()
    {
        Controls.Clear();
        input = new TextBox();
        this.Controls.Add(input);
        lineBreak = new Literal();
        lineBreak.Text = @"<br />";
        Controls.Add(lineBreak);
        displaymessage = new Label();
        this.Controls.Add(displaymessage);
    }
    protected override void RenderContents(HtmlTextWriter writer)
    {
        writer.Write("<br/>");
        input.RenderControl(writer);
        writer.Write("<br/>");
        displaymessage.RenderControl(writer);
    }
    public override bool ApplyChanges()
```

```
    {
        try
        {
            //validation logic

            //if ValidationSuccessful
            ZipCodeWebPart part = (ZipCodeWebPart)WebPartToEdit;
            // Update the custom WebPart
            part.ZipCode = input.Text;
        }
        catch (Exception exc)
        {
            //error handling
        }
        return true;
    }
    public override void SyncChanges()
    {
        input.Text = ((ZipCodeWebPart)WebPartToEdit).ZipCode;
    }
}
```

To associate the editor part with your Web Part, you will need to override the *CreateEditorParts* method in the Web Part where you will create the instances of the editor parts. An example of this is as follows:

```
public class ZipCodeWebPart : System.Web.UI.WebControls.WebParts.WebPart
    {
        protected string _zipcode;
        public ZipCodeWebPart()
        {

            ...
        }
        [Personalizable(PersonalizationScope.Shared), WebBrowsable(false),
        WebDisplayName("ZipCode"),
        WebDescription("The ZipCode")]
        public string ZipCode
        {
            get { return _zipcode; }
            set { _zipcode = value; }
        }
        public override EditorPartCollection CreateEditorParts()
        {
            ArrayList editorArray = new ArrayList();
            ZipCodeEditor edPart = new ZipCodeEditor();
            edPart.ID = this.ID + "_editorPart1";
            editorArray.Add(edPart);
            EditorPartCollection editorParts =
              new EditorPartCollection(editorArray);
            return editorParts;
        }
```

```
    protected override void RenderContents(HtmlTextWriter writer)
    {
        …
    }
    protected override void Render(HtmlTextWriter writer)
    {
        …
    }
}
```

Building Workflows in WSS 3.0

Every organization has its own business processes that must be reflected by the systems its employees use. Routing content through the organization for approval or feedback or automatic archiving of documents for audit purposes are just a few simple examples.

You can now build business processes (workflows) by using Windows Workflow Foundation and then deploying them in WSS 3.0. Most of the time, these workflows will be document- or list-centric.

There are two types of workflows: sequential and state-machine.

In sequential workflows, the actions occur in a specific order. You can use branches and loops, but you will always have a starting point and an ending point. An approval process is an example of a sequential workflow.

In a state-machine workflow, when the event arrives, the workflow decides what needs to be done.

WSS 3.0 comes with a simple built-in workflow called the Three-State, which you can use to track list items. SharePoint Server 2007 comes with several additional workflows such as Approval, Collect Feedback, Collect Signatures, and Disposition Approval.

To enable a workflow for a list or document library, you need to go to its settings and select Workflow Settings. There, you will be presented with a list of the active workflows that you can add or remove, as shown in Figure 18-1. After you enable a workflow, you can start it manually or automatically when a new item is added.

You can use four types of forms with a SharePoint workflow: association, initiation, task edit, and workflow modification. These forms can be implemented using ASP.Net or Microsoft Office InfoPath. Figure 18-2 shows an example of a SharePoint workflow initiation form.

You can build workflows for WSS 3.0 by using Microsoft Office SharePoint Designer 2007 or Microsoft Visual Studio. SharePoint Designer offers a declarative workflow design experience. A wizard helps you define your workflow.

Visual Studio is more powerful than Office SharePoint Designer 2007, but it requires coding experience. It provides you with a graphical design interface for the flow and code level support. I recently built a collection of very complex WSS 3.0 and SharePoint Server 2007 workflows, and SharePoint Designer simply would not cut it. Therefore, I had to go the route of developing them in Visual Studio.

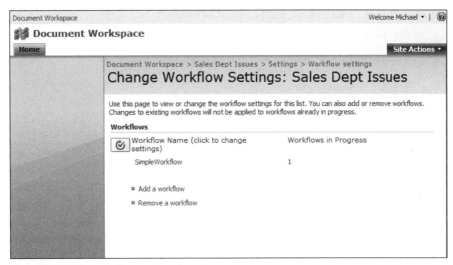

Figure 18-1 The workflow settings for a list.

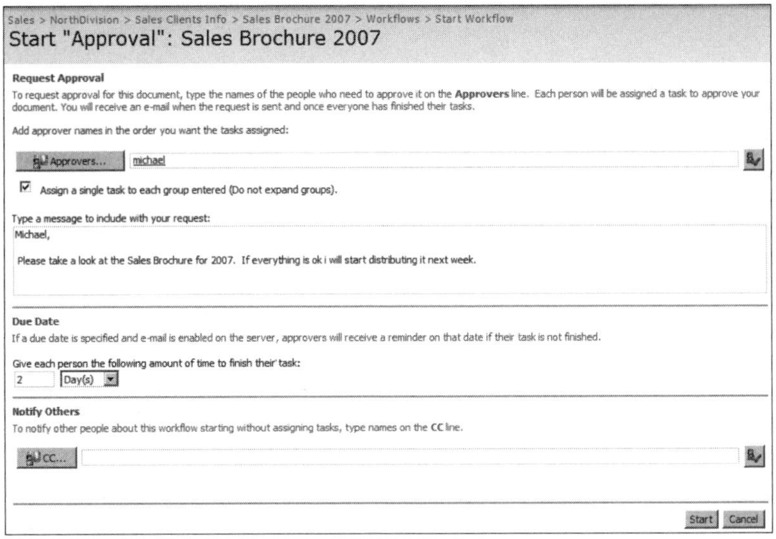

Figure 18-2 An initiation form.

Building Workflows with Visual Studio 2005

Each workflow is a set of steps. Each step is called an activity. You can choose to build an entire workflow in Visual Studio, or you can build just some specialized activities that you can later plug into an existing workflow. First you must install Visual Studio 2005 extensions for .NET Framework 3.0 (Windows Workflow Foundation), which will provide a graphical interface to design workflows. Once you also install the WSS Software Development Kit (SDK), you'll have some SharePoint workflow templates available for when you want to create a new project.

Chapter 18

It usually takes four steps to build a workflow:

1. Model the workflow.

2. Design the forms.

3. Implement the workflow.

4. Deploy the workflow.

Implementing a workflow is not an easy task. Before you start coding, check how Microsoft implemented similar workflows. To do this, download the Enterprise Content Management (ECM) Starter Kit, which provides workflows and activities samples.

> **Note**
>
> The ECM Starter Kit, which is included in the SharePoint Server 2007 SDK, can be downloaded at *www.microsoft.com/downloads/details.aspx?familyid=6D94E307-67D9-41AC-B2D6-0074D6286FA9&displaylang=en.*

Using the samples from the kit, you will learn how to implement a workflow as well as how to design the forms and prepare a workflow for deployment.

Customizing Site Definitions

A site definition describes the look and feel as well as the core functionality of a WSS 3.0 site. The appearance and the functionality of a site definition are described in a collection of files that can be found at *ProgramFiles*\Common Files\Microsoft Shared\web server extensions\12\TEMPLATE\SiteTemplates\.

A site can't be instantiated directly from a site definition. Instead, a site definition contains configurations that can be site templates. One site definition can contain several site templates.

WSS 3.0 comes with some preinstalled site definitions. One of those site definitions is STS, which provides site templates for common sites such as team sites, blank sites, and document workspaces. The other site definitions you'll find in that folder provide templates for blogs, Wikis, meetings sites (MPS), and of course, Central Administration.

You should not confuse site definitions with site templates. A site template contains a customization of a base site, and it has a .stp extension. If the solution you want to implement consists of only a set of customizations (such as adding some libraries, lists, and so on), you could use a site template.

If your solution contains custom Web Parts, workflows, events, master pages, and resource files, you should package it in a site definition.

INSIDE OUT   Ghosting site template files

When you create a site based on a site definition, WSS 3.0 does not copy a complete set of Web pages into the SharePoint content database. Instead, it ghosts or uncustomizes the pages in the site definition. This means that if you create a hundred team sites, those sites would behave as if the content database contained a hundred copies of the team site pages. But in fact, all one hundred sites would share one set of pages, and that set of pages would reside in the Web server's file system. This avoids the overhead of storing, retrieving, and caching duplicated pages in the content databases.

Of course, when someone opens an individual site and uses a program such as Share-Point Designer to customize one of its pages, the SharePoint server can no longer ghost that file for that site. The page becomes unghosted or customized, and the changes are stored in the database.

In WSS 2.0, the entire page is copied in the database. In WSS 3.0, because only the modifications are persisted, along with the performance improvements comes the possibility to revert to the original uncustomized page.

Taken as a unit, the files that make up a site definition describe every detail necessary to create a new site. A site template, however, contains only the differences between a site definition and the state of the site at some later time (with or without list and library content). When you create a site from a site template, WSS 3.0 creates a site based on the site definition that created the original site and applies any changes that the site template specifies.

Working with Site Definition Files

When you first install WSS 3.0, a file named WebTemp.xml identifies each site definition. (*Temp* in this context means template, not temporary.) You can find this file at C:\Program Files\Common Files\Microsoft Shared\web server extensions\12\TEMPLATE\1033\ XML, where 1033 is the current locale ID. A version of this file (with greatly shortened Description values) is as follows:

```
<?xml version="1.0" encoding="utf-8"?>
<!-- _lcid="1033" _version="12.0.4518" _dal="1" -->
<!-- _LocalBinding -->
<Templates xmlns:ows="Microsoft SharePoint">
     <Template Name="GLOBAL" SetupPath="global" ID="0">
          <Configuration ID="0" Title="Global template"
          Hidden="TRUE" ImageUrl="" Description="This template is
          used for initializing a new site." >
          </Configuration>
     </Template>
     <Template Name="STS" ID="1">
          <Configuration ID="0" Title="Team Site" Hidden="FALSE"
```

```
        ImageUrl="/_layouts/images/stsprev.png" Description="A
        site for teams to quickly organize, author, and share
        information. It provides a document library, and lists
        for managing announcements, calendar items, tasks, and
        discussions." DisplayCategory="Collaboration" >
        </Configuration>
        <Configuration ID="1" Title="Blank Site" Hidden="FALSE"
        ImageUrl="/_layouts/images/blankprev.png" Description="A
        blank site for you to customize based on your
        requirements." DisplayCategory="Collaboration"
        AllowGlobalFeatureAssociations="False" >
        </Configuration>
        <Configuration ID="2" Title="Document Workspace"
        Hidden="FALSE" ImageUrl="/_layouts/images/dwsprev.png"
        Description="A site for colleagues to work together on a
        document. It provides a document library for storing the
        primary document and supporting files, a tasks list for
        assigning to-do items, and a links list for resources
        related to the document."
        DisplayCategory="Collaboration" >
        </Configuration>
    </Template>
    <Template Name="MPS" ID="2">
        <Configuration ID="0" Title="Basic Meeting Workspace"
        Hidden="FALSE" ImageUrl="/_layouts/images/mwsprev.png"
        Description="A site to plan, organize, and capture the
        results of a meeting. It provides lists for managing the
        agenda, meeting attendees, and documents."
        DisplayCategory="Meetings" >
        </Configuration>
        <Configuration ID="1" Title="Blank Meeting Workspace"
        Hidden="FALSE" ImageUrl="/_layouts/images/blankmwsprev.png"
        Description="A blank meeting site for you to customize
        based on your requirements."
        DisplayCategory="Meetings" >
        </Configuration>
        <Configuration ID="2" Title="Decision Meeting Workspace"
        Hidden="FALSE" ImageUrl="/_layouts/images/decisionmwsprev.png"
        Description="A site for meetings that track status or make
        decisions. It provides lists for creating tasks, storing
        documents, and recording decisions."
        DisplayCategory="Meetings">
        </Configuration>
        <Configuration ID="3" Title="Social Meeting Workspace"
        Hidden="FALSE" ImageUrl="/_layouts/images/socialmwsprev.png"
        Description="A site to plan social occasions. It
        provides lists for tracking attendees, providing
        directions, and storing pictures of the event."
        DisplayCategory="Meetings" >
        </Configuration>
        <Configuration ID="4" Title="Multipage Meeting Workspace"
        Hidden="FALSE" ImageUrl="/_layouts/images/multipagemwsprev.png"
```

```
        Description="A site to plan, organize, and capture the
        results of a meeting. It provides lists for managing the
        agenda and meeting attendees in addition to two blank
        pages for you to customize based on your requirements."
        DisplayCategory="Meetings" >
        </Configuration>
    </Template>
    <Template Name="CENTRALADMIN" ID="3">
        <Configuration ID="0" Title="Central Admin Site"
        Hidden="TRUE" ImageUrl="" Description="A site for
        central administration. It provides Web pages and links
        for application and operations management." >
        </Configuration>
    </Template>
    <Template Name="WIKI" ID="4">
        <Configuration ID="0" Title="Wiki Site" Hidden="FALSE"
        ImageUrl="/_layouts/images/wikiprev.png" Description="A
        site for a community to brainstorm and share ideas. It
        provides Web pages that can be quickly edited to record
        information and then linked together through keywords."
        DisplayCategory="Collaboration" >
        </Configuration>
    </Template>
    <Template Name="BLOG" ID="9">
        <Configuration ID="0" Title="Blog" Hidden="FALSE"
        ImageUrl="/_layouts/images/blogprev.png" Description="A
        site for a person or team to post ideas, observations,
        and expertise that site visitors can comment on."
        DisplayCategory="Collaboration" >
        </Configuration>
    </Template>
</Templates>
```

Each <Template></Template> block identifies a set of similar Web site definitions. Within each <Template> tag is:

- The Name attribute, which supplies a mnemonic name.

- The ID attribute, which supplies a unique identifier.

Within each <Template></Template> block, there's one <configuration> tag for each site definition. Within this tag is the following:

- The ID attributes, which provide a unique identity within each <Template> node.

- The Title, ImageUrl, and Descriptions fields, which specify values that the Template Selection page will display when a team member creates a site.

- Display category, which is the tab on which you want the name of the site to appear when you create a new site. You can specify one of the existing ones (Collaboration or Meetings) or specify a new one.

- Hidden, which determines whether the site should be shown to the users.

- Image URL, which is an image that will be shown when the configuration is selected.

- RootWebOnly and SubWebOnly, which show whether the site could be created only as a top-level site or only as a child site.

Working with Onet.xml Files

Further information about each site definition appears in a file named Onet.xml. Because the WebTemp.xml file specified several template names (STS, MPS, Blog, Wiki, Central Administration), there are more Onet.xml files. To find these files, first navigate to C:\Program Files\Common Files\Microsoft Shared\Web server extensions\12\ TEMPLATE\SiteTemplates\ and then to these locations:

- \Blog\XML\onet.xml

- \CENTRALADMIN\XML\ONET.XML

- \MPS\XML\ONET.XML

- \sts\XML\ONET.XML

- \Wiki\XML\ONET.XML

Each Onet.xml file defines a series of common elements for individual sites to use. These include the following:

- Navigation bars such as the Top Link Bar and the Quick Launch

- List templates

- Document templates

- Configurations

- Modules

Several types of tasks can be performed in Onet.xml to customize a site definition:

- Specify an alternate cascading style sheet (CSS) file, JavaScript file, or ASPX header file for a site definition.

- Modify navigation areas for the home page and list pages.

- Add a list definition as an option to the Create page.

- Define a configuration for a site definition.

- Specify the lists, modules, files, and Web Parts to be included when a site is instantiated.

WSS 3.0 brings another site definition file, called the Global Site Definition, which can be found at C:\Program Files\Common Files\Microsoft Shared\web server extensions\12\ TEMPLATE\GLOBAL\XML\ONET.xml. This file contains provisioning information for every site definition such as base types, base master page, and so on. This is an improvement from the last version, in which a lot of redundant data had to be inserted in the Onet.xml file for every site definition.

Project is the top-level element in an Onet.xml file.

```xml
<Project
  Title="Site Definition"
  Revision="1"
  ListDir=""
  xmlns:ows="Microsoft SharePoint">
  <NavBars/>
  <ListTemplates/>
  <DocumentTemplates/>
  <BaseTypes/>
  <Configurations>
        ...
        <Configuration
          ID="0"
          Name="Default">
                <Lists/>
                <Modules>
                        <Module
                          Name="Default" />
                </Modules>
                <SiteFeatures>
                        <Feature
                        ID="00BFEA71-1C5E-4A24-B310-BA51C3EB7A57" />
                        ...
                </SiteFeatures>
                <WebFeatures>
                        <Feature
                        ID="00BFEA71-4EA5-48D4-A4AD-7EA5C011ABE5" />
                        ...
                </WebFeatures>
        </Configuration>
        ...
  </Configurations>
  <Modules>
        <Module Name="Default" Url="" Path="">
                <File Url="default.aspx" NavBarHome="True" />
        </Module>
        ...
  </Modules>
  <Components>
        <FileDialogPostProcessor ID="BDEADEE4-C265-11d0-BCED-00A0C90AB50F" />
  </Components>
</Project>
```

NavBars defines the top and side navigation bar. This node can contain additional *NavBar* elements, and the links can be added using *NavBarLink* elements.

```xml
<NavBars>
  <NavBar Name="SharePoint Top Navbar" Separator="   "
```

```
       Body="Label body" ID="1002">
   </NavBar>
</NavBars>
```

The Document templates elements describe what document templates will be used in document libraries.

```
<DocumentTemplates>
<DocumentTemplate Path="STS" DisplayName="Financial Report" Type="10001"
Default="TRUE" Description="Some description">
        <DocumentTemplateFiles>
<DocumentTemplateFile Name="doctemp\word\frep.doc"
TargetName="Forms/frep.doc" Default="TRUE" />
        </DocumentTemplateFiles>
   </DocumentTemplate>
</DocumentTemplates>
```

The *ListTemplates* section specifies the list definitions that are part of a site definition. The *ListTemplate* element also specifies a display name for the list definition and whether the option to add a link on the Quick Launch appears selected by default on the new page. In addition, this element specifies the description of the list definition and the path to the image representing the list definition, which are both displayed on the Create page. Configurations are the actual site templates. They are the structure that describes an individual site definition.

A site definition can have one or more configurations, which must also be referenced in WebTemp*.xml. The lists, modules, site features, and Web features that will be created together with the site are referenced as follows:

```
<Configurations>
        ...
        <Configuration
          ID="0"
          Name="Default">
              <Lists/>
              <Modules />
              <SiteFeatures />
              <WebFeatures />
        </Configuration>
        ...
</Configurations>
```

Lists are identified using globally unique identifiers (GUIDs) and if desired, you can use the Collaborative Application Markup Language (CAML) to override some of their properties.

> **To learn more about CAML, you can read the article titled "Introduction: What Is CAML?" at** *http://msdn2.microsoft.com/en-us/library/ms948028.aspx.*

A module is a block of XML code that specifies all the files associated with a definition and the location of those files in the new site. In the case of a Web Part page, for example, the module definition specifies not only the Web Part page file, but also the specific Web Parts, list views, and files to include on the page.

You can use the *Url* attribute of the *Module* element to provision a folder as part of the site definition.

The *Components* element specifies components to include in sites created through the definition.

```
<Components>
    <FileDialogPostProcessor ID="BDEADEE4-C265-11d0-BCED-00A0C90AB50F" />
</Components>
```

Working with Schema.xml Files

Another XML file, named Schema.xml, defines the views, forms, and fields for each type of list. The file for any of the standard list types resides at a location such as C:\Program Files\Common Files\Microsoft Shared\web server extensions\12\ TEMPLATE\FEATURES\AnnouncementsList\Announce\schema.xml.

Customizing Site Definitions

Making changes to the WebTemp.xml, Onet.xml, and Schema.xml files that come with WSS 3.0 is not a best practice. There are two main reasons for this:

- Microsoft considers these to be system files. As a result, any reinstallation, repair, or upgrade to WSS 3.0 might replace them and overlay any changes you may have made.

- Any site created from a site definition continues to use the WebTemp.xml, Onet.xml, and Schema.xml files indefinitely. Therefore, an incorrect change, even if it works for new sites, could break hundreds or thousands of existing sites.

The correct approach, therefore, is to create new site definitions rather than change existing ones.

Creating a New Site Definition

You can use Visual Studio 2005 to help create a new site definition. This application provides you IntelliSense, schema validation, and post-build events. It also helps to package the site definition to be delivered to a client.

Start this process by creating a class library project. The next step is to create a folder structure (Resources, Template, and so on) and add files such as Onet.xml, WebTemp*.xml, ASP.NET pages resources, and so on.

When you add the Onet.xml, it is recommended that you copy one from a WSS 3.0 site that most closely resembles your solution and then modify that. The end result, for a simple site definition, may resemble Figure 18-3.

After the site definition structure is ready, you must deploy the site definition. You can do this with Post-Build events or you can create a package.

If you choose the first option, you can use the *xcopy* command like this:

Figure 18-3 A folder structure for the Sales site definition.

Xcopy "YourVSSolutionLocation\WEBTEMPSALES.xml" "C:\Program Files\Common Files\Microsoft Shared\web server extensions\12\TEMPLATE\1033\XML\" \y

This will copy the WebTemp file. Add more *xcopy* commands like this to copy all the solution files to where they belong in the WSS folder.

For the second option, you will have to build DDF files and use MakeCab.exe. Instead of creating a new class library project, you can choose another way that is much easier. After you install the Visual Studio extension for WSS 3.0, a new Team Site Definition template appears in Visual Studio when you want to create a new project.

This template adds references to the necessary dynamic link libraries (DLLs) and creates a temporary SNK file. Figure 18-4 shows an example of the folder structure for the Sales site definition created with a template provided by VSeWSS. The Onet.xml file will be created together with a master page for the new site definition and a class file that inherits from *SPFeatureReceiver*. In that class, I can override events that are triggered when the feature is either installed, activated, deactivated, or uninstalled.

Figure 18-4 A folder structure for the Sales site definition created with a template provided by VSeWSS.

Choosing Between Site Templates and Site Definitions

With site templates and site definitions available to your organization for creating and designing sites, consider the following issues when deciding which method is best:

- **Ease of Use** Site templates are easy to create and deploy. You can find or create a site with the features you want, save it as a template, deploy the template, and start creating new sites—all without leaving the browser interface or SharePoint Designer.

  Creating a site definition requires working with XML code in a text editor. Then, when you deploy it, you must do so on each front-end Web server in the same farm. Without a doubt, site definitions are harder to create and deploy.

- **Who Will Perform the Work?** Any SharePoint Web designer can create a sample site and save it as a template. Then any site collection administrator can deploy it.

  Because site definitions require access to the Web server's file system, development requires administrative access to test Web servers, and deployment requires the cooperation of production server administrators.

- **Resource Dependence** Site templates do not include all the information required to create a site. Instead, they specify a site definition to use as a starting point and then a list of changes to apply. If that site definition isn't present, or if it's the wrong version, the site template will fail.

  Site definitions, by contrast, completely describe the sites they create, without dependence on any other site definition. This makes site definitions more attractive to software developers, server administrators, and third-party suppliers.

- **Extent of Modification** A site template can override many aspects of its underlying site definition, but not all. A site template can, for example, modify logos, menus, means of navigation, and default lists and libraries. But it can't incorporate new data types, new file types, new view styles, or new drop-down edit menus.

  The more your site needs to differ from any of the default site definitions, the more likely it is that you should go with a new site definition.

- **Maintainability** Once you create a site from a template, modifying the template has no effect on that site. This gives you the freedom to change a template and thereby add, remove, or modify features in future sites. Because templates reside in the configuration database or in a site template gallery, a single command deploys them for an entire server farm.

  Once you've deployed a site definition, there's no safe way to delete or change its features. This is because sites created from the site definition refer to it on an ongoing and active basis, and they depend on it remaining constant. If a site definition is no longer adequate, you can only add features or create a new site definition.

- **Performance** Web pages "ghosted" from a site definition run faster than pages that reside in a content database. This is because:

  - The Web server's file system is faster than a SQL Server database.

- ○ Caching files from the Web server's file system is more efficient than caching them from a content database.
- ○ The fewer cache hits, the more often ASP.NET must compile any ASPX pages. Each compilation incurs a performance penalty.

When you create a site solely from a site definition, none of its pages physically resides in the content database, and performance will be at its peak. Thereafter, the new version of each page you customize resides in the content database and incurs a performance penalty.

When you create a site from a site template, each page that differs from the underlying site definition resides in the content database and therefore incurs the performance penalty. Initially, a site created from a template will have one or more pages in the content database, and a site created from a site definition will have none.

If you create a site from a site definition and then modify some of its pages, the modified pages then reside in the content database. Depending on the number of unghosted pages, a site created from a site definition could run slower than, at the same speed as, or faster than a site created from a template.

In practice, the performance difference between sites created from a template and sites created from a site definition usually isn't noticeable. Nevertheless, these factors may be worth considering in a large-scale environment.

Reverse Engineering a Site Definition

SharePoint Solution Generator is a tool included in WSS 3.0 Tool: Visual Studio 2005 Extensions. It enables you to reverse engineer a previously created site or list definition. The output is a Visual Studio project file.

The site definition reverse engineering process has the following steps:

1. Copy the base site definition.
2. Copy the base site properties.
3. Update the site definition.
4. Copy the base list definitions.
5. Update the list definitions.
6. Generate the provisioning code.
7. Create the Visual Studio project.

> Note
> Not all the WSS 3.0 site templates can be reverse engineered.

TROUBLESHOOTING

Reviewing supported and unsupported scenarios for working with custom site definitions and custom area definitions in SharePoint (WSS, SPS, and MOSS)

Supported scenarios

When you work with custom site definitions or custom area definitions, the following scenarios are supported:

- To create a custom site definition or a custom area definition, you copy an existing site definition or an existing area definition, and then you rename and modify the new site definition or the new area definition. For more information about this supported method, visit the following site: *http://msdn2.microsoft.com/en-us/library/ms868598.aspx.*

- You modify the XML files and the ASPX files in a custom site definition or in a custom area definition before you create new sites or new portal areas by using the custom site definition or the custom area definition.

- You deploy the custom site definition or the custom area definition. That is, you create new sites or new portal areas by using the custom site definition or the custom area definition. To modify the new sites or the new portal areas that you created, you use one or more of the following three supported methods:

  ○ You modify the site by using the user interface in WSS, in SPS, or in MOSS.

  ○ You programmatically modify the site or the portal area by using the WSS object model or the SPS object model.

  ○ You modify the site or the portal area by using FrontPage 2003.

Unsupported scenarios

When you work with custom site definitions or custom area definitions, the following scenarios are *not* supported:

- You modify one of the default site definitions or one of the default area definitions that are included in WSS or in SPS. Microsoft does not support modifying the default set of site definitions or area definitions that are installed when you install WSS and SPS. Additionally, Microsoft does not support modifying the XML files or the ASPX files in the default site definition or in the default area definition.

- You modify a custom site definition or a custom area definition after you deploy the custom site definition or the custom area definition. Microsoft does not support modifying a custom site definition or a custom area definition after you create a new site or a new portal area by using that site definition or area definition. Additionally, Microsoft does not support modifying the XML files or the ASPX files in the custom site definition or in the custom area definition after you deploy the custom site definition or the custom area definition.

- You modify the Webtemp.xml file or the Webtempsps.xml file that is located in the following folder: *Drive*:\Program Files\Common Files\Microsoft Shared\Web Server Extensions\60\Template*LCID*\XML.

- With one exception, Microsoft does not support modifying the Webtemp.xml file or the Webtempsps.xml file. The exception is the Webtemp.xml file. Microsoft supports modifying the Webtemp.xml file only if you want to hide a specific template. To hide a specific template, you modify the Hidden parameter of that template in the Webtemp.xml file.

- Microsoft does not support modifying files that reside in the _layouts folder. Microsoft reserves the right to update these files in software updates or service packs at a later date. This may cause the custom changes to be lost. You must always back up files that you have changed so that you can restore them at a later date.

In Summary...

This chapter explained advanced design techniques that you can use when designing your SharePoint sites and solutions. The techniques will assist your organization in developing SharePoint solutions in a best practices manner that makes them more stable, more robust, and more easily governed.

The next chapter will cover topics designed to assist you in beginning Web Part development for your organization.

Beginning Web Part Development

With the flexibility of powerful prewritten Web Parts, Web Part pages, custom lists and libraries, browser-based editing, SharePoint Designer-based editing, data sources, Web Part connections, and connectivity to Microsoft Office applications, it's amazing how much you can do with Microsoft Windows SharePoint Services 3.0 (WSS 3.0) without programming. Inevitably, however, no tool—or set of tools—can do everything. And with software, that's the time to think about writing your own code.

In a SharePoint environment, writing your own code usually means writing solutions such as Web Parts, custom workflows, and master pages. These items integrate smoothly with the rest of your SharePoint site, leveraging its existing appearance, organization, security, and data management. What's more, these solutions are reusable. You can write them once and use them for as many pages as you would like.

Web Parts work differently from ordinary ASP.NET pages and much differently from legacy ASP pages. As a result, developing and deploying a Web Part requires a different mindset and a somewhat different tool set than does developing other kinds of server-based Web components. With that in mind, this chapter explains the essence of how Web Parts work and what software you need to develop them.

The purpose of this chapter (and Chapter 18, "Advanced Design Techniques") is to introduce Web Part programming. This chapter assumes you already have some experience with .NET programming and with Web-based programming in general. Once you learn the added skill set of developing solutions for SharePoint, you will become one of the most valuable developers your organization has working for it.

Configuring Your Development Environment

Configuring a good development environment and using the right tools are essential factors for a pleasant (and more important, productive) WSS 3.0 development experience.

The basic requirements are WSS 3.0, Microsoft Visual Studio 2005, Windows Server 2003 (Windows Server 2008 when it is released), and SQL Server. WSS 3.0 can be downloaded from the Microsoft Web site. Microsoft Office SharePoint Designer 2007 is not required, but it is a good tool to have at your disposal.

INSIDE OUT   When possible, make sure to use SharePoint Designer

As we have discussed in previous chapters of this book, SharePoint Designer helps you to create and customize SharePoint Web sites, as well as build workflow-enabled applications based on SharePoint technologies. SharePoint Designer provides professional tools for building interactive solutions on the SharePoint platform without writing code, for designing custom SharePoint sites, and for maintaining site performance with reports and managed permissions.

Visual Studio has several versions. If you are an MSDN subscriber, your subscription includes licenses for the Visual Studio Standard and Professional versions. If you wear the hat of a small Independent Software Vendor (ISV), you can enroll in the Microsoft Empower ISV program where—for a reasonable fee—you will receive licenses for Windows, Visual Studio, SQL Server, and other useful tools. And, of course, you can also buy the products right off the shelf.

Note

Visual Studio 2005 has a free version called Visual Studio Express. This can be downloaded at *http://msdn2.microsoft.com/en-us/express/default.aspx*.

Setting Up Your Development Infrastructure

You can use several different configurations for your WSS 3.0 development environment. If your organizational budget allows, it is recommended that you use more than one machine so that you can have WSS 3.0 on one machine and the SQL Server residing on another.

Note

Install Visual Studio only on WSS machines that are used as development servers. For production servers, if debugging is necessary, you should use Remote Debugging, which is discussed later in this chapter.

Additional machines add extra cost to the development process, so in many cases, using virtual machines is preferred. You can use virtualization tools from Microsoft (Virtual PC or Virtual Server) or from VMWare. Recreating your WSS 3.0 topology in a virtual environment is simple, and this next section will show how this is accomplished using Microsoft Virtual Server 2005.

Recreating WSS 3.0 in a Virtual Machine Environment (VM)

To recreate your WSS 3.0 topology in a virtual environment by using Microsoft Virtual Server 2005, perform the following steps:

1. Install Microsoft Virtual Server 2005 (the latest version is Virtual Server 2005 R2).

    Because you will run multiple operating system instances on this virtual machine, it needs to have plenty of memory (2 gigabyte [GB] RAM minimum), a fast hard drive (a 7200 or 1000 RPM SATA; SCASI is even better), and a fast processor (use a multicore one).

    > **Note**
    >
    > For the virtual machines, you should use a hard drive that is separate from the operating system. Also, if you run the VMs from an external drive (when you use a laptop for development), use one with at least Firewire or SATA interface (USB transfer rate is slow).

2. Create a base image. This base image, with Windows Server 2003, will be used whenever you need to create a new virtual machine. Windows Server 2003 should be installed with all available service packs and security updates.

3. You should then install Virtual Machines Additions. This is a tool that enables you to easily move the mouse out of the virtual machine. It also gives you copy and paste support, access to the host machine folders, and higher video resolution.

    Take a backup of this base image with these components installed and use this as your organization's base development image.

4. Prepare the base image for cloning. Before you can use this image, you need to prepare it for cloning by using Sysprep utility. Sysprep.exe assigns a unique security ID (SID) to each destination computer the first time the computer is restarted. Sysprep configures the operating system to use Windows Welcome or MiniSetup to run the first time the user restarts the computer. Sysprep is a valuable utility even if you do not use disk duplication. You also can create an answer file for Sysprep if you want to automate the process (it will contain the computer name, product key, and other various settings).

5. Start creating the virtual machines to replicate the WSS 3.0 topology. Create a new virtual machine with the Attach A Virtual Hard Disk Later option selected. Copy the VHD from the base image that was syspreped to the folder where the new image is located and add it as a disk. Figure 19-1 shows the Virtual Server 2005 main windows from which you get an overview of the virtual machine's status.

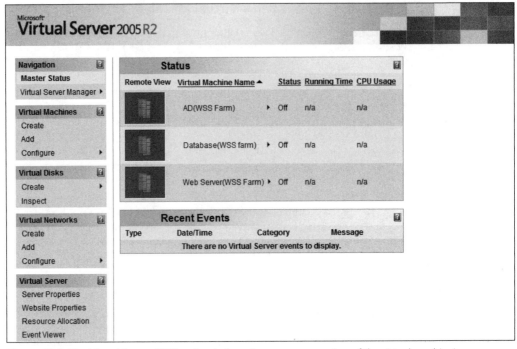

Figure 19-1 The Virtual Server 2005 main window gives you an overview of the virtual machine's status.

> **Note**
>
> It is important to test this new virtual environment before deploying and using it. You should spend adequate time making sure this WSS 3.0 virtual environment solution is as close to your production environment as possible to avoid surprises.

> **Note**
>
> You can download preconfigured virtual hard disks from Microsoft's Web site. They contain preconfigured trial images of applications and operating systems such as Exchange Server 2007, ISA Server 2006, Team System, and SQL Server 2005. This is a fast way to learn a new product without having to go through the software installation and configuration process. For more information on this, you can go to *http://technet.microsoft.com/en-us/bb738372.aspx*.

A variety of tools, add-ins, and resources can help you build a powerful WSS 3.0 solution for your organization. Here are some of them:

- WSS Software Developer Kit (SDK), which provides information about the languages, protocols, and technologies used to customize a deployment of Windows SharePoint Services.

- Visual Studio Extensions for Windows SharePoint Services, which provides tools for developing custom SharePoint applications: Visual Studio project templates for Web Parts, site definitions, and list definitions; and a stand-alone utility program, the SharePoint Solution Generator.

- Visual Studio Extensions for Windows Workflow Foundation, which provides developers with support for building workflow-enabled applications using Windows Workflow Foundation.

- Internet Explorer Developer Toolbar, which provides a variety of tools for quickly creating, understanding, and troubleshooting Web pages. It will prove helpful when you customize the appearance (for example, layouts and cascading style sheet [CSSs]) of the WSS master pages.

- Web Development Helper, which is an Internet Explorer plug-in that provides a set of useful tools for Ajax/JavaScript script diagnostics and HTTP tracing facilities.

- Windows PowerShell, to administer your SharePoint environment with powerful scripts.

- Fiddler HTTP debugger, which inspects HTTP traffic.

How Web Parts Work

WSS 3.0 comes packed with a lot of Web Parts that can be used with little configuration. They should meet most of your business requirements, but inevitably at some point you will want to create your own.

In WSS 3.0, the Web Part infrastructure has been radically improved; it is now built entirely on top of ASP.NET 2.0. The WSS 3.0 infrastructure uses the classes from ASP.NET 2.0 as base classes. SharePoint's *WebPart* and *WebPartManager* classes are still there, but they now they inherit from *System.Web.UI.WebControl.WebPart* and *System.Web. UI.WebControls.WebParts.WebPartManager.* (This process of changing the base for a class is called rebasing.)

You can build your Web Parts by inheriting them from the ASP.NET 2.0 Web Part or from the SharePoint Web Part. The ASP.NET Web Part (*System.Web.UI.WebControls.WebParts. WebPart*) can be used in most cases. The SharePoint Web Part (*Microsoft.SharePoint. WebPartPages.WebPart*) provides additional functionality for connected Web Parts, client-side functionality, and data-caching infrastructure.

For each ASP.NET page on which you want Web Parts, you also need to have a *WebPartManager* class that manages the lifetime of *WebPart* instances at run time and one or more *WebPartZone* objects (locations on the page where the Web Parts will be placed).

WebPart Manager maintains the instances of the Web Parts, serializing and deserializing them to and from the database. Figure 19-2 shows a diagram representing a WSS 3.0 page with Web Part zones and Web Parts.

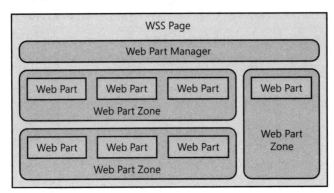

Figure 19-2 WSS 3.0 page with Web Part zones and Web Parts.

A Web Part is a special type of Web control that can be deployed inside of a Web Part zone control. In ASP.NET terminology, a server control is a software component that runs on the Web server as part of one or more ASP.NET Web pages. This provides a way of breaking complex Web pages into manageable pieces, and of using the same component on multiple pages. There are two kinds of ASP.NET controls: user and custom.

- **User controls** These controls consist of two parts:
    - A file that has an .ascx file name extension and that contains sample HTML.
    - The program code that executes on the Web server. This code, plus the code for all other ASP.NET pages and user controls in the same application, is usually compiled into a single dynamic link library (DLL) that resides in the application's bin folder. However, it can also reside in source form, within the ASCX file.

Most developers find user controls fairly easy to create. This is because the developer (or even a Web designer) can use a visual designer to create the sample HTML, and because programming a user control is very much like programming an ordinary ASP.NET page.

User controls, however, can be difficult to deploy widely. When a change occurs, someone must:

- Identify each Web site that uses the control.
- Install the new ASCX and source code files on each Web site.
- Recompile all the source code on each Web site.
- Copy the revised ASCX file and the recompiled code to each production Web site.

If Web Parts were user controls, deploying a new Web Part (or upgrading one) would require recompiling and reinstalling the program code for every Share-Point site that uses the Web Part. That's why Web Parts aren't user controls.

- **Custom controls**   These controls consist entirely of program code. There's no HTML template like the ASCX file for a user control, and consequently no way of using a What You See Is What You Get (WYSIWYG) editor to design its HTML. A programmer must write code that emits each scrap of HTML that the control needs to display output.

  The advantage of custom controls lies in deployment. Each custom control (or, if you choose, each logical group of custom controls) has its own DLL, and at your option you can install this once per physical server or once per virtual Web server. This is the model that Web Parts use. All Web Parts are, in fact, ASP.NET custom controls.

Web Parts can also be used outside of the SharePoint environment, in an ASP.NET 2.0 Web application, but you will not be able to use the rich features of the WSS 3.0 platform such as security framework, templating framework, and the WSS Web Part gallery's management capabilities.

Let's create the simplest HelloWorld Web Part. We can do this in two ways: create a class library project or use Visual Studio 2005 Extensions for Windows SharePoint Services 3.0.

First, let's explore creating a class library project. The steps are quite easy to follow:

1. Create a class library project.

2. Add references to System.Web.dll.

3. Create a class that inherits from *System.Web.UI.WebControls.WebParts.WebPart*.

4. Override the *Render* (and *CreateChildControls*) events.

5. Create a Strong name key and sign the assembly.

The output will look like this:

```
using System;
using System.Collections.Generic;
using System.Text;
using System.Web;
using System.Web.UI.WebControls;
using System.Web.UI.WebControls.WebParts;

namespace ACMECompany
{
    public class HelloWorldWebPart : System.Web.UI.WebControls.WebParts.WebPart
    {
        public HelloWorldWebPart()
        { }
        protected override void Render(System.Web.UI.HtmlTextWriter writer)
```

```
        {
            writer.Write("Hello world!");
        }
    }
}
```

TROUBLESHOOTING

WSS 3.0 support: Visual Studio 2005 Team Foundation Server

The release version of Microsoft Visual Studio 2005 Team Foundation Server relies on WSS 2.0. To enable the release version of Visual Studio 2005 Team Foundation Server to support WSS 3.0, you can install a hotfix along with some additional configurations. For more information on this hotfix, go to *http://support.microsoft.com/kb/932544*.

Using Microsoft Visual Studio 2005 Extensions for Windows SharePoint Services 3.0

VSeWSS is a set of Visual Studio projects and item templates that can help a developer complete a lot of repetitive tasks in quickly, building the foundation for projects such as the following:

- SharePoint Web Parts (adding references, creating .snks and so on)
- SharePoint field controls
- SharePoint content types
- SharePoint list definitions
- SharePoint site definitions

Note

Windows SharePoint Services 3.0 Tools: Visual Studio 2005 Extensions can be downloaded at *http://microsoft.com/downloads/details.aspx?familyid=19f21e5e-b715-4f0c-b959-8c6dcbdc1057&displaylang=en*.

VSeWSS requires WSS 3.0 and Visual Studio 2005 to be installed on the target machine. Without them, the setup will fail. Once you install VSeWSS, the templates become available in Visual Studio. Figure 19-3 shows the templates that the Visual Studio Extensions for Windows SharePoint Services 3.0 add-in installs, and Figure 19-4 shows the other item templates that the VSeWSS add-in installs.

After VSeWSS is installed, choose to create a new project and choose the Web Part template.

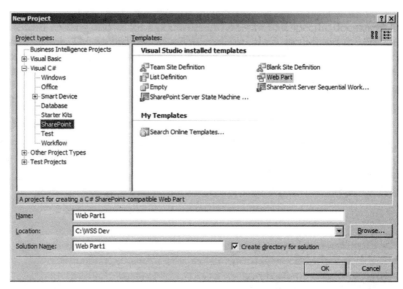

Figure 19-3 Templates installed by the Visual Studio Extensions for Windows SharePoint Services 3.0 add-in.

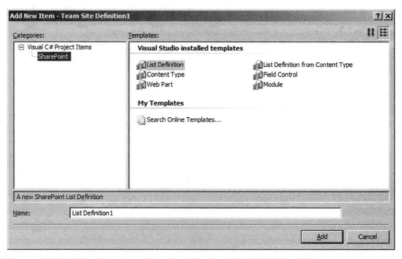

Figure 19-4 Other item templates installed by the VSeWSS add-in.

To find the components of the new project, you can look in the following directories:

- The Project Templates directory, which is located at: C:\Program Files\Microsoft Visual Studio 8\Common7\IDE\ProjectTemplates\CSharp\SharePoint\

- The Item Templates directory, which is located at: C:\Program Files\Microsoft Visual Studio 8\Common7\IDE\ItemTemplates\CSharp\SharePoint\

> **Note**
>
> One of the most powerful features in VSeWSS is the ability to create a site definition from an existing SharePoint site. The SharePoint Solution Generator (SPSolGen) takes an existing site definition or list definition from WSS and automatically reverse engineers it into a Visual Studio 2005 development project.

Web Part Life Cycle

To understand a Web Part life cycle, we need to know the methods that are executed before the Web Part is rendered, as well as the role of each one. The first one is *OnInit*, and the last one is *RenderContents*. Table 19-1 lists the methods that are executed prior to a Web Part being rendered, along with their roles.

Table 19-1 Web Part Methods Executed Prior to the Web Part Being Rendered

Event	Description
OnInit	Initialization of the control
OnLoad	Load event
CreateChildControls	Creates the child controls that are used
EnsureChildControls	Ensures that the child controls have been created and can be referenced
OnPreRender	The event handler for the *System.Web.UI.Control.PreRender* event that occurs immediately before the Web Part is rendered
PreRenderComplete	The *PreRender* is complete
Render	Renders the HTML that the Web Part will display
RenderContents	Renders the content of the control

WSS 3.0 applications run in a virtualized site context using the content database. This means that the Web Parts exist in the database. When they are serialized/deserialized, they are processed by the SharePoint Safe Mode Parser and are added in the page's life cycle later than declarative controls.

The SharePoint Safe Mode Parser checks the code that is run in WSS 3.0. It checks to see, for example, if the code has been configured as trusted, or if the code has the permissions necessary for the operations it is trying to execute. This is why it is so important to check to see if a Web Part has the necessary rights. Otherwise, the user might receive an error screen.

Creating a Web Part

As mentioned previously, Web Parts use the ASP.NET infrastructure. Therefore, if you have ASP programming skills, learning and using the Web Part interfaces, attributes, and development models will be a straightforward prospect.

Every time you have to implement a new Web Part, begin with documenting its functional requirements and overall high-level design. Decide the properties that your part will expose, the interfaces that need to be implemented, the operations the Web Part will need to handle, the necessary security rights it will need, and the deployment scenarios it will require. If you have the option, always try to focus on the security and performance of the Web Part as a top priority.

As an example for this section, we will implement a Contact Form Web Part, which you'll be able to use in an extranet site to collect feedback from your anonymous users.

Let's start with the design. Once we know we want a Web Part, there are really two choices: to inherit from the ASP.NET Web Part or from the SharePoint Web Part (which also inherits from the ASP.NET Web Part). After that, we will design the fields and the operations that are best suited as a base class. In this case, because our Web Part will have a simple functionality, we will go with the ASP.NET option.

Our form will have three text boxes in which the user will be able to fill in name, e-mail, and feedback content. There will also be two buttons: one to send the feedback and one to clear the fields. In addition, you'll find a label to display miscellaneous messages to users.

We will also expose a property in which the site administrator will enter the e-mail address where the feedback will be sent. This is just one possible action. For example, you could add the feedback content to a WSS 3.0 list on a site.

We will model our Web Part using UML class diagrams. UML is the Object Management Group's (OMG's) most-used specification. If you don't "speak" UML yet, it would be good to learn it! It's a language that can be easily understood by other developers.

> **Note**
> When you design the user interface (UI) for a Web Part or for a larger solution, you should develop a model (a simple sketch) in Visio or another modeling tool of what the UI will look like. This will be useful when you have to make decisions such as what elements the master pages will contain. Doing so will also enable you to get early feedback from your customer base regarding the usability aspect of the solution.

Figure 19-5 shows the UML class diagram for the Contact Form Web Part. Let's start by creating a new project and choosing the Class library template. Give your project a meaningful name such as ContactFormWP.

Figure 19-5 The UML class diagram for the Contact Form Web Part.

Add a reference to the *System.Web* namespace. (Right-click the References folder. Click Add Reference and the .Net tab, and then select System.Web. Click OK.) You need to add the reference to *System.Web* because the *WebPart* class is defined in that namespace:

```
namespace Yourcompany.WSS
{
    public class ContactFormWebPart : System.Web.UI.WebControls.WebParts.WebPart
    {
    }
}
```

Designing the Web Part Properties

A Web Part can be configured from the WSS 3.0 site interface, using the properties that it exposes. For the Web Part properties to be visible on the site, they have to be decorated with attributes such as *WebBrowsable*, *Personalizable*, *WebDisplayName*, or *WebDescription*.

Commonly used property attributes are:

- **WebBrowsable** Determines whether the WSS property editing pane can access the Web Part property. You will set it to false when you don't want users to have access to it or if that property will be accessed using a custom editor part.

- **Personalizable** Decides whether the Web Part property value can be set up once for all site visitors or individually for each user. Its values can be *PersonalizationScope.Shared* or *PersonalizationScope.User.* Personalization has an associated performance cost. It's better to use the same properties for all the users (*PersonalizationScope.Shared*).

- **WebDisplayName** The property name that will be displayed in the WSS default editor part.

- **WebDescription** The property description.

```
[Personalizable(PersonalizationScope.Shared),
WebBrowsable(true),
WebDisplayName("Email address"),
WebDescription("The email address where the feedback will be sent")]
public string EmailAddress
{
    get { return emailAddress; }
    set { emailAddress = value; }
}
```

> **Note**
> This is just an example. However, in real life scenarios, you should always validate the input value.

Rendering the Web Part

The Web Parts UI is rendered using code, exactly like an ASP.NET server control. To render our Web Part, we will have to override the *CreateChildControls* and the *RenderContents* methods from the Web Part base class.

In *CreateChildControls*, you create instances of the controls that will be displayed, set up their properties, and at the end you add them to the *Controls* collection. If you have controls that will respond to PostBack events, the event handlers for those are as follows:

```
protected override void CreateChildControls()
{
    this.btnSend = new Button();
    this.btnSend.Text = "Send";
    this.btnSend.Click += new System.EventHandler(this.btnSend_Click);
    ...
```

```
txtName = new TextBox();

...
Controls.Add(btnSend);
Controls.Add(txtName);

...
}
```

After you create this method, it is a good time to write the event handlers:

```
protected void btnSend_Click(object sender, EventArgs e)

{
...
}
```

The *RenderContents* method renders the content of the control:

```
protected override void RenderContents(HtmlTextWriter writer)
{
    writer.Write("Name");
    writer.Write("<br />");
    txtName.RenderControl(writer);
    writer.Write("<br />");

    ...
    btnSend.RenderControl(writer);

    ...
}
```

Let ASP.NET render the controls by using HtmlTextWriter. Although you can do it your-self, adding and closing HTML tags, it is time consuming, and ASP.NET usually does it better because it knows how to render the controls depending on the client type.

> **Note**
>
> I recommend that you render your user interface embedded in *<table/>* or *<div/>* ele-ments. It will help you to control the layout of your Web Part and add CSS classes to elements. WSS 3.0 uses *<table>* elements to render its pages, although more and more often, the World Wide Web Consortium (W3C) recommends *<div>* and *<span>* be used instead of tables. Choose the elements that you like best and are more proficient at.

Planning the Deployment

During the development process, you'll probably deploy, on a regular basis, the Web Part DLL file(s) directly to the WSS site folder, without packaging it first. It's faster and easier to debug. Your DLL file can be:

- Signed with a strong name and deployed to the Web site bin folder.

- Signed with a strong name and deployed to the Global Assembly Cache (GAC).

From a security point of view, the best option is to sign your DLL and deploy it to the site bin folder. If the DLL is deployed in the GAC, then your Web Part will be available to all the sites in your WSS farm, and in some cases, you will not want to do that. Plus, it will operate with full trust.

When deployed in the bin folder, the Web Part is affected by the trust level set in the Web.config file for that folder. By default, it is running under the *WSS_Minimal* policy.

WSS_Minimal doesn't allow for accessing objects from the WSS 3.0 object model or connecting to a database. To raise the trust level for the Web Part, you need to create your own custom policy file and add it in the Web site's Web.config file.

Adding the *AllowPartiallyTrustedCallers* Attribute

If you want to deploy your Web Part to the bin folder, you'll have to set the *AllowPartiallyTrustedCallers* attribute to it. This is due to the fact that the bin folder is a partial trust location. Open AssemblyInfo.cs and add:

```
[assembly: System.Security.AllowPartiallyTrustedCallers()]
```

Signing the Assembly

You will realize several benefits if you give your DLL a strong name (that is, sign it). For example, if you deploy it to GAC, then you can have support for side-by-side versioning, file security (ACLs), and so on. To sign the assembly, perform the following steps:

1. Right-click Solution Properties. Then click Open, Signing Tab.

2. Select the Sign The Assembly check box. In the Choose A Strong Name Key File list, select <New...>.

3. Choose a name and then uncheck Protect My Key File With A Password.

4. Click OK.

Because you'll need it later, you should extract the public key token. To do this, perform the following steps:

1. Start the Visual Studio command prompt.

2. Type **sn.exe –t yourassembly**.

You can also extract the public key of your DLL after it has been deployed to GAC by going to C:\WINDOWS\assembly folder (all the files added to the GAC are copied there) and checking the DLL properties. Figure 19-6 shows the public key token of the DLL.

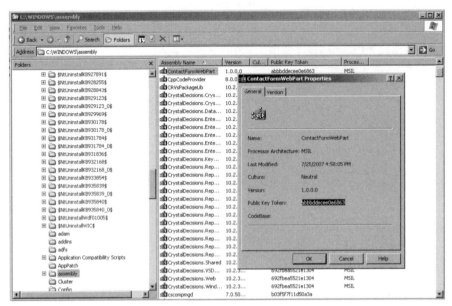

Figure 19-6 The public key token of the DLL.

Adding the Safe Control Entry

When a Web Part is deployed to GAC or bin folder, you need to allow it to run in WSS 3.0 by adding it as a SafeControl.

Locate the Web.config file of your site and open it. You'll notice two sections like these:

```
<sectionGroup name="SharePoint">
   <section name="SafeControls"
type="Microsoft.SharePoint.ApplicationRuntime.SafeControlsConfigurationHandler,
Microsoft.SharePoint, Version=12.0.0.0, Culture=neutral,
PublicKeyToken=71e9bce111e9429c" />
   ...
<sectionGroup/>
```

And:

```
<SafeControls>
   <SafeControl Assembly="System.Web, Version=1.0.5000.0, Culture=neutral,
PublicKeyToken=b03f5f7f11d50a3a" Namespace="System.Web.UI.WebControls"
TypeName="*" Safe="True" AllowRemoteDesigner="True" />
   <SafeControl Assembly="System.Web, Version=1.0.5000.0, Culture=neutral,
PublicKeyToken=b03f5f7f11d50a3a" Namespace="System.Web.UI.HtmlControls"
TypeName="*" Safe="True" AllowRemoteDesigner="True" />
   ...
</SafeControls>
```

The *SafeControls* section contains all the assemblies that WSS 3.0 allows to run. Before using the Web Part, you will have to add a similar entry for it.

Using PostBuild Events

Use PostBuild events to ease your workload and have the DLL automatically deployed to GAC or copied to the site \bin folder during the development process.

Deploying to bin Folder

To automatically deploy the DLL to the bin folder, you can set as Post-Build event the following command:

```
xcopy "Yourdll" "Yoursitelocation\bin" /y
```

Or in the project Properties, select the Build tab and set the Output path to "Your_WSS_Site_Location\bin".

Deploying to GAC

To deploy to the GAC, perform the following:

1. Open the project Properties and go to Build events.

2. Set the Pre-build event command line to:

```
"C:\Program Files\Microsoft Visual Studio 8\SDK\v2.0\Bin\gacutil.exe" /u
$(TargetName)
```

3. Set the Post-build event command line to:

```
"C:\Program Files\Microsoft Visual Studio 8\SDK\v2.0\Bin\gacutil.exe" /i
$(TargetPath)
```

When you compile a new version, before building the project, the existing Web Part will be removed from GAC. Then, once the build is successful, the new Web Part will be installed.

Using the Web Part in a Site

The first version of your Web Part has successfully compiled and has been added to bin (or GAC). The *SafeControl* tag is in place, and now the Web Part is ready for a test drive. You need to add the Web Part to a Web Part page. To add your Web Part to a WSS 3.0 page, perform the following steps:

1. Open the WSS 3.0 site to which you would like to add the Web Part.

2. Go to Site Actions and then Site Settings. Then click Modify All Site Settings and select Web Parts.

3. In the Web Part gallery, click New and browse to the new Web Part. Select the Web Part and click Populate Gallery to add it to the Web Parts gallery.

4. On the Site Actions menu, click Edit Page.

5. In the Web Part zone in which you want to add the Web Part, click Add A Web Part.

6. In the Add Web Parts dialog box, select the check box for the Web Part that you want to add to the page.

7. Click Add to finalize adding the Web Part to the page.

Debugging Web Parts

The debugging process for a Web Part is quite simple. Debugging a Web Part is similar to debugging a server control. After you deploy the Web Part and set breakpoints in the code, you just need to attach to the process responsible for rendering/executing the WSS 3.0 pages (w3wp.exe).

> **Note**
>
> When you try to attach to the w3wp.exe process, you may see several instances of this process in the list. You can attach to all of them (use Ctrl to select more than one) or try to find the correct one (attach to the one that runs under the privileges of your WSS 3.0 application pool user). If you used a local account for WSS 3.0 try an *IISRSET* command and after that, browse the WSS 3.0 page where the Web Part is located. This operation will spawn a new w3wp.exe process.

Remote Debugging

If necessary, you can remotely debug a WSS 3.0 instance installed on another server. This usually happens when you have to debug sites that are already in production. You will first need to prepare for remote debugging by following these steps:

1. Set up an account, which will be in the domain Admins (if you're using a Microsoft Active Directory directory service) or in the Administrators group (if you're using local accounts). This account—let's say SPDevDebug—must be listed in the Log On As A Service policy list.

2. You will then need to make sure that Visual Studio 2005 components are installed on the remote server.

3. Add Full Control permissions for the newly created user on the following folders. Then share them:

   o C:\Program Files\Common Files\Microsoft Shared\ web server extensions\12\ISAPI\

   o C:\Inetpub\wwwroot\

4. Create a folder on drive C, such as C:\SPDebug. Then copy the content of C:\Program Files\Microsoft Visual Studio 8\Common7\IDE\Remote Debugger\x86\.

5. On the remote machine, run the Visual Studio Remote Debugger Configuration Wizard. Follow the steps in the wizard to set up remote debugging as a service.

6. You must then configure a project for debugging and start the operation.

Creating a New Web Part Solution

Previously, we deployed the Web Part to the bin folder by using Post-Build events. Although this is a good solution for development scenarios, it cannot be applied when we want to deploy it to one or more customers.

One of the available solutions is to create a solution package, which usually contains a manifest file (manifest.xml) and the assembly file we need to deploy. The manifest file describes what we want to deploy and where we want to deploy it. Here is an example:

```
<Solution xmlns="http://schemas.microsoft.com/sharepoint/"
    SolutionId="081F7F9F-77BF-446d-BE6F-6507707F0584">
<Assemblies>
<Assembly DeploymentTarget="WebApplication" Location=" ContactFormWebPart.dll">
        <SafeControls>
                <SafeControl
                Assembly="ContactFormWebPart.dll, Version=1.0.0.0, Culture=neutral,
PublicKeyToken=xxxxxxxxxxxxxxx"
                Namespace=" Yourcompany.WSS" Safe="True" TypeName="*"/>
        </SafeControls>
    </Assembly>
</Assemblies>
</Solution>
```

Here are descriptions of some of the components:

- **SolutionId** Unique identifier of the solution: Global Unique Identifier (GUID).

- **DeploymentTarget** Specifies where the assembly will be deployed. This can be WebApplication (deploy it to the bin folder) or GlobalAssemblyCache (deploy it to the GAC).

- **SafeControl** This element will add an entry in the Web.config file in the *SafeControls* section.

To create a new solution package, perform the following steps:

1. Open the Web Part solution in Visual Studio.

2. Add a new CAB project. This can be done by clicking File, Add, New Project. Then, under Other Project Types, select Setup And Deployment Group, CAB Project.

3. Give a name to the CAB project.

4. Right-click the CAB project in the Solution Explorer and choose Add, Project Output.

5. In the AddProjectOutputGroup window, select the In The Project combo box and the name of the ContactForm Web Part project.

6. Select Primary Output in the list that is displayed. In the Configuration combo box, choose ReleaseAnyCPU and then click OK.

7. You will then need to go back to step 4 and choose Content Files to begin to add the Manifest.xml file to the CAB. Follow step 4 all the way through this step to add the Manifest.xml file to the CAB. Click OK to build the CAB project.

8. Change the extension for the newly created file to .wsp. The solution package is now ready for deployment to your WSS 3.0 environment.

Next, you'll need to add the solution package to the solution store and deploy it. To accomplish this, perform the following steps:

1. From the command prompt, run **Stsadm.exe -o addsolution –filename YourWSPFile.wsp.**

2. On the Operations page of SharePoint Central Administration, click Solution Management and select where you want to deploy your solution.

> **Note**
> You can also add a solution to the Solution Store by using the WSS Object Model.

From the Solution Management page in Central Administration, you can manage your solutions. You can control their scope by deploying them globally or only to certain Web applications, which is much more elegant and safe than copying, one by one, each of them to the \bin folder of each Web application where they are needed.

Adding Custom Events to SharePoint Lists

WSS 2.0 has events receivers (that is, Event sinks), but those events are only supported by document libraries and are asynchronous. WSS 3.0 comes with both asynchronous (after-the-fact) and synchronous (before-the-fact) events, support for events in lists, and content types.

For example, you can catch the *ItemDeleting* event to cancel an item deletion in a list. All you need to do is to write a class that implements *SPItemEventReceiver* and then override the *ItemDeleting* method. Once the code is ready, write a feature that will activate the event handler. This is how the code might look:

```
public class CancelDeleteHandler : SPItemEventReceiver
{
    public override void ItemDeleting(SPItemEventProperties properties)
    {
     if (condition)
        {
string message = "You are not allowed to delete contact details";
            properties.ErrorMessage = message;
            properties.Cancel = true;
        }
    }
}
```

By using a feature file, you can bind the receiver to a list type. The feature file will look something like this:

```
<Feature Scope="Web"
   Title="Deleting Event Handler"
   Id="GUID"
   xmlns="http://schemas.microsoft.com/sharepoint/">
   <ElementManifests>
        <ElementManifest Location="Elements.xml"/>
   </ElementManifests>
</Feature>
```

The elements file associated with the feature may look like this:

```
<Elements xmlns="http://schemas.microsoft.com/sharepoint/">
   <Receivers ListTemplateId="104">
        <Receiver>
                <Name>DeletingEventHandler</Name>
                <Type>ItemDeleting</Type>
                <SequenceNumber>10000</SequenceNumber>
                <Assembly>
                        CancelDeleteHandler, Version=1.0.0.0, Culture=neutral,
PublicKeyToken=a26b5449ac4a4cf3
                </Assembly>
                <Class>DeletingEventHandler.DeletingAction</Class>
                <Data></Data>
                <Filter></Filter>
        </Receiver>
   </Receivers>
</Elements>
```

The feature will activate the event handler for all the lists that have the *TemplateID* value specified in the Elements.xml file. In this case, *TemplateID* is 104, which is the Announcements list ID. If you have more handlers for the same list, you'll add an individual *Receiver* element for each one. The available list template types are displayed in Table 19-2.

Table 19-2 **List Template Types Available in WSS 3.0**

List Template Type	Template ID
Custom list	100
Document library	101
Survey	102
Links list	103
Announcements list	104
Contacts list	105
Events list	106
Tasks list	107
Discussion board	108
Picture library	109

These IDs can be found in the Features directory of WSS 3.0. The Features directory is located at C:\Program Files\Common Files\Microsoft Shared\web server extensions\ 12\TEMPLATE\FEATURES. For example, for the *AnouncementList* type, go to the AnoucementList folder, where you'll find *Type=104* in the Announcements.xml file.

This method of binding events has some limitations. Feature.xml cannot bind events to a specific list instance or a specific content type, and the event handlers can be activated only at the site level (not at the site collection level).

To overcome this, you can bind your events programmatically by using the WSS 3.0 object model. All you need to do is to provide the code for the *FutureActivate* method that runs before the feature is activated.

TROUBLESHOOTING

A WSS 3.0 hotfix package that resolves a feature install issue along with three other known issues

Microsoft has released a WSS 3.0 hotfix package that resolves four issues:

- The error message when you try to install a feature in Windows SharePoint Services 3.0: "The 'UserSelectionMode' attribute is not allowed": *http://support.microsoft. com/kb/934613*

- The Web File Properties dialog box displays incorrect properties for a document that is saved in a Windows SharePoint Services 3.0 document library: *http://support.microsoft.com/kb/934253*

- A file that is attached to an e-mail message is not put in a Windows SharePoint Services 3.0 document library: *http://support.microsoft.com/kb/934882*

- Issues that may occur when you use the volume shadow copy service (VSS) reference writer in Windows SharePoint Services 3.0: *http://support.microsoft.com/kb/935605*

More information can be found on this hotfix package at *http://support.microsoft.com/ kb/934790.*

Overview of the SharePoint Object Model

Over the past several years, WSS has evolved into a rich platform for application development. A comprehensive set of namespaces allow for programmatic access to most of the features of WSS 3.0.

The WSS 3.0 application programming interface (API) offers two majors interfaces: an object model and a set of Web services.

The WSS object model is spread throughout 30 public namespaces included in 10 assemblies. One of the most exciting new features in WSS 3.0 is support for workflows. WSS 3.0 comes with few built-in workflows, and it also offers the possibility to build your own workflows.

Table 19-3 lists the most important namespaces and contains a short description of each.

Table 19-3 The Most Important Namespaces in the SharePoint Object Model

Name	Assembly	Description
Microsoft.SharePoint	Provides types and members for working with a top-level site and its subsites or lists	Provides administrative types and members for managing a WSS 3.0 deployment
Microsoft.SharePoint. Administration	Provides types and members for performing backup and restore operations on SharePoint sites	Provides types and members for importing and exporting content between WSS 3.0 Web sites
Microsoft.SharePoint. Administration.Backup	Provides types and members for customizing the navigation structures and site maps of SharePoint Web sites	Provides a set of code access permission and attribute classes designed to protect a specific set of resources and operations. For example, access to the Windows SharePoint Services object model, the ability to do unsafe saving on HTTP Gets, and enabling point-to-point Web Part connections
Microsoft.SharePoint. Deployment	Provides utilities for encoding strings and processing user information	Provides types and members for associating, initiating, and managing workflow templates and instances
Microsoft.SharePoint. Navigation	Provides types and members for working with a top-level site and its subsites or lists	Provides administrative types and members for managing a WSS 3.0 deployment
Microsoft.SharePoint. Security	Provides types and members for performing backup and restore operations on SharePoint sites	Provides types and members for importing and exporting content between WSS 3.0 Web sites

Table 19-3 The Most Important Namespaces in the SharePoint Object Model

Name	Assembly	Description
Microsoft.SharePoint. Utilities	Provides types and members for customizing the navigation structures and site maps of SharePoint Web sites	Provides a set of code access permission and attribute classes designed to protect a specific set of resources and operations. For example, access to the Windows SharePoint Services–object model, the ability to do unsafe saving on HTTP Gets, and enabling point-to-point Web Part connections
Microsoft.SharePoint. Workflow	Provides utilities for encoding strings and processing user information	Provides types and members for associating, initiating, and managing workflow templates and instances

For the most basic operations, you will set a reference to the *Microsoft.Sharepoint.dll* assembly.

Site Collections and Sites

The WSS object model is hierarchical and is easy to navigate from top to bottom. Here are a few facts to keep in mind:

- Each *SPSite* object represents a site collection and has members that can be used to manage the site collection. The *AllWebs* property provides access to the *SPWebCollection* object that represents the collection of all Web sites within the site collection, including the top-level site. The *Microsoft.SharePoint.SPSite. OpenWeb* method of the *SPSite* class returns a specific Web site.

- Each site collection includes any number of *SPWeb* objects, and each object has members that can be used to manage a site, including its template and theme, as well as to access files and folders on the site. The *Webs* property returns a *SPWebCollection* object that represents all the subsites of a specified site, and the *Lists* property returns a *SPListCollection* object that represents all the lists in the site.

- Each *SPList* object has members that are used to manage the list or access items in the list. The *GetItems* method can be used to perform queries that return specific items. The *Fields* property returns an *SPFieldCollection* object that represents all the fields, or columns in the list, and the *Items* property returns an *SPListItemCollection* object that represents all the items, or rows, in the list.

- Each *SPField* object has members that contain settings for the field.

- Each *SPListItem* object represents a single row in the list.

The *Microsoft.SharePoint* namespace, used in most situations, has more than 220 public classes, 9 interfaces, and more than 70 enumerations.

You can use the API to:

- Get the current site collection:

```
SPSite site = SPControl.GetContextSite(Context);
```

- Enumerate the sites in a site collection:

```
SPSite currentsiteCollection = SPControl.GetContextSite(Context);
SPWebCollection sites = currentsiteCollection.AllWebs;
foreach (SPWeb site in sites)
{
    Console.WriteLine(site.Title + " ");
}
```

- Access list items:

```
SPWeb currentsite = SPControl.GetContextWeb(Context);
SPListCollection lists = currentsite.Lists;
foreach (SPList list in lists)
{
    //Console...
}
```

> **Note**
>
> When you write code for WSS 3.0, you usually instantiate objects such as *SPSite* and *SPWeb*. These objects should be disposed of after they are used. Otherwise, you may encounter performance penalties. A good resource on this topic is the article "Best Practices: Using Disposable Windows SharePoint Services Objects," which can be found at *http://msdn2.microsoft.com/en-us/library/aa973248.aspx*.

In Summary...

This chapter explained the basics of how Web Parts work and what tools you need to create Web Parts of your own. It then explained the basic programming techniques you need to successfully create and deploy custom Web Parts.

The next chapter will provide guidance on SharePoint best practices, governing your WSS 3.0 environment, and how to define the proper content types and metadata for your enterprise.

Additional SharePoint Best Practices

This chapter introduces a questionnaire that you can use in your requirements-gathering initiatives for implementing Microsoft Windows SharePoint Services 3.0 (WSS 3.0) in your organization.

This chapter also discusses how you can properly define content types and metadata for your organization as well as how you can use the Microsoft Best Practices Analyzer for WSS 3.0.

Best Practices Planning: Using a SharePoint Questionnaire

When you start to plan the approach to your new WSS 3.0 initiative, it is helpful if you think about all aspects of the deployment prior to implementing a solution. Over the past six or seven years, I have been involved in a large number of SharePoint projects all over the United States. I have developed a best practices approach to high-level requirements gathering by putting together a questionnaire to assist me in making sure I cover as many aspects of the client's organization as possible. This questionnaire is divided into four parts: Infrastructure, SharePoint Specific, Other Systems, and Security Specific.

This questionnaire has saved me countless hours of extra work because I can pass it to a large number of the client's resources and ask them to provide me as much information as they possibly can. Usually there is not one single person within an organization who is able to answer these questions. Getting more people involved in this process can help on the public relations (PR) side of the fence as more people feel involved in the process. In the past, I have also created a SharePoint survey of this questionnaire within a proof-of-concept environment if one is available to the project team.

The first section of the questionnaire concerns your organization's infrastructure. These questions should get you going in the right direction, but keep in mind that every organization is different, so you may need to modify the questions accordingly. Some of the questions are centered on organizations that already have SharePoint Portal Server 2003 (SPS) or WSS 2.0 installed and are looking to migrate into the new version of SharePoint. If you have not yet implemented SharePoint, you should keep the items that do not yet apply to you in mind and make note of them so that they are on your radar screen during the planning and implementation phases of your project.

Infrastructure-Related Questions

If you do not have SharePoint implemented at all within your organization, please keep infrastructure-related items in mind when planning your deployment and mark the items that do not currently apply to you as N/A. The following is a list of infrastructure-related questions for your organization. These questions will assist you in your deployment planning.

- How many data centers (will or are) being used for the SharePoint environment?
- If you currently have SharePoint implemented, what are the current SharePoint environment names (for example, Development, UAT, Production)?
- If you currently have SharePoint implemented, please go into detail about the current environments.
  - How many servers are in each environment (Web servers, search servers, database servers, and so on)?
  - Are there separate servers for WSS, SPS, or SharePoint Server?
- What software is currently being used to back up the actual SharePoint Servers (for example, VERITAS)?
- Is Shared Services configured within the environment?
- If applicable, how does the extranet environment differ from the intranet environment?
- What drives are currently being used on the environments?
  - Are the local C drives being used to store the Internet Information Services (IIS) metabase?
  - Are all files being written to the storage area network (SAN) or other locations?
  - What space is or will be available for this initiative?
- What performance monitoring tools are currently being used within the environment?
- What load balancing hardware is currently being used within the environment (for example, Cisco, F5, Windows Server 2003)?
- Within the organization, are there any high latency/low bandwidth sites that use SharePoint?
- How is the SharePoint Search infrastructure configured?
- Do administrators have full Admin rights to all front-end Web servers and search/job servers?
- Do SharePoint administrators have full access to the SQL Server environments?
- What current version of SQL Server is your organization using?

SharePoint-Specific Questions

This section of the questionnaire is about SharePoint-specific questions for your organization. If you do not have SharePoint implemented at all within your organization, please keep these SharePoint-specific items in mind when planning your deployment and mark the items that do not currently apply to you as N/A. The following is a list of SharePoint-specific questions for your organization. These questions will assist you in your deployment planning.

- If you currently have SharePoint implemented, what is the current total user base, or what will the future user base be?
- What are the disaster recovery policies and procedures for the current solution?
- Will there be a separate Disaster Recovery (DR) environment for SharePoint?
- Do you have paper copies of your other systems' disaster recovery policies? (That is, if SharePoint is down, will you have the DR documents you need for other systems?)
- Is SharePoint currently used for your organization's intranet solution?
- Does corporate communications or marketing play a major role in content promotion of the current intranet?
- Are any third-party tools or solutions implemented within the organization (for example, CorasWorks, AvePoint, Quest)?
- Are any knowledge management initiatives being managed within SharePoint?
- Is there a current site that I should look at that could assist me in master page development for the new WSS 3.0 implementation?
- What are the current Microsoft FrontPage or SharePoint Designer modifications within the environment?
    - Are there any existing unghosted pages within the environment?
    - Please go into detail about how FrontPage or SharePoint Designer is used within the organization.
- Please briefly cover the overall hierarchy structure of the portal(s).
    - Is it departmentally, functionally, or organizationally structured?
    - Do departments each get their own team site?
- Is any SQL Log Shipping taking place on the SharePoint SQL Server databases?
- Have any custom workflows been identified?
    - If so, who will develop them?
    - Do you have an internal resource identified for this type of activity?
    - Do you have any partnerships with external consulting firms to assist in custom SharePoint development?

- How are the current site collections configured?
- Are team sites created using the out-of-the-box templates?
  - Have any sites been created using the command-line options?
  - Are any database naming conventions being used for SharePoint team sites?
- What service packs are currently rolled out for the environment in relation to SharePoint?
- What is the current governance model for the portal?
  - Does a content approver group or a power user group exist to help with site management task delegation?
  - Is My Site currently being used within your organization?
- What are the current branding standards for the portal?
- What custom Web Parts are deployed within the portal?
  - Please discuss each Web Part and its main function.
  - Are these developed in .NET 1.1 or .NET 2.0?
  - Are any custom .NET applications being used within SharePoint?
- What is the current content type/metadata model for the portal?
  - Are there core metadata fields that must be captured within each document library or list?
- Are any file types specifically excluded from SharePoint (for example, MP3, MP4)?
- At what level is the file upload quota for SharePoint currently set?
- Are any third-party tools being used to back up or migrate SharePoint data (for example, AvePoint's DocAve, Commvault)?
- Is any anonymous access configured within the SharePoint environment?
- Are any Microsoft Office Outlook Web Parts (Calendar, Mail, tasks, and so on) being used within the portal?
- How do users currently request new sites?
  - Are any chargebacks being sent to the departments that are requesting these new sites?
- Are folders being used within document libraries, or are any limitations set as to how deep users can go with folders?
- Who currently manages the SharePoint backup scripts?
  - What is the procedure for adding new sites to these scripts?
- Do any SharePoint 2001 or 2003 environments exist within the organization? If so, was there a 2001 to 2003 migration?

- Does a Microsoft Project Server 2003 or 2007 environment exist within the organization?

- Please go into detail about the current help desk policies and procedures for SharePoint.

  ○ Describe the FAQ lists.

- What is the current help desk ticketing tool that captures SharePoint issues (for example, Remedy, Heat)?

- What external sites or content sources are crawled within SharePoint's search?

- Is a change management (CM) process currently in place for SharePoint concerning content, code, and so on?

- Is iFilter currently being used to crawl PDF documents?

- Are any Business Objects XI/SharePoint initiatives within the organization?

- What are the current crawling times for SharePoint search?

- What is the process for adding future organizational acquisitions to SharePoint?

- Is there a scalability plan for adding new divisions, users, and so on?

- How many separate content databases exist for SharePoint within the organization?

- Will your organization use the Business Data Catalog (BDC)?

- Will we need to connect to other external data sources (Siebel, PeopleSoft, SAP, and so on)?

For more information regarding governing your WSS 3.0 environment, refer to the section titled "Site Governance Best Practices" in Chapter 5, "Creating SharePoint Sites, Workspaces, and Pages."

Other Systems-Related Questions

This section is about other systems-related questions. If you do not have SharePoint implemented at all within your organization, please keep these other systems-related items in mind when planning your deployment and mark the items that do not currently apply to you as N/A. The following is a list of other systems-related questions for your organization. They will assist you in your deployment planning.

- What other systems in the company are tightly integrated within SharePoint?

- Is there an implementation of Documentum, LiveLink, DocuShare, or a similar content management solution within the organization?

- How is an average SharePoint user's machine configured (for example, Windows XP with Service Pack 2 (SP2), Windows Vista, Microsoft Office 2007)?

- Are any Macintosh (Mac) machines with Safari accessing the portal?

- How large (speed/size) are the organization's current network pipelines that SharePoint is using?

- Is Office Communicator 2007 implemented within the organization?
    - What instant messaging tools are being used?

- What version of Microsoft Exchange Server is currently deployed within the organization?

- What development tools are being used within the organization to develop .NET Framework applications (for example, Visual Studio 2005)?

- Are there currently any SharePoint development standards within the organization?

- Is SQL Reporting Services rolled out and if so, is it being used for SharePoint?

- Please go into detail regarding any SAP or PeopleSoft/SharePoint interoperability that may be required.

- Please go into detail regarding any Sarbanes-Oxley (SOX) requirements that SharePoint may be required to support.

- Are all users within organization on Microsoft Office 2007?
    - Are there currently any Office 2003 users?
    - Will Microsoft Office InfoPath be used within the environment?
    - Do all users within the organization have Office InfoPath installed on their computers in their Microsoft Office installations?

- Are any other search tools being used within the organization?

- How many domains currently exist within the organization?

- What is the current architecture of the SQL Server environment?

Security-Related Questions

This section covers security-related questions about your organization. If you do not have SharePoint implemented at all within your organization, please keep these security specific items in mind when planning your deployment and mark the items that do not currently apply to you as N/A. The following is a list of security-related questions for your organization. They will assist you in your deployment planning.

- How do the current Microsoft Active Directory directory service security groups map to SharePoint's hierarchy?
    - Is there a need to add individual users to cover those groups that do not encapsulate an entire department or project team?
    - How are Active Directory groups managed within the organization?

- Are tools available for administrators or power users to use to enable them to add or manage users within existing Active Directory groups?

- What is the current lag time between Active Directory controllers (for example, 15 minutes)?

Defining the Proper Content Types and Metadata for Your Organization

Content type functionality in WSS 3.0, as discussed in the section titled "SharePoint Content Types" in Chapter 2, "Introducing Microsoft Office SharePoint Server 2007," offers your organization a robust solution to capturing metadata. Content types are a collection of settings you can apply to a specific category of content. Content types are also regularly referred to as metadata. You can also apply retention schedules to content types, which allows you to keep the content you are required to retain and to remove or eliminate the content you no longer need within your organization.

The size of your organization will determine how difficult defining the proper content types and metadata will be. Smaller organizations have a much easier time defining this because they don't have as many departments, projects, and operating companies that they need to consider when designing the organization's file plan.

WSS 3.0 automatically captures some system-generated metadata behind the scenes, so you should focus on other organizationally specific attributes that need to be captured. The following attributes are automatically captured by SharePoint:

- **Date Created** The date and time that the file or content was created or saved

- **Version** If this option is enabled within a list or library, it will create a version of the file each time it is edited

- **Created By** The user who created or saved the file or content

- **Modified** The date and time the file or content was last updated or modified

- **Modified By** The user who last updated or modified the file or content

- **Checked Out To** The user who has locked the file or content for editing

There is, however, one thing all organizations can plan in this realm—a core set of content types or metadata. If you can have the business owners agree on one main set of metadata that all departments, projects, operating companies, and users must populate prior to saving content into SharePoint, it will give you a firm foundation on which to build. Content types configured within your organization can be viewed and managed in the Site Content Type gallery, shown in Figure 20-1.

Chapter 20

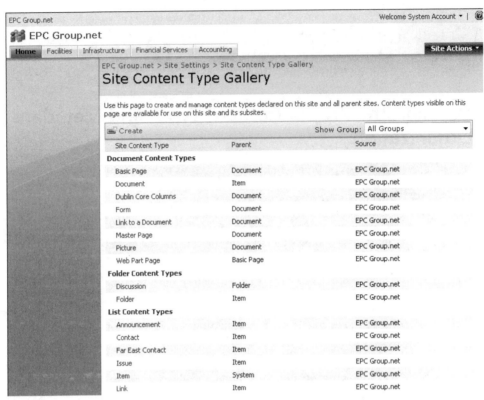

Figure 20-1 The Site Content Type gallery enables you to create and manage content types.

For example, if the new WSS 3.0 implementation is for a new intranet portal solution for your organization, you will more than likely have a number of departments that need representation within this portal. In this example, let's say this new portal is going to have representation from information technology (IT), legal, finance, sales, and marketing. Each of these departments will have their own ideas about which content types or metadata they want to capture in WSS 3.0 to help save and retrieve content. This is a good thing, but you first want to communicate to these departments that there will be a core set of content types or metadata that will be captured by default. Then you can work with the individual departments to add a few additional tailored content types or metadata values that are focused on their specific requirements.

Identifying a core set of content types or metadata also allows you to ensure that all of the site templates you make available to your users or departments will have objects, such as their lists and document libraries, that contain these core attributes.

For more information about planning the appropriate content types for your organizations refer to the article titled "Plan Content Types (Windows SharePoint Services)" at *http://technet2.microsoft.com/windowsserver/WSS/en/library/267ab7e5-35f6-46c9-ba64-2c63d6a0dbc01033.mspx?mfr=true.*

Using Microsoft Best Practices Analyzer for Windows SharePoint Services 3.0

The Microsoft Best Practices Analyzer for Windows SharePoint Services 3.0 and the 2007 Microsoft Office System is a tool that analyzes your current implementation and creates a report to help you configure WSS 3.0 to achieve greater performance, scalability, and uptime. It programmatically collects data and settings from different repositories such as Registry, Performance Monitor, and SQL Server, and it analyzes them using a set of rules.

> **Note**
>
> The Best Practices Analyzer for WSS can be downloaded at *http://microsoft.com/down-loads/details.aspx?familyid=cb944b27-9d6b-4a1f-b3e1-778efda07df8&displaylang=en.*

Once you have downloaded the Best Practices Analyzer, you can install it by running its setup program (BestPracticeAnalyzer.exe). The tool can be used only from the command line: sharepointbpa.exe -cmd analyze -substitutions SERVER_NAME *CentralAdministrationServer*, where *CentralAdministrationServer* is the server name for SharePoint Central Administration.

It is important to include *SERVER_NAME* capitalized in the parameters and to replace *CentralAdministrationServer* with the server name that is running SharePoint Central Administration, for example, sharepointbpa.exe -cmd analyze -substitutions SERVER_NAME WSSSERVER1.

The output is an HTML file called SharePointBpa.report.htm, located in the same folder as the tool. To view its content, open it in a Web browser. (ReportXslTransform.xsl and FormatXslTransform.xsl are used to render the report. If you want to change its appearance, then modify these two files.)

Adding the <Substitution Name="SERVER_NAME">*FILL_IN_YOUR_SERVER_NAME* </Substitution> tag to the SharePointBpa.config.xml file—in the Configuration node—enables you to run the utility with fewer parameters: *sharepointbpa.exe -cmd analyze.*

You can include a third parameter, *reportformat xml*, to get the report in XML format. The output file will be sharepointbpa<*number*>.report.xml.

The tool is based on rules definitions. The basic rules are contained in the SharePointBpa.config.xml file, so you can create your own rules and add them in the configuration file. It is recommended to run the tool on a regular basis and correct the problems that are found.

In Summary...

This chapter explained how to use a questionnaire to assist you in gathering information about requirements for your SharePoint initiatives. I also described how your organization can properly define content types and metadata, and how you can use the Microsoft Best Practices Analyzer for WSS 3.0.

The next chapter will explain how to launch your SharePoint environment and keep it as a thriving and viable system to all the users within your organization.

CHAPTER 21

Getting SharePoint off the Launch Pad

Once you have gathered the requirements for your new Microsoft Windows SharePoint Services 3.0 (WSS 3.0) environment, have the physical hardware in place, have the information architecture built out, and have the sites designed and in place, you are very close to taking the environment into production. You will need to develop the proper training materials for your users, develop a training and communication strategy, and make sure everything is thoroughly documented.

This chapter will discuss items to assist you and your organization in successfully launching your new WSS 3.0 environment.

Developing Training Materials

When developing training materials for your organization, you first need to identify which audiences you would like to train. In this book, we have discussed operations that will be performed by standard everyday users, power users, site owners, and site collection administrators.

Which of these roles does your organization want to train? Do you want to develop large paper training manuals to hand out to these users? Will you develop labs that users will need to follow online along with the manuals? Every organization has a preferred way of training the user base.

Personally, I prefer a combination of several different training mechanisms. I have found that the most useful training mechanism is developing voiceover videos that can be played in applications such as Windows Media Player. Developing these videos on a variety of topics for each of the roles you would like to train in your organization allows you to have CBT (computer-based training) available 24/7, which lessens the workload on your help desk, SharePoint administrators, and change management resources.

Several third-party programs are available to assist you in developing this type of training video. Camtasia Studio by Tech Smith has been one of my favorite video capturing programs over the past few years. Picking up a reasonably priced microphone from an electronics store and spending a few hundred dollars on a software license for a video capture application gets you ready to start recording helpful and cost effective training videos for your organization.

For more information on Camtasia Studio, go to the Tech Smith Web site at *www.techsmith.com.*

For the development of paper training materials, I would start with at least two different courses for your organization: end-user training and SharePoint administrator training.

End-User Training

End-user training should cover topics such as the following:

- An overview of SharePoint within the organization

- An introduction to the version of SharePoint that is implemented within the organization (for example, WSS 3.0 or Microsoft Office SharePoint Server 2007 [MOSS])

- SharePoint's hierarchy of sites

- Basic SharePoint functionality

- Lists and document libraries

- Overview of security and permissions in SharePoint

- Metadata and content types

- The organization's information management strategy

- Version control, check-in, and checkout

- SharePoint's integration with Microsoft Office applications

- SharePoint's notifications and alerts

- The organization's SharePoint governance model

- SharePoint's support structure: Service Level Agreements (SLAs) and support contract information

- A glossary of SharePoint terms

Because every organization is different, you should modify or expand this list as you see fit.

SharePoint Administrator Training

Administrator training should cover topics such as the following:

- An overview of SharePoint within the organization
- SharePoint's overall hierarchy
- The organization's overall security model
- The management of SharePoint's metadata and content types
- Site and workspace templates
- SharePoint's support structure and SLA requirements
- Quick Launch and Top Link bar management
- Web Parts management
- Search management
- Site design constraints
- Master page management
- My Site management (MOSS only)
- Developing custom lists and libraries
- Notification and alert management
- Site provisioning
- Backup and restore; disaster recovery
- SharePoint Central Administration: Operations page
- SharePoint Central Administration: Application Management page
- The organization's SharePoint governance model
- Developing custom views
- SharePoint extranet management (if applicable)
- Reporting, management, and statistics
- Web application and site collection management
- SharePoint database management
- SharePoint performance management

Because every organization is different, you should modify or expand this list as you see fit.

Developing the Proper SharePoint Communication Strategy

When developing a communication strategy for SharePoint, several different areas must be identified and addressed. For new SharePoint implementations, the business or executive sponsor should send out a message to the user base letting them know about this new initiative.

I would recommend putting together a detailed e-mail or Microsoft Office PowerPoint presentation that describes what SharePoint can do for the organization as well as promotes and identifies the areas that you will need to be successful in to accomplish this initiative.

INSIDE OUT   Communicating SharePoint's launch

For a new SharePoint initiative, a business or executive sponsor can use e-mail communications and Office PowerPoint presentations to promote SharePoint within the organization. An example of this follows.

What Is SharePoint?

- A gateway to company information, services, and applications based on the following principles:
    - ○ SharePoint offers a consistent look and feel
    - ○ SharePoint promotes organizational branding
    - ○ Navigation is intuitive and easy to use
    - ○ It enables the organization to promote a clear and understandable message to all employees
    - ○ It promotes information management
    - ○ It eliminates duplicate efforts and redundant or contradicting content
    - ○ It allows for powerful notifications and alerts to users based on specific criteria

Communicating the keys to success to the overall audience can assist in accomplishing your goals.

Keys to SharePoint Success:

- Clear and defined SharePoint objectives
- Management backing from our organization
- Formation of a SharePoint advisory committee
    - Include representatives from as many departments as possible
    - Involve this committee early on in this initiative
- SharePoint makes it easy for departments to collaborate within their site
- Define clear SharePoint standards and governance

Once SharePoint launches and is in production, communication should go out to the entire user base. An example of this communication might look like the following.

To: All Users

When you log in to your computer tomorrow morning, your browser's home page will display our organization's new SharePoint solution. This is an exciting time for us because this (intranet/extranet) platform has been designed to provide a consistent look and feel along with user-friendly collaborative features that will enable you to quickly find the content you need to successfully do your job. To help you get familiar with this powerful new platform, we have developed several training videos that are available for your viewing anytime at (*URL*).

This solution will enhance collaboration within our organization and provide access to vital information provided by departments across the company. Please take time tomorrow morning to test out this new solution that will be an integral part of our day-to-day activities and will provide a new central location for content management.

Thank you,

The SharePoint Executive Sponsor

Documentation, Documentation, and Documentation

As with any project, it is extremely important to document all aspects of your SharePoint initiative. You need to cover everything from hardware configurations to the overall site hierarchy to disaster recovery and training materials. You should document any customizations that were made as well as all custom code development (custom workflows, master pages, site definitions, and so on) and even down to how many document libraries are in each site and what their names are.

The new backup features in WSS 3.0, along with templates, make it easier than ever to have records of your environment. Nevertheless, going the extra mile and documenting granular configuration steps is a best practice. In several years, when a new version of SharePoint is released, it will be that much easier for you to take on that project with a great amount of success.

TROUBLESHOOTING

Have hard copies of your organization's documentation—both SharePoint and non–SharePoint related

I have worked on several projects where the client's documentation of their SharePoint environment was very impressive and its popularity was such that it became the primary document storage mechanism for the organization. This is what we are really trying to achieve, right? What happens when, for one reason or another, SharePoint goes down, you have a hardware issue, or you are performing a disaster recovery test on the environment? What happens if you need to troubleshoot something and all the sudden you don't have access to any disaster recovery or mission critical documents because the environment is temporarily down?

For all mission critical documents, I would suggest that you print out paper copies of them and have them in binders for easy access. This may seem like a no-brainer, but you would be surprised at how many organizations don't perform this easy task and it comes back to bite them in the long run.

In Summary...

This chapter covered training topics and strategies your organization can develop to assist in the proliferation and success of WSS 3.0 in your organization. I also covered some communication examples that I have had success with in previous SharePoint projects to ensure the greater user audience is aware of and kept in the loop about the product's launch.

This book introduced and explained every major aspect of WSS 3.0, including the browser interface, integration with the Microsoft Office system, advanced design with Microsoft Office SharePoint Designer 2007, installation on Windows Server 2003, use with Microsoft SQL Server 2005, complete administration and configuration, and custom programming with Microsoft Visual Studio 2005. This is an impressive range of topics, and it clearly indicates how popular SharePoint has become and continues to be on a daily basis in organizations throughout the world. SharePoint occupies an extremely strategic position among Microsoft technologies.

Hopefully my experience in SharePoint implementations and the lessons I have learned over the years will assist you and your organization in implementing this powerful software with great success. I work in SharePoint every day, have worked on some of the largest SharePoint projects in the United States, and am amazed at how popular this product has become. I look forward to Office 14 and its next release to see what Microsoft has up its sleeve. Good luck with your site, and I hope we meet again in the future.

Index to Troubleshooting Topics

Index

About the Author

Errin O'Connor has been working as a consultant on Microsoft solutions for the past nine years and has worked on enterprise implementations at companies such as Lockheed Martin, ConocoPhillips, Fannie Mae, UBS, and Chevron. He has worked with the Microsoft SharePoint Products and Technologies suite since 2001 and has probably worked on more SharePoint implementations than any other consultant in the United States.

Errin is the founder and senior SharePoint architect of EPCGroup.net, a Houston-based SharePoint implementation and custom .NET Framework–based applications consulting firm. He is focusing his efforts on rolling out SharePoint in organizations throughout the country as a true content management solution, an intranet solution, an internet-facing solution, and a centralized platform on which organizations can house all of their .NET Framework–based applications.

When not working on SharePoint implementations, Errin enjoys exotic cars and attending professional sports events. He founded HTownExotics, a Houston–based exotic rental car and timeshare company, where he enjoys the interaction with his clients and being able to share his passion for these unique automobiles.

A Message from the Author

I am happy to hear from any reader, whether you had a pleasant experience or are less than satisfied. Please note that I can respond only if you write in English. The e-mail address at which you can contact me is:

insideout@epcgroup.net

I'm most interested in your impressions of this book: what you liked or disliked about it, what questions it did or didn't answer, what you found excessive, and what you'd like to see added in the next edition. I'll post errors, omissions, corrections, frequently asked questions, and free Web Parts and solutions for readers on my company's Web site at:

www.epcgroup.net/wss-iso/

There is also a MySpace page for this book, where you can become friends with other readers. This page can be found at:

www.myspace.com/wss_iso

Even when I can't answer your e-mail messages directly, I find it instructive to learn what problems users like you are experiencing—and therefore how I can make this and future books more useful to everyone.

Please understand that due to my schedule, I can't provide technical support or debugging assistance, even for readers. Please try other channels, including the IT Pro Community SharePoint Newsgroups at:

http://www.microsoft.com/technet/community/newsgroups/server/sharepoint.mspx

and Microsoft's Advanced Search page at:

http://search.microsoft.com/AdvancedSearch.aspx

If you're getting an error message or error number, try searching for that exact phrase or number, plus the word *SharePoint*. If you're having trouble with a specific feature or component, try searching for the name of the component plus, again, the word *Share-Point*.

If you are interested in professional SharePoint consulting from me or my organization, you can contact EPCGroup.net via e-mail at:

sharepoint@epcgroup.net

Or visit us on the Web at:

www.epcgroup.net

What do you think of this book?

We want to hear from you!

Do you have a few minutes to participate in a brief online survey?

Microsoft is interested in hearing your feedback so we can continually improve our books and learning resources for you.

To participate in our survey, please visit:

www.microsoft.com/learning/booksurvey/

...and enter this book's ISBN-10 or ISBN-13 number (located above barcode on back cover*). As a thank-you to survey participants in the United States and Canada, each month we'll randomly select five respondents to win one of five $100 gift certificates from a leading online merchant. At the conclusion of the survey, you can enter the drawing by providing your e-mail address, which will be used for prize notification only.

Thanks in advance for your input. Your opinion counts!

*Where to find the ISBN on back cover

ISBN-13: 000-0-0000-0000-0
ISBN-10: 0-0000-0000-0

0 00000 000000

Example only. Each book has unique ISBN.

Microsoft®
Press

No purchase necessary. Void where prohibited. Open only to residents of the 50 United States (includes District of Columbia) and Canada (void in Quebec). For official rules and entry dates see:

www.microsoft.com/learning/booksurvey/